SWINGING THE MACHINE

SWINGING the MACHINE

MODERNITY, TECHNOLOGY, AND

AFRICAN AMERICAN CULTURE BETWEEN

THE WORLD WARS

JOEL DINERSTEIN

University of Massachusetts Press   *Amherst & Boston*

LC 2002013897
ISBN 1-55849-373-5 (library cloth); 383-2 (paper)

Designed by Richard Hendel
Set in Matra, Gill, and New Baskerville types
Printed and bound by Thomson-Shore, Inc.

Library of Congress Cataloging-in-Publication Data

Dinerstein, Joel, 1958–
   Swinging the machine : modernity, technology, and African American culture
between the World Wars / Joel Dinerstein
      p. cm.
Includes bibliographical references (p.) and index.
   ISBN 1-55849-373-5 (cloth : alk. paper) — ISBN 1-55849-383-2 (pbk. : alk. paper)
   1. African Americans—Intellectual life—20th century. 2. African Americans—
Music—20th century. 3. Swing (Music)—History. 4. African American dance—
History—20th century. 5. Swing (Dance)—United States—History. 6. United
States—Civilization—African American influences. 7. African Americans in
popular culture. 8. Popular culture—United States—History—20th century.
9. Technology—Social aspects—United States—History—20th century.
10. City and town life—United States—History—20th century.   I. Title.
   E185.6 .D5 2003
   305.896'073'009043—dc21

2002013897

British Library Cataloguing in Publication data
are available.

FOR MY MOTHER,

who calls swing "my music"

and opened my ears to the

soundscape of the world.

CONTENTS

ILLUSTRATIONS

ACKNOWLEDGMENTS

This project developed in fits and starts throughout my graduate education, and my first debt is to Shelley Fisher Fishkin, from whom I learned that scholarship is more a conversational process than a solitary endeavor. She encouraged its ungainly interdisciplinarity from the start and was an unswerving supporter of this work. Jeff Meikle introduced me to the history of technology and the study of its cultural effects; the germ of this work emerged in a caffeine-driven rant about big bands and trains I wrote to prove to him such a relationship existed. Much of my theoretical framework here I first discussed in long conversations with Gena Caponi-Tabery, whose combined historical and musicological expertise helped disabuse me of many romantic ideas about popular music left over from my years as a rock critic. Gena read much of this work as it came off the printer and always encouraged me to strive for clarity; I shall also never be able to repay her hospitality.

Sheila Walker introduced me to the anthropological discourse of African diasporic traditions in music, dance, and religion, and encouraged me in my attempts to understand the Yoruba cultural system in particular. Bob Abzug challenged me to think through my historical connections more clearly, especially regarding the relationship between African American music and American popular culture. Desley Deacon shared her frustrations with me concerning the inadequate historical context of the pre-1945 jazz discourse, and she encouraged me to assert bold claims in this work.

During my research I was privileged to have long conversations with two of the country's finest musicological minds. Albert Murray spent four hours with me one January afternoon in his apartment in a classic encounter between master scholar and junior seeker which I will always treasure. I had a similar encounter with Charlie Keil at El Sol y La Luna in Austin, Texas, and subsequent conversations with him at his home in Buffalo and at a conference in Washington, D.C. Charlie calls this field of study "grooveology" and its scholars "grooveologists." May these terms become common parlance one day. I hope my work helps provide historical context for both Keil's and Murray's theories on the social functions and vernacular aesthetics of American and African American popular music.

The American studies community in Austin, Texas, has enriched this work and my life. Kim Hewitt has taught me a great deal about consciousness, identity, gender, and performance; our friendship has changed the way I view the self in the world. Siva Vaidhyanathan and I pray to the same musical gods, but it is our generational debates about popular music and its embedded meanings (and groovings) that made this a better work. Concurrent with my research, Carolyn de la Pena and Christina Cogdell were making similar connections about bodies, machines, and ideologies of energy, and our intellectual paths crisscrossed often and created a set of permanent friendships. Bill Pugsley taught me an incredible amount about the history of trains; in a better world, he would be the official storyteller of Texas. Ina Szekeley and Cary Cordova were stalwart compadres during the gestation of this work, which was also enriched by my friendships with Alicia Barber, Kathie Tovo, Sheree Scarborough, Jonathan Davis, and Julio Tavares.

My postdoctoral fellowship from the Woodrow Wilson Foundation made this book possible, and I am especially indebted to Dominick LaCapra for his support of my work during my time as a fellow at Cornell University's Society for the Humanities. I would also like to thank Judith Pinch at the Wilson Foundation. Important support for my research came at crucial times from the Pew Foundation, the Mellon Foundation, and the University of Texas.

My immersion into big band swing culture resulted from roaming the stacks of records and CDs at the Institute of Jazz Studies at Rutgers during the summer of 1997. I owe an immense debt to Vincent Pelote and director Dan Morgenstern for letting me hole up in one of their cubicles and listen to music (and read) all day. At the Newberry Library, JoEllen Dickie was especially helpful in my research on trains and on Sherwood Anderson. I am thankful to the archivists and librarians at the New York Public Library for their assistance with the New York World's Fair collection and at the Lincoln Center for the Performing Arts for its dance collection.

The University of Massachusetts Press is a class operation top to bottom. Special thanks to my editor, Clark Dougan, who believed in this work from the start; a pretty sharp historian himself, Clark is a good friend and a stand-up guy. My hat's off as well to my copy editor, Joel Ray, who helped me clarify the argument at every turn and reined in my verbiage without ruining my narrative voice.

Finally, to quote writer Michael Ventura, "I *am* my friends." I have shared so much of my life with my sister Adele and my *bucha*, Kenny Fass, that I cannot imagine my life without their love and friendship. Dave Weinraub is my soul brother and is always there for me. That's true as well for Jeff Schanzer, a great friend (and fine musician) who even reads my fiction. Shaianne Osterreich helped me at several crucial junctures in the completion of this manuscript, intellectually and organizationally; she is a sharp reader and an even better friend. Naeem Inayatullah and I became friends by discussing how music works in culture, and our talks about grooveology kept me excited about this project as I wrapped it up. Last but not least, for their long-distance love over the years, my deepest thanks to Janet Chasin, David Fisher, Barbara Gerber, and Donna Badome.

SWINGING THE MACHINE

INTRODUCTION

BODIES AND MACHINES

"They got all this machinery, but that ain't everything;
we the machines inside the machines."
—*Lucius Brockway to the narrator of Ralph Ellison's* Invisible Man

When the preeminent modernist architect Le Corbusier visited New York, the preeminent modern city, in 1935, he marveled equally at the skyscrapers and at African American music and dance. "Jazz, like the skyscrapers, is an *event*. . . represent[ing] the forces of today. *The jazz is more advanced than the architecture.* If architecture were at th[is] point . . . it would be an incredible spectacle." By "the forces of today," the architect meant industrialization and mass production. Many European observers considered jazz and skyscrapers the most significant vernacular cultural productions of the United States, but Le Corbusier must be considered an expert witness on the aesthetic impact of machines in modern society, as he had based his artistic revolution on calling the home "a machine for living." He made a crucial connection at the crossroads of American music, machine aesthetics, modernism, and architecture. "I repeat: Manhattan is hot jazz in stone and steel."[1]

Le Corbusier perceived that African Americans had successfully integrated music and technology: "The Negroes of the USA have breathed into jazz the song, the rhythm and the sound of machines." The architect's analysis of this relationship took up seven pages of a memoir of his first trip to the United States, appearing under the title "The Spirit of the Machine, and Negroes in the USA." He rhapsodized over Louis Armstrong's ability both to reflect and to contain the chaotic rhythms of the urban, industrial soundscape. "He is mathematics, equilibrium on a tightrope," Le Corbusier exclaimed. "Nothing in our European experience can be compared to it." He was amazed by the continuous rhythmic flow of tap dancers and how they embodied precision on the body. "The popularity of tap dancers shows that the old rhythmic instinct of the [African] . . . has learned the lesson of the machine." These observations have usually been dismissed as primitivist and essentialist, yet Le Corbusier's admiration here for jazz and tap seems unequivocal and even collegial. He concedes that these art forms reveal an adaptation to modernity through aesthetic attention to sound, flow, and mechanical rhythms missing not only from his own field of architecture but from the "European experience." "New sounds . . . the grinding of the streetcars, the unchained madness of the subway, the pounding of machines in factories . . . [f]rom this new uproar . . . they [African Americans] make music!"[2]

The process by which African Americans stylized machine rhythms and aesthetics through inquiry, experiment, and social experience is the launching point of this work. Le Corbusier's insights must be taken at face value if scholars are to understand the global power and success of West African–derived American vernacular music. The architect who made modernism a concrete reality perceived a machine aesthetic in jazz and tap dance that was "far more advanced than the architecture." Only a year earlier, the pioneering technology critic Lewis Mumford had warned that Americans were enslaved to their machines and that society's greatest challenge was to meet technology on human terms: *Our capacity to go beyond the machine rests upon the power to assimilate the machine.* In his manifesto of industrial design, *Horizons* (1932), Norman Bel Geddes likewise claimed that Americans were not yet "at ease" with the machine, owing to the speed with which the industrial revolution had changed everyday life. Total embrace of the machine would only occur when "the person who would use a machine must be imbued with the spirit of the machine."[3]

At the exact cultural moment that Mumford and Bel Geddes perceived a society out of balance regarding the priorities of humans and machines, big-band swing was on the verge of taking the nation by storm, and tap dance had become one of the nation's most popular artistic forms (to watch *and* perform). Americans realized with their senses, perhaps unconsciously, that swing music and dance stylized the increased pace of urban, industrial life, torqued up individual metabolic rates to the faster social tempo, and assimilated machine aesthetics into two of the primal cultural forms of human expression: music and dance.

West African societies perform their value systems in public rituals whose primary goal is the integration of music and society through rituals of social bonding.[4] African American jazz musicians and dancers, working within such a sociocultural imperative passed down through oral tradition, constructed a similarly functional dance-hall ritual for a nation that had built its identity on technological innovation.[5] Through contact with Euro-American musicians and cultural elites, as well as with black workers and the urban soundscape, African American artists integrated the speed, drive, precision, and rhythmic flow of factory work and modern cities into a nationally (and internationally) unifying cultural form: big-band swing.

The global triumph of swing's modernism was duly noted by Henry Luce in his famous "American Century" speech of 1941, as he tried to persuade Americans to trade their political isolationism for an already-potent cultural internationalism: "There is already an immense American internationalism. American jazz, Hollywood movies, American slang . . . [and] American machines . . . are in fact the only things that every community in the world, from Zanzibar to Hamburg, recognizes in common."[6] Sixty years ago, Luce recognized a global popular culture informed by technology and African American popular culture. As the historian Lewis Erenberg commented recently, "To everyone's surprise, American popular music, mass youth culture, and the democratic arts in general were reborn in the Depression."[7]

The historian of science Emily Thompson calls the new sonic barrage of the early twentieth century "the soundscape of modernity," and shows the "dramatic transformation" in the urban aural experience between 1900 and 1933. In 1896 the noises of the cities were still agrarian and natural: horse-drawn vehicles, animals, churchbells, peddlers. In 1929, according to a comprehensive report compiled by the Noise Abatement Commission of New York, the top ten most unpleasant noises for urbanites were "machine-age inventions": trucks, car horns, trolley cars, pneumatic drills, riveters, radios (in stores and homes). Nearly two-thirds of residents' specific complaints fit under three categories: traffic, transportation, and radios. "The air belongs to the steady air of the motor," declared a writer in a 1925 essay simply entitled "Noise." The musicologist John Blacking has famously defined music as "humanly-organized sound"; jazz musicians were the artistic innovators who organized the noise of machine-age civilization into artistic form.[8]

Jazz was the nation's popular music in the Machine Age (1919–45) because its driving, syncopated rhythms reflected the speeded-up tempo of life produced by industrialization in the American workplace and the mechanization of urban life. Jazz also reflected the hopes of African Americans for finding a new life outside the South.

When big-band swing became the nation's most popular music in the mid-1930s, it was both a morale boost for a nation in depression and a reflection of the relative freedom African Americans felt in New York, Chicago, Detroit, and Los Angeles. But whereas 1920s small-unit jazz was expressive, peppy, and polyphonic, big-band swing was propulsive, fast, fluid, and precise: it reflected the networked systems of large-scale industrialization, whether of Henry Ford's assembly lines or cross-country express trains. Through what Albert Murray calls "locomotive onomatopoeia"—the sounds and rhythms of trains—African American bandleaders put machines into American music. At a time when workers and social critics complained of the overwhelming roar of machine-driven factories, big-band swing *made sense* of factory noise, and the lindy hop gave the opportunity to *get with* the noise. Swing musicians stylized mechanical repetition, creating and controlling propulsive rhythms capable of jump-starting fatigued bodies and depressed spirits. Euro-Americans watched and mimicked African American swing dancers, whose fast, dynamic whole-body dances modeled one method of rejuvenating American bodies.

The United States was the international center of modern technology and mass production for the hundred years following the Civil War, and yet scholars maintain that European artists and architects established a "modern high culture" to reflect the Machine Age.[9] Through the testimony of contemporary observers, my present inquiry challenges the paradox of a nation seemingly unable to produce cultural forms to match its technological innovation. When Louis Armstrong, Duke Ellington, and Coleman Hawkins toured Europe in the early 1930s, Europeans perceived in their music the electrical energy of the age, the controlled power of its propulsive rhythms, the advent of innovative techniques and aesthetics, the virtuosic control of musical dynamics, and a renewal of individualism generated by "dissociat[ing]" the performer's interpretation from the written score and the conductor's orders. Jazz was an inspiration to the Surrealists, and "the staple musical nourishment . . . [of] all the intelligent and cultivated youth of Europe," noted the Belgian poet and critic Robert Goffin in 1934. He called on Americans to appreciate Armstrong, Hawkins, Earl Hines and others, who were "surely of more importance than sky-scrapers and Fordism." Since a jazz artist must both "have ample scope for independence and spontaneity of expression" *and* contribute to the overall texture and momentum of the music, jazz "requires *more* of its executants," Goffin suggested, than do other art forms.[10]

In 1970 Ralph Ellison famously described American culture as "jazz-shaped," and claimed that "most American whites are culturally part Negro American without realizing it."[11] What did he mean? First, that aesthetically the "abrupt starts and stops" in black cultural forms (jazz, basketball, the fast flow of black storytelling) constitute a large part of any American claim to being an "accelerated" culture. "Without the presence of Negro American style, our jokes, our tall tales . . . [and] our sports would be lacking in the sudden turns, the shocks, the swift changes of pace." Second, the educative and philosophical bases of these forms were as important as the aesthetics. Blues, folk tales, dance, sports, slang—all perform "a tragic-comic attitude toward life" communicating the idea "that the real secret of the game is to make life swing."[12] My goal here is to show how and why an *aesthetics of acceleration*—these "swift changes of pace"—is the basis of swing culture (and in fact remains an aesthetic core of American popular culture).

Much of the scholarship on adaptation to modernity focuses on artists mediating the systemic shift to industrial society through the visual media of literature, painting, and photography, but it is probably more true that "the twentieth century was built for the ear." To understand the transformation from an agrarian to an urban society, from a natural to industrial workplace, from acoustic to electric instruments and mechanical reproduction, we must explore what scholars of the Machine Age call *machine aesthetics*, and then "plug in the headphones and listen—to cable cars . . . Jupiter rockets, surgical banter, steam locomotives, punch clocks: the work songs of the whole carbon-based enterprise." The enormous aural adaptation required of the human system has eluded scholars in part because "sonic memories are at once more primal than visual ones . . . and more evanescent."[13]

Although I focus primarily on the machine aesthetics in swing music and dance, a specifically African American inquiry into the nature of human life in technological society began with the collective creation of "The Ballad of John Henry" in the 1880s. "Technological" here refers not only to industrial innovations and mechanical rhythms, but also to the ongoing changes in human perception brought on by the experience of modernity.[14] The social function of nearly all African American musical practice before 1945 was to create a public forum that provided the following: social bonding through music and dance, an opportunity to create an individual style within a collective form, and a dense rhythmic wave that imparts "participatory consciousness" to the audience. All three combine into a set of practices that the musicologist Charles Keil simply calls "grooving."[15] A generation before the development of a musical vocabulary for instruments that were themselves machines (electric guitars and basses)—and a generation before *musique concrète*—jazz musicians had tamed the industrial soundscape into a drive-train for a national dance pulse.

Machine Age Modernism, European and American

Historians of technology assume the canon of Machine Age modern art to be mostly European: the manifestos of the Italian futurists; the paintings and sculpture of artists such as Francis Picabia and Marcel Duchamp; Bauhaus and International Style architecture as practiced by Le Corbusier, Walter Gropius, and Mies van der Rohe; the paintings of Ferdinand Leger and the Russian constructivists; the American precisionist school of painting (for example, Charles Sheeler and Charles DeMuth); films and novels that project fears of overmechanization, such as *Metropolis, Modern Times*, and *Brave New World*.[16] But European Machine Age modernists were artistically motivated more by machine worship or modernist rebellion than the goals of aesthetic integration and continuity. The Italian Futurists were "obsessed with breaking away from the past" and envisioned the future as a powerful automobile speeding away from European artistic traditions and social conventions.[17] Gropius and Le Corbusier dreamed of mass-producing houses as Henry Ford produced cars; in 1920 Le Corbusier referred to himself as an "industrialist." The French modernist painter Francis Picabia saw in the machine "a model for his own behavior," and famously sketched individual Americans *as* machines (his "Portrait of a Nude American Woman" is a spark plug). For these artists, machine aesthetics were embraced as new social values in themselves, and "technology involved a commitment to such values as order, precision, power, motion, and change."[18]

The unifying aesthetic principle of Machine Age modernism was "flow," or rhythmic flow. The art historian Terry Smith has analyzed the process by which painters and photographers rendered machine aesthetics beautiful to the eye, and the dance scholar Hillel Schwartz has shown how machines influenced the emergence of a new "twentieth-century kinesthetic" in dance. Whether in Taylorist time-and-motion studies or motion pictures, in the assembly line or automatic phono-graphs, in the ideals of modern dancers or the graceful, banked curves of an airplane in flight—these scholars perceive a quest for continuous, efficient, flowing, forward motion. "In each case, one sought a natural, fluid transition from step to step, frame to frame, task to task, bar to bar," Schwartz observes. By 1930, for example, modern dancers and pro-gressive educators dismissed the staccato motion of nineteenth-century physical training methods such as gymnastics and ballet as "antique, highly technical" and too "mechanically systematic"; they were forms that "promot[ed] not autonomy, but automata."[19]

The model for industrial flow in the early twentieth century was the assembly line, which was the centerpiece of the enormously pop-ular tours of the Ford Motors River Rouge plant in the 1920s. Before the assembly line, mechanics worked in teams around a workbench. Then between 1908 and 1913 Ford's production engineers and senior mechanics realized that if you placed benches end to end and ran a conveyor belt across them, you could create a more uniform pace for workers: it would speed up the slow workers and slow down the fast ones. The same ideal of rhythmic flow was already present in motion pictures, and Smith sees the assembly line as itself cinematic: work-ers are framed in a single, specialized job and then sequenced, just as individual photographic frames become motion pictures. In 1913 a writer from *American Machinist* began his description of the assembly of Model Ts with the disclaimer that it could only be rendered accu-rately "with a modern moving-picture machine."[20]

In a similar quest for rhythmic flow, Bauhaus architects and the cre-ators of streamlined design eliminated all ornament from their work to emulate the clean, straight lines and flowing masses familiar to func-tional engineering forms such as grain elevators, ocean liners, and the steel skeleton of Chicago School skyscrapers.[21] Gone were the ginger-bread bric-a-brac of the Victorian aesthetic, the exposed industrial work-ings of the machines from the "gear-and-girder" era, or the regal, brick-solid symmetry of Beaux-Arts architecture. Machine Age modernist photographers and painters then "aestheticized" the machine by "still-ing [its] motion . . . excluding the human, implying an autonomy to the mechanical, then seeking a beauty of repetition, simplicity, regularity of rhythm, clarity of surface."[22] For example, in his influential paint-ings *Classic Landscape* (1930) and *American Landscape* (1931), Charles Sheeler represented the rational centralized power of mass production of Ford's River Rouge plant through precise, flat renderings of smoke stacks, steel pipes, trains, and even mounds of industrial slag. In displaying the new mechanical order, both Sheeler and fellow painter Charles Demuth nearly always "omitted people from their technological landscapes."[23]

Was there any way for human beings to *participate* in these new technological landscapes? Only Diego Rivera's murals and Lewis Hine's photographs integrated human beings into artistic visions of industrial society in this period. In Rivera's immense murals of the River Rouge assembly line, the workers are individuated (many were the artist's friends), rendered with dignity, clothed in distinct styles, and shown cooperating within the bowels of the great industrial machine. The central mural on the south wall at the Detroit Institute of Fine Arts features an enormous stamp press producing fenders out of long sheets of steel while workers attach cylinder-head covers and other parts to the engine block. Produced in 1931, Rivera's mural interweaved machines, workers, and foremen as if they were the intestines of a freshly minted Meso-American body politic reigned over by Aztec gods who were supervising the unification of the four races (white, black, red, yellow) in the same way industrial processes turned raw materials into mass-produced goods. In envisioning a productive synergy of the natural and mechanical orders and a unification of the "North" with the "South," Rivera's work was a rare optimistic vision of New World humanity in the Depression built around what he called "the collective hero, man-and-machine."[24] Less cosmically, Lewis Hine's acclaimed photographs of the Empire State Building's construction workers suggested human beings at home in the immaterial ether. Sitting on girders suspended in space, the workers entrance us with visions of skyscraper castles in the air; they converse, eat lunch, and weld steel at altitudes most people are still thrilled simply to look out from.

Rivera and Hine provide visions of men at work, not at play or in creative engagement with the new technological regime. But many people participated in technological landscapes in riding trains, trolleys, and cars, and in using such common devices as sewing machines and telephones. At the turn of the twentieth century Thorstein Veblen theorized that by their work as "attendants" of machines, Americans by necessity adapted to machine imperatives.[25] In *The Octopus* (1901), for example, Frank Norris implies that any California farmhand running a thresher sat at a new human-machine interface. "Underneath him was the jarring, jolting, trembling machine; not a clod was turned . . . that he did not receive the swift impression of it through his body, the very friction of the damp soil, sliding incessantly from the shiny surface of the shears, seemed to reproduce itself in his finger-tips and along the back of his head."[26] Not through art or play, not through choice or volition, but through the workplace and life in the industrial city people learned (they *had* to learn) to adapt minds and bodies to machines.

Yet human work directed by a machine threatened something essentially human and offended workers across class, gender, ethnicity and epoch. The Lowell "factory girls" of the 1840s despised the "ceaseless din" of the belts, wheels and springs in constant motion; the skilled machinists of the 1890s loathed the stopwatch of the Taylorist consultant; the striking General Motors workers of the 1930s resented the tyranny of "the line." Even the prosperous, unionized Cold War assembly-line nine-to-fivers who enjoyed the lifestyle made possible by well-paid factory work always complained of working at "the machine's pace."[27] Such dissatisfaction peaked in the Depression as the economic reality of what was then called "technological unemployment" dimmed the national pride in technological progress.[28]

Early industrial researchers referred to the body as "the human motor" in the nineteenth century; doctors called it simply "the human machine" until 1940. Industrial research into work-related fatigue focused on how to maximize productivity over a ten- to twelve-hour shift.[29] Businessmen were concerned only with how to get the most out of the human machine, or of the factory "hand." (In this revealing trope the body part is both reduced to a mechanical aid and becomes a metonym for the whole human being.) Two crucial philosophical questions were rarely raised by these nineteenth-century professionals: How can a human being reclaim his or her *human* motor from workplace demands, and how can a person integrate the newly revved-up, machine-driven human motor into the entire human organism? In looking back at the obsession with speed at the turn of the twentieth century, James Gleick astutely perceived the subtext: "Why not change the speed of the human machine as well?"[30]

The American technological analyst Stuart Chase first began to see and hear Machine Age modernism in 1929. In *Men and Machines* he identified the machine aesthetics in modernity that cultural forms needed to reflect and contain: "mass, size, speed, fleeting images, repetition, sharpness of line; oral experiences of the staccato, precise timing, and rhythm of completed operation." These then are the elements of machine aesthetics: *power, speed, repetition, precision, efficiency, rhythmic flow*. Chase quoted an American art critic who found "the interaction of the machine on art" in forms such as cubism, futurism, streamlining, jazz, skyscraper bookcases, "modern plane and angle furniture, and new color combinations in factories," and these forms remain the touchstones of the era. Chase was tentative about these forms but admitted that skyscrapers, photography, motion pictures, automobile design, airplanes, and mass-produced goods suggested some hope for "art . . . in the Power Age."[31]

When trying to locate the "modern" visual aesthetic in the first third of the century, Terry Smith kept in mind this key question: "What makes something look old?"[32] Certainly the airplane, the assembly line, and motion pictures made Victorian culture seem staid and obsolete. But African American music and dance made nineteenth-century Euro-American forms of music and physical movement, that is, kinesthetics, look old as well. The term "kinesthetic" here refers to an aesthetic of bodily movement—the felt, sensory experience of continuous physiological movement, whether in dance, work, or physical gestures (such as walking). Obviously the kinesthetic of the turkey trot is quite different from that of the waltz. The cultural reasons for the emergence of the former at the expense of the latter in ballrooms across the nation—especially among Anglo-American upper-class youth in the early 1910s—have less to do with primitivism than with the need to swing the human machine. Through rhythmic nuance and sophistication, through more inclusive (and holistic) aural and bodily engaged frameworks, through a synthesis of European and American song forms and dances, African American musicians and dancers cracked open restrictive classical forms of music and ballet. Big-band swing, tap dance, and the lindy hop were public models of humanized machine aesthetics.

In the popular culture between the wars, Americans hungered for displays of human mastery of machine aesthetics. In the chorus lines of the Ziegfeld Follies and Harlem revues, in Busby Berkeley's rotating *fantasies* of female abundance, in the quick metallic snap of tap dance and the whirl of the lindy hop, Americans wanted to see the machine mastered. The Italian Futurists hailed the twentieth century's new addition to aesthetics—the thrill of speed—and wondered how human beings could embody the thrill they found in automobiles, trains, and planes. In "Manifesto of the Futurist Dance" (1917), Fillipo Marinetti declared the need for dance in which people "imitate the movements of machines with gestures," reflecting the power of "wheels, [and] pistons, thereby preparing the fusion of man with the machine"; the aspiration of any "futurist" dance should be the "ideal *multiplied body* of the motor." Where did he then find it? "We Futurists prefer [modern dancer] Loie Fuller and the 'cakewalk' of the Negroes."[33]

In the next two decades, jazz and its associated dances provided popular cultural forms that were both participatory and dynamic. What were the solutions that jazz artists provided? First, as machines speeded up hands, hearts, and minds, individuals had to engage these new aesthetics on the body. Second, take the loud, harsh, repetitive rhythms and mix them down into a groove centered in the torso, hips, and thighs; get your ass into it (as in the turkey trot), get your shoulders (shimmy), your neck, your feet (tap) into it. Now slide across the floor, release your partner, strut your stuff, and show the world who you are.

Kathy Peiss has shown that dance was the social activity most enjoyed among working-class women between 1900 and 1920. Regardless of work fatigue, young women geared themselves up to go dancing even on week nights. In her classic study of 1920s college youth, *The Damned and the Beautiful*, Paula Fass identified dance as "unquestionably the most popular pastime" among upper-class white students. Jazz dances represented rebellion, sensuality, and sexual liberation; despite pressure from college authorities to curtail lascivious dances, Fass reports that no college editor ever condemned jazz or dancing. A typical editorial in the University of Illinois paper proclaimed, "A college existence without jazz would be like a child's Christmas without Santa Claus." The dance critic Lucille Marsh traveled fourteen thousand miles in the early 1930s to make a record of American social dance by region, class, and ethnicity, and she declared it "the national pastime."[34] Jazz and its dances provided the cultural forms of reinvigoration.

The cultural hunger for physiological engagement helps explain the global importance of social and commercial dance in this period. Between 1910 and 1940, dance enjoyed a higher profile in the humanities than at any time in American history. "Dancing and building are the two primary and essential arts," the doctor and sexologist Havelock Ellis declared in *The Dance of Life* (1923); dance manifests the felt experience "in the human person" and architecture the public and social expression "outside the person." Since dancing came first, it was "the supreme symbol of spiritual life." Why was dance so important to self-expression and social expression between the world wars? The transformation from agrarian to industrial work brought forth a need for dynamic physiological engagement and cultural resistance—taking one's body back from machines.[35]

Swing music and dance have been omitted from modernist discussions of rhythmic flow in part because African American musicians and dancers did not theorize about what was then simply called "the machine." Duke Ellington, for example, never mentioned the liberating or debilitating effects of the machine; he did, however, write often about music's role in social relations and about the necessity of reflecting social and cultural forces. When Ellington stylized train sounds and rhythms in musical compositions, his approach derived not from machine-driven modernism but from two *functional* imperatives of African-derived musical practice: that music is (functionally) for dance, and that it must aesthetically render the common environment in sound.

One goal of this book is to show how these forms fit into the experience of modernity, and to recognize the aesthetics and values within such artistic production. For example, when Gropius and Le Corbusier declared the need to humanize the functionalism of engineered forms through the "texture, tones . . . light and shadow" of the architect's craft,[36] I find this analogous to swing-era musicians bringing texture and depth to 1920s jazz through a more powerful rhythm section, a richer variety of tone colors, and a more subtle use of dynamics. Certainly the heavily arranged jazz of big-band swing also reflects the mass production of music, and reduces the jazz musician's individual freedom to specialized function.[37] As for the stripping of ornament to create clean, flowing lines, big-band arrangers eliminated the collective improvisation and raucousness of the New Orleans style in favor of smoothness, rhythmic flow, controlled masses (instrumental sections), and powerful motion. Music scholars often used the term "streamlining" to express the shift from 1920s jazz to big-band swing.

As for dance, the crucial new element in the lindy hop was a smooth motion located in the hips, a sense of horizontal flow that white Americans had a great deal of trouble mastering at first. Similarly, the "narrative" of a tap artist's solos derives from the rhythmic flow of individual sequences seamlessly sutured together, and the fluidity, precision, speed, and execution of clean lines.

Gazing at Rhythmic Mastery

A major factor in the aesthetic revolution of modernism in music, architecture, painting, and modern dance was the revaluation of rhythm in human existence: the biological rhythms of the body, the rhythmic line in art, the creation and maintenance of a driving rhythmic beat in music and dance. Prime instances were Stravinsky's *The Rites of Spring* (1913) and the Zuni-influenced rhythmic earth-stamping of Martha Graham's *Primitive Mysteries* (1931). Long devalued aesthetically in Western culture as equivalent to repetition, boredom, and elemental simplicity, rhythm was associated with uncontrolled sexuality and a lack of self-control. For this reason, many scholars and historians still cannot literally see (or hear) the aesthetic elements in jazz and jazz dance.

But the half-century after the Civil War saw the emergence of several new theoretical schools of physical movement. Two of them—the Dalcroze system (of Emile Jacques-Dalcroze) and the Alexander technique (of F. Matthias Alexander)—are still taught today; the former remains a popular method for training dancers, the latter a more rarefied approach to self-conscious body awareness, which John Dewey, for example, practiced his entire adult life. A third, the Delsarte system (of François Delsarte), was the theoretical basis for the dance strategies of Ted Shawn and Martha Graham, and Ned Wayburn used it to train the chorus lines of the Ziegfeld Follies. Championed by modern dancers searching for ways to reinvigorate white bodies in the face of industrialization and Victorian emotional repression, these rhythm theorists are not quaint figures from a bygone era. The dances and kinesthetic movements of Euro-American bodies looked old in the face of modernity, and it was dancers who first perceived the need for a new kinesthetic. For themselves and their audiences, modern dancers gravitated to a new grammar of physical gesture, graceful motion, and mind/body integration. This *lack* in white culture is one motivating force for what has been named "primitivism."

The vogue for primitivism went hand in hand with the alienation from industrial imperatives. Lewis Mumford perceived the relationship between bodies and machines, between primitivism and the technical civilization. Intellectuals, artists, and the "mechanically disciplined urban masses" of the civilized world needed to counter the increasing rationalization of machine imperatives with a more emotional, expressive range of physiological activity; Americans found "the machine, which acerbically denied the flesh, was offset by the flesh." They found relief in sex, social dance, folk arts, sculpture, and "the erotic music of the African negro tribes." For Mumford, "negritude" was the flip side of the machine worship of Italian Futurists and French architects, and "the Congo maintained the balance against the motor works and the subway." But Mumford himself could not see rhythm except as boring repetition, so he perceived only the opposition of black dance and technology, not the dialogue or the critique.[38] As the historian Lewis Erenberg has noted about swing, "Awareness of the African roots of black music may be widespread today, but in 1938 it was still uncommon."[39]

In the 1920s, by performing modernized plantation dances such as the Charleston or the Black Bottom, Americans broke down encrusted patterns of stiff movement and emotional repression. "Looseness . . . is an essential characteristic of jazz dance," a dance scholar asserts. "Hips, shoulders, wrists and ankles should be free to engage in . . . loose-limbed, carefree . . . improvisational action."[40] These 1920s dances energized all the limbs and shifted the center of gravity downward to the hips from the chest or solar plexus of the waltz and ballet. They were sexual, energetic dances to a jerky, nervous two-beat, in direct opposition to the smooth, clean lines of machine aesthetics.

By the early 1930s, however, the best tap dancers (John Bubbles, Fred Astaire, Jack Donahue, and Bill "Bojangles" Robinson) had incorporated the smoothness, speed, precision, and rhythmic continuity of machine aesthetics. Throughout the decade, led by the child-actor Shirley Temple, Americans rushed to learn tap. At the same time, the lindy hop (or jitterbug) synthesized energy *and* control, pattern and improvisation; black and white dancers alike came to embody the kinds of theoretical principles then being taught by Dalcroze, Alexander, and others. Black dance was in such demand between 1910 and 1940 (and met with such resounding response) because here were artistic, aesthetic, and kinesthetic survival skills for human participation.

Scholars have recently reclaimed rhythm as an aesthetic force of cultural expertise and continuity within a long, venerable tradition of music and dance. Rhythm re-energizes the body and creates the conditions for participatory activity, kinesthetic lightness, and grooving. "The power of the rhythm [surges] through the body, energizing and vitalizing all its parts," the musicologist Jon Michael Spencer explains. "All other aspects are anchored by its solidity, stability, and repetitiveness. It is not enough merely to hear the groove; you must be drawn inside it, and it must penetrate to your inner core."[41] To engage machine aesthetics, Americans of all ethnicities appropriated a West African-derived cultural aesthetic. The elements of such a specifically Afrodiasporic cultural aesthetic as articulated through music and dance practices have recently been analyzed by the American Studies scholar Gena Caponi-Tabery: (1) rhythmic and metric complexity; (2) individual improvisation and stylization; (3) call-and-response—that is, active engagement of the whole person and the whole community; (4) social commentary or competition through indirection and satire; and (5) development of a group consciousness or sensibility.[42] And, of course, rhythm has remained the sine qua non of American popular music, from ragtime to hip-hop.

"I got rhythm/I got music/I got rhythm/who could ask for anything more." Ethel Merman launched her career with this song, the show-stopper of the 1930 Gershwin musical, *Girl Crazy*. But it was only one of literally hundreds of songs between the wars that spoke of rhythm as a kind of magic elixir that would help Americans survive the Machine Age through participatory activity.[43] Why was rhythm the *élan vital* itself? Because rhythmic activities presume participation, body-centered motion, hand-clapping, dancing, singing. One listens to symphonies; one dances to rhythm.

Let me return to Havelock Ellis's idea of dancing and building as poles of modernist engagement. Herbert Muschamp recently summed up the modernism of New York's cityscape as beholden to an ideal of "escaping gravity and heaviness without losing touch with the ground"—as, for example, in the Brooklyn Bridge, the Chrysler Building, and the Seagram Building.[44] But what of the *human* structure? The regrounding of what Julia Foulkes calls "modern bodies" came through the global impact of African American dance.[45] African dance is earth-centered: one faces the ground, not the heavens as in ballet; the dancer uses all parts of the body, not just arms and legs; vigorous African shoulder and hip movements energize the body, and the angular bending of knees and elbows symbolize engagement with everyday life. What Barbara Glass calls the "Africanization of American movement"—the (white) embrace of rhythmic fluidity, hip-centered motion, individual creativity within a set pattern, and the loose carriage of the body—reached a certain peak during the swing era.[46]

How could people participate in technoscapes? By dancing the industrial changes generated by big-band swing machines into their individual systems. One contemporary writer who heard the interplay among big bands, human bodies, and machines was Otis Ferguson, the jazz critic of the *New Republic*. Upon leaving a Benny Goodman show in New York in December 1936, Ferguson recalled that he could still hear the music "ringing under the low sky" and pulsating beneath his feet, "as if it came from the American ground under these buildings, roads, and motorcars (which it did)." The Goodman band created a "clangor in the ears" that pumped "the air . . . full of brass and of rhythms you can almost lean on." The veteran swing bassist Gene Ramey riffed on the big-band machine this way: "No [big] band was great unless it had a strong rhythm section. It had to have a motor."[47]

In combining the fields of popular culture, intellectual history, African American music and dance, modernism, and the history of technology, I acknowledge an immense intellectual debt to Ralph Ellison's and Albert Murray's analyses of the functions of black music in this period. I owe the greatest debt, however, to jazz musicians. In swing's aesthetic power and communication, and through the commentaries of Sidney Bechet, Jo Jones, Gene Krupa, Duke Ellington, and the musicians of the Count Basie Orchestra, I became aware of a musico-philosophical pragmatism at the core of pre-bebop jazz. Swing musicians crystallized an emergent aesthetic tradition of American Machine Age modernism; in so doing, they created a genuine popular art that mediated the need for both accommodation and resistance to the technological society.

Jazz, Cities, and Machines

More than seventy years after its creation, big-band swing remains "the music nobody knows."[48] The triumvirate of jazz, cities, and machines was a cliché between the world wars and is the key to what Lewis Erenberg calls "the rebirth of American culture" in the swing era. Classical musicians, music teachers, clergy, and cultural guardians of the 1920s repudiated jazz for its fast tempos and rough sounds.[49] But many Americans (and Europeans) frankly admired jazz's ability to capture the feel and spirit of urban, industrial life. In an obscure short book on jazz called *Syncopating Saxophones* (1925), one symphony musician observed that "jazz is . . . the music of new cities. . . . It is the music of hot-dog wagons and elevated trains, the music of morning papers published at nine in the evening, the music of the quick lunch and the signboard and the express elevator." A fellow classical musician added, "It is the spirit of today, of us. It is jazz. . . . It is the fact about which our theorists have no theory."[50] Here's my theory.

West African–derived musical practices assume a sociocultural imperative to integrate all the sounds and rhythms in the natural landscape into the percussive mix. In other words, African and Afrodiasporic musicians make sense of the universe through the medium of sound, and the aesthetic element of rhythm; machines were simply another kind of rhythm to integrate. The previously unappreciated qualities of aesthetic beauty which machines brought into industrial society were speed, precision, flow, power, and continuity.[51] All are hallmarks of West African dance and drumming, and all have become trademarks of American vernacular music. Thus the success of big-band swing and dance was due to the *machine aesthetics* inside the music: again, *power, drive, precision, repetition, reproducibility, smoothness.* Le Corbusier contended that only Americans had a taste for precision in art in the 1930s, as he watched numerous audiences galvanized by big bands and tap dancers: "In America, the rigor of exactitude . . . is a pleasure."[52]

Swing's speed, power, and drive helped reenergize a sense of human capacity in a period of machine worship, both through watching musicians and dancers and through participation. Siegfried Giedion famously suggested that the assembly line was the dominant image of American life between the world wars. In its relentless, continuous motion were the assets and liabilities of what contemporaries simply called "the machine": quiet, controlled power, but monotonous repetition; continuous rhythmic flow, but also large-scale integration that isolated workers as cogs in *its* network; high-paying jobs, but menial, repetitive work. During the same period, swing music and dance constituted significant social practices of cultural resistance that helped Americans regain a sense of their own individual bodies set against assembly line realities. In dancing, we not only adapt our bodies to new environments, but "create" new bodies by becoming aware of our movements, strengths, possibilities, and limitations.[53]

What cultural resources and historical contingencies influenced the creation of swing music and dance? Owing to their lack of control over land and even of their own bodies in slavery, African Americans created *portable* cultural forms such as music, dance, and slang—a set of mobile structures that Cornel West calls "New World African Modernity." During slavery, blacks were faced with an enemy whose ideology was dependent upon the racial unity of whiteness. Despite the diversity of African cultures, slaves were seen as simply "black," and this forced them to distill a set of African-derived pidgin languages for speech, music, and dance. Out of the contributions of hundreds of African peoples, black Americans created a core set of modern African *American* cultural forms based on unifying rhythms and sounds. The dance scholar Katrina Hazzard-Gordon has shown that cultural kinship was first worked out in the antebellum period in response to the "universal influence" of "king cotton." Cotton culture "synchronized bondsmen's work rhythms across previously diverse regions . . . affected language by adding to the daily vocabulary, daily routines and yearly schedules . . . and modified the tools as well as the materials from which the folk culture was created." Nathan Huggins says of this period of African Americanization that slaves "help[ed] create a new world . . . becom[ing] the founding fathers and mothers of a new people."[54] The southern black vernacular culture codified by the 1890s was then transformed during the black migration of 1910–40, and during that period tap and the lindy hop represented a move away from the plantation dances of cotton culture to the machine aesthetics of the urban, industrial North.

Between 1870 and 1939 African American musicians created a set of propulsive rhythmic idioms—ragtime, blues, New Orleans jazz—that eventually smoothed out to a steady 4/4 rhythm which today undergirds nearly every form of Western popular music. The first and third beats of a bar were emphasized in brass-band marching music and ragtime, while the second and fourth beats of a bar were stressed in the blues and black church music. The Count Basie Orchestra best synthesized these two rhythmic approaches—seen as "eastern" and "western" by Basie's drummer Jo Jones—into a 4/4 in which each quarter beat was articulated by the drummer, bassist, and guitarist. What became the national beat was perfected by Kansas City jazz musicians in the early 1930s, where the Basie band developed a tempo so steady and physiologically satisfying that it was quickly "picked up by musicians elsewhere as if it had been in the public domain all along." The "inexhaustible 4/4" was a tempo created in dialogue with public dance needs and the industrial soundscape, and it is an American masterwork, copied the world over. Musicians did not create the swing pulse out of "the direct expression of personal feelings," as primitivists would have it; these musicians grew up within a West African–derived cultural aesthetic based on rhythmic mastery and manipulation. Albert Murray insists that "African drummers had to serve a long period of rigidly supervised apprenticeship before being entrusted with such an awesome responsibility as carrying the beat!" Swing tempo is an African American stylization of the concept of "industrial time"; in fact, when jazz musicians today say, "Play straight time," they mean the steady, balanced 4/4 perfected in the swing era.[55]

Among the many narratives of the 1870–1939 industrial epoch there are two that run parallel to each other, like train tracks. The first is the story of the industrial revolution and technological innovation, with its attendant centralization and urbanization. The second is the cultural influence of the black migration. Southern African Americans went north (and west) and in the process of defining themselves as Americans created the nation's portable cultural forms; they drew on Afrodiasporic cultural practice, their own historical experience, the promise of social equality, and the excitement of a vibrant industrial American society. In making sense of their new soundscape, African American musicians and dancers used the sounds and symbology of the train journey to create a rhythmic center for American music. In this book I explore an ongoing dialogue between white technology and black culture during a period that "mark[ed] the rise of an entire people."[56] If "speed was the cry of the era" for Machine Age artists and designers, then "jazz it up"— i.e., speed it up, make it more lively—was the response of African American musicians.[57]

Euro-Americans did not realize their primal need for powerful, portable cultural forms until the combination of an economic depression and fears of overmechanization dulled the national faith in progress. The union of the nation's messianic impulse with technological progress was first consummated in the antebellum era. As the nation became united through canal building, railroads, and interstate business growth, mill owners, political leaders, and civic leaders created a rhetoric of productivity to rationalize their industrial wealth under the rubric "Christian stewardship."[58] Significantly, the first utopian writings began in the antebellum period, drawing on technological invention, steam power, and interstate commerce; the vision of American resources changed from a "closed system" of farmers and scarce land to an "open system" of abundance and manufacturing.[59] J. B. Jackson uses the image of the "pilgrim" (from John Bunyan's *Pilgrim's Progress*) to show the transformation in national consciousness from individual salvation to technological redemption. Where once Americans envisioned themselves as lone Christian pilgrims on an arduous journey in the hope of personal salvation, now technology would bring salvation en masse if Americans would simply meet science halfway. I call this melding of technology and religion "techo-progress."[60]

In 1934 Lewis Mumford labeled the nation's machine worship a "mechanical faith," or simply, our "mechano-religion." After the Civil War, during the "age of energy" (1865–1915), so many inventions, energy sources, and technological innovations came into industrial society (car, telephone, airplane, electricity, cinema) that hope for the future became secularized into technological futurism. Christian hopes for human perfection became transmuted into machine dreams of redemption; the paradigmatic text for these cultural tensions is Edward Bellamy's novel *Looking Backward* (1888). Bellamy's protagonist, Julian West, time-travels to the Boston of 2000, a city where mass production has eliminated hunger, poverty, dirt, disease, and menial work, and yet no machines are visible; the individual "pilgrim's progress" had been transmuted into the social faith I call techno-progress. During the Depression, however, Americans attacked "technological unemployment" as a crucial factor in their loss of purpose and livelihood. The composer W. C. Handy astutely observed in 1941, "We [African Americans] have known for years how to laugh under trying circumstances, how to go on living with nothing but song to sustain us. But it took a woeful depression to teach this trick to white America." David Stowe has convincingly shown that Euro-Americans drew more on black culture in the swing era than at any time since blackface minstrelsy a century earlier.[61]

To simplify a bit, for effect, in this seventy-year industrial period Euro-Americans created the nation's *technology* while African Americans created the nation's *survival technology*. Albert Murray uses the term "survival technology" in passing; I develop it here as a critical term for American expressive culture.[62] Survival technology consists of public rituals of music, dance, storytelling, and sermonizing that create a forum for existential affirmation through physicality, spirituality, joy, and sexuality—"somebodiness," as some African American preachers call it—against the dominant society's attempts to eviscerate one's individuality and cultural heritage. In the "Saturday night function," for example, African Americans created a special secular space—a weekly suspension of social convention—to reclaim their bodies from the boss and "the Man," to enjoy emotional release and experimentation, to assert their "somebodiness" in a world that daily denied it. At a time when the nation's clergy and cultural observers were still suspicious of frivolous enjoyment, this ritual was "to be enjoyed solely as an end in itself."[63] Just as important, African American musicians and dancers could not revert to any specific folk tradition since there was no cohesive African past to hang onto; they played and danced the tempo of the time, and created the future in (musical) time and (physical) space.

In the late 1940s a few cultural historians picked up on the dialogic relationship between black music and the industrial revolution. In *Made in America* (1948), John Kouwenhoven claimed that Louis Armstrong and Benny Goodman had solved the single most challenging problem of "industrial organization"—the relationship of the individual to the group—with the artistic model of the big band. It presented opportunities for individual soloing, precise section playing, and contributions to collective drive. In *Jazz: A People's Music* (1948), Sidney Finkelstein argued that in jazz, black musicians rebelled against being deprived of a voice in the society; jazz was the "free, creative and humanly expressive music" set against "the chains of mechanical production." The music was a group rebellion against intransigent racism and demoralizing work, but it also allowed solos in which the music "bears the stamp of his [the musician's] mind and personality." However astute these observations, Kouwenhoven ignored the importance of dance to the music's power (and its very creation), and Finkelstein set the individual against the mechanical, a trope of jazz scholarship that still prevents scholars from hearing the train power in big-band swing.[64]

The links among jazz, machines, cities, and modern bodies have since been lost to scholars, as is evident in recent cultural histories of swing. In *Swing Changes* (1994), David W. Stowe expands our historical understanding of swing's cultural context and social practices, as explored through "audience, performance context, ideology, and mass media." In *Swingin' the Dream* (1998), Lewis Erenberg provides a corrective to jazz history that has cast swing as a commercialized, less artistic form of jazz. Swing was a vernacular musical culture emphasizing "central American values": "spontaneity, individual freedom, and group cooperation . . . [the] antidote to urban, machine-driven, and success-obsessed New York."[65] Neither work discusses mass production or technology, or explores the African American cultural practices and aesthetics inside these art forms. When Berndt Ostendorf claims that "jazz is the idiom of American modernism," he refers more to literary modernism and the increasing visibility and influence of jazz than to the everyday experience of Machine Age modernity. Jazz was not only the nation's popular music for nearly four decades (if one includes ragtime);

it was the nation's representative artistic form internationally. Only American mass production and technology impressed Europeans more than jazz as a thrilling, terrifying cultural force in the world.[66]

In Whitney Balliett's famous phrase, jazz is "the sound of surprise." Besides improvisation, the essential elements of jazz are rhythmic flow and flexibility, two hallmarks of all modernist art at the turn of the century. "The secret at the heart of all jazz is rhythm," Will Friedwald offers in *Jazz Singing*, "[and] keeping in time, in jazz, is even more important than keeping in tune." In saying a singer can "swing," Friedwald defines a jazz musician as one "[who] can get tremendous effects out of the most subtle beat manipulations—dropping behind the pulse puts that extra spin on the ball for a ballad, racing ahead of the band makes an up-tempo number that much hotter." Such improvisation puts audiences on alert: you must be prepared to follow the band wherever it goes. In other words, such rhythmically sophisticated music, by its very nature, puts audiences literally and figuratively on their toes.[67]

If ever Kenneth Burke's famous definition of philosophical practice—"the dancing of an attitude"—had national implications and embodied form, it was during the period Reyner Banham once dubbed "the jazz decades."[68] The seemingly unrelated designations, the swing era (1930–45) and the Machine Age (1919–45), need to be considered together.

Taking the "A" Train to Tomorrowland

This book is not a history of the industrial period from 1865 to 1939, but an inquiry into the strategies and symbols that sustained national identity in a period of rapid social, technological, and cultural change. The musicologist Christopher Small argues that African Americans were the first modern people in the world. "Africans . . . enslaved in the New World were the first of the world's peoples to experience the full dehumanizing impact of modern industrialism." It is not simply that Africans were violently uprooted and dislocated from a preindustrial world and forced to perform alienating work in the service of an implacable enemy. In every New World colonial situation, Africans continually integrated their artistic and aesthetic traditions with those of the colonial powers they came in contact with, and in the process, constructed a functional culture for industrial society. I am suggesting here a reconsideration of a cultural "American exceptionalism" through two fields in which vernacular accomplishment outpaced the world for a century: technological innovation and African American–derived popular culture.[69]

In the first half of this book I put early jazz musicians into historical, artistic, and technological context, and in the second, jazz and commercial dance and dancers. In chapter 1 I explore the fear of over-mechanization rampant in the 1930s. I have identified a tempo-of-life discourse among liberal intellectuals and artists who wondered if the restless, speeded-up American tempo would obliterate human dynamics. I suggest that jazz musicians provided the solution of swing tempo to this social problem. If the tempo of life was out of control, as many writers claimed, the masters of tempo reined in the abundant new energies and focused them on the dance floor.

In chapter 2 I discuss how jazz musicians put a specific machine—the train—into the music, and I analyze the stylization of its power, drive, repetition, and flow into a veritable musical grammar. Big-band swing's totemic symbol was the train, and blues guitarists, female blues vocalists, country harmonica players, boogie-woogie pianists, tap dancers, swing drummers, and arrangers all found creative ways to employ "locomotive onomatopoeia." As an anthropologist once observed, "Man echoes the soundscape in speech and music."[70]

In chapter 3 I theorize a cultural tradition of resistance to technology in African American expressive culture, including folk tales and toasts, blues songs and performative practices: what I call the techno-dialogic. I also suggest a few ways in which the function of ritual in West African societies might have provided some basic philosophical premises and cultural practices for African American musicians. From the man vs. machine inquiry of "The Ballad of John Henry" to the full-throttle sonic barrage of Ellington's "Daybreak Express," I examine the symbiotic relationship of machine aesthetics and individual artistic power in the African American oral tradition.

In chapter 4 I explore the impact of two public symbols that manifested the human-machine interface and caught the industrial zeitgeist: streamliner trains and big bands. Buoyed by Franklin Delano Roosevelt's leadership, Americans needed new symbols of industrial power to show their renewed faith in the future. Streamliners and swing music burst upon the national scene in 1934–35, and the humanized machine aesthetics inherent in these icons were a major factor in their popularity.

In chapters 5 and 6 I analyze the enormous success of two separate pop-cultural displays of modern bodies rhythmically engaged with machine aesthetics. On the one hand, the aesthetics of mass production and industrial organization underlie the chorus lines and fast pacing of the Ziegfeld Follies and the musicals of Busby Berkeley. In these female-powered dynamos, the individual element is an anonymous beautiful woman lacking both identity and voice who is pressed into service as a cog in a pleasure machine that produces fables of abundance. The antithesis of Ziegfeld's and Berkeley's luxurious tableaux was the individual tap dancer who rivets an audience's attention with only his or her body and the sound of rhythmic metallic taps on wood or a Bakelite floor. Fred Astaire and Bill Robinson synthesized several traditions to show that being "human" is about grace, humor, balance, improvisation, surprise, and flow—and not just menial work, industrial time, and consumerism. The inquiry that first took shape with John Henry—what is human vs. what is machine—is restaged in a challenge dance between Fred Astaire and a series of three machines in *Shall We Dance?* (1937). In this rhythmic dialogue Astaire shows exactly how American artists had learned to swing their machines.

One path by which the elements of Astaire's victory can be seen in American youth culture is through the impact of the lindy hop, the subject of chapter 7. At Harlem's Savoy Ballroom, Whitey's Lindy Hoppers, a group of teen-aged dancers, brought machine aesthetics to black dance, combining smooth, horizontal motion, fast tempos, quick spins, torque, and aerial flips in a dynamic dance requiring precise timing and control; the Savoy was a tourist "must" in the 1930s, in part for their artistic display. I analyze the lindy's enthusiastic reception at the Harvest Moon Ball, an annual amateur dance contest at Madison Square Garden that started in 1935. Hosted by Ed Sullivan, the ball was a major cultural event attended by movie stars, and dancers were judged by prestigious dance impresarios. By 1943 Betty Grable concluded her overseas USO show every night by jitterbugging with a different soldier.

The concept of "embodiment," as discussed by cognitive anthropologists, focuses attention on "a return to the sensuous quality of lived experience." In other words, acculturation between groups during cultural crises will have physiological consequences. According to Berendt Ostendorf, the literary term "mimesis" (meaning imitation or representation) originally meant "the incorporation of the Other through dance"; surely this is a process that recurs every generation in American youth culture (for instance in ragtime, jazz, swing, rock and roll, funk, and hip-hop). "What is embodied is always some set of meanings, values, tendencies, orientations, that derived from the sociocultural realm." Europeans often comment that white Americans move and speak more like blacks than like Europeans, and this appropriation of African American aesthetics and kinesthetics needs to be seen as a crucial cultural exchange.[71] The popularity of dance between 1910 and 1945 signals a cultural (and physical) hunger for rhythmic engagement in response to the industrial landscape, and Americans chose to incorporate African American aesthetics and kinesthetics into their mindful bodies.

Chapter 8 is a case study of the dialogue between technology and survival technology at the New York World's Fair of 1939–40. Known for its motto, "The World of Tomorrow," this fair is well known to cultural historians for its technological utopianism and for the "Futurama" exhibit of General Motors (a giant diorama of a suburban future complete with superhighways). But many visitors felt the fair was too serious and elitist; it spoke *to* them, not for them, and there were complaints about a lack of spaces to relax, dance, listen to music, or get a cheap meal. As E. B. White observed drily, "Gaiety is not the keynote of Tomorrow. . . . There is no talking back in Tomorrow."[72] I tell the stories of two buildings—the Hall of Music and the Savoy Ballroom—to highlight the popularity of swing culture. I will show why big-band swing, the lindy hop, and tap dance should be considered artistic hits of the fair as human-powered exhibits whose popularity subverted the messages of technological utopianism.

Throughout this book I discuss the factors that have blocked the recognition and celebration of what W. E. B. Du Bois called the "gifts" of African American culture. In 1933 the American composer George Antheil suggested that a "racial terror" gripped European artists in the mid-1920s as they began to realize the modernist debt owed to African and African American music, dance, art, sculpture, and performative ideas.[73] An even stronger American backlash occurred in 1943: the brutal treatment of black GIs in the American army; race riots in several American cities; the "whitefacing"—and thus, economic takeover—of big-band swing and the lindy hop, and consequent loss of jobs among black musicians and dancers; the temporary closing of the Savoy Ballroom; the abrupt elimination of tap from Broadway and film due to a backlash from teachers and performers of modern dance and ballet. And in 1947, readers of *Downbeat* voted to rename jazz "crewcut music" or "Ameri-music," a clear signal of white America's inability to cope with their African American cultural roots.

Many cultural observers and musicians referred to the explosive popularity of swing music and dance as "swing religion," and I wish to oppose that term to Mumford's idea of the nation's "mechano-religion." Through a public display of individual expression and collective drive within a precisely drilled 14-to-18-man unit; through a fusion of musical communication, improvisation, grace, humor, and style into a powerful, dynamic sound; through the model of African American dances (and dancers) that encouraged the physical participation of audiences in this dance-hall ritual, vital aspects of human life returned to American culture. Big-band swing music and dance humanized the cold, rational, machine-world created and fetishized by technical, corporate, and even artistic elites in the early twentieth century.

The historian Warren Susman suggests that the representative figure of the 1930s was Mickey Mouse, not Franklin Roosevelt. Then at the cutting edge of cinematic technology, Mickey Mouse—as a symbol—is simply a white face on a black body, a totemic figure who is as innocent (and white) as Euro-Americans see themselves, yet as agile and resilient (and black) as African Americans were in the 1930s. In "The Sorcerer's Apprentice" sequence from *Fantasia* (1940), Mickey seems overwhelmed by the constant changes in the environment he has willed, the consequences of technological magic. Technological change is out of control, and so is the tempo of life. Helpless to control these changes, Mickey is eventually rescued by the Sorcerer himself. But between 1935 and 1945 Americans engaged machine aesthetics through the primal human cultural forms of music and dance. Mickey Mouse represents this generation's survival and the "white-facing" of the nation's democratic arts—a term used by a music scholar as early as 1930 to refer to "a phenomenon . . . almost as old as the nation itself."[74] Perhaps Mickey Mouse continues to thrive as an unconscious tribute to the Machine Age black-white composite of technology and survival technology.

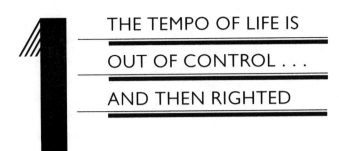

THE TEMPO OF LIFE IS
OUT OF CONTROL . . .
AND THEN RIGHTED

In the early 1920s Henry Ford called for Americans to forsake jazz
dances and bring back the European dances of the nineteenth century
(for example, the waltz, quadrille, schottische, and square dance). Ford
imagined that he could separate the private, residential sphere from the
public, industrial one: that engagement with machine aesthetics and
power in the latter might mean a desire for old-fashioned relaxation in
the former. As radical as Ford was in bringing modernity into American
mass production and mass consumption, his conservative, *anti*modern
ideas did not resonate outside of upper-class white elites, and in retrospect they can be considered cranky and reactionary (akin to his anti-
Semitism).[1] Chronicler Mark Sullivan astutely perceived that Ford's
dance activism was literally out of step with the times and his own products. "The very fiber of America seem[s] to have been *attuned to a new
tempo,* to which the Model T was more adapted than the graceful sweep
of the quadrille."[2]

In his 1931 study of the phenomenon of this new American tempo,
The Tempo of Modern Life, the historian James Truslow Adams wrote that
the average American now experienced "*more sensations and of a more varied sort*" than preindustrial human beings. Drawing on industrial research, Adams suggested that because sensory inputs had increased in
volume and pace, Americans now reacted and processed changes more
quickly. Americans made "*a far greater number of adjustments to the universe*"
every day, resulting in a "speeding-up process in human life." This was
his definition of "modern life," and this information barrage and subsequent adaptation remain primary indices of modernity. Adams speculated that the "mental life" of Americans had increased to four times

its previous rate, "each time the wave length of the force growing shorter, the vibration more rapid." This "speeding-up process" had become "embedded in the universe."[3]

Americans would have to adjust their mental and physical rhythms to the new tempo. "A change in rhythm, whatever it may be in reality," Adams wrote, "is for us a change in essential nature." Indebted to a scarcity theory of human energy, Adams believed that the individual human body, as processing unit, had reached its capacity for taking in new information. Since the nation's business culture was aligned, for better or worse, with scientific progress, Adams began to have apocalyptic fears: "Scientific discovery . . . cannot be halted without a complete collapse of our civilization." His only hope was that new technology and new sources of energy might solve the very problems they had caused. "We must now go on, seeking new inventions, new sources of power, or crash—a civilization in a nose dive."[4]

Adams's focus on technology, cognition, and physiology as sites of industrial modernity differs from the intellectual discourse derived from Marx, Baudelaire, or Walter Benjamin, all of whom concentrate on the loss of individuality, community, and dignified labor. The machinery was "the master," according to Marx, and the worker an "automaton" within an efficient industrial organization controlled by scientists and engineers. In the factory system, it is "the movements of the machine that he [the worker] must follow." Marx does note "the speed with which machine work is learnt by young people," suggesting that bodies adapt to mechanical imperatives regarding tempo and repetitive motion, but there is no sense of physiological adaptation: the factory simply "transform[s] the worker, from his very childhood, into a part of a specialized machine." As technology is a tool of capitalist industry, it has no aesthetic attraction; "the machine" instead becomes the metaphor for social enslavement. The focus of European intellectual and political protest in the late 1800s thus becomes "the resistance of the individual to being . . . swallowed up in the social-technological mechanism." Until Filippo Marinetti's Futurist manifesto of 1909 celebrating "the beauty of speed," European intellectuals by and large did not address the aesthetic influence of machines on everyday life.[5]

In 1904 the American sociologist Thorstein Veblen called attention to "the *cultural* incidence of the machine process," implying a more open and ongoing set of changes. The culture-bearers were businessmen, whose ownership of technology put them at the cutting edge of modernity. Most new technologies of the late nineteenth century were first utilized for business purposes, either in urban office buildings (for example, the telephone, electricity) or at factories. But nearly all aspects of everyday American life were changed by machine processes: to adhere to the schedules of railroads undercut individual autonomy; mass-produced goods of "equal grade and gauge" eliminated the "rule of thumb" of handicraft; to use a telephone or telegraph was to participate in communication networks that deemphasized the nuance of language for the facts of the message.[6] Due to the influence of industrial capitalism, the tempo and flow of human life had been transformed.

> To make effective use of the modern system of communication in any or all of its ramifications (streets, railways, steamship lines, telephone, telegraph, postal service, etc.), men are required to adapt their needs and their motions to the exigencies of the [machine] process. . . . The service is standardized, and therefore the use of it is standardized also. Schedules of time, place, and circumstance rule throughout. The scheme of everyday life must be arranged with a strict regard to the exigencies of the [machine] process.[7]

For Veblen, workers were not slaves but "attendants" or "assistants" to machines, and such constant exposure to "regularity of sequence and mechanical precision" taught mental discipline and concentration (for better or worse). Those who worked with machines had to learn "to keep pace with the machine process"; following Veblen, Mumford noted that Americans had developed "the mechanical habit of mind."[8]

In the same period, the machine worship of middle-class white American males was at its peak, as revealed in popular culture. The engineer was a cultural hero in popular fiction throughout the industrial period, and John Kouwenhoven claims that as early as the 1870s "mechanization was an American folkway." Marshall Berman points to the original name of baseball's Brooklyn Dodgers—the Brooklyn Trolley-Dodgers—as an instance of the urban American dialectic of resistance and accommodation to machines. I take my cue from the historian John Kasson, who shows convincingly how at Coney Island Americans mediated their overly mechanized jobs by engaging industrial objects for dynamic leisure. For example, coal carts were put into service as roller-coasters and gear-wheels enlarged into ferris wheels.[9] In 1928 Carl Jung theorized that the international popularity of jazz and jazz dance were manifestations of the need for individuals to physically adapt to "the Western world['s] . . . more rapid tempo—the rapid *American* tempo."[10] The increased tempo of life—literally, the faster pace of everyday existence and work—had changed the quality of human life and consciousness.

Adams's *Tempo of Modern Life* is an integral part of what I call the "tempo-of-life discourse," a specific set of American responses that peaked in the early years of the Depression (1929–34).[11] Why did this musical term for "pace" emerge as a central trope for the most troubling aspects of American industrial life? What did cultural observers mean when they declared that the tempo of life was out of control?

They meant that the machine, a nonhuman element, was driving social change, and that the nation's priorities were set neither by its traditional leaders (clergy, intellectuals, politicians, artists) nor according to a traditional agrarian economy attuned to natural and seasonal rhythms. Cultural observers from John Dewey to Martha Graham commented that the faster American tempo of movement and thought reflected the presence of machines in the soundscape, at the workplace, and in transport networks (cars, trains, trolleys, trucks, elevators). Machine sounds and rhythms dominated the aural environment and helped ratchet up the pacing of American theater, film, and music. "The Machine Age has influenced practically everything . . . from the arts to finance," George Gershwin wrote in 1933, "[especially] in tempo, speed and sound."[12]

In this chapter I analyze the tempo-of-life discourse and its articulation of both the society's fears of mechanization and the need to integrate the power and presence of machines into cultural life, social consciousness, and individual physiological movement. Now what does the tempo of life mean at the individual level?

I'll start with a personal anecdote. I was born and raised in Brooklyn, New York, and after spending my undergraduate years in Buffalo I returned to Manhattan one late spring day by train. Walking on the streets, I felt knocked around by New Yorkers; I had adapted to a slower tempo and sparser street life, and Manhattan seemed fast, harsh, and abrupt. I sat down to reflect on the experience at a coffee shop, and I realized that I was simply not "in gear"—that was the term that came to mind. I was depressed to be out of step with my hometown, but the solution was easy: I threw myself into a different, forward gear and bopped back onto the street.

Getting into the New York groove required changes in the posture and motion of my whole body. My head tilted forward off my torso and I looked toward the earth rather than the sky or straight ahead. I was bent more at the knees, walking in a more crouchlike position. There was more of a bounce to my step—that vertical head-to-toe walking flow we used to call "the New York bop." In this new position, my body was poised and ready for quick tempo shifts, to sprint across streets ahead of cars and red lights, to slip fluidly through crowds yet be able to slam to a halt to avoid someone. This position recalls basketball players at the tip-off: mentally alert, partly crouched, and ready to spring in any direction depending on where the ball goes. This set of in-body techniques was an important piece of my Brooklyn cultural heritage; I learned them growing up on the streets by imitating others and responding to fast cars and pedestrian traffic. You had to be *thinking* about walking to surf the city's concrete terra firma; you had to be *aware* of all the flowing movement around—people, cars, sudden shifts—and be able to adapt to the changes.

The vernacular phrase "a New York minute" is not simply a metaphor but an expression of felt experience. In *A Geography of Time* (1997), the sociologist Robert Levine demonstrated that every city has a different tempo, comprising work rhythms, "cultural values," the degree of industrialization, the "speed of the [local] economy," "concern with clock-time," and the relationship of work to play. Levine measured cities by timing individuals in their daily rounds: by their speech patterns, walking speed, driving speed, work pace, and, for example, the length of time it took before people became irritated by waiting. He identified five factors that contribute to a fast cultural tempo: people move faster in places "with vital economies, a high degree of industrialization, larger populations, cooler climates, and a cultural orientation toward individualism."[13] New York City qualifies on all counts.

In studying the rhythm of New York, Levine found that the city's inhabitants assume a more rapid pace in movement, in quick business exchanges, in response to new stimuli. New Yorkers are proud of the rush of their lives; it makes them feel their lives are important, that they have places to go. They literally enjoy the *rush* of living, walking, being, speeding through New York.[14] On that day twenty years ago, for the first time, I felt the New York tempo as an outsider would. Luckily, I had an "overdrive" gear to shift into; I knew the terrain and the kinesthetic moves required to navigate it.

According to Levine, "first and foremost, the pace of life is a matter of tempo." The American urban tempo between the world wars derived from the new, seemingly abrasive soundscape of subways, cars, and trolleys, from the shared experience of factory work that demanded discipline, speed, and repetition, and from a more constant rush of sensory impressions (visual, aural, and physiological) to which human minds and bodies had to adapt.

Walt Whitman did not quite name the problem of tempo, but he called for Americans to integrate machines into their cultural traditions. In *Democratic Vistas* (1871) he praised the speed and power and "practical grandeur" of machines, but he worried about the soulless, relentless quality of machine-driven progress. Machines were creating a "restless wholesale kneading of the masses." He believed only poetry and the arts could stem the new forces of energy and materialism building at "steam-engine speed" across the country, and "everywhere turning out . . . generations of humanity like uniform iron castings." For there to be any meaning in American life, the forces of speed, standardization, and mechanization had to be met with a "tremendous force-infusion" of the arts for the "purposes of spiritualization . . . conscience, [and] for pure esthetics." If culture was unable to contain these new energies, the whole project of "our modern civilization . . . is in vain, and we are on the road to a destiny . . . of the fabled damned."[15]

Whitman's critique was picked up by Henry Adams in his famous essay "The Dynamo and the Virgin," and, after the creation of the assembly line in 1913, by those worried about the standardization of human beings slotted as mass-produced tenders of the factory system. Until the later tempo-of-life discourse, Whitman's call for an artistic engagement that admits an admiration for machines without conceding to their relentless force lay dormant. In 1933 Hart Crane updated Whitman's call for artistic engagement of technology, declaring the need for a new functional organic poetry. "Unless poetry can absorb the machine, i.e., *acclimatize* it as naturally and casually as trees, cattle . . . and all other human associations of the past, then poetry has failed of its contemporary function." Crane called on poets to create a new machine-based "architecture" of "contemporary human consciousness." Simple admiration of machine aesthetics did not amount to integration, as such "romantic speculation on the power and beauty of machinery keeps it at a continual remove."[16]

Crane's plea was echoed the following year by Alfred H. Barr, Jr., the director of the Museum of Modern Art. In announcing the 1934 exhibit of "Machine Art," Barr suggested that if "we are to 'end the divorce' between our industry and our culture we must assimilate the machine aesthetically as well as economically."[17] Philip Johnson, the curator of the exhibit, identified the same aesthetic elements in ball bearings and mass-produced silverware as were found in modern architecture: repetition, rhythm, beauty of surface, functionality. Johnson wrote in the exhibit catalog that a machine aesthetic always "implie[d] precision, simplicity, smoothness, reproducibility."[18] A primary objective of the Machine Art exhibit was to show the beauty of machines, but it was only accomplished by abstracting the products from their production systems of noise, motion, dirt, and labor.

Integrating machine aesthetics into human life would require a physiological adjustment—a new tolerance for speed, noise, and standardization. "There has been a change of tempo brought about by the machine," Martha Graham warily noted in "The American Dance" (1935), but it remained unanalyzed. Americans had embraced the machine-driven future without an "involved philosophy," and in the excitement of the age had "not yet arrived at a stock-taking stage." Graham was at a loss to explain how to adapt to the new pace, but she suggested that it was imperative to do so. "We can only express this tempo [right now]," she admitted, and she advised dancers to take into account this "characteristic time beat" as it spun the country into "a different speed."[19]

Graham specifically separated the American kinesthetic from all European articulations and from the angular, jagged movement of European machine dances of the 1920s (for example, Gertrude Bodenheiser's "The Demon Machine" and expatriate George Antheil's *Ballet Mécanique* [1926]).[20] For European dancers, according to the dance critic John Martin, the machine was "still a matter of wonder and excessive sentimentality," and so-called machine dances combined inharmonious, jagged rhythms with metallic costumes and jerky motions.[21] "Some sort of machine dance is a staple of every European dance repertory," Graham observed. "But to the American[,] sentimentality for the machine is a lie." For Americans, machines were tools with which to create their societies and themselves. For Graham, "the machine" was a fact of American life—unanalyzed, perhaps, but a permanent collaborator in society. "No American dance I know represents the machine. The dancer of America does not glorify mechanized movement, which so completely concerned the ballet. *He no longer considers protests against the mechanization of life.* He sees the machine as one of the many products of human skill, and then considers its work. This is simply one of the fundamental characteristics of our country." Like Whitman and Crane, Graham called for the integration of machine aesthetics and kinesthetic needs. "The machine is a natural phenomenon of life [for Americans]. . . . Make use of it. Suit it to our needs. Integrate it into our activities."[22]

Graham believed the nation's spirit was embodied in its cultural and kinesthetic choices. "The psyche of the land is to be found in its [physical] movement. It is to be felt as a dramatic force of energy and vitality. We move; we do not stand still. . . . In the dancer is to be mirrored the tempo and essential rhythm of his country." Any genuinely American dance needed to reflect this speeded-up, rootless, dynamic motion. Graham's response was to integrate the spare, pounding rhythms of the Shakers and the Indians of the Southwest, rejecting imitative mechanical rhythms for "narrow, stamping dancing that emphasized the polarity of earth and sky."[23] (She did not mention jazz dances of any type.)

To William Saroyan, the physical motions of Americans had become palpably mechanical. People imitated "implements, gadgets and so on," and "the machine rhythm runs through this whole age." The machine rhythm wasn't "a bad rhythm," just boring and lacking in beauty; its archetypal public display was "the kicking and turning of Follies girls," an anonymous chorus line of dancers who kicked out "the American rhythm, the tempo and calculation of American life."[24] Saroyan's 1939 play *The Time of Your Life* was a John Henry–type story whose climactic scene centers on a working-class kid trying to beat a pinball machine; the whole neighborhood cheers him on as if their humanity depended on this man vs. machine battle.

Sherwood Anderson frankly admired the machine's tempo in the controlled factory environment, where it "work[ed] so freely, so swiftly, so beautifully." The factory was a model of "absolute precision and order," with machines "mov[ing] at terrific speed." In comparison, the small factory towns were shabby, full of "cheaply constructed houses," the streets strewn with the refuse of mass production such as "rusty tin vegetable cans and old newspapers." He observed that southern farmers preferred mass-produced "cheap New York clothes" to handmade ones, canned food to fresh, and consumer goods (especially cars and radios) to farming and nature. Even small towns were "becom[ing] factory towns," he lamented. Anderson perceived a social challenge in the contrast between the "tired puzzled look in the eyes" of Americans and the awe-inspiring vision of controlled power in the factories. "The machine dominates American life," he concluded with a mixture of awe and trepidation.[25]

For John Dewey, this loss of individual control owing to the focus on "non-human modes of energy" and the industrial application of machinery "constitute[d] the 'modern.'" Dewey also argued in *Art as Experience* (1934) that society must contain mechanical forces through a more vital, energetic, participatory art manifested in daily life.[26] Similarly for Reinhold Neibuhr, the lack of integration between human-centered modes of thought and industrial organization was the basis of the "spiritual" malaise of the early 1930s, which he attributed to "the mechanization of modern life." It caused the "destruction of [the] religious imagination," and it fueled the more realistic but "essentially religious vision" of Communism.[27]

Even before the Depression added the factor of economic despair, Dewey believed the disruption of human needs by technological imperatives was the great problem of the age. "It is a commonplace that the problem of the relation of mechanistic and industrial civilization to culture is *the deepest and most urgent problem of our day.* [And] if interpreters are correct in saying that 'Americanization' is becoming universal, it is a problem of the world . . . although it is first acutely experienced here."[28] The economic effects of large-scale industrialization presented the nation with distinct social dilemmas requiring both a rearticulation of individual possibility and some sense of a shared unified culture. Dewey's famous dictum, "Science is the handmaiden of art," is a plea that needs to be historically contextualized.[29]

Lewis Mumford stated unequivocally that the challenge to human society of machine-driven progress was an issue of tempo.

> The problem of tempo: the problem of equilibrium: the problem of organic balance: in back of them all the problem of human satisfaction and cultural achievement—these have now become the critical and all-important problems of modern civilization. To face these problems, to evolve appropriate social goals . . . instruments for an active attack upon them . . . here are new outlets for social intelligence, social energy, social good will.

In 1934 Mumford was optimistic; he believed the speed-up would ease due to human correctives applied to a technical civilization. Society would find it "necessary to lower the tempo" to integrate an efficient lifestyle with an organic one. The rapid American tempo was the result of an exceptional period of technological innovation that would soon subside, leaving only "the temporary fact of increasing acceleration."[30] Yet seventy years later Americans continue to demand increased speed in business, entertainment, and electronics, as James Gleick has recently shown in his cultural survey, *Faster: The Acceleration of Just About Everything.*[31]

In *Taming Our Machines* (1931), the mechanical engineer Ralph Flanders dissented from these liberal critics and suggested that Americans passively accept the machine's accelerated pace. Any attempt to put a brake on technological innovation would be a disaster, he prophesied, and he called instead for a goal of constant acceleration. Besides, there was already an agent of technological adaptation in place: the automobile. "The whole habits of the race, the instinctive bodily reactions, have in a short generation been completely reconstructed to adapt them to the pace of these ubiquitous vehicles." Through driving, Americans developed a desire for fast tempos, an addiction to change, a taste for instant gratification, and a seemingly permanent restless quality. Americans would become attuned to their machines little by little, but in the meanwhile, "our only safety lies in perpetual advance, and that preferably at an accelerated rate."[32]

Intellectuals who embraced American society as a technical civilization in the 1920s were, by decade's end, challenged by the problem of creating a new set of human values to oppose to machine values. Charles Beard believed new artistic forms needed to contain the speeded-up energies of "power-driven machinery which transcends the physical limits of its human directors." Machine values were "highly dynamic," and technological innovation led to a social value placed on novelty and renewal and "contain[ed] within itself the seeds of constant reconstruction." In 1928 Beard was optimistic, as "the machine age is young," and he claimed to see all around him "signs of a new art appropriate to speed, mechanics, motion, [and] railway stations."[33]

Reflecting on the confluence of ideas around "time, work and tempo" between the world wars, the American sociologist Nels Anderson highlighted the 1920s writings of German historian Werner Sombart. For Sombart, "the tempo problem" emerged from urbanites responding to "the mechanized environment" and the sensory stimulus of "the inherent cosmopolitanism of modern life." The machine-driven tempo reflected a feverish effort to *feel* some kind of progress, and people hurried out of a compulsion to keep up. When slowed down, one felt guilty—or worse, inefficient. "This lust for activity [was] so great that the Western[er] seems without balance," Anderson wrote, "and the values of literature, art, and nature vanish into nothing." According to Sombart, in the 1920s, the Western[er] "ha[d] no time"—a compelling parallel to being "out of one's time," or out of step, a factor for both industrialists and workers. He ended his book with this admonition: "'Tempo! Tempo! That is the watchword of our time.'" What had started with the European obsession with clocks, and was ingrained through the Protestant values of thrift, hard work, and discipline, had come to influence monetary values, social values, and the very tempo of life.[34]

But if a person's "felt" time was out of sync with a new social rhythm, life became nervous, frantic, rushing, restless. Historians refer to the "nervous generation" of 1920s intellectual and social elites.[35] A later age would call this drive to attune one's subjective and social rhythms "the rat race." But as early as 1873 one German observer understood that the tempo of life was now dictated by the machine, and that citizens of industrial society had to get on board or be left behind. "The railways have the effect of great national clocks. . . . Clearly, he who wants to keep up in life has to leave behind all individual desires, place himself at the disposal of the fast pace, of the general conditions of the long-distance."[36]

Machines had in fact changed the very experience of time. In 1883 the railroad industry implemented a new temporal order—the "standard time" of our present four time zones. The new industrial order served a national transportation system increasingly reliant upon efficient connections for the distribution of people and goods. Neither Congress nor the clergy nor the popular vote created standard time; the new industrial order was literally railroaded into American lives by industrial fiat. (Congress passed accompanying legislation only thirty years later.) In service to the nation's largest and most influential machine, the sun officially lost its time-telling authority on November 18, 1883; that day, the sun's time conceded to "train time." The mechanical landscape superimposed its will on the natural, as church bells and courthouse clocks lined up behind the standard time kept at the local train station. William Carlos Williams rendered sunlight itself a prisoner in the wrought iron windows of large train terminals: "A leaning pyramid of sunlight . . . [even] moves by the clock."[37]

Clockwork was Western culture's ruling metaphor of creation itself in the industrial period (with God as clockmaker), and its dissemination became complete through the wristwatch. The clock gradually became an external monitor whose authority displaced the rhythms of the body.

"The cycle of the mechanical organism dispossesses that of the body; the heartbeat . . . loses its autonomy to the beat of the machine [that] . . . has to move with the regularity of a clock."[38] In the Machine Age, artistic attacks on the mechanical rigidity and efficiency of clocks were common: a huge factory clock dominates the opening credits of Chaplin's *Modern Times* (1936) and Harold Lloyd hangs from a large public clock that watches over a small town in *Safety First* (1923). Industrial time, business efficiency, and mechanical regularity were foreign—even alien—to human experience, according to such films. "There remains within the human heart a longing for the uncertain, the incalculable, the chaotic," Anthony Aveni reflected recently. In a world where "time is money," perhaps non-measured time might be considered "the sacred, symbolic turf . . . to which we might escape."[39]

By 1900 the machine's time—that of the train or the industrial clock's standard time—had taken precedence over the traditional agrarian and religious hours. The very time of day now adhered to man-made industrial rhythms; you were only "on time" if you wore or carried *a machine that manufactured time* on your wrist. When wearing a watch, an individual brings industrial time onto the body, marking one's self off from nature's time (and church time); the wristwatch is the first human-machine interface. Well before the assembly line created a workplace driven by machines, the needs of machines were privileged over those of human beings.

Howard P. Segal has coined the term "technological plateau" to refer to periods in which public demand for improvements of a "social, economic, cultural [and] political" nature outweighs its excitement over the products of technological progress.[40] Segal points to the anti-space-race rhetoric of the late 1960s and to the reaction in the late 1980s after the Challenger explosion, but I believe the early 1930s marked the first "technological plateau" in American history. The Depression temporarily ended the reign of mechanization and techno-progress as social doubt about the role of machines in the nation's future outran the cultural myths indebted to "technological futurism."[41] Polls showed that more than half of all Americans blamed machines for the economic depression and the phrase "technological unemployment" was a byword of the period. "There was . . . an ongoing sense that things were not quite right, in the natural order, in the moral order, in the technological order," according to Warren Susman, "and most especially in the relationships among them."[42]

In 1936 the prominent historian Carl Becker even declared the social doctrine known as "progress" to be moribund. Moreover, he asserted it had never been anything but an Enlightenment-derived secular religion whose apocalypse had arrived. The concept that "the world moves forward" toward some positive outcome or greater happiness had lost power for Americans; this loss of faith in progress also cast doubt upon associated concepts such as "process," "development," and "evolution." For two centuries, progress had been "a species of religion" that had muted the loss of faith in Christian salvation, but in the 1930s it was simply "a . . . philosophy of human destiny" with few believers outside of scientists.[43] Significantly, the early 1930s also marks the end of the first phase of utopian fiction and of the classic period of skyscraper building—cultural signs of a less confident techno-progress.

Industrial progress and scientific invention had reordered everyday existence without bringing happiness (or jobs); the concrete results of scientific materialism had cast doubt on the efficacy of religious forces to make sense of the world. One must feel "the 'reasonableness' of one's society . . . of its aims and methods," Kenneth Burke wrote in 1937, "[which] comes to a focus in symbols of authority"—all of which were in flux.[44] Massive unemployment and the collapse of business leadership in the early 1930s brought on a deep crisis deemed "spiritual" by many intellectuals. According to Frederick Lewis Allen, many of the nation's cultural myths died during the Depression, and dependable icons such as the businessman, the engineer, and the scientist lost their authority.[45] The loss of such icons can bring about what Clifford Geertz calls spiritual "chaos." Such a period is the result of "a tumult of events which lack not just interpretations but *interpretability* . . . [that leave a person] at the limits of his analytic capacities, at the limits of his powers of endurance, and at the limits of his moral insight."[46] It is a moment when society cannot explain itself to itself. By the mid-1930s, technological salvation, the assumed superiority of rational thinking, rugged individualism, and the idea of "civilization" itself were all under suspicion.

When Terry Smith and Siegfried Giedion refer to the assembly line as the dominant image of American society between the world wars, they draw attention to the workplace reality of people being subjected to mechanical imperatives. Factories were machine-driven worlds that left little room for socializing, eliminated autonomous behavior, and overpowered the individual human voice. Liberal intellectuals believed mechanization made intolerable demands on the traditional organizing frames of human life (work, religion, individualism, social values, and human nature) and left Americans without a sustaining set of beliefs. I will digress for a moment to explore how factory work itself was part and parcel of the disruptions of modernity, affecting the human body through noise, machine rhythms, repetitive motion, and a lack of autonomy.

Noise and Readjustment: Bodies on the Line

As early as the 1850s, Charles Dickens, Herman Melville, and Rebecca Harding Davis wrote major literary works critiquing factory realities and the toll of noise, speed, and repetition on factory workers. Already in this period industrial researchers in Europe spoke of "the human motor" and its limitations, and there was a "widespread fear that the energy of mind and body was dissipating under the strain of modernity."[47]

The roar of machines functioned as an index of early industrialization. In 1845 Elizabeth E. Turner, a "factory girl" in the Lowell mills, claimed her job had two intolerable aspects: a lack of mobility on the job and the "ceaseless din" of the machines. "Must I always stay here, and spend my days within these pent-up walls, with this ceaseless din my only music?" John Kasson has described the aural environment of "the buzzing and hissing and whizzing of pulleys and rollers and spindles and flyers," and how women defied the noise and repetition by "distancing themselves . . . through private thoughts and daydreams." Contemporary journalist Fanny Fern remarked that factory owners considered the workers as just that—"sewing *machines*"—and that upper-class women would not last "five minutes in that room where the noise of the machinery used is so deafening, that only by the motion of the lips could you comprehend a person speaking."[48]

Herman Melville indicted the factory environment in his two-part sketch "The Paradise of Bachelors and the Tartarus of Maids" (1855). Melville's anonymous narrator first imagines the machines of a New England paper mill as huge, dynamic, impressive, and noble.[49] The beauty and power of machines increase, however, only to the extent that workers—specifically, female workers—become dull, mechanical and listless. Melville's narrator articulates the archetypal fear of critics of industry: that machines are the new master beings and humans their slaves. "Machinery—that vaunted slave of humanity—here stood menially served by human beings. . . . The girls did not so much seem accessory wheels to the general machinery as mere cogs to the wheels."[50]

The narrator observes no conversation (or collegiality) among workers, only "the low, steady, overruling hum of the iron animals." He is terrified by this inhuman work environment: "Not a syllable was breathed. . . . The human voice was banished from the spot." The narrator had, in fact, heard his way to the factory: in the deep wilderness he heard "a whirling, humming sound . . . like an arrested avalanche," and turned to see "the large white-washed factory." When he is shown the "great machine" that produces the noise, he compares its long, huge "iron frame-work" to an as-yet-undeciphered "Eastern manuscript." The steam engine's mysterious shuttles, rattles, and spins came from "all sorts of rollers, wheels, and cylinders, in slowly-measured and increasing motion." In the repetitive movements of a nameless "tall girl" at her loom "feeding the iron animal," the narrator observes that the "rosy cheeks" that should color the woman's face instead color the "rose-hued note paper." To the narrator, "virtue" had been stolen from human beings and given to the nation's machinery. "I looked from the rosy paper to the pallid cheek, but said nothing."[51]

In *Life in the Iron Mills* (1861), Rebecca Harding Davis uses the industrial roar of her childhood home of Wheeling, West Virginia, as a backdrop for her story of labor, frustrated ambition, and class conflict. From her long walks observing the mill workers, she remembers how "the unsleeping engines groan and shriek, the fiery pools of metal boil and surge." Quiet only on Sunday, "the great furnaces break forth with renewed fury, the clamor begins with fresh, breathless, vigor, the engines sob and shriek like 'gods in pain.'" In one scene, she depicts the new industrial soundscape through the ironworker protagonist Hugo Wolfe's female companion, Deborah, a hunchbacked, overworked woman who sews by day. At 11 p.m., Deborah walks a mile from town to bring food to Wolfe. Even in the heavy rain, "the noise of these thousand engines sounded through the sleep and shadow of the city like far-off thunder." She gives Wolfe his dinner then takes a nap on a slag heap while listening to "the monotonous din and uncertain glare of the works," mechanical rhythms that make the heavy rain just a "dull plash . . . in the far distance."[52]

Both Davis and Melville were influenced by Charles Dickens's *Hard Times* (1854), the novel that staked out the industrial village ("Coketown") as a literary subject. To live in Coketown was to breathe smoke (not air) and hear machines (not the sounds of nature). "It was a town of machinery and tall chimneys" with constant "serpents of smoke" and slag-dirtied waters ("a black canal . . . and a river that ran purple"). The factory's mechanical rhythms displaced the natural ones: "There was a rattling and a trembling all day long, and . . . the piston of the steam-engine worked monotonously up and down." When the daily train came through, the noise of "the Express" barely registered, "little felt [as it was] amid the jarring of the machinery, and scarcely heard above its crash and rattle."[53]

The factory roar made workers half-deaf and forced physiological adjustments. Because factory hands "work[ed] with eyes and hands in the midst of a prodigious noise," their faces took on a dazed countenance. Dickens compared one worker's facial expressions to the "concentrated look with which we are familiar with the countenances of the deaf—the better to hear what . . . [was] asked." He also takes the metaphor of "factory hands" to its logical endpoint, classifying his worker-saint Stephen Blackpool as from the class "generically called 'the Hands'—a race who would have found more favor . . . if Providence had seen fit to make them only hands."[54]

Eventually a set of machine aesthetics evolved because humans need to make sense (and beauty) of any environment. Victorians found it difficult to conceive of machines as objects of artistic beauty; triumphs such as the Corliss Engine and the Crystal Palace were seen more as feats of engineering than artistic stylizations. Observers felt what David Nye calls the "technological sublime"—awe in the face of unimaginable and, for a time, inconceivable power—because they had no aesthetic vocabulary (or theory) to understand it.[55] Machines were still associated with materialism, dirt, capitalism, noise, and physical exertion. But in the transformation of an agrarian society to an industrial one, as the language began steaming up with mechanical metaphor, it was pragmatic to learn not to be *dis*pleased by noise, power, and repetition, and to adapt to the new demands upon the human organism. One Lowell worker of the 1830s wrote that "the noise of the machinery . . . [is] not displeasing"—if only she worked eight hours instead of thirteen.[56] Forced to adapt themselves to the pace, power, precision, and repetition of machines, workers gradually came to (or were forced) to admire mechanical qualities and the merits of mass production.

The terms of factory work did not change dramatically until Ford's engineers developed the assembly line. The most famous literary rendering of the assembly-line experience appears in the French novelist Louis-Ferdinand Céline's *Journey to the End of the Night* (1934). Céline, a doctor, spent time investigating the Ford assembly line at River Rouge in the late 1920s, and he fictionalized his impressions in the experience of his protagonist, Ferdinand Bardamu. Describing his first day on the job, he is engaged by the twitching, nervous men hopeful for work outside the factory gates. The factory roar invades his consciousness as soon as he enters: "All about one, and right up to the sky itself, the heavy many-sided roar of a cataract of machines, shaping, revolving, groaning." After being examined in a "sort of laboratory," he is told not to think too much. "What we need is chimpanzees," the doctors tells him of Ford's preference for workers. "We will think for you, my friend." Then all the men return to "where the vast crashing sound of the machines came from."[57]

Bardamu equates the physiological experience of the factory roar to possession by a mechanical god. "The whole building shook, and one['s] self from one's soles to one's ears was possessed by the shaking, which vibrated from the ground, [through] the glass panes and all this metal, a series of shocks from floor to ceiling." The constant, overlapping mechanical rhythms created dense layers of noise that constituted the workers' aural reality. This is the industrial soundscape—neither repetitive enough to become hypnotic nor relevant enough to physical motions so that it might provide a groove to which to align one's work (like a work song). Instead there was only a constant, random roar, "a thousand little wheels, and hammers never falling at one time, their thunders crowding one against the other." Workers kept their heads down not from shame or exhaustion, but due to the overwhelming aural environment: "You give in to noise as you give in to war."

The factory roar obscured Bardamu's thoughts and even his heartbeat: "You long to stop it all and be able to think about it and hear your heart beating clearly within you; but . . . it's impossible." The assembly line threatened to turn him "into a machine" through the repetitive motion of the work and the sonic assault. "The whole of one's carcass quiver[s] in this vast frenzy of noise, which filled . . . [the] inside of your skull and lower down rattled your bowels, and climbed to your eyes in infinite, little, quick unending strokes." Even the critical way a worker holds onto a sense of self—"the three ideas" one still held "behind your forehead"—became ground into the machine's rhythms. And then memory went, and fantasy, and finally whatever you "remember . . . has hardened like iron and lost its savor in your thoughts."

Céline's authority as a physician makes these passages especially powerful as historical documentation. At the end of the day, when "everything stops," he recalled, "you carry the noise away in your head." He was so possessed by the factory soundscape that "a whole night's noise and smell of oil" remained in his mind after work. After one day, he felt as if he had "been fitted with a new nose, a new brain for evermore"; he warned that machines would turn workers into a new kind of human being. Bitterly and playfully he claimed that after the "renunciation" of his old self, through Fordism, "bit by bit I became a new man—a new Ferdinand." Like a soldier drilled to survive on the front line, a factory worker had to adapt his mind and body to a new regimen.

In "On the Assembly Line," a 1937 *Atlantic Monthly* article, Gene Richards begins and ends his description of factory work with the jarring physiological experience of the noise.[58] "The Noise is deafening: a roar of machines and the groaning and moaning of hoists; the constant *pssfft-pssfft* of the air hoses. One must shout to be heard." Echoing Céline, Richards claims that "after a time the noise becomes a part of what is natural and goes unnoticed." The only instance of resistance Richards recalled happened when the workers were forced to work overtime. Significantly, they registered their dissent by raising their voices above the machines: "We take to hollering to build up a morale which will help us lick the last hour."

Richards provides an interesting synthesis of Veblen's and Céline's analyses of the machine process. He, too, feels as if his mind has been rebuilt by tending the machines. "I have gained one thing from this hell. I have learned discipline. I can concentrate for an hour on one subject." The cost, however, has been a partial loss of his own mental direction and an emotional distancing, a new layer of disengagement. "My efforts are fast losing direction. I have lost contact with anything to think about."

After work, Richards recalled the workers' laughter, of a type "sincere but weary." Perhaps the workers experienced the same kind of anomie and isolation that black slaves felt in the cotton fields; their personal "cry" had been shut off, and they felt emotionally isolated. They had the blues and needed the survival technology called the blues—as song form, personal narrative, field holler, work song, validation of "somebodiness," and as a cultural form that integrates the expression of individual experience within a group consciousness.

The idea of singing aloud on the assembly line struck the contemporary chronicler Mark Sullivan as absurd. "A worker who would have sung at his task, and made the swing of his tools conform to the rhythm of the song, would have been a startling phenomenon along the Ford assembly, and would have been regarded by the efficiency engineer as having no place in industry." Here we have a new kind of group work and group work rhythm but no work songs. On the assembly line, "heresy . . . was excess of motion, the flourish that was the exuberance of spirit in an artisan finding joy in creative work." In the great factory roar, the human voice—as speaking voice, as inner voice, as singing voice—was overruled by the machine's. For this reason, the battle between the human and the mechanical would not take place on the machine's home turf.[59]

The New American Tempo

While white liberal intellectuals and artists of the 1930s despaired that the "tempo of life" was out of control, they were generally blind to the ways Americans were already adapting to the machine age. Two years before James Truslow Adams's study of the modern tempo, the advertising consultant Robert Updegraff published a prescient little book of advice for businessmen entitled *The New American Tempo* (1929). Updegraff chided them for lagging far behind the public taste in terms of style and aesthetics. The daily lives of Americans were already informed by the American tempo, and its pace made former advertising guidelines obsolete. Updegraff warned that the new American tempo was more important to business than "materials, machinery, processes, labor, capital, and . . . competition of other men in the same business." The crucial element was "the speed factor"; the speed of change— social, economic, technological, and cultural—subverted all previous business principles. Nothing stood still any longer: not public taste, not sales, not the structures of industrial organization. Giving advice common enough in business today, Updegraff advised businessmen to include flexibility and improvisation as part of the corporate ethos, especially in its public relations and advertising.[60]

Updegraff's book suggests that Americans had already adapted to the new tempo. If businessmen did not adjust to the public's speed-loving style, their companies would lose the interest and business of savvy American consumers. Updegraff's expert (and only) witness was the entertainment impresario Steve Roxy (born Samuel Lionel Rothafel), owner of the successful Roxy Theater and an innovator in the creation of movie palaces in the 1910s.[61] The speed factor was the result of new technology, but Updegraff's dependence on Roxy implied that business needed to take its cues from *show business*. Show business—the business of show, illusion, and up-to-the-minute narrative—approximated the new tempo first.[62]

Roxy stressed the need in advertising for innovative combinations of "style, color, change, light, brevity, contrast, sweep, motion." There must be constant novelty and flashiness to attract the public's attention. In other words, *the accelerated experience of modernity could be conveyed through manipulating aesthetics*—standard practice today in advertising, packaging, and filmmaking. Businessmen should thus emphasize marketing (process) over product and aim at the public's desire for novelty rather than appeal to traditional values. A sense of modern style could be communicated through "the swing of color," "the craze for speed," and the creative use of texture, style, and smoothness.[63]

When John D. Rockefeller bought out the Roxy Theater, he gave Steve Roxy full artistic control over the crown jewel of Rockefeller Center: Radio City Music Hall. Originally the artistic center of the skyscraper complex was to be a new metropolitan opera house; here is a revealing instance of the transformation of public taste from European to vernacular culture, and of an American vanguard in twentieth-century aesthetics. The tempo of American life was best reflected in its popular culture, its music, dance, and theater.[64]

A second show-business tributary of the new American tempo came from the mass culture lessons learned at Coney Island. The architect Rem Koolhaas points out that "Manhattanism" developed organically from the "culture of congestion" first successfully negotiated at Coney Island.[65] On a summer afternoon in the 1890s, the amusement park and resort was one of the most populous places in the country, and it boasted a more sophisticated infrastructure than any other city besides Chicago and New York. At Coney Island "the metropolitan condition . . . [of] hyper-density" was first organized for consumer application as a fantasy world. To Koolhaas, Luna Park was "the most *modern* fragment of the world" when it opened in 1903. *The Guide to Coney Island* boasted that its thirty-eight acres contained "its own telegraphic office, cable office, wireless office . . . [and] telephone service," and were illuminated by "1,300,000 electric lights." The architect and designer Fredric Thompson's phantasmagoric display of illuminated towers at Luna Park (1,221 of them by 1906) prefigured the New York City skyline as an icon of modernity, and his crowd control techniques antedated those of urban railroad terminals such as Grand Central. Nearby at Coney Island's

Steeplechase Park, the amusement expert George Tilyou created rides of startling speed and disorientation, such as the Leap-Frog Railway where two trains hurtled toward each other until one climbed onto a separate track at the last moment. The developer William H. Reynolds opened Dreamland in 1906, the largest ballroom complex in the world. Its 25,000 square feet was so capacious it swallowed the subtle grace of ballroom dancing and led to roller-skate dancing—another example of the human machine's desire for a new kinesthetic of rhythmic flow. "In the technological frenzy of the time, the natural movement of the human body appear[ed] slow and clumsy," Koolhaas speculates, whereas by roller skating, couples displayed "speed and curvilinear trajectories" that created "fresh and random rhythms." Such ideas, rides, and thrills pioneered by Thompson, Reynolds, and Tilyou were copied throughout the country; temporary "electric cities" and dynamic thrills produced a "psycho-mechanical urbanism" even on rural sites. When Thompson bought an entire city block in midtown Manhattan to build the Hippodrome Theater in 1905 (Sixth Avenue, between 43d and 44th Streets), and later when Reynolds developed the Chrysler Building, they helped midtown Manhattan become "a *theater for progress.*"[66]

For show-business experts, the primary catalyst for bringing this machine-driven tempo to Manhattan's night life was the boisterous instrumental attack and propulsive rhythms of New Orleans jazz. Vincent Lopez, New York's second most popular hotel society orchestra in the 1910s and 1920s (next to Paul Whiteman), recalled in his autobiography that "the advent of Dixieland on Broadway changed the fabric of the entertainment world." During the same theatrical season of 1917, the debut of the Original Dixieland Jazz Band (ODJB), a white New Orleans quintet, at Reisenweber's restaurant in New York City was the event of the season (helped along by their million-selling record, "Livery Stable Blues").[67] The factors that distinguished the ODJB from previous small jazz units were the frenetic pace of their songs, the interweaving polyphonic instrumental lines that seemed chaotic and out of control, and the novelty sounds they wrested from their instruments (including imitations of barnyard animals, often called "hokum").[68] (Sidney Bechet claimed that the ODJB appropriated the style of New Orleans blacks well enough, but not the meaning of jazz or the historical experience inside the music.)[69]

The musicians of the ODJB made no pretense to art or virtuoso musicianship, and their brash, unpolished style "closely mirrored

America's carefree World War I mood" and speeded up Broadway's already lively tempo. After hearing them, Lopez immediately transformed his orchestra's repertoire. "In a week, we made the switch from schmaltzy music with heart appeal, to the drive of Dixieland that does something to the adrenal glands!" Though classically trained, Lopez believed the rhythmic innovations of jazz rejuvenated bodies and spirits. "Like the Renaissance, the new music brought a quickening of thought for all show business." Twenty years later, as an instructor at New York University, Lopez taught his students that swing (even more so than New Orleans jazz) was "the perfect expression of the tempo and atmosphere of the machine age in which we live."[70]

Paul Whiteman, the so-called King of Jazz of the 1920s, had a similar conversion experience, and machine rhythms were even more central to his analysis of the Jazz Age aesthetic. "The rhythm of machinery became the rhythm of American civilization," Whiteman recalled in *Jazz* (1926), "a clanging, banging, terrific rhythm, full of an energy that promised accomplishment."[71] An ex–symphony violinist, Whiteman was an entertainment giant in the 1920s, appearing on the cover of the annual review issues of *Variety* in 1921 and 1922 as an unofficial entertainer of the year. Whiteman ran a national network of more than one hundred and fifty "Paul Whiteman Orchestras," and was celebrated by English royalty throughout the decade. By 1922 his jolly, rotund, tuxedoed figure was a national icon, and the screen musical *King of Jazz* (1930) cemented his position as "Pops" in American music before Louis Armstrong stole the name. Whiteman's conversion to jazz happened at a dive in San Francisco's Barbary Coast in 1915, where he probably heard the trumpeter Freddie Keppard's early New Orleans unit.

Whiteman's first impression of jazz was as a set of machine rhythms, as if "the whole tempo of the country had speeded up." He reflected that this only made sense in a country where "wheels turned like mad."

Every factory was manned by day and night shifts. Americans—and the term included Slavs, Teutons, Latins, Orientals, welded into one great mass as if by the gigantic machines they tended—lived harder, faster than ever before. They could not go on without some new outlet. Work was not enough and America had not yet found out how to play. The hard-pressed, hard-working young country had no folk songs, no village dances on the green. . . . [But] brewing in New Orleans [was] a restorative for the national nerve complaint. The great

American noise, jazz, was then just drifting out of the shanties and tango belt to begin its ascent into the ballrooms of the cultured.[72]

It is important to note the evolutionary artistic paradigm in the last sentence. Whiteman's orchestra was the main conduit of that ascent, and he reaped the economic rewards. Throughout the 1920s Whiteman claimed he had "made a lady of jazz," and his rhetoric harped on his triumph in bringing artistic (that is, white, European) control to this unruly, machine-driven, African American (black, folk) creation.

Whiteman created a hybrid genre called "symphonic jazz," a large-unit, heavily arranged style that left little room for improvisation. Whiteman thought about music through the written score, not through hearing musical ideas expressed by individuals. As Gunther Schuller points out, it was thus not "a jazz concept": it's not jazz if the musicians do not improvise, do not create a spontaneous musical conversation, and do not aim individually to create a distinctive signature sound on their instruments. Whiteman appropriated from New Orleans blacks their syncopated rhythms and innovative vocalized quality of horn playing, but for his upper-class white audiences he brought in more classical qualities: "excellent intonation, perfect balances [of sound], and clean attacks."[73] The cultural critic Gilbert Seldes called Whiteman's orchestra a "mechanically perfect organization" but one that had sacrificed the soul of jazz's revolution: improvisation and "the element of surprise."[74]

In closing off the music's spaces for individuality and improvisation and creating a symphony-derived hierarchical structure, Whiteman was something of an industrialist of jazz. Rehearsals were as "thorough and frequent as in any symphony . . . [since] the discipline of the orchestra must be complete."[75] Gilbert Seldes called Whiteman's band a "dynamo" that had smoothed out the clashing polyphonic lines of New Orleans jazz. "The modern jazz orchestra is an efficient arrangement. Every member knows exactly what he is to play every minute of the time. Even the smears are indicated in the music."[76] For the best Euro-American jazz artists of the 1920s, such as Bix Beiderbecke, Whiteman's orchestra was too rigid. Still, Whiteman's bands were immensely successful and influential across class and region and spread a muted form of the American tempo into all sectors of society (sometimes mocked as "the businessman's bounce").

In his autobiography Whiteman omitted any mention of African American musical traditions and singled out only white jazz musicians for praise. He often went to see Duke Ellington and the Washingtonians at the Kentucky Club in New York in the mid-1920s, though, and he always put a big tip in the pianist's jar. He gave only "collective" credit for the creation of jazz to African Americans, writing that blacks did not realize the importance of the music or the need for an artistic form to evolve. Jazz "bid[ed] its time among the black laborers in the cotton fields . . . [and] lounging in the sunshine along the New Orleans levees." Still, Ellington wrote with respect of Whiteman's orchestra, as did Armstrong.[77]

Despite his stereotyping and the anxiety of influence, Whiteman perceived the cultural forces at play inside the music, the human integration of the mechanical. As the music came out of New Orleans, "it had lost none of its primitive African swing through mingling with the clanging of the machinery, the broken crashing rhythm of Whitman's poetry, the gigantic steel and stone of the skyscrapers."[78] Here in 1926 is early recognition of the dialogue of African American music with the industrial soundscape.

The same aesthetic elements that excited Whiteman and Lopez often repelled social and artistic elites. They disparaged jazz for its fast rhythms, mechanically repetitive beat, and sensual dances. Nor were they comfortable, writes Kathy Ogren, with the fact that marginal groups of "blacks and entertainers" had become the cultural leaders in "help[ing] white Americans with diverse social backgrounds [to] explain their world."[79] The three main groups aligned against jazz were educators, clergy, and classical music professionals; for example, Daniel Mason, then the dean of American composers, emphasized its soulless, mechanical qualities.[80] Such critics saw in jazz rhythms both unfettered sensuality *and* mechanical qualities: the steady, pronounced pulse of drummer, banjo, and tuba suggested both sexual rhythms and those of the subway. Jazz became associated with crime, sexual freedom, primitive behavior, and licentiousness, largely owing to its association with African Americans and with New Orleans bordellos. Summing up the anti-jazz discourse, one historian noted: "On the one hand, jazz was made to stand for the devolutionary forces of sensual blackness against which 'culture' has always struggled, [and] . . . on the other hand, paradoxically, some critics perceived jazz as the anti-music of robots and riveting machines, the technology of urban civilization."[81]

The dominant Victorian music aesthetic posited an elitist, sacralized art to be used as an escape from "the noise, bustle, and materialism of city life." Classical musicians were at odds with traitors such as Lopez and

Whiteman. "Art ought to be a relief from modern civilization," Mason wrote, "as opposed to "reflect[ing] its defects." Engaging machine aesthetics amounted to lowering the sacred to the vulgar and mechanical. Beethoven might use "the sounds of country life in a symphony," but noise itself was "antimusic, or 'anarchy' in Matthew Arnold's use of the term." In Ernest Bloch's *America* (1926), the composer represented jazz as "Material 'prosperity'—Speed—Noise—'Man slave of the machines.'" George Gershwin was among the younger, jazz-influenced (and immigrant) composers influenced by the urban soundscape, and he saw a cultural need to synthesize the new tempo and human emotion. "Mechanism and feeling will have to go hand in hand, in the same way that a skyscraper is at the same time a triumph of the machine and a tremendous emotional experience, almost breathtaking." The inspiration for *Rhapsody in Blue* (1924) came "on the train, with its steely rhythms, its rattle-ty-bang. . . . I heard it as a sort of kaleidoscope of America—of our vast melting pot, of our . . . national pep, of our blues, our metropolitan madness."[82]

For Stuart Chase, this debate was about human nature, opposing those who thought human values were adaptable creatures to those who believed in "transcendent value[s]."[83] In *Men and Machines*, Chase argued that Victorian artists had failed, in their social roles, to engage industrialization. The lone exception was in the field of music, and specifically the evolution of the symphony orchestra in Germany. "The symphony orchestra made its bow to the world, arm in arm with the first power-driven factories. It flourished and grew strong along with looms, locomotives and milling machines. . . . What is an orchestra but a cunningly articulated, and thoroughly standardized, factory of sound?" For Chase, the massed sections and power of symphonies enabled them to reflect machine realities, an artistic fact that possibly "saved the [human] race from drowning through all those dreadful early years." Listening to a symphony, Chase would "sample the [music] waves which reach my ears, and compare them to the currents from a rolling mill." Jacques Attali points out that classical music is seen by contemporary middle-class audiences as ennobling, contemplative, ethereal; but it is hard to imagine the dynamic volume—and the experience of awe, terror and noise—that must have characterized the premiere of a Beethoven symphony. For example, Beethoven's Third Symphony, the "Eroica," is now considered a calming pastoral work, but it "excited, puzzled, and disturbed its original audiences in about equal proportions."

The work's controlled, passionate urgency spoke to a rising European middle class rebelling against aristocratic authority with the aid of "the deafening splendor of orchestral noise," but it now speaks for a middle class that "is the defender, not the assailant, of the status quo."[84]

Lewis Mumford likewise theorized a cultural relationship between the orchestra and industrialization. He compared the composer and symphony orchestra to "the industrial engineer or designer" and a new machine. Machine techniques transformed musical instruments "for the purpose of achieving greater accuracy and range," leading to new families of brass instruments that utilized valves and pistons. "The symphony orchestra comes into existence as a contemporary of the modern factory," Mumford wrote, echoing Chase. Both believed that only music remained relevant to the industrial experience of the nineteenth century as "industrialism had undermined most of the traditional arts and depleted their vitality."[85]

Cultural analysis of the development and reception of the symphony orchestra sheds further light on its role as an aesthetic "order-maker" of the new bourgeois society. For Attali, symphony musicians were analogous to factory workers, while the rising bourgeois class identified with the conductor, "the creator of the order needed to avoid chaos in production." To the Bulgarian novelist and social theorist Elias Canetti, the unquestioned power of the conductor to lead an obedient regiment of musicians foretold the possibility that Germans might follow a demagogue lockstep into military ambition and conquest. To jazz clarinetist Mezz Mezzrow growing up in Chicago in the 1920s, the symphony orchestra was "assembly-line music" imposed by a "pompous director . . . [who was] mechanical as an epileptic metronome." In the window display of a Wurlitzer piano store, Mezzrow once saw an "animated-doll symphony . . . run by some hidden electrical clockwork," and there was the "whole philosophy [of classical music] on display." It was all mechanical time: "one-two, one-two—take their clock away and they'd go around in circles, like travelers without a compass."[86]

This battle between classical and jazz worlds was represented in popular culture in one of Disney's "Silly Symphony" shorts of the 1930s, a Romeo and Juliet story entitled "Music Land" (1935). The saxophone-shaped son of the King of the Isle of Jazz (shaped like Paul Whiteman) falls in love with the violin-shaped daughter/princess of the Land of Symphony. The two island nations then have a naval battle on the Sea of Discord over this illegal courtship. The Land of Symphony's cannons are church pipe organs that emerge from cathedrals; the Isle of Jazz is a steamboat that blows its projectiles through trombones and the bell of saxophones. The jazz prince is imprisoned within a guardhouse shaped like a metronome, and its rigid rhythm drives him crazy. He escapes and tries to go to his princess; when the lovers nearly drown, a truce is called. The two kingdoms are united through the cooperative building of a "Bridge of Harmony" between their nations and the marriage of classical and jazz worlds.[87]

Using Chase's argument and Disney's light-hearted romp, we can see the Machine Age continuity between the symphony orchestra and the big band. The main artistic form for engaging modernity had been music because of its relationship to the industrialization of time, to the need to be "on time," to the underlying insistent beat of the clock. "Music is our chief art because of its beat," Chase declared simply.[88] If the symphony orchestra reflected the large-scale organization made possible by steam-driven industrial applications, big-band swing symbolized a cultural resistance to assembly-line workplace realities by emphasizing rhythmic propulsion over harmonic density, and seamless continuity between short melodic phrases over linear narrative. Big-band swing was more rhythmic, more fluid, and more horizontal in the relationship among musicians (than between conductor and orchestra); the music also left aesthetic room for individual self-expression and the participation of dancers. The big band itself, as an icon, did not represent the hierarchical music of a successful middle class looking to create a new order, but a grassroots vernacular music created by socially mobile ethnic groups that had integrated European-derived chords and harmonies with Afrodiasporic rhythms and performative approaches: European hardware, African American software.

Jazz is a Machine Age modernist art form as well as a vernacular response to modernity. According to Leonard Bernstein, in the 1920s and 1930s jazz influenced the symphony orchestra in several musical areas: "melody, harmony, rhythm, form, counterpoint, and color." Bernstein called the contribution of jazz "unconscious" and rhythm-derived, because he too failed to see the African American aesthetics at play. From 1895 to 1920 there was a vogue among American classical composers to create a national music from folk themes, whether Native American, African American or Irish American. "[Americans] were not Indians . . . any more than they were all Poles or all Irish. . . . [T]o what indigenous folk-material could they all respond in common?" Apparently to African

American material—so long as people *called* it American and white-faced its artists. In other words, if the composer effaced its black heritage, jazz allowed the American composer to be both "original" and "American." In Bernstein's words, "here at last was a musical material which was everyone's bread and butter."[89]

The 1930s was the decade when composers "owe[d] the greatest debt to jazz," Bernstein recalled. Jazz captured something of the American spirit after the stock market crash, and "something *inner* in jazz . . . entered into our serious music." Such qualities included "the glorious instrumental color that derives particularly from Negro wind-playing, the healthy, optimistic percussiveness of youthful gaiety, or the neurotic percussiveness of the American citizen when he is on a spree." Big-band swing became popular even without cultural promotion because of its rhythmic drive, blending of musical tones, and solo improvisation—all of which symbolized the democratic society. As Bernstein declared, "A national music is national in direct proportion to how close to its home audiences feel."[90] Yet despite the popularity of jazz in the 1920s, most American intellectuals could not see (or, more accurately, hear) their indigenous culture dancing a new attitude. The tempo of big-band swing had a different velocity and feel from the jazz of the 1920s.

The Artistic Creation of the
Swinging American Tempo

Recalling the 1930s, the African American poet and journalist Frank Marshall Davis speculated that the omnipresence of big-band swing was the result of a cultural need for a functional art form to respond to the new tempo of life. "Railroads and new inventions accelerated the tempo of living. . . . Since African traditional music is functional, it was only logical that an oppressed minority would mix what it valued of the music of the majority with its own concepts and extend the personal protest of the blues into the united protest of . . . jazz music." Jazz was devalued at the time as inferior music since it "originated among an 'inferior' people," but once white men could play it well enough, the democratic interplay, the rhythmic vitality, and the defiance of European musical rules were all embraced. "In 1936 America got swing religion," Davis reflected, "[and] the messiah who fed and then converted the multitudes was Benny Goodman."[91]

The transition from the 1920s ODJB-style group to the swing bands was "startling," according to Marshall Stearns. Swing bands were double the size of New Orleans–inspired units, yet maintained their power, speed and drive. The expansion of the size of the band (at first to ten or eleven) brought a double-edged challenge to arrangers and musicians: how to play in a unified groove that also left spaces for improvisation. Considering the technical challenge of the expanded format, still "the music sound[ed] smoother, fuller, more flowing, and paradoxically, simpler." The powerful flow, the simple, clean lines, the smooth aural quality, the legato fluidity of the best soloists meshing with the background sections—these were not the qualities of 1920s jazz, whether the jerky, reckless, anarchic quality of the ODJB, Louis Armstrong's Hot Fives and Sevens, or of Whiteman's muted dynamo.[92] Whiteman may have influenced the size of the bands and even the early voicings of the sections, but the pianist and bandleader Fletcher Henderson created the blueprints for big-band composition and performance, and the Count Basie Orchestra later added depth and speed without sacrificing control, creating a "simplicity of format, simplicity of texture."[93]

What had happened? In the mid-1920s Henderson and his alto saxophonist Don Redman realized that a big jazz band created an artistic "problem," so they set out to "solve the problem." In small-unit New Orleans jazz, musicians collectively improvised; every musician played a separate line. When a band had upwards of seven or eight pieces, the music became difficult to dance to and often anarchic. As the house band at New York's Roseland Ballroom throughout the 1920s, the Henderson orchestra had plenty of time to experiment. Henderson or Redman would write out a melodic line conceived in a jazz style, and then harmonize the line for the members of a section (say, the three saxophones). The arranger would then contribute a short, punchy, rhythmic counterphrase (a riff) as a response for the brass section (trumpets and trombones). The saxophone section was one voice, the brass section the second voice. Drawing on the West African practice of call-and-response, Redman and Henderson kept the sections "answering each other in an endless variety of ways." Once the theme and battling riffs were established, a soloist improvised on top, and the arrangers composed suitable background riffs as variations on the initial theme.[94]

A similar process, by way of the African American oral tradition and the frontier mix of blues and ragtime, was going on simultaneously among the "territory bands" of Kansas City, Texas, and Oklahoma.[95] Many musicians in the orchestras of Count Basie or Andy Kirk could not read music, so new songs were often composed collectively, worked out by the band during rehearsals. Any musician might bring in a melodic idea, and the different sections would go off into separate rooms to construct their riffs and harmonies for a given song once the idea was set— what was called the "head arrangement."[96] Later Benny Goodman and other classically trained musicians (black, white, and immigrant) brought to swing an emphasis on classical elements such as precision and accurate pitch, and Goodman's success influenced soloists and bands to value control and efficiency.

Swing musicians thus had multiple roles in the band. Any musician needed to be able to play clearly, loudly, and precisely to be heard over the sections, but also needed to be able to swing the section. The sections had to swing as a group and not lose their voice during the call-and-response battles. The best jazz musicians would later profess their preference for small-band playing, where they were able to solo more; but they remembered the swing era fondly as a period when you had to learn teamwork, blend with your section, and contribute to the band's powerful drive. "It meant endless rehearsals, a comparative loss of identity (except for the solo stars), and high-level teamwork."[97]

Hitting the right tempo for dance audiences was perhaps the most crucial element in a big band's success. "Tempo was always a very important thing in the big band days," the pianist and bandleader Earl Hines recalled from his sixty-year jazz sojourn. "When it was a vocal number, I told all the guys to watch me directing, but when it came time for dancing, I had to have an understanding with the drummer as my main man." Hines meant that the drummer had to extrapolate the right tempo *from* a given audience—not provide it. "'Don't you set the tempo,'" he mimicked his directions to the drummer. "'The people and dance acts set the tempo and you keep it.' Some nights they don't feel like dancing too fast." Hines had the band's new songs "arranged with the people in mind," and he told his arrangers "to make it [a new song] flexible, so if we wanted to change the tempo it would still have the same feeling." The audiences set the tempo; the drummer matched it and "kept it." Hines even watched the response of the dancers' feet. "I was always out front and watching, almost looking down their throats! I watched the singer's mouth and his expression, and I watched the people's feet."[98]

The arranger, trombonist, and electric guitarist Eddie Durham worked with both Count Basie and Glenn Miller, and he too equated the right tempo with swing success. "You can't get away from the tempo. It hits the human [part]—when it hits one human, it generally hits thousands. . . . The tempos mean everything. If you can get the tempo exactly what the public want, you can get the hit."[99] There was a general "swing" feeling among musicians, and even among dancers, recalled the alto saxophonist and arranger Eddie Barefield (a veteran of the bands of Bennie Moten, Cab Calloway, Fletcher Henderson, and Ella Fitzgerald). "In those days . . . [e]very man played with a beat," he recalled, and "when you went to a dance you could hear the feet on the dance floor." His reflections echo Earl Hines: "Everybody was beating in time, it was one of those things, you could hear the patting of the feet right along with the music. And this made a lot of the momentum in the swing more predominant."[100]

The drummer Jimmy Crawford, of the enormously popular Jimmie Lunceford Orchestra, explained his relationship to Lunceford in similar terms: "Lunceford [brought] . . . his stick down for the opening beat, but from then on the drummer had to control the tempo, make the transitions, watch the music, the feet of the dancers, the gestures of the singers, and everything. . . . [If] I didn't look at the dancers' feet as well as the music, I couldn't make those transitions right."[101]

In fact, black dancers in the South often stomped off the tempo *they* wanted. African American bandleaders learned to take their cues for tempo and rhythm from the dancers, and in this way incorporated the demands of what intellectuals of the 1930s might have called "the people."[102] "A group [of dancers] always would come around the bandstand and request something," recalled the Kansas City big-band leader Andy Kirk. "'Play so-and-so,' they'd say, so I'd say, 'Where do you want it, Man?' . . . And they'd pat off the tempo they wanted [with their feet]." Here is one reason why the idea of a "national tempo" must be taken seriously. This southern practice migrated to the North and was common at dance halls such as Harlem's Savoy Ballroom. "Dancing was about the only pleasure [blacks had]," Kirk recalled. "And there were dance halls of every type in the South."[103]

Count Basie's trombonist Dicky Wells had similar experiences with the lindy hoppers in New York. "You might say we composed while they danced—a whole lot of swinging rhythm. That's when we invented new things and recorded them the next day." Such experimentation was common in swing-era dance halls that functioned as African American community institutions, such as the Savoy and Chicago's Grand Terrace. "When you've got people out on the dance floor and dancing, you know what they like—you got 'em!," Wells remembered. "Tommy Dorsey told me he could . . . tell when he had a hit because that floor stayed packed." If recording engineers could only "screen the bandstand with glass . . . at a place like the Savoy, and record while the band could still see the dancers, they'd get a wonderful effect," Wells imagined. "[It] would help the musicians a lot. . . . Without them [the dancers], and you just sitting up there playing a concert, it's pretty cold. There was more soul when jazz and dancing went together."[104]

Hitting the right tempo was so important to the swing era that bandleaders, bassists, and drummers sometimes had fights over who had the authority to "read" the tempo desired by individual audiences. "I remember many a fight between the bass player and the drummer about who was right and who was wrong," Eddie Barefield recalled. "Because everything predominantly in those days was played for people to dance by. So [even] the worst dancer in the audience would tell when the band got off, you know."[105] The term "got off" here refers to the band's ability to enjoy itself, and to communicate that joy to the dancers; when the band "gets off," it provides that sense of uplift generated by what African American musicians call the "foundation" quality of the music. The goal of these bands was to "send" the audience—a newly minted musicians' slang term that meant "to arouse the emotions" or make one "joyful." In 1942 Zora Neale Hurston noted that in Harlem a "sender" was "someone who could really get to you."[106] Ralph Ellison described the "sender's" role within the dance ritual of early 1930s Kansas City: a musician would "send you at some big dance . . . into the ecstasy of rhythm and memory and brassy affirmation of the goodness of being alive and part of the community."[107]

One of the more famous disputes between bandleader and drummer over tempo leadership led to Sid Catlett's dismissal by Benny Goodman. Catlett was a drummer's drummer, a universally respected musician and human being. He was renowned for asking each musician in the band for his preferred rhythmic background and then providing it. One night Goodman thought a certain song wasn't swinging, so he whistled at the bass player, John Simmons, to play quieter, and he then tried to rush Catlett. Simmons described Catlett's reaction:

He started rushing things, you know, like 'Make it faster, make it faster.' . . . So when they come off the stand, Sid collared him. . . . 'Looky here, Pops, you give me the downbeat. I'm supposed to keep that tempo. . . . [Y]ou know it's unprofessional to change the tempo once the dancers are on the floor. . . . And all that rushing you're giving me, that doesn't mean a thing to me as far as swinging the band.'

Goodman was angry, but rather than fire Catlett he made it impossible for him to stay. First he fired Simmons, Catlett's good friend, without apparent cause. A few days later, at the band's next recording date, Catlett found a different drummer had been hired for the session—a direct insult. He quit the next day.[108]

When jazz musicians create a dance groove through their own internal dialogue, they do so by playing slightly "out of sync." Playing together on the beat would have a precise military feel and suggest metronomic time; jazz musicians play "in phase, but out of sync," to use the musicologist Charlie Keil's succinct phrase, creating overlapping textures that suggest an openness of musical structure. And the musical "space" between the instruments *provokes the participation* of listeners and dancers. Played for dancers, such open rhythm allows their movements to add visual and kinesthetic flare to the sound; played for listeners, it allows one's brainwaves to en-*trance* with the music. Keil calls this process among rhythm-section musicians "participatory discrepancies"—also, "relaxed dynamism" or "creative tension." The groove is both created and maintained collectively, and in the maintenance of such imperfect, overlapping rhythms, a listener or dancer finds "the juice, the groove, the funk, and the delights of music, and of life." Keil believes participatory discrepancies promote a "basic worldview that says the universe is open, imperfect, and subject to redefinition by every emergent self."[109]

The ways jazz musicians "sync up" with each other and create a groove, and the way human beings have their own dance moves—with the music, and with their partners—makes the swing dance-hall ritual an important forum whereby an individual can link his or her subjective time with the social tempo. "Every individual on the planet has a different time feel, just like everyone has a different signature and everyone dances differently."[110]

In *Art as Experience* (1934), written just before the swing era began, John Dewey claimed the dualities of mind and body, intellect and emotion, higher and lower natures, vulgar and enlightened were all obsolete, and had always been based on two issues: the fear of change and of our bodies. Dewey argued that the integration of animal instincts would not "reduce man to the level of the brutes"—the Western fear of "going native"—but would instead help "make possible the drawing of a [new] ground-plan of human experience." Such a "ground-plan" required a new idea of individuality, Dewey postulated, one that replaced the obsolete mind/body duality with "mind-body integration."[111]

That ground plan was a dance floor, and on it, individuals could attack any and all outmoded dualities—including the opposition of human and machine.

Coda: Swinging the New World

If the machine-driven tempo of life was out of control—if that was a major factor creating social "chaos"—then the public display of a humanly driven and organized tempo could provide a social bonding ritual essential to the reaffirmation of human values. Big-band swing's underlying popularity lay in the need for a public display of the mastery of the tempo of life.

Big-band swing *was* the social tempo of the time. It featured mechanical repetition, brassy power, and precision section playing. Swing dancers responded to such machine aesthetics by choosing relaxed tempos with their bodies and feet, which were extrapolated by African American musicians throughout the country. Swing-era dancers did not choose mechanical rhythms—as in disco or techno music, to take two examples—to reflect their cultural values. "To swing is to affirm," a Catholic priest (and jazz fan) suggested, explaining that when a jazz musician solos, he or she provides a public display of how to forge an individual style and hold one's ground against "depersonalizing social structures and dehumanizing machinery."[112]

The ethnomusicologist John Blacking theorizes that it is necessary for a belief in human possibility "to show that the real sources of technology, of all culture, are to be found in the human body and in co-operative interaction between human bodies."[113] Calling people to dance by providing tempos in which artistic performance was driven by public demand, swing-era musicians began the project of adjusting the physiological, aesthetic, and earthly rhythms of Depression-era Machine Age Americans to what Duke Ellington would call in his 1943 suite "New World A-Comin'."

THE JAZZ TRAIN AND
AMERICAN MUSICAL
MODERNITY

And mothers
with their babes asleep
go rockin' to that gentle beat
the rhythm of the rails
is all they dream.
—Steve Goodman, *"City of New Orleans"*

Starting in the late 1920s, the train began to be seen as the nation's fore-most *nostalgic* symbol of progress—the totemic subject of the country's experience of industrialization. Many histories of the train often discuss only the demise of the railroads relative to the automobile in this period and note the industry's two swan songs: the streamliners of the 1930s and the massive troop movements on trains in World War II.[1] Regardless of the industry's fortunes, however, swing-era Americans read their history through the train as through no other single object, symbol, or metaphor. "John Henry" was celebrated as the "greatest folk ballad in American life" in the 1930s, and several books and plays about the folk hero appeared, including a Broadway production starring Paul Robeson. Another Broadway play, "Heavenly Express" (1940), celebrated the folklore of railroad men and their hobo opposites.[2] The Baltimore and Ohio (B&O) Railroad's "Fair of the Iron Horse" and the Chicago Railroad Fair drew huge crowds in 1927 and 1948—surprising even their promoters—and railroad industry exhibits were mainstays of national expositions such as the Chicago Century of Progress of 1933–34 and the New York World's Fair of 1939–40. A *New York Times* drama critic wrote of the "Railroads on Parade" exhibit at the latter fair, "A good deal of the romance of human progress has been caught in this hour of railroad spectacle."[3]

Despite the nation's worship of aviation, the first roar of the automobile age, and a depressed railroad industry, the most popular (and beloved) songs of the swing era were about trains. If two songs could be said to best represent the genre of big-band swing, they might be the Glenn Miller Orchestra's "Chattanooga Choo Choo" (1941)—his theme song and one of the earliest million-selling records in American history—and Duke Ellington's "Take the 'A' Train" (1941), a best-seller that replaced "East St. Louis Toodle-Oo" as that band's theme song. A generation before rock and roll's "big beat," train-powered big-band swing made the "locomotive" quality of Americans—restless, on the move, longing for a better future—available in musical form. The stylization of train sounds and rhythms in American popular music also brought to swing what I call "the hum of machinery" in muted horn riffs.[4] Big bands smoothed out industrial noise and overwhelmed mechanical cacophony with massed blowing power under human control, as rendered by trumpet, saxophone, and trombone sections.

This chapter centers on the train as an icon of historical experience in the interwar years, and on the process by which African American musicians employed train sounds that evoked certain unconscious beliefs connecting the *retro*-promise of the industrial past to the uncertain Depression-era present. The actual locomotive onomatopoeia in big-band tunes and blues songs—propulsive rhythms, steam whistles, station bells, freight-car clanking, cross-tie clacking—resonated with American listeners and dancers, and I explore its sonic place in several musical genres, such as boogie-woogie piano, blues, harmonica pieces, and big-band swing.

Why songs about trains, and not airplanes or cars? Because trains vibrated in the American body first and helped unify the nation geographically, technologically, sonically, physiologically. On a train, a passenger sees a larger swath of the terrain, senses the topography of a region, and gets fleeting glimpses of other lives. Here was the first experience of a montage of impressions, an epic narrative at once real and ephemeral. For many Americans, train sounds were the music of techno-progress itself: the rhythmic drive of technological change and the promise of social mobility. In the words of one scholar, "Unlike air travel with its coldly detached view of the world, trains . . . keep us close to the ground, linked to the land's every rhythm and subtlety." Even Charles Sheeler, America's premiere Machine Age artist, employed the word "power" for only one work, a photograph of a stilled huge locomotive wheel, at rest but ever-ready to roll (*Rolling Power* [1939]). The historian Lewis Erenberg has suggested that the 4/4 swing rhythm itself "derive[s] from the pistons of the locomotive driving ahead."[5]

It would be hard to overstate the influence of trains (as discrete objects in motion) and railroads (as industrial organizations) on American history and culture. As a fast, mechanical means of travel, as a circulatory system of tracks, as a capitalist enterprise that created an American industrial aesthetic, and as the first twenty-four-hour-a-day business, railroads remain the nation's primordial symbol of unity. Well before the Golden Spike linked the nation in a continuous transportation network in 1869, railroad promoters of the antebellum period praised the machine's ability to connect cities and regions at a time of discordant sectionalism. Later, consumer dreams were fed by the romantic glamour of sophisticated, aristocratic style aboard express trains such as the Twentieth Century Limited. The nation's first malls were the huge train depots of New York's Grand Central and Washington's Union stations. Railroad corporations were the model of industrial organization for venture capitalism and multinational corporations. Some historians argue that the railroad was the nation's formative social institution; others, its prototypical corporate lobby and political agent.[6] At the Baltimore and Ohio Railroad museum honoring the first fully functioning passenger railroad (the B&O), placards proudly inform tourists of the railroads' role in nineteenth-century American life: "The railroads and the national economy were one and the same."[7]

The historian John Stilgoe has shown that the "metropolitan corridor" in most American small towns was the combination of train station, telegraph shack, and factories just on the outskirts of town; this was the real—and sonically determined—path to modernity.[8] The railroad clock hung proudly at the stations as the most efficient clock in town. Major architects designed even small-town depots, often combining Victorian elements, masses of stone and brick, and landscaping ideas derived from English gardens into a vigorous, masculine style known as Richardson Romanesque. Despite economic and political wars between railroad companies, and the smoky, dirty experience of riding the earliest trains, "the railroad was universally celebrated . . . because it provided a link with the wider world, an anodyne for isolation."[9] This link had a melody, a set of train-whistle riffs, a musical modernity. The whistle's initial function was as a cautionary sound, a way for the conductor to signal the brakeman or to alert the train crews or pedestrians to get off the track. But by the late nineteenth century each engineer developed his own "occupational signature," and the train-whistle became something of a musical instrument.[10]

The railroad historian George Douglas believes that the modern American tempo of life is itself train-derived. Trains "determined the essence of life in our cities—governance of the clock, the hurried step, the quick exchange of luggage, and the electric transfer of information." Inexpensive railroad travel helped create an American "desire for movement and escape to some other place," as well as giving "birth to our sense of the diversity of places—of cities, of suburbs, of leisured resorts." The automobile was a "johnny-come-lately in this game," and historians often give credit to the automobile for elements of modernity that were actually pioneered by the railroad industry: for negotiating the elements of vehicular traffic flow and efficiency, and for making possible the settlement patterns of suburbs and malls. The first "temples of progress and achievement" were not skyscrapers but "the great urban terminals."[11]

Not only did the railroads bring people and places closer together, but passengers were the first industrial subjects; cultural observers before 1850 complained that a human being was no more than "a parcel" processed and distributed by this impersonal system of mass distribution. More so than the telegraph, the steam-driven train gave emergent industrialized societies their first taste of a mechanical future world: fast, powerful, smooth, mobile, man-made, portable, impersonal. Train symbology mediated the shift from a natural to a mechanical world, from the traditional mindset characterized by comparing human behavior to plants, animals, water, and sky, to an expanded sense of possibility determined only by human dreams and techno-progress. By the 1860s the railroad had taught the industrialized world the thrill of speed and power and noise—of "flying," as one observer said—and disrupted agrarian-based patterns of stability with experiences of rupture, flow, speed, and forward momentum.

The first generation of railway passengers in the 1830s and 1840s often commented on the train's ability to "annihilate time and space."[12] Watching the landscape from a train altered the visual frames of industrial societies, and an appreciation for machine aesthetics slowly dawned on artists, leading to a new visual regime based upon shifting planes of light, rapidly dissolving "evanescent" snapshots, and shimmering views of landscapes. A group of early Impressionist painters embraced the train as the most dramatic subject of the era, meeting often along the approaches to Paris's Gare des Batignolles, a station Edouard Manet spent an entire year painting. Claude Monet's *Arrival of the Normandy Train, Saint-Lazare Station* (1877) rendered the drama of a train arriving majestically in the new glass and steel shed, steam pouring out from above and below, attendant well-dressed travelers scattered insignificantly around the mechanical agent. The Lumière Brothers used Monet's painting as a model for their influential thirty-second silent film, *Arrival of le Train at La Ciotat* (1895).

The number one star of silent film was also the locomotive, as Lynne Kirby has convincingly shown in *Parallel Tracks: The Railroad and Silent Cinema*. At first, directors focused on the locomotive's potential for speed and power, its visual effects of steam and smoke, its precedent as a shaper of visual perceptions. But they also realized that the experience of riding trains was a prototype of consumption and could be related to watching moving pictures in a theater: in both cases, a "passive consumer" watches shifting landscapes flattened by speed and encased in a frame.[13] Significantly, it was in *The Great Train Robbery* (1903) that the director Edwin Porter first demonstrated the potential of the cinematic medium to capture motion and excitement, teaching directors in the process "how to cut, how to edit, how to place the camera in the establishment of scenes, how to get a story line to move."[14] The symbiotic cluster of relationships among trains, movies, national unification, and cultural identity was also key in such popular and influential films as Buster Keaton's *The General* (1926) and John Ford's *Iron Horse* (1924).

As early as the 1850s Americans referred to themselves as "a locomotive people." James A. Ward attributes such self-identification to early railroad promoters for such trade publications as *The American Railroad Journal*, where editors D. Kimball Minor and Henry Varnum Poor linked railroad tracks to "iron bonds" uniting the nation in a symbolic human body or family, a "circulatory system" of pulsating industrial blood vessels. These railroad enthusiasts were peddlers of techno-progress and speculators of the American spirit, testing out new metaphors for a young nation with few unifying symbols. They found that Americans liked what the train reflected back to them: youth, power, speed, mobility, single-mindedness, bright prospects, novelty, connection. A British tourist of the 1850s wrote that "there must be some natural affinity between Yankee 'keep-moving' nature and a locomotive engine. . . . It is certain that the 'humans' seem to treat the 'ingine,' as they call it, more like a familiar friend than as the dangerous and desperate thing it really is." In 1846 Minor wrote that "we are preeminently a locomotive people and our very amusements are locomotive—the greater the speed, the greater the sport."[15] The railroads appealed to Americans as, paradoxically, "both centrifugal and centripetal": ideas, merchandise, and human beings spread into the country, and those on the frontier had access to markets and goods otherwise shut off.[16]

Cultural engagement of machine aesthetics via locomotive onomatopoeia began to appear in music, folklore, and the penny press as early as the 1840s. New songs such as "The Railroad Quickstep" (1854) and "The Railroad Gallop" (1850) indicated that the machine was calling the tune now (and the tempo of life). Slaves in the South with little experience of trains had already begun to sing about a "heavenly train" by the 1840s. W. C. Handy remembered African Americans singing about particular trains and identifiable steam whistles in the 1870s; trains were part and parcel of every journey in his life, and "always in the rumble of trains there had been the echoes of something sweetly sad."[17] Both the harmonica and the pedal-steel guitar found their American voices in train sounds, and blues singers found their totemic symbol in the train. If in 1873 Jules Verne rendered the excitement of "a new sense of world unity" by propelling a British gentleman around the world in eighty days,[18] American musicians collapsed distance through sound, recreating this "annihilation of time and space" through an *aural* rendering of the mechanical presence in the landscape through textures, rhythms, power, riffs, and repetition.

Whether in work songs, railroad ballads, dance steps, or blues, "no other popular art was more closely allied to the railroad than that of popular music." Trains were the sonic embodiment of modernity. The famous "clackety-clack of trains riding the rails" inspired songsters and balladeers, yodelers and harmonica players, blues guitarists and boogie-woogie pianists. More than a symbol of technological power and the pioneer experience, the train provided the foundational rhythms for moving forward and getting a move on, as well as for an almost obsessive need for power, rhythm, and locomotion—in other words, for the American tempo of life.[19] Americans are a rootless, mobile, speed- and acceleration-hungry people. The automobile has long since come to symbolize—and concretize—these values; but all were present first in the train.

Music was the cultural form that codified and artistically rendered the place of trains in American society. Why is this historically significant? Contrary to the presumption that culture diffuses from the center to the periphery, in this case the subcultural practices of a low-income ethnic group *colonized* the musical practices of the nation (and the world). The nature of this process—integrating the sound of trains into music and culture—began in the antebellum period, and it reached a level of almost total diffusion when the national media network unified in the 1930s around big-band swing culture.

Playing the Train

When the drummer Jo Jones, later the heart of the Count Basie Orchestra's nonpareil rhythm section,[20] was a journeyman in the 1920s, he learned an important lesson from one of the Southwest's finest drummers, A. G. Godley of the Alphonse Trent band. "Young man, you got to learn to play 'the train.'" The "train" was a basic drum pattern (Godley probably didn't invent it) that stylized the rhythm of a steam locomotive pulling out of the station, first accelerating and then rolling down the tracks. Jones replayed "the train" on record in 1966 as he remembered it, first hitting slow, deep, powerful "booms" that mimicked the steam's initial bursts during departure, and then steadily accelerating the pattern, echoing the train as it pulled away. Jones "spoke" the pattern as he played it. "I *think* I *can* . . . I *think* I *can* . . . I *think* I *can* . . . I *think* I *can*," he intoned slowly as the engine pulled out, and then "IthinkIcan IthinkIcan IthinkIcan IthinkIcan," kicking the steam-train rhythm into a higher gear, first something like a gallop and then snickering into the smooth sound of a train cruising rhythmically over the cross-ties. Jones then gave a virtuosic display of how Godley used "the train" as a basic dance pulse to which he added other rhythmic figures and interpolated drum accents, all the time maintaining the clackety-clack of the tracks underneath.[21]

The Alphonse Trent Band was one of the best African American big bands of the 1920s, idolized by black musicians throughout the South and Southwest for its polish, precision, and success. The twelve-piece Trent band was the first to hold down a long-running steady gig in a prestigious white hotel (Dallas's Adolphus), and the musicians were famous for their camel-hair coats and silk shirts. As the Trent band's clientele was the white Dallas elite, we must assume "the train" brought people onto the dance floor.[22] Trent's band recorded only a total of eight songs at a time when drums were kept away from the recording horn so as not to disrupt the mix; there is thus no documentary evidence of Godley's "train," but its evolution into the big-band train can be heard in the live recordings of Jo Jones's band.[23]

During a month-long engagement at the elite Hotel William Penn in Pittsburgh in early 1937, the Count Basie Orchestra enjoyed a remote hook-up that sent the jazz train into living rooms all over the country.[24] For example, "St. Louis Blues" begins with thirty seconds of locomotive onomatopoeia. A song traditionally associated with steamboats, "St. Louis Blues" here begins with ten seconds of a mellow, almost soothing, muted riff for the saxophone section, as of the rhythm of a train at night cruising at high speed. Then the band slowly increases the volume and tempo until the train seems to bear down on the listener. The unison riff starts to mirror the clackety-clack of the wheels while Jo Jones keeps the "train" rhythm on the high hat. Then the brass section begins to scream like so many train-whistles or like people waving and shouting out from grade crossings. After the first instrumental chorus, trumpeter Carl Smith plays a growl trumpet over a bolero rhythm. The singer Jimmy Rushing then takes the first verse, listeners and dancers hearing the first words after a full ninety seconds of instrumental narrative.[25] When Rushing finishes the verse, the brass section returns to the tracks, screaming unison-voiced train whistles at the top of their range—suggesting the train is now at top speed and warning all humans and vehicles of its presence—while this time the saxophones mock the brass from the lower ends of their register. The reeds seem to sob happily "wah" and the brass screams back "WAH," and for five or six seconds, it sounds like: "wah . . . WAH . . . wah . . . WAH." After the exciting attack and counterattack that revs up the band (and no doubt the audience), the trumpets play a high, thin riff that builds to a climax that suggests the sound of air-brakes.

The jazz train makes many appearances during the Basie stand at the William Penn. There is a five-second build-up of train rhythms to open the song "Swinging at the Daisy Chain," and on "Yeah! Man," fifteen seconds of that "wah . . . WAH . . . wah . . . WAH" call-and-response between brass and reeds.[26] After the end of the fast swing standard "King Porter Stomp," the radio announcer tries to pin down the exact speed of the band's driving power: "Now they slow down to sixty miles per hour and present 'I'll Always Be In Love With You.'"[27] In his autobiography, Count Basie declared he loved everything about trains and attended closely to their sounds. The train "was music" to him in all its aspects: "whether they are up close or far away . . . the way the bell claps and . . . all the . . .

things they do with the whistle . . . [and] the way they feel when you riding them and hearing them from the inside." One of his favorites was the Super Chief, a train Basie honored in a 1939 song of the same name, "one of those express coast-to-coast trains that used to go streaking across the Kansas plains like greased lightning."[28] Basie's orchestrations of train sounds and rhythms became instrumental parts of the set pieces of big-band swing for two decades.

There were a variety of train-derived swing riffs, but the ten-to-fifteen-second musical portrait of a steam train leaving the station occurs often as a standard opening for big bands; I call it *the locomotive ball of sound*. Forever immortalized for the Depression and World War II generation by the opening seventeen seconds of "Chattanooga Choo-Choo," this motif—the slow whooshings of the steam, attendant acceleration, clackety-clack rhythm, and trumpet-screaming train-whistles—kick off not only Fletcher Henderson's much earlier "Sugarfoot Stomp" (1926) but even such mainstream pop songs as "Lullaby of Broadway" (1938). Duke Ellington composed more thorough musical delineations of train sounds in compositions such as "Daybreak Express" (1933), "Happy-Go-Lucky Local" (1946), and "Take the 'A' Train" (1941; written by Billy Strayhorn), as did Count Basie, with "Super Chief" and "9:20 Special" (1941), Jimmie Lunceford with "Lunceford Special" (1939) and "Jaznocracy" (1934), and Artie Shaw with "Streamline" (1937).[29] American dance audiences apparently loved the jazz train: its drive and flow, its power and speed, its acceleration and repetitive rhythms, its aural associations and continuous flow from past into the present.

The locomotive ball of sound functioned as a sonic social cement binding industrialization, vernacular music, and dance audiences. Here's my impressionistic analysis of this popular tonal portrait of the steam-train-leaving-the-station. There is a kind of collective success to this motif, something like an aural rendition of Sisyphus, if he'd been successful: it is as if the band and its audience dislodged a huge boulder and set it rolling under its own power. First there's the hard steam-breathing—the exhales—of the train as it begins to leave the station, as if the various musical engineers have put their instrumental "levers" to work and gotten the train moving. Second, the machine begins to roll and the band pushes it forward: the marked acceleration of the tempo communicates the idea that we're "getting somewhere," or at least *going* somewhere. And then quickly, the train is moving under its own power: the mechanical boulder is rolling down the road.

Such an opening telescopes the narrative of the nation's secular myth of techno-progress. Americans felt they worked hard to build this industrial society, this technical or machine civilization. Once a train as beautiful and powerful as the aptly titled "Twentieth-Century Limited" gets rolling, one might as well get on board, and hope for the best down the line. Instead of "If we build it, they will come," this swing motif suggests "We built it, so let's see where it goes." Variations of the motif kick off Jimmie Lunceford's "Rhythm Is Our Business" and "Four or Five Times," Fletcher Henderson's "Wild Party" and "Hotter Than Hell," the Mills Blue Rhythm Band's "Ridin' in Rhythm," and many more tunes.

Such a concentrated essence of the rolling power of the train grew out of the musical depiction of train rides that began in the mid-nineteenth century and were "a staple of 1920s' blues recordings." Programmatic music (imitative compositions) rendering train rides were a "well-established tradition" among the symphonic jazz orchestras of Paul Whiteman and Vincent Lopez in the 1920s, and were apparently conveyed "with considerable realism."[30] But these so-called sweet bands never produced the rhythmic power and drive of the big-band train; their intent was less propulsion than narrative subtlety and harmonic extension. Just as big-band swing was a synthesis of New Orleans small-unit jazz and symphonic jazz, Ellington's fully developed train songs combined the narrative quality explored by the larger symphonic bands with the African American trope of the train.[31]

In 1976 Albert Murray theorized that the rhythmic basis of *all* African American music is "locomotive onomatopoeia."[32] Murray's thesis has remained underexplored owing to a cultural lag only recently overcome in cultural histories of popular music and technology. For example, two generations of jazz scholars and folklorists proceeded from an outmoded primitivist dialectic with "human/preindustrial" on one side and "mechanical/commercial" on the other; they valorized African American music such as blues as "expressive" and "authentic" in opposition to the "commercial" and "popular" songs made possible by mechanical production and distribution.[33] Murray's theory instead reflects Le Corbusier's mid-1930s epiphany, and his resonant phrase needs to be understood literally: nearly all beat-driven American popular music emerged from the imitation, stylization, repetition, and resonance of the clackety-clack of train rhythms, the screaming of the train whistle, the patterning of the station bells that signaled arrival and departure, and the felt experience of riding the rails. The basic elemental propulsive force and rhythmic riffs that together create the American groove—in blues and country, in rock and roll and electrofunk, in hip-hop and techno musics—depend upon many unnamed musicians whose African-derived practices "made the freight train boogie" (to quote a 1947 country song).[34]

What makes American popular music *modern* lies in the cultural potency and aesthetic attractions of the rhythms, sounds, and symbols derived from the public's embrace of the train—the loudest, fastest, most powerful machine in the landscape in the formative period of American nation building. According to Murray, the two "definitive" influences on blues musicians were "the down-home church" and "the old smoke-chugging railroad-train engine." With these two institutions as a base, African American musicians philosophically and aesthetically made the transition from West African practices to the American techno-dialogic. "What may once have been West African drum talk has in effect . . . long since become the locomotive talk of the old steam-driven railroad trains as heard by down-home blackfolk on farms, in work camps, and on the outskirts of southern towns."[35] What Murray omits is that rural white Americans were equally attached to the sound and symbol (and romance and metaphor) of the steam train. Country musicians also stylized locomotive onomatopoeia, and in fact, "Take the 'A' Train" was also the theme song for Bob Wills's seminal western swing band.

By putting the train into the music, musicians enabled listeners and dancers to "wear" their cultural identity through an embrace of technology, optimism, speed, and power in the form of big-band swing. Why did Americans respond so strongly to the jazz train? It gave artistic form to their childhood landscapes (and soundscapes), to their dreams of geographical (and upward) mobility, and to their hopes of both finding out what was over the hill and arriving in style. The fast, fluid, powerful sound of the big bands provided a sense of history, familiarity, and hope to Americans at a culturally precarious moment of technological pessimism. Train-driven big-band swing allowed Americans to keep their faith in techno-progress without leaving their old selves and experiences behind.

Two classic early investigations into African American folklore came to the same conclusion as Murray and reinforce his theorization. In 1925 Dorothy Scarborough declared that the train was a "real being" to southern blacks, as alive metaphorically as mechanically. The train appealed musically to them in many ways. In the "rhythmic turn of [the] wheels," African Americans were inspired to "a rhythmic turn of phrase." She found the "regularly recurring noises" of the train to fall into alternate groupings of two and three—"iambic or trochaic like the Negro's patting of foot or clapping of hand"—not like a horse's gallop, which were "dactylic or anapestic." (Alternations and combinations of two- and three-beat phrases is a central tenet of much African music.) Scarborough wrote that blacks heard the complexity of locomotive rhythms as simultaneously "diabolic and divine . . . gratif[ying] [their] sense of the dramatic with its rushing entrances and exits." Despite her primitivist rhetoric, Scarborough's identification of the rapid shifts of tempo, the personification of technology, and locomotive onomatopoeia stands up well in light of our more thorough knowledge of African American practices today.[36]

In 1947 John and Alan Lomax declared that without discounting all the ballads and folk songs about trains, "it is in the texture of our popular music . . . that the railroads have left the deepest impression." Since most Americans lived "within the sound of the railroad," inside African American music "you'll hear all the smashing, rattling, syncopated rhythms and counter-rhythms of trains of every size and speed." It was in the "rolling bass" left-hand technique of boogie-woogie pianists, in the "steady beat" of jazz, in the "silvery breaks" of blues musicians. "What you hear back of the notes is the drive and thrust and moans of a locomotive. . . . [T]he distinctive feeling of American hot music [i.e., jazz] comes from the railroad."[37]

W. C. Handy remembers both his father and his fellow minstrels imitating train sounds and rhythms as early as the 1870s, often getting the necessary drum sounds by striking knitting pins on the fretboard of a violin. Handy felt fortunate if someone had a harmonica so he and his siblings could "imitate the railroad trains"; the kids used "for drums . . . our mother's tin pans and milk pails."[38] I can only imagine children all over the nation were doing the same. The rhythm of the drum *drove* the imitative melodic sounds of the train whistle.

Locomotive phraseology existed even in children's stories. Jo Jones's use of the now-famous phrase "I think I can" from the classic *The Little Engine That Could* (1930) suggests it may have been a well-known onomatopoetic sequence long before that book was published. If so, the association of social mobility and individual uplift—"I think I can"—with train rhythms further consolidates the myth of techno-progress. Whether in model trains, children's stories, the miniaturized steam railroad encircling Disneyland, or the train trope in American popular music, the symbolic connection between Americans and trains survives to this day. Americans don't enjoy listening to the sound of cars—even one car, in a pastoral landscape—but "people still like to watch trains go by, listen to the sound of the far-away whistle, the groans of the engines."[39] In urban areas the train is now a minor factor in the aural industrial landscape, but once it was the whole kit and caboodle.

The Empire Builders and DeFord Bailey

How closely did Americans attend to the sound of trains? NBC went to inordinate time and expense to accurately reproduce the sounds of trains for "The Empire Builders," a popular radio drama underwritten by the Great Northern Railway that ran from 1928 to 1931 and is considered the first "adventure program" on radio.[40] Broadcast live from Chicago in the largest broadcast studio in the world, the show was supervised by Harold M. Sims, the assistant to the president of Great Northern. The popular show had an audience of millions, for whom the company built a "track machine" to scale, around which "a speeding miniature train br[ought] the listener the clickety-clack of a transcontinental train as it pound[ed] its way through the night." To capture the full range of sounds, rhythms, and textures produced by the steam, wheels, and whistles, a full orchestra backed up the electric trains with kettledrums, whistles, several kinds of bells, and "the hiss of steam."[41]

The show's stock-in-trade was the vast repertory of train sounds produced by the engineers. Sims himself recorded trains in all kinds of weather, over all kinds of terrain, accelerating downhill and lumbering uphill; he recorded the change in the wind as trains passed other trains, and the sound of the engine pulling coal cars or passenger cars. "There is probably as much difference between the sounds of different trains as there is difference between flakes of snow," he declared. The sound of trains changed with "the atmosphere, the time of day, whether [it] . . . is going upgrade or down, whether it is picking up speed or slowing down, [and according to] the length and weight of the train, its speed, [and the] power of the engine."[42]

The show employed five "sound-effects experts" and several engineers; together they aimed not simply to reflect reality but to improve on it, to create "a synthetic effect . . . even more colorful than the real." (See fig. 1). The warning bells at grade crossings came up and faded, as did the clicking of switches and the sound of "passenger flyers passing

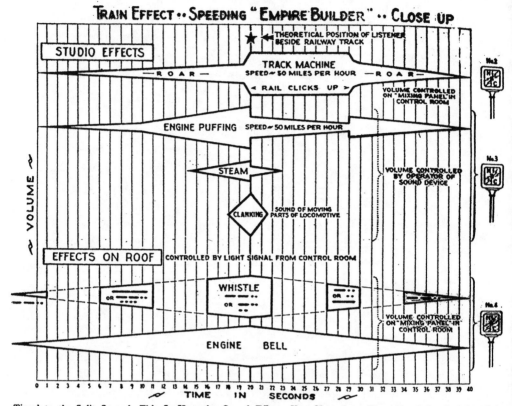

Figure 1. "Empire Builder" sound effects, 1931. This graph maps the overlapping layers of locomotive onomatopoeia produced in the studio to simulate the passing of the Empire Builder, on NBC's popular radio drama of the same name. (Reprinted from *Popular Mechanics*, May 1931. © The Hearst Corporation. All Rights Reserved.)

. . . box cars"; the whistle came from "one of the Great Northern's monster locomotives," as did its standard call of "two long and two short toots." To maintain the "proper balance" of sounds, the sound-effects experts "calculated by seconds what the dominant sounds should be" while maintaining the overlapping layers and textures of locomotive onomatopoeia in proportion to real time. Most shows began in a railroad telegraph office where a professional telegraph operator sent a real (that is, comprehensible) message by Morse code, and the show worked from a set of specially created charts and schedules of "arriving trains, departing trains, freight trains." The combined technological innovations of radio, recording, communication, and sound effects made it possible to bring the small-town world and the natural landscape into homes across the nation.[43]

A few years before the radio drama aired, the first African American star of the Grand Ole Opry, DeFord Bailey, rose to national fame through his ability to conjure up the sound of the train in the landscape with just a harmonica. Known as the "harmonica wizard," Bailey was an Opry favorite second only to Uncle Dave Macon. Requests poured in every night for "Pan American" or "Dixie Flyer Blues," and Bailey performed twice weekly and twice on Saturday (more than any other performer); "Pan American" was one of the Opry's early signature themes. Bailey received thousands of letters of fan mail and became a spokesperson for a number of products. Recording "The Pan-American Express" and "Pan American Blues" in 1927, and "Casey Jones" and "John Henry" the following year, Bailey remains linked to trains in the memory of the older Opry audience. One listener admitted sixty years later he "still remember[ed] the sound of DeFord's train . . . [i]t sounded so real that you could almost see it coming down the track."[44]

Bailey was "playing the train" before he ever saw one, and the first one he saw scared him. "It was the biggest thing I'd ever saw. It got bigger and bigger as it came toward me . . . I was half scared of it." But he slowly got to know the train by meeting the Dixie Flyer every morning at eight; the engineer would "blow round the corner to see if I was there . . . [and] blow that whistle at me—two longs and two shorts." Then Bailey would lie under the trestle with his foster sister, "and put something over my eyes to keep cinder out of my eyes. We'd listen to the sound and then I'd play that sound all the way to school." "The Pan American Express" took its name from the passenger train from Cincinnati to New Orleans (with a stop in Nashville) which was simply "the fastest around."[45]

Bailey worked for years to get each part of the train down perfectly. He first "got the engine part," and then later the train whistle. "It was about, I expect, 17 years to get that whistle [right]." Like Sims, he noticed that trains made distinct sounds on different tracks, and learned "how to make a harp sound like it was going over a trestle or a deep curve . . . [or like] when you in the mountains and going through a tunnel. . . . I'd listen to everything." He figured out how to make the cautionary low sound of the train whistle "when cattle was on the track and all that kind of thing . . . a distressed blow." But he wasn't just imitating the train literally: "I got that whistle so it would have a double tone to it, a music tone." As Samuel Floyd has pointed out, Bailey imitated "the whistle, the movement of the wheels, the escaping steam, and the train's increasing speed." To be original musically "takes years," he said simply.[46]

As I theorize in the next chapter, West African–derived sociomusical practice involves *re-presenting* the soundscape in rhythmic phrases, not in correctly playing a written score through notes; in other words, Afro-diasporic musicians render the universe intelligible through sound. DeFord Bailey's biographer rightly perceived that his "fondness for 'sounds' rather than individual notes meant that he was ceaselessly experimenting with various unorthodox chords or what fiddlers would call 'double stops.'" Bailey's immersion in black vernacular practice was also a factor in his affinity for abrupt tempo shifts, and he was "a master of dynamics, swooping in one phrase from a loud, braying trainlike phrase to a gentle, fluttering arpeggio."[47]

Bailey was proud of his ability to stylize and re-present any sound, even in the agrarian environment. "I caught all that. Sheep. Cow. Chicken. Dog. They got music in 'em. . . . You can get a heavy bass from a cow."[48] He would lie in bed and hear dogs howling, or wild geese honking as they flew overhead, or the wind as it blew through the house, and he would play any and all of it. "You know there's some music in everything. . . . If we couldn't find nothing else, we could always blow in a jug or beat on some skillets and pans." As a child then, Bailey was already repeating, revising, and replicating his environment, making sense of his universe through sound. Once he played his harmonica from inside of a toy airplane; the toy had a wheel that spun inside its plastic shell and with the harmonica blowing through, Bailey thought it sounded like a real airplane. "I'm just like a microphone," Bailey once said. "I pick up everything I hear around me."[49] In other words, Bailey was a master practitioner of the techno-dialogic: a musician creating a dialogue among culture, music, and technology.

"Some people can play the train, but they can't make it move like I do." Opry audiences loved Bailey's train because he registered the felt experience of riding and watching trains. "Most of theirs [other musicians' trains] sound like they're running, but the sound is standing in one place too long. You can tell my train is moving. Every time I blow, you can tell I'm getting further. It's moving out of sight as I blow. The sound of their train is moving, but staying in sight too long. I'm always reaching out. When I get about 115 miles an hour, I can feel it. my normal speed is 95 miles an hour." Bailey's accomplishment was to make the steam sounds and whistle cries while simultaneously "keep[ing] the wheel-mimicking rhythm going."[50]

Of his two most famous trains, Bailey considered the "Dixie Flyer" a completely different piece from "Pan American Blues." The latter was a generic train, "natural whistle, natural sound." But the Dixie Flyer was "a slick train" (an express) and he especially worked on the "pretty brass bell" the engineer rang when he blew through small towns. "It was the prettiest thing you ever seen. Shiny. When that train came through, that bell'd be ringing. I can see it now. It was running so fast, the smoke would be laying down, jumping out of the stack and curling around on top of the coaches. When they'd see that track was clear, they'd shift into the last gear, and throw that throttle wide open."[51] Bailey's experience of the landscape and soundscape rendered by that train was a profound aesthetic experience, one most of his radio audience clearly shared. His trains were steam trains; though he added a diesel whistle after a train trip to Chicago in the mid-1930s, he never liked the sound much.

The real-life whistle of the Pan American Flyer was literally the signature sound of the Opry in the mid-1930s. WSM in Nashville took advantage of the location of its transmitter next to the L&N (Louisville and Nashville) tracks near the Brentwood, Tennessee, radio station. An engineer thought to "plac[e] an open mike by the track to catch the Pan American as it left Nashville, headed for New Orleans," and every day, "like clockwork," when the train known as "the Pan" blew its whistle approaching the station, "the sound would go out over WSM." This was one of the station's most popular features, and it "formed a real-life counterpart to the favorite piece by the station's favorite harmonica soloist."[52]

"The Ballad of John Henry" was one of Bailey's favorite songs (and an Opry favorite), and in his use of music, props, and rhythms to create the setting of this ballad, he created a matrix of technology, music, and storytelling. Bailey used two steel bars as props to mimic John Henry's hammer as he blew his harmonica. He placed the steel bars in a rack around his neck and "hit the bars with a hammer in time to the music, imitating the steel hammer in the song." He sometimes added other effects "to simulate the clanking of metal as . . . [John Henry] pounded feverishly away," or simply "clacked sticks and bones together with one hand" while blowing to set up an alternating rhythm. Such added textures enhanced the ambience of the story and its message.[53]

Euro-American and African American cultural practices reveal quite different approaches to the symbolic representation of the train. The Euro-American approach was now infused with machine technologies. The production of "The Empire Builders" reveals that popular culture producers were dependent *on* the machine to *reflect* the machine. But DeFord Bailey took on the machine with the tool he had mastered (the harmonica) in order to humanize machine aesthetics, adding only found objects (steel bars, toy airplanes, wooden sticks) to recreate a more textured soundscape. Bailey meditated on the train from every direction—as if looking at the *aural* planes vibrating in the landscape—and created a train as real to his listeners as that in "The Empire Builder." This is the social and artistic objective of the techno-dialogic: to re-present the universe as humanly organized sound through aesthetic practices.

Trains Are Us

Before returning to the jazz train, let me digress to show just how important the locomotive was as a mediator for American masculine identity, and for a male/machine interface in the late nineteenth century.[54] The train was the first idealized *mechanical man,* a prominent cultural image embedded in the American male desire for machine aesthetics.

In 1868 a robotlike character known as the "Steam Man" appeared in Edward S. Ellis's dime novel *The Steam Man of the Prairies.* The ten-foot-tall grinning steel servant, first referred to in the story as "the Gentleman," the Steam Man represents the American male cultural desire to integrate machine aesthetics with human form. Basically a superhero who might well have been named "Train Man," Steam Man is described as "a sort of peregrinating locomotive." His boy-inventor, Johnny Brainerd, explains that the mechanical man works "on the same principle [as a locomotive], except that it uses legs instead of wheels." In one scene Steam Man runs alongside a train—shocking the passengers—and the narrator entreats the reader to admire his mechanical power: "Like a locomotive, he seemed to have acquired a certain smoothness and steadiness of motion."[55] Yet when the Steam Man is first spotted by two stock comic figures of American folklore, the practical Yankee and the superstitious Irishman, they don't know whether to run for their lives or indulge their curiosity.

Their reaction was consistent with society's crisis regarding the presence of machines in American society. What if a train got up and walked like a man? How would humans defend themselves against such power-ful creatures? Yet it was almost cultural blasphemy in the late nineteenth century to express anxiety over technological change. These factors led Steam Man to be presented not as a powerful human-hybrid superhero, but as a servant—just as cars and consumer appliances would become domesticated machines a half-century later. He is also black in color; as with blackface minstrelsy, white men could only express their desire for machine aesthetics by putting a mask—a black face—on it. Steam Man is thus the color of coal and of the slaves emancipated just three years earlier.[56]

As a hybrid of man and train, Steam Man prefigures Superman, the "Man of Steel," who in 1938, by the end of the industrial period, ap-peared over the skies of Metropolis. As American men became more comfortable with the dreams of techno-progress, the human-machine interface changed from the black servant of Steam Man to a Janus-faced white man, part shy small-town journalist and part robot (complete with x-ray eyes, an airplanelike body and, of course, "more powerful than a locomotive"). Though an alien from another planet, the "machine man"—Superman—became an official American icon between the world wars.

As with any kind of cultural exchange, a desire for the Other (in this case, the mechanical Other) is a desire for acculturation. In Steam Man, pulp writers produced the first character built out of a human-machine interface, which is now common to popular culture. (To take a few ex-amples: the films *AI, Robocop,* and *Inspector Gadget,* R2D2 and C3PO from *Star Wars,* the *Bionic Man* and *Bionic Woman* television shows, humanized androids such as *Star Trek*'s Data and *Blade Runner*'s replicants.) Dime novels pressed machines into the service of the same American male fantasies that are today rendered much more palpable by special effects. The Steam Man stories featured not only boy-inventors and robots, but "armored flying vessels, electrified wire, and remote-control weapons." Such technological fantasies were almost totally separate from the "means of production revolutionizing the industrial system."[57] In other words, regarding economic change, these pop-cultural texts repre-sented neither resistance nor accommodation, but a specifically male desire for machine capabilities.

The nation's best writers were similarly moved by locomotive ono-matopoeia and train symbolism. Walt Whitman addressed the train as a co-conspirator of modernity in "To a Locomotive in Winter." To rouse

Americans to democratic action, Whitman called for the "fierce-throated beauty" to "roll through" his poetry with its rhythmic power and "lawless music." Whitman's "chant" was filled with references to train rhythms: "thy measur'd dual throbbing and thy beat convulsive"; "the train of cars behind, obedient, merrily following . . . now swift, now slack, yet steadily careering"; "thy madly-whistled laughter, echoing, rumbling like an earthquake,/rousing all." For Whitman, the train *embodied* modernity: "Type of the modern—emblem of motion and power—pulse of the continent."[58]

William Carlos Williams's "To Freight Cars in the Air" (1914) is composed almost entirely of locomotive onomatopoeia. At first one hears "the slow/clank, clank/clank, clank" that seems to come from out of the blue, from "above the treetops." Then one hears "the/wha, wah/of the hoarse whistle/[and] pah, pah, pah/pah, pah, pah, pah, pah, pah," as the train courses forward "trippingly," a sound that lingers in the landscape "long after the engine/has fought by/and disappeared/in silence." In "Overture to a Dance of Locomotives" (1921) Williams attempts to capture the whole railway journey. He begins with the bustle of the terminal, where "the domed ceiling" creates an industrial cathedral, and instead of church-bells, "the hands of its great clock/go[ing] round and round!" carry standard time. Then one proceeds to the train "poised horizontal/on glittering parallels" enticing passengers to a comfortable journey, called to attention by "the whistle!" blown in "twofour" time. Once the train is in motion, a passenger's sense of time, space, and distance gets rerouted, just as nature had been straightened and reshaped to accommodate the coming of the train: "rivers are tunneled: trestles/cross oozy swampland," and the spinning wheels run "forever parallel/[and] return on themselves infinitely."[59]

Many of the nation's most famous folk ballads came from legends of trains, engineers, and the railway journey: "Casey Jones," "Railroad Bill," "The Wreck of Old 97," "The Ballad of John Henry," "I've Been Working on the Railroad." There were also several genres of work songs related solely to building the railroad—track-lining songs, hammer songs, drill songs, "tamping" songs—and the legacy of these work songs permeates blues, country music, and western swing.[60]

Black railroad workers—track gangs, "gandy dancers"—made their own train poetry by literally singing the track into the ground. Of the black gangs "who laid so many rails in the South and West," one railroad historian noted that "singing as they drove in their spikes was . . . as necessary as eating and breathing."[61] As work songs directed such group-based work as unloading ships or corn-shucking, so "work chants . . . direct[ed] railroad crews who line[d] heavy steel tracks." As workers lifted the heavy rails or cross-ties, a caller would direct their moves. The caller functioned as a work-conductor, whose expertise included rhythmic steadiness, verbal dexterity, improvisation, and a management ability to focus a diverse crew of laborers on tasks requiring great collective effort. Moving steel tracks was dangerous work, and men had to work together; any laxity on the part of an individual put more strain on the rest of the crew and unbalanced the load. Loss of life and limb was quite common.

As railroad construction has specialized jobs, a good caller directed different work with distinctive chants and rhythms. Rhythms that were right for the tamping crew would be wrong for the lining crew—a common West African practice based on the functionality of different rhythms for specific actions. Such traditions may have existed for other ethnic groups, but there are no recordings of them. For example, although there were many Irish songs *about* working on the railroad such as "Drill, Ye Tarriers, Drill"—which would seem to be a hammer song—there are no recordings of Irish work songs, meaning songs created as accompaniment for the work. Norm Cohen, author of the definitive study of railroad folk song, *Long Steel Rail,* calls the former "occupational songs" and the latter "worksongs." All known field recordings of railroad work songs are by African Americans.[62]

Cal Taylor, who led railroad crews in the Mississippi Delta for fifty years, told William Ferris "how on each beat the [lining] crew slowly moved heavy rails into position." Taylor sang three verses with identically structured seven-line calls, where only the first two lines changed. The new "story" of a verse might be, "Oh, I got a letter from Haggis Town,/East St. Louis/was burning down," followed by the chorus: "Ha ha, way over/Ha ha, way over/Poor boys, pull together/Track'll line better/Whoa!" Some of the verses were explicitly sexual; as Taylor commented, some verses "for track lining . . . got bad stuff in 'em." He sang one of those, too: "Oh, talking about a pretty girl, you oughta see mine/Great big titties and a broad behind/Ha ha, way over/Ha ha, way over/Poor boys, pull together/Track'll line much better/Whoa!"[63] Such songs reveal the interconnection of work and play in African American cultural practice, and a continuum leading from preindustrial work rhythms to those of modern industrial society.

As for the musical quality of African American work songs, the composer W. C. Handy once said that the "shovel music" his gang of steel workers made in Florence, Alabama, in the early 1890s would have "stopped almost any Broadway show . . . [if we could have brought] our brigade before the footlights." Up to a dozen men "pass[ed] the time" by beating the shovels against the "iron buggies" in rhythm, and altering pitch and tone by "withdrawing or thrusting forward the metal part [of the shovel] at the point of contact." Handy compared it to the technique of playing the musical saw. As music that was created to pace work, and purely as participatory entertainment, "it was better to us than the music of a martial drum corps, and our rhythms were far more complicated."[64]

Railroad culture also produced one of society's most enduring anti-heroes of techno-progress in the hobo, a free radical of American society celebrated because the machine served *his* enjoyment. An escapist from the work ethic, the hobo was imagined unproductively riding the rails, a figure of adventure and freedom. Hoboes first appeared in great numbers after the Civil War and represent a male desire for machines that serve their fantasies of leisure time rather than those that supervise their work in factories. Like the tramp and gamin in Chaplin's *Modern Times,* the hobo lived on the outskirts of industrial society. As a safety valve for hostility towards industrial capitalism, the hobo represented a dream of nonparticipation in machine-driven modernity.

Dancing the Engine

Americans had two different ways to engage encroaching mechanization: to worship and emulate machine abilities through fantasy, or to artistically stylize machine aesthetics, which had the advantage of physiological engagement.

For example, the locomotive ball of sound had a dance analogy in a warm-up exercise for tap dancers known as "Dancing the Engine." (See fig. 2.) Just as in the jazz train, the steps were done to mimic "the sound of an engine leaving a railroad station. The chugs of the engine start slowly and evenly. They gradually go faster and faster until they become one continuous sound." Once the dancers picked up enough speed, one no longer heard the individual beats but rather a continuous rhythm.[65]

"Dancing the Engine" was a simple enough four-step routine which any reader can do right now. First, you slide the left foot forward and

The Engine

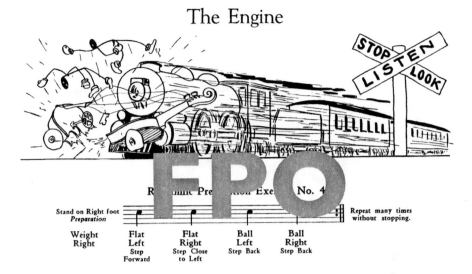

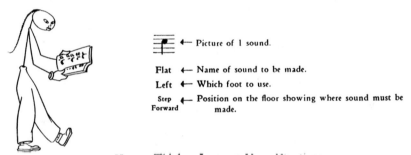

Notice above how the *pictures* of the *sounds* (Notes) are written on the staff to show *how many sounds* are to be made. The *directions* for making *Tap* sounds are written in a *column* directly *underneath each note* and should be *read* from the *top down* like a Chinaman reads sentences.

← Picture of 1 sound.
Flat ← Name of sound to be made.
Left ← Which foot to use.
Step Forward ← Position on the floor showing where sound must be made.

How to Think or Interpret Above Directions
(Reading from top down)

On the "Flat" of the "Left" foot "Step Forward"—or—"Step Forward" on "Flat" of "Left" foot.
(Say "Flat Flat Ball Ball" aloud as you dance)

How to Practice and Enjoy Dancing the Engine

Did you ever hear the sound of an engine leaving a railroad station? The chugs of the engine start slowly and evenly. They gradually go faster and faster until they become one continuous sound.

That is the way to practice. Start slowly and evenly, taking care to tap correctly. Later go twice as fast. Increase the speed until you have almost a continuous sound. Say "Sh" aloud with each tap. Make the "Flat" taps as loud as possible and the imitation of an engine will be perfect.

This dance is very clever when accompanied by a pianist who can follow the dancer slowly, then faster and faster until the tempo becomes an exciting race.

First National Institute of Allied Arts
FIRST NATIONAL INSTITUTE BLDG.
SOUTH BEND, INDIANA

Figure 2. Instructions for "Dancing the Engine." In this simple tap routine the dancer imitates the sounds of a steam train leaving the station, getting up to speed, and then cruising along at a smooth, steady rhythm. (From Ruth Stryker's *Tap Dancing*, vol. 1, 1938.)

drop the heel, then slide the right foot forward and drop the heel. Next, you draw the ball of the left foot back, then the same with the right foot. If you do it quickly, your feet make the standard chukk-a chukk-a chukk-a chukk-a chukk-a chukk-a chukk-a rhythm of a steam engine. As the drummer does with the train rhythm, a dancer should "start slowly and evenly . . . [then] later go twice as fast. . . . Increase the speed until you have almost a continuous sound." And just as Jo Jones combined speech and music to mirror the rhythmic figure of the train with "I think I can," the tap instructor Ruth Stryker suggested that the dancer emit the "'sh' [sound] aloud with each tap." If one also "make[s] the 'flat' taps as loud as possible . . . the imitation of an engine will be perfect."[66]

A more widely disseminated train-derived dance step was the "chug," a basic one-sound tap maneuver probably named after the quick sound of steam released from the engine. The dancer simply "jump[s] or slip[s] forward keeping foot in contact with the floor." This loud, precise slide is "always accented," and the quick dropping of the heel displaces the air under the shoe as if to release the steam. The step is described in nearly all tap manuals of the 1920s and 1930s.[67]

The stylization of industrial aesthetics in music and dance during the interwar years reflects a confident engagement within popular culture that looks back to the transition from natural and agrarian metaphors to industrial and mechanical ones.[68] For example, the 1850 song "Railroad Gallop" marked the transition from the horse to the train; the fastest moving body in the landscape was no longer an animal but a machine. Like the familiar Native American designation, "iron horse," the title reflects a transitional moment of continuity and change. Land travel had been limited to "that of a galloping horse," and the railroad "represented the first quantum leap" toward the technological transformation of the felt experience of time, space, and speed. In the process, railroads "provided the human frame, the human spirit, [and] the human imagination, with the first and most shattering mechanically-induced shock they had ever experienced . . . [a] shock [that] was both sudden and universal."[69] Just as the figure of the centaur reflects an ancient desire for men to be half horse, the machine now embodies the collective desires for qualities such as speed, power, and excitement. The 1854 march called "The Railroad Quick-Step" similarly suggests that the machine now dictates the tempo of life.[70]

African Americans incorporated the train into social dance steps as early as the 1890s. "Ballin' the Jack" was a hit song, a dance, and a vernacular term that brought music and dance together. "Jack" refers to the locomotive—an update of its black vernacular use for "the indestructible donkey or jackass" (similar to "iron horse")—and the term "ballin'" was derived from "high-balling," a hand signal given by the engineer to start the train rolling. According to a southern folklorist, "'Ballin' the jack' means traveling fast and having a good time."[71] The song was written by two black songwriters, Chris Smith and Jim Burris, and published in Harlem; Florenz Ziegfeld bought the whole routine and brought it downtown for the Ziegfeld Follies of 1913.

In *Psychology of Music* (1938), a landmark musicological work of the period, Carl E. Seashore began his chapter on rhythm by asking readers to recall the rhythm of the train riding over the rails. When lying in a "Pullman sleeper [car]," a traveler often connects up "the successive beats coming from the crossing of rail joints" into a "crude" rhythm sufficient for humming or singing popular songs. This common experience was Seashore's launching point for defining "the perception of rhythm," which he theorized as a twofold cognitive experience: first, "an instinctive tendency to group impressions in hearing"; second, the ability to "do this with precision in time and stress."[72]

Seashore presented himself as Exhibit A. He remembered a journey in which he was "haunted" by an old "plantation melody"—"What kind o' a crown you gwine to wear? Golden Crown?"—that was surprisingly well-served by the train's repetitive, driving rhythm. As he relaxed into "the imagery of the melody," the clickety-clack seemed to become increasingly buoyant, and "the accentuation of the click of the rails became very prominent and satisfying as rhythm." In retrospect, it seems no accident that the song was a variant of an African American spiritual, whose rhythm may have originally been influenced by locomotive onomatopoeia. Seashore concluded: "The rails seem . . . to beat the time emphatically into measures."[73]

The Blues Train

Along with literature, work songs, dance steps, and dime novels, an important element in building the jazz train was the blues. As blues emerged as a genre in the late nineteenth century, musicians brought the train into their songs literally, figuratively, and onomatopoetically. The transition from spirituals to blues in this period represents a transition from the collective spiritual struggle of emancipation to the personal, corporeal, day-to-day challenge of survival in the Jim Crow

South.[74] The soprano saxophonist Sidney Bechet, born in 1897, put it this way: "Both of them, the spirituals and the blues, was a prayer. One was praying to God and the other was praying to what's human. It's like one was saying, 'Oh, God, let me go,' and the other was saying, 'Oh, Mister, let me be.'"[75] Casting their lots pragmatically, blues musicians transmogrified the "glory train" of the spiritual to steel-blue steam trains, vehicles they had actually seen, heard, and ridden.

In researching early spirituals, John Lovell Jr. was surprised to find the early integration of train sounds and symbols in African American musical thought. The South had less than a third of the nation's track miles before the Civil War, and slaves had little opportunity to examine this new machine up close. "Yet before 1860, many spiritual[s] . . . exploited the train, its seductive sounds, speed and power, its recurring schedules, its ability to carry large numbers of passengers at cheap rates, its implicit democracy." Between 1865 and 1873, according to Samuel Floyd, the metaphysical train took over from the metaphysical chariot in spirituals such as "Swing Low, Sweet Chariot." In this period, thirty thousand miles of railway track were laid, an act of empire construction of which black gang workers were an integral part. The "horse-drawn heavenly chariot" might take souls to their final reward as liberation from earthly torment; "its steam-driven, land-borne, rail-riding descendant" carried the blues of individual African Americans.[76]

By 1925 blues trains had company names, distinctive whistles, and a cast of archetypal characters including the engineer and the fireman. A sampling of songs recorded by blueswomen between the world wars include: "He Caught That B&O," "TN&O Blues," "I Hate That Train Called the M&O," "Panama Limited Blues," "The L&N Blues," "The Cannonball," and more generic titles such as "Freight Train Blues" and "Railroad Blues." Samuel Floyd points out that these blues trains "have names, whistles that blow, and engines that break down. . . . Some are slow, and some are fast . . . they take away lovers . . . and never bring them back."[77] In blues songs, the train functions as the metaphorical conveyance of choice for African American movement, with a cluster of associations even beyond the energy, technology, and forward progress it represented for most Americans. The train represented freedom for ex-slaves: *literal* freedom, the right to locomotion under one's own power.

The first blues song was not recorded until 1920, and by then musicians had fully incorporated the train and all its symbolic associations into the music. The train-as-journey, the sonic train, the train as symbol of industrial power and energy, the train as romantic escape from hardscrabble living and static lifestyles—all such musical trains were ripe for riffing in Clara Smith's "Freight Train Blues" (1924), Blind Willie McTell's "Travelin' Blues" (1929), Lonnie Clark's "Broke Down Engine" (1929), and Booker White's "New Frisco Train" or any boogie-woogie piece fashioned after "Pine Top's Boogie Woogie" (1928). Hazel Carby has shown how the train was a totemic symbol of freedom for blueswomen, who serenaded it as an agent of change and escape or cursed it for taking their man. Bluesmen created the trope of being a "broke down engine" with either a useless "driving wheel" or an engine that "ain't got no drive at all."[78]

Trixie Smith's "Choo Choo Blues" (1924) utilizes twenty seconds of locomotive onomatopoeia to set up the singer's ride. What sounds like a genuine station bell clangs unaccompanied for five seconds to mark the venue (a train station) and the singer's predicament (her man left on a train). Then an anonymous musician slowly scrapes an unidentified percussive instrument, perhaps a washboard, and then increases the tempo, producing an early version of the locomotive ball of sound. When this raw rhythm approaches the train's cruising speed, two horns squawk a train-whistle in unison. The horns cede the musical space to a honky-tonk piano, which then softens the rhythm for the singer's entrance.

Clara Smith's "Freight Train Blues" is an early anticipation of the big-band swing train. The opening is a recognizable version of the locomotive ball of sound. Lacking a big band's power, Smith's five-piece band re-creates carnival sounds, circus riffs, and even a calliope. The train whooshes steam heavily three times to start off, then slowly accelerates; once rolling, the singer has a rhythmic platform from which to perform. The song's rhythm accelerates from silence to a slow, chugging tempo in about twelve seconds.

In a confessional blues such as "Freight Train Blues," the opening suggests that the listener get on board with the singer to join her for this emotional journey. Smith wrote the lyric and role-plays the experience of a woman meditating on her man leaving home. The nonlinear narrative refers to the train as both an agent of freedom and an agent of male mobility, and it ends with one of the most famous blues couplets for signifying the differences between men and women: "When a woman is sad, she goes to her room and cries/when a man gets the blues, he catches a freight train and rides." Yet the song's ending belies this message, for the singer gets on the train—making it an agent of female mobility as well. Musically the song ends with a five-second refrain of the train motif: two big whooshes of steam and one whistle suggesting departure.[79] Smith recorded "Freight Train Blues" again in 1938, and to compare the two versions is to realize just how much the blues train had become "streamlined" into the big-band swing train. The rhythm is smoother and more powerful, the introductory train-station ambience is omitted, and Smith's vocal conveys a more assured sense of urbanity.

Blind Willie McTell's "Travelin' Blues" (1929) shows the central role of the train in the soundscape and features a musical conception of alienation. The song simply describes a hobo's average morning. The narrator feels hungry walking down the road and gets fed by an elderly woman. Back on the road, he creates an internal dialogue with the sounds of the train. First he hears the train whistle "getting off" (a common jazz term for "taking a solo") and mirrors this sound on his guitar. Then he hears "the old bell . . . getting off like this," and rings out a few harmonics to complete the verse instrumentally. In the next verse the narrator "hear[s] the whistle blow" and translates the sounds into spoken cadences: "Lookee yonder," he intones, alternating slide-guitar elisions and single-note repetition; "lookee yonder," he repeats, lining up voice and guitar. "At the women," comes the punchline, "at the women," he repeats, as if that's what the train-whistle has on its mind.[80]

Having made locomotive onomatopoeia the main content of his morning, McTell then presents the engineer in his ritual role as apologist for The Man, using blues couplets then in common usage. He asks "Mr. Engineer" if he can "ride the blinds" (meaning the space between the locomotive and the mail car). The engineer says he would like to help him out, "but you know this train ain't mine." McTell plays the train whistle on his guitar, a distinctive "long and [then] short," and then repeats the riff with bent notes that emit a more lonesome wail than any of his previous instrumental breaks. The shift in tone suggests the singer's awareness of his narrative's emotional progression. The narrator then curses the fireman and the engineer; he's not hurting anyone, just trying "to hobo my way." This line is mirrored by a slower slide-guitar riff that suggests a more resigned, moanful motion, as if the narrator has slowed to walking speed and given up on the train ride.[81]

Another conduit between blues and the swing train was the genre of boogie-woogie piano. Meade Lux Lewis's "Honky Tonk Train" (1937) is only the most famous piece in a blues genre that first caught fire with Pine Top Smith's "Pine Top's Boogie Woogie" (1928).[82] The eight-to-the-beat left-hand rhythm "represents the moving train's wheels" and the right-hand thematic improvisations a "variety of whistles." As the pianist shifts motifs and rhythmic emphasis, the train seems to speed up and slow down, and listeners of the time might have heard "various whistles . . . and even different sets of wheels."[83] The boogie power of these solo virtuoso pieces suggests the kind of powerful, dynamic music that fifteen train-driven musicians could provide swinging together.

By 1934 the train had thus been thoroughly absorbed and integrated into African American "musicking": repeated and revised, mimicked and stylized, blessed and cursed, personified and transmogrified. Both Euro-American and African American musicians took the train about as far as it could go riding one instrument, whether harmonica, fiddle, guitar, or piano. Here we have a set of black vernacular practices—West African–derived, techno-dialogic, and blues-individualized. Blues guitarists such as Blind Willie McTell traveled all through the South, trading music for money. Clara Smith, Bessie Smith, Alberta Hunter, and other blueswomen mixed blues with vaudeville in nightclubs around the nation, hitching an independent female perspective on gender relations to a mobile music, and bringing a new vocal power and confessional honesty into the American musical aesthetic. DeFord Bailey blew his train into American homes across the nation. Meade Lux Lewis and Albert Ammons eventually took their boogie-woogie piano trains to Carnegie Hall for the "Spirituals to Swing" concerts in 1938.

How did the blues train become incorporated into the swing train? The men who became African American swing bandleaders, many of them raised in southern middle-class families, found their best career opportunities in popular music. Atlanta-born Fletcher Henderson, unable to get a job even with his B. S. in chemistry from Fisk University, came to New York in 1921 and became the house pianist at Black Swan records. What he didn't know about blues, he learned accompanying Ma Rainey and Bessie Smith on their early records. Duke Ellington, from the still-southern town of Washington, D.C., deferred taking an art scholarship at Pratt Institute and began creating "tonal portraits" at the Kentucky Club in New York in 1924. Alphonse Trent, another chemistry major, muted the blues backgrounds of a crack band of south-western musicians to play propulsive dance music for white society. Memphis-raised Jimmie Lunceford, an instructor at Fisk University, took his best students up to the then thriving and cosmopolitan industrial center of Buffalo, New York, and created one of the period's smoothest big bands. The blues train swung its way powerfully north, gathering up American dreams and disappointments, absorbing the rampant industrial energy let loose over four generations, and reflecting the tempo of American life. All this musical work was completed before Benny Goodman's triumphant emergence; and all that train-work in the music was ready to be tapped and adapted, co-opted and appropriated, made more precise or more melodic for a whiter American musical aesthetic.

Jazz *Is* a Train

The central importance of the train to the African American historical imagination would be equally hard to overstate. For example, the last piece of music composed by Fletcher Henderson, the major architect of big-band swing, was a theatrical score entitled *Jazz Train* (1950), for a revue performed at New York's Bop City and Paradise nightclubs. Co-created with the writer Mervyn Nelson and the lyricist J. C. Johnson, *Jazz Train* comprised a series of six musical vignettes, each one called a "car" (a train car) and proceeding chronologically.[84] The first car was called "Congo" and featured two dance numbers (one was Henderson's 1926 hit, "Stampede"). The second car was called "Plantation" and featured plantation dances, and the third "Laughter" and featured a mini-minstrel show. The fourth was called "New Orleans" and featured characters named "Lady Blues" and "The Man with a Horn." The fifth car was called simply "Passengers" and highlighted the contributions of great black musicians. Actors played the roles of Bessie Smith, Louis Armstrong, Ethel Waters, Jimmie Lunceford, and Buddy Gilmore (the drummer for James Reese Europe and the Castles); "The Roarin' 20s" was also a character, as was "Porgy and Bess." The sixth and final car was called "Journey's End." Henderson had crafted a history of the African American experience through the reality *and* metaphor of the train journey as embodied in the big-band jazz train.

In a 1934 "soundie" (an early music video) entitled "Cab Calloway's Hi-De-Ho," the jazz train is rendered visually.[85] As the house band at the Cotton Club, Calloway's band was then arguably the most popular big band in the nation. The ten-minute narrative was produced by Adolph Zukor and widely distributed for all audiences. (Two years earlier, the animated figure [and real voice] of Calloway co-starred with Betty Boop in three influential and revolutionary animated shorts, by Max and

David Fleischer, each on par with the best Disney work of the period. These films and the soundie were shown in theaters to boost business when Calloway came through town.)[86] The film opens in the early morning hours on a train busting through the countryside; the foremost sound is the train's clickety-clack rhythm. A steam whistle blows, and the Pullman porter wakes Calloway to give him a telegram that informs the audience that this is a private car on the Chicago Limited en route to New York City. "Must change opening number Cotton Club . . . by morning," reads the message from Irving Mills (Calloway's real-life manager). The bandleader wakes up the musicians. They are shown slowly getting out of their sleeper compartments; as a joke, the bass player is shown sleeping with his arm around his bass, as if it were a woman. The musicians warm up in their pajamas.

When Calloway counts off the beat, they blast into action. First, the entire ensemble creates a foundational beat, a three-note steam-powered riff—boohm-BOOHM-boohm boohm-BOOHM-boohm— that mimics the clickety-clack but in a higher timbre, playing the low-register propulsive rhythm with steam-whistle sonorities. Then the clarinetist plays a short two-bar solo over the chugging ensemble.

Suddenly all the instruments stop—and allow the train itself to take a solo. The steam whistle of the train they're riding hits and holds a high note for about five seconds. When it fades, the band waits one beat and then Calloway leads the band's response to the train's call, a snaky, slightly dissonant riff. The band repeats the riff three times and then explodes in terms of both speed and power. They play the next section at a furious pace: if the initial riff was played at 140 beats per minute, the new section is played at 240. The first riff has responded to the train's rhythm on the tracks, but the latter responds to the locomotive itself. The brass and reed sections scream at each other, building up more excitement through counterrhythms; the bass player pounds out the even quarter-notes that ground swing tempo; a short baritone saxophone solo tunnels into the collective drive, followed by a trumpet solo that soars over the top. After about one minute the music suddenly ceases. In the silence, the clickety-clack rhythm takes back the night.[87]

Jimmie Lunceford's band, one of the most popular with white audiences, was known as the "Harlem Express" and was labeled by chronicler George Simon as "without a doubt the most exciting big band of all time."[88] Lunceford's first hit, "Flaming Reeds and Screaming Brass" (1933) reveals the band playing at a blazing up-tempo pace in the style of the (white) Casa Loma Orchestra: fast, precise, and driving, though with few train-whistle sonorities. "White Heat" (1934) and "Jazznocracy" (1934) show evidence of train power, the former seemingly influenced by Ellington's "Daybreak Express" (1933). Lunceford's arrangers, Sy Oliver and Clyde Wilcox, quickly latched on to the locomotive ball of sound and used it to open several pieces, especially the hit song, "Rhythm Is Our Business" (1934). In 1941 the band recorded "Lunceford Special," a train with the leader's name on it.[89]

Nearly a half-century after Fletcher Henderson's *Jazz Train*, Wynton Marsalis celebrated the same cluster of associations in his hour-long composition, *Big Train* (1998). Before its premiere at Lincoln Center, the opera star Beverly Sills interviewed Marsalis. "Why a train?" she asked first. "Why a train instead of, say, a plane or a bicycle?" Marsalis replied, "Jazz music actually is a train."[90]

"The shuffle [rhythm] is a train," said Marsalis as he sat down at the piano, laying down a 1–2–3–&–4–& shuffle rhythm that emphasized blue tonalities in the right hand and open fifth and sixth chords in the left. "Then you got the train whistle," and he played broken octaves in the right hand while continuing the shuffle in the left hand. "Then you got the engine," and he steadied the rhythm to an even count (1–2–3–4, 1–2–3–4) that surged forward almost imperceptibly. With the Lincoln Center Jazz Orchestra providing musical illustrations, Marsalis explained the meanings of the jazz train as musical grammar, "I'm a musician . . . I don't want it to be literal like . . . chick-uh-chick-uh chick-uh-chick-uh woo-WOO," and he emphasized the importance of "metaphysical trains—the underground railroad, the gospel train."

In recalling the sound of the train as it went by his boyhood home in New Orleans, Marsalis hoped to craft an epic statement about everything the train represents as a carrier of history and as the collective African American journey in the United States. Many African Americans point to black music as a cultural carrier of their historical experience. Nelson George claims he has heard some version of the following sentiment his whole life: "You can tell where black people are at any given point in history by our music."[91] The role of the jazz train is part and parcel of the story of African American music in its intertwined functions of dance music and history, of aesthetic statement and cultural newspaper, of memory and metaphysics.

"The heart of the train is the drum," Marsalis explained to Sills. To illustrate, his drummer Herlin Riley played a solo that combined the low rumbling of the tom-toms, rhythmic figures echoing train whistles on the cymbals and cowbells, and occasional press-rolls on the snare drums. Riley always maintained the surging chug-chug-chug rhythm underneath with the bass drum and high-hat, just as A. G. Godley and Jo Jones had before him. Marsalis claimed he heard the drum solo for the composition first; next came the clackety-clack "go[ing] puh-POM-puh-POM . . . the sound of the train on the tracks."

"Then there's the train call and response [of the whistles]—'wah-WAH . . . wah-WAH,'" Marsalis mimicked, using two different figures to express the train's passage: a quick "wah-WAH wah-WAH"—for a train speeding through—and a more gradual crescendo and fade, "wahhhh-hhh-WAHHHHHHH-wahhhhhhh," mirroring the whole sequence of a train passing through the landscape. Then there was the train's wake which required muted trumpets to create a soft wash of color. "The train is loud, the train is soft too. . . . When that caboose is leaving, it's one of the softest sounds in the world; you ain't never heard a loud caboose. . . . It's a nostalgic sound."

At the beginning of the piece, with only the shuffle rhythm established, the drummer Riley calls out to the imaginary passengers:

> Somebody tell me. . . .
> Does anybody know. . . .
> Where-uh-huh-where
> Where-uh-huh-where
> Where-uh-huh-where
> Does the Big Train go?

In repeating the same phrase three times, he varies the message of the single word "where" as he draws it out melismatically to "where-uh-huh-where." First, it's just a literal question: where is this train going? The second time, he inserts into the phrase his personal cry, one of the basic tenets of African American music. It's not just a physical journey, but a metaphysical one: he wants to know, really, where is *he* going? The third time, he's thrown in his lot with the other passengers: where are *we* going?

Riley's answer, musically speaking, is to get the train-rhythm going, get the passengers on board, and we'll figure it out as we go. Marsalis answers with a solo trumpet passage, a train-whistle screech that sounds like WAH-WAH-wah. The trumpet section plays at the top of its range, not at all in rhythm, varying unison passages and dissonant rhythmic phrases. This opening cacophony seems to relax the drummer-conductor Riley, who yells out more calmly and evenly, "All Aboard"—as if to say, everyone relax, we're on our way.

"The big train is about the relationship between the individual and the group," Marsalis concludes. Ten minutes into the composition, the train has been aurally (and collectively) created, and it is up and running. Now it's time to give the band's individuals some space to speak their piece to the collective since "people soloing is a part of the train." For three or four minutes, the band engages in call-and-response: solo calls and full big-band responses. Marsalis then deemphasizes the band's propulsion, focusing on complex harmonies with conscious Ellingtonian tonal colors for the ensemble brass and reed passages. Two minutes later, we've moved from swing to bebop: Riley plays some subtle rhythmic figures while Marsalis converses with him, soloist and drummer cut free from their timekeeping responsibilities.

The end of Big Train's first section is signaled by Riley's reprise of the opening question: "Does anybody know where the Big Train go?" He is answered first by an expressive growl trumpet solo, which suggests the pain and lonesomeness of the journey; Riley responds by simply keeping the steady train-rocking rhythm going. Next, the brass section shouts riffs at the drummer, approximating the sound of steam pouring from the locomotive, punctuated puffs of sound that lend a visual quality to the rhythm. Then a high screeching by trumpets and soprano saxophones creates the once-familiar dissonant sound of air brakes as the train comes into the station.

Wynton Marsalis is a protégé of Albert Murray, and his self-conscious use of locomotive onomatopoeia in *Big Train* is a tribute to Murray's theorization, as well as to Ellington's "Daybreak Express" and Basie's "Super Chief." In Murray's best novel, *Train Whistle Guitar,* the Alabama boy Scooter idolizes the local blues guitarist and "rounder" (wanderer), Luzana Cholly. The bluesman embodies Scooter's two central passions—music and trains—and functions as an archetypal American man on the road (or on the railroad): he has no family and always arrives in town by "coming up that road from around the bend and . . . the L&N railroad bottom." When improvising on guitar, Cholly's musical train of thought sounds like a train-whistle. He "play[ed] the blues on his guitar as if he were also an engineer telling tall tales on a train whistle, his left hand doing most of the talking including the laughing and signifying as well as the moaning and crying and even the whining, while his right hand thumped the wheels going somewhere." Murray used

Luzana Cholly to represent how bluesmen had inscribed the train into the nation's music as a leitmotif of American male wanderlust.[92]

Stephen Henderson uses the term "mascon" for vital words and phrases that carry historical and metaphysical associations in the African American oral tradition. Such a mascon as the word "train" carries a "massive concentration of black experiential energy."[93] Not only were there freedom trains and trains to glory, but such associations carried both spiritual and concrete experience into jazz. Thus a post-swing jazz classic such as John Coltrane's fourteen-minute "Blue Train" carries all the train's meanings in its wake (including the jazzman's nickname, "Trane"). The jazz train functions musically and metaphorically for a journey both individual and collective; its propulsion renders the journey profoundly dramatic and spiritually purposeful.

Two major African American composers of different generations in fact experienced emotional epiphanies while riding trains at key moments of mourning. Duke Ellington wrote his most personal work shortly after his mother's death. In 1935, during "one of th[o]se one-nighter tours of the South," Ellington began to reminisce about his mother, and the memories mixed with the rhythms of the train. He sat down to write his then-longest composition, "Reminiscing in Tempo," (1935) and remembered feeling that "the past . . . was all caught up in the rhythm and motion of the train dashing through the South." The train gave voice to feelings "I could never have found words for." The title recognizes the train's role: "Reminiscing in Tempo" means to the train's tempo.[94]

On the night that the African American bandleader James Reese Europe died, the sound of the subway haunted W. C. Handy with a "ghostly [sound] like the rumble of train wheels out of the past." Handy realized his life had been full of "melancholy journeys, filled with trains rumbling through the night." He recalled the freights that took his gospel quartet to the Chicago World's Fair in 1893, and the trains that carried his minstrel-show troupe across the country. "Always in the rumble of trains there had been the echoes of something sweetly sad, something lost perhaps," Handy reflected, thinking of his "Railroad Song" and other pieces.[95]

Trains held deep, complex meanings for southern blacks, and this "sweetly sad" or "bitter-sweet" or "happy-sad" trope rolls through musicians' autobiographies. Charles Keil suggests that one crucial function of all music is to yoke opposing realms of feeling into an artistic unity, whether combining politics with poetics or transmuting opposition into complementarity. For Keil, blues and soul musics are "about emotional mixes in people's minds," and they represent a "resistance-accommodation dialectic." Public ritual focused on music and dance mediates social and aesthetic tensions, which for Keil is exactly the power "beneath the Apollonian-Dionysian distinction" theorized by Nietzsche. Many African American musicians suggest that the train-as-machine symbolized a yearning for mechanical power tempered with a sense of loss of community—that is, an increase of individual potentiality and a decrease of communality.[96]

For example, Lionel Hampton, Benny Goodman's vibraphonist and an excellent drummer, described the role of the train in the lives of African Americans of Birmingham, Alabama, around 1910 as "a major form of entertainment." With blacks unable to afford diversions like the circus and excluded from participating in organized sports, "the trains let us dream about faraway places." Hampton remembered how "people sat along the railroad tracks on summer afternoons and watched the train go by." At six o'clock every evening, "hundreds of people" gathered to watch the Special pull out, "and cheer[ed] the spectacle." As the train pulled out "in slow motion . . . you could see every detail." From a seventy-year remove he lingered over every detail: "the dining car with its white tablecloths, the coaches filled with passengers, the berths being made up for the night." The "star" of the show was the locomotive, which was subject to the same caste regulations as the rest of southern life. "The engineer, who was always white, blew the whistle. The fireman, who was always black, rang the bell." There was no hostility in the recollection, just a flash of pride in connecting African American life with the modern technology of the locomotive. "How proud I was when the fireman was my grandfather, mastering the biggest engine in the world."[97]

Train imagery permeated African American religion, politics, and work in the industrial period, adding layers of metaphorical and historical meaning to mainstream meanings.[98] The underground railroad was the slaves' own pathway to freedom; the "freedom train" and the "train to glory" were vehicles that took supplicants from the secular realm to the sacred; the Brotherhood of Sleeping Car Porters was the first labor union run by and for African Americans.[99] That the train had long been an important symbol of freedom and power in African American oral tradition and history dovetailed with its role in national unification. Swing musicians and fans alike caught the sonic association. The jazz critic Otis Ferguson described swing bands at the Savoy Ballroom as "dominating the hall and bearing down on it, inexorable, all steam and iron, like freight trains."[100] Dizzy Gillespie attributed swing's popularity with dancers to the "chug-chug-chug" of the rhythm section.[101]

Stanley Dance refers to the years between 1931 and 1934 as Ellington's "train period." Until 1930, Ellington had been writing "jungle"-themed music to feed the primitivist desires and plantation fantasies of Cotton Club audiences. As the band began to tour more in 1931, he wrote songs that engaged his new traveling environment and reflected its sonic textures and forward drive. As evidence of the transition, on the same day in 1933 that Ellington recorded "Daybreak Express," the band also recorded two plantation melodies and a ballad: "Dear Old Southland," "Delta Serenade," and "Solitude."[102] In the early 1930s the Ellington band was energized by a new momentum in its rhythm section that anticipated the propulsive swing then coming out of Kansas City bands. The guitarist Freddy Guy steadied the rhythm with straight quarter notes, the bassist Wellman Braud began to play more of a walking bass figure behind soloists, and the drummer Sonny Greer began to vary his repertoire of rhythmic figures.[103] Such changes made the new pieces "capable of the most delicate shades of tone and the most blasting power."[104]

The veteran clarinetist Barney Bigard described how closely Ellington attended to the sounds of trains in composing "Daybreak Express": "Duke would lie [in the baggage car] resting, and listening to the trains. Those southern engineers could pull a whistle like nobody's business. He would hear how the train clattered over the crossings, and he'd get up and listen to the engine. He'd listen as it pulled out of a station, huffing and puffing, and . . . start building from there. . . . He had the whistles down perfectly."[105] Ellington imagined it this way: "You're lying in bed at daybreak, somewhere down South, and you hear this train rushing by as swift as the wind. It's passing up stations like a son-of-a-[gun], and you know that that one 'ain't stoppin' no place'! It's just the opposite of the 'Happy-Go-Lucky Local,' which rattles along with a boogie beat." Similarly, the drummer Sid Catlett often stood outside on the observation car to attend more closely to the train's sound-world; he would point out specific sounds to his bassist-partner John Simmons, who recalls hearing these sounds integrated into Catlett's rhythmic pulse and his solos.[106]

Albert Murray claims that train sounds were once "pictures" inside the music—visual metaphors—as in "Daybreak Express." "Now," he says simply, "it's just the way we play music." He calls the train rhythms at the base of African American music the "dead metaphors" of American popular music. In other words, even though train sounds are no longer the most exciting in the landscape, they still contribute an overall forward drive to American popular music. The train instilled a get-a-move-on quality to the blues, and this drive is now present in all American music. The historian Lewis Erenberg asserts something similar when he calls swing "the music of the black migration": train-powered music conducted by newly urban (and urbane) African Americans, offering aural encouragement for southern blacks to come north, to "get a move on" to where life was better.[107]

Stanley Dance remembers "Daybreak Express" as "the most thrilling of the jazz trains. Fourteen men say so much in three minutes. . . . [T]o those who traveled on the rushing expresses in those days the piece has more than evocative significance."[108] "Daybreak Express" was a landmark in jazz composition and ensemble playing. It was an unprecedented technical performance in terms of power, tone color, textures, unison section playing, and the interplay between solo instruments and collective drive. It was also, in its time, a "stunning lesson" in how well the jazz medium could "equal or better anything . . . being done in classical program music." For Gunther Schuller, Ellington's fourteen-piece band created more drama and drive than a classical orchestra of seventy-five musicians.[109]

What's more, Ellington's orchestra *swung* this machine. In 1923 the German composer Arthur Honegger's six-minute "Pacific 231" became something of a classical hit song in Europe. A powerful but ponderous machine when accelerating into the landscape, once up to speed "Pacific 231" became a frightening mechanical monster. The climax of Honegger's piece contains Hitchcock-like musical elements of suspense through tortured dissonance, screeching violas, and gnarled brass—as if the train is going to crash. The piece reveals the great difference between European and American attitudes toward technology.

Yet in a forum on the future of American music, "Daybreak Express" went unmentioned by composers George Gershwin and Roy Harris. Both were excited about bringing the industrial soundscape into music. Gershwin made enthusiastic reference to "Pacific 231," his own use of taxi horns in "An American in Paris," and George Antheil's metal-and-machine potpourri in *Ballet Mécanique*. Harris called for American composers to reflect "America . . . [and its] smoking, jostling, clamorous cities of steel and glass and electricity dominating human destinies." Both mentioned jazz in the abstract, but neither mentioned Ellington or African American music in any form. Harris condemned jazz as "an unimaginative commercial routine which serves only crystallized symmetrical dance rhythms."[110]

Yet Harris was quite specific about the nation's distinctive musical character—its rhythmic complexity—and he gleefully pointed out the inability of European composers to employ the jazz idiom. Compositions by Stravinsky, Ravel, and Milhaud did not swing because these composers had not grown up in a culture where rhythmic fluidity and improvisation were part and parcel of musical life. "Our rhythmic impulses are fundamentally different from the rhythmic impulses of Europeans," he wrote, and consequently the rhythms "generate different melodic and form values. . . . European musicians are trained to think of rhythm in its largest common denominator, when we are born with a feeling for its smallest units." In other words, classical composers attempt to create harmonic complexity at the expense of micro-rhythmic figures and rapid tempo shifts—which they cannot handle. "Anyone who has heard the contrast between a European dance orchestra and an American . . . playing in the same dance hall cannot have failed to notice how monotonous the European orchestra sounds."[111]

Harris waxed poetic about the "American rhythmic talent" obvious even in American children. "Children skip and walk that way . . . our conversation would be strained and monotonous without such rhythmic nuances." In the United States, a "unique rhythmic sense" had been created, the "develop[ment of] a different feeling and taste for phrase balancing.[112]

In fact, even the white swing train required African American rhythmic elements to maintain the representation of the train-driven soundscape. "Chattanooga Choo Choo" achieved its wildest distribution in the hit movie *Sun Valley Serenade* (1942), a Hollywood vehicle for the Glenn Miller band. In the movie sequence, the band does not play behind any narrative action, but behind the virtuosic tap-dancing duo of the Nicholas Brothers, who perform in front of a cardboard backdrop of a train. A promotional still showed the Nicholas Brothers in their final pose, smiling and throwing their hats in the air in front of a nineteenth-century Pullman car made of wood and featuring Victorian decorative elements.[113] Tap dance was a swing idiom, and its percussive virtuosity was on a par with that of swing drummers; yet the Nicholas Brothers are neither named nor recognized for their art in the film. In fact, their presence as entertainers in service to white society is underscored by the song's opening lines: "Pardon me, boy/is that the Chattanooga Choo Choo/Track 29/I got to get me a shine."[114] The "boy" is no doubt a black porter, and the shoeshine will be applied by a black man as well.

Thus do the opening lines of "Chattanooga Choo Choo" establish a foundational social narrative at the train station by referring to African Americans in reassuring subservient roles in the South. The white swing train needed jazzing up by black tap dancers, but the white audience continued to respond to African Americans as lower-caste citizens. A further irony, of course, is that African American musicians helped fuel Miller's rise. His first big hit, "Tuxedo Junction" (a song about the street-car terminus in Birmingham, Alabama) was a cover of an Erskine Hawkins song already popular with African American dancers, and the black arranger Eddie Durham was one of Miller's hit-makers (with "In the Mood").[115]

Again and again, three elements are intertwined in big-band swing culture: African American musical practices integrate locomotive onomatopoeia; the machine aesthetics of music and dance help fuel the nation's imagination; and social (and caste) stratification reify the exclusion of blacks in the nation's songs and movies. Even the first western swing bands were train-powered for their all-white audiences. In a live recording of Bob Wills and His Texas Playboys' "Steel Guitar Rag," Wills kicks it off by announcing, "Now let's get on this train." In the Sons of the Pioneers' "When the Golden Train Comes Down" (1937), a white gospel train comes down from heaven at full steam. The rapid bowing of the fiddle mimics the clackety-clack of the tracks while the pedal steel lets off train-whistle riffs.[116]

Why did the jazz train resound in so many genres and into the far reaches of the national consciousness?

In the jazz train, African American musicians accomplished what the Futurists never quite conceptualized: they stylized mechanical elements into a living aesthetic tradition that humanized the machine and accepted it as a factor in industrial society. Jazz itself carries the bittersweet journey of the train—constantly driving ahead into the future but full of a sense of loss—in a "happy-sad" music full of longing, locomotion, and physiological engagement. The New Orleans clarinetist Louis "Big Eye" Nelson summed up the jazz aesthetic this way: "Keep a lively tempo but shove in [that] crying wherever you get the chance."[117] The personal cry in the cotton fields, the lonely wail of the alienated slave or share-cropper, becomes a jazz solo calling for collective response. The presence of the blues cry means that even the person farthest down the ladder can lend his or her voice to the national music. By yoking West African musical practice to machine aesthetics, black musicians have made the African American historical experience part and parcel of all the popular music that Americans will ever create.

Coda: The American Music Train Rolls On

The last railroad exposition was the 1948 Chicago Railroad Fair, which, like its predecessors, exceeded expectations in attendance and interest. At the fair, two major producers of the American mythos passed the torch of train-centered nation building into the postwar era. First, Edward Hungerford wrote and produced the fair's featured dramatic show, "A Parade of Transportation," a historical review of transportation from the horse to the Conestoga Wagon to the stagecoach to the train. Hungerford was responsible for every train-based costume pageant of the period, from the B&O Railroad Centennial in 1927 to "Railroads on Parade" at the New York World's Fair of 1939. After several historical locomotives went by along the railroad tracks, a series of 1947 cars followed alongside, with carefree young Americans leaning out of convertibles. The message was clear: the railroads had built the nation and driven its industrialization, but from now on consumers would drive their own cars.[118]

More importantly, Walt Disney claimed he got the idea for Disney-land at the Chicago Railroad Fair. Disney was a train fanatic and once referred to driving the legendary DeWitt Clinton locomotive as the greatest thrill of his life; he thought it comparable to shaking hands with George Washington. (That makes for a nice triangulation of imagineering.) When Disney first imagined his theme park, he told his nephew, "I just want it to look like nothing else in the world. And it should be surrounded by a train." First opened in 1955, Disneyland was a concrete expression of nostalgia for the preindustrial American small town, a place where there was only *one* machine roaming around: the train. To ensure the realism of the soundscape, Disney underwrote the "most elaborate steam railroad preservation project in American history," 5/8th-scale versions of real historical trains to circle Disneyland.[119]

Whether in a cutting-edge production like "The Empire Builders" or in the one-man-with-harp virtuosity of DeFord Bailey, the train as sound and symbol strengthened its hold on American ears, hearts, and minds during the very nadir of the railroad industry, between 1929 and 1934, and so the train as a nostalgic symbol of techno-progress overrode the economic vagaries of the industry itself. Having by the Depression survived the heavy historical weight of robber barons, strike-breaking, price-gouging, and political corruption, the train was a machine with nine lives. The locomotive familiarized Americans with the potential of machines right where they lived, as a new embodiment of power, speed, strength, purpose, and continuity. If the train provided the master experience and symbol of American industrialization, locomotive onomatopoeia became the syntax of the American beat.

AFRICAN AMERICAN MODERNISM AND THE TECHNO-DIALOGIC

FROM JOHN HENRY TO DUKE ELLINGTON

Gilbert Seldes identified a conundrum about jazz in a 1926 *Dial* article. If jazz reflected the American tempo—its energy, its machines, its restlessness—then how could an ethnic group perceived to be lazy, childlike, and primitive produce music that expressed the powerful, reckless spirit of American life? Seldes began his argument from the minstrel-derived theory of blacks: "The Negro . . . holds to a pace and a rhythm different from those of our large cities; he still loafs, is carefree, avoids business a little." But, he wondered, how would this stereotype "explain the snap and surprise of current jazz?"[1]

"It is a rough generalization that the rhythm of jazz corresponds to the rhythm of our machinery," Seldes wrote, restating a truism of the 1920s. Yet if black musicians managed to absorb machinery into their musical traditions, "we cannot say that a simple civilization (the African) by accident hit upon a complex one (our own)." Seldes had been reading the most recent analyses of African American music, as well as European studies of African art. Armed with Henry H. Krehbiel's breakthrough studies of African American folk songs and West African drumming, Seldes leapt the cultural divide. "If we can hazard that the African civilization preserved for us in their art was of a high order, and that ours is of an equal intensity, expressed in the complication of machinery, we can suspect a parallel which would make the suitability of African rhythms not at all surprising." For Seldes, machinery and West African rhythms swung together to create the jazz aesthetic.[2]

For African Americans, music is the cultural form that mediates between oppositional and assimilationist trends, between resistance and accommodation.[3] Pre-1945 jazz qualifies as "modernist" art within

European ideas of artistic experimentation, social defiance, and self-expression; but its artists created music with an entirely different social and aesthetic agenda. *African American swing-era modernists did not consider themselves separate from their audiences,* nor in defiance of bourgeois taste or archaic artistic convention. Their goal, more often than not, was to encourage a unifying spirit in a public dance-hall ritual more indebted to a West African aesthetic than to either a folk, classical, or vaudeville tradition. The artists' most rewarding moments came in-the-moment: when audiences of ordinary people responded with emotion, enthusiasm, and physical grace to their art, it made them play harder and better for that temporary community. As with the goal of much West African ritual, the swing dance-hall ritual yokes seemingly opposite social demands together: in this case, a rebellious modernist defiance in aesthetics combined with the unifying act of social dance.

African American arts are no longer referred to as primitive, folk, or unconscious, yet even such an astute scholar as Martha Bayles refers to African American musicians and dancers as "culturally innocent" of "the attitudes and beliefs of modernism." This is true only if we accept exclusively European ideas and ideals of modernism; wouldn't it be more useful to examine the commonalities between African American and European modernisms? Marshall Berman defines the experience of modernity as "a life of paradox and contradiction," one that involves being dominated by "immense bureaucratic organizations," which modernists must "be undeterred . . . to fight the change." How can African Americans be "culturally innocent" of such an experience? Berman admires Marx and Dostoevski for speaking to the necessity of "embrac[ing] the modern world's potentialities without loathing and fighting . . . its most palpable realities." For African American artists, such a stance was literally a matter of survival, at both an individual and cultural level.[4]

Swing music and dance express precisely this very modern tension, but African American bandleaders attempted to communicate with a *popular* audience. Black musicians and dancers created and performed within an aesthetic tradition they felt strongly about honoring, not rebelling against. Thus the cultural production and artistic experimentation of what one might call "African American popular modernism" emerged from a non-European set of cultural practices and artistic intentions.

Duke Ellington's artistic goal was to establish two-way social and aesthetic communication with his audiences. "If a guy plays something and nobody digs it, then he hasn't communicated with the audience. And either he goes somewhere to an audience that does dig him, or else he adjusts what he's doing to the audience that he has." This is not a modernist attitude but a culturally democratic one. When Ellington wrote "improv" or "ad lib" on his scores for the trumpeter Cootie Williams or the altoist Johnny Hodges to create their own solos, he believed he worked in service to the musicians and audiences. From a Western perspective that valorizes the individual artist, such cooperation makes him a lesser composer; from an American perspective, such an approach seems democratic and populist in striving to create functional music that mediates tension between the individual and the group. "The music of my race . . . [is] something which is going to live, something which posterity will honor in a higher sense than merely that of the music of the ballroom today."[5]

Louis Armstrong articulated more precisely the artistic tension of individual style and popular acclaim, of call and response. In a short 1932 piece written to promote his London performances (which sold out), Armstrong declared that "the famous musicians and bands all have a style of their own. I determined from the start to cultivate an original style, and . . . I tried out all sorts of ideas, discarding some, practicing others, until I reached, not perfection, since that is unattainable for the true musician, but the best that was in me." Therein lies his artistry, but communication results only if the audience resonates with that created style. "The real test is entertainment. Does it interest your audience? Of course, you can gradually teach them to appreciate new styles and absorb new ideas, but it must be gradual and they must have no idea that you are 'teaching.'" The call-and-response of Afrodiasporic music contains this performer-audience aspect: the artistic call must earn the audience's response, or else no conversation is taking place.[6]

Ralph Ellison best expressed this innovating-traditionalist approach of swing-era jazz musicians. In the 1930s, Ellison was an aspiring swing trumpeter and jazz composer. Classically trained at Tuskegee Institute, he always insisted jazz was an American "institution" and that the interwar period marked the high point of its artistic functionality at the center of the dance-hall ritual. "The artistic interchange between the orchestra and a moving audience was quite exciting and creative . . . [as] a communal experience. . . . There used to be groups of people who made the public dance part of a total experience." It is no accident that

Louis Armstrong is the underground hero of *Invisible Man*, the artist whose "familiar music . . . demanded action" of the protagonist in the novel's prologue. "My strength comes from Louis Armstrong and Jimmy Rushing, Hot Lips Page and . . . Duke Ellington," Ellison maintained in a 1976 interview.[7]

Ellison grew up in Oklahoma City, the home-base of the influential territory band, the Oklahoma City Blue Devils; he was also a close personal friend of Jimmy Rushing, the band's vocalist, and a regular at their performances and jam sessions. Anchored by the bassist Walter Page, the trumpeter Oran "Hot Lips" Page, Rushing, and the tenor saxophonist Lester Young, the Blue Devils effectively merged with Bennie Moten's band in Kansas City between 1932 and 1935 to form the Count Basie band. I must quote at length to honor the passion (and acute analysis) of Ellison's homage to his hometown heroes:

> These jazzmen . . . lived for and with music intensely. Their driving motivation was neither money nor fame, but the will to achieve the most eloquent expression of *idea-emotions* through the technical mastery of their instruments (which . . . some of them wore as a priest wears the cross). . . . The delicate balance struck between strong individual personality and the group during those early jam sessions was a marvel of social organization. . . . *The end of all this discipline and technical mastery was the desire to express an affirmative way of life through its musical tradition* and . . . this tradition insisted that each artist achieve his creativity within its frame. *He must learn the best of the past, and add to it his personal vision.* Life could be harsh, loud and wrong if it wished, but they lived it fully, and when they expressed their attitude toward the world *it was with a fluid style that reduced the chaos of living to form.*[8]

If that is not the point of artistic endeavor—and if experimentation with new forms was not a modernist ideal—then the term "modernism" is meaningless. Gunther Schuller adds that all black bands knew their limited "options for professional survival" and balanced artistic and aesthetic concerns with "economic and social" ones. They knew that "a music which cannot attain and then *maintain* an audience also cannot survive.[9]

For example, Louis Armstrong often declared that he was here on earth "in the cause of happiness," as did Duke Ellington, and neither had in mind the archaic stereotype of childish, natural, innocent, primitive joy. Their performative styles reflected both an awareness of their roles as conductors of functional public rituals meant to uplift the collective spirit, and a sense of musical *work* in service to the "cause" of collective joy. Sonny Greer, Ellington's drummer, proudly declared, "I was part of an organization that made millions of people happy." Armstrong's contemporary and fellow New Orleans virtuoso Sidney Bechet expressed this sentiment more profoundly: "My race, their music . . . it's their way of giving you something, of showing you how to be happy. It's what they've got to make them happy."[10]

A hundred years earlier, Frederick Douglass came to much the same conclusion when distilling the function of music among slaves: "Slaves sing more to *make* themselves happy, than to express their happiness." Slaves were "relieved by" their songs, which contained within "boisterous outbursts of rapturous sentiment . . . ever a tinge of deep melancholy." Douglass believed that any white American who would "thoughtfully analyze the sounds" of blacks singing to and for themselves—"in the deep, pine woods," for example—could never believe these were the songs of an innately happy and simple people. Six years before the Civil War, Douglass wrote that the songs of African Americans "would do more to impress truly spiritual-minded men and women with the soul-crushing . . . character of slavery" than reading "volumes" of abolition literature.[11]

What Douglass said about spirituals was addressed in more modern fashion by the blues. The unsettled, mobile, out-of-control feelings common to southern blues musicians at the moment of its creation (the 1890s) still contribute to its success as a musical form. Being alienated and isolated, "the sense of being a commodity rather than a person," feelings of displacement, rootlessness, and a lack of control—such were the limits of African American possibility for sharecroppers of the Deep South. African American blues singers sang this state of mind into being, and this "crying tone" is ingrained in American musical practice. The folklorist Alan Lomax believes the blues are "the best-known tunes humans have ever sung," and he calls the past century "the century of the blues."[12]

African American music contains the moans of daily struggle inside a groove expressive of collective trust that makes self-expression possible in a dangerous society. Think of the individual-collective tensions in a gospel choir, Muddy Waters' electrified city blues, or Miles Davis's lyrical trumpet solos washing over the buoyant musical platform provided by the bassist Paul Chambers and the drummer Jimmy Cobb on *Kind of Blue*. "What connects that sadness and joy is the courage to live," Sterling Stuckey reflects, "the capacity to confront tragedy without wincing . . . [which] allow[s] the human spirit to assert itself undiminished."[13]

The European modernist aesthetic stands opposed to both commercial product and folk styles, and assumes an artist in rebellion against tradition and convention. As Kathy Ogren has argued convincingly in *The Jazz Revolution,* the most important and influential jazz musicians of the 1920s were *those who left* their hometowns, musicians who went where the musical (and commercial) action was. Nearly all New Orleans musicians had a deep, abiding affection for their hometown. But it was Louis Armstrong, Jelly Roll Morton, and Sidney Bechet—the travelers—who brought jazz to the world and the world into jazz. New Orleans musicians who toured and returned, talented men such as the trumpeter Freddie Keppard or the clarinetist Lorenzo Tio Jr., were first-rate artists but not modernists. Louis Armstrong was thrilled to be crowned "King of the Zulus" in the 1949 Mardi Gras parade; but he lived in Chicago and New York in the 1920s, in Los Angeles and New York in the 1930s, and in Queens, New York, for the rest of his life. Duke Ellington left Washington, D.C., for New York in 1923, and later reflected that Harlem and Paris were the modern artistic centers of the day. Sidney Bechet spent the 1920s in Harlem and Paris, and he claimed Harlem in the 1920s and Montmartre in the 1930s were the artistic centers of the world. "Everybody had a kind of excitement about him. Everyone, they was crazy to be *doing*." As well-traveled modernist artists, jazz musicians in such testimony add to our understanding of modernism.[14]

Arguably, jazz was a modernist form before it left New Orleans. New Orleans was one of the most cosmopolitan cities in the world in the nineteenth century, a multicultural, multiethnic mix of people as renowned for its Dionysian revelry and distinctive food and cultural mores then as now. What early jazz musicians often simply called "New Orleans music" was cooked up out of blues, French dances, Italian operatic arias, American brass-band music, Haitian rhythms, Spanish flourishes, military drill, "Latin tinges" from the Caribbean, Afro-Cuban music, and the dramatic shifts of the tango. Jazz was already the result of a musical exchange of lower-class African Americans and middle-class, often French-educated Creoles—a literally "creolized" music in which blues-based self-expression appropriated European musical structures to create new musical forms. In the mid-1910s, when Freddie Keppard's band first played the bars of San Francisco's Barbary Coast, audiences didn't know if the music "was for dance or sing or listen," Bechet recalled.[15]

Perhaps even more importantly, jazz musicians increased the range, technique, and tonal palette of every instrument in the orchestra—trumpet, violin, clarinet, contrabass—certainly one of the hallmarks of any modernism. Early jazz musicians imitated everything from trains to barnyard animals on their instruments, and they attempted to make their instruments "talk." They extended the range and expressive abilities of every instrument in order to capture African American vocal qualities, dynamics, cadences, and speech patterns.[16] This "vocalization" of instrumental music—the talk, the moans and hollers, the "cry," the spoken phrase—first occurred among blues musicians, and it is one major conduit through which blues practices became part of the jazz musician's tool kit. Here, European musical instruments were pressed into service to speak in black voices and tones about African American emotional and historical experience.[17]

Louis Armstrong's "incomparable sense of swing" changed the rhythmic approach of nearly all popular music in this century; he literally taught the world to swing. His expressive, playful, often gravel-toned singing remains the most revolutionary vocal style in American history, influencing everyone from Billie Holiday to Frank Sinatra to Chuck Berry. Indeed, Gunther Schuller says that he "added a new school or technique of singing to Western music." And that's all besides the influential innovations on his instrument: his hitting one hundred high C's at the climax of a performance, a note trumpeters had never hit; his "upward rip" to begin a solo, which defied every European idea of tonal purity and attack; his use of exaggerated vibrato and the "shake" of his trumpet to bend the notes and distort the sound waves (just as blues guitarists do). And that's just Armstrong.[18]

A personal, individual, signature sound (or tone) is an aesthetic imperative for jazz musicians, without which one is not by definition a jazz musician. Olly Wilson calls the African American musical ideal "a heterogeneous sound ideal," meaning that musicians do not value purity or perfection, and, when playing together, blend their sound with others but not by playing the same tone in unison. The arranger and guitarist Eddie Durham worked with both Count Basie and Glenn Miller and perceived these contrasting ethnic musical approaches to instrumental playing. "[In] the white bands, the musicians play one or two tones, the vibrato tone and the straight tone. . . . And that's why any white musician can sit down and play in Glenn Miller's band. . . . But the black musicians can get eight or ten different tones on his horn, so when he gets in a band, that's why it's hard for him [initially] to fit." Bandleaders might hire a new musician for his individual sound, but in big bands he had to learn to blend in; "[you] got other[s] on the team with you, you've got to stay in line."[19]

The conductor Leopold Stokowski remarked in the late 1920s that "the jazz players make their instruments do entirely new things, things finished musicians are taught to avoid. They are path-finders into new realms." The ethnomusicologist Ingrid Monson solved the long-standing problem of transcribing African American "rips, slurs, swoops, slides" into Western musical notation by adding eight additional markings that approximated how musicians "talk" through their instruments and play with or against the rhythm. In 1919 a French brass band that encountered James Reese Europe's famous World War I band insisted on exchanging instruments to see how the musicians had altered their horns to get such original sounds. In other words, jazz musicians "Africanized" European musical instruments, aesthetic ideals, and rhythms.[20]

During his tour of the United States in the late 1920s, the German philosopher Count Hermann Keyserling wrote in the *Atlantic Monthly* that "nothing America has created so far can bear comparison with the convincing power of negro dancing and music." According to Keyserling, "the negro dance, the jazz music, those songs which sweep every American audience" were not the creations of "natural" Africans, but of *modern Americans.* Jazz and jazz dance were "self-expressions of the emancipated negro, of what the black man has developed into . . . since the Civil War." These are not observations within a primitivist frame of reference; Keyserling even referred to blacks as a "much more convincing [American] . . . than any living white type." Unlike the imitative music of Euro-Americans, blacks had created "all [the] expressions of American emotionalism." Keyserling recognized very early the global impact of jazz and its dances: "His [the African American's] convincing power has asserted itself all over the earth."[21]

The American modernist composer George Antheil frankly declared the 1920s "a Negroid epoch." He located the roots of African American musical power in musical and cultural practices then diffusing with great speed throughout the world. He singled out the habanera beat (three beats against two) as a "signature," a musical DNA code identifying Africans throughout the diaspora in Latin, Caribbean, South American, and African American musics. "The Negro music, like the Negro, absorbs, but does not become." As a favorite composer of literary modernists, Antheil, too, must be considered an expert witness. His famous Machine-Age composition, *Ballet Mécanique,* was performed at Carnegie Hall in 1927.[22]

The American architect Claude Bragdon also referred to big-band swing as a modernist form. The crucial new factor in popular music was "improvisation"—in Bragdon's translation, "greater freedom within set forms, or the breaking down of set forms altogether." Is this not the definition of a modernist aesthetic? In his 1940 lecture "Art and the Machine Age," Bragdon maintained that the best big bands produced more "exciting" art than classical musicians and composers by virtue of "the active exercise of the *intuition.* . . . [Here was] a group . . . able to energize as a unit, dominated by a common consciousness." Swing was the tempo of the time. "Boogie-woogie and swing take precedence over Bach, Beethoven, and Brahms . . . [because they] sound the modern note and move to the current tempo."[23]

To dismiss the enthusiasm of these modern artists for jazz as primitivist (and therefore racist) is to reject their appreciation for the music's artistic achievements, its existential affirmation, its emotional expressiveness, and its noticeably non-Western approach to music and public ritual. When Europeans embraced jazz, the artistic elites of New England and New York were shocked. They may have considered Europe a decadent "parent" culture in need of New World redemption, but "no one expected its [Europe's] musical community to turn away from 'sweetness and light' as an ultimate ideal." The Victorian aesthetic had been exploded by World War I. "Negro music made us to remember at least that we still had bodies which had not been exploded by shrapnel," Robert Goffin wrote in 1932, "[and] that life had been going on a long while and would probably go on a while longer."[24] The existential affirmation of African American survival technology could now be appropriated by any society in crisis.

Jazz owes a great deal not only to West African rhythms but to the region's musical and cultural practices. As stated at the outset of this work, West African musical practices presume a sociocultural imperative to recreate the world in sound. Every detail in the soundscape must be repeated, revised, represented, and stylized in public rituals to recognize and rechannel its power. I use these terms to draw a parallel with Henry

Louis Gates's theory of "signifyin(g)" and to draw attention to the philosophical assumptions beneath such a strategy. Western composers of musique concrète began bringing random sounds and electronically manipulated collages to music in the late 1940s, and the use of sampling among hip-hop DJs makes such an approach obvious today: any sound can be (and is) replicated and tossed into the mix.[25] But even using acoustic instruments, Afrodiasporic musicians assume they can re-create (and then stylize) any sound. To quote an old ad for the Yellow Pages, "If it's out there . . . it's in here."

In *African Music: A People's Art* (1975), the Cameroun guitarist and composer Francis Bebey declares that all African musicians "experiment with unusual sonorities" to create all kinds of sounds, including "muted, nasal, or strident" tones. To get the intended effect, an African musician may use "metal jingles . . . attached to [the] instrument," or drop "dried seeds . . . in the sound-box to add their dancing rhythms." The overriding purpose of such artistic experimentation is "to bring the music as close as possible to the actual sounds of nature." For example, West African musicians create buzzed tones—what classical musicians would call "impure" or "dirty" instrumental sounds—to reflect such sounds in nature, where growls, cries, whistles, and abrasive sound textures are the norm.[26] In African and African American music, "European standards of beautiful vocalization are not applicable . . . [v]ocal grunts, rapid text delivery, whispers, and special interjections or explosive sounds are not unusual." The notion of a "pure" note, a "perfect" harmony, or a "correct" way of playing are equally inapplicable.[27]

According to the anthropologist John Miller Chernoff, legend has it that African stevedores first "understood a machine to be the white man's music." Or as a Western-educated Dagara drummer and shaman similarly observes, "Indigenous people find their rhythm in nature. Westerners . . . seem to seek meaning in the realm of the machine." These machine rhythms reflect the "ceaseless movement" of Western culture at least since the Enlightenment, when material changes, industrial transformation, and technological innovation became a measure of social progress.[28] In contrast, West African musicians pride themselves on knowing the defining rhythms of neighboring cultures. Master drummers must play at functions where different groups are in attendance, or at marriages that bind two separate peoples; the drummer plays the fundamental rhythms of each ethnic group to give "face" to each person present. The Dagomba master drummer Ibrahim Abdulai told an anthropologist that he could play the rhythms of every people within a hundred miles; he could not play the white man's rhythms because "he had not seen his drums."[29] If, for argument's sake, the machine can be conceived of as the white man's drums, than in the country where white technological innovation was the most advanced, Afrodiasporic musicians would be likely to integrate the machine into their own traditions.

Duke Ellington made the practice of rendering the soundscape in music explicit for jazz. He theorized that sociorhythmic stylization is in fact the music's primary function. "Jazz is a matter of onomatopoeia," he said; "the question is, what are you imitating?"[30] Ellington's musicians were renowned for their ability to talk on their instruments, but here the composer means something different. He was referring to his aesthetic intent to render the *felt experience* of a physical landscape in music. Ellington had a story line, or sketch idea, for many of his compositions, and he called such works "tonal portraits." For example, "Main Stem" was intended as an aural portrait of walking down Broadway (in Harlem vernacular, the "main stem"); the function of the composition was to remind the listener how it felt to walk down Broadway on a Saturday night. "Harlem Air Shaft" (1940) was an impressionistic portrait of all the sounds one heard through the dumbwaiter of a Harlem apartment building.

> You get the full essence of Harlem in an air shaft. You hear fights, you smell dinner, you hear people making love. You hear intimate gossip floating down, you hear the radio. . . . You see your neighbors' laundry. You hear the janitor's dogs. The man upstairs' aerial falls down and breaks your window. You smell coffee. . . . One guy is cooking dried fish and rice and another guy's got a great big turkey. . . . You hear people praying, fighting, snoring. Jitterbugs are jumping up and down always over you, never below you. . . . I tried to put all that in *Harlem Air Shaft*.[31]

Ellington cited the influence of his star trumpeter Bubber Miley, the man whose "growl trumpet" gave the Ellington orchestra its early signature sound in the late 1920s. Miley often told a story before his solos, in effect painting his picture in words, then music. Ellington recalled an example: "'This is an old man, tired from working in the field since sunup, coming up the road in the sunset on his way home to dinner. He's tired but strong, and humming in time with his broken gait—or vice-versa.' That was how he [Miley] pictured 'East St. Louis Toodle-oo.'"[32] For Ellington, such musical stylization of everyday life was a primary function of jazz composition.

Ellington was less interested in form and musical architecture than "he was enthralled by sound," according to one biographer. The actual subtleties of the brass mutes, the tone colors, the voicings made possible by a big band—of this "he had . . . made himself one of the great masters." Perhaps Americans responded to not only the propulsive quality of Ellington's compositions, but to the fact that "everything was in motion."[33] One early reviewer wrote of Ellington's compositions, "He thinks not in chordal blocks but in moving parts, and the resulting harmony . . . derives . . . inevitably from the fluent weaving of contrapuntal lines."[34]

If Ellington provided propulsive tonal portraits for a big band, the alto saxophonist Charlie Parker could be a one-man techno-dialogic, an artistic bridge between self-expression and the technological soundscape. "Bird was the most receptive being," reflected the bassist Gene Ramey, a boyhood friend of Parker's and his bandmate in Jay McShann's excellent big band. "He got into his music all the sounds around him—the swish of a car speeding down the highway. The hum of wind as it goes through the leaves." Even as a struggling teen-aged musician "everything had a musical significance for him," Ramey recalled. "He'd hear dogs barking, for instance, . . . and say it was a conversation . . . [and] portray that thought to us." They might be riding in a car and "he'd have some sound" for a certain "country lane and . . . the trees." If an attractive girl walked past the bandstand, "something she might have would give him an idea for something to play on his solo." The drummer Elvin Jones recalled Parker quoting the melody of "A Pretty Girl Is Like a Melody" in the middle of a solo, at which point all the musicians quickly located the beautiful woman being referenced. Band members remarked about "how fast his mind worked," as Parker spontaneously "imitated sounds echoing in from the street—engines, backfiring trucks, auto horns—and work[ed] them into musical phrases."[35]

Jazz musicians use the trope of "catching" a musical or physical gesture to communicate the same idea. To "catch" (musically) means to hear and respond to a gesture in a timely fashion. Any good drummer had to catch the moves of a tap dancer to keep in step with the dancer's rhythmic messages; drummers had to catch the action while in the orchestra pit of silent movies, or in circus bands, or of other soloists.

Dancers at the Savoy Ballroom loved Dizzy Gillespie for his ability to respond to their individual gestures with quick musical jabs and riffs. According to the trumpeter Rex Stewart, many African American chorus-line dancers preferred Big Sid Catlett to all other drummers for his ability to "make the rhythms visible" (to use Jacqui Malone's phrase).[36]

If an alto saxophone can reflect the way a car speeds down the road, or a drummer can catch an expressive act as subtle as a hand gesture, then a big band of sixteen people can produce human-powered music as loud, dynamic, thrilling, and terrifying as industrialization itself. As African American musicians toured the nation, first in minstrel bands and later in jazz bands, they came into further contact with Euro-American rhythms, both ethnic and industrial. Train rhythms, train whistles, and station bells were the common aural-industrial coin of the nation, and black musicians must have found that the train resonated across race, class, gender, and generation. And, of course, they also felt the speed-up of American culture. If African American drummers could catch the quicksilver tap-dancing of Baby Laurence or John W. Bubbles, they could certainly catch a train.

The techno-dialogic contains West African rhythms, the industrial soundscape, European song structures, and African American musical practices, or so the drummer Gene Krupa, the journalist Frank Marshall Davis, and Prince Effin Odok all perceived at the time. Davis reviewed a set of six ten-inch West African field recordings called *African Music* (1939) in his column in the *New York Amsterdam News* and suddenly perceived "the great dependence of our dance tunes upon intricate African rhythm." He found the rhythms so familiar (from swing) that he "half expected to hear Cootie Williams and Barney Bigard" launch into solos, and he also recognized "rhumba and tango" rhythms. To Davis, these West African rhythms survived intact in the musical practices of even white swing drummers. Gene Krupa's "Jungle Madness" sounded like a "continuation of 'War Song' by the Malinke tribe." "Big Noise From Winnetka," the best-selling duet record of drummer Ray Bauduc and bassist Bob Haggart, showed percussive affinities with "'Dance Song' by the Benin tribe."[37]

When Krupa heard these records, he intuited that West African drummers integrate the "beats" of other cultures with their own. One rhythm clearly derived from the "beat of a regimental drummer of an English army," and others reflected "the sounds of civilization." For example, in one common "quick, pattering rhythmic pattern," he heard "the putt-putt of a motor boat." Despite the rural sources of the field recordings, Krupa heard "a rhythmic beat which sounds strangely reminiscent of the gasoline age." Having played with West African drummers during the New York World's Fair of 1939, Krupa wrote that "American jazz owes much of its origin to African influence," as did "many rhythms of North and South America."[38]

Krupa later composed songs that made "use of basic African beats," and he saw that rhythm in music was similar to a heartbeat in a healthy human; he theorized that drumming began as a way for human beings to replicate their heartbeat externally.[39] According to Marshall Stearns, Krupa's concept of music and drumming was "essentially African." And so a good deal of the "Africanization" of American music occurred in the swing era because of a white drummer, the "gum-chewing, tousled-haired Gene Krupa, the frantic idol of the bobby-soxers of the 'thirties.'"[40]

"Swing . . . is nothing but an imitation of native African music," declared Prince Effin Odok, an immigrant musician from southern Nigeria then living in Harlem and running a dance troupe. Dances such as the "Suzi-Q, trucking, Big Apple and other stage and so-called modern dances" were West African dances, all of which were "the results of the peculiar rhythm and melody . . . characteristic of native African music." Odok presented several dance recitals between 1939 and 1942, combining African and African American dancers in performances that he directed, conducted, and led from his drums.[41]

The master drummer Babatunde Olatunji came to Atlanta on a college scholarship straight from "Yoruba-land" (southwestern Nigeria) in 1950. He was not then a master drummer—"in the old sense of knowing all the village rhythms"—nor even a musician, and he was unfamiliar with American popular music. But the first time he turned on his radio in Atlanta, he was "stunned" by a generic rhythm-and-blues song. "Hey, that's African music," Olatunji thought, "it sounds like what's at home. . . . [Then] the same thing happened when I heard gospel music. So I joined the campus jazz combo." Early rhythm and blues was little more than a stripped-down, electrified version of big band swing with a heavier backbeat.[42]

At an early age, the Grateful Dead drummer Mickey Hart found himself fascinated by a set of cultural practices in which "the drum—scorned by European melodic music—was the dominant driver." In *Drumming at the Edge of Magic,* Hart dubbed them "the African Counterplayers" to pay tribute to the master drummers who preside over public rituals and cultural events. "If you build a town and there is no master drummer, then it is not a town," runs the proverb of the Kpelle of Liberia. Among the Akan of Ghana, the drums are considered instruments of social expression, not self-expression, and "as a rule . . . [they] are owned corporately."[43]

Hart made the connection between West African rituals and American popular music. "By separating the music from its religious intent, the century-long gestation began that would ultimately produce the dominant popular musical styles of the twentieth century—jazz, the blues, rhythm and blues, and rock and roll." The power of the rhythms—their "binding" quality, their ability to soundtrack generational experience and technological change—comes from "the severing" of the secular from the spiritual in African American musical culture.[44] The difference between West African and African American approaches is that the former is conceived in rhythmic sequences, and the latter in terms of a steady pulse, owing to the encounter with European meter. For example, the steady backbeat of early jazz and rock and roll does not exist in traditional African music. Strong-beat and weak-beat (on-beat/off-beat) notions are related to the "1 and 2 or 3 and 4 in European music," notes a Nigerian scholar, but "the African neither makes nor comprehends his music in terms of numerical beats."[45]

"The times are always contained in the rhythm," according to Quincy Jones, and the Jamaican reggae poet Linton Kwesi Johnson says likewise that "the beat must shift as the culture alter." The swing era trumpeter Rex Stewart reflects that music always "mirrors the tempos and sociological attitudes that exist within the framework of that particular period."[46] To be modern—of the moment, able to speak to present audiences—African American music and dance had to absorb the metronomic rhythms of machines. "The drumbeats of Africa . . . survived industrialization, with its staid rhythms," notes the musicologist Jon Michael Spencer, "that, although percussive, beat counter to the asymmetry, multimetricism, and improvisation of African time."[47]

Over and over again in the last 125 years, African American musicians transmuted the "propulsive rhythms" germane to the ritual and functional music of African music and yoked it to one of the nation's fundamental identifying traits, technology. African American music is not only about *surviving* but about the survival of African and African American cultural values in a society bound to destroy them. Treated as human labor machines during slavery, the ex-slaves turned the tables, confronted "the rational god" and tamed it.[48] By incorporating the dominant society's machines into music, African Americans both guaranteed the survival of their cultural heritage and provided aesthetic solutions to the problems of an overrationalized culture.

The African American Inquiry into Technology Begins: The Ballad of John Henry

In the late 1930s Kenneth Burke wondered whether certain individuals hear "the new qualities" represented by a cultural shift before such new factors come under mainstream discussion. "Might not the *single song of one poet,* under certain conditions, put us on the track of something that the *typical platitudes of a group* could give us no inkling of?" I believe the collective folk creation of "The Ballad of John Henry" put Americans on the track of a new inquiry: the challenge of machines to the individual male in the workplace. Perhaps this is why the story of John Henry retained its resonance through the 1930s.[49]

"The Ballad of John Henry" pays tribute to the grind of the railroad workers who blasted holes into the mountainous rock of West Virginia to create the Big Bend Tunnel in 1870, a two-and-a-half year project that produced the then-longest tunnel (a mile and a quarter) ever attempted.[50] In the midst of oppressive heat, with the constant fear of cave-ins and personal injury, workers swung a ten-pound hammer through the air and pounded a six-foot drill held by the "shaker," who sat on the ground turning the drill a quarter-inch after each hammer blow. The objective was to dig holes deep enough to drop dynamite in and blast out the rock. To ease the monotony of the labor, and help set a rhythm for the heavy, exhausting work, black workers made up "hammer songs," a rich genre that came to incorporate John Henry's battle:

> This old hammer—WHAM!
> Killed John Henry—WHAM!
> Can't kill me—WHAM!
> Can't kill me—WHAM!

Phallic puns must have accompanied hammer songs, and the folklorist Alan Lomax believes John Henry's sexual prowess with his wife (or "the woman in red") is integral to his legendary hammering heroics. The more compelling question for my argument remains: Why did a big

African American man—six feet tall, two hundred pounds, "of pure African blood"—become the nation's emblematic worker in the battle against machine abilities and technological unemployment?[51]

When a new force appears in society, one logical response is to send an expert out to assess its powers. Post-Emancipation blacks migrating into the industrialized North sent their best man (so to speak) against the machine. The ballad often states that John Henry was *born* with a hammer in his hand, born to drive steel. The ballad was composed collectively just after the steam drill was introduced into railroad construction; the new machine challenged the worker's strength and threatened him with technological unemployment. "It was de flesh ag'in' the stream," as one folk singer later explained. John Henry actually defeats the machine in the ballad—drilling fourteen feet to the steam drill's nine—but his superhuman effort proves fatal. "John Henry" remains the nation's most "widely known [and] . . . recorded [ballad], has stimulated more printed commentary, [and] . . . inspired more folk and popular literature" than any other.[52]

For southern blacks, folk tales and ballads were important educational media for the transmission of cultural values. It is in this light that we must view John Henry. Unlike the cagey intelligence of Brer Rabbit, or the spiritual dignity of High John de Conquer, John Henry took on the Euro-American male's most lethal weapon: his technology, and the work based on that technology. And he did it as an equal, as a co-worker on the frontier long before social equality existed. In performance, the singer almost always lingers over the line, "A man ain't nothing but a man," which resonates in terms both of the man vs. machine frame story and the black man vs. white man subtext.

I am suggesting an alternative interpretation of this ballad. The African American oral tradition valorizes heroes who bring important social knowledge. John Henry's message was simple: the machine's rhythm could only be matched physically at the cost of one's life. The moral of the story?: Learn to live with machines. John Henry was a *sacrificial* hero, a symbol uniting Christian suffering with industrialization. He provided essential "equipment for living," for coping with an industrial society.[53] He was thus rewarded in the ballad with fame, food, whiskey, and women, each element sometimes praised with the same detail as his battle with the machine. Such knowledge was so essential that white workers took up the ballad almost immediately.[54] John Henry is "the definitive folk song of American working-class history" because there is racial solidarity in a ballad "sung about . . . the man who was better than a machine and who died trying to prove it."[55]

Ralph Ellison reflected that "in spilling out his heart's blood in his contest with the machine, John Henry was asserting a national value as well as a Negro value."[56] What was that national value? John Henry brought this important message of spiritual uplift: a man cannot defeat a machine in terms of production, but at the end of such a battle, the human spirit demonstrated in the effort reinvigorates the collective will. The steam drill survived the battle because it was a machine; no human being can outlast a machine at the level of stamina. (For example, we use the vernacular phrase "he's a machine" to signal both praise and something not quite human about the person's effort.) John Henry's herculean effort was judged a triumph by the balladeers and thus he was showered with rewards. W. C. Handy recalled hearing the song all his life, in many variations, including "the simple melody I heard in the rock quarry when I was a kid." Handy was born in 1873, which would put him among the workers in the early 1880s. "Colored laborers sing about John Henry all over the nation," he recalled.[57]

The lesson gained from John Henry's battle was a simple one: machine aesthetics had to be integrated into art, culture, and everyday life. In the late 1800s, however, the dominant aesthetic attitude of highbrow Anglo-American culture was indebted to Matthew Arnold's call for "sweetness and light." In Arnold's vision, art and music were catalysts for contemplation, aesthetic vehicles by which the individual mind was transported into ethereal communion with a higher power; "art" was meant to function as an "alternative to the disorderly outside world." Such a vision was at odds with the gross materialism of industrialization and commercialization of the Gilded Age. With the important exception of the locomotive, artists rarely celebrated or engaged workplace machines, though both Mark Twain (in *A Connecticut Yankee in King Arthur's Court*) and Walt Whitman (in "Passage to India" and "Song of the Exposition") celebrated machines abstractly.[58] By the 1930s this lack of artistic guidance in coping with industrial transformation led to an intellectual crisis in which not even the critics of mechanization and capitalism could envision a future without machines, and in this period the story of John Henry enjoyed its greatest popularity. The subject of two scholarly studies in 1933, a popular novel, and a Broadway play, the story of John Henry "permeated all genres of American lore— . . . fiction, drama, art, stage musical."[59]

Ellison perceived the accommodation/resistance dialectic in a distinctive African American inquiry into techno-progress. "What we [blacks] have counterpoised against the necessary rage for progress in American life (and which we share with other Americans) will have proved to be at least as valuable as all our triumphs of technology." Or as poet Sterling Brown wrote in 1930, "John Henry, ideal hero of the railroad men [and] steel drivers . . . died at his triumphant task of 'beating the steam driver down.' To the more 'philosophical' he served as a tragic symbol of Man in his losing fight against the Machine."[60] John Henry is an American Hercules, born to serve the national psyche in a crucial test of physical wills.

Only African Americans seem interested in John Henry today. At least seven new versions of the John Henry story have been written over the last twenty-five years in the field of children's literature. In Colson Whitehead's recent novel *John Henry Days* (2001), a West Virginia town exploits John Henry's legacy for tourism, displaying little knowledge about the industrial struggle he symbolizes. The protagonist is a pulp journalist named J. Sutter (John Henry Sutter) who generates forgettable content for websites at pennies per word and decides one day to try and break the record for continuous corporate junkets. As he grinds out short, disposable copy for the global media machine, Sutter's ironic anomie seems an even heavier existential burden than John Henry's.[61]

The scholar Julius Lester's children's story *John Henry* (1994) makes of the legendary figure a national hero of the industrial era, rendering his hammer as a musical instrument wielded with power, music, grace, and style. John Henry's hammering creates "a rainbow around his shoulders . . . shining and shimmering in the dust and grit like hope that never dies." When he falls dead, the crowd quiets; but in the silence, they collectively realize that "dying ain't important . . . what matters is how well you do your living." They all then applaud John Henry's victory loud and long. In the morning, a train takes the worker's body to the nation's capital and he is "buried on the White House lawn while the President and Mrs. President was asleep." But if you stand still late at night by the White House, you'll hear a "deep voice" singing an old hammer song: "I got a rainbow/RINGGGG! RINGGGG!/Tied round my shoulder/RINGGGG! RINGGGG!/It ain't gon' rain,/No, it ain't gon' rain./RINGGGG! RINGGGG!" Lester equates the folk hero's struggle to contribute to emergent national ideals with those of Martin Luther King Jr.; both were cultural leaders who had the "courage to hammer until our hearts break" and brought a bittersweet victory, "leav[ing] . . . mourners smiling in their tears."[62]

As Alan Lomax wrote in 1960, John Henry was the industrial heir of "Old John, the trickster-slave," and yet he managed to become "the hero of the hard-working . . . guys who opened up the modern South." From the mouths of workers the message traveled along the rails that "men are always more important than the machines they build."[63]

Up from John Henry

In 1913 the man vs. machine story of "John Henry" became explicitly racialized in the bawdy epic toast of "Shine," a black boiler-tender who survives the crash of the *Titanic*. The *Titanic* was advertised as one of the greatest technological achievements of the age, and the arrogance of such a claim, as well as the tragic sinking of the ship, called forth countless verses by white and black balladeers alike. The tragedy caught the African American imagination, and colorful narratives appeared in many genres, none more so than "Shine," which mocks the white man and his technology.

One legend about the *Titanic* was that the shipowners denied passage to the black heavyweight champion Jack Johnson. In fact, Johnson never attempted to get on board the *Titanic,* but the rumor provides an interesting juxtaposition: the nation's most famous black man denied access to the finest product of white technology. The bluesman Huddie Ledbetter (aka Leadbelly) believed the legend and wrote a song about it. Johnson was an attractive subject since he was a real-life "bad nigger" (to use Mel Watkins's term) who transgressed every boundary set up for black men. The heavyweight champ married three white women, drove flashy cars, and trash-talked white boxers as he humiliated them in the ring. The idea of denying Johnson access to the *Titanic* called forth a new formulation of the human vs. machine inquiry: it was now the black man vs. the white machine; or the black male worker-body vs. the white technological machine-body.[64]

The plot of the toast is straightforward: as the lone boiler-tender of the *Titanic*'s mighty engines, Shine notices before anyone else that the ship is taking on vast quantities of water. He warns the captain, who simply invokes the ship's specifications: "It can't sink . . . it's got 99 pumps." Shine continues to give the captain updates of the rising water ("up to my knees," "up to my ass," and so on) but is ignored. As the ship begins to sink, passengers beg Shine to save their lives—millionaires, businessmen, pregnant women, even the captain himself. Shine turns them all down with scorn, sarcasm, and rich, bawdy language. The businessmen offer money; the women, including the captain's daughter, offer their bodies. But Shine exacts revenge in verses combining confidence in his survival skills with the joy of transgression: "Pussy on land, there's pussy on the sea," Shine sings pragmatically, "But the pussy on land's/the pussy for me."[65]

The excluded, mistreated, invisible man "Shine"—the name itself a racial slur denoting a dark-skinned African American—thus has his revenge on the wealthiest slice of white society. Shine suggests they all swim for shore, as he will. He may be "trapped in lowly service deep within the interior of a white vessel," but the captain is likewise trapped in the "blind confidence in his machines."

As an idealized black everyman, Shine embodies truth-telling, physical skill, arrogant self-confidence, and the importance of a good time; the white captain, on the other hand, stands for pompous hypocrisy and a nearly religious faith in technology. Like Jack Johnson, Shine is spirited, determined, and cocksure of his skills. When he jumps overboard, he takes pleasure in taunting and outswimming his new competitors, the fish. Ripping through the ocean, he boasts to the dolphins, sharks, and whales: "You may be the king of the ocean,/the king of the sea,/but I am the swimmingest motherfucker/you ever did see." When news of the *Titanic* tragedy hits shore, Shine is drinking at a bar in Times Square, as if the human grapevine can outrun the telegraph and telephone as well. Ishmael Reed has dubbed Shine "black America's Ulysses."[66]

Shine can be seen as a synthesis of the hard-working culture hero John Henry (shared by all Americans) and the more overt black cultural style and rebellion of Jack Johnson. In the "bad man" ballads popular at the turn of the century (for example, "Stagolee"), the "bad nigger" nearly always winds up dead after exacting revenge. Shine's achievement is that "he defies white society and its technology and he triumphs."[67] The toast appeared soon after the *Titanic* sank, yet it was one of the three most popular toasts in the postwar era and remained current on the streets of black neighborhoods through the 1960s. I suspect the toast retained its power so long due to the continuation of the man vs. machine trope that began with John Henry. The promise of machines resonated differently for blacks as their cultural identity was tied less to techno-progress than to social progress.

The Techno-dialogic

The *techno-dialogic* is my term for revealing how the presence (or "voice") of machinery became integral to the cultural production of African American storytellers, dancers, blues singers, and jazz musicians. I hope to draw parallels both between authors and musicians as social agents of change, and between literary, folkloric, and musical practices as indices of change in any dynamic culture. In highlighting the dialogue of music and technology, I want to suggest that American popular music can be read historically just as literature can: as a record of the emergence and prestige levels of ethnic groups, as a mapping of shifts in social hierarchy and cultural values, as the ongoing artistic mediation of commercialization and professionalization.[68]

The literary theorist Mikhail Bakhtin considers the novelist an artist who "orchestrates" the roles of social groups (and individuals) into a coherent polyphony of voices as they compete for the attentions of the dominant society. Readers can thus view the changes in society at a given moment for a given text through an evaluation of the relative salience and prestige of competing jargons and discourses (for example, occupational, conceptual, and ethnic). The dialogue between groups in a given novel of a historical period reflect and record the "heteroglossia" (overlapping layers of reality) of modern societies. An excellent example is Marshall Berman's study of the archetypal confrontation in nineteenth-century Russia between lowly clerk and army officer on the Nevsky Prospect in St. Petersburg, as represented in Russian novels over the course of nearly a century.[69] Thus the appearance of a new political force in society (such as the working class) reveals itself over time; novelists recognize a new social force by giving voice to its presence. The prestige of a new force, whether a rising social group or a technological invention, can be seen by its power and presence in a given text at a given time. When any musician or dancer integrates the sounds, rhythms, and aesthetics of machines in a live performance, the artist embodies the techno-dialogic.

For example, in her travels through southern jook joints in the late 1920s, Zora Neale Hurston recorded a classic call-and-response she often heard, "a favorite jook song of the past" usually sung by a dark-skinned blueswoman. The woman would sing, "It ain't good looks/ dat takes you through this world," to which the audience responded, "[Then] what is it, good mama?" And she brought home the punchline, "Elgin movements in your hips"—she probably made an erotic gesture—"twenty years guarantee." Elgin was then a popular watchmaker that boasted of its product's precise mechanical movement, and in 1929 the company introduced an "American Efficiency Series." "Elgin movement" becomes a pun that mixes eroticism and precision, mechanism and human undulation, making into poetic bawdiness the admiration for those machine qualities (precision, accuracy, and repetition) that might serve human sexual relations best. When singing this song, any blueswoman embodies the techno-dialogic. As for how the song resonated with audiences, Hurston noted that "it always brought down the house."[70]

When Bessie Smith compares her ex-boyfriend to an "old wagon" and her new man to an automobile, she calls attention to the dialogue between personal and technological change. She accuses one man of being out of style, unmodern, technologically extinct; "You're a good ole wagon/but honey you done broke down."[71] In this rendering of the human/machine interface, Bessie Smith recognizes and registers the values of techno-progress in society—though the fickleness of lovers will continue. The novelist John Edgar Wideman defines the African American aesthetic tradition as one that stays focused on "the necessity of remaining human, defining human in its own terms, [and] resisting those destructive definitions in the Master's tongue." Wideman describes "black music" as a "moveable feast, fluid in time, space, modality," and capable of "the fullest possible range of relationships, including the power and independence to . . . reverse the hierarchy, [to] *be* the dominant order."[72]

In machine worship (as in the stories of Steam Man and the figure of Superman), or in the fears of overmechanization (as in the tempo-of-life discourse), there was little integration of technology and human dynamics for ordinary individuals. In the blueswomen's songs above, superior mechanical skill is recognized, but with humorous admiration it is integrated into physical gesture and human behavior. Such a cultural approach suggests a confidence in the adaptability and plasticity of human beings that is not readily apparent in Euro-American attempts to humanize machine aesthetics during the Machine Age. I am not making an essentialist or primitivist argument, but suggesting only that African American ritual performance had opened a public space for the engagement and performance of new forces.[73]

The African American musician is thus a conduit for the historical and emotional experience of the community. In Ben Sidran's formulation,

"the musician *is* the document . . . [he or she] is the information itself."
In performance, an African American musician conducts the black audience through an emotional experience; his or her job is "the skilled
evocation of extreme emotional and mental states." The performer must
engage the audience in call-and-response and communicate the idea
that he or she *represents* this audience; as the poet Larry Neal suggests
about blues singers, "when they say 'I,' they mean 'we.'" The musician—
"whether a gospel shouter, a blues singer, or a jazz shouter"—is a priest,
or perhaps "medium" is a better word. Unlike the individual artist of the
Western tradition, "the Afro-American musician . . . is elevated chiefly as
a conduit for the expression of communal emotion and experience."[74]

For example, blues carried the techno-dialogic to the North and West
during the black migration. In April 1924 at Chicago's Grand Theater,
Gertrude "Ma" Rainey, the godmother of blueswomen, began her set
from inside a giant victrola. She sang the first verse of the first song from
inside the huge cardboard replica, and then emerged in a glittering
gown; according to her pianist Thomas A. Dorsey, "the crowd went wild."[75]
At that moment she was the "machine inside the machine," to use Ellison's phrase. As much as any blues singer, Ma Rainey's songs helped heal
and soothe the emotional disruptions of the black migration to northern
cities. Her concerts sold out instantly in Chicago; people moaned and
sang with her throughout.[76] Sterling Brown's "Ma Rainey" (1932) expresses the interaction of performer and audience at her shows:

> O Ma Rainey,
> Sing yo' song;
> Now you's back
> Whah you belong,
> Git way inside us,
> Keep us strong . . .
>
> O Ma Rainey,
> Li'l an' low;
> Sing us 'bout de hard luck
> Roun' our do';
> Sing us 'bout de lonesome road
> We mus' go.[77]

Within her role as one who conducts the emotional states (and experience) of her audience, Ma Rainey knew that her presence was superior

to any mechanical recording. To be the audience's representative, however, she had to embody the best of their cultural aspirations but not present herself as superior to them. She had to embody both "I" and "we" feeling at the same time and create an interactive flow of information between performer and audience. In Brown's poem, the crowd arrives in all kinds of conveyances, from "river settlements . . . blackbottom cornrows and from lumber camps." People are in good spirits, looking forward to hearing Ma Rainey sing, "waitin' wid deir aches an' miseries." Listening to a song about a flood, the crowd all "bowed dey heads an' cried." The narrator of the poem mentions a fan who explains, "She jes' catch hold of us, somekindaway."

The function of the giant victrola was to communicate the message that technology was simply a tool which collapses distance. It was as if Rainey were saying, "You listen to my records because I'm not around; when I'm here, we don't need the machine to talk to one another." No doubt Rainey also used the record player as a prop to mark her prestige as a recording artist in the new "race market" of a comparatively new record industry. But for a performer with a community base, her presence was a signal for a public ritual, and the interaction must be in-the-moment, a reestablishment of ethnic and experiential bonds. Charles Keil found such an attitude among both blues artists and audiences and Polish polka artists and audiences from the 1920s through the 1960s. There were no "live" albums by any blues or polka artists in this period. When artists performed live, the music had to have its "own integrity," and "the recorded thing is just a memory device." For these two ethnic groups, the recorded version of a given song was simply a reminder of the performer's songs—a "clean" version to listen to at home, "not an intensification . . . [but] a kind of distillation."[78]

In *Mumbo-Jumbo* (1972), Ishmael Reed's re-envisioning of black culture in the 1920s through the influence of African American music and dance, the author pays tribute to the emergent techno-dialogic. Benoit Battraville, a visiting priest of the Yoruba-derived vodun religion, tells a group of black Americans that a new "loa" (deity) has been born. "No one knows how a new loa is formed," Battraville admits, but when one is, it demands to be "fed" with prayer, offerings, music, and dance.[79] The priest explains that during World War I, a "radio loa" emerged that fed on "static"; in the subsequent years, this new deity had come to be symbolized as a radio with a "Yellow Back to symbolize its electrical circuitry."[80] New media, new sources of energy and power, and new methods of communication had created a new energy grid. A new technology deity had to be fed—and honored, and danced with—on a regular basis so that its power could be understood and integrated into everyday life. Battraville compares the feeding of a loa to the collective financial, emotional, and spiritual support given to "Ragtime and Jazz" artists who embody the forces of the loas in public rituals.

To live in cities required seemingly contradictory "demands for improvisation on the one hand, and discipline and coordination on the other." The sociologist Charles Nanry claimed that jazz answered those contradictory demands and embodied the nation's cultural coming of age. "Pluralism and jazz represent the survival of the parts within the whole: the hard work of forging an organic unity out of mechanistic disparity."[81] Regarding music and dance, the United States is "the most integrated society in the world," notes the folklorist Gene Bluestein. "White people apparently cannot live without black music . . . [and they] adopt every black dance as it is created in . . . African-American communities."[82] Jazz musicians worked in all kinds of venues (night clubs, vaudeville, movie theaters, circuses, dance halls, even a few elite hotels) for all kinds of audiences. Until bebop their artistic ideal was not oppositional but instead cumulative and accretive. African American musicians brought the power of machines under artistic control and thus modeled the possibility of individual style within a technological society.

Powerhouse Musicians

With the exception of motion pictures, jazz was the first cultural form capable of containing a machine civilization. Speed and repetition were the hallmarks of late 1920s jazz; by 1930 a European jazz scholar could point to the "precision of gradation, [and] inexorable rhythm" of black big bands such as McKinney's Cotton Pickers.[83] Paul Whiteman claimed he could hear steamboats, locomotives, and electricity in the music. Jazz was "the sound of riveting," H. L. Mencken mocked, while the *New Republic* saw even in ragtime that locomotive American quality, an "underlying rhythmic progress toward a vague nowhere." Jazz fans and critics "equated it with the noise of cities like New York."[84] Irving Berlin claimed in 1924 that jazz was the "rhythmic beat of our everyday lives," and the music's "swiftness is interpretive of our verve and speed and ceaseless activity." The composer Daniel Mason attacked jazz as "ultra-modernistic" in its "relentless mechanical efficiency," claiming only that "if robots could make a music of their own, it would be jazz."

One constant criticism of jazz in the 1920s was that it reflected "the me-chanical speed-up commonly associated with industrial production and urban life."[85]

Paul Whiteman's pianist, Leopold Godowsky, analyzed the power dif-ferential between the instruments of jazz and classical music. "We have computed [that] one baritone saxophone is equal in sonorousness to a section of 9–10 cellos; that one alto saxophone is equal to sixteen first violins or twelve second violins; that one tenor saxophone is equal to eight violas." Whiteman thus needed only twenty-five instruments to "get the volume of an 80-piece symphony orchestra." In a sense, the sax-ophone replaced the violin as the lead instrument in American music of the 1920s; it was an icon of jazz's rhythmic drive and power, and it sym-bolized the Jazz Age. The saxophone was the "king of the jazz orchestra," while the drummer provided rhythm and texture, working "a dozen noisy devices." Godowsky judged the jazz band as a musical agglomera-tion "somewhere between the symphony and the military."[86]

By the late 1930s "powerhouse" was a term used by some jazz musi-cians to refer to the rhythm section of big bands. This piece of American vernacular entered the language as a reference to the building that housed the electrical power which provided current to the railroads.[87] The powerhouse rhythm section mediated the human energy of big bands as they interfaced with dance audiences on any given night.

Eudora Welty's "Powerhouse" (1939) refers to the title character, a jazz pianist fashioned after Fats Waller. The story is unlike any other in the Welty oeuvre, and renders jazz's black cultural style with accuracy and admiration. Welty had seen Waller perform in New York and was awestruck by his musical power, Rabelaisian humor (and body), and control of dynamics. Powerhouse is the epitome of energy: with his "pis-ton legs," his nonstop talking, and his "rhythmic kicks against the floor to communicate the tempo," he sends the band and "everybody into oblivion." Welty's narrator at first believes such energy in human beings is simply wrong, irrational, untidy, unruly: "He is in motion every mo-ment—what could be more obscene?" She compares him to an ice skater who never stops or a rower on an endless river—"he's going all the time."[88]

Welty sets Powerhouse in concert at a white dance in Alligator, Mis-sissippi, in part to show him off as a new force in American society. For Welty, he threatens to be the very "new man" dreamed of by Whitman, Crevecoeur, and others—though perhaps not what they had in mind.

"You can't tell what he is," the narrator exclaims, "'Nigger man'?—he looks more Asiatic, monkey, Jewish, Babylonian, Peruvian, fanatic, devil." The narrator contrasts Powerhouse to the timid, slow-moving Mississippi blacks who follow him around at a distance, awed, and laugh at his jokes. Meanwhile Powerhouse and his fellow musicians ("his Tasmanians") walk around town, drink beer, and engage in collective storytelling about a stock comic cuckold named Uranus Knockwood. Welty fuses together the performative conversation of jazz, the individual and collective artistry that goes into the creation of the groove, and the inseparable black cultural elements of language, music, and storytelling. Here are the southern roots and new emancipated fruits of African American culture. Here also is the subtext of Waller's real-life resentment that white audiences could "cheer their heads off" while he was on stage but deny him a citizen's access to restaurants, hotels, and bathrooms.[89]

At the end of the story, Welty reveals Powerhouse's awareness of white America's love-and-theft affair with black music. The last song he plays at the dance is "Somebody Loves Me." In the midst of "twelve or fourteen choruses" on the piano, Powerhouse calls out occasionally, "Somebody loves me? Somebody loves me, I wonder who!" And he teases the audience, "Maybe . . . ," he ponders and plays some pianistic trills, "maybe . . . ," he repeats, toying with those leaning forward over the bandstand. Then suddenly he becomes serious and "a vast, impersonal and yet furious grimace transfigures his . . . face." And Powerhouse shouts, "Maybe it's you!" In one line, Welty recognizes both the pianist's self-conscious jazz artistry and his lack of social recognition.

A companion song to Welty's story might be Fats Waller and Andy Razaf's big-band favorite "Christopher Columbus" (1936).[90] In a period when white intellectuals were obsessed with creating a "useable past," Waller and Razaf turned the nation's very foundation myth rhythmside up. The song picks up Columbus en route to the New World, partially lost, "sail[ing] the sea/without a compass," with a mutinous crew about to "begin a rumpus." The explorer needs a new compass, just as the society did.

Columbus gets an idea to calm the crew, which Waller sings in a humorous falsetto: "There's land somewhere/until we get there/we will not go wrong/if we face it with a song." Waller's vocal mocks the patriotic schoolbook version of the valiant, fearless explorer, keeping sight of

him as half captain, half conductor. In his mocking Rabelaisian baritone, Waller advises the crew to stick to the rhythm:

> Since the world is round-o
> We'll be safe and sound-o.
> 'Till our hold is bound-o.
> We'll just keep rhythm bound-o.

Columbus establishes rhythmic control of his ship and the sailors calm
down. "No more mutiny," Waller sings, "with diplomacy/Christy/made
history." This is one of dozens of songs from this period suggesting that
society rejuvenates itself through rhythm.[91]

> Mister Christopher Columbus . . .
> He used rhythm as a compass.

For three hundred years, and throughout the African diaspora,
white observers have noticed that when black workers improvise work
songs, the caller often comments on any and all objects in the immediate landscape. In virtually every case, workers improvise verses that
comment on every person in the landscape, including (and especially)
visitors and observers.[92] What if we think of big bands as work groups
(which they were) and their work as providing physical engagement and
play for American audiences? One jazz scholar notes that "in jazz, a composer's or player's meaning and uniqueness depend greatly upon his
choice of significant sound patterns and ideas from the common cultural environment."[93] Machines were central to "the common cultural
environment"; they just needed to be invited onto the dance floor.

Thirty years after he first heard the Jimmie Lunceford big band, the
jazz critic Ralph J. Gleason remembered "the great roar . . . from the
brasses and the amazing cohesion of that sax section," as well as
"the incredible dynamics of the band, [and] the way it could whisper."
Here are those machine aesthetics of the techno-dialogic: the human-
powered roar to match the mechanical noise of the factories, the precision of the sax section, the varied tempos and sonic contrasts from
industrial instruments built of valves and pistons. Gleason found it almost "impossible to believe" that the band had only sixteen members,
nor that it could produce both a "wild, throbbing sound" yet be in such
control of "its subtlety and its insinuating rhythm." For Gleason, the
band's only peers for character, power, and dignified ensemble playing were Duke Ellington and Count Basie. "We dug them deeply . . .

before the verb 'to dig' [existed] . . . What I mean is, we hardly listened to anything else."[94]

The Lunceford band had no peers in the area of what was then called "showmanship," which often featured precise choreography. One trick was alternating facing one way and then the other; another feature was the "up-and-down motion of the sections in unison . . . the back row going one way, the front row visually going the other." Such tricks were stolen by the Glenn Miller band and several other big bands. "Visually, it was the greatest," Gleason wrote. And in the middle of this rolling power, "hunched behind that great battery of equipment" now known as the trap-set, sat the drummer Jimmy Crawford, "pounding out that pulse."[95]

Gleason worshiped the Lunceford men and thought they carried themselves like the nation's native royalty. "They walked and they talked and they played like men who had been touched with a very special thing. . . . They looked regal. . . . And, of course, they were." But white swing fans knew almost nothing about the facts of life for African American swing musicians: how they traveled on the road every night in beat-up buses, were nearly always denied hotel accommodations and restaurant service, and yet all the while spread spiritual uplift and the techno-dialogic across the nation. They were "soldiers of music," to use David Stowe's term. "I think now these men were heroes," Gleason wrote thirty years later. "Then I only knew they were magicians."[96]

"Magic" is a common term used when an analyst lacks the knowledge or aesthetic criteria by which to evaluate another culture's art and philosophy. The "magic" of technology has often been compared to the "magic" of non-Western religious belief and power; here, *the magic is the music*. Jimmie Lunceford's band was an ensemble of professional musicians working within an unrecognized (and admittedly, often unarticulated) aesthetic tradition that had synthesized its own elements with the cultural and sonic forces of the dominant culture.

Glenn Miller indirectly captured the essence of the techno-dialogic in responding to criticism of his Army Air Forces Band that entertained troops during World War II. A veteran commander of the previous world war expressed his indignation that Miller had replaced that era's martial music with big-band swing. "We played those Sousa marches straight in the last war and we did all right, didn't we?" the officer asked. "You certainly did, Major," Miller responded. "But tell me one thing: Are you still flying the same planes you flew in the last war, too?"[97]

Coda: The Social Conductor

Unlike the mythic Romantic or modernist artist, African American swing-era musicians were *social* artists. These musicians created music to function socially—that is, in cooperation with an audience attuned to such African-derived practices as call-and-response, collective and individual movement, and a nonverbal understanding that musician-conductors would lead them through "extreme emotional and mental states." The musician-as-priest is a cliché, but that does not make it less true. Until the bebop revolution, the best African American musicians regarded their job as one of spiritual uplift: to make people dance, to create the atmosphere to rejuvenate one's spirits, to help tell the social blues in a secularized sacred space. The Ghanaian author Ayi Kwei Amah suggests, profoundly, that "poets are bandleaders who have failed."[98] For Duke Ellington, Count Basie, and Louis Armstrong, to gain an audience's attention was the first rule of artistic purpose; artistic success came from exciting that audience and making them happy on a given evening.

In 1937 Kenneth Burke succinctly theorized about cultural prestige that "class morality functions as cultural lag." An inability to recognize important artistic triumph often occurs when a "class of people arises whose situation is not accurately located by the . . . [conventional] frame."[99] Blacks occupied the lowest rung of the socioeconomic ladder between the world wars, and they were not considered wholly "American" or equally human by white Americans. Because a low-prestige ethnic group brought the artistic "news," their arts and aesthetics were effaced and dishonored. Otherwise the nation's system of racial supremacy and cultural hierarchy would have been thrown into disarray. Lawrence Levine points out that jazz musicians have always ignored any and all distinctions among classical, folk, and dance music; they have always appropriated any sounds they found useful and thrown them into the mix. In the process, "jazz musicians . . . revolutioniz[ed] not only music but also the concept of culture."[100]

The modernists George Antheil, Claude Bragdon, and Le Corbusier nearly grasped the innovating-traditionalist approach of this modernism. They did not recognize the dialogue between music and technology, nor the importance of the music/dance axis for rejuvenating Machine Age bodies. But their analyses, and that of Gilbert Seldes, Count Keyserling, Gene Krupa, and Frank Marshall Davis provide evidence that the means for understanding the techno-dialogic was present before World War II.

Significantly, Bragdon and Le Corbusier were architects, and their understanding of structure and form possibly gave them an advantage in being able to "see" the structural and functional aspects of African American music and dance. Big-band swing and architectural modernism are arguably the two most successful Machine Age forms and enjoy the most permanent legacies. The aesthetic element common to both arts is rhythm, and ideas of line, proportion, sequence, and pacing are crucial to both. The rhythm that held together a powerful big band, or seemingly frenetic dancers, is analogous to what holds together a structure as a discrete artistic entity in relation to its site and environment.

A famous nineteenth-century phrase connecting these two art forms is often attributed to both Goethe and Schiller: "Architecture is frozen music." In 1938 Duke Ellington wrote a short article comparing individual black entertainers to corresponding skyscrapers. In the "Chrysler Tower, [and] the Empire State building" he saw "the lives of [the comedian] Bert Williams, [and the actress] Florence Mills." Such "immortals" of entertainment represented African American experience, elegance in performance, and humor through "simplicity, sincerity . . . [and] a rigid adherence to the traditions of our own people." Such stars "tower as far above their fellow artists" as the skyscrapers above other buildings. In comparing New York's "marvelous sky-line to our race," Ellington might have included himself, "the man-orchestra . . . the genius of cohesion," as an early French jazz critic labeled him. And perhaps if we could slowly melt the Empire State Building, the stone and steel and glass and electrical wiring would dissolve into the strains of "Take the 'A' Train."[101]

SWINGING THE

MACHINES

BIG BANDS AND

STREAMLINER TRAINS

If I were the American Stalin, I'd build a giant dance hall, with a negro orchestra[,] in every town in America. That would be my church.
—Sherwood Anderson, Kansas City, January 1933

In 1993, before the swing revival, one summer night my girlfriend and I went to see the jazz veteran Illinois Jacquet and his eighteen-piece big band at the Tavern on the Green in New York's Central Park.[1] For white couples from the World War II generation, Jacquet's appearance was a nostalgia show, and the crowd was well-dressed, as if for dinner and dancing on a cruise ship. We were easily the youngest people in the room by thirty years. The room sat about three hundred at banquet tables horseshoed around a hardwood dance floor in front of which fourteen gleaming brass instruments lined up in formation. When the first song kicked in the band nearly blew me out of the room; before the first chorus I had no idea how loud eighteen instruments could sound, nor that a seventy-year-old Texas tenor saxophonist (and many other senior citizens) could rock my socks off.

I was a rock critic in my early twenties, and I liked my music loud, dynamic, chaotic, electric, riveting, thundering. I fought battles with my parents (and other adults) who seemed unable to hear even lyric-driven mid-tempo rock and roll such as Bruce Springsteen and Bob Dylan as anything but noise—to the point of putting their hands over their ears. And so I turned to my seventy-year-old listening companions expecting some perceptible discomfort, scrunched-up faces suggesting they turn it down. But the bald man next to me just started tapping two fingers rhythmically on the table, and his wife tilted her head slightly from side to side on the beat. I looked around the room and there was more of the same: calm, rapt attention; digits and toes tapping; smiles as if someone had welcomed them home. During the first mid-tempo ballad the dance floor filled up.

When I started researching swing as a historian, I was astounded by the number and variety of big bands playing every night in every town of more than fifty thousand. I tried to imagine an average Wednesday night in Salina, Kansas, in 1931 when Lester Young played with Art Bronson and the Bostonians for fifteen hundred dancing couples at the armory—the kind of statistic that only makes sense before television, when entertainment was to be found largely outside the home. But watching people the age of my grandparents lap up music of the same volume, power, and speed as rock and roll was a musical (and scholarly) conundrum. Now I know better: teenagers and young adults adapt to shifts in American culture through the popular music of their time. A given popular musical idiom speaks for you (and to you) in part because it reflects the soundscape of one's youth; any generation's aesthetics and values continue to reside inside the music as in no other cultural form. Marketing consultants still define the "Depression cohort" as one that "saves for a rainy day," is "intolerant of immorality in sexual matters," and whose favorite music is "big band." The raw volume and sheer blowing power of big-band swing were functional artistic forces: the daily lives of Americans had been filled with the noise of cars, trucks, radios, and workplace machinery for over a century.[2]

After three or four songs, I went to work in my rock critic mode. I noted the precision of Jacquet's sections, the joyful call-and-response of the brass and reeds, the way the trombone section might pump a riff for the soloist to work against, how the drummer fed the soloist his own distinctive supporting rhythm. A particular musical thrill came at moments when all the brass instruments would suddenly drop out, leaving only the rhythmic engine underneath, that smooth, flowing, buoyant 4/4, a veritable platform of sound. I felt the physiological impact of big-band swing: first a pulsing somewhere around the solar plexus; then those powerful brass *voices*—human breath amplified by metal, tubing, and electricity—swelled just below my collarbone; I felt the bass in my heart, as if it helped the blood pump, as the drummer worked to rivet my spine into better position. My body was soon attuned to the big-band machine.

In writing this book I solved that night's conundrum, at least for myself. I now believe the techno-dialogic has been the driving force of the global influence of American popular music since the swing era (maybe even since ragtime). Why? Next time you get in your car, roll the windows down and keep the radio off; listen only to the steady machine rhythm of the engine. It is not displeasing, but neither is it music. To *hear* the music in it, musicians needed to stylize machine aesthetics. Between 1870 and 1940, human beings raised to enjoy natural rhythms, whose bodies were adapted to a horse-powered world, found their bodies thrillingly—and terrifyingly—rattled first by trains and later by cars. Farmers rode on motor-powered vehicles every day; factory workers were immersed in the industrial soundscape. The bodies of urbanites—including millions of immigrants from southern Europe and Mexico, rural Euro-Americans, and African Americans—adapted to the steady rollicking of trolleys and streetcars, buses and subways.

But the felt grandeur of the American technical civilization lost its luster during the Depression when the benefits of industrialization could no longer be pressed into ideological service as a vision of a more convenient and enjoyable, technologically enabled, higher standard of living. For example, there were more automobiles in the United States in 1929 than in the rest of the world combined. As one in five Americans came to own "a machine"—then simply slang for a car—the democratization of technological progress seemed assured; the future promised a continuous flow of new devices.[3] But during the Depression the connotations of the term "the machine" began to take on a far more sinister cast. The assembly line became a common metaphor for an impoverished, brutal work life, and mass production an analogy to unindividuated persons—what H. L. Mencken once called "human Fords."[4] Machines kept increasing in complexity and beauty, while human beings were driven by Taylorist scientific management and the Fordist industrial model to perform up to mechanical standards.

In this chapter I trace the cultural work of big bands and streamliner trains in rejuvenating American imaginations and bodies. I contrast it with the more familiar historical model of the period, theorized by Roland Marchand (among others), that corporations restored popular faith in the machine-driven future through the sophisticated image-making of industrial designers. Exhibit A of this top-down model is Norman Bel Geddes's "Futurama" exhibit for General Motors at the 1939 New York World's Fair—the Fair's most popular industrial exhibit for its theme "The World of Tomorrow." As fairgoers rode gently in carts, two-by-two, over a giant diorama of a miniaturized 1960 suburban utopia featuring interstate highways and green, spacious landscapes, their experience of this virtual future helped *create* that future; they in turn fell victim to corporate agendas of suburban prosperity.[5] With Futurama, Bel Geddes adapted core national myths, first promulgated by railroad promoters of the antebellum period, in the service of the newer automobile industry. Futurama synthesized the hope for peaceful, clean abundance with a more lofty set of ideals from the era's social planners; in so doing, it updated an earlier upper-class fantasy of bloodless social transformation, Edward Bellamy's utopian novel, *Looking Backward, 2000–1889* (1888).[6] In 1939, after ten years of economic depression, the American faith in techno-progress—and in the world of tomorrow—depended upon a novel combination of materialism, mobility, and technological pastoralism.[7]

Corporate manipulation, however, cannot explain what the historian Lewis Erenberg calls the "rebirth of American culture" during an economic depression in which so many cultural myths and icons temporarily lost their power. The extent of public alienation from capitalism in the middle of the decade brought on a marketing crisis for American corporations. In a series of influential speeches, the advertising executive and marketing consultant Bruce Barton assured corporations that their main weakness was image, not efficiency or product quality. "Business says to itself, 'We have created most of the comforts and satisfaction of modern life'—but it does not say this to the 130,000,000 in language they can understand," he told manufacturers. Executives needed to communicate "the greater mission" of their individual corporations, and of capitalism itself. Businessmen soon shifted their public relations to market themselves as responsive to workers, consumers, and "the people." Corporate executives made "confessions" concerning their lack of attention to consumers in ads and employee magazines.[8] Most importantly, at industrial expositions and world's fairs, they spent vast sums to create user-friendly exhibits that would make science and the manufacturing process accessible to audiences.[9]

By the time Futurama opened in 1939, a cultural revitalization had *already* taken place in the previous five years, a process possible to trace through the cultural work of two public symbols that still define Depression-era American culture: big bands and streamliner trains. As an aesthetic object, the new streamliner became a symbol of the nation's industrial past retooled for the future, a gleaming new physical body blending human and machine attributes. The big band was itself an icon of humanized machine aesthetics: it generated waves of musical energy that served to rejuvenate human agency and a sense of renewed physicality in the face of human obsolescence. Big bands and streamliners signified as public figures against a forbidding ground of overmechanization.

When the cultural myths of society are shaken, symbolic order is often created at the grassroots level, not from the top down. According to Clifford Geertz, a public symbol reflects how individuals think *socially;* that is, it functions as an emblem of a cultural thought-pattern.[10] The rhythmic drive of big-band swing derived from train rhythms and sounds, fusing past experience with mechanical power, and blending culture, identity, and artistic engagement. The swing dance-hall ritual enabled Americans to dynamically and expressively engage the unnerving increased tempo of everyday life. How big was swing? In the mid-1930s, with the help of a new invention, the jukebox, swing saved the recording industry from bankruptcy (its worst year was 1932). Big-band swing accounted for nearly 50 percent of all record sales in the late 1930s.[11]

Significantly, neither contemporary observers nor historians have adequately explained the sudden popularity of either swing or streamliners. Reflecting back on the streamliner's explosive debut into national consciousness at the Chicago Century of Progress Exposition in 1934, the editors of *Business Week* wrote in 1940 that "something clicked in Mr. Average Man, and the streamlined era had arrived."[12] Similarly, "something surprising and *not-altogether* explicable" occurred at the Palomar Ballroom in Los Angeles in August 1935, on the last night of Benny Goodman's unsuccessful and demoralizing cross country tour. To the band's surprise, the same hard-swinging jazz that had drawn boos in many cities suddenly clicked. The club held Goodman's orchestra over for four weeks, it returned triumphantly to Chicago and New York, and the word "swing" soon appeared in the mainstream press. The swing era had arrived.[13]

The Human Dilemma of Mass Production

The closest the United States has ever come to projecting an official culture was in the world's fairs and expositions from Philadelphia's Centennial Exposition of 1876 through the New York World's Fair of 1939.[14] In 1933 the nation's preeminent advertisement for itself was named for techno-progress: the Chicago Century of Progress Exposition. The two-year exposition's motto clearly placed the needs of American machines above that of human beings: "Science Finds—Industry Applies—Man Conforms." In granting technology both autonomy and extrahuman agency, the expo's mission statement anthropomorphizes science as the national deity served by the secret priests of technological determinism: "Science discovers, genius invents, industry applies, and man adapts himself to, or is molded by, new things. Science, patient and painstaking, digs into the ground, reaches up to the stars, takes from the water and the air, and industry accepts its findings. . . . Individuals, groups, entire races of men fall into step with the . . . movement of the march of science and industry."[15] There is no better delineation of American cultural ideology in the Machine Age. The musical metaphor is telling as well: the "march" of science and industry is a militaristic lockstep that all human beings (not just Americans) must "fall into step with."

So Americans were semiofficially enslaved to technology, and their physical and mental abilities were found wanting in comparison. As one historian put it, "In 1833, Technology was understood as one of Man's tools; by 1933 it had become his acknowledged master." The exposition's iconography confirms such a reading. In the main corridor of the Hall of Science, the centerpiece of the exposition, stood a sculpture with three figures that embodied the exposition's motto. A life-sized man and woman stood cringing, seemingly helpless, "hands outstretched as if in fear or ignorance." Between them stood "a huge angular robot nearly twice their size . . . with an angular metallic arm thrown reassuringly around each."[16] (See fig. 3.)

The enthrallment of American business and political elites to the technological god reverberated internationally. Several European intellectual and artistic works of the late 1920s pictured the United States as a nightmare of mass-production values and overmechanization, a society where the enlightenment of individualism was eliminated by menial jobs and mindless leisure. Though Fritz Lang's film *Metropolis* (1927) illustrates those fears against a German backdrop, it was inspired by his visit to New York City the previous year. The entire opening montage is a visual meditation on the vertical city as Lang experienced it in 1924 from a ship "docked somewhere on the West Side of New York." Lang recalled, "I looked into the streets—the glaring lights and the tall buildings—and there I conceived *Metropolis*." The film was then the most expensive European movie ever produced. Lang later told the American director Peter Bogdonavich that "it was a picture in which human beings

Figure 3. Sculpture at the Century of Progress Exposition, Chicago, 1933–34. The sculpture stood in the atrium of the Hall of Science, the exposition's most popular exhibit, and was one of the icons of the exposition. (A Century of Progress Records [COP neg. 39], Special Collections, The University Library, University of Illinois at Chicago.)

were nothing but part of a machine," and that he believed his prophecy had come true by the mid-1960s.[17]

Aldous Huxley's dystopic *Brave New World* (1932) mocked mass production as a Fordist religion based on the American system of manufacture. Huxley's novel is set in the year A.F. 632 ("After Ford," where the year 1 corresponds to the date the first Model T rolled off the assembly line). Feudal lordships had become corporate "Fordships," and people crossed themselves with "Ts" (for the Model T); in the future, Ford's mass-production values would replace those of Christendom. Huxley's novel points up European fears of a Fordist cultural hegemony, which John Dewey had bemoaned two years earlier: "Quantification, mechanization, and standardization: these are then the marks of Americanization . . . conquering the world.[18]

Such fears were presented within the context of the debate on "technological unemployment" in the United States but found little articulation in popular culture outside of labor union publications.[19] Chaplin's *Modern Times* (1936) is the major exception; but it was not a popular movie (it grossed 30 percent less than Chaplin's previous three films) nor was it primarily received as a critique of industrialization. Some critics and audiences felt that a silent film in 1936 was simply old-fashioned (that is, technologically obsolete).[20] Techno-progress was the nation's "faith"—as Mumford pointed out, it was a secular religion, a mechano-idolatry—and could not be rejected without an equally potent countermyth.

Throughout the interwar period all major government reports agreed that scientific progress was "inevitable" and that "society had no option but to change and to accommodate." American economic, intellectual, and technological elites considered the challenge of the 1930s to be "cultural lag," not overmechanization. Rural Americans especially needed to be brought into the machine age, requiring "a speeding up of social invention." Businessmen and scientists promoted the idea that scientists discovered laws and converted the knowledge into consumer technologies. According to the historian of technology Carroll Pursell, such "rhetorical flourishes" were met with "widespread agreement" by the public.[21]

The grandiose vision of the benevolent machine at the Chicago exposition was undermined by the desperate rhetoric of the nation's business leaders on the eve of the exposition's second year. Alfred P. Sloan Jr., the president of General Motors, convened six hundred of the nation's leaders to help "contradict the philosophy that progress was a thing of the past and [to] paint a picture of the next century as one of scientific marvels"—such as atomic energy, solar-powered motors, and color movies. The *New York Times* covered the meeting as though it were a world summit, with two columns on page one and a full page inside. The article contained a three-paragraph transcription of a telegram sent by President Roosevelt to encourage the business leaders, and the coverage was akin to that of a presidential visit during a domestic crisis. What seems most surprising in retrospect is that two full columns were devoted to a transcription of a literary fantasy written by Walter S. Pitkin, a Columbia University English professor who "painted a picture of the future in Edward Bellamy style." Claiming to use "the hyperzootic ooze controls of a time broadcaster" of 2034, Pitkin reassured the people of 1934 that economic salvation was near at hand. In 1949, he assured his audience, the largest twenty corporations would begin to offer cradle-to-grave security for a flat monthly payment: "complete equipment for living . . . food, clothing, a home, an auto, a plane, television, and a world travel ticket good on all trains and boats." Without explaining how such corporations would turn a profit, Pitkin's time broadcaster claimed that by the early 1960s "governments became rapidly obsolete . . . [and] politics died out. . . . People had everything they wanted. They felt secure from birth to death."[22]

Sloan, Pitkin, and the *New York Times* were engaged in highbrow hucksterism, trying to sell techno-progress via "the rhetoric of the technological sublime" (to use Leo Marx's term). The headline was telling: "Science Will Liberate All Mankind in Next Century, Leaders Predict."[23] To a severe crisis of technological faith, business leaders and academics responded with recycled literary fantasy and the promise of consumer technologies. To end the Depression, business and cultural elites could only imagine top-down fantasies dependent on technological deliverance satisfying consumer demands.[24]

The nation's vision of its own future, as well as its cultural identity, had been dependent on technological innovation for a full century. The fruits of technology—sewing machines, cars, radios, home appliances, "a flood of consumer durables unprecedented in history"—seemed more miraculous than the fruits of nature.[25] In the 1920s the emergence of networks of power that created access to electricity, telephone service, and radio stations encouraged the rhetoric of continuous progress. Sociologists attributed cultural shifts more to technology and applied science than to politics; change came through "mass production, urbanization, birth control, the typewriter, education." The novelist William Gibson reinscribes such a position today when he claims that "all cultural change is essentially technologically driven."[26]

The rarely asked question was whether Americans could embrace machine aesthetics—speed, precision, efficiency, and flow—without discarding (or demoting) the preindustrial past. What of the legacy of Western culture and supposedly universal human values? Could they be integrated with machines? According to James Truslow Adams, the nation was caught between emergent mass production values and Christian-derived "higher values" based on noble models of human behavior. The society's purpose was now to keep its machines running in an alienating system causing social "chaos . . . [that] will drown our human personalities in a dehumanized whirl of production and consumption of things without human values."[27] Mass production values led to "mental withdrawal," John Dewey wrote, "[and] the failure to face the realities of industrialized society."[28] Even the heroes of Chaplin's *Modern Times* are tramps who choose not to participate in industrial society but instead are "spiritual escapees from a world in which he [Chaplin] saw no other hope."[29]

Dewey called for leadership among intellectuals to help Americans cope with the social chaos brought on by industrial transformation. "[If] at least one group of individuals [would] recover a social function and so re-find themselves . . . [it would be] a first step in a more general reconstruction that will bring integration out of disorder." Sherwood Anderson tried to develop a dramatic work that would celebrate both human and mechanical energies. But for a play concerning "the relationship of man and the machine" and the "march of machinery across American life," the renowned Anderson could interest only one producer, who backed out before rehearsals.[30]

In two books about his travels in the American heartland, *Perhaps Women* (1931) and *Puzzled America* (1935), Anderson meditated on the relationship between human beings and machines. Alone among American writers, he brought together the problems of human obsolescence, lost individuality, and mechanical intimidation. He observed that many white American men saw themselves as failures, as obsolete pieces of equipment; men he picked up on the road began to talk with "an apology. . . . 'I've failed in this American scheme. It's my own fault.' . . . that's the tone." And he repeatedly contrasted the fast, clean, powerful machines of the factories with the haggard, worn-out human beings he observed and spoke with: "That curious contrast, the care lavished on the machines, the carelessness about human lives." The machines emasculated individuals. Anderson himself confessed, "They are too complex and beautiful for me. My manhood cannot stand up against them yet."[31]

Anderson thus identified the individual male body as a crucial site of Depression-era despair. In the physical movements of American men—

how they walked, stood, shook hands—he observed a lack of energy that was in inverse proportion to the vigorous machines.

> American workmen, so often now thrown out of their place in our social and economic scheme by the modern machine, so often robbed of something peculiarly vital to their feeling of manhood—this I keep thinking the most important thing of all. . . . The machines themselves apparently becoming always faster and faster, more and more efficient—the man in the street can see it with his own eyes in the increased beauty, speed, and efficiency of the automobile.[32]

A former factory-hand himself, Anderson wrote often of men's bodies during his career. A close friend recalled Anderson as "extremely aware of his hands as tools . . . [and] always conscious of his body as an instrument of expression." But in the 1930s he saw only worn-out hands and frustrated faces throughout predominantly rural America.[33] In fact, the thesis of *Perhaps Women* is that only women could lead the nation into the coming technical civilization because men were physically and mentally worn out.[34]

Many liberal intellectuals speculated that the world was in the birth pangs of a new kind of machine civilization.[35] What most worried Anderson was that people no longer remembered how to enjoy their own *humanness*. He encountered spirited people rarely, and usually among newly unionized workers. Like Dewey, Anderson also challenged artists to go into the factories and mills and help Americans appreciate both the beauty and terror of our machines: "the old question—to make men rise in nobility to the nobility of the machines."[36]

The art historian Terry Smith has analyzed the works of the American artists who did go into the factories and portray the beauty of the machines: Charles Sheeler's paintings, Margaret Bourke-White's photographs, the sharp, half-toned workplace photographs in *Fortune* and *Time* magazines. Smith points out that there are virtually no human beings in any of these works; machines alone live in these landscapes, "implying an autonomy to the mechanical." Ironically, these art works feature machines at rest, their motion stilled; the viewer's gaze is directed to gears and engines as embodiments of "repetition, simplicity, regularity of rhythm, clarity of surface." In these works, machine aesthetics are fetishized for corporate elites; what Smith calls "the gaze of management at leisure."[37]

Sheeler's paintings of machines and interlocking systems were especially lionized by the corporate elite, his canvases bought by the likes of

Edsel Ford and Mrs. Abby Aldrich Rockefeller. In an extensive *Fortune* photo-essay, the editors praised Sheeler's works for helping to neutralize business elites' fear of overmechanization by bringing out the hidden *cerebral* beauty of machines. Machines were "not strange, inhuman masses of material, but exquisite manifestations of human reason." As Renaissance artists registered everyday beauty through the form of the human body, in the Machine Age "the modern American artist reflects life through [machine] forms . . . forms that are more deeply human than the muscles of the torso because they trace the firm pattern of the human mind as it seeks to use co-operatively the limitless power of nature." Machine bodies, being superior to human ones, were now more worthy of representation since their speed, power, precision, efficiency, and lack of fatigue symbolized a more perfect embodiment of rational thought processes and man's dominance of nature. According to *Fortune*, a shift had occurred in the ideal body from the Renaissance admiration for the human (such as Michelangelo's *David*) to the industrial revolution's worship of the machine. *Fortune* wrote about Sheeler's photos and paintings, "Nature was never quite like [this], so luminous, so fiercely beautiful, so rich in design."[38]

Streamlining into the Future

The human body was obsolete, not up to mechanical specifications. Yet ironically the train became the public symbol that helped Americans transmute the country's industrial past—and, in some way, human values—into a restored faith for the future; such is the conflicted role of technology in a nation whose civil religion is techno-progress. The train *body* was a better representative of the American past than Americans themselves. The only historically based exhibit at the New York World's Fair of 1939 was the popular "Railroads on Parade"—a giant spectacle which paraded twenty real locomotives on stage, showing the evolution of the train body via tableaux of the American past.[39] This transformation of *the train as symbolic individual body* held a spellbinding power for Depression-era Americans.

The streamliner burst into national consciousness at the Chicago Century of Progress Exposition in late May 1934. Throughout the previous months, crowds gathered throughout the territory of the Chicago, Burlington, and Quincy Railroad to see the first streamliners. Then on May 26, 1934, at dawn of the same day that Alfred Sloan convened his summit meeting, one of the first diesel-powered streamliners, the

Burlington Zephyr, began an exciting nonstop dawn-to-dusk run between Denver and Chicago, a marketing stunt thought up by Burlington's president, Ralph Budd. By the time the Zephyr arrived at dusk to celebrate the reopening of the exposition, it had cut the land-speed record nearly in half. Excited crowds stood and watched the sleek silver streamliner power across the Midwest at an average speed of 77.8 miles per hour, and Chicagoans showed up in great numbers to greet the train, breaking the previous year's opening-day attendance by one-third.[40]

The Zephyr was represented as a sentient being in the next day's *New York Times;* not a single person was mentioned in the first ten paragraphs of the newspaper's coverage of this "silver king." To use Langdon Winner's phrase, the trope of "autonomous technology" prevailed—as if a locomotive were a self-contained, self-sustaining, self-propelling machine powered by energy systems neither understood nor open to question.[41] Over the next year, fifteen million Americans went to see the streamliners on tour; the chronicler Frederick Lewis Allen observed how "crowds surged through [them], entranced: here was a symbol of the new America they wanted."[42] The term "streamliner" soon became synonymous for "train," and "streamlining" became equated with a technological "modern" style—meaning anything that "improves economy or efficiency."[43] The Zephyr's bold run was immortalized in film almost immediately in *Silver Streak* (1935); apparently the streamliner was the kind of charismatic leader Americans were looking for.

Streamlined design emerged from aerodynamics, the study of how an object moves through space. Ideally, an object moves forward smoothly and with the least resistance ("minimal drag") from decorative encumbrance. Stylistic elements such as long horizontal lines, backward parabolic swoops, uncluttered masses, and metallic colors emphasized speed and forward motion both visually and functionally. Regardless of function, though, streamlined design came to add a patina of progress to any new appliance, whether toaster or refrigerator or washing machine. It came to symbolize "frictionless flow into the future."[44]

Streamlined design hid the industrial workings of the machine under a smooth, flowing, hard shell, and its success was due to a cultural shift. Americans had lost their pride in observing the inner workings of machines, the industrial triumphalism of what Cecilia Tichi calls "the gear-and-girder world."[45] With the workings of machines hidden under a brilliant surface, Americans could ignore the tensions and contradictions of machine-driven modernity. The simple, elegant, metallic beauty of streamlined design symbolized a shift to an aesthetic of *controlled power.* Before its redesign, the shell of the Pennsylvania Railroad's GG-1 locomotive, for example, was a patchwork of uneven steel plates riveted together, and the powerful motion of the wheels was visible to all. The industrial designer Raymond Loewy designed a new unified shell—assembled on the ground and lowered onto the chassis—and added a steel skirt to quiet the wheels. The shell was not only easier to keep clean, it muffled the train's sound so effectively that horizontal gold bands were painted on to enable track-workers to see the train coming.[46]

Considering the American fascination with aviation in the 1930s, logically streamlined design should have *flown* into the public's heart. But instead it "rode" in as a new sleek, hard shell for a vehicle of the past. In part, the style fit the vehicle: sleek lines and smooth surfaces created a fast, forward-moving horizontal flow that underscored the train's power on the ground. Airplanes still seemed "futuristic and fanciful," according to one historian, while the retooled streamliners "seemed to have a firm grip on the immediate future"; the railroad "was here, it was now . . . it was alive, it was healthy."[47] And, of course, the train had been the prime mover of global modernity: as early as the 1840s, the locomotive had surpassed the steamboat "as the dominant symbol of the new civilization's mobile energies."[48] In the nineteenth century "the railroad was the center of attention, the forerunner of prosperity, the augur of progress," and until at least 1920 the train was the most powerful machine—and spectacle—in American life.[49] The Century of Progress Exposition celebrated the hundredth anniversary of the founding of Chicago, but it might well have been celebrating one hundred years of train-powered industrial unification.

In the 1920s the United States economy was built around the automobile and its cultural dreams around aviation; by 1930 the railroad industry was in severe decline, carrying almost 70 percent below its 1920 capacity.[50] Where once the railroad industry imposed its will on the national economy and local landscapes, the train itself now seemed more like an old friend from simpler times. It was a nostalgic symbol of the nation's successful industrial expansion, its technological manifest destiny, its sectional unity. And of course railroads remained central to American industry: even in 1939 they carried 65 percent of all freight traffic and purchased 20 percent of the nation's coal, fuel oil, iron, steel, and lumber.[51]

I am suggesting here that the parallel obsolescence of train bodies and human bodies underlies the popular embrace of the new streamliners. The transformation of a noisy, inefficient, smoke-pouring obsolescent mode of transportation into a light, fleet, dashing silver streak was living proof (so to speak) that the worn-out industrial-era physical body could be retooled for the Machine Age. When the dime-novel character Steam Man first appeared in 1868, he represented the conflicted American desire to integrate machine aesthetics into a human body. His appearance was connected to the role of the train in unifying the nation just as Superman's appearance in the late 1930s represents the first dreaming of the integration of the human body and the airplane.[52] The crucial difference is that the train had an American past; the airplane did not.

In the 1930s human obsolescence became a serious topic of discussion. In an extensive 1932 photo-essay entitled "Obsolete Men," *Fortune* bemoaned the human costs of a machine civilization (especially the inevitable technological unemployment), though the adulatory ten-page photo-spread of the enormous industrial machines then displacing the workers undermined the editorial sympathy.[53] The following year, the industrial researcher Elton Mayo likewise worried about the costs of the needed social transformation: "The worker, as we at present conceive him, [is] no longer needed by industry . . . [what is occurring is] the development of a society in which there will be no place for the illiterate or the ignorant."[54] The noisy, smoke-belching train symbolized the obsolete, unneeded American; the streamliner was a faster, quieter, more efficient and flowing train-body symbolizing a retooled American for the uncertain future. (See fig. 4.)

Langdon Winner asks a key historical question about Americans' relationship with their machines: "When old technologies die, do we mourn?" Focusing on nostalgia for such products as the album (LP) and the manual typewriter, Winner claims that Americans do not understand their emotional investment in inanimate objects. What he terms "the pain of technical change" is more clearly seen in children's stories and toys, in model trains or the stories of Paul Bunyan. The emotional investment of Depression-era Americans in the train body is clear, for instance, in the 1930 children's classic, *The Little Engine That Could.* This story of human resilience featured male and female trains, but no human characters; yet two of the trains are so human that they conk out from mental and emotional exhaustion.[55]

Figure 4. Model of the Zephyr. This promotional photo reveals that the Chicago, Burlington, and Quincy Railroad thought about its new streamliner through an evolutionary paradigm. (Courtesy of The Newberry Library, Chicago.)

The story gets going when the wheels of a red female local seize up, stranding her load of books and toys, who then try to hitch a ride over the mountain. "Rusty Old Engine," a friendly, steam-pouring, industrial male, wants to help, but he is used up. He declares in a pique of existential despair: "I can not . . . I can not . . . I can not." Two powerful male trains refuse to stop and help; the "shiny new engine" passenger train must get his businessmen to work on time and the powerful black freight train must get his goods to market on time. Both of these trains value industrial needs over human ones. The heroine is a small, cheerful, older blue female from the local valley who admits she has never been over the mountain and confesses her self-doubt about the trip. Agreeing only to try her best, she slowly revs up to speed; when her momentum carries her over the mountain into the next town, she beams with pride, seemingly as proud of her own inner resources as for serving her passengers. The local girl-train-next-door represents the self-image of rural Americans infused with industrialized train energy; it is a vision of the American self retooled for modern society.

Winner's point about technologies is quite relevant to the late 1930s. Americans often measure their historical moment—their *progress*—by the technological inventions of the age. But the pain of adjustment to machine-driven change is revealed during a technological plateau. Virginia Lee Burton's classic children's stories of the period reveal similar tensions to *Little Engine*. In *Choo-Choo* (1937), "a beautiful little engine" named Choo-Choo forsakes her productive life of carrying passengers and freight, having "tired of pulling all these heavy coaches." While her engineer, fireman, and conductor are having coffee, she takes off down the track by herself, without a schedule or a destination—call it a mental-health day. Ringing her bell and tooting her steam whistle, she causes disorder in rural areas (scaring cows and horses) and in cities (causing pileups at grade-crossings and terminals). She eventually loses her coal tender and winds up fuelless on a long-abandoned track; meanwhile her engineer and fireman commandeer a new streamliner. "What about my schedule?" asks the conductor. "Never mind your schedule," answers Jim the engineer, suggesting that our machine "friends" are more important than industrial time and productivity. The streamliner with Choo-Choo's attendants aboard find her run-down and pull her back to the roundhouse where she is given a clean bill of health (and a new tender). In Burton's *Mike Mulligan and His Steam Shovel* (1939), the symbiotic pair of man and machine known as Mike Mulligan and Mary Anne (the steam shovel) find themselves out of work due to the efficiency of gasoline engines and faster, electric-powered shovels. Having dredged canals, blasted through mountains, and dug foundations for skyscrapers, this inseparable duo of American male and steam-powered machine get one last job offer. In the vein of John Henry, Mulligan bets that he and Mary Anne can dig a foundation for a new town hall in Popperville in one day. Of course they succeed, but in the process they literally dig themselves into a hole from which there is no path back to ground level. The solution? Mary Anne's steam engine becomes the furnace of the Popperville town hall and Mike is hired as the janitor, a tribute to the technological folklore of American industrial culture and the human/machine interface.[56]

There is an uncanny real-life analogy. In 1994, Chicago's Museum of Science and Industry received funds to restore the streamliner that excited crowds at the Chicago's Century of Progress Exhibition. Officially opened in 1997, the Burlington Zephyr is now the centerpiece of a permanent exhibit entitled "All Aboard the Silver Streak" in the basement of the museum.

Refueling and Regrooving American Bodies

The subtext of these works of children's literature speak to an inquiry into human vs. machine that neither Sherwood Anderson nor John Dewey managed to articulate: How could Americans retool and rejuvenate their *physical* bodies? How could they restore confidence in the grace, dignity, and expressiveness of the human body? The streamliner was a symbol of the new age, a humanized machine carrying a century's worth of technological progress on its back and combining human and mechanical traits (and energies). It was still, however, a machine. On the other hand, the most admired human body on display in American culture had always been the black male body, whether in the conflicted love-and-theft of blackface minstrelsy, the admiration of southern slave-owners, or professional sports today.[57] But until at least the 1960s African American kinesthetics had been devalued as animalistic and primitive, and historians have only recently theorized an African American cultural aesthetic.[58]

Owing to Christian associations of the body with base instinct and sexuality, as well as to the Cartesian bifurcation of (intelligent) mind and (instinctive) body, Euro-Americans had always been conflicted about the relationship of their bodies to both intelligence and noble human values. The primitivist view enabled Euro-Americans to admire and imitate nonwhite bodies without honoring them as equally human. Primitivism was a search by Europeans and Euro-Americans for alternative value systems after being jolted awake to "the self-destructive capacity of machinery and weaponry" in World War I. The psychiatrist Robert Coles suggests that it be contextualized as an internal critique of "Western civilization . . . disavow[ing] . . . materialism, scientific thinking, faith and progress . . . over other more human modes of thought and feeling."[59] In other words, primitivism functioned as a corrective for white elites overinvested in rational modes of being. A historian of psychiatry viewed the interwar period as one of transition for upper-class Euro-Americans from a "controlling to a releasing symbolic" as elites began to admire emotional outlet over the Protestant work ethic and emotional repression. According to Philip Rieff, "The upper classes . . . lost this most fundamental of all class struggles by their admiration for the 'vitality' of the lower."[60] Primitivism can be seen as an identity politics practiced by white elites intent on preserving the terms "civilized" and "rational" for themselves while confessing a lack of human resources for rejuvenating body and spirit. Caught between racist assumptions of human difference and a mechanistic ideal of the body, Depression-era Americans had an unconscious desire for a new relationship to their bodies.

Many scholars are now investigating the inadequacy of mind/body dualism as a depiction of cognition. In studies of "embodiment," for example, cognitive philosophers, neuroscientists, and anthropologists consistently find that "sensori-motor experience" influences not only *what* human beings think but *how* they think and how aesthetics expand the boundaries of thought. In *The Body in the Mind* (1987), the philosopher Mark Johnson declares at the outset that "as animals we have bodies connected to the natural world . . . [and] our consciousness and rationality are tied to our bodily orientations and interactions in and with our environment. . . . [M]eaning and rationality are tied to bodily experience."[61] As mentioned in chapter 1, John Dewey called for a new plan of "mind-body integration" in 1930, and Richard Shusterman finds that Dewey missed an opportunity to delineate an embodied philosophy in *Art as Experience* (1934). In a key chapter, "The Organization of Energies," Dewey called for a renewed appreciation of the organizational principle of rhythm in painting, in music, in the workings of our bodies, and in everyday life—what he termed "esthetic recurrence." But in discussing the importance of rhythm for a renewal of social energies, Dewey felt it necessary to distinguish the noble qualities of rhythmic line and proportion from both "the 'tom-tom' theory" of rhythm (with its model of "the beat of the drum of the savage") and "the 'tick-tock' theory" (the clockwork model).[62] Still, Dewey's prophetic text must be contextualized within the Machine Age call and the swing-era response.

Dewey's disavowal of the rhythm of popular music as useful for social renewal suggests the low prestige of jazz among American liberal intellectuals, and an avoidance of its artistic and aesthetic implications in

American life. Although several studies of jazz appeared between 1936 and 1944 by American and European critics[63]—a testament to the immense impact of swing in particular on American culture—the aesthetic element of rhythm remained undertheorized by musicologists of all kinds. The musicologist Carl E. Seashore published a research paper in 1918 called "The Sense of Rhythm as a Musical Talent," as if that were a new idea. As jazz swept the nation in 1917, the *New Orleans Times-Picayune* described rhythm as the element of music that resides "in the basement," near "the servants' hall." It was as if rhythm, melody, and harmony were parallel to the evolutionary stages of primitive, agrarian, and industrial societies. The exploration of rhythm as an aesthetic force in classical music began in earnest with Stravinsky's *The Rite of Spring* (1913), a composition whose rhythmic emphases and variation caused a riot among the Parisian upper classes but also "led many composers to realize how underdeveloped rhythm had been in Western art music." As late as 1955, Henry Pleasants wrote that "of the basic musical elements . . . rhythm . . . has been the least highly developed and the least systematically exploited in European music."[64]

Rhythm was not simply the driving force of African American popular music; in the first four decades of the century it came to represent the primal force itself, what Bergson called the "élan vital." Anthropologists noted the importance of rhythm to work among nonindustrial societies, and painters and composers saw in rhythm the steady pulse of the heartbeat. "The rhythm of the body was the root of all art," the historian Anson Rabinbach notes, and "the repetition of figures, of movement, of forms was the source of aesthetic pleasures."[65] Duke Ellington connected the biological experience of rhythm (breath and heartbeat) with the role of rhythm in jazz. "Our very lives are dependent on rhythm, for everything we do is governed by ordered rhythmic sequences: that [good] dance music . . . is completely rhythmic is only in accordance with the natural law." In contrast to the role of the piano in a symphony orchestra, Ellington declared that the role of the pianist was "to feed the band with rhythm."[66]

Early rhythm theorists often prefaced their arguments by declaring that human life was dependent upon the rhythms of the heartbeat and the breath. Nor is this equation simply rhetoric. Composer John Cage walked into a soundproofed vacuum chamber in 1947 in search of pure silence; what he found instead was a pulsating inner soundscape. With all external sound removed from the environment, he heard two unusual sounds. The engineer informed him that the "high" noise was his "nervous system in operation," and the lower tone his "blood in circulation." At a time when technology had made it possible to create "perfect" silence, a Western composer discovered he was rhythmically engaged at all times. "Try as we may to make a silence, we cannot," Cage concluded.[67] Black musicians and dancers had always made connections between musical and bodily rhythms. The drummer C. Scoby Strohman put it dramatically: "Your heart is your drums: and when it expires, you're dead."[68]

From a different point of view, by the late 1920s there had already been two decades of debate regarding the physiological needs of factory workers; to some extent, the debate was about whether to "work that body" or "rest that body."[69] But the debate over the role of "play" largely ignored the crucial environmental factor of noise. If, as discussed in chapter 1, noise was one of the most disorienting sensory experiences of industrial society and modern cities, then artists who transformed that noise into music and created accompanying social dances could well become cultural heroes. (See figs. 5, 6, 7.) Factory workers were equally disturbed by performing jobs at the machine's pace, a complaint that transcended generation and economic status. Skilled machinists complained of it to the 1912 U.S. House of Representatives Special Committee to Investigate the Taylor and Other Systems of Shop Management. Striking General Motors assembly-line workers in 1936–37 were more frustrated by the "speed-up" of the line than any other factor of job dissatisfaction besides wages. Even unionized Cold War factory workers despised working at "the machine's pace."[70] If American culture was built upon a mechanical (rather than "natural") foundation, then artists and cultural producers would have to take such a new set of sensory-motor experiences into account to keep up aesthetically with social needs. If human beings need to integrate rather than escape those dynamic forces they encounter, then perhaps big bands grew in size and volume in response to a need for louder, more humanly organized noise.[71] Considering the expressive forms of swing culture—tap, the lindy hop, big-band jazz—within a context of rapid industrialization, it becomes easier to understand why Americans admired the dramatic spectacle of humanized machine aesthetics as displayed upon a musical foundation.

The innovative quality in jazz that would enable big bands to reflect the industrial soundscape was itself called the *foundation* or *foundation*

Figure 5.
Selmer advertisement in *Metronome*, 1936. (Courtesy of Selmer.)
The ads on the next three pages feature some of the first dignified images of African Americans ever presented in the national media: jazz musicians dressed in suits and featured as artists, media stars, and representative Americans.

Figure 6. Conn and Martin advertisements in *Metronome,* 1940. (Reprinted with permission of United Musical Instruments U.S.A., Inc., a subsidiary of Steinway Musical Instruments.) These ads for C. G. Conn and Martin Band Instrument Company appeared opposite each other in *Metronome.* Johnny Hodges and Grady Watts, of the Duke Ellington and Casa Loma Orchestras respectively, are framed with equal dignity and without any racial markings as spokesmen for these manufacturers of musical instruments.

Figure 7. Gretsch-Gladstone advertisement in *Metronome*, 1940. (Courtesy of Gretsch.) Besides Joe Jones, other African American drummers featured in similar full-page ads for Gretsch included Chick Webb and O'Neill Spencer (Gene Krupa and George Wettling were white drummers given the same treatment). Some full-page ads for Selmer, Conn, and Martin featured a dozen or so musicians in small square yearbook-style photos, black and white men and women side by side—all framed as equals.

quality by jazz musicians. The pianist and composer Jelly Roll Morton defined the crucial elements of jazz as accurate tempos, strong riffs, breaks in the music for solos, and a sense of open musical space. He defined a ragtime piano riff as "what you would call the foundation, as like you would walk on." W. C. Handy was more philosophical: "We [African Americans] look for truth in music . . . What we want in music is something to build on." Duke Ellington declared simply that any "Negro musician" uses "the black beat [as] his foundation" to reflect the aural environment. White musicians used the term as well. The role of the band pianist, according to Benny Goodman, was to "play solid foundation [harmonies and rhythm figures] as well as be able to get off on solos." Jazz musicians refer to this foundation quality as a palpable physical presence, as if sound waves created a platform to build a temporary structure to dance on. Significantly, the jazz rhythm section—piano, rhythm guitar, bass, and drums—was created and perfected in the swing era. Even the best 1920s jazz bands had "no bottom," according to one of the decade's best arrangers, and the drummer was considered simply a time-keeper.[72]

The emergence of individual identities for the string bass and the drummer, and of a new relationship between the two, created swing's stronger rhythmic foundation. "The foundation . . . is rhythm . . . and this is between the bass violin and the bass drum, between the two of them," explained Panama Francis, Cab Calloway's drummer. "[They] set the pulsation for people to pat their feet and dance to."[73] Milt Hinton and John Simmons, two influential swing-era bassists, took up the bass precisely because it had no identity in 1920s jazz; they enjoyed the challenge of creating its sound. Like the drums and saxophone, the bass often functioned as a noisemaker or a novelty instrument in the 1920s, "a personality [thing] . . . slapping the bass, you know," recalled Hinton, "single slap, double slap, triple slap, spin the bass."[74] The guitarist Eddie Durham recalled how Count Basie's bassist Walter Page pumped up his attack to back the brass instruments. "Without amplification, a lot of guys weren't strong enough on bass . . . [b]ut Walter Page you could hear! He was like a house with a note."[75]

The drummer's job was to uplift the band to "lift that band, just lift it right off the floor and push it."[76] As New Orleans drummer Baby Dodds put it: "You can't get into a locked house without a key, and the drum is the key to the band."[77] The drummer Cozy Cole explained that a drummer had to get to know every musician in the band in order to play a personal rhythm for the musician to work with: "I'm not going to play solo drums behind your solo, but I'm going to feed you a certain foundation that will make you feel good while you're playing."[78]

The Italian Futurists recognized even before World War I that a rise in the noise level of industrial society had produced a cultural hunger for more noise in music. In "The Art of Noises" (1913), Luigi Russolo contrasted the aesthetic ideal of the late nineteenth century—"purity, limpidity and sweetness of sound"—to modern demands for "dissonant, strange and harsh sounds . . . *noise-sound.*" The aesthetic shift was due to "the multiplication of machines, which collaborate with man on every front." Cities produced a "roaring atmosphere," but also "in the country . . . the machine today has created such a variety and rivalry of noises that pure sound . . . no longer arouses any feeling."[79] But the Futurists had no training in a rhythmically sophisticated aesthetic tradition and did not produce any lasting works, popular or otherwise. In Afrodiasporic cultures, on the other hand, there is a sense of a specifically rhythmic power to heal inherent in playing "a rhythmic cycle . . . over and over" until there is "a foundation you can build on. The stronger the groove the higher the building you can erect."[80]

Tricia Rose suggests that the crucial difference between European- and African-derived music has been their approach to "the inevitability of repetition." To the Yoruba of southwestern Nigeria, for example, repetition first represents "stability and predictability," and in drumming it can be experienced as "a steady, unbroken flow." It is first and foremost a grounding. In classical music, rhythmic repetition is considered boring and static, in contrast to the goal of "harmonic resolution" and linear melodic narrative. "Rhythm and polyrhythmic layering is to African and African-derived musics what harmony and the harmonic triad is to Western classical music," Rose asserts. Afrodiasporic cultures instead perceive repetition as "circulation, [and] equilibrium"; there is a constant return to the original rhythm "with a signal difference"—that is, each time something new is added to "the rhythmic and percussive density and organization."[81] Maintaining a dense percussive layer for the purpose of stability provides the conditions by which new rhythms and sounds can be "mixed in." Just as African master drummers learn and synthesize the idiomatic rhythms of neighboring peoples, African Americans have created unifying idioms that are recognized as "black" music and dance, yet that continue to absorb other cultural influences and develop aesthetically.

The 1930s is the moment when African American musical and cultural practice completed its appropriation of Euro-American popular music and dance at two levels: that of individual self-expression and that of the mindful body. In writing about hip-hop, Rose theorizes that the Afrodiasporic stylization of repetition through flow, layering, and disruption enables that musical form to best reflect postmodern fragmentation; for similar reasons, African American music was best equipped to swing the machine.[82]

African American cultural forms were created in the crucible of an existential dilemma: how to affirm a meaningful individual—and group—identity in the face of a dominant society bent on one's cultural destruction. The machine, as the creative source of the emergent technical civilization, had some of the qualities of a relentless adversary to the individual. In a period in which Euro-Americans needed a new plan of mind-body integration, one that included a vision of humanized machine aesthetics, was it not logical that Euro-Americans would borrow—or appropriate (or steal)—from African American survival technology?[83] The elements of African American survival technology had been worked out by the mid-nineteenth century. Through secret religious services, the telling of folk tales and proverbs, through music, humor, and dance (individual and social), African Americans participated in collective rituals that shut out the dominant society.[84] These portable strategies to affirm individual human dignity were rooted in a rejuvenation of human bodies as agents of joy, improvisation, empowered self-expression, and "reaffirmation and continuity in the face of adversity."[85]

Two recent inquiries into the foundations of artistic production focus on the body as a site of existential affirmation, pleasure, cognition, and aesthetics as a corrective to Western culture's distrust of emotion and its devaluing of physiological engagement. Karol Berger's *A Theory of Art* changes the question "What is art?" to "What is art for?," implying that art always has a function beyond transcendence and that artists always create to communicate something explicit (they are "for" something). Richard Shusterman's *Pragmatist Aesthetics* takes Dewey's *Art as Experience* as a starting point toward a philosophy grounded in everyday life and experience. In both I find analogies to the West African musical and philosophical imperative of "functionality"—that art forms have specific social objectives. Albert Murray begins his trenchant analysis of African American music by adapting Kenneth Burke's apt phrase "equipment for living" to the blues aesthetic. The entire set of primitivist tropes set up in opposition to an overcivilized and overrationalized Western culture—the fantasy of a more natural mode of existence that might provide more emotional and physical outlets—clearly suggests an awareness on the part of Euro-Americans of a need in white culture for some new survival technology ("equipment for living") to undo the damage of a century of physiological repression and mechano-idolatry.[86]

Swinging the Machine

Despite big-band swing's enormous popularity, there is little cultural analysis of why bands nearly doubled in size (from an average of eight to an average of sixteen), why the section superseded the soloist in importance, why the groove was smoothed out. "Swing music was the answer for the American—and very human—love of bigness," Marshall Stearns theorized in 1955. Thirty years later, James Lincoln Collier added only that "it was a time when leaders and fans liked a lot of power."[87] Why bigness? Why power? Because the tempo of life was increasing as mechanical rhythms pervaded the workplace and urban environments. It seems logical that Americans would choose music—"the temporal art par excellence," as one anthropologist calls it—as the art form to cope with this shift.[88]

There were two major structural changes from small-unit jazz to big-band swing: first, the different massed sections (trumpets, trombones, saxophones) "talked" back and forth, building up rhythmic tension only to release it; second, the rhythmic underpinning became much more sophisticated.[89] As arrangers, Don Redman and Fletcher Henderson perfected the call-and-response of the sections by the late 1920s, but smoothing out the rhythmic groove took about six years (approximately 1928–34). There were three main elements in this change: string basses replaced tubas; guitars replaced banjos; and drummers such as Jo Jones transferred the time-keeping from the heavy, thudding bass drum to the light, shimmering high-hat cymbal.[90] By the time this groove revolution was complete, says one jazz scholar, dancing to Count Basie's rhythm section was like "riding on ball bearings."[91]

One veteran trumpeter of the early 1920s defined "swing tempo" as "*feeling* an increase in tempo though you're still playing at the same tempo." A jazz critic of the time defined swing as "an exhilarating rhythmic feeling created around a fundamental pulse that suggests—but does not actually realize—a quickening of tempo."[92] In other words, swing tempo is deceptively fast, a musical illusion produced by playing, as jazz musicians say, "on top of the beat," as if pushing the music forward. Swing tempo was also called "the push beat" or the "kick-your-ass beat." Albert Murray has called it the "velocity of celebration."[93] This illusion was provided by a resilient, flexible rhythm section playing four even beats to the bar, freeing soloists to soar away from the ground beat; the jerky two-beat syncopation of the 1920s dissolved into "a more flowing, streamlined four-beat rhythm."[94]

Big-band swing was the fastest popular dance music in American history. This is observable through the measurement of beats per minute (bpm). March tempo is 120 bpm, and ragtime also hovers around this rate. A fast rock-and-roll song might be taken slightly faster, at 140 bpm. The bpm measurement was created in order that disco-era DJs could create seamless dance grooves; but disco rarely surpassed 140 bpm. Yet there were dozens of swing tunes above 200 bpm, and Chick Webb's "Clap Hands, Here Comes Charlie" (1936) clocked in at 260 bpm.[95] Two new terms were coined by musicians for these superfast songs: "flag-wavers" and "killer-dillers."[96] Harlem's Savoy Ballroom became a must-see tourist stop in the 1930s in part because Euro-Americans wanted to see how African American lindy hoppers danced gracefully to such fast music.

As for precision, the instrumental sections reflected gear-and-piston efficiency. In addition to the rhythm, the horn section was the key structural innovation of big-band swing, and a musician had to learn how to blend in without losing his or her own voice.[97] The average song was only "25% solo" and "to 'swing the sections' was the most important part."[98] For example, three trumpets would stand up and play an ensemble passage and try to achieve a sonorous blend of tones. Other sections stood up to play in turn, like different parts of the machine kicking into gear. A major technical advance of the average 1930s musician was in proficiency and precision. Meanwhile the arranger, who scored the sections, became one of the most important members of the big band (and often the highest paid).[99]

The swing band was also a *visual* icon: it was, in a sense, a machine built of human beings. Swing bands embodied dynamic order visually and musically; from fourteen to eighteen men in identical suits sat calmly in sections behind musical desks monogrammed with the company name waiting to explode in a controlled fashion.[100] One fan recalled the excitement of seeing the big band rise out of the orchestra pit as the movie ended at the Paramount: "The stage lights burst aglow and out of the pit rose this marvelous ark filled with 16–20 men, gleaming golden instruments flashing in the spotlights. . . . [T]he band was already pulsating with life, the front sax section filling the hall with sweet notes, the brass setting your ears afire . . . [drummers] flailing their snares, tom-toms and cymbals, a row of trombonists executing precision drill."[101] The big band was a machine whose human "workings" were visible to all. It was also a machine whose working humans often appeared to enjoy their work. Musicians claimed that they were as thrilled to hear Billie Holiday or Chick Webb or Benny Goodman every night as the audiences were, and that they looked forward to what the band would produce on any given night.[102]

Musicians and social observers caught the connection between the stylized mechanical rhythms of swing and its enormous popularity. In 1938 the columnist Damon Runyon wrote that swing music's dynamic noise echoed "the sounds of the machine shop," and that this "violent" strain in the music was an important element in its cross-generational popularity. Runyon didn't like swing but had to admit it was "the most tremendous vogue of any style, form, or system of noise-making in the history of the USA." American youth were "lunatics on swing music . . . [and] old folks, too, are pretty much swing-minded." Like many other observers, Runyon was shocked to find that swing bands outdrew the movies at urban cinema palaces, and that young swing fans hooted for the movie to end. After watching a Mae West movie lose out to "the huffle-scuffle of Mr. Goodman's following," Runyon quipped that it was the first time "Miss West ever ran second to a slide trombone."[103]

Benny Goodman, the so-called King of Swing, recalled the crucial aesthetics of the first wave of swing popularity: "The essence of swing was drive and power." What Runyon called "the sounds of the machine shop" Goodman called "high-pressure powerhouse thumpings." The new swing-era rhythm section "hammered out" the "power of swing," and chased the sweet music of the early Depression away; the band "pounded away at the audience" using massed sections of instruments and "jungle-style drums." The music was made more exciting by its unpredictability, by "the sound of surprise," and "the excitement of improvisation transmit[ted] itself to the audience with the certainty of an electric spark." What Damon Runyon called the swing "vogue," Goodman called "the swing gospel."[104]

"Swing is the tempo of our time," the *New York Times* declared enthusiastically in 1938, and the nation's third controversy on jazz was engaged.[105] Was the music a healthy, vigorous outlet or a "manifestation of . . . restless hysteria"? If everyone agreed that swing was "a reflection of the American emotional state," did that indicate a healthy exuberance and energetic optimism?[106] Or were Americans irrationally drawn to repetitive sounds and mechanical dances, motor behavior that suggested trancelike passivity? Or did swing instead represent the exact opposite, "a *protest* against mechanization," as one psychologist claimed, "a *release* from the drab monotony of the machine age?"[107] The answer can only be yes.

Big-band swing represented a synthesis of the rhythmic drive of New Orleans music with Paul Whiteman's "symphonic jazz" of the 1920s. Whiteman muffled the New-Orleans–based syncopation to achieve a grander symphonic vision that retained only what was then called the "businessman's bounce." In 1924 Gilbert Seldes approved Whiteman's achievement: "All the free, the instinctive, the wild in negro jazz, which could be integrated into the music, he has kept; he has . . . worked his material until it runs sweetly in his dynamo, without grinding or scraping. It becomes the machine which conceals the machinery."[108] Just as streamlined design hid the industrial workings of the machine, Whiteman's symphonic jazz hid the self-expression and call-and-response of jazz in its muted horns, soft rhythms, and lack of improvisation. On the eve of Benny Goodman's triumphant 1938 Carnegie Hall concert, the *New York Times* was quite specific about what symphonic jazz had hidden in order to rise to respectability: "It had disowned and erased from its memory its forebears . . . the darky workers on the levees of the lower Mississippi, the hell-holes of New Orleans, the riverboat bands . . . Memphis and the blues, the sawdust and smoke-beery air of the Chicago joints."[109]

The musicians of one of the best white big bands of the 1920s, the Jean Goldkette band, were torn between players who preferred the Whiteman style and those who "had a looser style." Arranger Bill Challis was on the "jazz" side of the argument, and summed up the schism this way: "You couldn't make the one [style] . . . go over into their [Whiteman] type of thing, which had been very, very successful." That is an understatement: Whiteman had an amazing 169 hits between 1920 and 1930, yet almost no hits after March 1936. By mid-decade, symphonic jazz had lost its hold on Depression-era Americans. Benny Goodman took the nation by storm with brilliant soloists such as Teddy Wilson, Harry James, Lionel Hampton, and himself, all grounded in the drummer Gene Krupa's "rock-solid foundation."[110]

The New Orleans jazz guitarist Danny Barker remembered the early 1930s as the time that small-unit jazz bands turned into big-band machines. In the 1920s, in small-unit New Orleans jazz bands such as King Oliver's band or Jelly Roll Morton's Stompers, the guitar players and banjo players participated as independent musical voices. The banjoist or guitarist helped the drummer keep the rhythm, but he also took as many solos or breaks as the clarinetists or cornetists in the melodic front line. One day, Barker looked around and noticed that "all the virtuoso guitar and banjo players weren't working"; they were "out there scuf-flin'" or scraping by "working in dives."[111] The new guitar stars were rhythm guitarists, such as John Trueheart in Chick Webb's band, "who was the master and boss of rhythm. Everybody remarked how great he was. . . . He was a master. He would never take a solo, maybe a little break." In the newer big bands, "you wouldn't be no virtuoso." The era of the rhythm section had arrived, and the guitarist had become a rhythm provider, or, to adapt African American musicians' vernacular, a "foundation-maker."[112]

"You sat down with the bass player, the piano player and the drummer," Barker remembered, "you got together and you had a machine going there." The big bands of fourteen or more musicians needed four instruments just to create enough strong, loud, steady, stylized mechanical rhythm to provide percussive grounding for the horn sections and keep them on task. Fletcher Henderson's band featured the guitarist Clarence Holiday (Billie Holiday's father), who was "no virtuoso, but . . . the pivot in the band; he was the solid foundation in the band." The new integrated function of the guitarist was to be one of the pistons providing enginelike power to drive the big band train.[113]

Sidney Bechet perceived the same set of changes less favorably. Big bands had turned his beloved New Orleans music into a flashy machine whose arranged power mattered more than the creativity and improvisation of the individual musicians. To Bechet, bandleaders sold their personalities rather than the music, and arrangements moved jazz toward musical practices based on written scores. "They've got themselves a kind of machine. And so to make sense out of whatever it is the machine is doing, they get a whole lot of composers and arrangers to write it all down, just the way the machine is supposed to run." Gone was the conversation of one musician to another of the small New Orleans units, "all that freedom, all that feeling a man's got when he's playing next to you." Bechet compared big-band arrangements to "running a ball through a pinball machine"; with fourteen to eighteen men, "you've got a whole lot of noise." For Bechet, the big-band sound removed the black historical experience from the music. "Those new musicianers, they lack the memory of it."[114]

It is significant that according to Barker and Bechet big-band swing was *not* New Orleans music; swing musicians were rather in dialogue with the cultural desires of the entire nation. The new musical role of the guitarist, for example, had social and cultural ramifications. "I found out that you keep appearance and watch the clock and be on time," Barker remembered about big-band success. "You had to be competent and you had not to be an obnoxious character." Musicians admired Clarence Holiday as much for his urbane style as for his guitar work: "He was immaculate . . . and neat and cool." Neither Holiday nor Buddy Johnson nor Trueheart had "much to say" on their guitars—that is, they did not solo much—but they played crisp, immaculate 4/4 rhythm, and kept the bands on track.[115]

The guitarist's new role was a crucial element in the transition from New Orleans jazz to big-band swing. For example, Count Basie's rhythm section was considered the best of all—the most fluid, powerful, and stable—and was dubbed "the All-American Rhythm Section." "Basie's rhythm section . . . was probably the most brilliant percussion combination in jazz history," the musicologist Wilfrid Mellers wrote in *Music in a New Found Land,* and "Basie's music . . . accepts the consequences of a machine-made world."[116] Yet despite the innovative virtuosity of the drummer Jo Jones, the bassist Walter Page, and Basie on piano, many band members believed the foundation of the band was guitarist Freddie Green. Green "holds things together," Basie admitted, and kept time in a lean, efficient fashion. Green's steadying role was as important as Jones's more famous sizzling hi-hat cymbal or Page's powerful walking bass.[117]

At a 1982 party, the bassist Red Mitchell expressed his respect for Green for playing "the most swinging quarter notes of anybody ever." He read this short ode to Green and his swing beat: "It isn't really rigid metronomic time that counts/It's sound and soul, communication, love, support and bounce." Green responded that he "couldn't have said it better than that." When Mitchell asked for advice, Green told him that no matter who is leading the melody, "the bass player has to live, has to sort of sleep with the groove, make love to it." To "make love" to a groove, mechanical or otherwise, cannot be confused with assembly-line work, despite the common qualities of repetitious motion. Such metaphors remain common among rhythm-section players today.[118]

The first band to combine raw speed and technical precision was the white Casa Loma Orchestra; it was also the only band *Downbeat* ever labeled as purveyors of "machine jazz." The Casa Loma Orchestra came out of late 1920s Detroit—the epicenter of American mass production—and its sound reflected machine aesthetics: fast tempos, precision execution, limited soloing, and a driving, though stiff, rhythm section that produced a "steamroller" effect.[119] The arranger Gene Gifford was a trained draftsman whose scores required a high level of technical expertise and exhaustive rehearsals, and the trombonist Billy Rausch intimidated the band members into playing with "machine-like precision."[120] Black bands admired them; Fletcher Henderson's Orchestra recorded their influential 1930 hit, "Casa Loma Stomp," and Chick Webb's trombonist Sandy Williams admitted that besides Ellington's band, only Casa Loma "really gave us a headache . . . I hate to say it, but they outplayed us."[121] Benny Goodman said they were "the band we had started out to buck." They may have been mocked as embracing "soulless efficiency and . . . military precision," but their stiff mechanical rhythm was central to the band's aesthetic, to their college fans, and to musicians aspiring toward technical perfection in the early 1930s. One incarnation of the band was even called "Glenn Gray and his Mechanical Marionettes."[122]

But by 1937 the Casa Loma Orchestra had shifted its emphasis to slow ballads. *Downbeat* pondered the change in white musical taste in a 1936 cover story: "Casa Loma's music is not the most relaxed swing . . . but they are one of the most brilliant ensemble groups that ever swung sixteen men in a single groove. . . . When did 5 brass or saxes phrasing as one, beautifully voiced and perfectly executed, cease to be [as] worthwhile as a solo man with a simple rhythm background?" My guess would be the middle of 1935, the period when Benny Goodman rose to fame. The key phrases here are "solo man" and "simple rhythm background." Reflecting on the band's career, *Downbeat* compared Casa Loma's peak in 1934, when fans admired its "brilliant precision" and the British press called them "white Ellingtonians," to its 1940 incarnation, when Casa Loma sounded "mechanical and devoid of feeling . . . repetitive . . . and stilted." With regret, *Downbeat* demoted the band in 1940: "They do not swing." It was as if once musicians could *replicate* machine aesthetics—noise, speed, precision, efficiency, relentless drive—

the need for human dynamics, and thus individual self-expression, re-asserted itself.[123]

Duke Ellington disdained the "soulless" quality and "continual churn-ing" of certain rhythm sections. Uninspired metronomic time-keeping caused "apathy in the section[s]," he wrote in 1931, and a loss of in-terest among the musicians, whose "performance becomes stodgy and mechanical." The most important element in dance music was the groove generated by the rhythm section of bass, drums, guitar, and piano; the pulse they generated kept the other musicians in gear, and thus in touch with the dancing audience. The rhythm section drove in-dividual soloists, kept the ensembles loose but precise, and allowed a live performance to embody the jazz ideal of "relaxed intensity." At the end of Ellington's first theoretical discussion of music, he stated simply, "Remember that your most important asset is your rhythm."[124] For African American bands, to have "good" rhythm had nothing to do with being mechanically perfect.

The Count Basie Orchestra was the prototype of a *soulful* metronomic swing groove, as Jo Jones replaced Krupa's heavier bass drumming and Casa Loma's mechanized speed. Having developed in Kansas City, far from the commercial styles of New York, the Basie band brought south-western vernacular practices of collective music making, blues-based in-dividual self-expression, and rhythmic sophistication into the American mainstream; the cultural history of the 1930s is incomplete without understanding the band's impact and aesthetic underpinnings. Bands from "the territory" (Kansas, Oklahoma, and Texas) prided themselves on the dynamic relation between expressive individualism and collec-tive power.[125] When Basie brought the loose, blues-based, "up-South" relaxed swing style of territory bands to New York in 1937, it gave a sec-ond boost to swing's popularity. The lindy hopper Norma Miller said of Basie's band, "We had never heard such tempos."[126]

The musical tension between Basie's soloists and the rhythm section publicly displayed a ritual fight between the needs of the individual and the needs of the group. "Basie's soloists are protesting against—or trying to hold their own against . . . the hard, sharp, predatory vigor of an industrial society, which barks in the brass, crashes and snaps in the percussion." (Listen, for instance, to how the tenor saxophonist Lester Young attempts to cut across the sonic challenges of the brass and rhythm sections in "Clap Hands Here Comes Charlie.")[127] Marshall Stearns summed it up best: "If Benny Goodman became the 'king of

Swing' in 1935, reaping all the publicity and profits, the man behind the throne was Count Basie. For it was the Basie band that gave depth and momentum to the whole swing era."[128]

The impresario John Hammond brought the Basie orchestra to New York from Kansas City in 1937 after hearing them on his car radio in Chicago. When he produced the "Spirituals to Swing" concerts at Carnegie Hall in 1937, the headliners were members of the Basie band. The scion of the Vanderbilts, Hammond spent the 1930s promoting swing as a vernacular art form. Jazz "expresses America so clearly that its readiest recognition here has come from the masses, particularly youth," he wrote in the concert program. "While the intelligentsia has been busy trying to water our scrawny cultural tree with European art and literary movements, this thing has come to maturity unnoticed." Swing had not been handed down by a genteel cultural elite to be studied by aspiring lower classes, but was an art form "warmly participated in by the people." Jazz was not only "uniquely American," but also "the most important cultural exhibit we have given the world."[129]

The tenor saxophonist Albert "Budd" Johnson, one of the few jazz musicians to make the transition from swing to bebop, saw a parallel in black musical and white technological traditions. He compared the creation of jazz as an art form to the invention of the airplane as an art form. "The Wright Brothers built the airplane. . . . Now you're going to the moon, but it's still an airplane, and it just keeps progressing and going on and on and on. . . . We [blacks] have built a great foundation . . . and I think jazz is . . . going to be going on and on and on, I don't care what names people put on it. . . . It's basically that old music that we started to play . . . they started off by calling it ragtime . . . but I mean you could take a guy that played a solo and put him behind a modern rhythm section and it would still sound good, and it would fit."[130]

Both music and technology (that is, toolmaking) are characteristic of all human societies, but a change in landscape and soundscape requires new cultural forms. As Budd Johnson noted, "Music is as old as the world itself. Music started out by the winds. Man tried to create the sounds of music by imitating the winds blowing through the trees, the waterfalls falling, making music. The grunts and groans of different beasts. That's music." But the new beats, rhythms, and everyday sounds were those of machines.

The condescension implicit in the stereotype that "blacks have rhythm" has deprived our national history of one of its fundamental truths: West African–derived American popular music made life in the Machine Age swing. (And it still does, as witness the swing-dance revival of the 1990s.) At the height of his fame, Glenn Miller admitted that no white band could touch the rhythmic mastery of "Negro bands." "I don't see how any white leader can be satisfied with his rhythm after hearing so many wonderful colored rhythm sections," Miller told *Downbeat* in 1939. "Even the second rate Negro bands have good rhythm." Rhythmic mastery derives from Afrodiasporic cultural approaches and aesthetics. The masters of rhythmic flow—the most important element in Machine Age art—were African American swing-era musicians. Since rhythm could not be copyrighted, white crossover artists simply used what they loved.[131]

The Corporate Whitefacing of Swing

Benny Goodman admitted that his band's popularity took off only after he purchased Fletcher Henderson's excellent arrangements, which were characterized by simplicity, open spaces in the orchestration, and a smoother rhythmic feeling.[132] Just as the streamlined style was not altogether new when it caught the public imagination with the train, black big bands (Fletcher Henderson, Duke Ellington, Alphonse Trent, and Bennie Moten) had put all the elements together three years before swing became mainstream with Benny Goodman. Goodman's success thus had as much to do with the conventions of the music industry, and American racial and ethnic frameworks, as with his musical prowess. The music industry would never have supported an African American band as it did Goodman's; a black band would not have been let in the front door of some of the nation's most prestigious venues. To Goodman's credit, he pioneered the breaking of the color line in music. With the insistence of his brother-in-law John Hammond, Goodman hired the pianist Teddy Wilson, the vibraphonist and drummer Lionel Hampton, and later the trumpeter Cootie Williams and the drummer Sid Catlett—all a decade before the celebrated changes in baseball and the armed forces.

Of course, the "whitefacing" of swing was one part of Goodman's success; techno-progress required a streamlined face and big-band swing a white one.[133] But Goodman was not simply the right man in the right place; he was a virtuoso clarinet player with flawless technique. Neither charming nor exciting, neither a personality nor a showman, he created music that communicated a feeling of "matchless control." Like Glenn

Miller directly after him, Goodman was also a rigorous taskmaster, and his success owed much "to his abilities as a strict and tirelessly demanding leader." As many people noticed, he looked like a high-school science teacher.[134] Once Americans were on the move, they needed a smooth, controlled soundtrack for their streamlined ride, played by someone who embodied their own hopes. As an ambitious first-generation Jewish immigrant, a talented musician, and an astute businessman, Goodman was the Horatio Alger of jazz.

Goodman was, in effect, a *musical engineer* and the conductor of the big-band swing train—a culture hero dedicated to the uplift of a nation during a technological plateau. If the conductor of the train was unimportant for the Burlington Zephyr or The Little Engine That Could, the conductor of the big band was of central symbolic importance to the swing machine. The bandleader conducted American leisure; the big band and the bandleader/conductor were symbols of orderly progress. Although big-band leaders were not trained classical conductors, almost all of them used the baton as a highbrow marker that validated the popular art-form's aspirations. Bands like Basie's and Ellington's often composed songs collectively and allowed soloists to create their own solos, but the nineteenth-century model of the conductor as the representative "order-maker" and "culture-preserver" in the world of art remained potent.[135] By embodying order, the big band became a model of corporate organization. (See fig. 8.)

Even in terms of visual presentation—both in photographs and on the bandstand—the bandleader was marked as the boss and the musicians as the employees. On stage, the bands were arranged in straight rows, behind musical "desks" which were monogrammed with the boss's name or initials.[136] Journalists referred to the musicians as if they belonged to the bandleader: Dorsey's Jo Stafford, Goodman's Hampton, Ellington's Tizol.[137] Publicity photographs changed to suit the new corporate style. In the early 1930s jazz bands were typically photographed standing in symmetric rows facing the bandleader in the center; David Stowe calls this "skyscraper-style." But in the later 1930s they were photographed at their monogrammed musical desks, workers in the employ of the corporate bandleader.[138]

The visual style may have reflected seamless corporate order, but the artistic dynamic was one of *controlled power,* in my view the predominant element of a distinctively American Machine Age modernism. A *London Times* reviewer noted Ellington's ability to ensure that rhythms

Figure 8. Woody Herman's big band, mid-1940s. (Courtesy of the Institute of Jazz Studies, Rutgers University.)

were neither too mechanical nor too wild; the music, he wrote, has "complete control and precision. It is . . . a scientific application of *measured* and dangerous stimuli."[139] Big bands symbolized orderly progress both symbolically and visually, creating sonic order out of industrial cacophony.

Not all big bands played fast-paced swing. The big-band format included a variety of styles, from the hard-driving swing of Count Basie to the accordion-led polka swing of Lawrence Welk.[140] There were three main types of bands: "hot" (swing) bands, "sweet" bands (soft, soothing music, lots of ballads), and "corn" bands (gimmick-based or novelty bands). A 1937 radio survey showed swing popularity divided into a third "hot" (or swing), a third playing both "hot" and "sweet," and a third playing either "sweet" or "corn."[141] That the better swing bands are the ones that have stood the test of time is not at issue here; rather, my point is that the machine-built-of-humans occupied a special place in the symbolic life of the 1930s and 1940s. The big band was a hierarchical organization headed by a well-known "brand name" and symbolized the orderly, almost militaristic direction of fourteen or sixteen men by the wave of a classical wand. Regardless of the music's aesthetic quality, all of these bandleaders provided Americans with live dance music, symbols of social mobility, and a shared piece of vernacular culture.

The Function of a Social Drummer

One last element of big bands needs to be pointed out. The leadership of the swing dance-hall ritual was actually split between the bandleader and the drummer. In the late nineteenth century, American audiences responded to drumming showmen in many areas of popular culture: in circuses, carnivals, and minstrel shows, in military parades and brass marching bands, and as creators of sound effects from the orchestra pit of silent movies.[142] Many swing drummers (for example, Jo Jones, Chick Webb, Buddy Rich, and Sonny Greer) began at such jobs or apprenticed with such a drummer.[143] As drummers helped develop swing's fast but buoyant tempos in response to unarticulated needs of American audiences, they became star instrumentalists. Gene Krupa was a teen idol in the Benny Goodman band and a drum guru for many aspiring musicians; Chick Webb was the bandleader and emotional flashpoint of the Savoy Ballroom's house band that launched the young Ella Fitzgerald. The biggest audience response at Cab Calloway's energetic concerts were for the drum-solo features of Cozy Cole, "Paradiddle" and "Crescendo for Drums."[144]

As drummers became the point-men for producing smooth, flowing rhythms that offset and evened out the brassy power of big bands, they began to take on roles akin to West African master drummers. In West African societies the master drummer must be a tempo leader, "ensemble conductor," philosopher, psychologist, "coordinator of dance and song," and the source of spiritual uplift.[145] One route of cultural transmission from the Afrodiasporic tradition into mainstream swing came through Baby Dodds and Zutty Singleton, the New Orleans drummers who moved to Chicago in the early 1920s. There a small band of young white musicians who later became famous—Goodman, Krupa, Eddie Condon, Mezz Mezzrow, Hoagy Carmichael, and others—spent their nights absorbing the philosophical underpinnings of New Orleans jazz at the "black and tan" cabarets. Krupa claimed he learned both technique and "drum philosophy" from Baby Dodds.[146]

Dodds thought of the drum as "sacred" and believed a drummer had to think about the rhythm constantly, with his heart as much as his mind. "To drum required a good thinking brain and a sharp ear . . . [and] to keep a sense of humor, for God's sake, so that if something didn't sound right I could always change it." As the drummer for King Oliver's band (featuring Louis Armstrong), Dodds remembered, "I would drum all night till about three o'clock and when I went home I would dream all night of drumming. That showed I had my heart in it, and the others had the same heart I did. We worked to make music and we played music to make people like it." Dodds often stressed that the band played for *all* the people in a given audience, not just blacks. A white New Orleans doctor who saw King Oliver's band in both New Orleans and Chicago, five years apart, complained that Oliver's band had "sold out" to the white audience in Chicago, diluting its rhythmic drive and polyphonic interplay.[147] Dodds understood the same process as absorbing a new "whiter" style of playing that enabled the music to include everyone in the audience. "You can't go along with a one-track mind and be a good drummer."[148]

In his weekly *Downbeat* column, Gene Krupa advised all aspiring drummers to "go out to clubs and study the negro drummer." African American drummers engaged the music holistically and had to control their emotions, so as to be able to guide the other musicians as well. "The drummer's job is to break down any demoralized feeling that exists in the band and prevent the listlessness," Krupa wrote. "Unless indifference or moodiness is overcome, the entire band may fail to find its groove. . . . [P]ersonal feelings (or lack of them) on the part of the drummer . . . must not interfere with the work of the band. . . . Don't brood—be happy." Since each night was a different emotional moment for the band—and the audience—Krupa advised the drummer to ignore the authority of the metronome and adapt himself to the moment and to the musicians. "The truly great drummer must . . . break down self-consciousness and eliminate top-hatted dignity . . . [and] proportionately must his self-control be built up." George Wettling, another prominent white swing drummer, wrote in his *Downbeat* column: "A dance band is as good as its rhythm section and its rhythm section is as good as its drummer."[149]

John Hammond recognized that the shared leadership of drummer and bandleader was the key to swing's rise to popularity through Benny Goodman. "Gene's musicianship and enthusiasm succeeded in welding together all of the sections, which hitherto had been at sword points. With Gene to send him, Benny was able to rise to new heights of musical inspiration." The drummer had to provide a sense of balance to each individual player and to the band as a whole. Goodman himself admitted that "from the time he joined us . . . Gene gave the band a solidity and firmness . . . it never had before." Krupa advised his *Downbeat* readers, "When the band screams, the drummer should be the essence of simplicity. . . . Someone has to become the 'bottom' while the brass or the reeds are taking off." This sense of lightening the sound of one's instrument to balance other, more powerful, instruments was common to swing-era jazz musicians, and has since become jazz lore. Krupa saw it as efficient energy use: "Cut down the speed of drumming as tempos increase . . . [which] suggests the saving of energy."[150]

Lightness, simplicity, efficiency, energy management, fluidity, unified direction: here again are the stylized, humanized machine aesthetics in big-band swing. In his autobiography *Night People*, the Count Basie trombonist Dicky Wells recalled that band's rhythm section as "so light and so strong that it was a real inspiration." Wells felt its elegant power as "nothing less than a Cadillac with the force of a Mack truck."[151] By 1935, jazz musicians had thus created cultural materials able to contain and reflect the new American tempo with rhythm-section engines that drove units with power, simplicity, precision, and elegance.

Coda: Self-Expression and Collective Drive

If the major social challenge of the 1930s was to create a political system in which the individual would not get lost within the group, big-band swing represented a rare cultural display of this possibility. David Stowe notes "swing's . . . quality of enabling the individual voice to contribute to the collective whole," an aesthetic and artistic quality that reflected the "cooperative commonwealth central to Franklin Roosevelt's vision of America."[152] As Otis Ferguson wrote of Goodman's band, "The band as a whole gets its lift from the rhythm men and the soloists as they take off . . . [but] it is built from the ground rather than tailored. . . . [It is] . . . the most beautiful example of men working together to be seen in public today."[153]

If Goodman was swing's Horatio Alger, the big band itself embodied the best of the American spirit as it "enabl[ed] the individual voice to contribute to the collective whole." The interactive display of self-expression and mechanical drive made the big band itself a star, and a successful big-band movie genre arose in the 1930s and 1940s, featuring Goodman in *Hollywood Hotel* (1938), Jimmy Dorsey's orchestra in *The Fleet's In* (1942), and Glenn Miller in *Sun Valley Serenade* (1942). Many of the later films were about "square" highbrows being transformed into hip, confident dancers by their girlfriends, with the assistance of Miller or Goodman. Clearly, the big band as a symbol carried some of the same "retooling" value as the streamliner.[154]

How did big bands regroove industrialized American bodies? As I suggest in chapters 6 through 8, through swing dance, especially tap and the lindy hop. The best lindy hoppers across the country proved that obsolete, rusted-out American bodies could indeed be "tuned up"; they executed fast moves with uncanny precision, pivoted as if on ball bearings, and timed their leaps to land on the beat and fluidly slide into the next step. This was hard work created for nonmaterial (and non-mechanical) ends and developed out of portable materials—the human body, acoustic instruments, interaction. Like big-band swing, the lindy hop featured both horizontal motion and machine aesthetics; it streamlined the bouncy vertical steps of such 1920s dances as the Charleston and the turkey trot into a dance that "flowed horizontally, with more rhythmic continuity," while still leaving room for the "break-away" step, when dancers would improvise in solo.[155]

Big-band musicians worked in the service of human needs: in the progress of the human body, so to speak, rather than industrial progress. The dialogue between musicians and dancers and the participation central to the dance-hall ritual developed out of an African-derived musical tradition, where one function of music was to reinvigorate people, at work and at play. "The aboriginal purpose of rhythm in African music," writes Martha Bayles, "was not to stir Dionysian passion, but to accompany work. . . . The better the rhythm, the sooner it revived the weary and reconciled the discordant. In both . . . ritual and work, the motive power of rhythm served a civilizing function."[156]

In 1981 the swing-era *Metronome* columnist and chronicler George Simon noted the affinity for sonic power between swing and rock-and-roll audiences. Through the lens of his swing bias, Simon contrasted how rock bands *overpowered* audiences while swing bands *integrated* dancers with the rhythmic power of the dance-hall ritual. Rock and roll's "electrified guitars and . . . basses . . . could virtually steamroller you," but big bands, he wrote, "didn't knock you down and flatten you out and leave you lying there, *a helpless victim of sodden, sullen, mechanized musical mayhem.* Instead they swung freely and joyously. And as they swung, *they lifted you high in the air with them,* filling you with an exhilarated sense of friendly well-being; you joined them, emotionally and musically, as partners in one of the happiest, most thrilling rapports ever established between the givers and takers of music."[157] This is the rhetoric of spiritual uplift in the words of a contemporary white chronicler who was unconscious of the African American cultural system to which he had become a joyous convert.

In his classic *Mechanization Takes Command* (1948), the architecture scholar Siegfried Giedion called for Americans to "reinstate basic human values" against the machine's encroachment into everyday life.[158] But Americans had by then already partly mediated the fears of a machine-dictated existence in the swing era. Streamliners and big bands functioned as grassroots public symbols of a restored faith in the future: the former, by evoking feelings of nostalgia while simultaneously acting as a symbol of a retooled human body; the latter, as an art form (and icon) that used machine power to serve the society's need for dynamic play. The appeal of both cultural forms was determined by a popular need for the humanization of machine aesthetics.

The historian Lewis Erenberg believes swing's forward-spinning tempo sent a message to southern blacks to move north. Calling swing "the music of the black migration," Erenberg claims the best African American big bands "transformed themselves into powerful locomotives, with all embellishments stripped away and movement the central function."[159] Swing tempo, however, had an equally important function for all Americans; like the frictionless flow of streamlining, swing tempo propelled Americans into the future when they danced or listened.

Otis Ferguson, the astute jazz critic of *The New Republic,* left to historians a challenge to unpack the meaning of big-band swing: "If you leave a Goodman show . . . no more than slightly amused, you may be sure that in the smug absence of your attention a true native spirit of music has been and gone, leaving a message for your grandchildren to study through their patient glasses."[160] What Ferguson did not then see were the African American aesthetics at the base of this spirit, nor the ongoing pattern of white-facing that has long characterized the "Americanization" of black cultural forms.

One on one, you could not beat the machine, as Sherwood Anderson confessed and John Henry discovered. But machines cannot improvise or provide aesthetic surprise; they cannot express individuality in work and still cooperate with each other to provide a larger message. Big-band swing was fast, precise, fluid, efficient—*and* displayed a larger message of fellowship while providing a dialogue with machine aesthetics. In big-band swing the soloist interacted with the sections and the sections argued with one another, all of it chugging along over the rhythm section's engine; such dynamic interplay did not exist in symphonic jazz or mechanical jazz such as that of Whiteman or the Casa Loma Orchestra. The swing bandstand was one workplace where Americans saw humans work as well as machines, but in service to the needs of the human body; it was also a place where Americans saw individuals who loved their work. No matter how fast the tempo of life might get, it could be matched by human physical effort, stylized into artistic moves and integrated into cultural forms. Bands could increase in size and power but keep their flexibility. (Count Basie said, "I wanted my fifteen-piece band to work together just like those nine pieces [of mine] did.")[161] Dancers likewise proved they could match the tempo of life and still find room for self-expression. Big-band swing was a functional dance music for a cautiously optimistic people.

THE STANDARDIZED WHITE GIRL IN THE PLEASURE MACHINE

THE ZIEGFELD FOLLIES AND BUSBY BERKELEY'S 1930S MUSICALS

On June 23, 1942, six months after the United States entered World War II, the Bendix Aviation Corporation held a celebratory banquet at the prestigious Waldorf Astorial hotel in New York City to honor its president, Ernest K. Breech. Later heralded for saving the Ford Motor Corporation (he became chairman of the board in 1957), Breech was being honored for his role in the success of Bendix's aviation instruments, then being used in every wartime aircraft. The title for the night's entertainment—"The Invisible Screw"—was company shorthand for its "insertion aviation instruments, accessories and controls," and the program featured the drummer Panama Francis and his swing band. The "Invisible Screw" was an umbrella term for five instruments then "serving with American fighting machines," each of which lent itself to sexual double entendres: the Stromberg Injection Carburetor, the Eclipse Direct-Cranking Starter, the Scintilla Aircraft Magneto, the Bendix Direct-Reading Compass, and the Pioneer Turn-and-Bank Indicator. On the printed program, each was pictured in an inset box and appeared to serve an erotic function; for example, the coils of the magnetos were drawn as a pair of disembodied breasts.[1]

The relationship of women and machines in Euro-American male erotic fantasy gets its full treatment in this program, dominated as it is by a graphic fantasy of clear skies filled with heavenly female bodies enjoying sexual relations with "insertion aviation instruments, accessories and controls." Eight goddess-sized naked women dominate the heavens as various mechanical phalluses make ready to pleasure them. One woman joyfully straddles a fighter plane; another gasps with pleasure at the carburetor injecting her upper thighs; the largest blonde figure sports a pressure gauge for a pubic triangle while also poised to throw a javelin-shaped phallic crank like a thunderbolt. Two brunettes lie on their back with their legs spread: one has her legs in the air, holding an air pressure gauge between her feet; the other sleeps unaware that two different "insertion aviation instruments" are sneaking up on her (both look like guns). One woman is shown happily bent over and prone, awaiting two large screws poised perpendicularly above her backside. Two women function as bookends for the scene on a smaller scale. On the bottom right side, a standing nude preens against an imaginary wall, her breasts pushed forward like weapons. On the bottom left, a relaxed, chummy blonde straddles the Bendix logo, leaning forward and offering her breasts for her country. The logo consists of cutaway airplanes with their noses in the air, repeating into infinity, and slants right (a graphic motif commonly used to indicate speed) to point to these words: "The Invisible Screw: Bendix Assignation Corporation."

There are no men in the graphic; only unmanned machines give pleasure to these women. But in fine print there appears a recruitment call for young men between the ages of 18 and 26 for "screw training" to learn how to "fly to victory with the U.S. Army, Navy or Marine Corps." Such heroic men would use the Bendix parts that "helped fliers put the finger on the Bottom" and assisted "the U.S. battle boys that blasted the 'Virgin' Islands." The erotica of machine aesthetics is quite clear in 1942: "In every duty, 'The Invisible Screw' is fast, precise, alert . . . [as] are the more than 40,000 trained workers of . . . Bendix." What are you waiting for, the subtext of this erotic fantasy fairly shouts, "Join America's invincible screw!"

The development of the American *pleasure machine*—that is, the techno-dialogic of eroticized popular culture—is the subject of this chapter.

In the 1920s the transformation of American society by mass production drew more intellectual bemoaning than constructive criticism regarding the loss of communal purpose, local traditions, individualism, and spiritualized virtue (to name a few romantic ideals). But a generation after Henry Adams perceived that "the machine" had replaced Christianity as the driving erotic force of Western civilization in "The Dynamo and the Virgin,"[2] white male liberal intellectuals such as

Mumford, Chase, Dewey, and Anderson did attempt to assess the social benefits and liabilities of machines, arguing for the need to reaffirm "human values"—for them, a self-evident concept comprising Enlightenment individualism, Christian piety, and a heroic masculine resistance to religious and political tyranny. Even in the 1920s, working-class Euro-Americans, African Americans, and immigrants—those without the luxury of nostalgia—were drawn to cultural forms that integrated machine aesthetics into their everyday lives. As I have suggested, one social adjustment came through the development of a new machine-driven tempo in music.

In this chapter and the next, I analyze two Machine Age dance formulations in which machine aesthetics and mass-production methods were displayed for popular consumption. Here I explore a "top-down" method in which a dictatorial impresario employed chorus lines of anonymous women to produce abstract geometric patterns. Florenz Ziegfeld was the American pioneer of what I call "mechanized choreography," and his most important heir was the director Busby Berkeley. The type of theatrical spectacle engineered by Ziegfeld was appropriate to the large-scale industrialization that characterized American economic organization. In the Ziegfeld Follies, and later in Busby Berkeley musicals, women functioned as cogs and punch cards in immense, mechanically-rotated tableaux of lavish fantasy. I call such spectacles "female-powered dynamos," and they reflected a specifically Euro-American male cultural hunger for more pleasure within a Machine Age modern aesthetic. These spectacles were a response to industrial repression and led to the mass production of the "standardized Ziegfeld [female] body."[3]

Ziegfeld's success derived in part from an "uncanny ability to combine the exotic with the familiar, the 'high' culture with 'low.'" His New York audiences were the social elites; his star performers were non-white or working class in origin, and his revues toured all over the country. He dressed chorus girls in the fashions of world-class designers; employed the classical composer Victor Herbert to write his scores; introduced "ballet elements into musical-comedy numbers"; and stylized African American social dances (the cakewalk, fox-trot, shimmy, and turkey trot) for elite consumption. One theater critic highlighted this mediation of classes and tastes in a review of the 1915 Follies: "It is a monster vaudeville pageant framed in plush, an organized comedy romp in a rose garden, a high-brow scenic revel shot with good low-brow fun."[4]

There was also a grassroots explosion of individual dance innovation. By screwing metal taps into shoes, tap dancers industrialized—and "metallicized"—the sound of the human body in motion. Each tap dancer worked to stylize speed, precision, repetition, smoothness, and rhythmic continuity into an expressive individual dance, and tap captured the American imagination as few dance forms have before or since. Every actor, singer, dancer, and comedian needed to be able to tap in the interwar period, and the best dancers were national celebrities: Fred Astaire, Bill Robinson, John W. Bubbles, Ray Bolger, the Nicholas Brothers, and Eleanor Powell (among many others) were known for their individual styles. Tap dancers embodied the possibility of taking the nation's speeded-up tempo onto the individual human body, and were symbolic of the conflicted technological desire to assimilate and resist machine aesthetics. If Ziegfeld and Berkeley nourished a certain need for the collective expression of a new mechanized order, tap reflected a hunger for individual, body-centered rhythmic engagement. Tap and mechanized choreography occupied opposite poles of industrialized dance between the world wars.[5]

I juxtapose Henry Adams and Florenz Ziegfeld to highlight a cultural rift in the dissemination of technological change between the rhetoric of political leaders and theatrical demonstrations by producers of popular culture.[6] For example, on May 24, 1844, Samuel Morse transmitted the first long-distance telegraph message from Baltimore to Washington, D.C., over newly laid cable along the Baltimore and Ohio Railroad's right of way. The words struck the proper note of awe and human transgression: "What hath God wrought!" The phrase was provided by the daughter of the commissioner of patents, and the event was attended by political dignitaries to confer the proper authority and import, just as such "elders" attended the ground-breaking of railroads between the 1830s and 1869. In 1844 there still existed the fear that humans were playing with forces of divine power; God therefore had to be invoked, even if ambiguously—as much to say "excuse our human arrogance" as to call for a blessing. Thus new technological power was conducted into society by politicians and industrialists employing Christian rhetoric concerning the nature of human capability and daring.[7]

In contrast, perhaps the best-known transcontinental telephone call was made by Florenz Ziegfeld to his wife Billie Burke. The first such call took place in 1914, and a famous one between Alexander Graham Bell and Thomas Edison on January 25, 1915. But the breakthrough was dramatized further every night at the 1915 Follies with a reenactment of a call between Ziegfeld and Burke of a month later. In a skit called "Hello, Frisco," the actor Bernard Granville (playing Ziegfeld) placed a call from New York to the actress Ina Claire in San Francisco (playing Burke), setting a large map of the United States in motion as "Ziegfeld girls," playing operators, rushed to make the necessary connections.[8] The industrial society was thus shown as unified for a constructive purpose: in effect, to create a system of spontaneous communication. The vignette symbolized both the magic of the telephone in annihilating space and, more importantly, the continued technological unification of the United States; it was a way for audiences to share in the achievements and hopes of techno-progress. "Hello, Frisco," was the most popular song of the 1915 Follies.[9]

That such a momentous technological innovation was conducted into public awareness by a theatrical producer and his actress wife symbolizes the *communicative* function of popular culture in American society, as well as the need for Americans to feel included in techno–progress. Of course, it signifies the new cult of celebrity and its vagaries of wealth as well. But Ziegfeld's well-publicized "embrace . . . [of] the spirit of modernity"—his constant use of "telegrams, machinery, public relations"—was another way the public learned to love the tempo of modern life rather than fear it.[10]

The 1915 Follies began the annual revue's golden age. First, it marked the debut of the architect and theater designer Joseph Urban, whose tableaux and mise-en-scène brought the "new stagecraft" of German theater to American stages. Second, dance itself became a "unifying element" of the Follies that year and "eight major dances were performed" (not including musical numbers with movement). Third, technology became a major theme through three vignettes: besides "Hello, Frisco," there was "Under the Sea," dramatizing the invention of the submarine, and a production number called "Radiumland," which featured "Radium girls."[11]

Increasingly, Americans with little stake in an idyllic New England past looked to the performers and impresarios of popular culture for human-powered visions of the Machine Age and the integration of machine aesthetics into their bodies and their lives.[12] For example, one popular vaudeville routine of the time consisted of a team of men stripping a Model T Ford and putting it back together again in ten minutes. According to Susan Douglas, "By 1910, the prevailing theme in vaudeville and popular literature was man's mastery of and alliance with technology . . . supplant[ing] western themes glorifying the white man's victory over the wild frontier."[13]

The battle I describe in the following two chapters is ultimately between the human being and the machine—more precisely, between the individual dancer and the camera. It is also a cinematic battle, between Busby Berkeley's vision of dancers pressed into abstract patterns to serve the camera, and Fred Astaire's insistence that the individual human body be filmed as a flowing, continuous entity.

In effect, both visions were popular with American movie audiences, and both transformed the cinematic depiction of dance. In the early years of talkies, directors often filmed pieces of the dancer's body— ankles, heels, knees, faces, torsos—in quick succession. The camera usually reflected the music through quick cuts of just the ankles or the legs from the hip down. Astaire believed this method was ill-suited to the visual and sonic expressiveness of dance—to its *rhythmic flow*. In the mid-1930s Astaire used his box-office clout and artistic prestige to demand full-body shots of his dancing numbers. Filming the "full figure of the dancer . . . retain[ed] the flow of the movement intact," he told an interviewer in 1937. Astaire forced his directors to place the camera "at approximately eye-level and . . . shoot the dance as 'straight on' as possible." Before Astaire, "the dance had no continuity, [and] the audience was far more conscious of the camera than the dance."[14] In disempowering the camera, what came to the fore was the grace, elegance, and controlled power of human motion through space. In forcing an artistic change of cinematic style, Astaire met machine aesthetics halfway and, in effect, won a social victory of individual human self-expression over the impersonally mechanical.

Ziegfeld's Dynamo

By 1920 the Ziegfeld Follies had earned a "permanent and definite" place in the theatrical landscape, the *New York Times* wrote, by consistently "hit[ting] the popular mark" and "not only keep[ing] pace with but anticipat[ing] the trend of the times."[15] Through a series of successful musical comedies, a seasonal bawdy revue called "Midnight Frolics," and annual editions of the Follies, the name "Ziegfeld" came to stand for a sumptuous theatrical visual style that blended vaudeville, variety, and burlesque into a glorified "girlie show." Its signature selling points were theatrical spectacle, vivid tableaux, and female chorus lines;

Ziegfeld, "a dreamer, a supplier of fantasies," began in 1907 to "breathe fire into a moribund vaudeville tradition."[16] The Follies mesmerized businessmen and cultural critics alike, and from 1910 to 1927 had New York's social elite happily fighting for opening night tickets for the theatrical event of the season.

In 1923 the cultural critic Edmund Wilson declared the Follies an "institution"—with all the "persistent vitality" and "stupidity" of institutions. The annual revue was a shimmering, superficial fantasy, "a glittering vision which rises straight out of the soul of New York." While providing "consistently gorgeous" women, spectacular tableaux, and lighting and costumes of "distinction and intensity," Ziegfeld also presented "first-rate performer[s]" such as Eddie Cantor and Bert Williams. The Follies' fast-paced skits, energetic dance and production numbers, precision drill chorus lines, and chaotic humor caught the energy, tempo, and recklessness of the 1920s. "Expensive, punctual, stiff, it moves with the speed of an express train," Wilson wrote. "It has in it something of Riverside Drive, of the Plaza, of Scott Fitzgerald's novels."[17]

The cultural critic Gilbert Seldes likened the Follies to a "dynamo" in its power, speed, "smoothness and balance." Like the dynamo, the Follies "aspires to be precise and definite[;] it corresponds to those de luxe railway trains which are always exactly on time, [and] to the millions of spare parts that always fit." He equated the revue's torrid pace with the split-second timing and interlocking systems characteristic of mass-production methods; a Follies "production runs smoothly and the parts are neatly dovetailed." Seldes thought the Follies best displayed machine-influenced artistic production in 1920s America; by way of comparison, he dismissed the Metropolitan Opera as both irrelevant and second-rate. Ziegfeld was the only theatrical producer artistically "in line with our [American] main development," and the Follies were theatrical productions consciously envisioned as "mechanically perfect organisms."[18]

Ziegfeld's artistic triumph lay in his role as a social interpreter of machine aesthetics. If "the machine" was the most dynamic cultural force then acting on society, the role of the artist was to engage it in dialogue. "We tend to a mechanically perfect society in which we will either master the machine or be enslaved by it," Seldes observed. "And the only way to master it—since we cannot escape [it]—will be by understanding it in every detail. This is exactly Mr. Ziegfeld's present preoccupation." For example, many critics thought the aesthetic of chorus lines cold and mechanical—too much like military drill—but Seldes believed that this was the point; the function of the Follies was "to be Apollonic, not Dionysian," and its aesthetic was *order,* not emotional release. For Seldes, even the Follies' orchestra was governed by a mechanical impulse: "Jazz or symphony may sound from the orchestra pit, but underneath is the real tone of the revue, the steady, incorruptible purr of the dynamo."[19]

I want to be more specific about the Ziegfeld "dynamo," since Seldes was not simply being rhetorical. One crucial element of the dynamo, speed, was the "essence" of the Follies, according to Ziegfeld: "Something must be happening every minute." The comedian Eddie Cantor recalled, "Every show we gave seemed to play with clock-like precision for the audience out front."[20] The intense, speeded-up tempo of the show, which reflected the urban soundscape, was palpable enough to its audiences that Wilson noted a revving-*up* of energy in the 1923 Follies. "The tempo of the show is now . . . the same as that of the life outside," he wrote. "This is New York in terms of entertainment—the expression of nervous intensity to the tune of harsh and complicated harmonies." The tempo was present in "the machine-like energy of Eddie Cantor," who joined the dancer Ann Pennington and the comedienne Gilda Gray as "the three highest-pressure performers in the city." The manic energy of these three performers provided an equilibrium between the energy of the streets and that of the theatrical stage. "When, afterwards, you take the subway home, it speeds you to your goal with a crash, like a fast song by Eddie Cantor," Wilson realized. "In the roar of the nocturnal city, driven rhythmically for all its confusion, you can catch hoarse echoes of Gilda Gray and her incomparable *Come Along!*"[21]

Like Seldes, Wilson also perceived the Apollonian, order-making impulse whirring in the Ziegfeldian dynamo as it rendered the chaotic urban intensity palatable to its audiences. In particular he found it in the methodical presentation of white femininity in the Follies' famous "beauty parades." This stage convention is familiar now from countless beauty pageants, but Ziegfeld apparently invented the form. Often the women did little but walk across the stage, or up and down steps, adorned in sumptuous fabrics and elaborate costumes; but they were trained to walk with their shoulders back, hips and pelvis thrust slightly forward, in a gait then renowned as "the Ziegfeld walk." This famous motion "was a kind of slow, flowing series of steps which emphasized the pelvis and raised shoulders . . . the women entered upstage and slowly walked downstage, a smile gradually forming in recognition of the audience."[22]

Ned Wayburn, Ziegfeld's dance director, claimed that overt sexuality was always downplayed in the Follies, with "dignity and impersonal pride" accentuated in carriage and demeanor. Wilson saw in this aesthetic the cold, mechanical qualities of a studied whiteness: "Ziegfeld's girls have not only the Anglo-Saxon straightness—straight backs, straight brows and straight noses—but also the peculiar frigidity and purity, the frank high-school-girlishness which Americans like." The intended aesthetic was expressly "*not* the movement and abandon of emotion"—which was left to ethnic performers of the day. Wilson complained of Ziegfeld's "ballet . . . becoming more and more like military drill"; he was unaffected by such Apollonian order in his female fantasies. For Wilson, "watch[ing] a row of well-grown girls descend a high flight of stairs in a deliberate and rigid goose-step" was neither erotic nor aesthetically appealing, but "too much like watching setting-up exercises."[23]

Ziegfeld himself used the term "girl" with great relish to suggest male fantasy rather than female experience or sexual power. He offered the men in the audience "a promise . . . of romance and excitement—all the things a man dreams about when he thinks of the word *girl*." The Ziegfeld "girl" Paulette Goddard (later Chaplin's co-star in *Modern Times,* and his second wife) commented on her passive role. Playing "the girl on the moon" in the 1925 Follies, Goddard had only to sit on a large crescent moon that descended from above the stage. "I could tap . . . but I was never given the chance. Ziegfeld used to say I was a great sitter. I sat, and I walked."[24] Ziegfeld girls only had to be beautiful, to walk gracefully, and to submit their erotic power to male direction (Ziegfeld and Wayburn) and the controlling male gaze.[25]

Wilson believed Ziegfeld hit the popular male fantasy of the time by shaping the American female ideal to "what the American male really regards as beautiful: the *efficiency of mechanical movement.*"[26] Ziegfeld did not attempt to make his chorus girls individually "as sexually attractive as possible, as [at] the 'Folies Bergère.'" They were not framed as individuals but as mass-produced "girls." Paul Derval, the director of the Folies Bergère for almost fifty years, perceived a similar difference between the two theatrical institutions. "[The] *chorus girl Americana* as a species . . . [is] mass-produced, like a Chevrolet or a tin of ham." In contrast, the methods and intent of the Folies Bergère were "entirely different," and Derval put "greater stress . . . on the personality of each individual member of a troupe. . . . [U]niformity breeds boredom . . .

I select my dancers in the hope that each will claim the attention of a certain number of spectators!'" The British authors of *The Natural History of the Chorus Girl* (1975) similarly noted the lack of individuality among American chorus girls compared to English "Gaiety Girls" and the Folies Bergère.[27] Here was an exciting consumer vision for American men: mass produced wholesome girls.

Ziegfeld's success in articulating his audiences' unconscious investment in mass production came from his own attitude toward technology, which was characteristically American: on the one hand, a desire for affordable abundance, and on the other, to be "always searching for the innovation . . . [to] delight the audience." This mass-produced quality of chorines prepared them to act as automata in skits about machine processes or technological innovation. A production number in the 1913 Follies highlighted the opening of the Panama Canal by presenting a huge ship on stage entering the locks while "the chorus poured out through the gates imitating the onrush of water." In the 1914 Follies, Eddie Cantor and Bert Williams celebrated the erection of the Woolworth Building in a skit called "The Skyscraper on the 1313th Story, in Course of Construction." Ziegfeld also experimented: with phosphorescent paint on costumes for lighting effects, with radium to provide a glow-in-the-dark look, and with 3-D glasses. He often brought scale-model airplanes and real cars onto the stage. Ziegfeld tapped the unspoken ideology of techno-progress by providing unifying cross-class symbols of American popular culture—telephones, skyscrapers, airplanes—and in so doing he helped domesticate and disseminate such technological ideas and inventions within epic spectacle.[28]

Ziegfeld girls occasionally also played machines. In the very first Follies (1907) women dressed up as telephone switchboards in one skit, and "each table connected . . . customer[s] to the switchboard of his choice." In another skit the girls dressed as dirigibles and each wore a "sweeping searchlight moving over them against a . . . background of a burning city." In the 1909 Follies there were celebrations of both the airplane and the battleship. In the airplane tribute, the chorus line dressed as aviators while Lilian Lorraine piloted a plane suspended on wires over the heads of the audience, scattering roses as she sang "Up, Up, Up in My Aeroplane." In a tribute to the United States Navy, forty-eight chorus girls dressed as different battleships, and each wore a battleship-in-miniature as a headdress. At the end, they provided a "special effect": the lights dimmed and "the illuminated ships appeared riding the waves of New York harbor with the city skyline in the background."[29]

The nexus of female beauty and new technology was not original to Ziegfeld; he simply enlarged the scope. For example, in the 1880s the Electric Girl Lighting Company rented out "illuminated girls"; dressed in filament lamps as hostesses for parties, such "electric girls" were trendy party favors. That decade's marriage of techno-progress and male fantasy "embodied both the personal servant of a passing age . . . and the electric light as ornamental object, a dazzling and opulent display of social status in a new age." Of course, the iconography of female-as-divine-light was codified by the Statue of Liberty's electric torch and crown in 1883.[30] By the 1925 edition of Ziegfeld's "Midnight Frolics," the "electric girl" could be historicized within an evolutionary model of light. One woman was costumed as "Sunlight," one as "Candlelight," one as "Lanternlight," and one as "Electric Light." To the more common male/machine interface familiar in figures such as Steam Man and Superman that celebrated strength, Ziegfeld added a female/machine interface around electricity.[31]

Even without specific technological props, the chorines of the Follies re-created mechanical processes by conforming to the fast, steady, seamless tempo of the show. Ziegfeld girls were not required to be energetic or to provide any individual moves; they represented precision, not individuality. Energized, dynamic, individualized motion was reserved for the ethnic stars. Seldes suggested that there was a *need* in white culture for the modeling of a reenergized body—one in step with the new American tempo—but that upper-class whites were loath to see "Anglo-Saxon" men and women selling themselves through chaotic motion, histrionic singing, or pointless silliness. Trapped within what Max Weber and Ronald Takaki have called emotional "iron cages," Euro-American elites preferred to be stirred by those adjudged as nonwhite, whether Jewish (Fannie Brice, Al Jolson, Eddie Cantor), black (Bert Williams), or even Irish (Marilyn Miller, Ann Pennington). (Cantor and Williams often appeared in blackface.)[32] As with the primitivist perspective, they preferred to see lower-caste ethnic entertainers perform the reenergized body, in effect maintaining the dominant position of observer while others performed the emotional mood of the body politic.

Machine Aesthetics of the Chorus Assembly Line

On the other hand, white chorines were straitjacketed into their roles as cogs in production numbers. Sitting in on a dress rehearsal for the 1925 Follies, Edmund Wilson perceived such elements in the steps and patterns of the Tiller Girls, a precision drill troupe from England. The finale featured Will Rogers's rope tricks and a cowboy song with the chorines creating precise geometric patterns. The Tiller Girls came on stage all in "white with purple leggings and sombreros," and proceeded to "make a swinging line: all together." The troupe "crack[ed] their whips all together . . . [then] circl[ed] about the pedestal, [creating] two rings, one inside the other and turning in opposite directions."[33] The two lines of women began to spin inside each other like gear-wheels.

Will Rogers entered the scene with his trusty lasso to establish control, "drop[ping] his lariat down about them, making it whirl in the opposite direction to the outer circle of girls." Chorines were often called "ponies" or "fillies" (especially by black musicians) and Rogers lassoed the two circles of women while singing the words "I would like to corral [you].[34] Once Rogers had the Tiller Girls lassoed, the music was torqued up into a whirling, nearly out-of-control tempo; the women stayed together in their circles and Rogers ably maintained his role as ringmaster. Rogers's persona here synthesized the engineer of mechanical order with the solitary Western loner.

Perhaps even more than the women, the *machine-as-social-force* needed to be corralled. Wilson described the escalation of tempo: "The beat has mastered everything; it pounds fast in a crash of orange. For two minutes in wheeling speed, focused in the green-gilt proscenium frame, they [the Tiller Girls] concentrate the pulse of the city." A final reminder of the beauty of controlled perpetual motion concluded the number. The performers did not stop; the curtain was dropped on the whirling tableaux still in motion, "on the girls and the turning lariat"; then, a minute later, the curtain was reopened to show "the rings . . . still turning." This dance coda suggests confident control over chaotic forces. Only after this last display of control over the human gear-wheels did "the circles draw in and halt."[35]

"*The beat has mastered everything.*" I wish to meditate on Wilson's phrase to reemphasize a point crucial to my argument. To stretch a metaphor, the "beat" is the cultural base of Ziegfeld's dynamo, while the mechanized choreography represents the cultural superstructure. Ziegfeldian spectacle—the conspicuous consumption of women and finery on display, the militaristic and geometric stylization of machine aesthetics, the nonverbal reinforcement of gender roles—was made possible by the cultural work done by the creation of "the beat" in American society.

Only after the beat had mastered everything could fluid geometric dance patterns be choreographed to reflect machine processes. Wilson understood this to be the primary function of the precision high-kicking of groups like the Tiller Girls: "[With] the strong urgent beats of their kicking they send home the strong beats of the music." The beat was the foundation that made the spectacle of abundance "modern" and reflective of its historical moment.[36]

Ziegfeld himself understood something of the rhythmic basis of his modern syncopated revue. For his production of *Show Girl* (1929), the impresario hired Duke Ellington's band to play for a cabaret scene—above and beyond the regular orchestra. A theater critic from the *New York World Telegram* questioned this duplication of musicians and Ziegfeld responded with a three-column reply in the same paper:

> It was probably foolish of me, after spending so much money on a large orchestra, to include a complete band in addition, but the Cotton Club Orchestra, under the direction of Duke Ellington . . . is the finest exponent of syncopated music in existence. Irving Berlin went mad about them, and some of the best exponents of modern [that is, classical] music . . . during rehearsal almost jumped out of their seats with excitement over their extraordinary harmonies and exciting rhythms.[37]

Ziegfeld understood the difference between "symphonic jazz" and the emergent big-band swing. The former was a melody-centered approach based on subsuming a dynamic rhythm in an orchestral tradition; the latter was (and still is) a rhythmic conception featuring the conversational call-and-response of instrumental sections, the interplay of solo improvisation and collective drive, and the creation of new tone colors from original orchestrations of brass instruments. Ziegfeld's praise was so important that the Cotton Club quoted it in full to advertise the Ellington residency there.

Jazz dancing—that is, African American social dance—was also a crucial ingredient of the Follies. Many kinds of dance were presented at the Follies over the years, including "traditional 'hoofing' numbers, acrobatic dances, popular dances such as the tango, shimmy, 'jazz dancing,' ballroom dancing, precision dancing, tap and ballet." But black dance was central to the Follies, even as it was often caricatured. For example, ragtime music and dance was the theme of both the 1910 and 1911 Follies; there were eight rags in the former ("Temptation Rag,"

"Franco-American Rag") and, in the latter, a presentation of "New Year's Eve on the Barbary Coast" (San Francisco's ragtime-driven cabaret district). The turkey trot was so popular nationally that it was presented, caricatured, and disseminated over a three-year period (1912–14). In 1914 the eccentric dancer Leon Errol taught the dance to a dressed-up urban throng of cops, garbage men, tramps, and horses in a skit entitled "Turkey Trottishness."[38] As far as individual dancers go, Ann Pennington danced the Black Bottom in her Follies tenure from 1913 to 1924; Gilda Gray danced the shimmy in the 1922 Follies; and Marilyn Miller tap-danced throughout the 1920s Follies.

According to scholars, the definitive edition of the revue was the 1919 Follies. The centerpiece of the first act was a depiction of jazz dancing and the shimmy that both celebrated and mocked black social dance. First, two men shimmied in a number called "A Shimmy Town"; the dance was then parodied by a chorus line called the "Shimmee Girls" and then by a group of children, the "Follies' Pickaninnies." Eddie Cantor followed with a song called "The Apostle of Pep," which led into the first-act finale, "a minstrel spectacular" entitled the "Follies Minstrels." As the star dancer Marilyn Miller impersonated the legendary (white) minstrel dancer George Primrose, performers in blackface provided commentary and song arranged in the standard semicircular minstrel format (with Eddie Cantor as "Mr. Tambo" and Bert Williams as "Mr. Bones"). In a typical Ziegfeld touch, the semicircular set of minstrel seats was covered in white, silver, and pink satin. The first act ended with Miller doing a fast buck dance accompanied by eight men and women from the chorus. Three years later the Follies featured a parallel white history of "theatrical dancing styles," from late nineteenth-century Scottish clog dances to the precision dance of the Tiller Girls—as if showing the industrial (r)evolution of raw individual expression to collective mechanized choreography.[39]

By 1928 Ziegfeld's chorus lines had influenced all of Broadway; in terms of energy and originality, his only competition came from "the Negro shows." White Americans had "learned a vast amount from negro dancing," Seldes wrote in 1924, and the black tradition had "touch[ed] the dance at every point in music." African American social and commercial dance styles were the crucial element "preventing the American dance from becoming cold and formal."[40] Seldes had little vocabulary for analyzing black dance, and he perceived in the huge hit *Shuffle Along* (1921) and other black revues only "the true frenzy," the Dionysian release, "elements . . . riotous and wild"—the antithesis of the meticulous control and discipline on display in Ziegfeld's shows.

Shuffle Along was almost solely responsible for bringing black tap dancers to the attention of theater critics and audiences. The show's chorus line was influential for its speed, precision, songs ("I'm Just Wild about Harry"), and comedy (Josephine Baker's star comic turn as the incompetent chorine at the end of the line). The pace of all-black revues captivated London and Broadway theatergoers till the end of the decade, from *Shuffle Along* to *Hot Chocolates* (1929), and at Harlem's Cotton Club and Connie's Inn. David Levering Lewis describes Cotton Club floor shows as "Ziegfeldian in their gaudiness, and almost too athletic to be sensuous, with feathers, fans and legs flying in time to Ellington's tornado renditions of compositions like . . . 'When My Sugar Walks down the Street.'" Speed was the cry of those revues, and "all great Harlem floor shows of the Twenties . . . [had] that quality [of] speed: a spectacularly frenzied pace."[41]

By the late 1920s Broadway had been so influenced by both the Follies and the black revues that dance directors were as important as writers and composers.[42] Their prestige was directly related to the increasing importance of the chorus line in theatrical production. The focus on the scantily clad female dancer and on dynamic movement—rather than on costume and drill—permeated Broadway. The cookie-cutter chorus line combined English music-hall traditions of costumed older women performing marches and drills, Ziegfeld girls' precise movements, and dynamic black dance movement to create "[the] precision chorus line of 'girls' dancing in unison with rhythm and a sense of swing."[43]

In 1928 an anonymous Broadway dance director declared chorus lines themselves to be an artistic manifestation of the Machine Age. "Our day . . . is a day of hop, skip and clockwork," he told the *Vanity Fair* critic Gilbert W. Gabriel. "Our art must be a grotesque vivifying of the rigid, steely architecture. . . .Our dance must evoke the dynamo, the axle worm, the crank-shaft, the clash of great, glinting metal rods in swiftly syncopating formation." These perceptions disturbed Gabriel, who was "awed . . . and depressed" by the associations. Like Wilson, he found the movements of chorus lines "joyless" and associated their coldness with overmechanization: their intensity, their group discipline, their unison kicks, "their torsos with . . . clock-like communality of spasm, their heads and arms with such a crack infantry precision."[44]

But to Gabriel the dance director's words shed light on a popular Broadway dance number in many 1928 productions. The routine was built on an old vaudeville slapstick bit where people simply stood and sat quickly, creating fast, chaotic, humorous patterns of movement. In the updated version, chorines stood and sat quickly—sometimes singly, sometimes in rows—and the repetition across rows of faceless women created a sense of interlocking mechanisms; their "alternate risings and squattings" came to resemble "the regularity achieved by a row of pistons." Gabriel recommended that readers go look at the "inner workings" of an eight-cylinder car to see the fidelity of "this simple evocation."[45]

In the 1930s the precision chorus line became institutionalized in the Rockettes. The in-house cultural ambassadors of Radio City Music Hall, the Rockettes emphasized mechanical execution, geometric forms, collective malleability, and female pulchritude. Their production numbers offered neither individuality nor improvisation, but instead a dance machine made out of human female cogs. "Love one Rockette, and you love them all," a British dance historian sneered, for "it is impossible not to connect them in the mind's eye with [an] interminable procession of cheerleaders. . . . The Rockettes seem to a European to exemplify the clean-limbed all-American girl at her brashest: each one, no doubt, able to step up front and recite her essay on Why America is Best." Born in 1925 as the "Missouri Rockets" and brought to Radio City in 1932 by Steve Roxy (and renamed the Roxy-ettes), the Rockettes are still promoted as "the quintessential American chorus line—an exciting precision drill team with great style," and they continue to embody the stylized machine aesthetics of abundance, repetition, standardization, and precision.[46]

Through music and dance, the female-powered dynamo brought the industrial soundscape into an artistic frame for its audience to ponder the new pulse of the city. With the machine process stylized into a driving rhythm, Ziegfeld could overlay, for a prosperous elite, the fantasies of abundance endemic to American technological utopianism. In the promise of hedonism and sex after the long industrial age of repression, in the reinforcement of traditional gender roles in dance and humor, in the assimilation of ethnic groups under one elite brand name, there lies a shift in cultural leadership from religion, politics, and the arts to popular culture. As for "the beat," Ziegfeld culturally appropriated it to create speed and chaos on the one hand and yet maintain mechanical regularity and control on the other.

Ziegfeld the Industrialist

Ziegfeld was thus a captain of industry working in theatrical production; he did his homework and found his niche. He sat through every production of the 1906 Broadway season and concluded that the musical comedy field "lack[ed] in costumes and girls." The formulaic production of the pre-Ziegfeld revue involved "about 20 girls, three changes of costumes, a pair of young lovers, a leading woman with a voice and reputation, a straight man, dancers, a dozen or so musicians in the pit and the inevitable boy-gets-girl plot." For Ziegfeld, plot did not matter; he would instead "overwhelm [the audience] with beauty and magnificence," doubling every commodity on the stage. Ziegfeld's formula was itself a "fable of abundance," to use Jackson Lears's phrase: "In place of 20 girls of varied ages, some of whom could sing a little, some dance a little, he would have 120 girls whose figures would be as provocative as their faces," wrote one biographer. "He would put 100 musicians in the orchestra . . . retain the greatest artists to design as many as 20 changes of costume for every girl. Where one comedian would amuse an audience, six would convulse it."[47]

A defining moment of Ziegfeld's early Machine Age vision occurred in a vignette known as "The Artist's Studio" in *The Parisian Model* (1906). Six women walked on stage wearing long cloaks and stood behind easels and then "suddenly the girls threw off their cloaks and the audience saw gleaming bare shoulders and curving bare legs." One contemporary recalled: "The psychology was perfect. . . .[T]he logic of the illusion proceeded like this: (a) this was an artist's studio; (b) artists paint beautiful young women in the nude; (c) hence . . . they were nude. They weren't. . . . They wore strapless evening gowns with the skirts and trains pinned up. . . .[but the audience] wanted to believe the girls were naked." This scene alone "lured men about town time and time again to the show." Ziegfeld's Broadway career began with a single female icon, the French musical-comedy star Anna Held. But he soon realized the audience's investment in abundance and repetition, and he allowed their fantasies to inform his theatrical productions. As one biographer put it, "[Ziegfeld] glut[ted] the gourmets of excitement with a feast of desire."[48]

Ziegfeld's investment in speed and precision, abundance and repetition, dictatorial control and mass distribution, and unified hierarchical organization and centralized refinement returns us to Seldes's astute claim that Ziegfeld was an artistic visionary then in line "with our main development." The show proceeded seamlessly, as each number ran "smoothly and the parts . . . neatly dovetailed."[49]

Ziegfeld was an industrial manufacturer of beauty, the Henry Ford of the theatrical world. The Ziegfeld girls were the standardized parts in his assembly line; he boasted that he interviewed fifteen thousand girls a year (an unlikely number—that would be about forty a day). The Follies' dance director Ned Wayburn claimed that Ziegfeld's objective was "to invent groups of girls that could be moved artistically [as parts]." The manufacturing process was complex yet unindividuated. First, the Ziegfeld girls were trained in dance and kinesthetics by Wayburn, using the then-popular Delsarte system of naturalistic movement. Then they were taught how to walk and wear makeup.[50] Finally they were costumed in the finest fabrics in order to be refracted in cutting-edge theatrical lighting. Ziegfeld girls came from all over the country but, except for the star performers, they were all stripped down into human canvases and rebuilt into products of fantasy. The process of what Ziegfeld called "glorifying the American girl" reflected the technology then dictating American life. As Veblen noted, the large modern organization "requires . . . that the labor force . . . be mobile, interchangeable, distributable, after the same impersonal fashion as the mechanical contrivances engaged. . . . [Workers must] be standardized, movable, and interchangeable in much the same impersonal manner as the raw or half-wrought materials of industry."[51] One admirer caught the quality of standardization in the Ziegfeld dynamo: "Ziggy was always looking for something different. But when he finally got through with it, it always looked like the same thing."[52]

The ten-minute opening sequence of Ziegfeld's first film, *Glorifying the American Girl* (1929), featuring a review of past Follies that adapts the famous beauty parades to the screen, reflects this industrial method. As the overture plays twenty years of Follies' themes (titles zing by, identifying "Glorifying 1919" or "Glorifying 1927"), a multitude of anonymous shapely women in every manner of dress march over a full-screen map of the United States: they are all heading for New York City. The girls march in a slow, perfectly regular step from points north, west, east, and south—akin to rivers or railroad lines—heading with calculated intent for Ziegfeld's glorification factory. This parade lasts for ten minutes, during which a huge bubble filled with a rendering of the skyline floats over the heads of the aspiring showgirls.

This is a model of industrial manufacturing. In New York City,

Ziegfeld drew upon the raw, unrefined American women from the farm and the frontier, subjected them to a military regimen (on stage and off), transformed the ore into manufactured beauty through the industrial process known as "glorifying," and integrated all the moving parts into a unified, fast-paced production that celebrated the nation's driving engine and ideological obsession: the machine.[53]

Ziegfeld's chorines also had to demonstrate the self-discipline their standardized roles suggested. As with the invasive surveillance of workers perpetrated by Ford's sociological department, Ziegfeld practiced paternalistic discipline, and it was part of his industrial appeal. All talking and kidding around during rehearsals were punished—and "during the rehearsals . . . [an] atmosphere of military discipline was retained." Eddie Cantor recalled that "no seminary students were ever under closer surveillance." Ziegfeld's principles were simple: "Don't get fat. . . . Don't stay up late. . . . Don't go to wild parties."[54] As Veblen had theorized, the discipline and efficiency imposed by the machine process would eventually infiltrate everyday life.

Just as Le Corbusier termed the modernist home "a machine for living," the Ziegfeld Follies can justifiably be called a machine built of female beauty. Lewis Mumford theorized that the first machine—in ancient societies—was the "human machine," which comprised masses of humans yoked together to build monumental symbolic forms such as temples or palaces. Human laborers themselves were the "motor power" of the tools, and the lines and proportions of the pyramids, for example, stand up well to modern standards of precision. In the building of the pyramids, slaves acted as human bulldozers, tractors, and prospectors, and there were at least fifty separate job grades within a sophisticated division of labor.[55] In the construction of the nation's transportation networks (canals, railroads, and levees), masses of ethnic immigrants and African Americans acted as collective steam shovels and human jackhammers to eliminate natural barriers so that goods could be moved to market.

In the Follies, sensual strength was built of masses of females that fetishized machine processes, reflecting beauty on both the power of machinery and on the manufacturer. The audience was to be "overwhelmed by the 'supreme glory of the spectacle.'"[56] Ziegfeld girls functioned as the beautiful *public face* of the new machine-driven theater, with its mechanical tricks, its rotating stage, its electrically controlled layers of curtains, its rising and falling orchestra pit. In running women through mechanical patterns for leisure, Ziegfeld and his competitors served to allay anxiety about mechanical power by dressing it up in beautiful female flesh.

Ziegfeldian chorus lines were thus *female-powered dynamos*, or *pleasure machines made of women*. In mechanized choreography, the individual female body functions only to serve a larger pattern. Ned Wayburn's job was to see that "the chorus functioned as decorative elements and performers and as agents of spectacle . . . their individual physical attributes were not emphasized; rather, the composite effect was given primary consideration." The women were combined in patterns to temporarily recreate mechanical processes uniting fantasies of flesh and machine, sexual abundance, and commodified leisure.[57] If the labor machine of the ancient world helped build the monumental iconography that emphasized visual reification and symbolic power, the female-powered dynamo helped audiences assimilate mechanical power through male fantasy.

Veblen's analysis of turn-of-the-century industrial organization is quite relevant here. Veblen distinguished the roles of engineer and businessman in order to valorize the former as the driving force of the machine process; he idolized engineers and called businessmen agents of "interstitial adjustment." To Veblen, the businessman was simply the human lubricant at the interfaces between technical and economic components. The industrialist was no more than a salesman overseeing—and standardizing, and combining—separate industrial processes to maximize profit.[58] Ziegfeld's biographers suggest that this was exactly the impresario's genius.

In making hundreds of daily decisions, Ziegfeld was an *aesthetic* captain of industry, despite having no technical skills as a dancer, actor, singer, choreographer, or set designer. What exactly did Ziegfeld bring to the Follies? According to Marjorie Farnsworth, "He gave the master's touch, the true entrepreneur's sense of proportion and timing, the quality that brought all these things into form and focus. . . . Ziegfeld had a formula . . . a changing pattern held within the basic confines of certain fundamental concepts . . . but within those confines [he kept the drama] fluid and moving." Another biographer added that Ziegfeld "revolutionized at every level: in the use of color in costumes and sets, in the blending of music with action, in the reduction of long comedy acts to sketches integrated with a whole work." One historian points to "the careful integration of all these elements into a unified whole that distinguished the revue."[59] And in the words of the best historian of 1920s musical theater, "The Ziegfeld touch lay in Ziegfeld's quality as ringmaster of talent."[60]

Ziegfeld's death in 1932 was an apt marker of the transition between the Jazz Age and the Depression, from upper-class celebration of opulence and techno-progress to the nervous fear of economic disorder and social strife. The last Follies, in 1931 (after a four-year hiatus), was unsuccessful; significantly, one review deemed it full of "waste" and "extravagance." The Follies was permeated with the values of the 1920s, "with its opulent style, and its chorus of 80 beautiful women." The Follies "symbolized a golden age" of prosperity, "when the United States was a land of opportunity, freedom, and progress."[61]

Ziegfeld transformed American theater by killing off the puritanical strain in the presentation of the female body and revealing upper-class elites to be as prurient as the vulgar working classes. During the Depression, Americans did not lose their taste for spectacle; fantasies of the wealthy were a major staple of films, for example, from *Grand Hotel* to *The Philadelphia Story* to the *Thin Man* series. But there was a distinct difference. In these films the lives of the rich—of luxurious consumption, of freedom from want—were the content. The leading female role was not that of a Ziegfeld girl presenting her body as an element in a fable of abundance.

Ziegfeld managed to impose order on sexual urges and fantasies of consumption for a passive theatrical audience in a mega-revue that reflected the values of prosperity and the processes of mass production. "He was at once witch doctor and organizer of tribal dances," according to one scholar. "Most American men were obsessed with dreams of glamorous sexual fulfillment, and Ziegfeld provided [them]."[62] Ziegfeld's taming of "the beat"—its speed and rhythmic continuity—to run his female-powered dynamo is itself an important contribution to machine-age cultural creativity. But his most enduring artistic legacy with regard to machine aesthetics was an ability to view human beings and theatrical performance as if through a camera lens—intuitively, as it were, without any skills as a photographer or director. This skill was picked up by his heirs, Busby Berkeley and Billy Rose, both of whom carried on Ziegfeld's tradition of mechanized choreography until World War II.

The Apotheosis of Mechanized Choreography: Busby Berkeley

Busby Berkeley's musicals remain our most familiar touchstone of mechanized choreography. In what Martin Rubin calls "the Berkeley-esque," the camera is the engine that drives production numbers.

Women, soldiers, bathtubs, pianos—everything functions as raw material organized for the production of imaginative kaleidoscopic patterns.[63] Behind Berkeley's "fanciful geometric patterns, his bizarre montages of camera angles, his famous overhead shots, his kaleidoscopic effects, his cascades of designs," was a fetishization of camera technique.[64] Yet, like Ziegfeld, Berkeley claimed no conscious artistic vision: "I'm completely at a loss to explain my method. . . . I can't be any help to you, I don't know anything about it."[65]

Berkeley's visions, too, are filled with female-powered dynamos. In a Berkeley film it would not be surprising if a man lifted off the streamlined cover of a washing machine and inside were millions of young, beautiful women spinning in place, acting as fans, belts, and gearwheels. The "Berkeleyesque" depends upon compartmentalizing human bodies, building abstract patterns out of repetitive elements, and then making the patterns—as opposed to the dancers—dance. "Berkeley's choreography isn't important for its movement of dancers," one scholar notes, "[but] for its movement of the camera."[66] Berkeley proudly claimed there was little actual dancing in his movies. "I work, I create, only for the camera," he confessed in 1966. "For me, if I dare to say it, it is the camera that must dance."[67]

For Berkeley, the camera had to be allowed to express itself—just as modern architects and industrial designers claimed "the machine" expressed itself in streamlined design or the Bauhaus style.[68] Unlike Ziegfeld, Berkeley consciously hired women who looked similar, who "matched just like pearls."[69] What is mass production besides repetition, precision, efficiency, and abundance? Reflecting back on the worst aspects of the factory system, the cybernetic theorist Norbert Wiener might have been speaking of the women in Busby Berkeley numbers: "When human atoms are knit into an organization in which they are used, not in their full right as responsible human beings, but as cogs and levers and rods, it matters little that their raw material is flesh and blood. *What is used as an element in a machine, is in fact an element in the machine.*"[70] What is most expressly and expressively mechanical about Berkeley production numbers are the precise, incremental motions the chorus girls must perform to achieve the aesthetic of live-action time-lapse photography.

Martin Rubin's *Showstoppers: Busby Berkeley and the Tradition of Spectacle* (1993) provides an excellent historical and genre analysis of the "Berkeleyesque." In contrast to most studies placing the choreographer/director within European avant-garde and surrealist traditions, Rubin grounds

Berkeley's aesthetic in the American stage tradition of "spectacle." A nineteenth-century "aggregative" theatrical form "based on creating feelings of abundance, variety and wonder," spectacle depends upon overwhelming audiences with a surfeit of entertainment; the idea is to provide so many acts and so much information that the consumer cannot process it all in a single visit. First codified in P. T. Barnum's "American Museum," the form took hold after the Civil War in burlesque, so-called "Tom shows," medicine shows, Buffalo Bill's Wild West shows, minstrel shows, and the Ziegfeld Follies. But Rubin rightly places Berkeley within the paradigmatic challenge of the 1930s artist—that of finding a middle ground between the individual and the group. Berkeley's work celebrates both through his "ability to shift fluidly from grandiosity to intimacy."[71]

Berkeley absorbed the tradition of spectacle in his five years as a Broadway dance director (1925–30) and later transferred it to the new medium of film. During his Broadway tenure, Berkeley's theater aesthetic combined polyrhythmic vertigo with mechanical order. An early success with small-ensemble geometric formations in *A Connecticut Yankee* (1927) merited a rare artistic profile by John Martin, the dance critic of the *New York Times*. Martin believed theatergoers were hungry for a refined artistic approach to the decade's obsession with speed and "novelty," and he claimed that Berkeley had "assume[d] the mantle of a minor prophet" by creating a kind of "high-brow' jazz dancing." Berkeley's Broadway work was marked by improvisation and collaboration (hallmarks of jazz practice), and he created his dance numbers on the spot. His inspiration came "from having the girls in front of him on the stage ready to work."[72]

Berkeley's dance numbers were so rhythmically complex that one Broadway conductor admitted he could not watch the dancers "for fear he could not move his baton to the required beat of the score." Martin perceived that Berkeley had "delv[ed] into the actual rhythmic structure of jazz to a degree that has not before been attempted."[73] Dancers were required to execute "contrary rhythms . . . to perform simultaneously, two rhythms counter to each other, and also [to] the music." In film, this would translate into lines and circles of women moving in different directions and at variable speeds. For example, in the "By a Waterfall" number in *Footlight Parade* (1933), each circle of a five-tiered fountain of women rotates at a different rate; in the "My Forgotten Man" number of *Gold Diggers of 1933*, different lines of men march in varying rhythms in the foreground and background. The maintenance of two or more distinct rhythms is a cardinal aspect of African music and a rarity in classical music or European-derived folk music; hence Martin's astute perception that Berkeley had "delved into the actual rhythmic structure of jazz." The dance critic was also awed by the abilities of "the *ordinary* chorus girl of today" in terms of her speed, precision, and rhythmic fluidity—skills which would have guaranteed "her elevation to stardom a few years ago."[74]

Martin could not imagine "kinesic progress" beyond the 1928 level: "Unless there are undreamed-of changes in the constitution of the physical universe, the human body cannot be made to move any more rapidly than it has already been trained to do for theatrical purposes."[75] What he did not see was that the human body is adaptive and plastic, and that Berkeley's syncopated geometric configurations heralded the next step in mechanized choreography.[76]

Along with the revolution in the American tempo created by jazz, Berkeley also had mechanical processes on his mind for the dances staged in *The Earl Carroll Vanities of 1928*. Taking his cue from a stage convention called "living architecture," in which women were literally embedded into large props, he arranged chorines in the shape of an airplane while Lilian Roth sang "I'm Flying High" above them and the dancer Dorothy Lull cartwheeled continuously to form the propeller. (He revived this motif in the film *Flying High* [1931].) In other skits women "form[ed] parts of columns, 'human fountains,' and layer-cake-like platforms," motifs that later became common to Berkeley films.[77]

That revue's most critically acclaimed number, however, was "The Machinery Ballet," in which the chorus line transformed itself into an assembly-line factory tableaux. Inspired by a visit to the Ford plant at River Rouge, Berkeley provided "lurid flashes of fire and smoke" to produce an expressionistic atmosphere that critics compared favorably to Fritz Lang's *Metropolis* (1926), Karel Capek's play *R.U.R.* (1923), and Russian constructivism. The chorines were dressed not as workers but as robots, and they wore "metallic robot-style costumes emblazoned with dials and switches." Nor did they pretend to perform any assembly-line work; instead they "shuttled and whirled mechanically in an endless circle," just as many precision line dancers did in the 1920s. On a high pedestal, one chorine performed continuous slow cartwheels that transformed her into a "living cogwheel." Here again is the human/machine interface with women as gears and cogs in the female-powered dynamo.[78]

Unlike European machine dances, "The Machinery Ballet" was a tribute to the automated factory and not a social critique of mass production. The number calls attention to the relationship between the female-powered dynamo and factory realities. In a rare nod to the performing arts, the *Journal of Electrical Workers and Operators* recognized the homage and printed a photograph with the following caption in December 1928: "Midst smoke and flashes of fire, as from . . . a furnace door, these dancers whirl and turn, rise and fall, leap and toss, in an ensemble, which . . . gives off the dizzy impression of a modern factory. . . . [S]o insistent is the pressure of wheels, pulleys, belts, endless chains of production, upon the playground of the world, that it [Broadway], too, begins to understand." It was high time, the writer noted, that "Broadway . . . Fifth Avenue and Wall Street" gave credit to the "machine civilization of which we all are a part."[79]

Ziegfeld's and Berkeley's Machine Age modern aesthetic depended on inhibiting desire for the beautiful half-naked women on display and heightening the vertigo effects of the production numbers. For Ziegfeld, his girls were like high-quality white photographic paper awaiting his patented form of processing (glorifying); he looked less for beauty than malleability. His interviews were like screen tests in which he visualized women in sensuous fabrics and flattering lighting, their faces and walks trained to his aesthetic. In *Ziegfeld, the Great Glorifier* (1934), Eddie Cantor credited Ziegfeld with being "the first to see girls *through a camera eye*—long before the movie people, who learned the trick from him." Cantor noted that Ziegfeld

> often accepted women from their photographs after actually rejecting them in person . . . in the magic of his clothes, the tint of his lights, and the effect of his ensemble, that same, plain-looking girl acquires something angelic and supernal. That was the Ziegfeld touch. 'Glorifying the American girl' was not merely a press agent's slogan—it was an actual process invented by Zieggy . . . even homely-looking comedians and burlesque clowns took on an aura of grandeur on his stage.[80]

The quality of his "camera eye" can be measured by the successful graduation from stage to screen of many Ziegfeld girls (among them Ruby Keeler, Barbara Stanwyck, and Paulette Goddard). A contemporary wrote that "his eye for detail was miraculous."[81]

In retrospect, Hollywood seemed a logical next step for Ziegfeld's kind of spectacle, but he had little interest in making movies. Broadway was then the most prestigious form of American culture, and Ziegfeld was its reigning monarch; he did not consider film a competitive medium until the advent of talkies in 1927. In part, Ziegfeld had no interest in learning a new medium; Cantor pointed out that early movies were weak "technologically in his strongest suits—lighting, color and sound." Nor was Ziegfeld threatened; after all, for the first two years of talkies, the filmed Broadway musical—"canned theater," Rubin calls it—was Hollywood's first successful genre. The movie-musical formula first found its own identity in *The Broadway Melody* (1929), and then Berkeley took Ziegfeld's legacy into the new medium.[82] As far as Ziegfeld was concerned, the movies crawled along in technological infancy while he painted epic spectacles on a huge canvas by focusing the efforts of first-rate artisans on hundreds of live women (and comedians, singers, and dancers).[83]

The Berkeleyesque depends upon treating women as the raw material for fantastic dream sequences, an approach pioneered by Ziegfeld that had little theatrical precedent. (Before Ziegfeld, the bare female leg itself sold tickets.) Berkeley's first movie, *Whoopee!* (1930), was a film adaptation of a successful 1927 Ziegfeld musical comedy; Ziegfeld also coproduced and lent his star comedian (Eddie Cantor) for the effort. A Western parody that "explicitly established the connection between Berkeley's film work and the Ziegfeldian stage tradition," *Whoopee!* utilized the latter's stage conventions in all three dance numbers. In the beauty parade of the "Song of the Setting Sun," chorines dressed as "Indian maidens" ride by slowly on horses and part their robes to reveal "skimpy but ornate outfit[s]." In "Stetson," Berkeley introduced his own "parade of faces" motif—close-ups on each chorine as she walked by—and shifted the focus from the female torso and legs to the face. In "Cowboy Number," Berkeley first employed his trademark top-shot to develop striking patterns of ten-gallon hats, focusing on the aesthetic element of repetition.[84]

Cantor also starred in Berkeley's next two films, *Palmy Days* (1931) and *The Kid from Spain* (1932); *Dames* (1934) was virtually a tribute to the Ziegfeld chorus lines and dancers, chock-full of "precision formations" that gave short-lived currency to the term "cinematerpsichorean." As early as 1933, the Hollywood columnist Louella Parsons declared that Berkeley had "revolutionized musical comedies and made it possible for the screen to feature girl revues comparable with the Ziegfeld Follies." On all these scores, Berkeley's debt to Ziegfeld is immense.[85]

Berkeley's aesthetic came from an unlikely combination of military drill, mass production, and jazz dance. In 1969 the *New York Times* reflected that "if there was no Busby Berkeley, Hollywood would have had to invent him." The stale rhetorical device aside, Berkeley *was* the perfect candidate for Machine Age worship of the camera, since he had no formal training or any artistic traditions, such as ballet, to draw upon. His only training in directing human bodies in motion came from military drill. As a second lieutenant under General John J. Pershing in France during World War I, he trained groups of twelve hundred men for parade drills and conducted aerial observations for a small army film unit. There he taught his battalion not only to march and drill to music but to do complicated maneuvers in absolute silence. Berkeley films are permeated with military drill and kaleidoscopic patterns, two activities dependent upon precise organization, repetition, and mechanical movement. He thus became an unconscious Machine Age modernist, "an outstanding choreographer who had never studied choreography, a . . . dance director who had never taken a dancing lesson, and a brilliant film maker who had given no thought to film-making until his first day in a studio." His real talent was "his ability to move great masses of people in strict time all over his stages."[86]

For example, in the "Shanghai Lil" sequence from *Footlight Parade*, James Cagney's search for a whore-with-a-heart-of-gold in a Chinese port ends with a bugle call for the sailors to get back on deck, and five minutes of military drill formations follow that would not be out of place today in a college football half-time show. The climax features soldiers and "Orientalized" call girls holding up placards that form the American flag, the face of President Roosevelt, and the then-famous blue eagle of the National Recovery Administration. There are similar salutes to military and naval academies in *Varsity Show* (1937), and several girls march with rifles and drums in *Gold Diggers of 1937*.[87]

The counterpoint to military drill is Berkeley's prominent use of blackface and minstrel-show motifs. In two films with Judy Garland and Mickey Rooney, *Babes in Arms* (1939) and *Babes on Broadway* (1942), Berkeley uses the minstrel show in the musical-within-the-musical that saves the day at the films' climax, and in *Strike up the Band* (1940), a white swing band saves the day; Rooney and Garland "black up" in *Babes on Broadway* (1941).[88] In these musicals, Berkeley appropriated African American music without recognizing either its creators or its function as a survival technology of rejuvenation and reaffirmation. Although jazz rhythms are central to the Berkeleyesque, the director rarely employed black musicians or dancers and ignored swing music and dance. Berkeley instead portrayed energy visually through his constantly changing kaleidoscopic fantasy-scapes, not through individual entertainers.[89]

The plot of *Roman Scandals* (1933) ironically sets out Berkeley's inability to honor the jazz rhythms on which his aesthetic is based. Eddie Cantor plays a lazy dreamer from the small town of West Rome, Oklahoma, who gets knocked out and finds himself transported back to ancient Rome as a slave. Accidentally given a mud facial while lying on a table, he wakes up and fluidly slips into minstrel mode; he is immediately mistaken for an "Ethiopian beauty specialist" and understood to be a court eunuch. Asked by two of the emperor's harem girls for beauty tips, he sings "Keep Young and Beautiful," a production number in which "real" (African American) female slaves act as servants who attend to the all-blonde harem girls: they wax their legs, brush their hair, dress them, and massage their arms and legs. When Cantor's blackface melts under steam, all the women chase him around. Visually, Berkeley had a "penchant for rendering the chorus into white-and-black patterns,"[90] and the contrast of black arms on white shoulders or black women set off against white women is used to vivid visual effect. But in presenting "real" African slaves in this sequence, the movie provides a dizzying racial masquerade: the character who liberates the empire from a corrupt, repressive regime is a Jewish American comedian in blackface masquerading as an Ethiopian eunuch who, in the film's longest production number, sings a 1920s jazz number while chorus lines of white and black women chase him and each other around a shimmering black and white stage set. The vortex of racial and cultural confusion in this plot is an apt metaphor for Berkeley's anxiety of influence regarding African American survival technology.

The Camera Dances

What makes Berkeley a Machine Age modernist was his subjugation of dancers to the camera, which allowed the camera to "assert its own presence as an element of autonomous display."[91] The dances in Berkeley's first few films were "stage-bound" because the choreographer was intimidated by the new medium. For months Berkeley groped for new ideas—and a new technique—while roaming around the Goldwyn studio lot in 1929. "I realized . . . [cinematic] technique was entirely different from the stage. In pictures you see everything through the eye of the camera . . . the director and his cameramen decide where the viewer will look. It was obvious to me that film musicals so far had been disappointing because no one thought of imaginative things to do with the camera."[92] While pre-1930 dance directors kept the camera rooted to the floor, conceiving a movie as if from the point of view of a theatergoer, Berkeley's cinematic breakthrough came from "spectacularizing the camera." He built a monorail for the camera to travel upon to create vertigo-inducing tracking shots; he utilized revolving turntables to make heavy, static objects like pianos "dance"; and, of course, he created the famous Berkeley top-shot.[93]

In *Palmy Days* (1931) Berkeley parodied the assembly line and the erotics of machinery in a production number at a donut factory. Set in a bakery where the "Goldwyn Girls" are live-in workers—reminiscent of nineteenth-century Lowell factory girls—the prologue finds the women "glorifying the American donut." The obvious bawdy jokes and double entendre aside, the production number connects up the machine aesthetics common to both assembly lines and chorus lines, and "satirize[s] the mechanistic precision and cookie-cutter interchangeability" of both.[94] The women cope with the pressures of their jobs through rhythmic physical exercise at the company gymnasium in scenes that combine machine aesthetics with female display. In the campy number "Bend Down Sister," the chorines perform "synchronized calisthenics," a reference to the various gymnastic systems of Delsarte and Dalcroze then in vogue. From the "synchronized chorus movements" to the "conveyor-like treadmills" to the "revolving machine-structures" and moving platforms constantly rotating and deploying actors, dancers, and chorines, the movie is a showcase for machine aesthetics.[95] But these assembly-line images function more as a general reference to the factory system than to anything resembling jarring, repetitive, exhausting factory work.

The machine aesthetic of the Berkeleyesque in the 1930s involved abstracting parts of women's bodies to render geometrical patterns and mechanical processes. For example, the fifteen-minute "By a Waterfall" number from *Footlight Parade* begins as a pastoral fantasy of a man (Dick Powell) resting by a waterfall and singing out for some companionship. When a water nymph (Ruby Keeler) sings back, the two meet and sing a duet. Powell falls asleep on Keeler's lap, whereupon she invites hundreds of her fellow nymphs to perform for him. Soon the scenery shifts from its "realistic" natural setting to an expansive, Roman-style Olympic-sized pool with multiple platforms, underwater lighting, and classical ornamentation. "What with all the water pumps, the hydraulic lifts, and the dozens of workmen, someone said the set looked like the engine room of an ocean liner," Berkeley recalled.[96]

In one section of "Waterfall," fifty or so women lie on their backs and, supported by hidden floats, intertwine their arms and legs to form "complex, rotating spokewheel patterns." They are like hubcaps spinning in the ether, and Berkeley lights them from underneath for an ethereal, disembodied effect. In another shot, the women's bodies are submerged, leaving only their heads and arms above water. As each woman extends one hand to rest on the woman's shoulder in front of her, the women transmute into vertebral sections of a long, undulating snake. Detaching themselves, they duck under water and clasp arms at the wrists to form alternate triangular and circular patterns, almost as if they were performing chemical combinations at the molecular level. "The overall effect is as if the chorus had exchanged their human forms for simpler, more elemental ones," Rubin suggests, "becoming cellular units in an overall body of abstraction." The number was the hit of the movie; at its New York premiere, audiences gave it a standing ovation, "some even throwing programs in the air."[97]

Many scholars have noted the erotic element—and the Freudian displacement of sexual desire—at the core of Berkeley's fantasies. For example: the suggestion of zipping and unzipping mimicked by dozens of pairs of interlocked womens' legs in "By a Waterfall"; his patented through-the-legs shots; and the common push-in-pull-out pumping of his kaleidoscopic images.[98] In all three cases, hordes of attractive, scantily clad women are engaged in symbolic sexual processes. As one film scholar succinctly put it, "Berkeley's production numbers provide a spectrum of images of women that range . . . from Reverence to Rape." Jack Cole, a choreographer who often worked with Berkeley, believed the dance director "reflect[ed] the erotic attitudes of the middle class." Just as Ziegfeld had made public prurience respectable for elite audiences in New York, Berkeley brought fetishized desire to Hollywood, taking "lots of blonde girls and photograph[ing] them in as many ways as were acceptable to the middle class . . . [not] completely nude, but . . . with their legs open and their breasts hanging."[99]

As a fellow choreographer, Cole was able to pinpoint the sexual aesthetic of Berkeley's camera eye: it was "all about looking at gorgeous women erotically with the camera as a penis substitute." The camera was anthropomorphized in Berkeley's production numbers—peeking around corners, looking up women's dresses—and this mechanical penis stood in for the biological one.[100] A single heterosexual male may be satisfied with one woman, but the machine has its own aesthetic needs: it requires abundance and repetition, rather than a sexual exchange it cannot enjoy. The Berkeleyesque depends upon "our perception that the women look remarkably alike," and as they are "line[d] . . . up behind one another . . . their multiplicity is subsumed in an image of apparent unity."[101] To follow the logic of machine aesthetics, a camera-penis would require hundreds of females, thriving on mass-produced girls rather than emotional fulfillment with one woman. Significantly, Berkeley's 1930s films feature mostly undistinguished male leads as opposed to the more popular virile males of the period such as Clark Gable, Gary Cooper, and Cary Grant. Rubin suggests that Berkeley chose actors such as Dick Powell precisely for "their charming innocuousness."[102] In effect, Berkeley uses the camera as the leading man, and it does not wish to compete for the womens' affections with a strong male actor.

In close readings of two ten-minute production numbers in *Dames* (1934), I conclude this chapter by teasing out the various intersections of the "Berkeleyesque," the techno-dialogic, Machine Age modernism, and the camera-as-mechanical-penis.

"I Only Have Eyes for You" and "Dames"

Three themes crucial to the techno-dialogic weave through these two musical numbers. First, the standardized girl appears to enjoy her work as a cog in an eroticized, fetishized pleasure machine that helps allay anxiety regarding the transition to urban, industrial society. Second, these numbers are cinematic fables of abundance, a rhetorical set of tropes founded in American advertising and focused on the idea of available and malleable young women.[103] Third, for economically strapped audiences the techno-progress of American society could here be enjoyed through technological innovation and continuous novelty. No plot background is required since the two numbers are self-contained vignettes unfolding as part of a musical within the movie.

A popular chestnut still recorded often, Harry Warren and Al Dubin's "I Only Have Eyes for You" (1934) was a ballad written for *Dames* that itself attempts to mediate the challenges of mass society: how to identify the distinctive qualities of one's romantic object and ignore the distractions and alienation of everyday modern life. Using the song as a theatrical platform, Berkeley made Ruby Keeler's face an icon of the decade by bringing the pastoral idyll of the previous year's "By a Waterfall" to the city. Instead of the actor Dick Powell dreaming of Keeler transformed into a fantasy of cavorting aqua-babes, the couple fall asleep together on the subway after Powell gets off work. Rocking to the rails, Powell dreams Keeler as the female life-force of the city: its vitality, its democratic populism, its industrial blood.

The scene opens with Powell selling tickets at a Broadway theater while Keeler waits for him ten feet away; he looks through all the customers and sings straight at her, "I only have eyes for you." The show sells out, Powell leaves his cage, and the couple hits the street with no apparent destination; Powell continues to sing as they walk in the midst of metropolitan crowds heading to their appointments. His devotion to Keeler is seconded by an Irish mailman (who takes a chorus) and an Italian couple who own a newsstand (each gets a line); the immigrant voices usher the couple to the subway station. Yet despite the urban millions, the dynamic soundscape, the rush of city life, even the subway's roar, mass society "all disappear[s] from view" when the love object is around. Berkeley makes this line cinematically literal twice: first when the couple stands in the middle of two intersecting streams of pedestrians and the crowds dissolve, leaving them alone on the corner, and second, after they get on a full subway car and Berkeley erases the other passengers.

The urbanite dreams not of the pastoral but of machine-made abundance. As Powell serenades her, Keeler falls asleep; Powell then sings to the female models in the subway ads around him—for cigarettes, hair-dye, and cosmetics—and each model's face morphs into Keeler's. After the third face turns into Keeler's, the ad's black background pulls Powell (and the viewer) inside it; suddenly we are all in the ad-space where Keeler's face floats disembodied in the ether. Rubin calls this typical Berkeleyesque dreamscape "spectacle space"—an immaterial, boundaryless, shifting space upon which the director projects his most imaginative cinematic creations.[104]

Keeler's face comes toward the viewer and then splits into several identical cutout placards that float downward single-file into the visual field. The placards multiply until dozens of Keeler faces are being marched around three different geometric groupings (a rounded triangular one and two trapezoids). Then for the first time we see human bodies; the placards fall, revealing chorus girls all of the same general size and shape as Ruby, all "coiffed and dressed exactly like Keeler." To make the message clear that these are standardized Ruby Ks, the chorus girls then pick up flat masks of Keeler's face and hold them to their faces.

A quick cut moves us to a multileveled edifice upon which the women wave their dresses and do little else. The all-white structure comprises three staircases, a revolving platform, and a half Ferris wheel; the women walk mechanically in their white gowns, sashaying their skirts right and left on different levels and in different directions.[105] The constantly circling camera meanwhile creates a sense of vertigo out of the music's intricate rhythmic crosscurrents, the female bodies in motion, the black and white patterns, and the gauzy, shiny fabrics. The only constant is Keeler, who is always in the middle of the fantasy somewhere; the camera often searches her out and dwells on no other face. The camera scans through all the mass-produced Rubies—the girls "matched like pearls" for the effect—but Keeler is the only subject.[106]

After two minutes of this parade, the women reassemble into a rectangular grid, all seated on the ground; they look like lily pads and flutter their arms oddly as if in a tableau of riverine life. After fifteen seconds, the women somersault forward and turn up new placards, each a jigsaw-puzzle piece that together form Keeler's face as seen through Berkeley's classic top-shot. The camera then penetrates the left eye of the puzzle and locates the "real" Keeler, who walks forward into a gilt-edged frame magically hovering in the air. For the moment Keeler becomes a live-action cameo: the ultimate elevation of the average Jane into Victorian womanhood. Extending the fantasy, the camera pans down to capture twenty women sitting and talking below on a gently curving, twenty-foot-long Victorian couch.

The women stand up and form a single file. They melt into one woman and then morph into a long, vertical handle that attaches to the gilt-edged frame to display Keeler alone in the blank black space. Keeler then steps out of the frame and miraculously the cameo shrinks to "real-life" size. She picks it up and holds it like a mirror. Then, signaling the audience to watch with her, Keeler turns the mirror toward the viewer and it has become a camera lens, through which we see Powell and Keeler sleeping on the subway. And we're back in real narrative space.

What's more, the viewer is returned to a surprisingly "real" depiction of 1934 America. The couple wake up in a silent, empty train yard, at the "end of the line" (so the subway sign says)—as if they are unsure where they live or what the future holds; it is the Depression, after all. The couple must climb down off the back of the train and into the abandoned train yard like hoboes. Behind them seven or eight trains stand sentinel in the shadows like industrial icons awaiting new marching orders. It is cold and rainy; Keeler shivers, and Powell chivalrously wraps his jacket around her. The camera pulls back into a long shot that reveals eight sets of rails gleaming in the moonlight, a symbol of exciting but uncertain journeys. Powell sweeps Keeler off her feet into his arms and resumes his serenade but with a more melancholic tone. He begins walking, crossing diagonally from the top right of the visual field to the bottom left; the camera remains still the entire time and frames the couple as only a minor aspect of the train yard. As Powell sings slightly mournfully "I only have eyes for you," holding Keeler in his arms, the couple crosses the threshold of train-powered modernity.[107]

This closing shot consummates the marriage of technology and survival technology as theorized in this work: the standardized modern white female, the (subway) train riding into the (uncertain) future, American popular music as the artistic currency of continuity. As Rubin notes, Keeler is "extraordinarily ordinary and infinitely replicable"—the average Jane apotheosized for proud average Joes who are lent voice and words by the great American songwriters of Tin Pan Alley and boosted by the foundation of the African American beat. Americans *need* these songs in 1934. The emotional costs of the industrial revolution, the anxieties of mass production, the mediation of the female-powered dynamo—they've all disappeared from *conscious* view. In the dreamscape, Berkeley's camera-as-mechanical-penis has eyes for hundreds of Ruby Ks; but the-male-viewer-as-Dick Powell only has eyes for *you*.[108]

Yet in "Dames," the very next number in the film, Berkeley delivers a surfeit of abstract patterns that only emphasizes the industrial subjugation of the female individual to larger impersonal machine dreams. The scene opens with Dick Powell imperiously directing a meeting of wealthy investors for a new Broadway show, and he rhetorically asks them: "What makes a hit show?" The white men debate vociferously—it's the songs, the story, the cast, the publicity—until Powell dismisses all these noble ideas with a wave of his hand. "Admit it," he sings, "it's all those cute/and cunning/young/and beautiful/dames." With the confidence of a Ziegfeld, Powell refuses several urgent phone calls—from wealthy investors, bank presidents, George Gershwin, successful playwrights—and waves in a bevy of chorus girls. As Powell takes cards from their elegantly gloved hands, Berkeley provides a typical parade-of-faces motif while the women are serenaded with "Dames." "Your knees in action/that's the attraction," Powell croons, somehow innocently. As the song-and-dance man presiding over a board room of rich investors, Powell might as well be the CEO of American interwar popular culture.

American pleasure has to be regulated, however, so Powell picks up an alarm clock and orders the girls home for morning rehearsals. Upon exiting, the women walk behind seven-foot-high cardboard clocks; here again the clock as icon signals the shift from nature's time to industrial time. Then the lights dim, the clocks roll away into the grooves of the stage floor, and five seconds later the lights come up on pairs of women waking up in nearly two dozen double beds, in white satin nightgowns.

The women wake each other with pantomimed shrieks of joy. First they push the canopied beds into an oval and perform bending, stretching, and kicking exercises (one on the bed, one standing beside it). They then rearrange the beds into three runways, and, four abreast, they link arms and parade down the center. At this point, two nearly identical platinum blondes fall intimately into the camera lens with cheesecake smiles for their favorite machine, a shot that kicks off what might today be a *Victoria's Secret* video. The shot wipes into a spectacle of twenty-eight free-standing bathtubs in a triangular pattern, each featuring a full-length neon-framed makeup mirror that glows against the black background; it looks like the skyline of a miniature city. Half the women bathe, the other half wait on them. When the camera zooms in too close on one woman's bubbles, she admonishes its mechanical desire, clouding the lens with a large sponge. The women towel each other off, then seductively stand and powder their skin. The mechanical penis has come to chorus-girl camp.

Next Berkeley references an iconic shot from King Vidor's *The Crowd*, one of the first American cinematic critiques of mass society and corporate culture. Vidor's original overhead shot (still used, most famously in Billy Wilder's *The Apartment*) frames a long open room filled with rows of desks to accentuate the lack of privacy and individuality in corporate culture.[109] Here, their morning ablutions finished, the women apply powder and lipstick at desk-shaped makeup tables lined up in rows similar to corporate offices of the time. But Berkeley's shot is the antithesis of Vidor's. Here the chorus girls happily, though mechanically, move their faces from side to side; then quickly they're out on the street, purposefully walking to work. The city streets are sexualized by this glorified crowd of young women, framed as the only workers in the city.[110]

Their function in this number is to eroticize the nine-to-five workday; and in their jobs as "dames," Berkeley presses them into industrial overdrive. They trade their stylish clothing for work clothes: white frilly blouses and black stretch pants, the raw material for Berkeley's geometrical time-lapse black-and-white graphics. First, they do jumping jacks lying down on a stepped stage of six horizontal rows; different rows kick in at different times, like parts of a machine starting up. The women then collapse into single file and Berkeley rotates the camera 180 degrees. The girls bend over, and the camera runs the gauntlet through their black-sheathed upper thighs as each face drops into view, and then pulls back—an act of mechanical penetration. The women then gather in four long rows that expand and contract like live paper dolls; a few shimmy, a few tap-dance, but it is only to break up the collective patterns.

Next, a hundred or so "dames" pack themselves tightly underneath a top-shot that frames them as an enormous white carnation. Out of the center of the flower, surreally, one girl flies up at the camera; she hovers, smiles, and returns. Then two more women fly up at the camera as if to kiss it. The fourth girl brings a black ball with her and gives it to the camera; the camera then drops the ball on the women, who scramble quickly into a complex geometric figure reminiscent of Parcheesi boards and marching-band formations. The camera drops the black ball on the women four more times, and each time the women spread into pulsating flower-patterns and mandalas.[111]

Now the mechanical penis reaches the climax of its fantasy. A new backdrop appears: a graphic diamond shape composed of alternating black and white patterns around a black center. Berkeley slowly peels back the two-dimensional graphic to reveal lines of women in black and white. The women are packed together and literally form the walls of a tunnel through which the camera moves slowly and inexorably toward its goal, the diamond-shaped black hole at the center. Berkeley rotates the camera slowly as it moves through the dozens of women toward its goal; leaving Freud aside for the moment (difficult as that is), such slow rotation gives the viewer a sense of vertigo and a proto-psychedelic sense of what Rubin calls "controlled disorientation." When the camera reaches the black core of the design, one woman miraculously appears in the black ether; after two seconds of silence, she begins to sing "Dames."

The camera then slowly pulls back, and we have a new cinemascape: a hundred women are arranged on a flat blank black artist's canvas in groups of three to seven in patterns seemingly culled from Greek urns. These standardized dames are the unifying, repetitive element in a Berkeleyesque cinematic painting. What happens last? This singing all-blonde pleasure machine is frozen into a wallpaper design that Dick Powell pops his head through to sing the last line of the musical: "To bring/you memories/of those beautiful/dames." Berkeley's dame is Ziegfeld's girl transmuted—from the 1920s glorified average-Jane-as-fashion-plate to 1930s Machine Age fantasy boilerplate. The cinematic transformation of Ziegfeldian stage conventions is complete: the standardized white female body, the fable of abundance, living architecture, mechanized choreography, and fetishized mass fantasy.

The message implicit in "I Only Have Eyes for You" suggests that to remove any woman from the "Berkeleyesque" would be to find her uniquely compelling and beautiful. Even on the chorus-girl assembly line, every woman is a jewel with stunning facets that need only a circling camera to reveal in the industrial light of day. Pull the girl off the line and she still has character; there's a universe in that woman as implied by the hundreds of placards and cookiecutter Ruby Ks. In this number, the Berkeleyesque is akin to the Fordist production line: the Machine Age woman will still be *your* baby, just as many Americans give their mass-produced cars pet names to personalize and individualize them. Berkeley here skillfully weaves what Rubin calls his grand "major key" themes—"spectacle, grandiosity, glitter"—with his "minor key" ones ("intimacy, banality, poignancy"). On the other hand, "Dames" reduces women to artistic lines for use in industrial graphics. Anchored by neither character nor function, these dames are used only to fetishize the workday and mass production, using the chorus girl as visual candy to render insignificant the plight of the average worker. Because "Dames" is the climax of the musical-within-the-movie *Dames*, it disturbingly reflects back on the optimism of "I Only Have Eyes for You." Taking the two together, Ruby Keeler seems less an object of romance than a commodified product for which the nation's corporations have endless replacements. As Rubin notes, "the dames of 'Dames' are all completely anonymous."[112]

Warner Brothers was at least indirectly aware that they were selling a female-powered dynamo. The trailer for *Dames* focused on the presence of "350 of the most gorgeous creatures on earth"; *Footlight Parade* sold itself as a parade of "300 of the world's Most Beautiful and Talented Girls."[113] In

Berkeley's vision of the machine of female beauty, these two production numbers communicated very different—and complementary—visions of hope that kept the concepts of progress and techno-progress alive.

Coda: The Missed Opportunity of Mechanized Choreography

In *Ziegfeld Girl* (1941) Berkeley finally produced a homage to the man he called "the master." The plot revolves around the struggles of three young female hopefuls (played by Judy Garland, Lana Turner, and Hedy Lamarr) as they go through the process of glorification. The movie reveals "how Ziegfeld girls were chosen, where they came from, how they behaved, and what . . . happened to them." The movie was "designed to out-Ziegfeld Ziegfeld," and in the climactic number, "You Stepped out of a Dream," Berkeley believed he finally had. Women walked up and around a gold-and-silver-adorned sixty-foot-high spiral staircase illuminated by the glittering light from a massive cut-glass chandelier, each girl encased in a filmy shroud only to emerge shimmering in sequins, as if dipped into a pool of silver. "With all due respect to the master," Berkeley proudly reflected, "Ziegfeld could never have done on a stage what we did in that finale."[114]

Only once did Berkeley deviate from his Ziegfeldian roots and use his cinematic aesthetic to create a trenchant piece of social commentary: "Remember My Forgotten Man" (from *Gold Diggers of 1933*). The opening production number of the film features women dressed only in necklaces of gold coins, singing "We're in the Money"; the women "appear as sparkling currency or 'canned goods' to be pried open for pleasure." Then, focusing all his trademark elements onto unemployed men, Berkeley poignantly evokes the lack of self-worth and feelings of failure of homeless veterans of World War I, especially that of the Bonus Marchers who had encamped in Washington, D.C., early in 1932.[115] After Joan Blondell sings the somber ballad, "Remember My Forgotten Man"—recalling the previous year's big hit, "Brother, Can You Spare a Dime?"—Berkeley uses repetition and his parade-of-faces motif to show a seemingly infinite number of gaunt, lean, somber, hungry male faces. In a montage of marching men, Berkeley first shows the soldiers returning victoriously from war; then men in a soup line; then men seemingly just "in line" somewhere, waiting, it's unclear for what. They seem to be waiting in ethereal space, going nowhere, disconnected from the nation.[116]

After the montage of aimless men, the scene dissolves into a dynamo-driven set and the men begin to march, singing a powerful battle cry. The camera pulls back to watch endless ranks of men marching on a huge semicircular three-tiered structure that looks like a cutaway section of the top half of an enormous wheel; the top two levels are arched slightly. As the soldiers march up and back—in contrasting directions, of course, and at variable speeds—from underneath the structure comes a dense phalanx of men, ten across, directly at the camera. The deep male voices gain strength and the polyrhythmic visual effect creates a sense of the potential power of the masses. Yet the large three-tiered structure also suggests machinery at rest, and still the soldiers seem caught in its power. The image projects a plea for a renewal of emphasis on human needs in the face of technological unemployment. But "Remember My Forgotten Man" contains the first and last of Berkeley's social commentary.

In creating a surfeit of images—in current terms, a sensory overload—that rolled nonstop at passive viewers, Berkeley mediated the tensions of the machine age. He combined grandiose dreams of mass-produced possibility with the vertigo of abstract kaleidoscopic patterns to produce lush fantasies mixing machine aesthetics and female abundance. Whereas Ziegfeld was a captain of industry, Berkeley was a creative technocrat. The aesthetic question for Berkeley seemed less, "How has the machine influenced human motion and audience desire?" and more, "How can machines provide us with interesting visual patterns of masses of people?" In the Berkeleyesque, audiences did not see individual bodies so much as masses of bodies in the process of creating, dissolving, and recreating images. But it's Ziegfeld's tradition: "The chorus girl spectacle of film musicals—the cookie-cutter line of leggy chorines—was a standard showstopper element directly inherited from . . . Ziegfeld."[117]

Ironically, Berkeley's favorite dancer was Fred Astaire. But their ideas about dancing (and dance on film) were diametrically opposed, and Berkeley never expressed interest in directing him. He rarely directed dynamic individual actors, singers, or dancers; not until *Lady Be Good* (1941) would he direct a single dancer with a distinctive style (Eleanor Powell) to power one of his grand production numbers. The individuality necessary to tap dancing was contrary to the "Berkeleyesque," whose aesthetic was expressed in the perpetual motion of masses in interlocking patterns.[118]

Tap dance was the Machine Age form that best displayed the rhythmic flow of an *individual* dancer, and is the subject of the next chapter.

TAP DANCERS

RAP BACK AT

THE MACHINE

In a 1941 profile of Fred Astaire, *Life* magazine declared tap the nation's "only native and original dance form," a democratic cultural form with its roots in "the people." *Life* declared Astaire the form's master and tap dance itself as "distinctive a species of U.S. folk art as the cowboy ballad, the Negro spiritual, or swing." Tap is "all about freedom," the dancer Chuck Green claims, "Tap . . . really is jazz itself."[1] Tap is the most individualistic art form of the Machine Age and best reflects the cultural hunger for an energized, revitalized, motorized body-in-motion.

The artistic message of an improvised individual tap routine is one of crucial importance to the rhythmic flow of modernity and human adaptation to change: *be light on your feet.* Tap is a democratic art form—anyone can learn a few steps—but the best tap dancers consider themselves "jazz percussionists who value improvisation and self-expression." Paul Draper, a white concert tap artist, puts it this way: "Being light on one's feet is a desirable characteristic whether one is a dancer or not. For the tap dancer . . . it is essential. A heavy-footed tap dancer is a contradiction in terms, since 'tap' means to strike lightly." The very names of tap steps suggest lightness in motion; every tap dancer builds combinations out of "steps, brushes, hops, slaps, shuffles, cramp-rolls, toe-taps, pull-backs and wings." Superlative tap dancing requires "fast, crisp shuffles, solid flat-footed stomps, staccato heel drops, and graceful cross-overs—all executed with a seemingly effortless lightness."[2] Being light on your feet is itself a modernist attitude, as it assumes an artist unencumbered by outmoded positions.

Just as the streamliner represented a light, fleet version of the nation's foremost symbol of industrialization, the tap dancer was a vision of the industrial body retooled for a rootless, mobile future. Stream-lined design appealed to the popular imagination by transforming heavy, clumsy, dirty, smoke-pouring industrial machinery into a vision of aerodynamic sleek lines emphasizing fast horizontal flow and metallic sheen. Similarly, the tap dancer took the speeded-up machine-driven tempo of life and the metallic crunch of cities and factories and spun it all into a dazzling pyrotechnical display of speed, precision, rhythmic noise, continuity, grace, and power. "Tappers made feet go like trip-hammers," one scholar suggests, and in so doing demonstrated how to "control the rhythms of life"; great tap dancing is "a testament to human competency and potential." Adds the tap artist Sandman Sims, "The greatest essence is time. Everything runs by time. You hear beats in time."[3]

Tap was the dominant professional and commercial dance style of the 1920s and 1930s, and arguably the most popular (and most participatory) American Machine Age art form. Le Corbusier caught the repetition and rhythmic flow in tap: "silent Negroes, as mechanical as a sewing machine, inexhaustible, holding your interest by beating out a rhythmic poem . . . with the soles of their shoes."[4] Marshall Stearns made the techno-dialogic connection long ago: "To his own people, Bill Robinson became a modern John Henry, who instead of driving steel, laid down iron taps."[5]

In this chapter I theorize the tap dancer as the embodiment of the human/machine interface. After reviewing tap's enormous popularity, I analyze the function of the tap aesthetic in historical context; I then do a close reading of Fred Astaire's dance with machines in a musical number entitled "Slap That Bass" from *Shall We Dance?* (1937). In a scene central to my thesis, Astaire challenges the machines of an ocean liner's engine room to an artistic duel—and wins! Much more than Chaplin's escapist vision in *Modern Times*, Astaire's dance heralds the emergence of a humanized machine aesthetic and contains an answer to the question first posed in John Henry: What is a human being *for* now that machines do the work? The scene marks an important turning away from the technological pessimism of the Depression, and represents the triumph of the techno-dialogic in popular culture.

The (Swinging) Men and Women of Steel

Tap dancing merits an examination with regard to Machine Age aesthetics for several reasons. First, tap dancers stylized machine aesthetics within the individual dancing body. Second, its golden age was between the world wars, especially the 1930s. Third, tap's primary message is one of *industrial power under individual control*. Fourth, tap dance brought the soundscape of the streets into American popular culture and onto the body itself. Fifth, the lindy hop picked up on the kind of "flash" steps, acrobatics, energy, and individuality pioneered by the best tap dancers. And finally, as "tap is primarily a swing idiom," so nearly all black big bands carried a tap dancer on tour in the 1930s and 1940s. "Tap . . . is the *master* dance," the dancer Willie Covan declared.[6]

What was the aesthetic objective of the "master dance"? The goal is to make and master "lovely noise," according to the veteran tap dancers Jerry Ames and Jim Siegelman. "[Tap dancers] want to blast out and express themselves in a blatant racket. They want to fight back against the roar of jets, the boom of factories, the whirr of air conditioners, the slamming of doors, the battering of jackhammers . . . [as well as] telephones, stereos, barking dogs, alarm clocks, screaming babies, ambulance sirens, whistling teakettles, banging garbage can lids." The aesthetic challenge for the tap dancer is to make sure "that 'noise' is transformed into a work of art, an aesthetic means of reaching other people."[7] The crisp, metallic rapping of steel taps against wood boards was one of the most popular sounds of industrialization within popular culture. Like swing drummers—with whom they often traded riffs—tap dancers turned the mechanical soundscape into elegant rhythmic patterns, helping to disarm the soullessness of mechanical regularity.

In 1928 a *Vanity Fair* critic discussed the aesthetics of four master tap dancers, the "clowns of extraordinary motion": Fred Astaire, Bill Robinson, Jack Barton, and Jack Donahue. "They have such swiftness and control and crazy grace, they turn their eccentricity into instants of thrill and beauty. . . . [They have] worked up into a full vocabulary of rhythms which swish and gulp, excite both eyes and ears—and humor, too—at running-fire time." Tap's appeal came from the stylization of machine aesthetics: speed ("swiftness . . . at running-fire time"), precision ("control"), flow, smoothness ("crazy grace").[8] Speed and control were so germane to tap that the dancer Pete Nugent judged any dancer incompetent "who couldn't duplicate with their feet any combination of accents you could make with your mouth." Many so-called flash acts were known for their "sheer speed and energy"; Frank Condos admitted that he and his brother were often exhausted after only sixteen bars of a song when "flash" dancing.[9]

The public was so hungry for tap's rhythmic sophistication that dancers performed tap on the radio and on records. Though that is an unthinkably dull concept today, the rhythmic organization of industrial noise was a crucial element of its success. The Nicholas Brothers, Buck and Bubbles, and Bill Robinson all performed their Cotton Club act on live remotes from that club, and were recorded accompanying big bands. The swing-era vocalist Kay Starr began her career as a tap dancer on the radio. Bill Robinson's tap routine to the song "Doin' the New Low Down" was listened to and copied by tap dancers across the country.[10]

Fred Astaire had a radio show, *The Packard Hour*, for which he tapped three or four numbers a show. The most popular routines were the quickest, noisiest, flashiest ones, a result of the studio microphones that kept his feet confined to a small four-foot-by-four-foot dance mat. "The only effective steps for radio were those with a lot of taps close together—a string of ricky-ticky-ticky-tacky-ticky-tacky taps." Growing up in St. Louis in the 1930s, Miles Davis listened to tap dancers on the radio and compared them to drummers: "I loved to look at and listen to tap dancers. They are so close to music in the way they make their taps sound. They are almost like drummers and you can learn a lot from just listening to the rhythms they get from their taps."[11]

By the late 1920s the metallicized sound of tap dance was already integral to Broadway shows, and the noisier the sound of their taps the more popular the routine. Chorus lines were often called upon to "tap on sharply crackling metal strips, on table-tops, and up and down stairs." One routine that graced several 1928 theatrical revues featured "20 young milliners [who] come in with tin hat-boxes, set them down, climb up and tap-dance on top of them." *Vanity Fair* declared tap the only feature of American musical comedy in the 1920s then "perfected and raised to the status of a very genuine, if very comic and contemporary, art."[12]

How popular was tap? Shirley Temple and Fred Astaire were always among the top five box-office draws of the late 1930s, the decade when "tap dancing . . . near[ed] its highest point of artistic achievement and popular acclaim." Between the breakthrough of the talkies in 1927 and the mid-1940s, all actors had to be able to do a few steps. Tap had its own pantheon of stars: James Cagney, George Raft, Ann Sheridan, Eleanor Powell, Ruby Keeler, Ann Miller, Ginger Rogers, Gene Kelly, Donald O'Connor, Buddy Ebsen, Ray Bolger, Mickey Rooney. (Rooney was a second-generation tap star; his father, Pat Rooney, was renowned as one of The Rooneys.) When Eleanor Powell came to New York as an aspiring actress in the late 1920s, the first question every agent asked her was, "Can you tap?" Powell couldn't, and quickly signed up for a package of ten lessons for thirty-five dollars.[13]

Powell's experience provides an excellent case study of the cultural transmission of West African–derived dance aesthetics. Frustrated by her first two tap lessons, Powell realized her ballet training gave her a methodological framework ill-fitted to tap. After the second lesson, her teacher, the legendary tap dancer Jack Donahue, spotted the trouble. "First of all, you're very turned out[;] tap dancing . . . makes all the different muscles *exactly* the opposite from ballet, *exactly opposite*. . . . You're also very aerial; in tap, you've got to get down to the floor." For her next lesson, Donahue brought in "a war surplus belt, the kind that you put bullets in," and filled each side of the belt with two sandbags of five pounds apiece. Powell felt stupid, but "with that belt on I couldn't move off the floor, and I haven't moved off the floor since. That's why I dance so close the ground, because Donahue started me with fundamentals, just as one would do scales on the piano." Tap's aesthetic ground is *literally* the ground, and a dancer makes an artistic statement with hips, legs, and feet more than with the upper body and the space above. The common term "hoofer" highlights tap's earthy, vital, proudly animalistic qualities; as Ruby Keeler claimed, "I'm what you call a hoofer because I work close to the ground."[14]

Tap dance is directly in line with a West African dance aesthetic in which the earth functions as an instrument (a drum, say) for the feet to play. West African dancers face the earth when dancing—often looking straight ahead or at their feet—and stomp, slap, pound, and glide on the earth. As an artistic form, it is "percussive, polyrhythmic . . . and dependent on the interrelationship of the dancer and musician." Tap dancers strive for many of the West African dance ideals identified by Robert Farris Thompson: speed, intensity, "strong expression," flexibility. Such qualities place tap at the opposite pole from ballet, which emphasizes verticality, an erect body, and the ability to "transmute mechanical function . . . into aesthetics." Ballet dancers and Scottish step dancers project upward into the air above them, and must consider how to use the space above them. Tap dancing is more rooted, more from the ground up, and is equally aural and visual. "Tap dance is percussive rhythms and the floor is the instrument which is played by the feet."[15]

The philosophical difference between tap and ballet lies in the difference between West African–derived and European-derived aesthetics: "One expresses the self, the other perfection."[16] Tap enabled dancers to both assimilate and resist the industrial basis of Machine Age America by rapping metallically back at the soundscape with revitalized individual expression. According to Sandman Sims, the tap dancer is "a free man" who shows his soul when dancing. Paul Draper describes tap as "your whole self, your way of living, and your expression of that way." The purpose of tap dance is "to make up a dance in terms of your own personality, your own dancing style and your own reactions to the world around you." Chuck Green expressed the sentiment this way: "You are free when you're doing rhythm dancing. The world is yours. . . . The rest—ballet, modern dance—you must do what the teacher tells you." Green made up a concise lyric to express this belief: "I got no maps . . . on my taps."[17] Like jazz, tap is an art form in which the individual artist improvises personalized statements (solos) within a set of artistic rules and concepts.

Many adult Euro-Americans must have felt as Shirley Temple did in *The Littlest Colonel* (1935), when she demanded imperiously of the sixty-year-old Bill Robinson after he performed his signature stair dance: "I wanna do that." The actor and dancer Gene Kelly once told the child-actress that every time one of her movies came out, new registrations for his family's chain of dance studios quadrupled. But only a child could publicly declare her desire to learn the secret of a relaxed, expressive, flow-centered art form embodied by a black man; an adult white actor or actress could not (and did not) show desire and envy for black artistic display. White adults never tap-danced together in 1930s movies with black adults. Fred Astaire's famous seventeen-minute tribute to "Bojangles of Harlem" (in *Swing Time* [1935]) is perhaps the most egregious example of tap segregation. First, Astaire blacks up; second, he performs a tribute more in the style of John W. Bubbles than Bill Robinson (as if all blacks dance the same); third, his dancing partners are silhouettes thrown on the wall—literally, shadows of "real" African American dancers—and a chorus of white women.[18]

The demands of southern theater owners prevented mixed dancing from appearing in any Hollywood studio picture. Instead, Robinson, Bubbles, the Nicholas Brothers, and the Berry Brothers often appeared in Hollywood films in routines not integral to the plot; black dancers were framed as guest variety acts, displaying rapid-fire acrobatic moves underneath big minstrel grins. In this way, studios were able to simply excise these sequences for southern theaters, which refused to show African American performers except in menial roles, such as those Bill Robinson played in Shirley Temple's movies (often set in the Civil War South). As Jacqui Malone points out, "Black dancers were depicted as excelling in creative energy but mindless."[19]

Tap Aesthetics and the Machine Age

Tap is an artistic synthesis of Irish clog dance, Scottish step dancing, African dance, African American buck dancing, and the American Machine Age soundscape; it was as popular among Irish dancers as black dancers at the turn of the century.[20] Jig and clog dancing contain complex footwork done in fast rhythms that allow for both improvisation and joyful noise-making (for example, the jig is performed to a triple rhythm). In this tradition, the sounds made on the ground are distinct and precise: no gliding, sliding, shuffling, or heel slaps. African Americans admired such dancing in nineteenth-century cities, where they lived with the Irish, and then added the qualities of African movement, bringing "torso fluidity, bending, and crouching" to tap, and allowing for more undulation through the hips and for full-body movement. They also added sliding, shuffling, and syncopation. Finally, buck dancing brought to tap a more percussive use of the heels in order to create expressive rhythmic sequences out of the contact of metal taps with the ground.[21]

Modern tap thus emerged from a synthesis of two separate trunk lines: jig and clog dance on the one hand, and African American performance aesthetics and rhythms on the other. The first professional American dancers were Irish; jig and clog dancers were common on the American stage by 1840. The artistic focus of these dancers was their speed and dexterity below the knee and the rapid manipulation of calves and ankles for distinct heel-to-toe movement. Arms were held close to the side, and the upper half of the body "stiffly erect" (still true, as in *Riverdance*). The first "American" dancers in this style were white (often Irish) minstrel performers. In the 1880s a British audience forced the American clog dancer Johnny Queen to pass his dancing shoes around for inspection, suspicious that his "phenomenally fast" dancing was either an optical illusion or mechanically assisted.[22] By then, the word "jig" had changed into a generic term for any African American dance (a backhanded recognition of black dance skill), and the term later became a generic epithet for an African American man.[23]

Until the 1890s, tap lacked metal taps and "*swing* in the jazz sense." There was no syncopation in the steps or the music, and improvisation via rapid tempo shifts was not essential to performance. African Americans grounded tap, speeded it up, added slides, and began to creatively imagine rapid rhythmic sequences as set solo pieces. Until 1900 or so, black tap dancers stayed in one place until King Rastus Brown began "travelin" (moving) across the stage. As tap evolved, dancers developed roles for individual parts of the body to effect more precise rhythmic communication. Bill Robinson brought tap up on the toes; Fred Astaire pioneered the use of arm movements and brought ballet movements to tap. John W. Bubbles created "rhythm tap" which brought a swing-time flow to tap dance, cutting the 2/4 rhythm of 1920s jazz to a smoother 4/4. Bubbles used his whole body, not just his legs, and he brought the weight, manipulation, and effect of the heels into play.[24]

Both white and black performers synthesized modern tap out of a blend of folk traditions that was then melding and overlapping among professional dancers in minstrelsy, vaudeville, and burlesque. John W. Bubbles knew the difference in cultural styles and audience preferences, and danced accordingly. In performing at both Harlem's Lafayette Theater and the Ziegfeld Follies in 1931, he danced "the same steps in both places . . . but with a different feeling." In Harlem, "you had to swing," and he danced "loose and rhythmic . . . flop and fling-flang." But "downtown," white audiences liked precise articulation, and he danced "simple and distinct."[25]

Tap's synthesis emerged due to its stylization of "the tempo, [and] the excitement of the Machine Age," according to the tap historian Rusty Frank. The revving up of American society resulted in tap dancers taking the industrial soundscape onto their bodies: "The clickety-clack of electric streetcars, the crash and pound of the subway, the riveting cry of buildings going up and coming down—all these modernistic sounds were echoed in the rhythms pouring out of thousands of hoofers' feet."[26] The combination of metallic rhythmic flow and tuxedoed elegance transmuted urban noise into urbane promise. Tap dance was a public expression of a new relationship between bodies and machines.

Willie Covan of the Four Covan Brothers was a crossover tap star in vaudeville who built his personal style on the mechanical rhythms of Chicago's streetcars. As a child of five in the first decade of the twentieth century, Covan used to wake up before dawn and sit outside on the curb: "From about five-thirty to six A.M., the city was absolutely silent except for one thing. The streetcars. I used to sit . . . and listen to those street-cars—*tchuk, tchuk, tchuk, tchuk, tchuket, tchuk, tchuk*—that clickety sound, that's where I first started hearin' it. That rhythm. That's when I first started dancin'. I took it right from the streetcars. . . . I never took a lesson in my life. . . . I taught myself from that streetcar in Chicago."[27]

Machine rhythms were integral to tap's appeal. Fred Astaire claimed that one of his most popular tap steps for radio was "a half-falling, half-standing flash [step] that sounded like a riveting machine." King Rastus Brown was said to have imitated the sound and power of a train through precise rhythmic tap composition. The signature step of the white tap dancer Frank Condos was a difficult wing step done with five taps that "come so fast—ta-ta-ta-ta-ta—it sounds like a machine gun." Astaire also performed to the rhythm of machine guns in *Top Hat* (1935).[28]

Like jazz musicians, black tap dancers believe they must be able as artists to stylize any tempo, sound, or rhythm. "We must learn to dance to anything, even if the tempo is odd," claimed Leon Collins, one of the few dancers able to keep pace with Charlie Parker's blazingly fast alto saxophone runs. Sandman Sims agreed: "I can duplicate any kind of sound I hear. I can do it with my feet. It's an ear thing; you hear it and you can do it." Again like jazz musicians, tap dancers embodied the swing aesthetic of *controlled power:* one reason for the disrespect of tap, artistically speaking, is because dancers make it look effortless. "People don't really know what tap dancing is," Sims explains, "they think it's just jump and hit some steps and make sound."[29]

Tap developed in touch with urban streets, literally "tapping" the new American tempo at the source. Black men (and a few women) often started their tap education literally on street corners, watching—and then participating in—"challenge dances" in American cities. The core elements of West African–derived musical practice were provided on the corner: hand-clapping to set the beat, vocal encouragement, competitive signifying, the importance of creating personalized combinations of rhythmic patterns. In the documentary *No Maps on My Taps* (1979), the veteran dancers Sandman Sims and Lon Chaney debated who would win a challenge dance between Bill Robinson and John W. Bubbles. Later in the film, we witness a phone conversation between Bubbles (then nearly eighty years old) and his closest artistic heir, Chuck Green (then nearly sixty). Bubbles gruffly asks Green if he has created any new steps lately. When Green stutters in response, Bubbles reminds him that creating new tap steps is the only worthwhile challenge and achievement in the art. Bubbles's tone is one of brusque affection, as to a son; Green is deferent—even shy and worshipful—in this discussion between mentor and disciple.

A striking dance sequence called "Industrialization" in the Broadway show *Bring in 'da Noise, Bring in 'da Funk* (1995) highlights the historical dialogue of tap dance and factory rhythms. The lights go up on a giant scaffold that looks like a cross between an assembly-line work station and a huge jungle jim. Loud, clanking, industrial rhythms seem to emanate from a steam-shrouded background of spinning wheels, steel pipes, and conveyor belts; it slowly dawns on the audience that all this noise is coming from the workers themselves, who "bang, beat, scrape chains, and swing [their tools] faster and faster . . . all to create the impression of a steam-filled factory in high drive." Like hand-clapping, these accompanying rhythms serve to launch each worker into a solo, each expressing himself with and against the factory rhythms. The scene suggests that within historical memory, tap emerged in response to the factory soundscape; the episode is clearly set between the world wars.[30]

Yet even tap-dance impresarios and educators devalued the cultural form and its creators. Rosalind Wade, the director of the BBC Dancing Daughters, a British tap-dance troupe, declared that both clog dancing and tap dancing were folk expressions created in response to separate periods of industrialization. "Just as the clog dances originated among the industrial workers [of England, Scotland and Ireland], so the negro cotton pickers . . . developed . . . [an] equally characteristic dance routine, which was gradually elaborated, and became the basis of American dancing." Nearly all the progressive characteristics of modern tap that Wade named—increased hip motion, smoother rhythms, "individual personality" in dance, "freedom of movement and grace of muscular expression"—stem from Afrodiasporic dance aesthetics. "Tap Dancing . . . is entirely a product of modern times," Wade declared confidently, duly noting the tap innovations of the late 1920s, especially the "comedy and personality . . . injected into the foot movements."[31]

Although Wade claimed that "colored dancers have undoubtedly revolutionized the dancing world," she dismissed their contribution within the common folk/fine-art paradigm of the time. Blacks had "an idea or basic routine, which the Western world . . . [has] gradually improve[d] beyond recognition"; in other words, African Americans had simply provided the raw material for European artistry. She compared the energetic intensity behind black tap dancing to religious fervor, and suggested that only ecstatic possession could explain the speed, precision, and passion of African American tap dancers. Wade claimed it was the European and Euro-American performers who transformed tap into an art that is "necessarily *the work of an individual*." Black dancers, apparently, were "quite unconscious of their own movements in the dance," although only a "trained observer could catch even a portion of the dance with sufficient accuracy to explain and reproduce the steps."[32]

John W. Bubbles showed just how conscious he was of his steps in recalling one of his youthful tap triumphs. In 1967 Bubbles recalled dancing the following routine to the song "Mammy o'Mine," at the Palace Theater in Louisville, Kentucky, in 1920: "I'd do a continued backslide on one foot, then a rhythm turn, then a double over the top, then a trench step called the figure eight, then forward and backward and to each side. . . . [Then] front two bars, back two bars, go to my left two bars, go to my right two bars. Then an over-the-foot step that had a continuous falling action, then a forward slide cakewalk, and go off with it!" Bubbles went off stage, came back to take a bow, and motioned to the orchestra "to whoop it up and . . . [I started again] in gallop tempo—da di, da di, doo-di, doo, di! I was gone, do you hear? I was gone!" Nor did Bubbles disclaim the contribution of white dancers in his proud development of an individual artistic style. "I took the white boys' steps and the colored boys' steps and mixed 'em all together so you couldn't tell 'em, white or colored. I made it *me*."[33]

If tap dancers spent their lives in artistic production, why have they been excluded from the canon of Machine Age modern artists? Eleanor Powell "lived and breathed dance" for three years; she and Fred Astaire both declared they "dreamed" their routines. The veteran tap dancer Jimmy Slyde spent many years teaching and performing tap in Europe in the 1970s. "Everybody there wants to tap dance. They see it as an American product, just like they look at jazz as an American cultural thing."[34] Why, again, has a cultural form valorized by Europeans as distinctively American—and as art—been dishonored in its own land? There are two obvious answers: the love and theft of black culture and Euro-American anxiety concerning African American influences.

Tap and Aesthetic Racism

Tap dance was so popular between the world wars that it was taught in public schools, dance academies, community centers, and even at the college level. More than three dozen tap manuals were published between 1920 and 1947, most of them written by female instructors in physical education departments of major universities (for example, the University of Chicago, New York University, and Teachers College at Columbia University).[35] Educators thought tap invigorated the muscles of the lower body, resulting, according to the physical director of Michigan public schools, in "more spring in the feet and . . . [an] ability to move quickly from one foot to another without loss of balance." There were commercial tap schools throughout the nation; one survey by a nationwide dance school showed that "interest in tap and step dancing . . . [had] increased to nearly 50% of . . . ballet work.[36] Taught and practiced at community centers and YMCAs, in settlement organizations and society groups, tap was valued as a pedagogical method for acquiring artistic grace and balance and as a tool for teaching creativity and motor coordination.[37]

Why did this cultural impetus leave such a poor legacy? Here are the key factors, according to Sharon Arslanian's excellent study of tap in education: cultural elitism, the continued disrespect of African American cultural forms, the valorization of modern dance in the late 1930s, the demise of tap in Hollywood films after 1945, and unacknowledged battles between European-derived and African-derived cultural production. A tap dancer herself, Arslanian analyzed nineteen tap manuals and interviewed all the living writers. These teachers said they wrote their manuals in response to widespread popular demand for tap instruction in part stimulated by tap in 1930s movies.[38] A short analysis of their rhetoric will help us understand the significance of Fred Astaire as the whitefaced John Henry of the swing era.

Most of the manuals referred to tap as an articulation of "the modern," and the authors stated as their mission the renewal of academic interest in grace, relaxation, physical dexterity, and body-centered joy.[39] "[Tap] is more popular, more spontaneously enjoyed, than many other activities in the physical education program," noted Mary Jane Hungerford in her groundbreaking 213-page tap history and methodology, *Creative Tap Dancing* (1939), and "it is also more responsive to the current of the times."[40] But these instructors believed that modern dance was the serious art form while tap was a simple, accessible, folk form—yet useful for teaching rhythm and grace. Many of the tap lessons were for group dances (not solos), a reflection of their interest in folk forms of dance rather than the individual human response which was tap's cultural stock-in-trade. Their recognition of tap artistry was at arm's length, and effaced the black contribution.[41]

Edith Ballwebber's *Illustrated Tap Rhythms and Routines* (1932) was one of the few manuals to explain the renewed importance of rhythm in Machine Age art. A University of Chicago professor, Ballwebber recognized tap as an artistic expression of rhythmic genius and identified its African American dance aesthetics, though not as such. Tap answered the "ever urgent demand of the rhythmic pulse," and she singled out the "synchronization of music and steps" as the crucial factor in creating routines. This combination gives the "feeling of dancing first with and then against the music," she wrote, in a nod to the influence of jazz rhythms on American dance. Ballwebber described a "rhythm buck" as a dance with a "blues quality," strong syncopation and lots of room for improvisation in the "breaks." Perhaps these coded terms for black dance were recognizable to her audience, but more likely they signaled readers that tap was a folk form and not art.[42]

I will use Anne Schley Duggan's *Tap Dances* (1932) as representative both because it was republished in 1947 due to popular demand and because its structure, strengths, and weaknesses are similar to those of the other manuals. Each chapter carries a set of instructions to plan a group dance for a class. Each routine contains the sheet music for the accompanying song, costume suggestions, a tap routine marked out in steps (complete with illustrations and instructions), and hints for performance. Each has a quick sketch of tap history. Duggan wrote that tap emerged from the Irish jig and Scotch clog dancing, as well as "other" folk traditions. She differentiated between Scotch-Irish clogging as a folk dance and modern American-style tap dancing as a commercialized art form (to the detriment of the latter). For Duggan, tap was easily the "more professionalized and intricate type of dancing . . . [with] emphasis . . . upon the variety of rhythms secured through rapid manipulation of the feet."[43]

Tap did not have much of a folk quality, according to Duggan, who distinguished modern tap by its "syncopated [time] . . . and a great many more tap sounds . . . achieved to each measure of music than those . . . [of the] slower, more even rhythms of clogging." Yet despite such references to polyrhythms and fast steps, she makes no overt references to genres such as levee dancing or buck dancing as African American. Tap was a modern cultural form that apparently "jes grew" out of nowhere, to use Ishmael Reed's code for white effacement of black cultural forms. Or, in Duggan's words, "To say . . . *exactly* where tap dancing begins and ends is a difficult matter."[44]

One image in Duggan's book neatly sums up the theft involved in the effacement of the artistic, aesthetic, and performative contributions of African Americans. The opening page of chapter two features only a photo, a title, and an epigraph. The chapter explains the tap steps necessary for a presentation of the song "Oh Lemuel," which would be appropriate for a "Buck [dance] for Solo, Duet or Group." The only sentence on the page states the most important skill required for this dance: "Dancers should feel characteristic rhythmic movements of the American negro."[45]

The photograph that takes up two-thirds of the page features a strutting man and woman in the midst of these characteristic movements. The young couple are dressed in minstrel-derived plantation costumes. The man wears overalls and the woman is dressed in the stereotypical garb of a southern mammy (bandanna, long dark skirt, white apron). The couple faces the reader in profile while walking off-page to the right, using the toe and heel positions of step four of the instructions. (See fig. 9.) The man has his hips thrust forward and his arms thrown back, perhaps to display the perceived looser walk of African Americans as opposed to the erect torso emphasized by Anglo-Americans. The man's right arm is back behind him, his left arm at shoulder-level, and his wide smile is outlined by white lips. The woman holds her arms in the same position as the man except that her right arm holds her skirt up slightly.

The man and woman are both blacked up: that is, they are white. The irony is almost overwhelming: apparently African American dancers were the wrong models for even their own dances. Their presence would, presumably, lower the prestige of the dance and thus the comfort level of white Americans who were excited to learn this form; photos of black performers might send the message to "emulate these people." Dancers *should* emulate the kinesthetic movements of "the American negro," Duggan writes, but somehow without integrating any of the culture or experience of African Americans. So an aspiring tap dancer must learn to "perform blackness" (to use W. T. Lhamon's apt phrase) but make sure never to integrate that blackness—by which I mean *the African-derived cultural heritage and the historical experience of African Americans in the United States*. To perform such "characteristic movements" without integrating any of the cultural values contained in

2: OH LEMUEL

Buck for Solo, Duet or Group

Dancers should feel characteristic rhythmic movements of the American negro.

OH LEMUEL

Toe-Heels in "A"
of Step IV

9

Figure 9. "Oh Lemuel" routine, page from Anne Schley Duggan, *Tap Dances*, 1932.

those movements reflects the kind of cultural schizophrenia this book addresses.[46]

Duggan captures a few core racial tensions in American history in these few pages. In her historical sketch, she effaces African American artistic creation. Then using the evolutionary model familiar at the time, she praises the genius of African American rhythmic movement in the most backhanded way possible. According to Arslanian, such disrespect for African American culture and artistry has left a legacy of "cultural appropriation in combination with denial and distortion of the same culture, and its contributions."[47]

For the academics who wrote these tap manuals, female modern dancers such as Martha Graham and Hanya Holm exemplified bodily control and, in so doing, recaptured the lost classical integration of mind, body, and spirit. The modern dancer's expressive aesthetic was "serious, tragic, austere"; in contrast, according to these manuals, tap imparted movements lacking any conscious content and provided only physical training. To be a good tap dancer, according to Duggan, is to continue the blackface tradition and simply let yourself go: cork up, imitate the African American rhythmic movements, and discover a new world of wild, uninhibited, primitive regression. The credit for tap thus became attached not to the dancer-as-artist—as in modern dance—but to the Euro-American educator.[48] Such an ideology followed in the footsteps (literally) of the dance stars Vernon and Irene Castle, who "educat[ed] Americans" during the 1910s on how to dance gracefully to African American rhythms. A generation before these manuals the Castles disseminated social dance for mass consumption, bringing "order out of the chaos [of black dance] without too much loss of the essential vitality of the movement."[49]

As Cole Porter wrote in the hit "Anything Goes" (1934), "day's night today, black's white today." Duggan's photo of corked-up white dancers performing "the characteristic movements of the American Negro" makes Porter's whimsical lyric almost literal. Black was white with or without blackface: black cultural forms had become important survival technology for white Americans in the Machine Age. But modern dance won the pedagogical war; by 1943 there was not a single tap course in the nation, and tap was displaced on Broadway in ballet-derived musical numbers.[50] Aesthetic racism excluded African American dancers and dances from being hailed as cultural carriers of a modernist American aesthetic.

Let's Face the Machine and Dance:
Fred Astaire in "Slap That Bass"

The most popular individual male body-in-motion of the 1930s was Fred Astaire, a dancer who synthesized tap, ballet, and ballroom into one of the most admired artistic styles of the century.[51] Astaire absorbed the artistic, aesthetic, and social traditions of African American dance from, among others, the choreographer Buddy Bradley, John W. Bubbles, and his close friend and choreographer Hermes Pan. At the height of his artistic powers and popularity in 1937, Astaire updated the story of John Henry at the culminating moment of the Machine Age. Only this time, man beats the machine by taking its rhythms onto the body.

On a back lot at RKO Studios during the shooting of *Shall We Dance?* Astaire passed a cement mixer and began to dance against the mechanical rhythm. Hermes Pan later claimed that Astaire created a spontaneous, well-structured tap routine right there on the spot, a version of which would appear in the film. As it happens, the film's director, Mark Sandrich, had recently returned from an ocean voyage with a similar idea after a tour of the ship's engine room. Sandrich was a methodical director, and in fact had a science background and had been a math major in college. "Every camera angle, every movement of the actors was planned before he came on the set. . . . [H]e sought ideas wherever he could find them." When Astaire suggested a dance with machines in the movie, Sandrich enthusiastically agreed.[52] The dance was integrated into the four-and-a-half minute musical number, George and Ira Gershwin's "Slap That Bass"; it is the film's first song after two extended tap sequences and occurs nearly twenty minutes into the movie.

Astaire's Anglo-American screen persona was ideal for Depression-era America. The characters he played in the 1930s were often temporarily broke or economically marginal: he plays a gambler who's lost all his money in *Follow the Fleet* and a transient hustler avoiding marriage in *Swing Time*. But even broke he looked sharp, and he combined an aristocratic front with everyday plain good looks and an urbane improvisatory spirit and wit. "He borrowed the elegance and style of Britain's aristocracy and America's wealthy and added the raffishness of vaudeville and the race track," one biographer wrote. "Beneath it . . . [was] his native shyness, his eagerness to succeed and please." In 1936, the novelist Graham Greene wrote in *The Spectator* that British audiences "considered Astaire one of their own."[53]

One function of the song-and-dance man in 1930s films was to re-
solve and mediate class differences in his role as well-dressed entertainer.[54] Astaire combined tuxedoed elegance with what the film scholar
Robert Sklar calls "a touch of the gutter"—an essential for Depression-
era male screen idols.[55] In real life, Astaire often cursed in public with
wit and verve, and he visited crime scenes to watch cops in action. James
Cagney once told him, "You know, Freddie, you've got a touch of the
hoodlum in you."[56] Similarly, tap dance helped Astaire mediate ballet
and jazz traditions; ballet aesthetics center on the upper body, those of
tap on the lower body. Graham Greene astutely observed that, in terms
of lower-body kinesthetics, "[only] Chaplin and Fred Astaire . . . have
really learned to act volubly from the knees down."[57] He didn't then
need to add "among white men."

I want to stress the importance of African American vernacular dance
to Astaire's style. According to Hermes Pan, his distinctive tap style came
from both "dropping his heels" and his predilection for "after-beats
and broken rhythm." Pan recalled that white tap dancers in New York in
the 1920s and 1930s danced on their toes and made light, delicate
sounds—"tip-tap," he called it. The style was "mechanical, but very intricate." Pan grew up in Tennessee, where the style was faster, more percussive, and used the whole foot. "I used to dance on my flat foot and
heel, which Fred does. . . . Fred and I used to call it 'gutbucket.'" The
first move Pan ever showed Astaire "was a broken-rhythm thing, and that
appealed to him. . . . [I]t's a black tradition, and I learned it from the
blacks in Tennessee."[58]

The musical concepts of "after-beats and broken rhythm" are both
African American; scholars credit John Bubbles as the first to drop his
heels. Bubbles claims to have given Astaire one dance lesson (for $400!)
in 1920, when the team of Adele and Fred Astaire were rising musical
comedy stars on Broadway. Astaire mentions only Bill Robinson in his
autobiography (and only in passing), which may be why scholars rarely
cite any black influence. But in a 1961 letter to Marshall Stearns, Astaire
named Bubbles as a dancer he had "always admired . . . tremendously."
Cryptically he claims to have "had some interesting meetings in dance"
with Bubbles and wrote that Bubbles had been "an inspiration to many
tap dancers." As for failing to cite Bubbles's influence in his autobiography, Astaire thought he had written of it but said it somehow "must
have fallen out in last minute editing . . . which I regret."[59]

Now to set up the human vs. machine challenge dance of "Slap That

Bass." Astaire plays a Philadelphia dancer named Pete Peters masquerading as Petrov, a famous Russian ballet dancer. Stricken with love at first sight for musical-comedy star Linda Keene (Ginger Rogers), Astaire is rebuffed in his attempts to court her. He follows Keene to England on an ocean liner, and the plot turns on Rogers's initial dislike for Astaire and his attempts to court her through dance. The usual complications from their work-lives—in this case, the press—keep the couple apart, giving Keene a chance to mock "Petrov" for his European ostentation and standoffish ways.

In the scene before the challenge dance, Astaire's manager, played by the veteran character actor Edward Everett Horton, is seen lounging on the upper deck in playboy ease and comfort. Horton's character watches a young male instructor teach ballet moves to a class of attractive young women while he sits in a smoking jacket surrounded by six bathing beauties attending to his every need. This character is a Depression-era buffoon—the indolent rich man who's out of touch—and the function of the scene is to locate Astaire outside of upper-class social and artistic conventions. Astaire is not to be found in any of the expected elite zones of the ship; he is not restricted by class, space, or rules. There is a suggestion, too, that ballet concerns the display of young, shapely women in tights for the entertainment and "enlightenment" of upper-class men.[60]

Where's Astaire? Ever on the lookout for ways to enrich his art, the adventurous dance-explorer is in the ship's engine room, meditating on some new dance moves suggested by machines and African Americans. As in the more recent *Titanic* (1997), the contrast lies between the wealthy young man being serviced by the ship's servants and the fun-loving young man displaying joie de vivre for the audience. As Horton enjoys the highbrow life on the upper deck, the egalitarian artist-type Astaire discovers the raw (primitive) folk life going on below decks, in the bowels of the ship.

The ship's engine room is a vast, gleaming open space of waxed floors seemingly about fifty feet long and with thirty-foot-high ceilings. The room is half-filled with shiny chrome and white ceramic machines that look more like the streamlined kitchen appliances of the day than a ship's engines. It is a fantasy of an engine room, "spacious, shiny, immaculately white, and preposterously unreal." Many of the smaller machines feature Art Deco touches: a motif of speed lines crowns the top of several unidentifiable devices, and chrome and white stripes are accentuated in geometric combinations of arcs and circles.[61]

The three machines that Astaire dances against churn their rhythms in the upper part of the stage set, fifteen feet or so above ground level. On the viewer's left, the first machine is an actual crankshaft for a ship's engine, albeit for a much smaller ship.[62] Three seven-foot-high vertical connecting rods rotate continuously on a platform five feet above this upper level. The second machine features three triphammers that produce a march rhythm. The machine has no ship-related functions, and is shown only in shadow; light is projected from underneath, and the viewer is separated by a six-foot-tall plate glass window. In real life, this machine might be used to open and close steam valves in sequence, but the small, tinny beat suggests it is being hand-cranked. The third machine (on the viewer's right) is a small belt-driven device that might be used for weaving fabric at an individual workstation. Belt drives are far too small to run an ocean liner, but the value of this machine may lie in the fact that something like it was familiar to American workers.[63]

The opening shot of "Slap That Bass" is a middle shot of the crankshaft, accompanied by the sound of its rhythms. For seven or eight seconds, that's all we hear—the crankshaft's connecting rods pumping out a repetitive mechanical rhythm. The camera pulls back and down to reveal five or so members of a black janitorial crew wiping the handrails on a set of steps leading downward to the engine room's ground level. The workers quickly set up a syncopated chant to accompany the work. In resonant bass tones, three workers begin to chant, "boomboom . . . buh-boom-boom, boom-boom . . . buh-boom-boom." Two of the workers wipe the handrails in perfect cadence to the pistons. Here we have, in twenty seconds of film, the techno-dialogic: black workers absorbing machine rhythms into a tradition of work song to lighten (and collectivize) the drudgery of menial work.[64]

The camera then pans down a level (five steps or so) where a second crew sets up a higher-pitched antiphonal response to the first crew. Within the chant, the first crew accentuates the strong beats while the second crew works the weak beats. Five seconds later the camera pans down to the ground level of the engine room where seven or eight more workers have formed an impromptu jazz combo. An upright bass and makeshift drums form the rhythm section; a trumpeter and tenor saxophonist make up the front line; the other four workers function as background singers. White movie audiences of the time would have assumed these were stereotypically lazy black workers, happy-go-lucky even at their dead-end jobs, imbued with the childish gift of joy and rhythm.

The work-song rhythm then fades into the background and is replaced by the groove of the rhythm section. The drummer plays on a fifty-five-gallon oil drum whose cover features the circular patterns of Deco moderne. His arm movements are mirrored by a spring-driven rocker-arm above him; the mechanical arm may have been used to regulate steam, but probably had no function in the engine room (except to add a visual parallel to the drummer's motions). The mechanism looks something like an industrial-sized electric mixer and is shown in parallel action with the drummer—the two rhythmic engines of American musical energies.

The camera moves slightly right and locates Astaire watching the combo appreciatively and intently: his hands tap the tops of his thighs, his left leg keeps the beat. Astaire does not look on as a spectator, as a raffish rich man slumming with the working class, but as someone trying to learn something. One worker mimes a scat solo into a fake trumpet in the style of the then-bestselling a cappella group, the Mills Brothers. A trumpet player and tenor saxophonist sit opposite the rhythm section and pretend to play a snappy riff that is clearly overdubbed.

The scene's minstrel elements now come into play as one of the janitorial workers, played by Dudley Dickerson, steps up to sing. With bulging eyes and an overwide smile, the nameless worker begins "Slap That Bass," a song about escaping the world's troubles through the rhythm of an upright bass. Dickerson first picks up the initial work chant, changing the "boom boom/buh-boom-boom" to "zoom zoom/zuh-zoom zoom." The first line after "zoom zoom" is "the world is in a mess," and the singer shakes his head at this thought, a minstrel gesture that might translate as "damned if I can understand the world." With the other workers providing backup vocals, Dickerson names several problems in the world, but then casts his worries away: "happiness/is not a riddle/when I'm listening/to that great big fiddle."

After two verses, and more than a minute into the scene, Astaire suddenly stands up, breaking the rhythm of the action both visually and aurally. The camera immediately places him front and center, framing his body as the agent of order here. The first thing Astaire does is command the bassist to keep the rhythm going: "slap that bass/keep it going/slap that bass." The bassist responds by exaggerating the "sambo" mask of childish happiness and unconcern. The other workers put on big smiles as well—emphasizing the minstrel aspects of his performance—as if to show the white "boss" how well music dispels gloom.

Astaire then picks up the "zoom zoom" phrase and repeats it several times; "zoom zoom" now comes to represent rhythmic joy in the Machine Age. The rest of the lyric suggests that rhythmic engagement is a crucial element for adaptation to modernity, even for authoritarian leaders: "Even dictators/would be better off/if they zoom zoomed now and then/today you can see/the happiest men/ . . . all got rhythm." Astaire sings all but these last three words in a standing, static position. But when he sings the phrase "all got rhythm," he bends at the knees and quickly soft-shoes to the viewer's right. This action is a diluted version of the "get-down" move, a physical gesture of crouching at the waist and bending the knee that historians assert carries a coded African retention signifying vital health of all the body's limbs.[65]

All of this musical grounding is necessary to launch Astaire into his solo challenge dance with the three machines. But first he (or the director Sandrich) makes an artistic miscalculation by cutting out the swing music and the contributions of the black workers. Slowly Astaire backs away from the workers and the insistent rhythm fades into an orchestral arrangement; meanwhile the drama of the song and its message dissipates. As the swing rhythm dissolves into generic orchestral music, Astaire is left foundering without rhythmic power. As one Astaire scholar points out, the first half of the dance sequence is unsuccessful, featuring only "fragmentary ideas . . . [and] flowery 'balletic' arm positions which Astaire hits and then pointedly abandons."[66] It's just Astaire and a huge gleaming wax floor, and the space swallows up his dance moves; he dances aimlessly around the white ceramic machines.[67]

The function of the first part of Astaire's solo routine seems to be to put distance—literally, to put space—between the refined Astaire and the black "folk." The African American workers are cut out in one shot: while backing away, Astaire tosses his sports jacket away (to the viewer's left) during a sweeping, balletic turn. With that cut, the black workers are socially and culturally (and cinematically) eviscerated. Their contribution to building the groove that Astaire commandeered has been effaced; the work song, the antiphonal response, and the syncopated song chant are all gone.

Astaire thus founders in the first half of the dance sequence because the workers no longer provide music or dance, support or handclaps, context or subtext. The work chant, the minstrel vocal, the swing rhythm—all are now framed as "folk" forms swallowed by the "fine" art of Gershwin's sophisticated harmonies. The dance has moved from a minstrelized African American performance model to a Hollywood model, with Astaire now the embodiment of all that historical rhythm-work encapsulated in the opening two minutes. He appears to be casting about for ideas—he literally pirouettes about—when we see him hit on an artistic solution. He quickly dances toward the steps leading up to the level of the machines.

With a precise hip vault worthy of a gymnast, Astaire swings himself up and over the handrail to a complete stop in front of the crankshaft. Suddenly the music stops. Astaire simply watches the rods and listens, nodding thoughtfully in time with the mechanical rhythms; in effect, he allows the pistons to take a solo break.[68] As he did at first with the black workers, Astaire watches and listens, engaging the machine's groove, getting this new rhythm into his bones. After ten seconds or so, he cautiously begins to echo the piston rhythms with quiet, soft-shoe taps: he is ready to dance with the machine.

First he matches the machine's precise, rigid rhythms in taps, mirroring its mechanical pattern. Then suddenly he bursts into a blurringly fast double-time step that quickly establishes who's the master here: *the human being has more energy than the machine.* After pausing for a second to allow the machine's rhythm to reestablish itself—and give him a rhythm to dance against—he begins a brilliant series of spins, falling steps, dropped-heel percussive effects, and heel-to-toe taps. Again Astaire stops to listen to the pistons' rhythm; he then mocks its rigid beats by marching stiffly, making exaggerated robotic limb movements, and putting on a Frankenstein-like expression.

He then dances over to the second machine, whose triphammers make a tinny, riffling sound like an old adding machine. Astaire mocks this rhythm with the face of a soldier in a fife-and-drum band as his legs march to the light snare-drum pattern. He again bursts out of the metronomic rhythms with a set of spins. Another message: a human being is more *expressively* energetic than a machine. Unlike a machine, a human body can display grace, elegance, humor, surprise, spontaneity, and rhythmic control.

In a full analysis of this dance, John Mueller misreads Astaire's intentions because he lacks an understanding of African American aesthetics. He finds the tap routine as unsuccessful as the balletic sequence: "Astaire, in front of various chugging machines, performs tap passages relating to their beat or supplies silly visual imitations of their workings." The key phrases here are "relating to their beat" and "visual imitations of their workings."[69] Astaire is not *imitating* the machines, but parodying their rhythms; in black vernacular terms, he *signifies* upon the machines' rhythmic "statements." In relating to their beat he establishes his ability to perform the machines' moves, while the machines cannot meet his challenge; Astaire's facial expressions make these intentions clear. Furthermore, in a jam session—or challenge dance—it is a common practice for the superior artist to dance (or play) back the style of each of the previous competitors before beginning his or her own improvisational statement.[70]

Astaire's next move occurs within such a framework. Having established mastery over the machines, he launches into a dynamic set of airplane spins up a ramp that ascends to an alcove attached to the ceiling of the engine room. It is as if he has beaten the machines in a cutting contest and can now use the remaining time to express his own dance ideas. The machines had a few good, albeit predictable, moves: precision, repetition, efficiency, perpetual motion. But Astaire can combine hundreds of tap moves into new combinations, and new expressive sequences, anytime he wants. Having taken the machine's rhythm onto his body, Astaire is energized by these new elements: he seems powered by the crankshaft right up the ramp, spinning to a place physically above the machines, above the black workers, above "work" even. He's not John Henry hammering with all his strength and skill, but an artistic John Henry demonstrating how this seeming enemy—the machine—can reenergize the human body.

Astaire spins up the ramp continuously like a top, using his arms for dramatic and metric emphasis; he then pauses before whirling into a turbo-driven set of spins so honest in its improvisatory joy, so in-the-moment, that Astaire seems flushed during his final flourish. He finally comes to a stop at a rail overlooking the engine room and extends his arms, as if throwing the dance over the rail to the black workers below, who greet the performance with seemingly honest and enthusiastic applause. The camera zooms back to include the workers and Astaire together for the first time in two minutes.

This final shot is as distinctive as the opening shot, and even more profoundly racist. It's a long shot (the only one of the scene) with the camera placed at the farthest point from Astaire in the engine room. It is as if we are seeing Astaire from the last row of a theater. He stands on the top level of the engine room, slightly higher than (but analogous to) the level of a Broadway stage. In the foreground, twenty feet below, we see the fifteen or so black workers distributed randomly around the deck, leaning on gleaming white machines. Although these unnamed workers provided the bases for the dancer's performance (and the crucial aesthetic and philosophical elements of his dance), they now must be content to applaud the master, the white man elevated on the stage. A spotlight even appears incongruously to highlight Astaire.

This shot sums up a century's worth of the love of African American culture and its economic theft by Euro-American performers. Here is Astaire the fine-artist, raised above the common black folk, acknowledging only the appreciation—and not the contribution—of those who provided the aesthetic materials of his art. (And who performed the menial work, and adapted their cultural materials *to* the menial work.) Unlike the survival technology created by African Americans to negotiate existential challenges that had little to do with material reward, here the economic worth of the fine-artist is all that is valued, displayed on a makeshift stage for money and an audience, and legitimated by stage semiotics and staged popular acclaim.

"Slap That Bass" encodes a classic primitivist framework. Astaire goes to the "lower" classes—the less-evolved, folk-primitive cultures—for the raw, instinctive passion lacking in "civilization." He first acknowledges the rhythmic genius of the African American workers by getting their stylized rhythms (and artistic affirmation) into his bones; then he's ready to sing a jazz-influenced popular song, converting raw material to refined popular art on the spot. Astaire can only see African Americans as naturally happy workers able to enjoy themselves even while performing menial tasks or heavy labor. He honors them with one of those classic interwar songs about how rhythm can save your soul and make you happy—"today you can see/the happiest men/all got rhythm." But there is no understanding of the concept in black work songs that music lightens heavy work, and there is the requisite minstrel overlay to the vocal, the "slap-that-bass" Uncle-Tomming of the bassist and the happy darkies.

Yet for all its limitations, "Slap That Bass" still manages to present a suggestive evolutionary narrative of how machine rhythms were integrated into American popular culture from the Civil War to the swing era. The techno-dialogic model unfolds: first, machine rhythms come into society, a brand new rhythm in the world; second, African Americans stylize these rhythms using only voices and percussion in work songs (as they did in railroad track-gangs, in hammer songs and ballads such as "John Henry"); third, the rhythm section of string bass and drums "catch" this new groove securely, freeing up the possibility of self-expression in the jazz solo and in tap.

There is no way to get from machine rhythms to Gershwinesque sophistication without recognizing all the intermediary cultural work of African American cultural production: of stylizing tempos, humanizing repetitive motion, creating the call-and-response of massed instrumental sections. In spirituals and blues, in the chants of work songs and the dances of jook joints, in the artistic competition of jam sessions and cutting contests, African American musicians and dancers integrated machine rhythms into their bodies and into American popular culture. For all its flaws, "Slap That Bass" recapitulated the techno-dialogic tradition, from the 1880s to 1930s.[71]

A last comment on the scene. Astaire transcended category as a dancer and musical-comedy performer; he was also an excellent singer, albeit of limited range. There were, however, a few African American artists of his caliber who never had the chance to grace a Hollywood romantic comedy. Euro-American audiences could not yet see a black man as an "American" whose skill, style, intelligence, and elegance might make of him an exemplar of the Machine Age American man. John W. Bubbles, for example, portrayed the original Sportin' Life in *Porgy and Bess,* but that was as good a dramatic role as he would ever get. The decade's only interracial couple in movies was Shirley Temple and Bill Robinson, a tribute to the strength of the plantation tradition.[72] The hugely popular pairing of the two recapitulated the Uncle Remus-indoctrinates-the-white-child plantation mythos: the old, nonthreatening black caretaker passes on a version of the cultural practices (and concepts) of African American storytelling and performance within a minstrelized framework. Robinson and Temple functioned as the shadow couple of Astaire and Rogers.

Coda: The Tap Legacy

In 1957, Beale Fletcher, a Hollywood dancer, teacher, and choreographer, called for a concert production called "The American Tap Dance" that would narrate the history of industrialization. His aim was threefold: to create a narrative of American history through a vernacular cultural form; to have Americans embrace tap as an original American artistic contribution equal to ballet and modern dance; and to popularize tap history as a phenomenon created by—and infused with—American ethnic diversity.[73] I quote at length since Fletcher brings together a number of historical connections in this work: popular culture, the tempo of life, machine aesthetics, the multicultural roots of tap dancing, and its importance in Hollywood movies.

> Tap Dancing is a cross section of America. It brings to us the footwork of the folk dances of Ireland, Scotland, England, and the Scandinavian countries. The Negroes of the Deep South, the jazz of New Orleans, the energetic clog dances of New England all contributed to its development. It carries the traditions of the American theater— Vaudeville, Minstrels, Ziegfeld Follies. It gained fame through Primrose and West, George M. Cohan, Bill Robinson, Fred Astaire, Paul Draper, Gene Kelly, Eleanor Powell, and many other dancing stars. It has been canned and put into moving pictures and sent all over the world. It is as much a part of our culture as the Western movie and the Manhattan skyscraper.[74]

A concert production, Fletcher thought, would serve to show how a unified cultural form was created out of the contributions of several ethnic groups and the local traditions of several major American cities (such as New Orleans, Hollywood, and New York). As opposed to modern dance and ballet, tap represented democracy, cultural diversity, and the tempo and rhythm of American cities.[75]

For Fletcher, tap was the cultural form best able to dramatically and artistically organize the industrial soundscape. Of course he had the benefit of twenty years' hindsight, but his enthusiasm should not be underestimated: "Visualize America with its factories, productions, assembly lines. Men and women marching to work, carrying boxes, twisting wrenches, making political speeches against a background of whirling wheels and machines that sing a rhythm more throbbing than the beat of a savage Tom-Tom. Tap dancing . . . could tell this story with dramatic staccato power the likes of which are seldom seen on the stage." For Fletcher, tap created a synthesis of modernism and the melting pot between the world wars.

In the mid-1990s tap began to enjoy a revival for many of the reasons Fletcher suggested. The Public Theater's long-running production of *Bring in 'da Noise, Bring in 'da Funk*, the Australian production of *Tap Dogs*, the celebration of clog dancing and the jig in *Riverdance*—all reflect a larger interest in the organized machine aesthetics in dance performance. Why is it back? Tap takes the hard, metallic ring of a technological society and makes "lovely noise" that talks back. The rhythmic display is the equal of a drummer's, but it is more expressive and holistic in its self-expression. Like the swing revival, the tap revival reflected a cultural need to reaffirm humanized machine aesthetics in the face of another technological revolution, that of the computer age.[76]

The Broadway producer and impresario George F. Wolfe and the tap virtuoso Savion Glover also believe that tap dance can tell the story of America—more precisely, the modern history of African Americans. That Fletcher, a white Hollywood dancer devoted to an ideology of the melting-pot, and Wolfe, a black impresario accused of Afrocentric nationalism, would both assume that tap could carry a two-hour theatrical narrative of American history speaks volumes about tap's expressive power and popularity.[77]

Finally, there is an important gender issue concerning the golden age of tap, a time when American men were overwhelmed by feelings of failure, assembly-line fatigue, and machine worship. Tap put the individual male body on display in the interest of sheer athletic and kinetic joy, and it converted raw strength and power into elegance. Although Eleanor Powell was considered a great tap dancer by her peers (Ginger Rogers was not, for example), tap was a male preserve, and represented a considerable transformation in ideas of virility among Euro-Americans. Paul Draper viewed tap in archetypally male terms: "The male is distinguished by his ability to take care of the ever recurring challenges of staying alive in a hostile environment, and by his ability to make valuable comments about how he does it."[78] The "hostile environment" of the Machine Age contained the threat of an overmechanized society.

So why did tap die? According to scholars and contemporaries, the primary factor was the return of ballet-derived dance to Broadway with Agnes de Mille's choreography in *Oklahoma!* (1943). That musical's triumph brought a synthesis of ballet and modern dance to theater; tap dancers complained of being "evicted" from Broadway. The success of *Oklahoma!* also produced a bandwagon effect for a new kind of Hollywood musical and spelled the end of black theatrical revues. Furthermore, in the mid-1950s the electricity and volume of rock and roll overwhelmed tap's metallic noise and put an end to the dialogue between tap dancers and big bands. Tap also failed on television, in part because of disagreements between union workers and network executives.

Tap also suffered from a lack of prestige and institutional support (as shown by the academic eviction of tap after 1945), as well as a deep-seated aesthetic racism that prevented Americans from honoring a non-white American art form. In the 1960s the drama critic Patrick O'Connor dismissed tap as a form that would "forever be a nostalgia thing." Lacking a narrative myth, tap "couldn't go anywhere." He compared it to ballet, "[which] is serious because it is based on the myths of Western culture: the beautiful, unattainable woman, the heroic prince, the rape of the peasant girl. The themes of ballet have always been Western myths, but tap is sort of just there on its own."[79] If one day Americans come to consciously embrace African American survival technology and the techno-dialogic, tap might be seen to have embodied a new myth: that of the "modern," industrial, multicultural American self.

Astaire's victory in the challenge dance of *Shall We Dance?* stands as the answer to the question first broached in "John Henry": What is the function of a Machine Age man in industrial society? In other words, what is the role of a working man in an industrial world that lacks dignified work, communal celebration, and an old-fashioned respect for male strength, and instead offers only alienated work, machine worship, and contribution through consumerism? What Astaire offered Machine Age audiences was the superiority of self-expression over machine aesthetics, while displaying an easy, humorous, off-handed elegance.[80]

AMERICA'S NATIONAL

FOLK DANCE

THE LINDY HOP

In 1930 the writer, photographer, and dance critic Carl Van Vechten observed that every decade or so, an anonymous black dancer creates a new step that so excites the African American dancing public that "it spreads like water over blotting paper" and quickly becomes observable at levees, jook joints, urban dance halls and even on street corners. After two years or so, a Euro-American dancer or dance director, witness to the excitement generated by the new dance believes he or she can cross it over for "white consumption" and "introduces it, frequently with the announcement that he has invented it." As this was the history of "the Cake-Walk, the Bunny Hug, the Turkey Trot, the Charleston, and the Black Bottom," Van Vechten predicted "it will probably be the history of the Lindy Hop."[1] He was right on all counts.

Then only three years old, the lindy hop had already been approved as a must-see "Harlem" dance by New York City's theatrical critics and gossip columnists, and the dance helped make the Savoy Ballroom a major tourist attraction. Throughout the 1930s, white tourists flocked to the Savoy; in 1935 the Savoy's best dancers, Whitey's Lindy Hoppers, thrilled a sold-out Madison Square Garden crowd in sweeping the lindy division of the first annual Harvest Moon Ball. Sixteen years after its creation, the lindy hop reached a certain pinnacle of mainstream recognition. On the cover of the August 23, 1943, issue of *Life*, a teenaged white couple leaned against each other with bizarre lascivious looks on their faces along the bottom edge of the cover ran the words "The Lindy Hop." A twelve-page photo spread was half devoted to the young white couple and half to a pair of Whitey's Lindy Hoppers. The headline inside the issue read simply: "A True National Folk Dance Has Been Born in the U.S.A."[2]

Van Vechten was unable to understand the moves of the lindy hop, as he lacked knowledge of African American dance aesthetics. He described the dance as "[a] certain dislocation of the rhythm of the Fox Trot, followed by leaps and quivers, hops and jumps, eccentric flinging about of arms and legs, and contortions of the torso only fittingly to be described by the word epileptic." Van Vechten didn't know a swing-out move from a turn-over Charleston, and there was then no awareness of African dance systems, whether Kongo-derived hip movements or Yoruba-derived head-and-shoulder movements (as in the shimmy).[3] Dance criticism was itself in its infancy, and the swift swoops and sharp tempo shifts of black culture—its accelerative and explosive qualities— were then unidentified.[4]

Yet despite the limitations of his gaze, Van Vechten honored the lindy hop's artistic qualities by comparing it favorably to European artistic technique. Individual dancers "embroider[ed] the traditional measures with startling variation, as a coloratura singer . . . would embellish the score of a Bellini opera with roulades, runs and shakes." The dance was so fast, rhythmic, and new to the eye that "it could be danced, quite reasonably, and without alteration of tempo, to many passages in the *Sacre du Printemps* of Stravinsky." Van Vechten believed the dance was a new synthesis that captured the tempo of the time; Marshall Stearns claimed that "the Lindy caused a general revolution in the popular dance of the United States."[5]

Van Vechten identified the lindy's revolutionary features: fluidity and perpetual motion; a noticeable lack of sensuality; startling dynamic shifts; and the importance of individual expression through improvisation. It was "a rite . . . [of] glorification of self," he suggested, an honor rarely (if ever) accorded to black dance. To distinguish the lindy from the assumed primitive sensuality and "natural" rhythmic ability of blacks represented a major breakthrough in the white gaze. "*The dance is not of sexual derivation,* nor does it incline its hierophants towards pleasures of the flesh . . . these couples barely touch each other, bodily speaking . . . and each may dance alone, if he feels the urge. . . . It is Dionysian, if you like . . . but it is not erotic" [emphasis added]. Apparently dancing the lindy, or even watching lindy hoppers, could reenergize Machine Age human bodies. "To observe the Lindy Hop being performed at first induces gooseflesh, and second, intense excitement, akin to religious mania."[6]

Pagan rites and religious fervor were Van Vechten's only benchmarks for intense energetic display, but the dance's very name unified machine technology and survival technology. The lindy was supposedly named after Charles Lindbergh, whose solo "hop" across the Atlantic was one of the heroic achievements of the 1920s. Recent research casts serious doubt on this myth, which was first promulgated by dancer Shorty Snowden; still the connection reflects a self-awareness of the techno-dialogic on the part of African American dancers about the individual breakthroughs of applied science and their inscribing on the body.[7]

The historian William McNeill has theorized that "keeping together in time" through such activities as dancing creates and maintains social cohesion in ways that go deeper than language. What he calls "muscular bonding" breaks down the boundaries of subject and object, and is a method of group cohesion "far older than language. . . . [T]he emotion it arouses constitutes an indefinitely expansible basis for social cohesion . . . moving big muscles together and chanting, singing, or shouting rhythmically." McNeill first extrapolated this theory from his own experience with close-order drill in the army, but he perceived similar unfying rituals in village dancing. Because participants share the "euphoric fellow feeling that prolonged and rhythmic muscular movement arouses," he maintains that village dancing may be as "political" as army maneuvers: it "smooth[s] out frictions and consolidat[es] fellow-feeling among the participants."[8]

McNeill asserts that rhythmic stimuli—listened to or danced to—can cause "boundary loss, the submergence of self to the flow." Until quite recently, there could be no more serious threat to the individual rational mind of the Enlightenment traditions than loss of self to the flow. Western scholars have been so focused on language there is as yet little research on "emotional response to rhythmic muscular movement in groups, nor even to choral singing."[9] But if the lindy hop (or jitterbug) was the national folk dance, perhaps it contributed toward putting at least a younger generation together "in time"—in their bodies, in their minds, in their bones. I am suggesting the lindy acted as an agent of biosocial bonding during the swing era.

The excitement of the lindy hop for the younger generation of the swing era is comprehensible only in context. Arguably, dance of all kinds—tap, ballroom, social, commercial, folk—was more important to mainstream *Euro*-American culture between 1910 and 1945 than at any other time in American history. Only in this period were dance halls such as the Savoy Ballroom or cabarets such as the Cotton Club major tourist destinations and celebrity haunts. Only in the 1930s could an annual ballroom dance competition (the Harvest Moon Ball) sell out Madison Square Garden every year within hours of putting tickets on sale, while another five thousand people stood around outside listening on the PA system. Only in the 1930s were there as many dancers among the top Hollywood box-office draws (Shirley Temple and Bill Robinson, Fred Astaire and Ginger Rogers, Jimmy Cagney and Ruby Keeler) as archetypal self-reliant tough loners (Clark Gable or Gary Cooper) or blonde bombshells (Jean Harlow). Only in the 1930s would a leading dance authority embark on a cross-country trip to investigate regional dance styles and conclude that "the social dance is . . . thoroughly established as the national pastime."[10]

In the 1930s dance helped unify a large industrial nation in a period of existential crisis brought on by machine worship and technological unemployment. When *Life* crowned the lindy hop the national folk dance, it was specifically acknowledging the enthusiasm that greeted Betty Grable every night as she ended her USO show lindying with a different soldier (of varied ethnicity). "A white movie star Lindy Hopping on a public stage with a black serviceman without, apparently, any innuendo—the dance was now much more than a hot and exciting black vernacular dance; it had become a symbol of America, the great melting pot."[11] Yet if dance symbolized melting-pot ideals, the history of its success reveals the tensions of the time as well. Havelock Ellis traced the outpouring of emotional energy after World War I to a hundred years of overproduction of material goods at the expense of biological needs. At seventeen, Ellis recalled thinking the world was itself a machine, "a sort of factory filled by an inextricable web of wheels and looms and flying shuttles, in a deafening din. That . . . was the world as the most competent scientific authorities declared it to be made." Ellis's interest in dance came from a personal rebellion against an overly repressive society; he embraced dance as joyous movement that enabled him to regain an aesthetic sense of beauty.[12] Americans used dance to reclaim the human body as a site of joy and *human* power, of athletic and aesthetic display.

Dance was already a culture-shaping social art form in the 1920s; if that decade had a national folk dance, it was the Charleston. According to the dance scholar Sally Sommer, the Charleston liberated American social dance from European styles "once and for all." In the place of statuesque postures and a focus on the upper body (from European culture) came an African American aesthetic featuring twisting hips, shimmying shoulders, the bumping, slapping, and sticking out of the buttocks, the undulating torso, the "rambunctious swinging of oppositional limbs," and other playful physical gestures such as rubber-legging. The Charleston's spirited syncopation and irregular rhythmic accents helped create a symbiotic relationship between musicians and dancers that owed more to West African dance aesthetics than to court, ballroom, or peasant dancing. Brought to the Broadway stage by the Harlem stride pianist and composer James P. Johnson in *Runnin' Wild* (1923), the Charleston was a dance rhythm he learned from blacks recently emigrated from the Carolinas; they stomped out the rhythm for him in a basement dance club and he used it as a basis for the hit songs in the show.[13]

The Charleston represented a turning point in American social dance: suddenly new Broadway dances were seen less as artistic spectacles than as new cultural forms *for participation*. Nor was there a "correct" way to perform the dance, so it allowed for individual interpretation. The Charleston became a hallmark of the Jazz Age, and its emphasis on the undulating torso and the lower body continued the American rebellion against the erect, rigid torso of European ballet and folk dance, suggesting a cultural desire for torsion, dynamic movement, and whole-body involvement. The Charleston also split the body into separate planes. The focus of the dance was from the waist down—on the pelvis, hips, knees, and ankles—and depended upon constant motion across the body: hands across knees, legs moving back and forth, high kicks into the air. The dance "shattered the body into separate limbs, swinging like a human mobile into a multiplicity of simultaneous but diverse rhythms."[14] All of these shifts predate the rock-and-roll revolution of the Twist and various animal dances, and continued the Africanization of American movement.

Unlike the Charleston, however, the lindy had no immediate southern antecedents. It was not derived from the African tradition of animal dances, nor did it contain the flat-footed shuffle of blues dances and the "slow drag." Without these features, the lindy calls attention to itself as something new in the black vernacular. According to the arranger and bandleader Jesse Stone, the lindy hop was not especially popular among African Americans in the South.[15]

In all West African cultures, and consequently in Afrodiasporic ones, the centrality of dance to group identity, self-expression, and moral instruction can only be compared to literature and philosophy in the

Western tradition. Equal parts oral tradition and embodied philosophy, West African dance always contains the possibility of individual expression within the group's circle. In the African diaspora, dance has functioned as a social structure that helps maintain African American humanity in the face of white domination and spiritual assault. Albert Murray refers to African Americans as culturally a "dance-beat oriented people," and emphasizes the affirmation of survival, joy, and individuality in the secular ritual of what he calls the "Saturday Night Function." The hallmarks of vernacular black dance are "improvisation and spontaneity, propulsive rhythm, call-and-response patterns, self-expression, elegance, and control." All of these qualities are present in tap and the lindy.[16]

The story of the development of the lindy hop has been outlined thoroughly by Marshall and Jean Stearns in their definitive *Jazz Dance*.[17] My intention here is twofold: to analyze the lindy's machine aesthetics and its reception among Euro-Americans. Danced to propulsive rhythms by partners across class and race, the lindy's fast, fluid steps demanded improvisation *and* precise motion. As it evolved, the articulation of moves became more efficient and precise, and the dance sped up. When Frankie Manning brought "air steps" into the lindy in 1936— and dancers threw their partners in the air and they landed, in step, back in the dance—he broke the plane of the floor and made good on the dance's aspirations to be airborne.[18] The lindy hop integrated the relentless power of machines by mixing speed, precision, and flow with human stamina and self-expression to display the *partnered* expression of dynamic control.

To review the lindy's reception, I first analyze eyewitness reports by three well-known cultural observers present at Harlem's Savoy Ballroom, and then focus on the role of the lindy at the annual Harvest Moon Ball in Madison Square Garden. Something of a dance olympics, the Harvest Moon Ball attracted huge sell-out crowds every year from 1935 to 1950, and the *New York Daily News* often gave it front-page coverage. Why would a dance olympics be front page news? The philosophy professor and lindy scholar Robert Crease might respond to the question this way: "How we dance, as Nietszche knew and Plato suspected, has a lot to do with who we are. And every time we experience that smooth feeling that accompanies moving in synch with jazz music—that *swing* . . . the Lindy has exerted its power over us."[19]

White Culture's Need for Black Dance

Between 1910 and 1940, millions of blacks left the South for the promise of better treatment, better jobs, and social equality. What I have elsewhere called the "swing hopes" of the black migration were manifested and expressed in big-band swing and the lindy—more for blacks than whites in the early years of the Depression—and embodied by conductors of the big-band swing train such as Duke Ellington, Fletcher Henderson, and Jimmie Lunceford. Stearns called the lindy "choreographed swing music," and it should be seen as a northern innovation expressing African American optimism in a new land.[20] Black dancers at northern dance halls registered the new soundscape in their language, bodies, feelings, and physical gestures. Created at the Savoy by African Americans in transition, the lindy expressed in dance an adjustment to a potentially liberating environment. The dance crossed over to Euro-American popularity in the mid-1930s when African American swing hopes fueled the rejuvenation of a younger white generation emerging from the dog years of the Depression. As Richard Wright observed in 1941, "Where we cannot go, our tunes, songs, slang, and jokes go."[21]

The new temples of dance built in the black neighborhoods of northern cities during a period of sustained migration might be usefully understood as southern "jook joints" raised up with white (often Jewish) capital. Zora Neale Hurston declared that "musically speaking, the Jook is the most important place in America"; it was the place where new dances were born, evolved, perfected, and then diffused into international popularity. Hurston named the Charleston, the Black Bottom, and the "slow and sensuous" grind as characteristic "[southern] Negro social dance[s]" that influenced physical motion around the world. The jook joint became the urban dance hall, and the petri dish for creating new dances reflective of modern life.[22]

Emile Jacques-Dalcroze, the renowned Swiss physical culture theorist and creator of the eurythmics method of dance training, echoed Hurston's observation in 1925. Surprised at the more sophisticated rhythmic fluidity of a younger generation of European children, he attributed their new agility and plasticity to the influence of African American dance: "Negro rhythms have had a salutary influence upon the development of our [European] sense of rhythm. Twenty years ago . . . our children were incapable of singing syncopations in the right time. . . . The freedom of jazz band rhythms, the extraordinary vivacity and variety of their cadences, their picturesque turns and twists, their wealth of accentuation and fanciful counterpoint: all these have certainly infused new blood into musical rhythm."[23] Modifications of tempo "come about gradually and quite naturally throughout the ages," Dalcroze wrote, and the new American tempo was carried by songs "cross[ing] the frontiers and . . . heard everywhere." Even at two removes from the source of jazz and jazz dance, syncopation changed the kinesics of European children.

Dalcroze's method of "musico-calisthenics" is still widely used to teach dance and physical movement. To call his perceptions "primitivist" or "essentialist," as contemporary scholars might, would admit a refusal to process the content of these statements, which are quite simple. Exposure to offbeat rhythms, creative rhythmic phrasing, sudden turns and shifts in tempo, and improvisational embellishment expanded the physiological skills and fluidity of European children. To dance to a music filled with rhythmic surprise (kinesthetically speaking, that is), the body must be alert and prepared to adjust to musical shifts, stops, and breaks. In European-derived patterned dances such as the waltz and minuet (and even in ballet), the body follows the music; in jazz dance, the body participates and interacts.[24]

As with all black vernacular dance, the lindy hop requires close attention to the music by the dancers. Robert Crease belonged to the New York Swing Society in the early 1980s, and he had an epiphany about swing dance when Al Minns, of Whitey's Lindy Hoppers, gave the members a lesson. Minns instructed them to listen to the music first and move their body to the music before doing any steps. Crease immediately realized this was a philosophical shift in the use of his body: to focus attention on the music rather than on the correct execution of the moves. "Suddenly we could see what dancing was all about . . . it had nothing to do with repeating patterns correctly, but with throwing your body into the music."[25]

The lindy hop as generally performed at the Savoy was an eight-count box-step syncopated on the offbeat, where the couple followed a circular path around a shared central axis. It began with an initial move called the "jig walk," where the couple connects by first walking toward each other, grasping each other's waists, and then spinning quickly in place, creating a torquelike motion across the hips. The "swing-out" move that follows involves the leader letting the partner out and away by extending the hand. At that point, either or both dancers can improvise. During this "break-away" step, partners literally break away to improvise steps of their own, or remain attached to their partner by a light touch.

The dance utilizes centrifugal force, torque, and momentum to keep the partners spinning smoothly; professional dancers could do this at a furious tempo. Good dancers then interpolate moves from other dances such as the Charleston, trucking, or the Suzi-Q. Some improvise spins, ecstatic solo leaps, and the fast, high kicks of African American "flash" dancing. To dance the lindy professionally required fast, constant side-to-side foot movement, the ability to follow your partner almost intuitively, and being comfortable with leaving your feet.[26]

The most artistic lindy hopper of all time, Frankie Manning, describes the dance as extremely horizontal and one that requires a certain "buoyancy." One needed to crouch to move quickly and smoothly across the floor; controlled sliding and gliding accentuated the fast, liquid flow. Yet the dance allowed for pauses to provide drama and self-expression. Manning claimed the dance evolved out of a step called the Collegiate in the late 1920s, a faster version of the Charleston but lacking a break-away step. As opposed to ballroom forms, the lindy had no "correct step," was danced to a 4/4 rhythm, and had the excitement of allowing dancers to be "together in the spirit" of the music yet "relating to the music on your own."[27]

What elements in the lindy appealed to all dancers of the Depression? The lindy hop represented a synthesis of European social dance traditions and the West African dance tradition of self-expression. European social dance contributed the pattern and the idea of couples dancing; from West African dance came the fast tempos, the use of the whole body, improvisation, and a lowered center of gravity (in the hips and thighs). Like big-band swing, it was a cultural form which displayed a dialogue between individual self-expression and collective drive (both from the music and from a partner). A white male dancer from Rhode Island recalled that the lindy "gave you that sharpness, that edge . . . that you had to say *I am*. It was the only dance that you could use the power of self-expression in. You personify it." Another contemporary lindy hopper recalled "the freedom . . . the marvelous freedom the Lindy Hop introduced into dance." As for the collective drive, white dancers were just as aware as black dancers that musicians and dancers were "artistic compatriots" who fed off each other's energy and rhythms. "We danced for them and they played for us," one white woman recalled.[28]

Now let's go to the Savoy to see what cultural observers made of the dance and the ballroom. In the 1930s, Harlem's Savoy Ballroom was a unique model of a public integrated space, arguably the *only* desegregated national institution. The *New York Amsterdam News* commented on the occasion of Greta Garbo's 1939 visit, "Perhaps no other spot in this great country is so symbolic of the American ideal. The Savoy is truly a melting pot—a cross-section of American life . . . [where] every night in the week, every race and nationality under the sun, the high and the low, meet and color lines melt away under the influence of the rhythms of America's foremost sepia bands." The Savoy drew capacity crowds of three to five thousand over the course of a given evening for Guy Lombardo as well as Duke Ellington, and many were turned away for the famous Benny Goodman–Chick Webb "battle of the bands" of May 11, 1937. Its main attractions were "ten-cent beer, twenty-cent wine, a reasonable entrance fee, Whitey's Lindy Hoppers, lovely congenial hostesses, and the best of swing music."[29] Actress Lana Turner pinned the nickname "The Home of Happy Feet" on the Savoy to honor the spiritual uplift of its mood and dancing, a slogan repeated nightly on live remote nationwide broadcasts.[30]

For all the Savoy's popularity, the white primitivist gaze at black culture stubbornly remained. In 1939 the Jewish novelist and humorist Leo Rosten went to the Savoy for the first time and left a depiction of the dancing that reveals the same combination of awe, primitivist viewpoint, and lack of vocabulary expressed by Van Vechten. Rosten cautioned readers about his shocking experience, warning them that "if the pale but desperate prose which follows seems impossible to believe, don't blame me. Just try the Savoy yourself once. Stronger men have been carried out of the place, babbling." First he was assaulted by the waves of musical power that greeted him upon entrance, "a battery of brasses blaring [the hit song] 'Flat Foot Floogie with the Floy Floy'," and then mesmerized by the sights on the dance floor. "Men . . . lifting women way up, throwing them down, flinging them over their shoulders, tossing them over their heads, hurling them to arm's length, yanking them back, shaking them like wet mops. . . . Hands flew out in all directions— waving, flaying, stabbing the air. It was a surrealist's nightmare."[31]

Rosten too used the rhetoric of religious fervor to express the emotive power, focused intensity, and circulation of energy in the room. "Frenzy ruled that ballroom," he wrote, noting the shouts of joy in the midst of improvisation. Rosten accurately identified the factors that made the Savoy Ballroom "the nation's leading ballroom" and a distinctive cultural institution.[32] There was the section of African American dancers who would "base" the best lindy hoppers with hand-clapping and shouts of encouragement, adding vocal and percussive layers to the big band's steady rhythm. There was the group of white "swing-addicts" who stood next to the bandstand listening to the music as if "in a coma." There were the circulating group of Savoy hostesses who provided men with three dances for a quarter, "gorgeous creatures . . . [who] carried themselves regally." There were several interracial couples, a sight that still enraged many white men even in New York.

At the height of an up-tempo tune, Rosten compared standing near the dancers to "being at the center of a particularly violent tornado." He was amazed at the dancers' self-control when, "at a [seemingly] secret signal and with marvelous precision, they slid into a slow-motion step, so slow it was hard to believe." Not thirty seconds later, they "went [back] into an acrobatic furor."

When one band ended its set, a collective sigh of disappointment went up, but a second band started up and "then someone yelled—and hell broke loose all over again. A man seized a woman . . . and [they] began to twirl as if he believed in perpetual motion." He swore he heard the band hurl a "long ecstatic 'YEeaaahHH!'" at the dancers, who responded with their "answering 'OoooohHH!'," and again "hundreds of bodies twirled and leapt and spun." He concluded with a prayer for the forces at play on the Savoy dance floor: "I had a premonition that if any of it stopped, for a single instant, the whole world would fall to pieces." His sentiment echoes the dance scholar Katrina Hazzard-Gordon's apt phrase for the goal of all Afrodiasporic secular dance: "dancing to rebalance the universe."[33]

Otis Ferguson, the unofficial jazz critic of the *New Republic,* wrote a more dramatic (and better-known) description of the Savoy's dancing. Ferguson compared being at the Savoy to being inside a drum: "When the band gets pretty well into it, the whole enclosure, with all its people, beats like a drum and rises in steady time, like a ground swell." He identified several overlapping layers of energy, a dense mosaic of speech, dance and music, and advised visitors to simply let all these waves of information wash over them. "You cannot see everything at once but you can feel everything at once, a sort of unifying outflow of energy, [and] you can almost see it burn."

For Ferguson, a "good dancer" was one who simultaneously kept the tempo of the song with one part of the body while improvising to a second rhythm (again, a West African–derived practice). Watching a black dancer off by himself swinging to the jukebox, Ferguson observed "the relaxed easy swing of the rhythmic pattern and along with it a drive of his own that runs along with the music and anticipates the restless urge of its lags, stresses, and sharp syncopations." A good dancer must, in effect, *wear* at least two rhythms and make them visible: he or she must register "the relaxed easy swing" of the song's pulse but also the musical riffs with individual, personalized limb movements. Ferguson, too, lacked a dance vocabulary; but he respected the dancing at the Savoy enough that even after describing the "hopeless[ly] intricate mass of flying ankles, swirls, stomps," he simply stated that it was "really beautiful dancing."

The initial explosion of a new musical idiom is a response to a collective cultural need for a set of movements that reflect the new historical "time." In other words, *one dances the new time,* and by dancing, inscribes it on the body. (Isn't this one way an American teenager becomes a member of his or her generation?) At the Savoy, sometimes the dancers led the musicians; sometimes the musicians led the dancers. When Savoy dancers would "forget dancing and flock around the [band]stand ten deep" to watch and listen to Teddy Hill's band pile up improvised choruses to "Christopher Columbus," the music had asserted leadership. The fans were trying "to register *the time* . . . with their bones and muscles . . . letting it flow over them like water," and get this new industrial power into their systems. "The floor shakes and *the place is a dynamo room,* with the smoky air pushing up in steady waves." When the dancers took the leadership, the musicians had to exert more rhythmic force to ground them. The function of the new swing rhythm section was to create a dense, powerful "beat of guitar-piano-string-bass-drum [to] nail all this lavish and terrific energy down to the simple restraints of a time signature." To inscribe Machine Age forces on American bodies required four rhythm instruments.[34]

Once bands could project that kind of power, dancers such as the young Malcolm X could take flight. Writing with both enthusiasm and expertise about the lindy, Malcolm X in his memoir retains the swing hopes of black possibility inherent in the dance. Almost a quarter of *The Autobiography of Malcolm X* centers on swing-era dance halls such as Boston's Roseland and the Savoy.[35] On his very first visit to Roseland, Malcolm X responded to the bandleader Lionel Hampton's "wailing" by "whirling girls so fast their skirts were snapping. . . . Boosting them over my hips, my shoulders, into the air. . . . Circling, tap-dancing, I was underneath them when they landed—doing the 'flapping eagle,' 'the kangaroo' and the 'split.'" He quickly became a strong enough dancer to stay on the floor even during "showtime," the last set in the evening "when only the greatest lindy hoppers would stay on the floor, to try and eliminate each other." All the nonparticipating dancers would create a circle for "showtime," with the hand-clappers "form[ing] a big 'U' with the band at the open end." This is a variation of the archetypal West African dance (and community) circle inside which dancers express themselves, only here it is more of an oval and the band is included within the round.

For Malcolm X, a successful lindy hop partnership depended upon reducing the friction between partners to increase speed and enhance the expression of horizontal flow. This was accomplished through a dynamic "push-pull" tension.

> With most girls, you . . . work opposite them, circling, side-stepping, leading . . . your hands are giving that little pull, that little push, touching her waist, her shoulders, her arms. . . . With poor partners, you feel their weight. They're slow and heavy. But with really good partners, all you need is just the push-pull suggestion. They guide nearly effortlessly, even off the floor and into the air, and your little solo maneuver is done on the floor before they land, when they join you, whirling, right in step.

But the key to the lindy's excitement was continuous motion, the ability of a couple to fluidly combine different moves without a discrete pause. Malcolm X brags of his ability to time his quick solo maneuver so as to finish the moment his partner returns (sometimes from the air), that moment "[when] they join you, whirling, right in step." His favorite partner, Laura, taught him the importance of lightness and flexibility. With Laura, Malcolm X only needed to "*think* a maneuver, and she'd respond." Twenty years later he still remembered clearly "her footwork . . . like some blurring ballet—beautiful! And her lightness, like a shadow!" He did not believe this lissome woman had the strength or stamina for the demands of the lindy hop at full throttle during what dancers called "Showtime"; but one night Laura wanted to compete and changed into sneakers. "They [Roseland dancers] never had seen the feather-lightness that she gave to lindying, a completely fresh style—and they were connoisseurs of styles." Her lighter, more balletic movements made them the heroes of the dance floor that night. "I turned up the steam, Laura's feet were flying; I had her in the air, down, sideways around; backwards, up again, down, whirling. . . . I couldn't believe her strength. The crowd was shouting and stomping."[36]

Boston's Roseland "look[ed] small and shabby by comparison" to the Savoy, Malcolm X admitted, and "the lindy-hopping there matched the size and elegance of the place." He also estimated a full third of the sideline booths were filled with white tourists who had come to "just watch the Negroes dance." Harlem residents had nicknamed the Savoy "the Track" (short for racetrack), a tribute to the ballroom as an arena of excitement. In the 1930s the racetrack still retained its glamour as one of high society's most exciting venues; it's where the action was. In swing-era jazz slang, "stallions" and "fillies" referred to young men and women; the "track" was a nickname honoring the action on the dance floor where the smartest, fastest human beings competed for the appreciation of the "connoisseurs" of elegance, speed, and motion.[37]

The Savoy was a must for New York City tourists, and "visitors from all the world over . . . attended the famous Savoy Saturday Swing Sessions or Tuesday night '400' Club initiations to see these amazing dance spectacles performed by talented, unbelievable fast action dancers . . . under the directorship of Herbert 'Whitey' White." The lindy hopper Norma Miller remembers the visits of Lana Turner, Greta Garbo, Marlene Dietrich, and Orson Welles. "Press agents saw the value of having the stars come to the ballroom," she remembered. "The boxes were reserved for them."[38] The Savoy claimed to receive ten million visitors between 1926 and 1940 (an average of two thousand a night). Nearly every big band recorded a version of "Stomping at the Savoy," and the equally popular ballad "Savoy" was the first song recorded by Judy Garland.[39]

The Savoy was a unique institution in American life: a multicultural public space without ethnic stratification where Americans learned to move together in time. The lindy's expansive use of the 30'-by-150' gleaming mahogany dance floor reflected the excitement of cultural democracy. Nearly a dozen American social dances were created at the Savoy. The ballroom was also a community institution and the most important public space in Harlem; it was famous for its interracial clientele and its egalitarian treatment, and was a symbol of social equality. When the Savoy was temporarily closed on trumped-up political charges in 1943, the lyricist Andy Razaf penned a bitter ode in his *Amsterdam News* column: "Yes, the Savoy is guilty . . . Guilty of impartiality/of healthy geniality/guilty of hospitality/Guilty of syncopation/of joy and animation . . . Guilty of national unity/of practicing real democracy/By allowing the races openly/to dance and mingle in harmony."[40]

For Afrodiasporic cultures, dance has always been more what Clifford

Geertz calls "deep play" than escapist entertainment or simple emotional outlet. Music and dance have a "quite different and incomparably greater significance" for Africans than for Europeans, wrote the musicologist E. M. von Hornbostel in 1928, and they do not fit "under the general headings of Art or Games . . . serv[ing] neither as mere pastimes nor recreations." Instead, music and dance are fitted to speech and to work rhythms, and they reflect "psycho-physical conditions"; these forms help free the body from heaviness and effort through repetitive action. The desired result is that "vitality is heightened above its normal state."[41]

African Americans "talk back" to their environment through imitation and dance. Among Afrodiasporic peoples, "mimicry is used to capture, restate, and control the *ashe* (soul force) of the object." In the cakewalk, for example, African Americans mocked the formal walk and mannerisms of the southern planter class. The dance served to neutralize the cultural power of upper-class culture through irony and derision, and it captured and restated such manifestations of economic power as a high-stepping, comic, joyful, controlled display of physical control within the archetypal West African circle.[42]

A similar ethos of mimicry underlies the stylization of machine aesthetics. In African American culture, dance moves have always "imitated the work routine."[43] In the late nineteenth century, former slaves remembered calling out such phrases as "pitchin' hay," "corn shuckin'," and "cuttin' wheat" to dancers performing the cakewalk.[44] Stevedores on the docks and track-laying gandy dancers used rhythm to stylize repetitive work. In the cotton fields, blues vocalization and song forms grew out of field hollers, turning work calls into personal cries that helped lessen the drudgery and neutralize the anomie caused by an implacable dominant culture.[45]

If the work routine suddenly centered on machines, then machines themselves had to be brought into the dance. If machines have too much power in everyday life (too much *ashe*), human beings must pump up their soul force to compete with the new power in order to survive. This is what the bandleader Vincent Lopez meant when he realized jazz in 1917 created an immediate shift in the tempo of show business from music of the "heart" to that of the "adrenal glands."[46] Lindy hoppers did not self-consciously stylize machine aesthetics into a hard-swinging artistic dance; but if Afrodisaporic dance traditions work within a philosophical framework based on signifying on the soundscape through music and dance, the new machine-driven tempo had to be aesthetically integrated. One has to ritually tame that which runs wild in the environment.

Within a tradition of propulsive rhythms, improvisation, and revitalization through dance, there is no reason to believe the machine represented an unintegratable set of rhythms and aesthetics. The host of a talk show once joked to Frankie Manning, "A ton of bricks could fall on you and you wouldn't lose the rhythm." Manning accepted the compliment shyly and replied: "Well, I don't know about that. . . . I think I might teach the bricks the rhythm."[47] The best African American dancers bring this attitude to the dance floor.

The Speed and Flow of the Lindy Hop

The most distinctive element in the lindy was the low-to-the-ground horizontal flow. Compared to the back-and-forth, up-and-down moves of the Charleston or the turkey trot, the lindy emphasized smooth, continuous, fluid motion. Frankie Manning danced from a crouch, bent low, his knees flexed, and he pivoted from this lower posture. "I like to dance slow, and have a buoyancy," he explained. "Other folks [that is, whites] dance upright—without getting their knees into it." Manning's crouch is the standard opening posture for the Yoruba people of southwestern Nigeria, and it is antithetical to the upright European posture. The upper torso is bent forward at an angle of ninety degrees to the thighs, which flex forward at the knees. In contrast to a statuesque ideal, such a relaxed posture prepares a dancer for intricate lower-body manipulation, large trunk movements, and propulsion from the pelvic center. As Stearns has pointed out, Africans dance with their center of gravity in the hips and pelvis, and the energy explodes out through the legs.[48]

Nearly all lindy hoppers dance from the crouch today, as one can see even in the popular 1999 television commercial for The Gap that anachronistically featured all white dancers. But in the 1930s there was a distinctive difference between white and black lindy hoppers. Howard Johnson, a sociology professor and former Cotton Club dancer, recalled that "the smoothness and flow was unfamiliar to whites."[49] Ernie Smith, a white lindy hopper from Pittsburgh and later a dance historian, recalled that young white middle-class dancers jitterbugged "more up and down, more staccato." Black dancers, "instead of hopping up and down, [made] everything [look] smooth. It's effortless dancing, really." The term "jitterbug" is thought to derive from black observers describing the jerky, up-and-down (vertical) accentuation of white lindyers, and it was codified in Cab Calloway's 1932 hit, "I'm a Jitterbug." According to Smith, white dancers "weren't what we call 'cool'"—a term also coined in the late 1930s ("a cool cat") that always contains associations with smooth motion, relaxed rhythm, and emotional control.[50]

The two most difficult characteristics of the lindy for whites to master were "the pelvic motion" ("the gyrating hips") and the polyrhythmic response of the body. "You have to sway forwards and backwards, with a controlled hip movement," Smith recalled, "while your shoulders stay level and your feet glide along the floor." A dancer thus must keep the shoulders squared, the hips rolling, and the legs and feet in constant motion. The pelvic motions felt "obscene" to Smith at the time, and whites generally "couldn't stand the gyrating movements." The lindy hop was a black dance; "even when whites are doing it, it's still a black dance."[51]

One can see the cultural difference in the photos of the white and black couples in the 1943 *Life* cover story. Almost every photo of Leon James and Willa Mae Ricker, of Whitey's Lindy Hoppers, capture the couple in step and yet in flux. In half the photos, one of the two dancers is airborne. In one shot, Ricker is flipped over in a 135-degree angle to the floor, yet her legs are straight and together. In a Gjon Mili photograph that later became famous, the dancers appear to be hanging in mid-air; exuberant smiles on their faces, bent in well-defined crouches, and attached only lightly by one hand, they seemingly defy gravity. By contrast, Stanley Catron and Kaye Popp, the white professional dancers on the magazine cover, feature barely bent knees and an upright orientation. When alleged to be showing the "swing-out" move and the "jig walk," they seem to be making only vaguely undulating movements; in the over-the-back move, Popp seems to be struggling not to land head-first on the floor. Certainly, according to all accounts, there were dozens of excellent white lindy hoppers. But the white dancers photographed in *Life* reveal none of the torque, whirl, and precision of Leon James and Willa Mae Ricker.[52]

The lindy was a social dance built for speed. Euro-American critics sometimes thought the fast numbers in a black band's repertoire—the "flagwavers" or "killer-dillers"—were gratuitously flashy, and lacking in precision and musical substance. But younger dancers requested these songs; according to Norma Miller, the goal was the "perfect attunement between dance and music." Miller enjoyed the competition and imitation of the white dancers at the Savoy. "We didn't mind that people came from downtown to watch us. No white kids could ever cut us up on the floor. But we liked that they tried. When they came close, *we'd just ask the band to up the tempo*." Her confidence belied a hostility related to the racial realities of the time: "They [whites] couldn't take this from us. They had everything else."[53]

More than speed and horizontal flow, the continuous motion of the lindy thrilled dancers and audiences. Manning worked with his partner Freda Washington day after day to create the first air step, the "over-the-back" move in which the couple locked arms and Manning pulled Washington over his head. The key artistic aim was to land in time with the music and continue through to the next move. When the couple could land on the beat every time—"Now I'm ready," Manning recalled thinking—they went to compete in the Saturday night Savoy contest. The moment after they completed the over-the-back move and powered through to the next step, the entire audience—dancers, musicians, spectators—stopped. "No one cared about the contest no more," Manning recalled with pride.[54] With the creation of a few more air steps like the "hip to hip" and the "side flip," the lindy's success was complete, and teams of professional lindy hoppers spread the dance through vaudeville, night clubs, and Broadway musicals.

The contrast of the vertical accents of the air steps with the smooth, continuous horizontal motion was thrilling, a mix of skyscraper aspiration and steady locomotive power. The dancers "toss[ed] each other around with what appeared to be fatal abandon," Stearns recalled, "[and] no matter how high a dancer soared, he hit the deck right on the beat and swung along into the next step."[55]

The lindy hoppers were "a kind of folk avant-garde," to use Marshall Stearns's term. They were often teenagers who worked for hours every day on their routines and on creating new steps. Norma Miller remembers that tourists thought the lindy was "a spontaneous exhibition by a regular group of dancers . . . [but] what they were watching was rehearsed and choreographed dance."[56] The lindy hop did not achieve its professional form overnight, but in conjunction with the growing rhythmic power and sophistication of big bands.

The machine aesthetics of the lindy helped devalue what the dance historian Sally Banes terms "the etherealized bodies of Euro-American culture."[57] An anthropologist who analyzed ballet as a white European ethnic dance form identified its aesthetic emphasizes: "the long line of lifted, [upward-] extended bodies," "the total revealing of legs," "[the importance] of small heads and tiny feet for women . . . [and of] slender bodies for both sexes." Of primary importance was "the coveted airy quality . . . best shown in the lifts and carryings of the female."[58] Airiness, petite bodies, lack of contact with the ground—a dance aesthetic that valorized such ethereal qualities could not hope to contain the energies of mass production or reflect a dynamic, speeded-up tempo of life. A *Vanity Fair* critic noted disparagingly in 1929 that "the classic ballet was the expression on tiptoe of a sigh."[59] Isadora Duncan claimed ballet was already sterile in 1900 because the goal of its dancers was "to create the delusion that the law of gravitation [did] not exist for them."[60]

African American dancers work with, not against, the laws of gravity, and the torque of the "swing-out" was functionally compelling because of its dynamic integration. Instead of a set pattern danced repetitively (as in a waltz) the lindy contained a common vocabulary of moves to be used in any order and improvised by each individual couple. The lindy's fast tempos and propulsive circular motion—the torque of it—added to the illusion of speed, generating a sense of smooth, dynamic motion. In African American communities, a new dance often precedes a new rhythm, and if necessary the dancers clap their own rhythms to cue the musicians. The dance director Lida Webb brought this practice to the Broadway stage in *Runnin' Wild,* having the dance chorus provide "hand-clapping and foot-patting" to "beat out the irresistible . . . rhythm in a veritable Charleston seminar for white Broadway audiences."[61] The musicologist Howard Spring has suggested that lindy hoppers *caused* the musical innovations of big band swing, that young black dancers "called" for a faster, more propulsive, more rhythmically sophisticated music.[62] According to Spring, lindy hoppers similarly created the impetus for the musical shift from the New Orleans two-beat to the articulation of an even four beats and swing tempo. A number of jazz musicians provide testimony supporting this possibility.[63]

The Harvest Moon Ball

The lindy hop entered a new phase of recognition and popularity when members of Whitey's Lindy Hoppers swept the lindy hop division of the first Harvest Moon Ball in 1935. Sponsored by the *New York Daily News* at Madison Square Garden between 1935 and 1950, the Harvest Moon Ball was a unique swing-era cultural event that highlights the importance of dynamic social dance to Depression-era young Americans.

The event sold out within hours every year, a fact that never failed to shock New York City's theater and entertainment professionals. The comedian Milton Berle hosted the program for the first two years; the *Daily News* columnist Ed Sullivan took over for the next six. Some seventy-five or so couples competed in six ballroom events (waltz, fox trot, tango, rumba, lindy) to live music provided by two name dance bands; the second band played expressly to accompany the lindy hoppers. The prize for the all-around champion couple, and each division champion, was a week-long contract to perform at the Loew's State Theater. The all-around champions received $750 and the division champs $250.[64]

The biggest stars of Hollywood and Broadway provided entertainment between rounds of the competition. In 1939 they included Judy Garland, Mickey Rooney, and the Andrews Sisters. Celebrity dancers, movie stars, sports figures, and political leaders sat in a row of celebrity boxes, and tap-dancing actors (George Raft in 1939, James Cagney and Ray Bolger in 1940) were known to give the crowds a quick thrill when called upon to dance.[65] The five-member panel of judges were "all world-renowned authorities in the professional dancing world." In 1935 they included the dance teacher Arthur Murray, the founder of the Rockettes, a senior producer at Radio City, and the owner of New York's Roseland.

The Garden not only sold out quickly every year, but more than five thousand fans often stood outside and heard the festivities over loudspeakers. Mayor Fiorello LaGuardia presided every year; at the end of the debut ball, he told a live radio audience it had been "one of the most interesting evenings of my life. . . . The quality of the dancing is far beyond what I imagined amateurs could do. . . . It is truly a splendid event."[66] Theatrical professionals were still shocked ten years later. "The pulling power of the amateur dance contest is no longer a novelty," the *Daily News* observed in 1944, "but it is still a source of amazement to veteran showmen."[67]

Owing to the event's partisan sponsorship, the ball has perhaps escaped historical scrutiny; no other city newspaper except the *New York Daily News* mentioned it. The *Daily News* covered it at the level of a major championship athletic event, and its staging had much in common with the boxing matches that made the Garden famous. The dancers competed in an enlarged boxing ring, a "raised platform, 30 × 40 feet . . . perched in the middle of the floor." The first Harvest Moon Ball was "charged with the gala air of a championship boxing battle."[68] The entire back page of the August 29, 1935, edition was taken up by a panoramic photograph of the Garden's interior showing the huge crowd and the central ring. Photos from the ball—of dancers in mid-step, of celebrities, of the crowd—dominated the tabloid's front page, back page, and centerfold every year until the outset of World War II. Even during the war, the "king and queen . . . of the ball" were often pictured on the front page beneath such headlines as "Laval, Nazis' Friend, Shot" (1941) and "Bomb 9 More Jap Ships" (1944).[69]

Nor was it a cheap event, or one just for "the bobby-soxers" or "the kids" (as teenagers were often termed). Prices for the first year were 55¢, $1.10, and $2.20 for box seats, at a time when a top price for a Broadway show was about $3.30. The average age of the audience was roughly twenty-three (if the winners are representative), and many of the winning couples were engaged, married, or planning to tie the knot. The marriage angle was a staple of the coverage, as reporters constantly asked the winning couples the status of their relationship. Winners were listed by occupation: clerk, bookkeeper, machinist, salesman, nurse, secretary, hairdresser.[70]

The event's origins are unclear. Norma Miller claims it was part of a series of responses to the Harlem race riot that took place in March 1935. The Savoy sustained some damage during the riot, and a meeting of the owner and managers resulted in the idea of a big dance. They met with the management of the *Daily News* and discussed "what could be done about the damaged property and the community's damaged morale" and "how to raise Harlem's tattered spirits and to restore the ballroom's business." They decided on a citywide contest as a way to popularize the lindy and restore morale. The city agreed to build a bandshell for two orchestras at Central Park and to provide a large dance floor. There was to be one white society band (first year, Abe Lyman) and one swing band for the lindy hoppers (Fletcher Henderson). Miller saw it as "our chance to put the Lindy on the map. . . . We were gonna let the world know about the Lindy and that it belonged to us!" Rehearsing for the ball "became the main focus of our lives."[71]

Certainly it is possible that community and municipal leaders believed the event would encourage young African Americans to spend their free time in the summer practicing for the competition. Moreover, all profits from the event went to the News Welfare Association to pay for two-week summer vacations for the city's underprivileged children, as administered by the Children's Welfare Federation.[72] But the coverage in the *Daily News* suggests the lindy was a late addition to the Harvest

Moon Ball. The idea to include "Lenox Avenue's favorite step" came at the insistence of James V. Mulholland, the supervisor of recreation for the Park Department (the municipal department supporting the event). Neighborhood competitions for the ball were held at outdoor dancing parties throughout the city that summer, and Mulholland witnessed "the enormous success of the city's first Harlem dancing party at Colonial Park" in mid-July. "The waltz, the tango, the rhumba and the fox-trot are all right, but what about the Lindy Hop? I never saw better dancing than . . . those couples doing the Lindy Hop in Harlem. It was a fine, well-behaved, carefree crowd, and we certainly want them represented in the contest." Mulholland personally requested the creation of a lindy division in the dance competition and "were we glad to oblige!," the reporter editorialized.[73]

Whatever the motivation for the first Harvest Moon Ball, the response took everyone by surprise. Called for Central Park on August 15, 1935, the first event drew a huge crowd of 150,000 people; because the police had no means to control such a crowd, the ball was postponed for two weeks and rescheduled for Madison Square Garden. Miller remembered the contrast between what she called the "ballroom people" and the lindy hoppers. "You couldn't imagine a bigger contrast. . . . First of all, the clothes: they had tuxes and evening dresses, and we were in sneakers and short skirts. Then there was the noise. The ballroom people danced silently, maybe swishing their gowns a little. But there's no such thing as a quiet lindy hop. We grunted and screamed, like martial arts people do today. We'd never seen people dance quiet before." Her memories are reflected in the *Daily News* coverage. Statuesque Anglo-Americans in "tuxes and evening dresses" usually won the overall competition, and were also the most photographed. But the crowd favorites were the hard-working, "grunt[ing] and scream[ing]" lindy hoppers in "sneakers and short skirts."[74]

Miller and her fellow Harlem teenagers were shocked to find out there would be *rules*—and *judges*—at the first Harvest Moon Ball. "We'd never heard of dancing to rules. We couldn't be away from our partners and had to have our feet on the floor. And the crowd didn't decide the winner [as at the Savoy]—they had all white judges and a point system!"[75] Miller points up the conceptual difference in European-derived and African-derived concepts of art, between classical training and an oral tradition of embodiment, challenge, and participatory consciousness. In the latter, the audience decides the winner and there is no correct way to dance; the audience chooses according to the excitement generated, to the syncing up of dancers to the music, to the physical control and execution of moves.[76]

The dancers first came out in a "grand parade." All the contestants were white except the lindy hoppers, yet the Harlem dancers drew the loudest cheers from the crowd, and "responded to the yells by swinging when we walked." Miller thought all the white dancers looked stunning in their formal gowns and tuxedos, and reflected that most of the dancers were working class with "low-income jobs . . . dancing was their way of escaping." She was surprised at how well the men fit their clothes, "carpenters and janitors . . . looked as if they were born for that attire." Yet when the same dancers began to lindy hop, she became belligerent: they "seemed clumsy to us . . . and watching them butcher our dance made our tempers flare." When the Fletcher Henderson band began to play, Miller recalled her competitive response. "Harlem came on . . . we were like a group of caged animals, ready to burst from the box."[77]

The lindy hop was always the hit of both the Harvest Moon Ball and the subsequent Loew's State Theater program. In 1936, the reporter Jack Turcott wrote that "it was the Lindy Hop which really set the audience on fire. Shoulders swayed and 22,000 pairs of feet tapped in unison as the competing couples swung into this infectious step."[78] In 1937, lindy hoppers "brought down the house with their wild gyrations."[79] In 1939, "The amusing Lindy Hop . . . brought down the house as usual, and the show closed with all the champions doing . . . the Conga."[80] Once the lindy hoppers repeated their debut success of 1935, they became, according to the *Daily News*, "the sole topic [of discussion] in theatrical circles."[81]

To recognize the dance's popularity in 1936, the second-place lindy-hopping couple also received a one-week contract to appear at the Loew's State Theater; no such offer was made to any other second-place couple. Beginning in 1938, the first *three* lindy-hopping winners were signed to one-week contracts at the Loew's; they "brought down the house" there, too, on a program that included a first-run movie, a music act, professional tap dancers, and comedy skits.[82] (See fig. 10.) Despite the importance of the lindy hop to these events, the dance and the dancers were noted only at the end of the articles in the *Daily News*. In 1940 Roger Dakin concluded his review of the Loew's program by saying it was a "must-see on the week's Broadway show list." "The fast-moving show closed, as usual, with the lindy hoppers from Harlem

Figure 10. Loew's advertisement featuring Harvest Moon Ball winners, 1941.

bringing down the house. Wilda Crawford and . . . Thomas Lee, abetted by the other speedy teams . . . [had] the audience on the verge of hysteria." He repeated the template the following year: "The swiftly paced lindy hoppers from Harlem [brought] down the house. . . . [They] had the audience on the verge of hysteria." In 1938 he had reported that for an "agreeable surprise" encore at the Loew's, the second and third place lindy couples (Joyce James and Joe Daniels, Bunny Miller and George Ricker) "brought down the house doing the Lindy Hop in slow motion with the champions, Miss Pollard and [Mr.] Minns."[83]

Not until 1940 did a *Daily News* reporter attempt to actually describe the lindy. All the dance genres had their points, noted William Murtha, but the one that "brought the audience to the edge of its seats was—you guessed it—the Lindy Hop." Murtha dismisses the dance as a cross between gymnastics and a sporting event. "They call it dancing, but it included everything from the old-fashioned airplane spin to something that looked like a baseball slide, preceded by a cartwheel."[84] The following year, Murtha described the dance within a familiar primitivist discourse. "The lindy hop [is] a bit of terpsichore that combined the best features of a windmill, a three-ring circus and a whirling dervish . . . legs, arms and midriffs flew dizzily with sundry bits of anatomy just missing your correspondent's writing machine. When it was over, three teams of colored whoop-de-doers bagged the prizes." Murtha did not call rumba dancers "whoop-de-doers," for example, referring simply to the "swishy, swaying strains of rumba band-leader Xavier Cugat."[85]

In 1942 Murtha equated the lindy with both childishness and insanity, the ultimate conclusion of the primitivist, "out-of-control" discourse. "After the tango came the *madhouse*, which is another way of saying jitterbug jive. In the name of rhythm . . . [couples] tossed each other around in a screaming array of shagging, pecking, big appling, Lindy hopping and any miscellaneous gyrations you care to mention. The crowd howled and all but fell out of the balconies as the jitterbugs did their stuff, and . . . [soon] the crowns of jive rested on the heads of three colored couples."[86] Murtha had learned enough about black dances to spot moves quoted by individual lindy hoppers ("shagging, pecking, big appling"), but clearly his new expertise did not upgrade the dancers (or the dance) to a level he felt bound to respect.

Every year the *Daily News* reported that the lindy hop brought down the house, and every year lindy hoppers appeared in the fewest photographs of all the contestants. All of the winners were designated by name, occupation, and age. Although many of the contestants had Irish, Spanish, Jewish, and Italian surnames, only the ethnicity of the lindy hoppers was listed (as "colored"). For example, in 1937 the three lindy hop couples were named and "all the winners named in this event were colored."[87] Again, despite the varying ethnicities of the winners, the most-photographed winners were statuesque Anglo-Americans often described as "king and queen" or the "royal couple" of the ball. The winning couple often graced the front and back pages of the paper, were inevitably dressed formally, and were photographed in ways that highlighted their attempts to look like English nobility or, at least, like Fred Astaire and Ginger Rogers.

Lindy hoppers appeared in at least one photograph a year, usually in demeaning poses or with minstrel gestures (eyes rolling, mouths wide open). The first year was an exception: 1935's lindy hop winners, Leon James and Edith Matthews, were depicted respectfully in two centerfold photos in the midst of their swing-out move; James was listed as "a superintendent" and Matthews as "a housemaid." In 1936 the lindy hop champs George Greenich and Ella Gibson were pictured "rehearsing" even though they were not dancing; Gibson hung from Greenich's arms and both smiled widely at the camera, as if they were just goofing around. In 1937 Joe Daniels was shown holding Joyce James nearly upside down, her feet high in the air and her thighs exposed. Third-place winner Norma Miller was shown almost completely upside down in 1938, with George Ricker bending over her; Miller's waist, buttocks, and legs hung in the air over their heads. That year's lindy hop winners, Mildred Pollard and Albert Minns, were photographed standing still with Pollard holding Minns high off the floor and their mouths hanging wide open. In 1938 all three winning lindy hop couples were photographed together, all bending forward with overly wide, unnatural, minstrel-derived smiles. There were no such corresponding photos of white dancers in any division.[88]

Not a single dignified photograph of an African American musician or dancer appeared in ten years. In 1935 Ginger Rogers was shown smiling and leaning over her box to shake Bill Robinson's hand. Robinson was also a movie star at the time but he was not seated in a celebrity box; nor was he described as a movie star but instead as "Harlem's #1 tap dancer." Rogers's engaging smile notwithstanding, the photo frames the two as mistress of the house and servant. In 1944 Robinson was shown "capering" for his long-time co-star Shirley Temple (who did not perform). In the newspaper's promotional articles, the black bandleader was never pictured, regardless of his local fame: neither Fletcher Henderson, a New York favorite since the early 1920s, nor Cab Calloway appeared in these articles. On the other hand, a photo of the white bandleader Abe Lyman appeared in a 1935 article.[89]

Two weeks before the 1938 ball, an article announced Billie Holiday's scheduled appearance with Artie Shaw. The headline declared "Billie Holiday to Be Harvest Moon Singer," but oddly the inset photograph was of an unidentified white woman named Mary Dee. The irrelevant caption underneath Dee's photo, "Waiting for Wednesday," only heightened the absurdity. The article respectfully (though inaccurately) called Holiday "the most exciting blues singer in America" and also "the undisputed queen of the blues since the death of Bessie Smith." Shaw's band was then the artistic equal of any in the nation; but Shaw's hiring of Holiday was itself a major act of racial transgression (and courage) in the 1930s—along with Benny Goodman's hiring of Lionel Hampton and Teddy Wilson—and was not approved in many business circles. Holiday "rate[d] tops with swing fans," and the newspaper promoted her "lilting vocals [that] jibe beautifully with the Shaw style," but the paper apparently would not print her picture.[90]

African American dancers took first place in the lindy hop every Harvest Moon Ball between 1935 and 1950 except 1943, when a summer race riot in Harlem generated political backlash from Mayor LaGuardia. Soon after the riot, the city padlocked the Savoy as LaGuardia used the police to punish Moe Gale, the Savoy's owner, and especially manager Charlie Buchanan, who was coeditor of *The People's Voice,* a socialist weekly antagonistic to the mayor. A broad range of community leaders protested the police action and the court injunction that followed, but to no avail.[91] Neither a black swing band nor a name band played at the 1943 ball, and Johnny Long and Enric Madriguera were the weakest bands in years. It seems as if local politicians and the *Daily News* intended to punish African Americans by withdrawing recognition of their cultural forms.

Ironically, on the day Italy surrendered—unlike Harlem, Italy *was* at war with the United States—an Italian American couple became the first nonblack champions of the lindy hop. The racial nature of the victory was duly noted: "For the first time in Harvest Moon history a white couple won the Jitterbug Jive."[92]

The Cultural Politics of the Lindy Hop

There is a clear division between the vested cultural interests of the *New York Daily News* and the stylized cultural forces that young dancers enthusiastically engaged. The newspaper was beholden to an older aesthetic regime and its cultural guardians. For example, the lindy hop was ignored by dance instructors until 1943. Yet as early as 1930 a radio-show host and writer for the magazine *American Dancer* was besieged with requests to learn the lindy, but was unable to find an instructor willing to teach it. He taught himself the dance and rented out the Roseland ballroom. A thousand people came to his first lesson.[93]

Professional dance instructors attacked the lindy hop as late as 1939. That year *Newsweek* and the mainstream press reported a "war on swing dance style" led by professional dance instructors intent on leading Americans back to old-fashioned styles, slower dances, and more discreet women's fashions. The Dancing Masters of America issued a "manifesto" at their annual convention "consigning the jitterbug to oblivion and predicting the speedy return of the gay '90s in the guise of the fabulous '40s." The sixty-eight-year-old president declared that the jitterbug had "no place in the[ir] instruction program" and claimed that dance instructors were hearing that people were tired of "the jumping dances . . . such as the 'Shag,' 'Big Apple,' and other athletic steps." The organization hired the dancing sweetheart of the early 1910s, Irene Castle, to be its spokeswoman. Labeled the "heaviest possible artillery in its war against rug cutters," Castle's promotional efforts coincided with the release of *The Story of Vernon and Irene Castle* (1939), starring Fred Astaire and Ginger Rogers. Dance educators also convinced journalists of the rising popularity of the "boomps-a-daisy," a dance invented by a British songwriter, at the climax of which partners lightly bumped each other's buttocks. These dance instructors, and the upper-class clientele they traditionally served, were literally out of step with their time—just as Henry Ford had been in the early 1920s. By 1941, most prestigious upper-class hotels featured hard-swinging big bands such as Count Basie.[94]

Why would a popular dance cause such a reaction? Why would a dance be taboo? Was it simply that dance instructors could not do the dance and were threatened economically? Perhaps. But they could have learned the dance and profited from teaching it to a rhythmically hungry dancing public. It took more than thirteen years for this to happen. Barring the lindy hop from dance studios was an act of cultural segregation and signified nothing less than culture war (and class war, and race war). "In its early days the Lindy flourished only in lower strata of society," *Life* reflected in 1943. "Negroes were its creators and principal exponents, and Arthur Murray would no more have taught the Lindy Hop than Rachmaninoff would have given lessons in boogie-woogie."

Life then recounted the rise in the lindy's prestige mediated by the whitefacing of swing by Benny Goodman and Glenn Miller. "With the renascence of swing, the Lindy *climbed the social scale*. New steps like the Suzy-Q, Trucking and Jig-Walk were invented. . . . And as they spread across the land, invading colleges and dance schools, the Lindy Hop attained respectability as a truly national dance." Dance instructors and educators were fighting to maintain white Eurocentric cultural and kinesthetic values over black Afrocentric ones. African American aesthetics won, but only under the mediated term "swing," and only due to popular demand.[95]

In his autobiography *Along the Way* (1934), James Weldon Johnson reflected back on Euro-Americans in thrall to Harlem nightlife in the late 1920s and early 1930s. In urban dance halls, "the Negro drags his captors captive." Johnson was "amazed and amused" to watch whites dance, "doing their best to pass for colored." Without resorting to blackface, Euro-Americans shed their white skins and obsolete kinesthetics for modern bodies in what has become a defining ritual for each white generation since. This cultural appropriation only became possible for large segments of young working-class Americans with the establishment of dance halls such as the Savoy rather than elite cabarets such as the Cotton Club. As Johnson rightly perceived, once the forms were appropriated they became subsumed under the term "American," effacing the black culture at its base and denying economic opportunities to the innovators and performers until "Negro secular music . . . was finally taken over and made 'American popular music.'"[96]

To take a salient example, in 1941 Whitey's Lindy Hoppers appeared in their last movie, *Hellzapoppin'*; both the choreography and cinematography of this scene make it the lindy hop's finest moment on film. Logically such dancers would continue to perform in movies, but instead, a white group, "The Jivin' Jacks and Jills," started to appear in films two years later. The Jivin' Jacks and Jills appeared in fourteen B movies between 1943 and 1955 while Whitey's Lindy Hoppers broke up and performed separately over the next few years.[97] In 1943 dance teachers finally began to teach the lindy, and white lindy hoppers began to find employment on Broadway. The cultural theft of the lindy hop by white performers signifies the unfair labor practices that prevented African Americans from enjoying economic equity and class mobility in every industry in the United States.

Technology and Survival Technology (Redux)

Katherine Dunham studied dancing in Jamaica, the West Indies, and Haiti in the 1930s. In comparing the dances of Afrodiasporic communities, she concluded that "the transition from tribal to folk culture" had three major effects: first, African ritual patterns, ideas, and values were imposed on Christian ideology; second, African dance lost contact with its original "meanings" or functions; third, Afro-Caribbean musicians meshed their secular musical patterns with those of "whatever European nation happened to dominate the territory."[98]

Upon her return in the late 1930s, Dunham easily identified African retentions in much of American social dance. She recognized "almost the entire pattern" of the lindy hop in Jamaican urban popular dances such as the sha-sha and mento. She identified "a practically pure Charleston step" in "possessed devotees" of Sanctified churches and in Melville Herskovits's field recordings from West Africa. The Big Apple dance then popular at the Savoy derived from the plantation Juba dance, one of an entire West African "category of 'circle' dances" featuring hand-clapping, individual self-expression within the circle, and contrasting rhythms for the group moving around the circle and the couple dancing inside it.[99]

Dunham proudly asserted in 1941 that the potency of African dances, rhythms, and gestures within American social dance were likely to "guarantee the persistence of African dance traditions." They had been "modified" more in the United States than the Caribbean, but African American cultural traditions had shaped American kinesthetics, physical gesture, timing, and rhythm. She celebrated the fact that African American cultural traditions existed in "a sound functional relationship towards a culture which is contemporary, rather than towards one which is on the decline.[100] The West African cultural legacy and the African American historical experience had been danced into the American mainframe.[101]

Why the African legacy and not the German or the Irish or the Jewish or the Native American or the Chinese? Owing to certain aesthetic affinities, African Americans had matched the *motor activity* of their cultural forms to the *motorized society*, a legacy still represented erotically in such song titles as James Brown's "Sex Machine," Parliament-Funkadelic's "Motor Booty Affair" and Prince's "Little Red Corvette."

The lindy hop was the "right" dance for its time, a demanding dance that made hard, fast-paced, precise work into a ritual act of deep play.

Martha Graham set these goals for the "American dance" in 1935: "No great dance can leave a people unmoved. Sometimes the reaction will take the form of a cold antagonism to the truth of what they are seeing. Sometimes an unbelievable response. What is necessary is that the dance be as strong as life itself, and of the life that is known in the country, that it be influenced by the prevailing expression of the people of a country, as well as by the geography of the land itself." Such a dance would be "powerful" and reflect the nation's energy and drive. "We look to the dance to impart the sensation of living in an affirmation of life, to energize the spectator into keener awareness of the vigor, the mystery, the humor, the variety, and the wonder of life."[102] Graham declared that such qualities would show "the function[s] of the American dance." She was right—but about the wrong dances; such were the functions of tap and the lindy hop.

The children of the new chugging, dynamic technical civilization valorized the human form moving through space *explosively*, not ethereally; *using gravity*, not defying it; having *fluid, continuous motion*, not abstract poses or "airiness." Swing-era dance culture broke down the European mask of sophistication; the lindy deemphasized the idea of good form or dance rules and empowered individual self-expression and the judgment of the audience. The lindy also furthered the development of a new youth culture, especially as women developed their own uniforms to enable more athletic dancing; the now-famous saddle shoes, full skirts, and sloppy sweaters evolved for dancing the lindy, not rock and roll.[103] The familiar cluster of youth culture—new slang, hip clothing, a new rhythmically driven form of music, sexual liberation—began with jazz and the Charleston in the 1920s but became codified through swing music and dance.

One recent historical study of jazz fans in Nazi Germany concluded that the lindy's embodied values were diametrically opposed to German lockstep, classical music, and rigid social planning. As early as 1917 an American journalist watching the German army march into Brussels described it as "mov[ing] . . . as smoothly and as compactly as an Empire State Express . . . [with] no halts, no open places, no stragglers." The German jazz fans of the mid-1940s valued the *opposite* kinesthetics in the lindy. In the dance's combination of self-expression, rapid motion, and fluid movement, they "discovered a living response to the terrorizing racism that lurked in the shadow of modernity. . . . As the dancers spun, broke away and turned they discovered an ethical understanding which valued the individual 'off-beat'—a syncopated sensibility." Perhaps we can ideologically embody the cultural values at stake between the United States and Germany as the lindy vs. the lock-step.[104]

Lindy hoppers displayed a mindful body capable of abrupt stops and starts, and of continuous dynamic, vigorous motion within a cooperative social pattern. Lindy hoppers took flight (like Lindbergh) and a moment later slid on the ground like diesel-powered serpents. West African–derived dance moves are a crucial aspect of global culture today and remain misunderstood as a force of modernity. Unlike ballet or modern dance, the lindy hop does not value body type itself but rather the dynamics and expressiveness of *the body-in-motion;* the idea that every individual can and will put some part of his or her self into the dance is an embodiment of democratic values.[105]

Coda: The Ruby (Dance) Slippers

I would like to conclude this chapter with a story you may recognize from 1939. On an infrequently traveled road in a mythical kingdom, three men paralyzed by their work lives—a scarecrow, a lumberjack, and a king who lacks self-esteem—are each in turn freed by a young woman newly arrived in their land. Each responds to this new freedom with a *solo dance of liberation* . . . and then joins a collective skip-march down the road toward the unknown. In "real" life, each man is a lowly Kansas farmhand trapped on the farm, and if you will, in obsolete, European-patterned folk dances; but in Munchkinland—that primitivist fantasy land of midgets—dance is a liberating force of anti-industrial play, a vehicle of self-expression. Significantly, the most powerful man in the dream kingdom does not dance, although he, too, is paralyzed by his work life. The ultimate wallflower, "the great and powerful Oz" is a pretentious, scared, knob-turning technological wizard who manipulates machinery in order to delude people into believing in his omnipotence.

What is the moral of this story? That we need more cultural history of music and dance. Then when someone such as Salman Rushdie notes the significance of Dorothy's "syncopated step" as she skip-starts down the yellow brick road, we will become more aware of the techno-dialogic of syncopation and skyscrapers on the road to the Emerald City.[106]

More to the point here, the actors who played the Scarecrow (Ray Bolger), the Tin Man (Jack Haley), and the Cowardly Lion (Bert Lahr) were all famous dancers of the period, and all three sat in Celebrity Row at the 1939 Harvest Moon Ball to promote *The Wizard of Oz.* (Bolger appeared again in 1940 and performed for fifteen minutes.) In 1964, Bolger, the most famous dancer of the three, claimed on the *Today* show that he invented the lindy hop in 1927 at the Hotel Coronado in St. Louis.[107] Again, we have a damning and embarrassing example of how the love and theft of black cultural forms and its subsequent appropriation are facts on the ground of American culture.

One of the few musical numbers cut from *The Wizard of Oz* was "The Jitterbug."[108] The Wicked Witch was to send "an evil advance agent—'a little insect'"—to sting Dorothy and her escorts, sending them into such an exhausting dance they would be unable to fight off the flying monkeys. This situation set up "The Jitterbug" routine, a song intended to be danced by the four principals with the participation of the trees of the Haunted Forest. The upbeat number broke the tension of the plot and was ultimately deemed inappropriate; it was dropped before release. The song is presented as a "frenzy," an uncontrolled set of steps resulting from emotional hysteria and having neither rhyme nor reason. But what if the jitterbug was not the response of a childlike, preindustrial people, but a sophisticated response to the disruptions of modernity? What if integrating power, precision, speed, flow, and control in modern bodies makes the lindy hop a most appropriate response to the challenge of a machine-centered society?

And what if we think of Dorothy's ruby slippers as *dancing shoes?* What if those erotic glittering blood-red shoes were the elusive cultural weapon for stepping *out* of American machined dreams into a new world cultural order that would include (and equally value) dance, sex, pleasure, individuality within a collective flow, and letting go? What if Glenda the Good Witch's statement to Dorothy—that she has always had the power to get home right at her feet—meant that she could "go home" and put these two worlds together into a new world where the primitivist fantasies of Oz were integrated into the emerald skyscraper cities of industrial civilization? In other words, what if Dorothy could have recognized what Christopher Small calls "a need in white culture" to make pleasure and joyful self-affirmation part of her everyday life, rather than retreat back into some puritanical, patriarchal sickbed down on the farm?

Then we might really be heading toward understanding the new cultural order threatening to burst through the industrial society and the attendant fantasy worlds of the New York World's Fair of 1939, which is the subject of the final chapter.

THE WORLD OF TOMORROW...

IN THE GROOVE

SWINGING THE NEW YORK WORLD'S FAIR, 1939–40

Nearly all of the historical examination of the New York World's Fair of 1939–40 focuses on the first year and its theme of technological utopianism, "The World of Tomorrow."[1] Since the London Crystal Palace Exhibition of 1851, international expositions had been celebrations of technology, but in 1940 the escalating war in Europe had punctured this Fair's optimistic view of techno-progress.[2] The national vision implicit in industrial exhibits such as General Motors's Futurama (which have concerned scholars most) could no longer obscure the demands of the present: in Europe the most sophisticated machines were once again being put to the task of human destruction. After the Nazi-Soviet pact of August 1939, the shape of the *real* world of tomorrow—politically, economically, geographically—was more unsure than ever.[3] In retrospect, the 1939 Fair's cryptic secondary slogan, "Time Tears On" (it appeared in huge blue block letters on its stationery) seems almost precious. By the Fair's second year, the excitement of technological futurism had ended for the moment. To freely adapt a common black vernacular phrase of the early 1940s, instead "*now* was the time."[4]

The World of Tomorrow had lost a significant amount of money in 1939. In an attempt to recoup its losses, the Fair corporation's board of directors altered its technological focus to promote the exposition's old-fashioned carnival aspects; its new motto, "A Fair for Peace and Freedom," spoke only superficially to political concerns. The symbol that best expressed the shift from socially engineered future to tense wartime present was the replacement of the Soviet pavilion with a shifting weekly program called "The American Common." An open space in the international Court of Nations, the Common was an open space built for ethnic groups to present their folk heritage and contribution to what would now be called the "gorgeous mosaic" or "tossed salad" of American culture. Every week a different ethnic group gave speeches, performed historical re-creations, and showed off their music, dance, and costumes. A few scholars mention the American Common in passing, as "an open area for occasional gatherings and celebrations," or a place where "various Americanized foreign groups . . . presented weekly programs of song and dance."[5] But it merits closer attention.

The official invitation to the June 1, 1940, dedication ceremony of the American Common declared that the ground was "dedicated to the people of every nationality, race and religion who . . . by uniting their unique contributions to the land of their adoption, built here a living, ever-growing democracy devoted to peace and freedom." Eleanor Roosevelt gave the dedication speech. The Fair vice president Robert Kohn advised her to emphasize President Roosevelt's recent statement that "we are all descended from immigrants," writing to the First Lady that "[we] must all realize how much each of us owes to those others of other cultures who have helped to make this country for us." In a press release, he encouraged members of each ethnic group to attend as many celebrations as possible, "to meet and celebrate their contributions to American democracy," so that groups were not simply preaching to their own.[6]

The American Common was *not* an example of melting-pot ideology, however, but of multiculturalism. The ideology of the melting pot presumes a goal of total assimilation into what scholars of ethnicity call "Anglo-conformity," not a proud declaration of ethnic identity. Jingoistic patriotism during both world wars made any public declaration of a hyphenated ethnic identity (such as German-American, Japanese-American, Jewish-American, or Irish-American) undesirable and often dangerous. In terms of survival skills, it was strategically important to publicly refer to one's self as "100% American," as first promulgated by the American Legion's constitution in 1919; asserting *any* ethnic cultural identity politically was uncommon until the mid-1960s. Looked at in this context, the American Common may lay claim to being the first quasi-official declaration of a vernacular American culture generated from various distinct ethnic contributions and acculturation.[7]

How important was the American Common to the Fair's projection of American cultural values and ideals? First, the Common was one of the few exhibits built by the Fair corporation itself, and at considerable expense; it featured a large music bandshell and stage, nearly four thousand seats, a giant flag pole ("the highest in the fair"), and a large dance platform "for Folk Dances and parties." Second, the stage was flanked by two large banners. On the left side hung a hundred-foot-long scroll, an honor roll of individual immigrant achievement, while on the right hung "two large maps portray[ing] . . . the racial strains of the nations from whence American immigration stems . . . [and the] locations of their [present] settlement." A press release explained the symbolism: "It is an effort to present for the first time on a nationwide scale the contributions made by America's foreign-born citizens to [our] development." Two groups specifically named as "hav[ing] made notable contributions to our living, ever-growing democracy" were "American Indians" and "Negroes"—groups that were not, in fact, "foreign-born" at all.[8]

In replacing the 1939 Soviet pavilion, the American Common symbolizes one end to the twenty-year romance of American liberals with Communism.[9] According to a Gallup poll, the Soviet pavilion was the most popular foreign exhibit in 1939, and the Russian presence provided the Fair's president, Grover Whalen, with an early diplomatic coup; the Soviet Union spent four million dollars on two separate sites, and their financial commitment elicited increased expenditures from other nations. The Soviet pavilion's most striking feature was a seventy-nine-foot granite column crowned by a stainless-steel statue of a Russian man known only as "Joe the Worker." The apotheosized proletarian everyman held a torch over his head, perhaps a response to Miss Liberty across the harbor. World's Fair crews nicknamed the muscular man in his work clothes "Big Joe" and "The Bronx Express Straphanger."[10] "Joe the Worker" might also be seen as a symbol of the "new man"—the mythical, politically conscious proletarian envisioned by Marxist ideology.

That the Russian worker was presented within the same conventions of monumental iconography as the fifty-foot-tall statue of George Washington just down the Fair's Constitution Mall is a fascinating historical irony. The artistic tensions (and pretensions) of Russia's eight-story-tall average Joe were matched in absurdity by the 1940 Fair's official American symbol, "Elmer"—a "rosy-cheeked, middle-aged middle-American" standing in for a nostalgic Rockwellesque vision of small-town American innocence.[11] These respective fantasies of the Great Man, the Great Worker, and the Great Average American were ignored on the American Common where a new national sense of self struggled to be born.

On the Common, the proletarian "new man" and the heroic "great man" were superseded by what I can only term "multicultural man." Four months into the Fair, on September 22, 1940, the Common dedicated a "Wall of Fame" to enshrine the contributions of six hundred immigrants to American society. Selected from an initial list of six thousand chosen by Robert Kohn's research staff, these Americans of "foreign birth" had their names inscribed on "sixteen wooden slabs, each bearing two columns of names." A capacity crowd of 4,500 witnessed the dedication of the Wall of Fame, and the *New York Times* deemed it "the major event on the Fair program" that Sunday. Eduard C. Lindeman, professor of philosophy at the New York School of Social Work, gave the dedication speech, and began by quoting Ralph Emerson's vision of multiculturalism: "The energy of Irish, Germans, Swedes, Poles, and Cossacks, and all the European tribes, and of the Africans . . . will construct [here] a new race, a new religion, a new state."[12]

Lindeman then used Emerson as a jumping-off point from which to declare a new American mission: a war of cultural diversity against ideals of racial purity. "Our future destiny will . . . be determined by this fact: either we demonstrate that strength may come from heterogeneity or we, too, succumb to the deadly rule of uniformity. And the testing time has arrived." Lindeman stressed this new version of good and evil to the audience. The American mission was diversity, represented by immigrant contributions; the new evil could be found in the master-race ideologies of the Nazis and Japanese, nations that annihilated and evicted the impure strains in their national makeup. Invoking a Whitmanesque idea of a "nation of nations," Lindeman claimed that Americans "are a mixed people," grown up from "transplanted stock," who were "as a people irrevocably associated with . . . [being] heterogeneous."

Lindeman then read aloud a short prepared statement from Albert Einstein, one of the nation's most well-known and best-loved immigrants. Only immigrants truly appreciated American citizenship, Einstein wrote, and he admonished Americans for their often condescending attitudes toward foreign-born citizens. The scientist then singled out the African American contribution to this "new race." He criticized the nation "for all the troubles and disabilities it has laid on the Negro's shoulders," and implied its "debt" was heavier for not paying due recognition to African American music. "To the Negro and his wonderful songs and choirs we owe the finest contribution in the realm of art which America has so far given to the world. And this great gift we owe, not to those whose names are engraved on this 'Wall of Fame,' but to children of the people." As remains typical of attitudes toward African American music and expressive culture, the *New York Times* printed Einstein's statement about racial oppression, but not his remarks about African American music.[13]

Among the six hundred accomplished immigrants honored on the Wall—including (in attendance) the broadcast mogul David Sarnoff, the poet W. H. Auden, the novelist Fanny Hurst, and the sociologist Max Weber—the nation's most popular "immigrant" turned out to be Bill "Bojangles" Robinson. The *New York Times* reported without condescension: "It was Bojangles' party. The veteran tap dancer attracted more autograph hunters than any of his fellow guests of honor who included eminent scientists, writers, educators and leaders in other fields."[14] Granted, Robinson was a movie star and perhaps the best known of those honored. Still, such public recognition and popular attention suggests the centrality of tap and the swing idiom in interwar American culture: its existential affirmation, controlled power, energizing rhythmic flow and portable self-expression, and its modeling of retooled and re-fueled bodies. Of course Robinson was not an immigrant; he was born May 25, 1878, in Richmond, Virginia, and raised by his grandmother (an ex-slave). *What had immigrated into the dominant culture of the interwar period was African American culture,* but it could only be honored in the minstrel guise of Bill Robinson.

In analyzing the now-failed political systems competing for control in 1940, William Irwin Thompson claims that jazz should be seen as the American cultural system that helped erode midcentury totalitarian ideology. "Both fascism and communism are hysterical systems of control, ones that cannot tolerate humor, ambiguity, complexity, and multidimensional topologies . . . all those qualities that are so richly present in jazz."[15] Black Americans had been living under totalitarianism in the form of white supremacy for most of their lives; jazz as a form helped provide a nonverbal forum for complex, coded social messages. As Duke Ellington famously said, "The music had to say what we couldn't say." So it is fitting that one of the first acts of public recognition for black cultural forms occurred on the Common.

During "Negro Week" on the American Common (July 23–29, 1940), spectators who bought a souvenir program read an essay entitled "The Negro in the Building of America." Written by Dr. Lawrence Reddick, the curator of Harlem's Schomburg Library, the essay predates by some thirty years Ellison's landmark essay, "What Would America Be Like Without Blacks?"—long recognized as a signal of ethnic pride in black vernacular culture. Reddick claimed not only that the African American political struggle had transformed the very *idea* of freedom (a fact now accepted by historians), but that black cultural forms were central to American identity and society.[16] "Would America be the America we know today, if the influence of the Negro were subtracted from our history? Concretely, what would American music be? The dance? The 'Cotton Kingdom'? The tradition of the struggle for human freedom? Would American life possess its present variety and richness minus the Negro? The posing of these questions suggests the answers."[17]

Reddick rightfully suggested that African Americans led the fight for social equality because they had "borne the brunt of . . . social denials" more than any other group and so "appreciate the value and meaning of them all." It was the African American "drive for liberty, security and for equality of opportunity" that represented the "broad struggle by and for the common man." Perhaps the most radical element in Reddick's challenge was his proud embrace of African American vernacular cultural forms as equal in significance with the historical struggle for social equality. He presented black vernacular culture and the African American political struggle as convergent streams, both of which fed—and continue to feed—American hopes and dreams.

The essay's fifth section, "Cultural Contribution," specifically lauded black music and dance for its function in humanizing an increasingly mechanistic society.

> The gift of the Negro to American music is the most known and accepted of the cultural contributions. Almost everyone agrees that it is one of the distinct elements of what might be called American culture. If the Spirituals are in essence folk melodies, the Blues and Jazz are, on the other hand, expressions of the urban way of life. Their secular, mocking, often sophisticated moods are characteristic of the city. Closely related are the free rhythms of such dances as the Cakewalk, the Pas Mala, the Charleston, Trucking and the Suzie Q. *Humor, merriment, song and dance, thus serve as a foil against the dehumanizing effect of the machine* [emphasis added].[18]

Although Reddick opposed the human to the mechanical, and did not see the machine aesthetics within swing culture, he understood that these New World African American portable forms were neither primitivist nor escapist but instead synthetic and syncretic.

These "cultural contributions" were the basis of Negro Week's largest program, "Jam and Jive Night at the American Common," on July 26, 1940. Here were the performances that celebrated "swing music's contribution to Negro Week": the composers James P. Johnson, W. C. Handy, and Eubie Blake played their best-known songs; the alto saxophonist Benny Carter led his big band through a short program; Maxine Sullivan and Alberta Hunter sang their hits; and Whitey's Lindy Hoppers danced. Even the "hip jive" of urban blacks was recognized; the evening's dance was called a "Rug Cutting Party" ("rug-cutter" was a black vernacular term synonymous with jitterbug and lindy hopper).[19]

Reddick even called historians to account for omitting the African American contribution, accusing white American history of being nothing more than identity politics. He envisioned a history where "no nation will be singled out as 'God's Country'. . . . Neither will any 'race' or class be glorified as 'the chosen people.'" He confidently predicted a time when "the story will be told in terms of the . . . interplay of all of the forces which have made for the upbuilding, the destruction and the rebuilding of civilizations and cultures. In this day of the future, written history will look more like the history that actually happened." Only in *that* world of tomorrow, Reddick implied, might Americans see that "the American Dream is the dream of the Negro."[20] And such a dream must manifest itself in the expressive culture of a people.

Reddick's confidence must be considered in the context of the global influence of African American music and dance between the world wars that resulted in the admiration of Le Corbusier and Count Keyserling, the jazz-derived works of Stravinsky and Ravel, the négritude movement, and the international stardom of Louis Armstrong, Josephine Baker, and Duke Ellington (as well as the Aryan master-race defeats of the Third Reich's "new man" at the hands of Joe Louis and Jesse Owens). As opposed to the technological utopia of the Fair, Reddick prophesied a "historian's utopia," when American intellectuals would recognize the nation's multicultural heritage.

In this final chapter I want to furnish a corrective to the discourse on the New York World's Fair by demonstrating the popularity of swing culture there, and thus point up its centrality to the American self-image at the outset of World War II. I argue that tap, big bands, and the lindy were artistic hits of the Fair, and I sketch the unknown story of the Fair's Savoy Ballroom and the Hall of Music, especially as the latter became home to the all-black cast of *The Hot Mikado*. The success of these cultural forms speaks to the failure of highbrow culture to provide survival technology for modern bodies.[21] Just as important, the racism of Fair officials points up the guilt and discomfort white elites felt at their investment in African American culture and shows Reddick's intellectual prescience regarding prevailing racial frames of the American mythos.

For example, the Fair's blazingly white theme center—the iconic Trylon and Perisphere, ideal Platonic forms of sphere and obelisk—remains a symbol of the *racially* white idea of techno-progress envisioned in 1939. Fair president Whalen in particular tried to keep blacks from tainting the vision of a white technological future. For three months in 1939, African Americans picketed against racial discrimination in hiring outside the Fair's corporate offices at the Empire State Building. The issue reached the state legislature, where Assemblyman William T. Andrews "castigated" Whalen in calling for a proportionate number of black jobs on this quasi-public project: "If the . . . World of Tomorrow is to be illustrated by its employment attitude toward Negroes, then there is no hope for democracy in this country."[22]

I want to make two points concerning the intertwined issues of racial politics, swing music and dance, and Machine Age aesthetics. First, while the New York World's Fair of 1939 is rightly known for rejuvenating American faith in techno-progress, the Fair planners and administrators failed to see the cultural need for humanized machine aesthetics and reenergized modern bodies in dialogue with technological forces. Second, swing's humanized machine aesthetics of controlled power were embodied by big bands belatedly hired after August 1, by Whitey's Lindy Hoppers, and by Bill Robinson's tap dancing in *The Hot Mikado* daily at the Hall of Music.

The icon of the energized modern body is still often a black male body, which remains, for better or worse, the most admired (and imitated) *human body-in-motion* in global popular culture through sports, music, and dance. Youth in every country learn and admire African-American cultural forms, and take onto their bodies the embedded aesthetics, style, and kinesthetics; Michael Eric Dyson refers to this cultural transmission as a "pedagogy of desire." Dyson coined the term in analyzing Michael Jordan's global impact as a "public pedagogue"—an aesthetic exemplar who communicates "[through] skill and performance, the . . . elements of African-American culture," and who in competition, "symbolically ritualize[s] . . . the ongoing quest for mastery of environment." In 1939, African Americans were barred from all major league team sports; blacks supported their own professional baseball and basketball leagues, but few white athletes at the time copied black athletic style. When the lindy hopper Frankie Manning reflects that "back then, we only had this one music," he suggests the centrality of swing culture to African American expressive culture. Certainly the display of black bodies in dance involved an overlay of primitivism and a projection onto the Other, but in embracing the performance of these dances, Euro-Americans registered their need and desire to master the urban, industrial environment through dynamic engagement.[23]

African American cultural forms, practices, and aesthetics are central to a global American popular culture (sports, music, dance, comedy, kinesics) that is now an international "lingua franca."[24] During a 1999 "Command Performance" broadcast from the White House featuring lindy hoppers and tap dancers, Hilary Rodham Clinton announced that these cultural forms were those the nation wanted to "take with us into the next millennium."[25] This aesthetic tradition is embodied by Michael Jordan, Michael Jackson, and Madonna; it is the basis for the enormous stylistic impact of African Americans in baseball, football, and especially basketball; and movies centered on black music and dance remain a staple of Hollywood and Broadway.[26] If the New York World's Fair was meant to show off machines as the key to the future society, African American dancers were the only performers then displaying individual expressive and aesthetic excellence.

One thing every visitor to the Fair was taking into the future was a body. I am suggesting that Americans wanted to see what those bodies might look like when they got there. At the New York World's Fair, all the nation's lindy hoppers—amateur and professional, black, white, Jewish, Hispanic, and Asian—displayed *the mindful body of tomorrow* (which is to say, today).

Remaking Americans for Modernity

According to the historian Warren Susman, the 1939 New York World's Fair was the most "self-conscious 'document'" of a society attempting "to create a culture on the basis of . . . Great Technology." The planners hoped to give Americans a cultural makeover so that a "new and yet democratic culture could be created with the aid of science and modern technology." The Fair itself was a kind of machine meant to transform raw human ore into machine-worshiping technocrats; it was "'a machine for display' [and] its product, a new set of social attitudes and understanding." The assembly-line products of Futurama were to be new forward-looking Americans, or more precisely, consumers. Citizens had a new civic responsibility: to become attuned to a mass-produced, machine-dictated world and forget whatever superstitious traditions and sentimental attachments they had.[27]

The payoff for forsaking tradition, folk heritage, and religious belief would be the leisure society. The idea of less work was an important element in selling the future since the Depression had dimmed the romance of techno-progress. In 1935, the Fair of the Future committee was quite conscious of the need to put a new spin on progress: "Mere mechanical progress is no longer an adequate or practical theme for a World's Fair; we must demonstrate that supercivilization . . . is based on the swift work of machines, not on the arduous toil of men." It was not enough to stress how new appliances and technological marvels "brought to the masses . . . better living and accompanying human happiness.[28] A supercivilization was one where an individual worked less (and less hard), and where leisure would be served by machines just as work had been.

The committee meant for Americans to "trade a useable past for a useable future," but the Fair's industrial designers offered no transition to modernity. With the exception of "Railroads on Parade," no industrial exhibit portrayed the past. Thus machines were not integrated into an understanding of the nation's history, nor did the Fair planners creatively imagine how machine aesthetics might be integrated into popular belief systems. The top-down message was for Americans to sit back, enjoy the ride, push the button, and be awed by the "engineer's utopia." E. B. White noted, "There was no talking back in the World of Tomorrow."[29] The Fair was mechanical pageantry, a demonstration of scientific power ultimately encouraging a passive public to line up and pay obeisance to King Technology.

The layout of the Fair displayed a symbolic order that captured the march of Western civilization. The shining white monumental structures of the Trylon and Perisphere represented both Platonic ideal forms and "the lovely white[-skinned]" ideal of the Enlightenment. There was a Roman sense of efficiency to the roads and the radial plan, with a sense of proportion and beauty in part derived from such aristocratic geometric gardens as Versailles; and there was an almost militaristic sense of order in the organization of the seven enterprise zones such as Transportation, Food, and Government. The industrialization of entertainment was represented by the awe-inspiring colorful electric lighting that turned the nighttime Fair into an upscale Coney Island. The final American touch was streamlining, the influential "national American style" that integrated the machine's unique qualities into architecture and design. Streamlined buildings emphasized horizontal flow and "the image of the machine with its attributes of speed, efficiency, precision, and *reliability*."[30]

This ground plan was the concrete ideal of utopia as imagined first by Edward Bellamy in *Looking Backward* (1888), a layout made possible by the marriage of the baroque garden-plan with mass-production methods and then applied to the distribution of people and goods across space. Its public face was president Grover Whalen, the symbolic American merchandiser of abundance, a man who rose to political power by way of the department store. Whalen was the longtime right-hand man to John Wanamaker, of Philadelphia's renowned Wanamaker and Company. Along with four of the nation's leading industrial designers—Norman Bel Geddes, Walter Dorwin Teague, Raymond Loewy, and Henry Dreyfuss—Whalen embodied the American marketing genius for making luxuries into necessities. The Fair "was a show window . . . for the industrial and scientific advances of our century," Whalen wrote in his autobiography.[31] These white men stood on the shoulders of all the ad men, magazine illustrators, theater builders, vaudevillians, and circus owners before them. Bel Geddes and Dreyfuss both came from theatrical backgrounds; their role at the Fair was to dramatize manufacturing processes for a Depression-weary public to keep up their faith in techno-progress.[32] "These works . . . represent almost the sum total of all that man has produced since history began," Whalen remarked on opening day.[33] In post-Depression America, techno-progress would be an American mythos for determining status, purpose, and happiness through an endless stream of mass-produced goods combining technological innovation, modern style, and middle-class leisure.

Whalen and the Fair planners were sure this industrialized "edutainment" would overwhelm prurient desires, so they placed the Amusement Area (AA) far away from the Fair's theme center and the Court of Nations. The positioning of the AA—itself a term of disdain—spatially suggests the Christian division between higher and lower natures. Only in the AA could one purchase a cheap meal, or indulge one's curiosities about human beings, or get a nonrational thrill. Fair planners wanted to deter fairgoers from indulging their biological drives and regressing to the superstitions of the past; instinct had to be sectioned off.[34] For the base necessities of food, clothing, shelter, and entertainment—not to mention the public display of near-naked bodies—you had to walk a long way. *Variety* singled out the AA as the Fair's "most dismal failure," describing it as "an elongated area stuck off in a distant corner of the grounds where only a small majority had the fortitude to traverse its length."[35] It was a long walk from the industrial exhibits and international buildings to the Fair's Savoy Ballroom, Aquacade, Frank Buck's Jungleland, and the Parachute Jump.

Inscribed in the ground plan of the World of Tomorrow was an ideology wherein the rational scientific intellect, embodied in technology, triumphed over emotion, tradition, history, sensuality, and any preindustrial articulations of human existence.[36] This was the new City on the Hill, which harkened back to the division between the neoclassical "White City" and its off-site Midway at the 1893 Columbian Exposition. How dangerous were pleasure and instinct to the Fair's ideals? The AA was administered by the "Amusement Control Committee," suggesting that amusements needed to be controlled or individuals would lose *their* self-control. For Whalen, the AA was associated with the frivolous pleasures (or sins) of the body, as opposed to the gravitas of the Fair's enterprise zones (manufacturing, agriculture, and so on).[37]

The actor Jason Robards was ten years old when he attended the Fair, and he confessed he was not sure if he was "fit" for "tomorrow." Could he rise to the challenge of this antiseptic machine-driven world? Would he too need a makeover? The question obviously resonated with Americans. A popular cartoon called "Going to the Fair" by the Fleischer Brothers (creators of Betty Boop, Popeye, and Superman cartoons) showed a young midwestern couple receiving a makeover in the Fair's rest rooms. In separate bathrooms, mechanical hands give them new hairdos, fit them with new clothes, and dispense perfume and cologne; with a new bounce in their walks, the couple float into each other's arms. At first they start to square dance, but then the music accelerates and they whirl into the lindy. Rebuilt for the world of tomorrow by machine technology and survival technology, the couple jump into their prefab convertible and, along with a new family dog, they are prepared to return home.[38] To enter the world of tomorrow, one had to submit to being remade; apparently preindustrial human beings had done nothing worth saving for humanity.

These inscribed cultural values—the opposed dualities of mind/body, higher/lower, civilized/primitive, evolved/regressed, white/black—affected the role of swing culture from the very first day of the Fair. For example, the AA was treated as a frontier outpost. Virtually dark and unpaved the first month, the AA's concessionaires complained of power, light, and maintenance problems; only three concessions were open. "That is the place Whalen forgot," the *New York Times* observed in mid-May, calling it a "segregated district" shrouded in "despondent darkness."[39] This treatment of the "play department of the World of Tomorrow" as a stepchild was so harmful that Whalen felt it necessary to officially recognize the AA separately two weeks later in a "reopening" ceremony.[40]

In his well-known costume of top hat and morning coat, Grover Whalen with his Anglo-American veneer masked an identity crisis of the body for Euro-American elites and technocrats, and a body politic now completely invested in African American cultural practices and forms. As the corporate image of techno-progress, Whalen stood for the white, civilized face of reason carrying forward an Enlightenment myth into the future. As the public face of the Fair and its corporate elites and sponsors, he represented the elite's inability to think outside of mechanical idolatry to envision the future.

This identity crisis of the white Euro American body was manifested in the Fair's prominent sculpture and statuary. Despite the Fair's futuristic theme, its well-promoted statuary featured neither pride in machines nor modernist abstraction (say, on the order of Brancusi or Giacometti); despite the decade's obsession with an abstract ideal of "the people," there were few, if any, realistic depictions of human beings. Instead there were predominantly naked human bodies stylized in academic classical modes. The statue of "Speed" did not portray Charles Lindbergh or a race-car driver, but Pegasus. Statues of "The Four Freedoms"—a distinctly American sociopolitical concept—were represented by huge thirty-foot classical statues of idealized nude Greek nymphs. *Architectural Forum* chided the Fair: "Even in the World of Tomorrow the great majority of sculptors will . . . be preoccupied with the threadbare legends of classical mythology." The magazine also mocked the Fair's "meaningless plaster effigies of the usual antique personalities" (George Washington,

Walt Whitman, Johnny Appleseed, Paul Bunyan).[41] Considering the artistic and intellectual interest in social realism and documentary photography at the time—with its emphasis on authenticity and verisimilitude in human expression—the Fair organizers must be seen as being out of touch with both popular and artistic sentiment.[42]

Machines were the kind of bodies upon which the Fair planners and industrial designers lavished the most care. The Fair represented the cultural moment when liberal intellectuals and artists admitted the beauty of machines.[43] Alexander Calder described his ballet of fountains and sprinklers as "written for fourteen nozzles . . . designed to sport, oscillate or rotate in fixed manners and at times as carefully predetermined as the movements of living dancers." He proudly claimed there were no human elements in his display.[44] Whalen pointed to the popularity of the fireworks choreographed daily with lights, colors, and music at the Lagoon of Nations. A prominent theater critic applauded the artist's ability to "win a place for himself among the . . . engines and the automobiles, the glass works and the big guns . . . [by] bringing color, light and drama into their very structure.[45]

Technology represented the higher nature of human beings as the embodiment of rationality—the human spirit as opposed to flesh. Consequently Whalen declared that there would be no nudity at the Fair, an unprecedented claim for expositions of this type. The impresario Billy Rose, whose Aquacade was the smash hit of the Fair (and which featured dozens of half-clad young men and women), warned Whalen to stay away from anything "too highfaluting," but Whalen ignored him. When polled, few Americans expressed either embarrassment or annoyance at this aspect of fairs. *Billboard*'s headline, "Skin Drawing at the Fair—Strip Shows Top Grossers," was clearly meant to embarrass Fair officials. Even *Life* mocked Whalen's prudish pronouncements against sexual exhibitionism: "The history of all major U.S. expositions shows that peep shows are their most profitable and memorable contribution to U.S. culture."[46] Whalen capitulated within a month of the Fair's opening, and by the first week of July there were "13 or more undraped girl shows operating" (according to *Variety*), including two produced by the industrial designers responsible for the Fair's best industrial exhibits.

But women's bodies too had to be redesigned for the future, as in Norman Bel Geddes's "Crystal Lassies" and Walter Dorwin Teague's "Living Magazine Covers."[47] These body-of-tomorrow concessions featured topless women fetishized by theatrical processes. Bel Geddes exhibited his "lassies" within a series of prisms that functioned something like a kaleidoscope; it created the impression of an abundance of women, or at least of one woman as a work of "art" to be appreciated from every aspect..Teague dressed women in metallic and synthetic materials and displayed them within metal frames, and often topless—a cross between a "living" magazine cover and a live statue.[48] They apparently gave no thought to redesigning the white male body; the industrial designers clearly did not think about their own bodies as objects. And neither Bel Geddes nor Teague could have imagined the African American body-in-motion as a model for the world of tomorrow. Bel Geddes's imagined racial future was a white one, indebted to an evolutionary ideal in which primitive races would become extinct, perhaps in a well-defined program of eugenics.[49]

To Grover Whalen and his progressive cohorts, black dance was frivolous "Harlem hotcha" (to use a phrase of the day) unrelated to the goal of transforming Americans into technocrats. Only those with scientific minds and a productive ethos would be pure enough to drive the clean-lined highways or live in the wholesome suburbs of General Motors's Futurama, to boldly control the forces of nature (such as the lightning reduced to electricity in the General Electric exhibit) or enter the brave new world of television (first introduced to the public at the Fair). Jason Robards recalled his youthful impression of the mood set by Whalen and the Fair planners: "These men were *serious* about the future." Perhaps a bit too serious, to judge by its financial failure and the complaints of fairgoers.[50]

Whalen attended the ground-breaking of the Fair's Savoy pavilion and allowed himself to be swung around by one of Whitey's female lindy hoppers, but he was hostile toward any black presence at the Fair. African Americans were routinely turned away by the Fair's employment agency and bluntly informed that only whites would be hired even for unskilled jobs. The only exception was a request "for Negro women to work as maids." Prior to mid-March 1939, only two nondomestic black workers were employed at the Fair.[51]

In a March 18, 1939, cover story, the *New York Amsterdam News* referred to Whalen as "the kingpin discriminator." Neither he nor the Fair personnel director Clarence Lee would grant a public hearing for their complaints about racial discrimination. Encounters with various Fair personnel led the *Amsterdam News* to conclude that "the 'boss' isn't bothered" by the issue. Whalen did not answer either calls or telegrams from

Reverend Adam Clayton Powell Jr., pastor of the Abyssinian Baptist Church, including one requesting "a change in his policy or a statement as to the reason for not doing so." Powell rebuked Whalen: "According to the desires of the erudite good Christians . . . promoting this endeavor, the Negro in the World of Tomorrow will be found in the toilets."[52]

African Americans picketed Whalen's office at the Empire State Building daily from April 3 until opening day (April 30)—two hours a day, with a twenty-four-hour round-the-clock march once a week. The Fair's Interracial Advisory Committee called for all rejected applicants to testify, and local labor-union locals and the Federal Writers Project gave their support. Various heads of Fair committees wrote letters to Whalen demanding a public hearing; he held to his claim that employment should be handled by private businesses. The Greater New York Coordinating Committee attempted to get a court order to block the opening of the Fair, claiming "the World's Fair corporation was a quasi-public corporation, aided by federal, state and municipal funds." Reverend Powell and the committee's counsel protested that under the LaGuardia-Norris bill, the Fair should not be allowed to open if its hiring practices were discriminatory. The order was rejected.[53]

Whalen never changed the Fair policy or made a public statement on this issue, but employment agencies quietly secured one hundred and fifty jobs for blacks as "carpenters, porters, ticket sorters and attendants." On opening day, five hundred picketers paraded for three hours and defied attempts by police to "shoo them away" during the afternoon's program of speeches. The picketers lowered their signs when President Roosevelt entered "in respect to him as an individual."[54] But the issue quietly faded after opening day. The *Amsterdam News* reported that black fair-goers were uniformly treated without discrimination at the Fair's eating places and exhibits.[55]

Apparently Whalen did not see the irony of a world of tomorrow in a democratic society that discriminated against blacks. Here again we have the familiar schism that allows Euro-Americans to embrace African Americans as performers but reject individuals as social equals and co-workers. How popular were African American entertainers? Just a month before the Fair opened, *Variety* ran a front-page article announcing the unprecedented recent success of all-black shows on Broadway. As of March 29, 1939, there were "more colored performers and colored shows on Broadway running concurrently than ever before in the history of show biz." There were two swing versions of *The Mikado* (the

Works Progress Administration's *Swing Mikado* and Michael Todd's *Hot Mikado*), Ethel Waters's first starring dramatic role in DuBose Heyward's *Mamba's Daughters,* a new Cotton Club show, and a revue then in rehearsal, "Sing for Your Supper." The *New York Amsterdam News* reported a record number of African Americans then appearing on "regular radio program broadcasts" as comedians, singers, and dancers, from the variety shows of Eddie Cantor and Rudy Vallee to such features as "The National Negro Hour." Both articles suggested a rising trend, and made reference to the recent theatrical successes of Orson Welles's all-black *Macbeth* (1936) and *Porgy and Bess* (1935). As the musicologist Charles Keil has written pointedly: "We want the music but we don't want the people."[56]

At the high-water mark of big-band swing's popularity, Fair planners pointedly chose to keep American popular music from tainting their vision of technological harmony. A number of opening-day visitors expressed a "need for a big dancing spot or open air pavilion for dancers, where mild spenders [could] enjoy themselves without [buying] expensive drinks."[57] Yet as the musicians' trade journal *Metronome* announced, "N.Y. Fair Nixes Name Dance Bands."[58]

The Fair corporation changed its mind about big bands in midsummer. First, the Fair was losing money; second, Benny Goodman drew a hundred thousand visitors in four days to San Francisco's competing Golden Gate Centennial.[59] On June 20, 1939, the Fair's board of directors approved the construction of a large, portable dance floor and a bandshell in the center of the Fair. The following week, it hired the Rockwell-O'Keefe agency to book bands for one- and two-week engagements.[60] To boost awareness of the Fair's swinging spirit, several white big-band leaders were given an official welcome by Mayor LaGuardia at City Hall. In a newsreel promoting the Fair's reformed outlook, Glenn Gray (of the Casa Loma orchestra) and Eddy Duchin waved to spectators as they hung out of convertibles circling in front of City Hall. A crowd of New Yorkers looked on; a few jitterbugged. In a fitting end to the story, the newsreel announcer intoned dramatically, "The world of tomorrow . . . *in the groove.*"[61]

During the first two weekends of swing's arrival at the Fair, newspapers trumpeted its new, festive spirit. *Variety* claimed that "Jitterbugs Up Fair Midway 20 to 500%" for individual concessionaires in the AA.[62] The three opening bands—Louis Prima's, John Kirby's, and Guy Lombardo's—had their music pumped out over loudspeakers and were credited with "instilling a more festive atmosphere, with swing music, [and] dancing in the streets."[63] By September 1 the upstart impresario Michael Todd had opened the "Mardi Gras Casino" featuring name swing bands and a large dance floor (provided free of charge) and a "gawking" area in which to buy drinks and watch dancers. The Mardi Gras Casino replaced the failed Textiles Building in the manufacturing zone; symbolically speaking, swing culture now existed cheek-by-jowl with American industry. The Mardi Gras Casino's presence scrambled the baroque order of the world of tomorrow; concessionaires in the AA complained they could not draw people to their far-flung district if they could dance for free in the main exhibit area.[64]

Later a successful theatrical and Academy Award–winning film producer (*Around the World in 80 Days*), Michael Todd was even more well known as Elizabeth Taylor's first husband. But he rose to fame at the New York World's Fair on the strength of the popularity of African American music and dance. He stole the Hall of Music from the upper classes and the *New York Times,* and the lindy hop from the Savoy Ballroom's satellite pavilion, then matched them together to popular acclaim.

Whose Hall of Music Is It, Anyway?

One of the few buildings constructed at Fair corporation expense, the Hall of Music as of June 20, 1939, became the home of an all-black version of Gilbert and Sullivan's *The Mikado,* officially called "Michael Todd's '*Hot Mikado.*'" Built to highlight the nation's cultural heritage, the Hall of Music was one of the Fair's most beautiful and expensive buildings; it was envisioned as a beacon of highbrow culture for the masses. The hall had a 2,500-seat capacity and was built to state-of-the-art acoustic specifications; its finishing touches were supervised by the conductor Arturo Toscanini.[65] It cost more than $350,000 to build, and boasted air-conditioning as an important selling point. *Architectural Forum* admired "its clean, spacious interior" and compared it favorably in quality and style to Radio City Music Hall, noting specifically its innovative use of an "arena-type plan" that allowed for good views throughout the house through an "elimina[tion of] the balcony."[66]

The Fair's Advisory Committee on Music was composed of wealthy patrons, communications moguls, and the directors of various cultural institutions. They chose as director Olin Downes, the music critic for the *New York Times.* In February 1938, the committee announced a "World Festival of Music" to include a Wagner cycle, "operas, operettas, concerts, ballets, choral singing, band music and folk presentations." The Fair corporation approved $350,000 in "preliminary expenses," but the board of directors was skeptical of its success.[67] The opening-night program was a benefit for the New York Philharmonic Society featuring a Chopin concerto and Beethoven's Fifth Symphony. Downes himself reviewed it, lauding the hall's acoustics and architecture and reporting with pride that "the audience was as resplendent as any . . . [for] New York's orchestra or opera. Leaders of society, business, finance and the arts filled the hall . . . and dress was formal." The Hall of Music was planned as an outpost of New York high society, and its original schedule included the Polish and Japanese national ballet companies, various national symphonies, and a Hungarian folk opera.[68]

Rival music critic Sigmund Spaeth thought that focusing an American World's Fair on classical and European folk music expressed an "inferiority complex" among American classical composers and musicians toward the overwhelming global influence of American popular culture. To Spaeth, the classical world had to display its elitism because of "the obvious *success* of our popular music . . . [which] emphasize[s] this lack of confidence in our more serious musical efforts." Spaeth did not mince words: "Our jazz and swing have been the envy of the whole world, and our Broadway revues and musical comedies have set a standard that no other country has recently equaled."[69]

The failure of Olin Downes's vision took less than four weeks. On May 25, 1939, Grover Whalen announced the closing of the Hall of Music at the request of the board of directors. The hall was "losing money consistently," and the high ticket prices "had failed to draw crowds." Individual events incurring big losses included a recital by the diva Grace Moore, an evening of orchestral music with Walter Damrosch, and a scheduled two-week stay for the Japanese Ballet. Whalen canceled the remainder of the schedule, promising that music with a "broad appeal," such as "swing bands, light operas and [theatrical] musical productions," would replace it. Putting his best corporate face on the hall's closing without conceding elitist ground, Whalen announced that "a more popular type of entertainment in the Hall of Music . . . [would] meet the public demand for popular and low-priced entertainment." *Billboard* summed up the hall's failure more concisely: "Classical fare did not meet with sufficient patronage to make it worth while to operate."[70]

Moreover, Whalen was bluffing about alternate programming; there was no backup plan. Archival materials reveal that Downes and Whalen were paralyzed by the flow of events; Downes did not even respond to an urgent telegram from his close friend Paul Whiteman, who was holding open his entire summer schedule for a pending July 9, 1939, all-Gershwin concert at the Hall of Music. The minutes of the board of directors reveal no references to popular music or theatrical productions before June 1939. The show that saved the Hall of Music financially, *The Hot Mikado,* was at that moment enjoying a successful off-Broadway run. Downes reluctantly resigned and expressed "deep regret" over the cancellation of the "exceptionally varied and interesting program."[71] Even at fifty-cent prices, the promise of a cool, elegant, sophisticated evening featuring imported culture—with near-perfect acoustics—failed to generate popular interest.[72]

The Fair's antagonism to popular music is fully revealed in its correspondence with popular musicians. From 1936 to 1939 the Fair was deluged with requests for bookings from a wide range of musicians, yet the society orchestras of Paul Whiteman and Leo Reisman, the legendary jazz pianists Jelly Roll Morton and Luckey Roberts, and the nation's largest music booking agencies (Rockwell-O'Keefe and Consolidated Radio Artists) were all rejected with near-equal aplomb. A few noted musicians and agents were referred to individual corporations and concessionaires.[73]

Ironically, society orchestras of African American musicians playing jazz-based dance music had dominated the world of New York's social elite since at least 1909 (in their homes, anyway). For example, the Harlem stride pianist Luckey Roberts ran a highly successful society orchestra from 1922 to 1939. He wrote to Grover Whalen looking for Fair booking, and was able to name three recent occasions on which Whalen had heard him play. Three lines embossed at the bottom of Roberts's stationery tell the story: "A recent survey indicates that Luckey Roberts and His Society Entertainers have[,] in the last two years, played more Social Registerite engagements than any other musical organization out of NYC such as debutante affairs, receptions, birthday parties . . . including the outstanding social event of the season, the Dupont-Roosevelt nuptials."[74] Roberts's popularity enabled him to headline Carnegie Hall for an August 30, 1939, benefit, playing a concerto of his own composition. Called by one local paper "composer, conductor . . . pianist and specialist in the field of syncopated music," Roberts was so secure in his niche that he had not given a public performance in seventeen years.[75]

In other words, maintaining an identity in association with white, European culture was (and still is) the basis for the invisibility that keeps the aesthetic power and social significance of African American cultural forms from being understood in Ellison's terms—that "most American whites are culturally part Negro American without realizing it." To underwrite a program of classical music at the Hall of Music was more an act of building highbrow prestige among New York's high society than a reflection of actual artistic preference or upper-class tastes. Classical music functioned more as a taste marker than noblesse oblige towards the fair-going masses.

The only venue where a fairgoer could see a big band for the first three months of the Fair was at the Savoy Ballroom, a satellite of Harlem's ballroom built by its owner, Moe Gale. There a young Dizzy Gillespie played in Teddy Hill's big band in a twenty-minute show called "Cavalcade of Negro Dance," whose finale featured an exciting, newly choreographed lindy hop for four couples of Whitey's Lindy Hoppers entitled "The Mutiny Swing." The show was critically acclaimed by every local newspaper and several national publications (*Life, Variety,* and *Billboard*) and was one of the Amusement Area's biggest hits. Norma Miller recalled, "We were the talk of the Fair [opening day], and we were the only all-black group there."[76] Audiences could not dance there, however; they sat on backless hard wooden benches to watch the alleged "evolution" of African American dance from Africa to jazz dance to the lindy.

Judging by the scant historical sources, the audiences apparently consisted mostly of white teenagers who, according to one usher, "sit up and shake their shoulders and like to pitch a fit sometimes."[77] The Savoy was so popular that a lindy hop contest was held there on May 21, 1939, and a *New York Times* reporter was surprised to find the white kids "had all the enthusiasm of Harlemites and just about their skill." He was stunned that these "jitterbugs" could dance to—and in fact requested—the torrid tempos the lindy demanded: "[They] demanded faster tempos from the band right from the start, and the reporter was shocked by this frenzied pace. . . . Many on the sidelines, who remembered the relatively peaceful rhythms of the Charleston era, shivered at the quickening pace of today and wondered what might happen when the jitterbugs literally invaded the World of Tomorrow."[78]

Despite its popularity, and being one of the few Amusement Area exhibits to be making a small profit, the Savoy closed in mid-August due to competition from Michael Todd's *Hot Mikado,* which also had a showstopping lindy hop routine featuring Whitey's Lindy Hoppers. Moreover, Todd stole the best lindy hoppers from the Savoy by offering better pay and a less strenuous schedule. The Savoy cost a quarter for twenty minutes; Todd's *Hot Mikado* cost 99¢ for a full theatrical show of seventy minutes that included Bill Robinson. Attendance dropped immediately after *The Hot Mikado* came to the Fair; by August, Gale deemed it pointless to stay open. He sued the Fair for breach of contract, claiming he had an exclusive in presenting "Negro dance," but to no avail.[79]

Given his own hostility to African Americans, for Grover Whalen to book an all-black theatrical production into the prestigious Hall of Music speaks volumes about economic pressures and his lack of options. Such theatrical productions conferred no prestige on their producers, only money from a public hungry for modern American cultural forms (and premodern stereotypes). Yet Whalen signed up the show within five days of the Hall's closing (May 30), renting it out to a brash young producer whose vision of culture was the polar opposite of Olin Downes's.

A confessed carnival man, Michael Todd believed in entertainment for entertainment's sake, and he dismissed the upper class as a minor demographic: "The carriage trade is good for only six weeks' business." Whalen announced *The Hot Mikado* gamely, as a true department store public-relations man might, citing it as "one of the outstanding New York attractions for scenery, costuming and novelty." *Billboard* reported bluntly that Whalen was simply trying "to make the Hall of Music pay."[80]

The Hot Mikado ended its off-Broadway run on June 17, and the Fair corporation turned over the Hall of Music to Michael Todd two days later; the play officially opened at the Fair on June 23.[81] The Board approved a one-month trial for the production and was so satisfied with its success after this grace period that Todd was granted a contract for the remainder of the Fair season. In its midseason review, the board praised "Michael Todd's 'Hot Mikado'" as one of only four or five shows "conceived on a magnificent scale worthy of this international exposition." On August 31, 1939, Todd was granted a personal option on the Hall of Music for 1940.[82]

Uncle Todd's Cabin and the Aquacade

Todd was a master of what a contemporary theater journal called "the art of 'speed-up.'" Thought egotistical and vulgar by other producers in 1939, he had neither a track record, respected partners, nor reliable funds, and was dubbed "a producer of somewhat obscure professional record" in one review.[83] Before *The Hot Mikado,* he had made and lost a few fortunes with novelty acts and "carny grift" (carnival acts).[84] Todd aspired to the position of Billy Rose, the impresario of Aquacade, the Fair's biggest moneymaker.

Rose's Aquacade can be thought of as a live version of a Busby Berkeley aqua-ballet: dozens of anonymous attractive bodies punch-carded into choreographed water routines of repetition, precision, and continuity. Rose gave the nation "bigness for its own empty sake" through visions of "human physical perfection." Rose admitted the Aquacade's primary selling point was "the girls . . . [in] tiny wet bathing suits," and he claimed "Listen, I'm no moralist. If I could get results with naked women, I'd put on naked women." But whereas Rose glorified the female body for the eroticized gaze, Todd was more interested in the American appetite for the excitement of the mindful body-in-motion.[85]

Both Rose and Todd were master showmen who had learned to read the American public's entertainment desires in the field. Both were proud of their roots in carnivals, of being the sons of Barnum; as Rose said late in life, "Belly-wheels, booze and beauties are my grift. . . . I'm an old carny man."[86] Both men aspired to (and received) highbrow recognition. Both had learned to overlay machine aesthetics and state-of-the-art production on carnival attractions and 1920s theatrical ideas. Like Berkeley, Rose glorified the nearly naked body through geometrically patterned spectacle; Todd was more interested in dynamic visual spectacle featuring expressive modern bodies.

Rose, like Berkeley, thought of himself as Ziegfeld's heir. The Aquacade combined Ziegfeld's chorus lines with Berkeley's "Before a Waterfall" to create yet another fable of abundance powered by the female dynamo. The only individual stars of Aquacade were Hollywood actors who had played Tarzan (Johnny Weismuller and Buster Crabbe) and female Olympic swimmers (one of whom, Eleanor Holm, later became Rose's wife). One feature of the exhibit was a chase scene with the male as predator and female as watery prey, "Johnny Weismuller pursu[ing] Eleanor [Holm] through . . . a three-million gallon stage while sixty other swimmers performed aquatic stunts."[87]

Why Tarzans? Because in 1939, these were the white male models of physical perfection. The actor-Tarzans were Hollywood's perfect white male bodies; the women were both attractive and athletic, and could be expected to give Tarzan a run for his (and the audience's) money. The formerly repressed values of the body as enjoyed through primitivism in the 1920s—vitality, open sexuality, instinctive desire—had become so important that Tarzan, a whitefaced primitive, was the ideal physical specimen.[88]

In contrast, Todd's *Hot Mikado* centered on Bill Robinson and Whitey's Lindy Hoppers, dancers that stylized and integrated machine aesthetics. Todd brought magnificent stage settings, costumes, lighting, and color to bear on the speed, energy, and graceful execution of black dance. Part of the show's appeal was also its special effects: "a mirrored floor, an erupting volcano [and] a waterfall of soapsuds."[89] Many critics also thought Nat Karson, an African American designer, deserved the year's award for best costumes and designs; Bill Robinson's diamond-studded all-gold costume was the crowning effect on a stage full of vivid colors and "gay carnival designs . . . full of bounce and originality."[90] Todd believed there could never be enough flashy effects, brilliant colors, fast motion, explosions, or beautiful women.[91]

African American dance was *The Hot Mikado*'s bread and butter. It was the pace of the production—the controlled speed and intensity of the dancers—that marked the show out to be a hit. *Variety* caught the synthesis of these elements in typical rhetoric: "[*Hot Mikado*] turns on the steam from the first beat and keeps the rhythm throbbing throughout."[92] *Time* called it "gaudy, glittering, foot-wise, fast"; a leading theater magazine referred to it as "typically slick, fast moving and continually enlivening." The *New York Times* favored its fast tempo and propulsive dance over the rival *Swing Mikado* production, noting Todd "substitute[d] Harlem frenzy for an amateur swing serenade."[93]

Theater professionals were well aware of the engine that drove Todd's rise to fame. A 1940 *Collier's* profile reported that when the first rave reviews came in for its off-Broadway run, "the Broadhurst Theater [was] immediately rechristened *Uncle Todd's Cabin*."[94] By surrounding black musical performance with state-of-the-art production values, Todd had updated the influential black revues of the 1920s—*Shuffle Along, Runnin' Wild, Lew Leslie's Blackbirds of 1928*—and synthesized the most popular aspects of 1920s theater: Ziegfeld-derived spectacle, first-class production values, special effects, and modern African American music, dance, and humor. "The dances are true to the best colored show tradition," wrote the *New York Daily News* critic Burns Mantle, and one review called it "the greatest all-colored show of all time."[95]

Like the more well-known white jazz impresarios of the time, Todd was able to make his fortune from the popularity of a modern African American cultural form because institutional racism closed employment opportunities for African Americans. With regard to big bands, often the larger share of the revenue was made by white (and often Jewish) agents, managers, or producers of African American talent, such as the agents Joe Glaser (for Louis Armstrong) and Irving Mills (for Duke Ellington and Cab Calloway). Many club owners and dance-hall proprietors refused to do business with black agents or managers.[96] Todd believed that swing was created by African American musicians, and he bragged that he had "ransacked the best bands in Harlem" for the pit band of *The Hot Mikado*. (The Broadway pit band was all-white; the World's Fair band featured black musicians.)

Todd also realized that white audiences had difficulty seeing African Americans in theatrical performance outside of minstrel or primitivist frames. He wanted audiences to view his *Hot Mikado* as serious theater in the comic vein, not minstrel-derived plantation humor based on malapropisms and comforting stereotypes. He hired a well-respected Broadway director (Hassard Short) whose very name insured a different type of response from the audience. He also claimed he had to teach the audience where to laugh.[97]

He did not, however, have to teach audiences to admire and appreciate African American dance. How important were Whitey's Lindy Hoppers to the show? Bill Robinson didn't appear until midway through the second act, and he made the show's drawing power clear: "Nobody had better mess with me or the Lindy Hoppers—*they* take care of the first act and *I* take care of the second."[98] The tap dancer Pete Nugent echoed this sentiment, recalling that the Lindy Hoppers "made it tough for everybody . . . [w]ith their speed and air steps they made all the other dancers look like they were standing still. . . . [T]hey dressed like a little-league baseball team, but they stopped the show wherever they appeared."[99] Yet theater critics made no mention of the lindy hoppers, who were generally subsumed under generic praise for the production numbers: "typically slick, fast moving and continually enlivening."[100] Only the *New York Amsterdam News* noted the "200 sizzling singers and jitterbugs and [the] large swing orchestra" that drove the production.[101]

The media preferred to focus on Bill "Bojangles" Robinson, the acknowledged star of the show. Robinson was singled out both for his dancing and his reassuring minstrel-derived presentation; nearly every review featured a publicity photo of Robinson's "rolling eye and beaming smile," and laid the success of the production at his feet.[102] George Jean Nathan in *Newsweek* called Robinson a "matchless hoofer," and *Time* hailed him as "still the noblest tap dancer of them all." The *New York Times* reflected that Robinson "has been a great man all these years in black dancing shoes and a black derby," and that it was "a grand thing to see him talking in tap." *Variety* wrote that Robinson's "grinning, gleaming, tap-dancing Mikado just about stands the audience on its head." *Theatre Arts Monthly* waxed poetic:

> The king of the evening is of course Bill Robinson. . . . Never has shoe leather beaten out such a variety of intricate patterns. Never . . . has one note been made to sing and soar, to whisper and to laugh, in such astonishingly complex rhythm. . . . [His] rolling eye and beaming smile, his masterly dancing, his kindliness and his vitality climax a gay evening and give it that extra lilt which comes from being in the presence of one of Broadway's most engaging and beloved comedians.[103]

Robinson was a movie star and the dancing partner of the 1930s' number-one box-office star, Shirley Temple. But this rhetoric is so inflated as to suggest other motives.

Robinson should be seen along with Louis Armstrong as a superb artist who enjoyed international success because he remained within a minstrel-derived framework in public performance. The photographed likeness of Bill Robinson was the sign of blackness that the mainstream media wanted to show. Brooks Atkinson of the *New York Times* called Robinson "the Master of Tap and the Good-Will Ambassador from Harlem to the Western World." The *Daily News* hailed him as "an unchallenged champion of the tap dancers . . . [and] also unchallenged in geniality and general likableness." Whether a white performer was "likable" mattered considerably less, and Robinson's convincing portrayal of the happy-go-lucky "darky" occasionally earned him the epithet of "Uncle Tom" among younger black performers; one black columnist called him "Shirley's Uncle." In contrast to the white media, the *New York Amsterdam News* focused its admiration only on Robinson's dancing: "a thing of beauty, balance, precision and brilliance." It was the rare review of *The Hot Mikado* that gave anything but lip service to other black performers, a telling omission not only with regard to the lindy hoppers but to Rosa Brown's portrayal of Katisha, the older woman intent on marrying the Mikado's son. Her shift from a comic spinster turn into "an eye-rolling, hip-shaking, torch-singing, Red Hot Mama" met with unanimous critical acclaim, but barely rated two lines in reviews.[104]

The media reduced the black cultural elements of *The Hot Mikado* to the sign of Bill Robinson's smile; Michael Todd simply effaced the sources of his success. He disingenuously declared in 1940, "The public wants broad theater, meat and potatoes, at a low top [price], and that's what I've been giving 'em." This became his well-known theater philosophy, and a longer version was printed in his 1958 obituary: "I believe in giving the customers a meat and potatoes show. Dames and comedy. High dames and low comedy—that's my message."[105] But *The Hot Mikado* was Todd's career breakthrough, and it was neither a "dame" show nor a "low comedy" (except that any all-black show might then have been deemed a low comedy). Such statements muted the impact and popularity of African American dance: its display of physical grace, elegance, and self-expression (as in Bill Robinson's tap routines) or of choreographed speed, power, and fluidity (as with the Lindy Hoppers). Todd never mentioned the African American contribution to the show nor gave credit to the dancers—not even to Robinson—but only to Hassard Short and the African American set designer Nat Karson. Todd was a colorful character, a producer who reveled in his Barnum-style antics and his self-declared genius for hucksterism. He made good copy all alone, and was only acting according to the conventions of the entertainment industry. Journalists had neither the interest nor the motivation to celebrate the cultural forms of an ethnic group lacking prestige.[106]

Despite his reputation as "tempestuous, erratic and often incorrigible," Todd's relentless work habits made him the dominant popular-culture impresario at the New York World's Fair over the two-year period, eclipsing in influence (if not in profits) even Billy Rose. In 1940, Todd became administrative director of the renamed "Great White Way," producing three of its most popular shows: "Gay New Orleans," featuring a troupe of African American female dancers;[107] "Streets of Paris," in the Hall of Music, with Abbott and Costello; and "Dancing Campus," a collegiate-themed outdoor dance pavilion featuring the most popular big bands, such as Gene Krupa and Harry James.[108] Todd took *The Hot Mikado* on the road after the World's Fair closed at two dollars a ticket, and there were plans (never realized) for a film. In 1940, *Variety* proclaimed Mike Todd the year's "new personality." Todd never did roll up the revenues of Billy Rose's Aquacade, but the trade journal claimed that he established "an important rep" with these shows.[109]

Todd's "Dancing Campus" deserves special note for shifting the lindy hop from a spectator dance, at the Savoy, to one of participation. At the Mardi Gras Casino in 1939, you could dance to the nation's best swing bands for a quarter—Gene Krupa's band was its breakthrough act—and for another twenty-five cents, there was "a gawker's terrace cafe (50¢ minimum)."[110] In 1940, Dancing Campus represented the triumph of the techno-dialogic on the grounds of the New York World's Fair. Whitey's Lindy Hoppers were in effect displaced by dancers who preferred to lindy themselves. This is an act of cultural significance that needs to be recognized: *the creation and modeling of a survival technology* able to swing Americans into Tomorrowland.

Coda: Humanized Machine Aesthetics

I conclude with an anecdote that suggests the complex tensions implicit in the Machine Age regarding what is "human" and what "mechanical." Reporting on the Fair for the *New Yorker*, E. B. White noticed an interesting come-on to attract business to the "Amazon" show (a "nudie show"). A tall "automaton" came out before every show, "dressed in white tie and tails, with enormous rubber hands," and fondled several topless girls. White described the visual effects as "peculiarly lascivious." The strange man's "gigantic rubber hands [on] the breasts of the little girls" revealed a chasm between natural and mechanical desire; next to the giant's rubber hands, the womens' hands were "by comparison so small, by comparison so terribly real." Yet the women put their hands "restrainingly on his, to check the unthinkable impact of his mechanical passion." In this contrast of hands, White perceived the tragedy of the nation's mechano-religion: "the heroic man, bloodless and perfect and enormous, created in his [Man's] own image, and in his hand (rubber, aseptic), the literal desire, the warm and living breast."[111] Thirty years later, the electrically reanimated automaton in Mel Brooks's *Young Frankenstein* (1972) would prove his humanity by tap dancing to Irving Berlin's "Puttin' on the Ritz" (1932); but the World's Fair automaton had only repressed desire to show for himself. Machine idolatry, as suggested by the human/machine interface of this automaton in 1939, has since been supplanted by *humanized* machine aesthetics.

Survival technology was an important draw at the Fair, especially if we view the Fair as a two-year project and not limit our gaze to the industrial exhibits of 1939. The Great Depression was ten years deep and still very much a fact of life; the geopolitical future grew more uncertain every day. Americans no doubt wanted to believe in the vision of techno-progress provided in Futurama; but their lives over the previous ten years had been much too uncertain for the platitudes of Grover Whalen to rejuvenate them. The humanized mechanical power of big-band swing, the adjustment of human bodies to the new American tempo, the ability to participate in a Machine Age modernist cultural form—such are the lessons of swing culture at the New York World's Fair. Americans needed both technology and survival technology to imagineer themselves into the unpredictable future.

CONCLUSION

THE CONTINUING
IMPORTANCE OF
SWINGING THE
MACHINE

In this "third machine age,"[1] Americans have sat themselves down to a new human/machine interface, and corporate advertisers pay to attract not citizens or consumers but "eyeballs" (a metonym like the factory "hand") to the computer screen. At the outset of the information age, technological enthusiasts, similar to the railroad enthusiasts of the 1840s, predicted computers would create a circulatory system of goods and information destined to revolutionize democracy and accelerate progress. Consumers were thrilled by the instantaneous access to people, information, and goods on the World Wide Web—similar to the first generation of train passengers' experience of "an annihilation of time and space." Meanwhile futurologists and cyberneticists studying artificial intelligence (or "AI") predicted a coming "age of spiritual machines" that will make human thinking obsolete within fifty years—just as manual labor was headed for obsolescence in the face of assembly-line innovations. The brain as computer continues to be a common metaphor for mind among psychologists, philosophers, doctors, and researchers of cognition, and it has become common to imagine the self as "hardwired" or "programmed." Revealing the vitality of the Cartesian and Christian traditions of the mind/body split, cyberpunk writers and programmers call the human body "meat" (or "the meat body") to distinguish it from mind or consciousness. Concurrent with all this computer-driven techno-progress came the first swing revival since the 1940s, and I would submit that vernacular survival technology resurfaced, in part, to dialogue with new technology.

I am not suggesting that swing reflects and contains the postindustrial soundscape—filled with the media barrage from television, Hollywood, and cyberspace, the sounds of machines in the home and on the street, and in part shaped by popular music and recording technology. The contemporary soundscape is reflected in hip-hop, techno, house, and electronica musics, and all of their subgenres, and is itself created on digital computer equipment. In these genres, musical artists use machines to swing the machines; or, more accurately, the machines are swung from the inside. For Afrika Bambaataa, one of hip-hop's pioneering DJs, the synthesizer and the Roland Drum Computer 808 were already "the primary rap instruments" in the late 1970s.[2] Today's DJs follow up on early rap's innovations, such as the transformation of turntables into expressive musical instruments and turning sampling into aural collage, in order to bring the soundscape directly into the musical equipment. Aspiring musicians now often "play with Roland grooveboxes, not Stratocasters," and layer grooves (not notes or chords) into electro-beats and tape loops. Even if (unlike Europeans) Americans have made few techno artists stars, these genres are omnipresent in television commercials, video games, and Hollywood soundtracks. More to the point, these are all functional dance musics, and "dancing is the key to the electronic aesthetic."[3]

In comparison to this electronic aesthetic, the swing revival seems like postmodern kitsch, a retro partner dance for young middle-class Euro-Americans rifling through the pop-cultural past for novelty effects, new combinations, and elements of pastiche. Yet set alongside rave culture, hip-hop, and techno, the swing revival represents another rebellion of the fleshly organism against overmechanization (this time at the data processing level). Again the physiological need for more feet-hips-and-shoulder-rocking arises to compensate for an increasingly sedentary work life centered on the monitor and a leisure life focused on the big, small, and flat screens. The mindful body's response to the mechano-religion of the computer age is another round of swinging the machine. Lewis Mumford's 1934 declaration in *Technics and Civilization* still rings true: "The machine, which acerbically denie[s] the flesh . . . [is] offset by the flesh." The dances of the 1950s and the sexual revolution of the 1960s certainly put an end to the need for primitivism, as did Elvis's whitefacing of black male performative aesthetics. So by 1976, the British rocker Graham Parker could sing matter-of-factly, "*You* don't mean a thing/if you ain't got that swing"—aptly updating Ellington's musical manifesto for self-affirming ends by suggesting that a certain sense of self-propulsive style is crucial to life in a technological society.

Thus does popular culture continue to perform cultural work and transmute music and dance ideas into *survival technology* (my update of Kenneth Burke's phrase "equipment for living"). The idea of a personal "swing" echoes the Machine Age search for the aesthetic element of "flow," and the ideal of being in the flow of one's mindful body has now generated thirty-five years of scholarship in psychology. In Mihaly Csikszentmihalyi's well-known *Flow* (1990), the psychologist singles out music and dance as two of the cultural forms most suited to making sense of any environment. "Music . . . is organized auditory information, [and] helps organize the mind that attends to it, and therefore reduces psychic entropy, or the disorder we experience." Just listening to music "can induce flow experiences," and dancing makes possible the felt experience of joy, groundedness, and self-affirmation. For Csikszentmiha-lyi, these cultural ideas are universal, and "the response of the body to music is widely practiced as a way of improving the quality of experience."[4] Such cultural practices were modeled by African Americans between the world wars, and when Ralph Ellison philosophized in 1970 that "the real secret of the game is to make life swing," he was underscoring how swing culture helped humanize the Machine Age.

Still swing remains the music nobody knows or respects. For example, the swing revival paid its African American artistic innovators lip service at best in the public sphere. In a popular 1999 television commercial for The Gap, more than a dozen beautiful young white Americans in white T-shirts and chinos radiated the athleticism, playfulness, flow, and grace of the lindy hop in a swirling exhibition of excellent swing-dancing. There are no African Americans in the ad and it is shot in radiant white light. The lindy hopper Frankie Manning could have been hired to lead the group; despite his age, he has been teaching swing seminars for the last ten years and his smooth, flowing moves remain as elegant as ever. The Gap ad might have used some African American dancers, or alluded in some way to the Savoy Ballroom. The Gap did create other historically minded ads for its chinos campaign, capitalizing on artistic icons such as Jack Kerouac and Miles Davis. But honoring an artistic tradition is admittedly more difficult than honoring an individual, especially if the audience is generally unaware of its cultural contribution. The Gap commercial marks dance as just "fun" and assigns neither swing nor the lindy any artistic valence.

This fun/serious dichotomy continues to haunt the study of popular music and social dance, as well as representations in film. The film *Swing*

Kids (1993), for example, focuses on the subversive thrills of the underground swing scene in Hamburg, Germany, where the "Judeo-Negroid music" of jazz was outlawed by the Nazis but represented freedom and democracy to German teens; although they called themselves "swing kids," in the film they appear to have no politics except dancing. The German swing kids are presented as being blissfully unaware of the transgressions of dancing a "Judeo-Negroid" music based on an interplay of self-expression and collective drive that is artistically and conceptually opposed to lockstep authoritarianism. Here Hollywood appropriates the victory of the lindy over the lockstep but strips the battle of its context, meaning, and black aesthetic. African American culture is invisible and appears only as the (aural) propulsion for the dance moves of white bodies and as markers of liberation in posters on the wall. (An additional set of ironies: the African American director of *Swing Kids*, Thomas Carter, says he was grateful to be given the chance to direct a film without overt racial themes.)

Perhaps the most egregious illustration of my point is that fifty-six years after *Life* proclaimed the lindy hop "the national folk dance" with a white couple on its cover, *Smithsonian* magazine ran a cover story on the swing revival featuring another white couple on the cover. The couple, New York City swing teachers Roddy Caravella and Angie Whitworth, do not seem to be in the midst of a dance move, although they are seemingly airborne. Judging by their expressions, they seem more interested in their attire than their movements. (Caravella wears yellow-and-black checked pants and suspenders, Whitworth an almost matching satin yellow blouse and yellow saddle shoes.) In a fold-out how-to section, two white couples model "floor steps" and "air steps" in a conscious tribute to the photographer Gjon Mili's "sequence of Lindy Hoppers for *Life* magazine . . . [updated for] a new generation of dancers." The writer, Doug Stewart, does refer to the dance's origins at the Savoy and quotes Frankie Manning as an artistic innovator. But there is no suggestion of swing dance within an African American tradition, and, as for swing's resurgence, Stewart suggests only that "everything old is new again" and perceives (rightly) that 1990s swing is a synthesis of big-band rhythm and the heavier rock-and-roll backbeat.[5]

In the same article, the commentary of swing musicians and dancers eerily echoes that of the swing era. Stewart describes the dancing at the Spanish Ballroom in Maryland's Glen Echo Park as a wild, dynamic display of athleticism with women "thrown through legs, snatched back the other way, flung upside down and spun around like lariats," while the crowd "whoops and shouts each time a body goes flying . . . [and] saxophones and trumpets blare in a syncopated crescendo." The bandleader Tom Cunningham claims his sixteen-piece band plays its best—and swings its hardest—when there are good lindy hoppers around. "We feed off their energy and they feed off ours." Speaking of the chic crowd at a New York club in their retro zoot suits and fedoras, a fifty-six-year-old big-band singer named Matt Carisi told Stewart, "Sometimes I look around and it feels like 1939." But if after rock and roll and the revolution of individual dancing, "swing dancing eventually went the way of all partner dancing, stigmatized as a nostalgic and decidedly uncool pastime," then why has it returned?[6]

Swing music and dance were participatory cultural forms that yoked then-assumed opposites together—the human and the machine—in a dance-hall ritual that helped dissipate the tensions of a technological society. James Gleick recently reflected on the self-doubt that continues to surge beneath the impending "wireless age." "The network knows where we are. The network is there, all around us, a ghostly electromagnetic presence, pervasive and salient, a global infrastructure taking shape many times faster than the Interstate highway or the world's railroads." The ghost in this machine is physiological resistance to technological determinism; thus today's generations *swing the network.* "Information everywhere, at light speed, immersing us—is this what we want? We seem unsure."[7] The swing revival, rave culture, hip-hop, techno, and clubbing continue a tradition of rebelling from the feet up—just as tap dancers did—as the mindful body asserts itself against American society's mechano-idolatry and an increasingly embedded faith in the salvation of technological progress.

Gleick's reference to "the world's railroads" as a proto-network is mirrored by the fact that locomotive onomatopoeia helped kick-start several contemporary musical genres. The German group Kraftwerk's fifteen-minute "Trans-Europe Express" (1977) was a seminal hip-hop, techno, and electronica recording. The DJs Afrika Bambaataa and Grandmaster Flash found the groove so satisfying they did not scratch over it or throw samples in it; they would just spin it and go take a break. Bambaataa thought of Kraftwerk's layered mechanical rhythms as taking "calculators and add[ing] something to it," and the group helped him see machines as a rich source of sounds and rhythms; "they really mastered those industrial type of machines." The name of Bambaataa's first group, "Soul Sonic Force" brought together signs of black music ("soul") and the potential power of mechanical rhythms ("sonic force"); Tricia Rose claims simply that "emotional power and presence in rap are profoundly linked to sonic force and one's receptivity to it." Grandmaster Flash's album, "The Adventures of Grandmaster Flash on the Wheels of Steel," set a new benchmark for aural collage in 1981, and calling turntables "wheels of steel" was an obvious visual and sonic connection to trains.[8]

Early techno hits such as Earth to Infinity's "Soylent Green" (1992) and The KLF's "Last Train to Trancentral" (1993) get rolling with nearly two minutes of ambient train sounds. In "Soylent Green," the listener first hears pastoral sounds of nature, which then cede sonic ground to train sounds and rhythms, which eventually dissolve into radio static and disperse into an audio collage of broadcast announcements reporting trips to the moon.[9] Thus the musical modernity of locomotive onomatopocia provides a kind of "start" date of the techno-dialogic now embedded in electronic music.

It would not be a stretch to claim that the musical trope of the train—its power, rhythm, drive, and relaxed propulsion—*evolved* from swing to techno, from the prototype rhythm of "the machine" to an early sonic map of "the network." Louis Jordan's various jump-band units (the Swingin' 7, the Tympani 5) defined the postwar rhythm-and-blues sound that later became rock and roll; Jordan had been a vocalist and alto saxophonist in Chick Webb's big band at the Savoy, and his breakthrough hit was "Choo Choo Ch-Boogie" (1947). Ten years later, Chuck Berry's archetypal guitar-playing rock-and-roll hero, "Johnny B. Goode," learned to play guitar by practicing to the beat of the passing train, absorbing the rhythm of the rails and the sound (and discontents) of a locomotive people.

> He used to carry his guitar in a gunny sack.
> And sit beneath the trees by the railroad track.
> Oh, the engineers used to see him sitting in the shade,
> Playing to the rhythm that the drivers made.

Johnny B. Goode's apprenticeship to the train-whistle guitar echoes DeFord Bailey's earlier attempts to "catch" the train on his harmonica. Growing up in Akron, Ohio, in the 1960s, Chryssie Hynde of the Pretenders remembered that the sound of the train outside her window *meant* rock and roll to her: it signaled adventure, musical motion, and rhythmic drive, and you can hear echoes of its relaxed propulsion underneath such hits as "Back on the Chain Gang" and "2000 Miles." Recent recordings of Los Lobos ("Everybody Loves a Train") and The Derailers ("Can't Stop a Train") continue this American sonic symbiosis.

Train songs, sounds, and rhythms were also essential to early country music, and train journeys remain one of the genre's central motifs. The same year as "Johnny B. Goode," Johnny Cash's version of "Casey Jones" (1957) began with an unaccompanied ten-second call of the train whistle. The whistle, almost as piercing on record as in the landscape, and the loudest call to modernity for the hundred previous years, seems to call forth the retelling of the legendary engineer's story. The train was the "most dramatic example of the industrial process," and an unparalleled symbol of power, mobility, modernity, and hope for Southerners. The country music historian Bill Malone sums up the train's sonic and symbolic power: "No one can document the number of people who have lain awake in quiet and darkened farmhouses listening to the lonesome wail of a distant freight train or have seen it belching smoke as it thundered down the mountainside and longed for the exciting world that the iron monster seemed to symbolize."[10]

The train was the original machine in the garden, but the original American inquiry into the human-machine interface was "The Ballad of John Henry." In 1939 the venerable folklorist John Lomax excitedly reported that a new verse had been added by anonymous folk singers. In his field recording of singer Arthur Bell that year there appeared a "stanza he [Lomax] had never heard before" in which John Henry's body is removed to Washington, D.C.

> They took John Henry to Washington
> and they buried him in the sand
> And the people from the East
> And the people from the West
> Came to see such a steel-driving man.
>
> Some say he came from England
> Some say he came from Spain
> But I say he's nothing but a Louisiana man
> At the head of a steel-driving gang.[11]

As "The Ballad of John Henry" posed a set of important questions about living in a technological society, folk singers promoted the "steel-driving man" to the status of a national hero of the industrial age.

To John Henry's call came the response of big-band swing, tap, and the lindy hop—adaptive cultural forms to mediate the threat of over-mechanization. The big band was a machine made up of working human beings; aurally and visually, it functioned as a human display of machine aesthetics—"efficiency, precision, control, and system"[12]—that cannot be located in any other modernist art form. The sonic textures and rhythmic depth of big-band swing emerged from the creation of new musical "parts"—the jazz rhythm section and the drummer's trap-set—capable of reflecting and containing the new soundscape within "the inexhaustible 4/4." Jazz musicians such as Benny Goodman and Danny Barker, as well as social critics such as Damon Runyon and Gilbert Seldes, perceived swing's popularity as dependent upon the power and drive of fourteen musicians playing rhythmically buoyant, seamless arrangements.

As for dance, specific West African gestures may have lost their original meanings, but the role of the dance in African American culture retained its function: to integrate music, movement, culture, and social forces into participatory consciousness. Dancing allows an individual to sync up with the social tempo. As the dancer and scholar Katherine Dunham noted at the time, American social dances of the swing era had engaged "the uniquely rapid industrialization of America." As earlier generations responded to the cakewalk and the Charleston as expressions of the "urbanization of the plantation folk-dances," tap and the lindy represented the ongoing process by which African American dancers integrated European traditions.[13] These dances were new artistic syntheses that left openings for improvisation; black dancers often interpolated older folk-dance gestures, such as the Texas Tommy or the Pas Mala, or moves from buck dancing, during the break-away step. Such a method allows for change within continuity, for innovation within tradition.

How did Americans adapt to the new industrial tempo and soundscape aurally, physiologically, and psychologically? They integrated technology into rituals of deep play by bringing it onto the dance floor, transformed locomotive onomatopoeia into odes on modernity, and tamed machines for leisure (rollercoasters, automobiles, luxury trains, radio, motion pictures). How does an individual rise to the challenge of the superior technical abilities of machines? Through an artistic display of speed, timing, humor, physical grace, flexibility, improvisation, and elegant noise. I would define the essence of a distinctly American

Machine Age modernism as *the controlled power of machine aesthetics in the service of self-expression*. The outright theft of the lindy hop by white professional dancers proves its success as a vernacular cultural form that was "right" for the Machine Age. Tap dance was even more expressive of the period, and Fred Astaire's besting of "the machine" in "Slap That Bass" was the culmination of the cultural inquiry opened by "The Ballad of John Henry."

In the worst years of the Depression, the tempo-of-life discourse was an indicator of the nation's first technological plateau. Within the context of massive overall unemployment, between assembly-line work realities and fears of specifically technological unemployment, the idea of techno-progress came under attack. Such fears of the early Depression were in marked contrast to the technological optimism of the 1920s, which drew on the prosperity provided by the automobile industry, the promise of new machines for leisure and convenience, and the international vogue for Fordism and Taylorism. When the French painter Francis Picabia visited the United States in 1915, he proclaimed that "the genius of the modern world was machinery," and that the machine had become the "very soul" of the American spirit; Picabia's influence on American painters, and the Bauhaus influence on American architects and industrial designers, led to a vision of a new city on the hill at the New York World's Fair of 1939. To fully enjoy this world, Fair planners and industrial designers suggested that Americans must cut their ties to past traditions.

Americans instead responded to swing culture as it livened up the technocracy of the Fair. At times of cultural transition and national self-doubt, people often "turn inward, searching for deeper life values," the jazz scholar Gunther Schuller reflected on the Depression, and Americans found them in swing, the nation's "popular music, its social dances and its musical entertainment."[14] I have shown how big-band swing's popularity was due in part to the attention bandleaders and drummers focused on the dancing public both as a sounding board and as a partner in the cultural practice of making sense of the universe in sound, dance, and time. Jazz was similarly influential internationally as the sound and symbol of adversarial resistance to totalitarian regimes, whether in Russia, Nazi Germany, or Czechoslovakia.

During World War II big bands helped maintain morale at home and overseas, and swing culture was honored for its artistic value by the media and the government. According to the swing chronicler Ernie

Smith, "American GIs, raised and nurtured on the swing-saturated environment of the period, spread the gospel of swing music and related dances, particularly the Lindy Hop, wherever they set foot. Newsreel footage of jitterbugging soldiers at overseas locations, at USO centers, in remote battlefield settings, at victory celebrations in the streets of Paris and London, were commonplace."[15] Glenn Miller's Army Air Forces Band functioned as the national band during the war, and swing replaced Sousa marches and precision drill teams as an international music that Europeans heard as expressive of freedom and democracy; Miller's untimely wartime death was mourned as a national tragedy. Perhaps the greatest tribute to swing's cultural importance occurred when Miller's Army Air Forces Band played a command performance at the National Press Club in Washington, D.C., upon its return in 1945 (under the direction of Tex Beneke). As General Dwight D. Eisenhower praised the band for its contribution to wartime morale, President Harry S. Truman spontaneously stood up to lead a standing ovation before the band played a single note.[16]

In 1943, the jazz journal *Metronome* celebrated its sixtieth anniversary by praising both the leadership of swing bandleaders and the consistently high quality of the music. "Some day, when their music has been established for many years as the magnificent thing it is, Americans will look back to Benny Goodman and Duke Ellington, to the Dorseys and Count Basie, Benny Carter and Coleman Hawkins . . . as the heroes of a Golden Age." *Metronome* called swing-era jazz musicians "the most brilliant group of musicians of our time," and insisted there was an "American national musical culture" in the early 1940s. The editors perceived in swing "a cultural rebirth" as important to "American democratic culture" as the "time of Emerson and Thoreau and Whitman and Hawthorne and Melville was to American literature."[17] At the popular level Americans have rediscovered swing-era artists such as Fred Astaire and Ginger Rogers, Count Basie and Benny Goodman, Louis Armstrong, Ella Fitzgerald, and Frank Sinatra, all of whom have become ensconced as avatars of vernacular American aesthetic excellence.

In 1969, Ralph Ellison reflected on Duke Ellington and Louis Armstrong as "stewards of our vaunted American optimism" who led the nation through an economic and cultural crisis. The jazz scholar Martin Williams claimed the nation owed a particular debt to Fletcher Henderson, whose architecture of big-band arrangement provided swing with its fundamental structural form. Swing music "carri[ed] millions of

Americans through a terrible Depression," and helped disseminate the existential affirmation at the functional core of African American musical practice. Williams interpreted the central message of big-band jazz in these terms: "'I will not succumb,' the music says. 'I will stay in touch with my essential humanity. And I will survive as a man.' . . . [F]or many of us . . . it affirmed the human spirit."[18]

The cultural work performed by swing music is today an essential part of musical practice. The techno-dialogic is a crucial survival strategy now embedded in American culture, a legacy of a social need to maintain a dialogue between art and technology. What began with jerky, rollicking ragtime rhythms and the functional repetition of work songs became orchestrated in the dance rhythms of New Orleans jazz and then transmuted into the controlled power of big-band swing: through an increase in the size and power of bands, in the smoother, cleaner, more flowing groove, in the power and precision of ensemble section playing (and interaction), and in overall improved musicianship. The techno-dialogic also explains one of the great conundrums of jazz history: the big-band blip. Before and after the swing era, jazz has generally been a small-band music. Before electric guitars and basses, and before dance halls had sophisticated amplification, fourteen to eighteen acoustic instruments were needed to blast out elegant noise to dialogue with factories and blast furnaces. The creation of electric instruments and amplifiers eliminated the need for big bands; the techno-dialogic of music and machinery passed on to rock and roll, funk, hip-hop, and electronica through synthesizers, drum machines, mixers, and MIDI technology. But big-band swing generated enough musical innovation that it split into three separate postwar musical forms: bebop, western swing, and rhythm and blues, each of which in turn carried the influence of swing into the present.

One final point. There is a crucial *economic* difference between swing and hip-hop; the latter has changed the rules of white economic appropriation of black musical innovation. African American hip-hop artists have crossed over and claimed roles in film and television, music producers such as Russell Simmons have become media entrepreneurs, and hip-hop has made a sonic home in the dense layers of recording technology that make it the music of choice for many Hollywood sound tracks. There is also considerable synergy among hip-hop, techno, heavy metal, and world musics. The love-and-theft economic cycle of African American musical revolution has been disrupted, and crossing over no longer leads immediately to whitefacing of the rhythmic idiom (with its varying degrees of artistry, mimickry, and dilution) nor to the exclusion of blacks from the largest share of profits and pop-cultural power.[19]

Such are the legacies of African American aesthetics in music and dance as they contribute to embodiment, cultural exchange, adaptation, and participatory consciousness. Call it *grooving*. The culture and history of these machine ages just don't mean a thing if we don't understand (the achievements and costs of) that swing.

NOTES

Introduction

1. Le Corbusier, *When the Cathedrals Were White* (New York: Reynal and Hitchcock, 1947), 160 (emphasis added). The memoir was originally published in France in 1936.

2. Ibid., 159, 164, 169. Le Corbusier calls Armstrong "a king" and "an imperial figure," and describes his playing as by turns "demoniac, playful and massive" (159). Le Corbusier wrote the manifesto of modernism, *Towards A New Architecture* (1927). For an alternative reading of this essay that places the architect in a more familiar primitivist discourse, see Mardges Bacon, *Le Corbusier in America: Travels in the Land of the Timid* (Cambridge: MIT Press, 2001), 219–26. Bacon links Le Corbusier to a larger European vogue for American culture between the world wars known as *américanisme*. Inspired by American skyscrapers, mass production, the urban energy of New York, and jazz and jazz dance, European architects and painters looked to the United States for postwar artistic renewal. To Bacon, Le Corbusier shared "the widely held European belief that they [blacks] were more primitive, more unspoiled, more noble, and open to new ideas" (226). On *américanisme*, see 6–14, 129–41.

3. Lewis Mumford, *Technics and Civilization* (New York: Harcourt, Brace, 1934), 363; Norman Bel Geddes, *Horizons* (Boston: Little, Brown, 1932), 4.

4. John Miller Chernoff, *African Rhythm and African Sensibility: Aesthetics and Social Action in African Musical Idioms* (Chicago: University of Chicago Press, 1979), 39–90; Robert Farris Thompson, *African Art in Motion: Icon and Act* (Los Angeles: University of California Press, 1974), 1–45; Yaya Diallo and Mitchell Hall, *The Healing Drum: African Wisdom Teachings* (Rochester, Vt.: Destiny, 1989).

5. Of course, there are and always have been many excellent white jazz musicians, but the cultural form, its values, and its practices were created by African Americans.

6. Henry R. Luce, "The American Century," *Life*, February 17, 1941, 65.

7. Lewis Erenberg, *Swingin' the Dream* (Chicago: University of Chicago Press, 1998), 5.

8. Emily Thompson, *The Soundscape of Modernity* (Cambridge: MIT Press, 2002), 1–2, 117–18, 149, 157–68; John Blacking, *How Musical Is Man?* (Seattle: University of Washington Press, 1973), 2–3.

9. Thomas P. Hughes, *American Genesis* (New York: Viking, 1989), 309–12; David A. Hounshell, *From the American System to Mass Production, 1800–1932* (Baltimore: Johns Hopkins University Press, 1984), 216–20.

10. Robert Goffin, "Hot Jazz," in *The Louis Armstrong Companion*, ed. Joshua Berrett (New York: Schirmer, 1999), 56–60. Goffin was one of three European intellectuals to write histories of jazz in this period, and in this 1934 article, Goffin specifically names as modernists Louis Armstrong, Coleman Hawkins, Earl Hines, Louis Armstrong, and Bix Beiderbecke. The better-known co-founders of *Le Jazz Hot* magazine in 1935 were Hughes Panassie, whose *Le Jazz Hot* (New York: Witmark, 1936) changed the American reception of jazz, and Charles Delaunay. For an excellent short analysis of the impact of jazz rhythms and dance on French choreographers, composers, and painters in the 1920s, see Constance Valis Hill, "Jazz Modernism," in *Moving Words: Re-writing Dance*, ed. Gay Morris (London: Routledge, 1996), 227–42.

11. Ralph Ellison, "What Would America Be without Blacks?," *Time*, April 6, 1970, repr. in *Going to the Territory* (New York: Vintage, 1986), 104–12. Before Lawrence Levine's landmark *Black Culture and Black Consciousness* (New York: Oxford, 1977), the typical white academic approach to black culture was still indebted to the Chicago School of Sociology. In 1974 the eminent sociologist Herbert Gans asserted that "blacks share the taste cultures created by whites, and their aesthetic standards, leisure and consumption habits . . . [according to] similar socioeconomic level and age"; he posited the beginning of a distinctive "black culture" in the 1960s emerging from the Civil Rights movement. Herbert Gans, *An Analysis of Evaluation and Taste* (New York: Basic Books, 1974), 100–101.

12. Ellison, *Going to the Territory*, 109–10. According to Ellison, the 1960s concept of "soul" stands for this philosophical approach to life. "It is its ability to articulate this tragic-comic attitude toward life that explains much of the mysterious power and attractiveness of that quality of Negro American style known as 'soul.' An expression of American diversity within unity, of blackness with whiteness, soul announces the presence of a creative struggle against the realities of existence." The same year Ellison's essay appeared, Albert Murray declared American culture "incontestably mulatto." Albert Murray, *The Omni-Americans* (New York: Avon, 1970), 39.

13. Alan Burdick, "Now Hear This: Listening Back on a Century of Sound," *Harper's*, July 2001, 70.

14. See, for example, Christoph Asendorf, *Batteries of Life: On the History of Things and Their Perception in Modernity* (Berkeley: University of California Press, 1993).

15. Charles Keil and Steven Feld, *Music Grooves* (Chicago: University of Chicago Press, 1994), 59–60 and 151–80. Hip-hop's DJs, dancers, and producers continue to soundtrack the pace of technological change through a rhythm-based set of African-derived aesthetic principles.

16. Hughes, *American Genesis* 314–46; Hounshell, *From the American System*, 216–20; Leo Marx, "The Idea of 'Technology' and Postmodern Pessimism" in *Technology, Pessimism, and Postmodernism*, ed. Yaron Ezrahi, Everett Mendelsohn, and Howard Segal (Dordrecht, the Netherlands: Kluwer, 1994), 20. A classic study of the American precisionists can be found in Abraham A. Davidson,

Early American Modernist Painting, 1910–1935 (New York: Harper and Row, 1981), 188–228.

17. See, for example, Pontus Hulten, ed., *Futurism and Futurisms* (New York: Abbeville, 1986), 552–53.

18. Hughes, *American Genesis,* 309, 317–21, 324–27, 331. Picabia believed the soul of the United States was its machines, and he freely adapted machine drawings from industrial catalogues for whimsical portraits of American life, sometimes depicting human beings as pistons or cylinders. Picabia helped the American painters Charles Demuth and Charles Sheeler see that the natural subject for the American artist was machinery. Significantly, Sheeler's "Self-Portrait" (1923) portrays a nondescript man cut off at the head standing behind a table, while his "head" (in the foreground) is a telephone; this is the first machine reference in Sheeler's body of work. See Susan Fillin Yeh, "Charles Sheeler and the Machine Age," Ph.D. diss., City College of New York, 1981, 48, 74.

19. Hillel Schwartz, "Torque: The New Kinaesthetic of the Twentieth Century," in *Incorporations,* ed. Jonathan Crary and Sanford Kwinter (New York: Zone/MIT Press, 1992), 87–90; Terry Smith, "Making the Modern," lecture/discussion, Austin, Texas, January 31, 1995.

20. For the best historical account of the creation of the assembly line, see Hounshell, *From the American System,* 228–56 (quote on p. 236).

21. See, for example, Jeffrey L. Meikle, *Twentieth Century Limited: Industrial Design in America, 1925–1939* (Philadelphia: Temple University Press, 1979), 172–79.

22. Terry Smith, *Making the Modern: Industry, Art, and Design in America* (Chicago: University of Chicago Press, 1993), 194. Cecelia Tichi coined the phrase "gear-and-girder era" to describe industrial aesthetics in *Shifting Gears: Technology, Literature, Culture in Modernist America* (Chapel Hill: University of North Carolina Press, 1987), xi–xvi, 4–16.

23. Hughes, *American Genesis,* 341.

24. Linda Bank Downs, *Diego Rivera: The Detroit Industry Murals* (New York: Norton/Detroit Institute of Arts, 1999), 92–104, 140–44; Smith, *Making the Modern,* 199–240; Diego Rivera, *My Art, My Life* (New York: Dover, 1991 [1960]), 111–22 (quote on p. 112).

25. Thorstein Veblen, *The Instinct in Workmanship* (New York: Huebsch, 1914), 302–13.

26. Frank Norris, *The Octopus,* in *Novels and Essays* (New York: Library of America, 1986), 679. Mark Seltzer analyzes the manifestations of industrial discipline on bodies in turn-of-the-century naturalist literature, using *The Octopus* as his primary American example; see Mark Seltzer, *Bodies and Machines* (New York: Routledge, 1992), 3–18, 25–35.

27. Elizabeth E. Turner, "Factory Girl's Reverie," in *Rebecca Harding Davis: Life in the Iron Mills,* ed. Cecelia Tichi (Boston: Bedford, 1998), 175. See also Thomas Dublin, "Women, Work, and Protest in the Early Lowell Mills: 'The Oppressing Hand of Avarice Would Enslave Us,'" *Labor History* 16 (1975): 99–116.

28. On "technological unemployment" and workers' fears of displacement through mechanization, see Amy Sue Bix, *Inventing Ourselves Out of Jobs?: America's Debate over Technological Unemployment* (Baltimore: Johns Hopkins University Press, 2000), 1–42, 80–142.

29. On the European development of the field of industrial research and the premise that a worker's body is a "motor . . . regulated by internal, dynamic principles," see Anson Rabinbach, *The Human Motor: Energy, Fatigue, and the Origins of Modernity* (Berkeley: University of California Press, 1992), 1–2, 51–52 and passim, and Bix, *Inventing Ourselves Out of Jobs,* 26–32. For the prevalence of the metaphor of human-body-as-machine in American medical practice, see the following: W. E. McVey, ed., *The Human Machine, Its Care and Repair* (Topeka, Ks.: Herbert S. Reed, 1901), an 848-page guide meant for home use; Frederic S. Lee, *The Human Machine and Industrial Efficiency* (New York: Longmans, Green, 1919), the 1918 Cutter Lectures at Harvard Medical School by a renowned industrial researcher; William H. Howell, *The Human Machine: How Your Body Functions* (New York: Funk and Wagnalls, 1924), a doctor's popular account underwritten by the National Health Council; and George B. Bridgman, *The Human Machine: The Anatomical Structure and Mechanism of the Human Body* (New York: Bridgman/Pelham, 1939), a book of drawings rendering parts of the body as levers (jaw, skull) and rotary mechanisms (shoulder, knee). The first work to explicate the human body through mechanical analogy was Julian Offray de la Mettrie's *Man, A Machine* (Chicago: Open Court, 1912 [1747]); La Mettrie celebrated the human body as "a large watch, constructed with . . . skill and ingenuity" and powered by "the heart as . . . the mainspring of the machine" (141).

30. James Gleick, *Faster: The Acceleration of Just About Everything* (New York: Vintage, 1999), 52. Gleick mentions experimentation with drugs such as cocaine (to speed up) or opium (to slow down), and the popularity of fantasies of time travel.

31. Stuart Chase, *Men and Machines* (New York: Macmillan, 1929), 248–49. Fred Colvin of *American Machinist* perceived the same aesthetic qualities in the assembly line at Ford's Highland Park facility in 1913: "principles of power, accuracy, economy, system, continuity and speed." Quoted in Hounshell, *From the American System,* 228.

32. Smith, "Making the Modern."

33. Filippo Marinetti, "Manifesto of the Futurist Dance," in *Marinetti: Selected Writings,* ed. R. W. Flint (New York: Farrar, Straus, 1972), 137–38.

34. Kathy Peiss, *Cheap Amusements* (Philadelphia: Temple University Press, 1986), 88–114; Paula S. Fass, *The Damned and the Beautiful* (New York: Oxford University Press, 1977), 300–306; Lucille Marsh, "A Survey of the Social Dance in America," *Journal of Health and Physical Education,* November 1935, 34–36, 62. Marsh was the dance critic for the *New York World* and the journal *Musical America.*

35. Havelock Ellis, *The Dance of Life* (New York: Modern Library, 1929 [1923]), 35. For an analysis of the "urban dance complex" as it evolved from rural societies and communal values, see Judith Hanna, *To Dance Is Human: A*

Theory of Nonverbal Communication (Austin: University of Texas Press, 1979), 119–229.

36. Hughes, *American Genesis*, 313.

37. For a similar relationship between industrialization and the rise of the symphony, see the discussion in chapter 1.

38. Mumford, *Technics and Civilization*, 359–63.

39. Erenberg, *Swingin' the Dream*, 120.

40. Walter Terry, *How to Look at Dance* (New York: Morrow, 1982), 114.

41. Jon Michael Spencer, *Re-Searching Black Music* (Knoxville: University of Tennessee Press, 1996), 69–70.

42. Gena Dagel Caponi, ed. *Signifyin(g), Sanctifyin' and Slam Dunking* (Amherst: University of Massachusetts Press, 1999), 9–13.

43. Richard Crawford, *The American Musical Landscape* (Berkeley: University of California Press, 1993), 220–22.

44. Herbert Muschamp, "A Rare Opportunity for Real Architecture Where It's Needed," *New York Times,* October 22, 2000, sect. 2, 38.

45. Julia Foulkes, *Modern Bodies: Dance and American Modernism* (Chapel Hill: University of North Carolina Press, 2002).

46. Barbara Glass, ed. *When the Spirit Moves* (Wilberforce, Ohio: National Afro-American Museum and Culture Center, 1999), 6–45; "What Is Black Dance?" in *One Hundred Years of Black Music and Dance* (Brooklyn Academy of Music program, 1992); Jacqui Malone, *Steppin' on the Blues* (Urbana: University of Illinois Press, 1996), 1–9; Robert Farris Thompson, "Aesthetic of the Cool: West African Dance," in Caponi, *Signifyin(g),* 72–86.

47. Otis Ferguson, *The Otis Ferguson Reader,* ed. Dorothy Chamberlain and Robert Wilson (New York: Da Capo, 1997), 72–73; Ramey quoted in Stanley Dance, *The World of Count Basie* (New York: Scribner's, 1980), 264.

48. James Dugan and John Hammond, "An Early Black-Music Concert from Spirituals to Swing" (1938), reprinted in *Black Perspective in Music* 2 (Fall 1974): 191–207. The music impresario John Hammond used the phrase "the music nobody knows" as a subheading for his program comments. Hammond was referring to the effaced roots of jazz, the "love and theft" that had allowed generations of white American musicians to appropriate black musical innovation. I am referring to something quite different: a set of Machine Age factors that contemporary intellectuals often perceived but cultural historians have lost.

49. Morroe Berger, "Jazz: Resistance to the Diffusion of a Cultural Pattern," in *American Music: From Storyville to Woodstock,* ed. Charles Nanry (New Brunswick, N.J.: Dutton, 1972), 11–44.

50. Alfred V. Frankenstein, *Syncopating Saxophones* (Chicago: Robert O. Ballou, 1925), 9, 39. Courtesy of the collection of the Institute of Jazz Studies, Rutgers University at Newark (hereinafter, "IJS"). See also Thompson, *Soundscape of Modernity,* 130–32.

51. In the industrial period under discussion, American classical composers were mired in a Victorian aesthetic that emphasized the pseudo-religious qualities of ethereality and tranquillity. There was no place in their

idea of culture for machines, commerce, and propulsive rhythms—the veritable enemies of Matthew Arnold's famous artistic dictum to produce "sweetness and light." Ethnic elements were appropriated, however. The Czech composer Antonin Dvorak's use of African American spirituals as leitmotifs for his "New World Symphony" (1893) led to a gold-rush mentality among American classical composers around the turn of the century to build a national music on native folk idioms. Symphonic works were built on Native American chants or dance rhythms, and on the plantation themes that romanticized African American life. See Macdonald S. Moore, *Yankee Blues* (Bloomington: University of Indiana Press, 1983), 3–5, 69–70 and passim.

52. For discussions of machine aesthetics in this period, see Sheldon Cheney and Martha Cheney, *Art and the Machine* (New York: McGraw Hill, 1936), 12–21, the chapters in Meikle, *Twentieth-Century Limited*, 19–38, and Richard Guy Wilson, Dianne H. Pilgrim, and Dickvan Tashjian, *The Machine Age in America 1918–1941* (New York: Brooklyn Museum/Abrams, 1986), 43–64. David Gelernter focuses on just two qualities, "power" and "simplicity," in his discussion of machine aesthetics in computer design; see David Gelernter, *Machine Beauty: Elegance and the Heart of Technology* (New York: Basic Books, 1998), 2–10. Le Corbusier, *When the Cathedrals Were White*, 160.

53. Siegfried Giedion, *Mechanization Takes Command* (New York: Oxford University Press, 1948), 121; Susan Leigh Foster, "Dancing Bodies," in Crary and Kwintner, *Incorporations*, 480–95.

54. Cornel West, *Keeping Faith* (New York: Routledge, 1994), xiii–xiv; Katrina Hazzard-Gordon, "Dancing under the Lash: Sociocultural Disruption, Continuity, and Synthesis," in *Africa Dance*, ed. Kariamu Welsh Asante (Trenton, N.J.: Africa World Press, 1996), 108–9; Nathan Irvin Huggins, *Black Odyssey: The African-American Ordeal in Slavery* (New York: Vintage, 1990 [1977]), 24, 55. For an analysis of the slaves' creation of a pan-African culture in the antebellum period, see Sterling Stuckey, *Slave Culture* (New York: Oxford University Press, 1987), 3–97.

55. Albert Murray, *Stomping the Blues* (New York: Da Capo, 1976), 106, 151; Ingrid Monson, *Saying Something: Jazz Improvisation and Interaction* (Chicago: University of Chicago Press, 1993), 52.

56. V. F. Calverton, "The Growth of Negro Literature," in *Negro*, ed. Nancy Cunard (New York: Frederick Ungar, 1970 [1932]), 82.

57. Industrial designer Norman Bel Geddes claimed "speed is the cry of the era" and needed to be visually expressed. Bel Geddes, *Horizons*, 24. There is a long debate on the origins of the term "jazz." I rely here on Sidney Bechet's testimony concerning the first generation of New Orleans musicians, who still called the music ragtime. "*Rag it up*, we used to say. You take any piece, you make it so people can dance to it, pat their feet, move around. You make it so they can't help themselves from doing that. You make it so they just can't sit still." Sidney Bechet, *Treat It Gentle* (New York: Da Capo, 1975 [1960]), 212.

58. According to John Kasson, faith in technological change itself made republican virtue possible in the revolutionary era, and he shows (along with Leo

Marx) that American Enlightenment figures combined religious, republican, and mechanistic values in a confused package of liberation. John Kasson, *Civilizing the Machine* (New York: Penguin, 1976), 1–51; Leo Marx, *The Machine in the Garden* (New York: Oxford University Press, 1964), 145–90. On the religious rhetoric behind "techno-progress," see Anthony F. C. Wallace, *Rockdale* (New York: Knopf, 1978), 394–97, and Kasson, 53–106.

59. Howard P. Segal, *Future Imperfect: The Mixed Blessings of Technology in America* (Amherst: University of Massachusetts Press, 1994), 4–16.

60. John Brinckerhoff Jackson, *A Sense of Place, A Sense of Time* (New Haven: Yale University Press, 1994), viii, 202–5. According to Jackson, Americans have a denatured relationship to both land and landscape. Just as Christian, the protagonist of *Pilgrim's Progress*, broke out of community pressures, local tradition, and daily earthly needs "in order to reach a distant, highly desirable goal: salvation," Americans rebel against local and community traditions in order to technologically improve their lives. Jackson's theory seems informed by Nathaniel Hawthorne's short story "The Celestial Railroad" (1843). Hawthorne was perhaps the first American writer to satirize the national faith in technological progress, and in "The Celestial Railroad" he contrasts those pilgrims willing to walk the long path to the "Celestial City," suffering hardship as they go, with those tourists who take the new train and ride comfortably alongside. The narrator's companion is a leading stockholder in the railroad known as "Mr. Smooth-it-away," a Luciferian character who disembarks before the final leg of the journey—a steamboat on the river of Death. Hawthorne here suggests the passengers have sold their souls for convenience and material comfort. See Kasson, *Civilizing the Machine*, 49–50.

61. The phrase "age of energy" comes from Howard Mumford Jones, *The Age Of Energy: Varieties of American Experience, 1865–1915* (New York: Viking, 1971). Lewis Mumford discusses the concept of "mechano-religion" in *Technics and Civilization*, 53–55 and 364–67, and again in *The Culture of Cities* (New York: Harcourt, Brace, 1938), 442; W. C. Handy, *Father of the Blues* (New York: Da Capo, 1969 [1941]), 232; David W. Stowe, *Swing Changes* (Cambridge: Harvard University Press, 1994), 14. In *The Culture of Cities* Mumford calls the faith in technological progress "mechanolatry"—meaning "mechano-idolatry"—and then, more precisely, a "mechanocentric religion." In the 1930s Mumford consistently argued for a new organic integration of machines into human social activity instead of the "bastard religion" of machine worship. For an analysis of how European intellectual currents were shaped by technological change, see Stephen Kern, *The Culture of Time and Space, 1880–1918* (Cambridge: Harvard University Press, 1983); for insight on the process in American popular culture, see the essays in Joseph Corn, ed., *Imagining Tomorrow* (Cambridge: MIT Press, 1986). An important attack on the philosophical underpinnings of progress in the period came from the Southern Agrarians; see Lyle H. Lanier, "A Critique of the Philosophy of Progress," in *I'll Take My Stand: The South and the Agrarian Tradition by Twelve Southerners* (New York: Harper and Row, 1962 [1930]), 122–54, esp. 148–49.

62. Murray, *Stomping the Blues*, 42.

63. Ibid., 16–20, 23, 38, 254, 257–58. On the concept of "somebodiness" in African American religion and music, see James H. Cone, *The Spirituals and the Blues* (Maryknoll, N.Y.: Orbis Books, 1972), 16–19, 105, 112.

64. John A. Kouwenhoven, *Made in America: The Arts in Modern American Civilization* (New York: Norton, 1967 [1948]), 218–22; Sidney Finkelstein, *Jazz: A People's Music* (New York: International, 1988 [1948]), 176.

65. Stowe, *Swing Changes*, 1, 9; Erenberg, *Swingin' the Dream*, 31, 91.

66. Berndt Ostendorf, "Anthropology, Modernism, and Jazz," in *Ralph Ellison*, ed. Harold Bloom (New York: Chelsea House, 1986), 145–72.

67. Whitney Balliett, *The Sound of Surprise* (New York: Dutton, 1959); Will Friedwald, *Jazz Singing* (New York: Scribner's, 1990), xiv, 66.

68. Kenneth Burke, *The Philosophy of Literary Form* (Berkeley: University of California Press, 1973 [1941]), 9; Reyner Banham, *Theory and Design in the First Machine Age* (New York: Praeger, 1960), 12.

69. Small argues that historical contingencies and artistic traditions combined to enable African Americans to create a modernist cultural form based in collective experience. Although not primarily focused on the United States, Robin Blackburn's history of the slave trade supports such a possibility in the opening chapter, "Slavery and Modernity." See Christopher Small, *Music of the Common Tongue* (London: Calder, 1987), 461–70, and Robin Blackburn, *The Making of New World Slavery* (London: Verso, 1997), 1–27. The definitive work on American exceptionalism in technology is Hughes, *American Genesis*.

70. Murray Schafer, quoted in Keil and Feld, *Music Grooves*, 143.

71. For an overview of the concept of "embodiment" and "the mindful body," see Andrew J. Strathern, *Body Thoughts* (Ann Arbor: University of Michigan Press, 1996), 177–204 (quoted material, 197–98); Berndt Ostendorf, "The Origins of the New Orleans Jazz Funeral," lecture, University of Texas at Austin, March 24, 1999, and e-mail communication, May 19, 1999. Ostendorf claims that "mimesis" refers to one culture's desire to imitate and incorporate the skills and attitudes (and even identities) of an alien culture, a mixture of admiration and distancing that Eric Lott, writing of the rise of blackface minstrelsy in the antebellum period, termed "love and theft."

72. E. B. White, "A Reporter At Large—The New York World's Fair," *New Yorker*, May 13, 1939, 26.

73. George Antheil, "The Negro on the Spiral," in Cunard, *Negro*, 214–18.

74. In Isaac Goldberg's *Tin Pan Alley* (New York: John Day, 1930), which chronicles the music industry, chapter 4 is entitled "Blackface into White." In the chapter on minstrelsy ("Pearls of Minstrelsy") he tortuously attempts to explain why "so many whites are trying to sing black ... [and some] blacks attempt to sing white" (32).

Chapter I

1. For an analysis of Ford's contradictions, see Warren I. Susman, *Culture as History* (New York: Pantheon, 1984), 122–32; for Ford's contribution to

machine-driven modernity, see Smith, *Making the Modern*, 47–51, 94–108, 147–51, and Hounshell, *From the American System*, 217–330.

2. Mark Sullivan, *Our Times: The United States 1900–1925, Vol. IV: The War Begins, 1909–1914* (New York: Scribner's, 1932), 232 n. 11 (emphasis added).

3. James Truslow Adams, *The Tempo of Modern Life* (New York: Albert and Charles Boni, 1931), 85–94 and passim.

4. Ibid., 93–94.

5. Karl Marx, *Capital, Vol. 1* (New York: Penguin Classics, 1990), 546–49; George Simmel, "The Metropolis and Mental Life," in *On Individuality and Social Forms: Selected Writings*, ed. Donald Levine (Chicago: University of Chicago Press, 1971), 324; Marinetti, *Selected Writings*, 41. Writing in 1903 about the urban metropolis, Simmel concluded that an individual "becomes a single cog as over against the vast overwhelming organization of things and forces which gradually take out of his hands everything connected with progress" (337).

6. Thorstein Veblen, *The Theory of Business Enterprise* (New York: Scribner's, 1904), 2, 10–16, 302–74; see also Veblen, *The Instinct of Workmanship* (New York: Huebsch, 1922 [1914]), 306–16.

7. Veblen, *Theory of Business Enterprise*, 13.

8. Ibid., 11–13, 324, 348, and Veblen, *Instinct of Workmanship*, 306; Mumford, *Technics and Civilization*, 53. Daniel T. Rodgers calls American workers between 1850 and 1920 "mechanicalized men." In the late 1800s, the excitement of technological progress merged with the quasireligious belief in the Protestant work ethic to create a mechanistic ideology in which the factory system was often seen as a social reformatory where workers learned discipline and rational thinking from their orderly machines. The primary spokesman was Commissioner of Labor Carroll D. Wright, who believed machines embodied rational thought and provided scientific models of cause and effect for the illiterate masses. Daniel T. Rodgers, *The Work Ethic in Industrial America 1850–1920* (Chicago: University of Chicago Press, 1978), 65–74. This social vision has its literary parallel in Mark Twain's *A Connecticut Yankee at King Arthur's Court* (New York: Norton, 1982 [1889]). The protagonist Hank Morgan is a Yankee inventor and foreman who believes the factory system promotes rational thinking and dispels superstition and aristocratic elitism. He builds a "Man-Factory" in sixth-century England and sends intellectually promising men there to become literate and to learn scientific principles.

9. On the engineer in the American imagination, see Cecilia Tichi, *Shifting Gears: Technology, Literature, Culture in Modernist America* (Chapel Hill: University of North Carolina Press, 1987), 97–170; John A. Kouwenhoven, *Half a Truth Is Better Than None* (Chicago: University of Chicago Press, 1982), 142; John Kasson, *Amusing the Million* (New York: Hill and Wang, 1978), 72–82; Marshall Berman, *All That Is Solid Melts into Air* (New York: Simon and Shuster, 1982), 160n.

10. C. G. Jung, "The Spiritual Problem of Modern Man," in *The Portable Jung*, ed. Joseph Campbell (New York: Penguin, 1971), 478–79.

11. In addition to the works discussed below, see also Joseph W. Krutch,

The Modern Temper (New York: Harcourt, 1932); Irwin Erdman, *The Contemporary and His Soul* (New York: Jonathan Cape, 1931), 1–19; the essays in Charles Beard, ed., *Whither Mankind: A Panorama of Modern Civilization* (New York: Longmans, 1928); and Mumford, *Technics and Civilization*, 198–99, 359–63, 432–33.

12. George Gershwin, "The Composer in the Machine Age," in *The American Composer Speaks*, ed. Gilbert Chase (Baton Rouge: Louisiana State University Press, 1966), 140–45. Without mentioning jazz, Gershwin referred to several famous contemporary compositions that integrated the sounds of machines, and suggested that machines "ha[ve] affected us in sound whenever composers utilize new instruments to imitate its aspects." He pointed to George Antheil's "aeroplane propellers, door bells, [and] typewriter keys" in *Ballet Mécanique*, Arthur Honegger's "Pacific 231," which was "dedicated to a steam engine [and] . . . reproduc[ed] the whole effect of a train stopping and starting," and his own use of "four taxi horns" in "An American in Paris" (140–41).

13. Robert Levine, *A Geography of Time: How Every Culture Keeps Time Just a Little Differently* (New York: Basic Books, 1997), 3–19; see also Eviatar Zerubavel, *Hidden Rhythms: Schedules and Calendars of Social Life* (Chicago: University of Chicago Press, 1981). Levine timed the same events in every city.

14. Levine, *Geography of Time*, 133–35, 146–47.

15. Walt Whitman, *Specimen Days, Democratic Vistas, and Other Prose*, ed. Louise Pound (Garden City, N.Y.: Doubleday, 1935), 327–28.

16. Henry Adams, *The Education of Henry Adams* (New York: Vintage Library of America, 1990[1907]), 352–62; *The Collected Poems of Hart Crane*, ed. Waldo Frank (New York: Liveright, 1933), 177–78.

17. Barr quoted in Susman, *Culture as History*, 189.

18. *Machine Art: March 6 to April 30, 1934*, exhib. cat. (New York: Museum of Modern Art, 1934), n.p.

19. Martha Graham, "The American Dance," in *Modern Dance*, ed. Virginia Stewart (New York: E. Weyhe, 1935), 103–4.

20. In "The Demon Machine," Bodenheiser called on her dancers to "move like pistons and turn like monstrous wheels" to show how humans were now enslaved to their machines. The futurist Filipo Marinetti wrote a manifesto on dance in 1917, calling for a choreography that was purposefully "Inharmonious—Ungraceful—Asymmetrical—Dynamic," and he suggested three dances: "Dance of the Autocar, Dance of the Machine Gun, and Dance of Shrapnel." Jack Anderson, *Art without Boundaries: The World of Modern Dance* (Iowa City: University of Iowa Press, 1997), 90–95, 107–8.

21. Martin thought such compositions superficial. There was "no essential difference between imitating the movements of a machine and those of a butterfly, for butterflies are equally contemporaneous"; the difference is "merely one of surface." These choreographers simply juxtaposed bodies and machines, and neither reconceptualized the interaction of bodies and machines nor conceived of any dialogic relationship. As Martin points out, the "deluge

of machinery dances" performed during the early period of modern dance resulted only from the mistaken belief "that nothing could be more modern than machinery." John Martin, *America Dancing* (New York: Dodge, 1936), 72.

22. Graham, "American Dance," 103–4 (emphasis added). From Karel Capek's *R. U. R.* (1922) to Aldous Huxley's *Brave New World* (1931), dystopic visions of mass-production futures came more often from Europeans than Americans.

23. Martha Graham quoted in Deborah Jowitt, *Time and the Dancing Image* (New York: Morrow, 1988), 176–77.

24. William Saroyan, "The Time of Your Life," *Theatre Arts Monthly* 23 (December 1939): 870–72.

25. Sherwood Anderson, "The Times and the Towns," in *America as Americans See It*, ed. Fred J. Ringel (New York: Literary Guild, 1932), 12–18.

26. John Dewey, *Art as Experience* (New York: Capricorn, 1958 [1934]), 337, 341.

27. Reinhold Niebuhr, *Moral Man and Immoral Society* (New York: Scribner's, 1932), 61–62.

28. John Dewey, *Individualism Old and New* (New York: Minton, Balch, 1930), 24, 33–34, 125.

29. Dewey theorizes on how to integrate scientific method into a revitalized and organic artistic vision in *Art as Experience*, 337–41.

30. Mumford, *Technics and Civilization*, 432–33. Mumford became increasingly pessimistic about the "megamachine" in the 1960s.

31. See also David Shenk, "Life at Hyper-Speed," *New York Times*, September 9, 1997, 29.

32. Ralph E. Flanders, *Taming Our Machines: The Attainment of Human Values in a Mechanized Society* (New York: Richard R. Smith, 1931), 52, 54, 81.

33. Beard, Introduction to *Whither Mankind*, 14–15, 18.

34. Nels Anderson, *Work and Leisure* (New York: Crowell-Collier, 1961), 56–61.

35. See, for example, Roderick Nash, *The Nervous Generation: American Thought, 1917–1930* (Chicago: Rand-McNally, 1970).

36. Quoted in Asendorf, *Batteries of Life*, 149–50.

37. Michael O'Malley, *Keeping Watch: A History of American Time* (Washington, D.C.: Smithsonian Institution Press, 1990), 121–27; William Carlos Williams, "Overture to a Dance of Locomotives," in *The Great Machines: Poems and Songs of the American Railroad*, ed. Robert Hedin (Iowa City: University of Iowa Press, 1996), 166.

38. Asendorf, *Batteries of Life*, 144. See also Mumford, *Technics and Civilization*, 12–18, and Alfred W. Crosby, *The Measure of Reality: Quantification and Western Society, 1250–1600* (New York: Cambridge University Press, 1997).

39. George Basalla, "Keaton and Chaplin: The Silent Film's Response to Technology," in *Technology in America*, ed. Carroll W. Pursell Jr. (Cambridge: MIT Press, 1981), 192–201; Anthony Aveni, "Time's Empire," *Wilson Quarterly* 22 (Summer 1998): 57. See also Kern, *Culture of Space and Time*, 110–11.

40. Segal, *Future Imperfect*, 33.

41. Everett Mendelsohn, "The Politics of Pessimism: Science and Technology Circa 1968," in *Technology, Pessimism, and Postmodernism*, 151–73.

42. Susman, *Culture as History*, 192. In summarizing the ideas and books that most influenced American intellectuals between 1900 and 1939, Malcolm Cowley emphasized the death of John Stuart Mill's "rational man" as an ideal of human behavior and the decline in respect for the self-reliant individual. Malcolm Cowley, ed., *Books That Changed Our Mind* (New York: Doubleday, 1939), 245–60.

43. Carl Becker, *Progress and Power* (Palo Alto, Calif.: Stanford University Press, 1936), 1–4.

44. Kenneth Burke, *Attitudes toward History* (Boston: Beacon, 1958 [1937]), 342.

45. Frederick Lewis Allen, *Since Yesterday* (New York: Harper and Brothers, 1940), 68, 124–29. See also Bix, *Inventing Ourselves Out of Jobs?*, 153–62, and Warren I. Susman, ed., *Culture and Commitment, 1929–1945* (New York: George Braziller, 1973), 194–97.

46. Clifford Geertz, *The Interpretation of Cultures* (New York: Basic Books, 1973), 99–100.

47. Rabinbach, *Human Motor*, 5–6. In the latter part of the nineteenth century, European social reformers and psychologists focused on the "fatigued" body as an important site requiring improvement in efficiency, energy distribution, and productivity.

48. Elizabeth E. Turner, "Factory Girl's Reverie" (1845), Fanny Fern, "The Working Girls of New York" (1867), and Anonymous, "My Experience as a Factory Operative" (1867), in Rebecca Harding Davis, *Life in the Iron Mills*, ed. Cecelia Tichi (Boston: Bedford, 1998), 159, 173, 175; Kasson, *Civilizing the Machine*, 78.

49. Herman Melville, "The Paradise of Bachelors and The Tartarus of Maids," in *Great Short Works of Herman Melville*, ed. Walter Berthoff (New York: Harper and Row, 1969), 202–22. Not until Sherwood Anderson's *Perhaps Women* (1931) and "Mill Girls" (1930) did a canonical American writer again portray the role of women in factories in such detail. Given the intervening success of American labor, Anderson wrote about a better-adapted female workforce and focused on the mill girls' leisure time, cultural resistance, and camaraderie.

50. Ibid., 215–16. Such a vision provides a contrast to the rosy fellowship Melville depicts in "The Paradise of Bachelors," where a group of English men separated from all manual work and family freely exchange ideas and experiences gathered from traveling around the world. These men are the financiers who invest in and profit from the mill; their every act involves paper. The men are something of a fraternal sewing circle, enjoying one another's company without competition or violence whereas the women are drawn as atomized, solitary slaves to both men and machines.

51. There are three basic interpretations of the "Maids" half of Melville's story: first, that the paper-making process mirrors the birth process; second,

that the landscape symbolizes a huge, archetypal woman, and the narrator's conflicts reflect Melville's conflicted relationships (sexual and otherwise) with women (especially as compared to "the paradise of bachelors"); and third, that the story is an indictment of industrial slavery. See Lea Bertani Vozar Newman, *A Reader's Guide to the Short Stories of Herman Melville* (Boston: G. K. Hall, 1986), 283–305. My interpretation has much in common with Marvin Fisher, *Going Under: Melville's Short Fiction and the American 1850s* (Baton Rouge: Louisiana State University Press, 1977), 70–94.

52. Davis, *Life in the Iron Mills*, 45–47.

53. Charles Dickens, *Hard Times* (London: Collins, 1959 [1854]), 22, 80.

54. Ibid., 63, 77. Lewis Mumford framed his critique of industrialization through Dickens's fictional Coketown and believed mid-nineteenth-century England was the nadir of Western technology in terms of its effects on workers and the natural environment. Lewis Mumford, *The City in History* (New York: Harcourt Brace, 1961), 446–50.

55. David E. Nye, *American Technological Sublime* (Cambridge: MIT Press, 1994), 33–43.

56. Anonymous, "My Experience as a Factory Operative," in Davis, *Life in the Iron Mills*, 172–73.

57. Louis-Ferdinand Céline, *Journey to the End of the Night* (Boston: Little, Brown, 1934), 222–25. Céline discusses the experience briefly in William K. Buckley, ed., *Critical Essays on Louis-Ferdinand Céline* (Boston: G. K. Hall, 1989), 323–24. One literary historian believes the account is simply hyperbole, and that Céline's experience was too short and superficial to be reliable as historical documentation; see John Sturrock, *Louis Ferdinand-Céline: Journey to the End of the Night* (Cambridge: Cambridge University Press, 1990), 17–19.

58. Gene Richards, "On the Assembly Line," *Atlantic Monthly*, April 1937, repr. in Susman, *Culture and Commitment*, 69–74.

59. Mark Sullivan, *Our Times: America at the Birth of the 20th Century*, ed. Dan Rather (New York: Scribner's, 1996 [1926–35]), 349. Perhaps the search for American work songs among folklorists in the first four decades of the century stems from the extinction of such songs through the removal of group consciousness in factory work. See, for example, Alan Lomax, *The Folk Songs of North America* (New York: Viking, 1947).

60. Robert D. Updegraff, *The New American Tempo* (New York: McGraw-Hill, 1929), 4–5, 7, 46.

61. Robert Sklar, *Movie-Made America* (New York: Random House, 1975), 44–47, 148–49.

62. The success of streamlined design in the 1930s was in part due to the influence of former theatrical set designers new to the field of industrial design, such as Norman Bel Geddes and Henry Dreyfuss. See Meikle, *Twentieth Century Limited*, 48–60.

63. Steve Roxy quoted in Updegraff, *New American Tempo*, 60–65.

64. Rem Koolhaas, *Delirious New York* (New York: Monacelli, 1994 [1978]), 208–19.

65. Ibid., 8–13.

66. Kasson, *Amusing the Million,* 57–112; Koolhaas, *Delirious New York,* 29–78 (quotes on 39, 61, 62); Woody Register, *The Kid from Coney Island: Fred Thompson and the Rise of American Amusements* (New York: Oxford University Press, 2001), 85–192. Thompson in particular helped transform the dynamic processes of industrial machinery into machine aesthetics for leisure and play. The son of a skilled ironworker, Thompson was enamored of mills and factories, and "had a taste for mechanics" as a boy. Much as Ford's River Rouge complex would later, the Hippodrome Theater featured its own transit system of train tunnels on each of its five levels for the movement of animals, actors, and props from stage to stage; such efficient movement enabled the audience to experience a seamless visual flow during the production. The Hippodrome featured departments of "engineering, carpentry . . . choreography, costumes, illumination, electricity, scene design, music," and Thompson thought of it as running like a machine with "no friction." For one production, Thompson had his designers visit a steel mill and recreate a working blast furnace. Register, *The Kid from Coney Island,* 15–18, 28, 163–69.

67. Vincent Lopez, *Lopez Speaking* (New York: Citadel, 1960), 132–36, 300; Kathy J. Ogren, *The Jazz Revolution* (New York: Oxford University Press, 1989), 93–94.

68. Gunther Schuller, *Early Jazz* (New York: Oxford University Press, 1968), 175–82.

69. Bechet, *Treat It Gentle,* 114–15.

70. Lopez, *Lopez Speaking,* 134–35.

71. Paul Whiteman with Mary Margaret McBride, *Jazz* (New York: Sears, 1926), 7.

72. Ibid., 16–17. For useful analyses of Whiteman's primitivist attitude toward African American music, see Gerald Early, "Pulp and Circumstance: The Story of Jazz in High Places," in *The Culture of Bruising: Essays on Prizefighting, Literature, and Modern American Culture* (Hopewell, N.J.: Ecco, 1994), 163–204, and Sieglinde Lemke, *Primitivist Modernism: Black Culture and the Origins of Transatlantic Modernism* (New York: Oxford University Press, 1998), 59–94.

73. Schuller, *Early Jazz,* 192fn21.

74. Gilbert Seldes, *The Seven Lively Arts* (New York: Harper and Brothers, 1924), 104–5.

75. Whiteman, *Jazz,* 243–44.

76. Seldes, *Seven Lively Arts,* 104–5; Whiteman, *Jazz,* 243–44.

77. Duke Ellington, *Music Is My Mistress* (New York: Oxford University Press, 1973), 103.

78. Whiteman, *Jazz,* 7, 9.

79. Ogren, *Jazz Revolution,* 8.

80. An important analysis of the antijazz discourse of the 1920s is Morroe Berger, "Jazz: Resistance to the Diffusion of a Cultural Pattern" (1947), in Nanry, *American Music,* 11–44.

81. Moore, *Yankee Blues,* 108, 158.

82. Cited in Moore, *Yankee Blues,* 151, 158.

83. Chase, *Men and Machines,* 19, 330. Chase welcomed Machine Age modernism as the cultural production of a more courageous artistic class. The new machine aesthetics reflected "oral experiences of the staccato, precise timing, and rhythm of completed operation—sharp and key noises definitively separated from the underlying matrix of monotonous and undifferentiable sound."

84. Chase, *Men and Machines,* 243; Jacques Attali, *Noise: The Political Economy of Music* (Minneapolis: University of Minnesota Press, 1993), 64–65; Henry Pleasants, *The Agony of Modern Music* (New York: Simon and Schuster, 1955), 139.

85. Mumford, "The Arts," in Beard, *Whither Mankind,* 292–93.

86. Attali, *Noise,* 66–67; Elias Canetti, *Crowds and Power* (New York: Continuum, 1981), 394–96; Mezz Mezzrow, *Really the Blues* (New York: Carroll, 1990 [1946]), 125.

87. Disney's "Music Land," www.teemings.com/shorts/Disney/years/ 1935/musicland.html. For a still-useful discussion on continuities between the symphony orchestra and the jazz band, see Pleasants, *Agony of Modern Music,* 137–51.

88. Chase, *Men and Machines,* 59–60.

89. Leonard Bernstein, untitled essay, in *Esquire's World of Jazz* (New York: Grossett and Dunlap, 1942), 176–79.

90. Ibid., 179.

91. Frank Marshall Davis, *Livin' the Blues: Memoirs of a Black Journalist and Poet* (Madison: University of Wisconsin Press, 1992), 223–28.

92. Marshall Stearns, *The Story of Jazz* (New York: Oxford University Press, 1956), 197–99; see also James Lincoln Collier, *The Making of Jazz* (New York: Oxford University Press, 1977), 181–91.

93. Gunther Schuller, *The Swing Era* (New York: Oxford University Press, 1988), 225.

94. Stearns, *Story of Jazz,* 200–204, 210–11; see also Ellington, *Music Is My Mistress,* 418–19. Goodman's first triumph in 1935 was with Henderson's arrangements. Significantly, he was playing in a large dance hall (the Palomar Ballroom in Los Angeles) with a lively, noisy crowd, and the band was afraid that the music would be swallowed by the room. Goodman needed the speed and power of the Henderson arrangements, and the crowd reacted immediately. "The first big roar from the crowd was one of the sweetest sounds I ever heard in my life." Benny Goodman with Irving Kolodin, *The Kingdom of Swing* (Harrisburg, Pa.: Stackpole Sons, 1939), 197–98. See also Collier, *Making of Jazz,* 261–62.

95. Thomas J. Hennessey, *From Jazz to Swing: African-American Jazz Musicians and Their Music, 1890–1935* (Detroit: Wayne State University Press, 1994), 103–21.

96. Ross Russell, *Jazz Style in Kansas City and the Southwest* (Berkeley: University of California Press, 1971), 135–36; Schuller, *Early Jazz,* 268, 365; Murray, *Stomping the Blues,* 120, 174.

97. Stearns, *Story of Jazz,* 199–201.

98. Earl Hines quoted in Stanley Dance, ed., *The World of Earl Hines* (New York: Da Capo, 1977), 86, 161.

99. Eddie Durham, interview by Stanley Dance, transcript, August 1978, Jazz Oral History Project (hereinafter "JOHP"), IJS: II:32–36.

100. Eddie Barefield, interview by Ira Gitler, November 20, 1978, JOHP IJS: 49.

101. Quoted in Stanley Dance, *The World of Swing* (New York: Scribner's, 1974), 124.

102. For a discussion of the potency of the idea of "the people" in this decade, see Susman, *Culture as History,* 114–15, 177–83.

103. Andy Kirk quoted in the documentary *Born to Swing,* dir. John Jeremy, BBC Productions, 1973.

104. Dicky Wells with Stanley Dance. *The Night People: The Jazz Life of Dicky Wells* (Washington, D.C.: Smithsonian, 1991 [1971]), 38, 41, 139.

105. Barefield, interview, 49.

106. Cab Calloway and Bryant Rollins, *Of Minnie the Moocher and Me* (New York: Crowell, 1976), 259; Zora Neale Hurston, "Story in Harlem Slang," in *The Complete Stories of Zora Neale Hurston* (New York: Harper Collins, 1995), 137.

107. Ralph Ellison, *Shadow and Act* (New York: Random House, 1964), 192–93. See also Mezzrow, *Really the Blues,* 387.

108. John Simmons, interview by Patricia Willard, January 1977, JOHP, IJS, I:71–77; Eddie Barefield, interview, 49; Whitney Balliett, *American Musicians II* (New York: Oxford University Press, 1996), 209–10.

109. Keil, "Participatory Discrepancies," in Keil and Feld, *Music Grooves,* 171.

110. Keil and Feld, *Music Grooves,* 98–100, 171. Keil once took two older couples polka-dancing, and although they had not polkaed before, within minutes each man (as leader) had created a distinctive dance step and had "sync'd up" with the new rhythm.

111. Dewey, *Art as Experience,* 22; Dewey, *Philosophy and Civilization* (New York: Minton, Balch, 1931), 299–317, 173–87 (these two key chapters are entitled "Body and Mind" and "Interpretation of the Savage Mind," respectively).

112. S. J. Gennard, "To Swing Is to Affirm," in *Jam Session: An Anthology of Jazz,* ed. Ralph J. Gleason (New York: Putnam, 1958), 219.

113. John Blacking, *How Musical Is Man?* (Seattle: University of Washington Press, 1973), 116.

Chapter 2

1. See, for example, John F. Stover, *American Railroads* (Chicago: University of Chicago Press, 1997), 167–244; Sarah H. Gordon, *Passage to Union: How the Railroads Transformed American Life, 1829–1929* (Chicago: Ivan R. Dee, 1996), 334–49; and Albro Martin, *Railroads Triumphant* (New York: Oxford University Press, 1992), 126–28, 241–43, 358–83.

2. Review of "Heavenly Express," *Theatre Arts Monthly* 24 (June 1940): 401–2.

3. Anticipating 18,000–20,000 visitors per day in late September 1927, "The Fair of the Iron Horse" drew 40,000–60,000 on average, and on one Saturday, 76,000. *The Catalogue of the Centenary Exhibition of the Baltimore & Ohio Railroad, 1827–1927* (Baltimore: Waverly, 1927), i; Brooks Atkinson, "Going to the Fair," *New York Times*, May 14, 1939, section 11, 1. There were also railroad industry exhibits at the Fort Worth Exposition of 1937–38 and the Great Lakes International Exposition in Cleveland, 1936–37.

4. For brass and reed riffs suggestive of machine rhythms, listen to the following: Fletcher Henderson, "Wrappin' It Up (The Lindy Glide)," "Tidal Wave," "Memphis Blues," "Wild Party," and "Limehouse Blues," Fletcher Henderson, *Tidal Wave*, Decca GRD-643, 1994; Count Basie, "Swingin' the Blues," "Jumpin' at the Woodside," and "Swinging at the Daisy Chain," Count Basie, *The Complete Decca Recordings*, Decca D217034, 1992.

5. Hedin, *Great Machines*, xvii; Lewis Erenberg, "News from the Great Wide World: Duke Ellington, Count Basie, and Black Popular Music, 1927–1943," *Prospects* 18 (1993): 494.

6. Martin, *Railroads Triumphant*, iii; Alan Trachtenberg, *The Incorporation of America* (New York: Hill and Wang, 1982), 57–60.

7. Placard at the B&O museum, Baltimore, Maryland, June 28, 1998.

8. John R. Stilgoe, *Metropolitan Corridor, 1880–1930* (New Haven: Yale University Press, 1983), 3, 339, and passim.

9. George H. Douglas, *All Aboard! The Railroad in American Life* (New York: Paragon House, 1992), 42.

10. Stover, *American Railroads*, 26.

11. Douglas, *All Aboard!*, 235–57, 375.

12. Wolfgang Schivelbusch, *The Railway Journey: The Industrialization of Time and Space in the 19th Century* (New York: Berg, 1979), 33–44; James A. Ward, *Railroads and the Character of America* (Knoxville: University of Tennessee Press, 1986), 111–15. In *Civilizing the Machine*, 110–35, John Kasson examined Ralph Emerson as a representative American figure going through a trajectory of curiosity, suspicion, fear of change, interest, excitement, and pessimism with regard to the revolution of the railroad in American life.

13. Lynne Kirby, *Parallel Tracks: The Railroad and Silent Cinema* (Durham: Duke University Press, 1997), 1–3, 11, 23–24, 250–51. See also George Bassalla, "Keaton and Chaplin: The Silent Film's Response to Technology" in *Technology in America*, ed. Carroll W. Pursell Jr. (Cambridge: MIT Press, 1981), 194–96.

14. Douglas, *All Aboard!*, 362–63.

15. D. Kimball Minor quoted in Ward, *Railroads*, 30; quoted in Kirby, *Parallel Tracks*, 201.

16. Ward, *Railroads*, 15; Marx, *Machine in the Garden*, 208–9.

17. Handy, *Father of the Blues*, 228.

18. Kern, *Culture of Time and Space*, 211–13. In *Around the World in 80 Days* (1873), Jules Verne dramatized the technological triumph of the collapse of distance. In the story, a wealthy, smug, British gentleman-hero takes advantage

of the transportation and communication revolutions to, as Kern points out, "project a new sense of world unity . . . as the railroad, telephone, bicycle, automobile, airplane, and cinema revolutionized the sense of distance" (213).

19. Douglas, *All Aboard!*, 353.

20. The Count Basie Orchestra's rhythm section produced the most powerful, yet relaxed, buoyant, and flexible groove of the swing era. See, for example, Schuller, *Swing Era*, 225–30; Collier, *Making of Jazz*, 273–74; Burt Korall, *Drummin' Men* (New York: Schirmer, 1990), 117–62.

21. Jo Jones, *The Drums* (1966), Jazz Odyssey 008, n.d., IJS. "I think I can" does not merely function here as a mnemonic device. The boundary between music and speech is a permeable membrane in nearly all West African societies. Within tonal languages, "talking drums" actually render vocal patterns native speakers understand; music and speech are not separate communicative media, but function in similar ways.

22. In the 1920s and 1930s white elites in the Southwest showed a great deal more interest in hard-driving dance grooves and brassy, expressive sounds than white northern elites. Whether in Kansas City, Dallas, or Tulsa, white Southwesterners were happy to pay for African American entertainment so long as the rigid caste system of the pre-civil-rights South maintained racial lines. Neither Duke Ellington nor Count Basie played a hotel of the caliber of the Adolphus until 1940. See Dave Oliphant, *Texan Jazz* (Austin: University of Texas Press, 1995), 92–93; Russell, *Jazz Style*, 18–20, 55–64; and Hennessey, *From Jazz to Swing*, 110–21.

23. The Trent band, which the Texas-born saxophonist Budd Johnson called "gods . . . in the twenties . . . just like Basie was later," scattered its best musicians all over the swing-era landscape (the trumpeter Peanuts Holland, the violinist Stuff Smith, the bandleader Terence Holder, and the legendary Jeter-Pillars band of St. Louis, featuring the tenor saxophonist Hayes Pillars and the alto saxophonist James Jeter). Schuller, *Early Jazz*, 299–303; Nathan W. Pearson Jr., *Goin' to Kansas City* (Urbana: University of Illinois Press, 1988), 43–45.

24. Count Basie and His Orchestra, *The Count at the Chatterbox, 1937*, Jazz Archives JA-16 (1974 [1937]). Frank Borden, a long-time journalist for the *Pittsburgh Courier*, recalled that the patrons of jazz bands at dance halls and nightclubs broke the color line in Pittsburgh in the late 1930s. The popularity of both black and white swing bands brought in a multiracial audience, and venues responded by maintaining color-blind entrance policies. Frank Borden, personal conversation, October 29, 1995, Pittsburgh, Pennsylvania.

25. In the 1920s the lyric was central to a song's popularity, especially on a number like "St. Louis Blues"; in the swing era the sound of the band was more important than the vocalist or the lyric.

26. One of the reed-section riffs in the second verse of "Daisy Chain" contains not only train-whistles but what I call "the hum of machinery," a mechanical murmuring that also appears in specific brass-section and reed-section riffs.

27. Six months later a different announcer says something similar about the Basie band's blazingly fast rendition of "The Count Steps In," played live at the Savoy Ballroom. "Oh mother, burn my Mackintosh!," he comments laconically; he then adds, "My, it's warm in here, isn't it?" The announcer's informal language completely subverts his radio persona, and his awe and excitement at the band's power is clear. *Count Basie: The Golden Years, Vol. 1, 1937*, EPM Musique CD. At the time, radio announcers for live remotes were always white men with uninflected, slightly nasal voices we tend to associate with the Midwest; such voices framed the exciting black music in a safe package for white consumption. The ad-libbed line "Burn my mackintosh" comes across as campy to contemporary ears.

28. Count Basie with Albert Murray, *Good Morning Blues: The Autobiography of Count Basie* (New York: Random House, 1986), 57, 240.

29. See, for example, Count Basie, "The Jitters" and "The World is Mad (Part II)" on *The Essential Count Basie, Vol. 3*, Columbia Jazz Masterpieces (1987).

30. Liner notes, *Honegger and Milhaud Conduct Their Own Music*, Pearl/GEMM CD 9459, East Sussex, England (n.d.); Schuller, *Early Jazz*, 321fn4; Schuller, *Swing Era*, 61–62.

31. For the train trope, see Samuel Floyd, *The Power of Black Music* (New York: Oxford University Press, 1995), 213–20.

32. Murray, *Stomping the Blues*, 117–26.

33. For example, Keil refers to African American music as a "non-machine tradition" until the 1970s. *Music Grooves*, 107.

34. The Maddox Brothers and Rose, "Freight Train Boogie," *Vol. 2—America's Most Colorful Hillbilly Band (1947–1951)*, Arhoolie CD 437.

35. Murray, *Stomping the Blues*, 118.

36. Dorothy Scarborough, *On the Trail of Negro Folk-Songs* (Hatboro, Pa.: Folklore Associates, 1963 [1925]), 238–40.

37. John A. Lomax and Alan Lomax, *Folk Song: U.S.A.* (New York: Duell, Sloan and Pearce, 1947), 245–50. The folklorist Norm Cohen dismisses the conclusions of Lomax and Scarborough (and, by association, Murray) as lacking in evidence—as "insubstantial as a whiff of smoke from a highballing coal-burner." Yet he does not offer an alternative explanation for the rhythmic drive of African American vernacular music. His *Long Steel Rail: The Railroad in American Folksong* (Urbana: University of Illinois Press, 1981) is a definitive work, a 700-page monument to train-centered nation building. He documents train imitations of all kinds, from the human voice and the harmonica to the fiddle and the pedal-steel guitar. Either Cohen is an old-school folklorist for whom folk song is a "pure" genre—and thus free from the taint of commercial music—or he underrates rhythm as a factor in railroad imitation.

38. Handy, *Father of the Blues*, 15.

39. Douglas, *All Aboard!*, xviii.

40. Jon D. Schwartz and Robert C. Reinehr, eds., *Handbook of Old-Time Radio* (Metuchen, N.J.: Scarecrow Press, 1993), 89.

41. "On the Air with the Empire Builder," *Popular Mechanics,* May 1931, 966–70.

42. Ibid., 967.

43. Ibid., 968–69.

44. David C. Morton with Charles K. Wolfe, *DeFord Bailey: A Black Star in Early Country Music* (Knoxville: University of Tennessee Press, 1991), xv, 51–55; Floyd, *Power of Black Music,* 213–22. W. C. Handy remembers such "harmonica masterpieces" dating back to the 1880s; musicians' two favorite subjects were "the fox and the hounds and imitat[ing] the railroad trains." Handy, *Father of the Blues,* 15. The bluesman Sonny Terry brought his own harmonica stylizations of train rhythms and sounds to Carnegie Hall for the "Spirituals To Swing" concerts. Dugan and Hammond, "An Early Black Music Concert," 215.

45. Bailey quoted in Morton, *DeFord Bailey,* 22–23, 74, 77–82.

46. Ibid., 77–78; Floyd *Power of Black Music,* 215–16. Bailey suggested that southern blacks were the nation's finest musicians at the time because whites didn't want to work that hard on music.

47. Morton, *DeFord Bailey,* 82.

48. Ibid., 21. A common African American musical term for being able to repeat and stylize a certain sound or rhythm is "to catch," as in "the drummer would catch every gesture of the dancers" and play some rhythmic figure to match it.

49. Ibid., 21.

50. Ibid., 78.

51. Ibid., 79.

52. Ibid., 80.

53. Ibid., 8, 58, 99.

54. Leo Marx produced a great deal of literary evidence for how the "machine"—meaning the locomotive—disrupted the Edenic "garden" of the American dream of pastoralism. Such fears line up with European resentment of machines, but Marx's only testimony comes from the New England writers of the American Renaissance. Yet even then, Emily Dickinson wrote of liking to see the train "lap the Miles/And lick the Valleys up"; she appreciated its rapid tempo shifts and how it would, "punctual as a Star/Stop—docile and omnipotent/At its own stable door." John Kouwenhoven countered Marx in an essay entitled "Who's Afraid of the Machine in the Garden?" and showed how, in dime novels and ballads, "mechanization . . . was literally an American folk way." Marx, *Machine in the Garden,* 227–319; John A. Kouwenhoven, *Half a Truth Is Better Than None* (Chicago: University of Chicago Press, 1982), 142.

55. Edward S. Ellis, "The Huge Hunter, or The Steam Man of the Prairies," in *Eight Dime Novels,* ed. E. F. Bleiler (New York: Dover, 1974), 114–17; E. F. Bleiler, "From the Newark Steam Man to Tom Swift," *Extrapolation* 30 (Summer 1989): 101–16. According to Bleiler, the character of Steam Man was based on a well-publicized invention of dubious merit by the inventor Zadoc P. Dederick of Newark, New Jersey.

56. Kouwenhoven, *Half a Truth,* 129–42; Trachtenberg, *Incorporation of*

America 46. Kouwenhoven argues that the black color of the Steam Man is insignificant, a projection of the soot, smoke, and coal of the industrial revolution and not of the need for nonwhite servants.

57. Trachtenberg, *Incorporation of America*, 46–47.

58. Reprinted in Hedin, *Great Machines*, 4, 5, 131, 166.

59. Ibid., 131–32, 166–67.

60. For one example of each, see Hedin, *Great Machines*, 6–14. "Tamping Ties" (anonymous) and "Railroad Section Leader's Song" (anonymous) were used for knocking in the cross-ties; "Take This Hammer" (Leadbelly) and "John Henry" were hammer songs. For a more complete discussion of work songs, see Cohen, *Long Steel Rail*, 530–95.

61. Douglas, *All Aboard!*, 353.

62. Cohen, *Long Steel Rail*, 647.

63. Quoted in William Ferris, *Blues from the Delta* (Garden City, N.Y.: Doubleday/Anchor, 1979), 34–35.

64. Handy, *Father of the Blues*, 139–40.

65. Ruth Stryker, *Tap Dancing, Vol. 1* (South Bend, Ind.: National Institute of Allied Arts, 1938), 5. To make the "tap engine" even more exciting, Stryker recommends that the dancer have a piano accompanist "follow the dancer slowly, then faster and faster until the tempo becomes an exciting race." Such a rhythm seems similar to the piano-and-percussion idea of the "Railroad Gallop." Here the percussion comes from the dancer.

66. Ibid.

67. See, for example, Edith Ballwebber, *Illustrated Tap Rhythms and Routines* (Chicago: Clayton F. Summy, 1933), 11, and Stryker, *Tap Dancing, Vol. 2* (South Bend, Ind.: National Institute of Allied Arts, 1939), 12–13. Postwar tap manuals often do not mention the "chug."

68. Cecelia Tichi identifies steam-era terminology now part of the American vernacular such as "I'm getting steamed" or "getting a head of steam on." Tichi, *Shifting Gears*, xx.

69. Nicholas Faith, *The World the Railways Made* (New York: Carroll and Graf, 1990), 1–2. The term "iron horse" came into the American vernacular in the mid-1840s and Thoreau uses it in *Walden* (1854). *A Dictionary of American English on Historical Principle, Vol. 3* (Chicago: University of Chicago Press, 1942), 1324.

70. Dee Brown, *Hear That Lonesome Whistle Blow* (New York: Holt, 1977), 4. On February 22, 1854, in honor of George Washington's birthday, the town of Rock Island, Illinois, celebrated the first train to cross the Mississippi into the West. Mixing business, technology, and national unity, a band at the new train station played "The Railroad Quick-Step," written for the event.

71. Marshall and Jean Stearns, *Jazz Dance: The Story of American Vernacular Dance* (New York: Da Capo, 1996 [1968]), 98; Willis Laurence James, *Stars in de Elements* (Durham: Duke University Press, 1995 [1945]), 47.

72. Carl E. Seashore, *Psychology of Music* (New York: Dover, 1967 [1938]), 138–39, 356–57.

73. Seashore rebuked music educators for spreading the idea that the "wildness" in African American singing derived from "the inability of the Negro to sing . . . with tonal precision." He speculated that Americans loved the emotional expressiveness in "the Negro's" singing, and that this license and freedom was one secret of the popularity of black song. The more musicological aspects of African American vocal practice included "soar[ing] through tonal regions with rhythmic movements, sharp syncopation, and liberal frills of adornment." Seashore, *Psychology of Music,* 139.

74. James Cone, *The Spirituals and the Blues* (New York: Seabury, 1972), 31, 61, 100, 113, 126–27; Angela Y. Davis, *Blues Legacies and Black Feminism* (New York: Vintage, 1998), 4–7, 127–28, 134–35.

75. Bechet, *Treat It Gentle,* 212–13.

76. On the comparisons of railroad construction in the North and South, see Stover, *American Railroads,* 50–60, 98–100, and 138–45. John Lovell quoted in Davis, *Blues Legacies,* 70; Floyd, *Power of Black Music,* 215–16.

77. Floyd, *Power of Black Music,* 214.

78. See Paul Oliver's chapter, "Railroad for My Pillow," in *Blues Fell This Morning* (New York: Horizon, 1960), 68–75; Hazel Carby, "It Jus Be's That Way Sometime: The Sexual Politics of Women's Blues," in *Unequal Sisters: A Multi-Cultural Reader in U.S. Women's History,* ed. Vicki Ruiz and Ellen Carol Dubois (New York: Routledge, 1990), 238–249; and W. T. Lhamon, *Raising Cain: Blackface Performance from Jim Crow to Hip Hop* (Cambridge: Harvard University Press, 1998), 90–113.

79. Clara Smith, "Freight Train Blues" (1924), *"Sorry but I Can't Take You":*
Women's Railroad Blues, Rosetta RR 1301 (1980). Many songs on this collection feature elements of locomotive onomatopoeia and the trope of the train as an agent of change.

80. Blind Willie McTell, *1927–1933 The Early Years,* Yazoo 1005 (1988).

81. McTell was a rare and distinctive musical performer who had mastered both slide technique and ragtime dance rhythms, creating a personal style blending thumb-picked propulsive rhythms with atypical narrative verses. One hears the bluegrass-like Piedmont style of Carolina blues and the cries, moans, and hollers of the Delta blues; but McTell sounds more "modern" than most blues musicians of this period. He keeps up an alternating bass rhythm while playing some startlingly fast—and original—picking patterns, all of which suggest a link to West African musical practices. First, each rhythmic phrase is a distinct entity and is not designed to fit into a larger structure; second, he "talks" with (and to) his guitar, voice and guitar carrying on as two separate voices; third, there are propulsive dance rhythms along with individual commentary; fourth, there are rapid tempo shifts, rhythmic dexterity, control, and improvisation. McTell's mélange of bluegrass licks, dance rhythms, scattershot picking patterns, slide-guitar vocalizations, and just plain talk speak of a "musical stream-of-consciousness." Liner notes, McTell, *1927–1933 The Early Years;* Samuel Charters, *The Bluesmakers* (New York: Da Capo, 1991), 121–31.

82. Collier, *Making of Jazz,* 207–8.

83. Floyd, *Power of Black Music*, 216.

84. Walter C. Allen, *Hendersonia* (Highland Park, N.J., 1973), 463–65. The show was not popular, though it drew a rave review from the *Pittsburgh Courier*.

85. "Adolph Zukor Presents 'Cab Calloway's Hi-De-Ho'" (1934), *Hollywood Rhythm: The Paramount Musical Shorts, Vol. 2—Jazz Cocktails*, Paramount Video, 1997. The short was reviewed as "generally pleasing," and noted for the "rehearsal in a Pullman," "its 'jump to a Cotton Club locale," and Calloway's "hot rhythm" backing up bathing-suited beauties at the club. "Shorts," *New York City Film Daily*, August 15, 1934, n.p. Courtesy of the Harvard Theater Collection.

86. Cab Calloway and Betty Boop co-starred in "Minnie the Moocher" (1932), "Snow White" (1933), and "The Old Man of the Mountain" (1933), cartoons written and directed by Max and David Fleischer. See Leslie Cabarga, *The Fleischer Story* (New York: Da Capo, 1988 [1976]), 63–64 and Jerry Beck, *The 50 Greatest Cartoons* (Atlanta: Turner Publishing, 1994), 94–101.

87. This minute of musical power is the artistic high point of the soundie. The ten-minute story of the film casts Calloway as a womanizing celebrity whose stardom and vocal power seduces women first over the radio and later in their homes. The story line promotes Calloway's sexual and vocal power, and displays a conflict around the trope of sexual "energy" regarding African American male performers. Calloway has an affair with the wife of the Pullman porter who first gave him the telegram, and he gives her jewels and furs. She falls in love with him, then goes to see him perform at the Cotton Club; later they cuckold the Pullman porter. The narrative is formulaic and titillating, a sop for Depression audiences fantasizing about hedonistic nights at the Cotton Club or romantic train journeys complete with freedom and celebrities on trains with names like "The Chicago Limited." The music, however, cannot be dismissed: the jazz train thundering through the night, sometimes the train soloing, sometimes the band soloing, sometimes individuals soloing—and all the while that driving clackety-clack rhythm, and those ecstatic and lonesome steam-whistles.

88. Simon, *Big Bands*, 329–33. One secret to Lunceford's success was the "two-beat" feel of the rhythm, a Dixieland jazz feel familiar to white audiences in the mid-1930s. The rhythm did not feel old-fashioned, however, because the drummer Jimmy Crawford superimposed this 2/4 on an underlying 4/4 beat, "propell[ing] a fantastically joyous swinging beat." The band's arranger, Sy Oliver, often argued with Crawford about the relative emphasis of the 2/4 or 4/4 feel. Crawford argued that on the superfast, full-ensemble "ride-out choruses," when the band was really going "full steam," he needed to stay in 4/4 to exert the right amount of driving power and rhythmic control.

89. Jimmie Lunceford, *The Classic Tracks*, Kaz CD 317 (n.d.); Jimmie Lunceford, *Harlem Shout (1935–1936)*, MCA-1305 (1980). The title "Jazznocracy" was a play on "Technocracy," a popular but short-lived social movement advocating a government run by engineers.

90. Wynton Marsalis, interview by Beverly Sills, *Live from Lincoln Center: Lincoln Center Jazz Orchestra with Wynton Marsalis*, PBS, WNET Channel 13, New

York, New York, July 1, 1998. Wynton Marsalis and the Lincoln Center Jazz Orchestra, *Big Train*, Sony/Columbia CD (1999).

91. Nelson George, *The Death of Rhythm and Blues* (New York: Pantheon, 1988), xvi.

92. Albert Murray, *Train Whistle Guitar* (Boston: Northeastern, 1989 [1974]), 8. Growing up a generation after Murray in a similarly small Alabama town, the French horn player Willie Ruff perceived the same train-powered drive in the drummer of his local Sanctified church. Ruff and his friends idolized Mrs. Nance, the solo bass drummer, and they'd "sit on the grass outside the church . . . [in] full view of the pulpit and our drum hero, whose beat gave her right arm the churning motion of a set of steam locomotive wheels." She played only a single bass drum with a mallet made out of a long-handled wooden cooking spoon wrapped tight with a sock—no "pedals, levers, cymbals, or gadgets"—and played all the polyrhythms Ruff later heard from bebop drummers with a complete trap set. Some of her technique is recognizably West African: she muffled the drumhead with the flat palm of one hand to create differences in pitch and timbre; she made the drum "talk," and Ruff heard the "instrument speak a clear and discernible 'Amen' or 'Hallelujah' or 'Thank you, Jesus.'" And her body was part of the performance, her arms making expressive swirls—"all circles and arcs, [and] figure eights"—before she ever hit a stroke. Ruff declared that "her reputation for inciting dance riots in the church was famous all over the Tennessee Valley." Willie Ruff, *A Call to Assembly* (New York: Viking, 1991), 42–43.

93. Stephen Henderson, *Understanding the New Black Poetry* (New York: Morrow, 1973), 44–46.

94. Ellington, *Music Is My Mistress*, 86.

95. Handy, *Father of the Blues*, 228.

96. The bittersweet mode is common to all genres of African American music. In Ralph Ellison's novel *Juneteenth*, Hickman makes several references to African Americans "learn[ing] to taste the sweet in the bitter" or understanding "many sides of the old good-bad"; an African American had to learn to "laugh at the 'laugh-cry' of it." Ralph Ellison, *Juneteenth* (New York: Vintage International, 1999), 223, 315. Keil and Feld discuss the "bittersweet" quality of the African American musical aesthetic in *Music Grooves*, 22, 166, 299.

97. Lionel Hampton with James Haskins, *Hamp* (New York: Amistad, 1989), 3–6.

98. Albert Murray, interview with the author, New York, New York, January 7, 1996.

99. For a discussion on the importance of the Brotherhood of Sleeping Car Porters, see Manning Marable, *Black American Politics: From the Washington Marches to Jesse Jackson* (London: Verso, 1985), 74–87.

100. Otis Ferguson, "Breakfast Dance in Harlem," in *The Otis Ferguson Reader*, ed. Dorothy Chamberlain and Robert Wilson (New York: Da Capo, 1997), 59.

101. Dizzy Gillespie with Al Fraser, *To Be . . . or Not to Bop* (New York:

Doubleday, 1979), 250. See also Benny Green, *The Reluctant Art: Five Studies in the Growth of Jazz* (New York: Da Capo, 1962), 86.

102. Ellington's environment always influenced his compositions, and "Daybreak" signaled the beginning of his "train period," a period of constant travel following a long residence at New York's Cotton Club. His cross-country touring, a triumphant trip to England, and the relaxed, undulating rhythms coming out of Kansas City spurred Ellington to move away from the plantation melodies and jungle themes he wrote to accompany Cotton Club revues (and satisfy audiences).

103. Schuller, *Swing Era*, 64–65.

104. Finkelstein, *Jazz*, 126.

105. Barney Bigard quoted in Stanley Dance, *The World of Duke Ellington* (New York: Da Capo, 1970), 85.

106. Ellington quoted in Stanley Dance, liner notes, *Duke Ellington, Daybreak Express* RCA LPV-506 1964 (1931–34); on Catlett, see Balliett, *American Musicians* II 209.

107. Albert Murray, interview; Erenberg, "News from the Great Wide World," 494–97. Ralph Ellison claimed that swing musicians were the most impressive male role models in African American life between the world wars—and maybe in mainstream American life. Ellison, *Going to the Territory*, 219–20.

108. Dance, liner notes, *Duke Ellington, Daybreak Express.*

109. Schuller, *Swing Era*, 64–65.

110. "George Gershwin, among other white composers, made a sincere attempt to distill from its [jazz's] folk qualities a concert type of music that would be acceptable to prosaic audiences," John Hammond observed in 1938. "It is doubtful . . . if this approach did anything more than suppress the genuine thing." Dugan and Hammond, "An Early Black-Music Concert," 191.

111. Roy Harris, "Problems of American Composers," in Chase, *The American Composer Speaks*, 147–60. Ravel's attempts to incorporate jazz rhythms into classical music were "studied . . . because he did not feel the rhythm in terms of musical phraseology." Such rhythms were not a bit of color for American composers; it was their very birthright. "The rhythms come to us first as musical phraseology," said Harris, "and then we struggle to define them on paper."

112. Ibid., 150–51.

113. George T. Simon, *Glenn Miller and His Orchestra* (New York: Thomas Y. Crowell, 1974), 257.

114. I am indebted to Gena Caponi-Tabery for her reading of this song.

115. Erskine Hawkins, interview by Leonard Goines, February 6, 1982, IJS. See also Gerald Early, *Tuxedo Junction* (New York: Ecco, 1993), xiii. White bandleaders increasingly turned to African American arrangers toward the end of the 1930s. Benny Goodman credits Fletcher Henderson for the very sound of his band, and claims that his arrangements were far ahead of all others (white and black) in 1934; Goodman also used Edgar Sampson's "Stomping at the Savoy" and "Don't Be That Way." Glenn Miller hired Eddie Durham away from Count Basie (Durham arranged "In the Mood," among others). The

jazz critic Ralph J. Gleason believed that Tommy Dorsey's leap into superstar status in the early 1940s could be traced to the day he hired Jimmie Lunceford's longtime arranger Sy Oliver.

116. "Steel Guitar Rag," *The Essential Bob Wills, 1935–1947,* Columbia Country Classics CK 48958 (1992); Sons of the Pioneers, "When the Golden Train Comes Down," on *Mystery Train: Classic Railroad Songs, Vol. 2,* Rounder C1129 (1997).

117. Quoted in Alan Lomax, *Mister Jelly Roll* (London: Virgin, 1991 [1950]), 93.

118. The guidebook from the Chicago Railroad Fair of 1948 and a clipping file can be found in the archives of the University of Illinois-Chicago.

119. Walt Disney quoted in Michael Broggie, *Walt Disney's Railroad Story* (Pasadena, Calif.: Pentrex, 1997), 25–29, 77.

Chapter 3

1. Gilbert Seldes, "The Negro's Songs," *The Dial* 80 (March 1926): 247–51; Moore, *Yankee Blues,* 144.

2. Seldes, "Negro's Songs," 251.

3. Brian Ward, *Just My Soul Responding* (Berkeley: University of California Press, 1999), 6.

4. Bayles, *Hole in Our Soul,* 96–97; Marshall Berman, "The Experience of Modernity," in *Design after Modernism,* ed. John Thackara (New York: Thames and Hudson, 1988), 35–36.

5. Ellington, "The Duke Steps Out," 49, and quoted in *Esquire's World of Jazz,* 200.

6. Louis Armstrong, "Greetings to Britain!," in Berrett, *Louis Armstrong Companion,* 47–48.

7. Ralph Ellison, *Living with Music: Ralph Ellison's Jazz Writings,* ed. Robert O'Meally (New York: Modern Library, 2001), xi, 139–40, 274–75, 286.

8. Ellison, *Shadow and Act,* 189–90 (emphasis added).

9. The modernist ideal of art-for-art's sake never arose for musicians with such limited economic opportunity in other fields, and "they all made their peace with compromise of one kind or another." Schuller, *Swing Era,* 213.

10. Louis Armstrong with Richard Meryman, *Louis Armstrong—A Self-Portrait* (New York: Eakins, 1971), 54; Sonny Greer, interview with Stanley Crouch, 1979, 88, JOHP, IJS; Bechet, *Treat It Gentle,* 3.

11. Frederick Douglass, *My Bondage and My Freedom* (New York: Dover, 1969 [1855]), 98–100.

12. Alan Lomax, *The Land Where the Blues Began* (New York: Delta, 1993), xiii.

13. Sterling Stuckey, *Going through the Storm* (New York: Oxford University Press, 1994), 44–45.

14. Ogren, *Jazz Revolution,* 49–50, 60; Bechet, *Treat It Gentle,* 111–24 and 144–51.

15. Bayles, *Hole in Our Soul,* 92–93; Finkelstein, *Jazz,* 84, 88–89; Bechet, *Treat It Gentle,* 111–12.

16. Schuller, *Early Jazz*, 56–59; Russell, *Jazz Style*, 33–40.

17. Sterling A. Brown, "Spirituals, Blues and Jazz," in Gleason, *Jam Session*, 17–26; Paul Oliver, *Savannah Syncopators* (New York: Stein and Day, 1970), 19–20.

18. Schuller, *Early Jazz*, 89–133.

19. Olly Wilson, "The Heterogeneous Sound Ideal in African American Music," in Caponi, *Signifyin(g)*, 157–71; Eddie Durham, interview, IJS, 1, 49.

20. "The Negro musicians of America . . . have an open mind, and an unbiased outlook. They are causing new blood to flow in the veins of music." Stokowski quoted in Calverton, "Growth of Negro Literature," in *Negro*, 81; Monson, *Sayin' Something*, x.

21. Hermann Keyserling, "What the Negro Means to America," *Atlantic Monthly*, October 1929, 444–47.

22. Antheil, "Negro on the Spiral," 215.

23. Claude Bragdon, *The Architecture Lectures* (New York: Creative Age, 1942), 89–90. Thanks to Christina Cogdell for pointing out this reference.

24. Moore, *Yankee Blues*, 70; Robert Goffin, "The Finest Negro Jazz Orchestras," in Cunard, *Negro*, 218.

25. Henry Louis Gates Jr., *The Signifying Monkey* (New York: Oxford University Press, 1988), xxv–xxviii, 65–68, 103–18; Olly Wilson, "The Significance of the Relationship between Afro-American Music and West African Music," *Black Perspective in Music* (Spring 1974): 3–22; Rose, *Black Noise*, 62–96.

26. Francis Bebey, *African Music: A People's Art* (Brooklyn: Lawrence Hill, 1975), 40–41. See also John Storm Roberts, *Black Music of Two Worlds* (New York: Schirmer, 1998), xxi–xxxvii.

27. Malone, *Steppin' on the Blues*, 17; Samuel Floyd, "Black American Music and Aesthetic Communication," *Black Music Research Journal* 1 (Fall 1980): 12.

28. Chernoff, *African Rhythm*, 35; Malinoma Patrice Somé, *Of Water and the Spirit* (New York: Arkana/Penguin, 1994), 178. On the evolution of technology as a measurement of a culture's intelligence and ability in colonialism, see Michael Adas, *Machines as the Measure of Men* (Ithaca: Cornell University Press, 1989), 4–7, 94.

29. Chernoff, *African Rhythm*, 35–36; Diallo and Hall, *Healing Drum*, 79–81.

30. The Ellington quotes were related to me by Albert Murray, and the subsequent commentary was part of the same conversation. Murray, interview with author, January 7, 1996.

31. Ellington quoted in Nat Hentoff and Nat Shapiro, *Hear Me Talkin' to Ya* (New York: Rinehart, 1955), 194–95.

32. Ellington, *Music Is My Mistress*, 106.

33. James Lincoln Collier, *Duke Ellington* (New York: Oxford University Press, 1987), 135, 137, 162.

34. R. D. Darrell, "Black Beauty," in Tucker, *Duke Ellington Reader*, 62.

35. Gene Ramey, "My Memories of Bird Parker" (1955) in *The Charlie Parker Companion*, ed. Carl Woideck (New York: Schirmer, 1998), 137–38;

Ramey quoted in Robert Reisner, *Bird: The Legend of Charlie Parker* (New York: Citadel, 1962), 186; Elvin Jones tells this story in the documentary, *Celebrating Bird* (1987), dir. Gary Giddins and Kendrick Simmons, Pioneer Artists, 1987; Gary Giddins, *Celebrating Bird* (New York: Beech Tree, 1983), 61.

36. Rex Stewart, *Jazz Masters of the Thirties* (New York: Macmillan, 1972), 166; Malone, *Steppin' on the Blues*, 2.

37. Frank Marshall Davis, "Rating the Records," *New York Amsterdam News,* January 6, 1940, 17. The late 1930s was the heyday of drum solo records, and Davis advised "every percussionist" in the nation to "listen closely" to the recordings to pick up on these performances by the "masters of syncopation and . . . intricate cross rhythms." The African recordings were originally supervised by Laura C. Bolton of the Museum of Natural History on the Straus West African Expedition in 1934.

38. Gene Krupa, "The Beat of the Drum," *Bandleaders,* July 1945, 12–13, 58–59. Here again is an early perception that African drummers rendered the environment in sound. "I believe that many of his [the African's] rhythms have been adapted from jungle noises and other sounds he hears." Krupa played with drummers who worked for Frank Buck's Jungleland at the 1939 Fair.

39. Ibid., 12–13.

40. Stearns, *Story of Jazz*, 14–15.

41. "Swing Is African," *New York Amsterdam News,* January 21, 1939, 16.

42. Olatunji quoted in Mickey Hart with Jay Stevens, *Drumming at the Edge of Magic* (New York: HarperCollins, 1992), 215.

43. Kao, master drummer, quoted in Ruth Stone, *Let the Inside Be Sweet: The Interpretation of Music Events among the Kpelle of Liberia* (Bloomington: Indiana University Press, 1982), 35; J. H. Nketia, *Drumming in Akan Communities of Ghana* (London: Thomas Nelson, 1963), 3–4. A master drummer is responsible for representing the tempo of the moment during rituals crucial to cultural identity, and for responding instantaneously to any change in that tempo. Although musicians, singers, and dancers share the responsibility of providing the rhythmic textures, the master drummer maintains order in the public forum, reacts to shifts in energy and momentum, and carries the burden of unification through the beat. A master drummer does not just keep time or add effects. He is analogous to the conductor of the classical tradition, but is more of a "player-coach" than a director. In public rituals and ceremonies crucial to cultural identity and stability, he is responsible for any and all of the following: reciting the history of his people, pacing the chief's walk, calling people to war, interacting with dancers, calling down the spirits, and performing a dialogue with any individual needing to dance a new attitude on a given day. See also Oliver, *Savannah Syncopators*, 28–53.

44. Hart, *Drumming at the Edge*, 210.

45. Felix O. Begho, "Black Dance Continuum: Reflections on the Heritage Connection between African Dance and Afro-American Jazz Dance," Ph.D. diss., New York University, 1985, 292, 307. West African musicians conceive of music "in measured idiomatic phrases," and it is more a language that is "syn-

tactically conceptualized." In other words, rhythms are functional and communicate translatable messages that the in-group can understand. It is always "more than just the *pulse* in a rhythm," and more akin to "a *message* as in speech."

46. Linton Kwesi Johnson quoted in Peter Lee, "The Beat Must Shift as the Culture Alter," *Living Blues* 96, March/April 1991, 2; Rex Stewart, *Boy Meets Horn* (Ann Arbor: University of Michigan Press, 1991), 220.

47. Spencer, *Re-searching Black Music*, 15.

48. Small, *Music of the Common Tongue*, 467–83. I have employed Small's term "the rational god" and applied his idea that "slaves themselves . . . were required, not just to serve machines, but actually to *be* machines" (462).

49. Burke, *Philosophy of Literary Form*, 409. To put it another way, artists put new cultural forces on trial. Samuel Butler put machines on trial for English society with *Erewhon* and *Return to Erewhon,* novels that presented an idyllic preindustrial utopian medieval culture that had destroyed its machines. *Erewhon* was a bestseller and helped set the terms of discussion in England.

50. That is the most accepted legend, although the name of the railroad, the location of the tunnel, and other details vary according to the version of the ballad.

51. For historical discussions of "The Ballad of John Henry," see Cohen, *Long Steel Rail*, 58–78; Levine, *Black Culture*, 420–27; and Alan Lomax, *The Folk Songs of North America* (New York: Doubleday, 1960), 551–55.

52. Lomax, *Folk Songs of North America*, 554.

53. The oft-quoted phrase "equipment for living" comes from Kenneth Burke, who believed the function of literature was to provide stylized behaviors, attitudes, and strategies for everyday life. Burke, *Philosophy of Literary Form*, 293–304.

54. Cohen, *Long Steel Rail*, 70–73. The earliest documented versions of "John Henry" (print and record) come from white sources, and they are clearly influenced by the Anglo-American ballad form.

55. George Lipsitz, *Time Passages* (Minneapolis: University of Minnesota Press, 1990), 115. This reading of John Henry challenges Lipsitz's argument that Euro-Americans appropriate black preindustrial values in music due to an African American value system that displays "resistance to alienated labor by contrasting it with leisure." See Lipsitz, *Time Passages*, 109–16.

56. Ellison, *Shadow and Act*, 270.

57. Harold Courlander, *Negro Folk Music, USA* (New York: Dover, 1991 [1963]), 110–15; Handy, *Father of the Blues*, 139–41. Citing the early 1870s construction of the Big Bend tunnel, most scholars believe the ballad began to penetrate into the lives of black workers in the 1880s. No documentary evidence exists prior to 1905, however; at that point a surge of interest among folklorists made people aware of John Henry.

58. Park Honan, *Matthew Arnold: A Life* (New York: McGraw-Hill, 1981), 346–47, 382–411; Lawrence Levine, *Highbrow/Lowbrow: The Emergence of Cultural Hierarchy in America* (Cambridge: Harvard University Press, 1988), 164, 176–77, 223–24, 244; Moore, *Yankee Blues*, 69–70.

59. Cohen, *Long Steel Rail,* 74.

60. Ellison, *Shadow and Act,* 270; Sterling A. Brown, "Never No Steel Driving Man" (review of Roark Bradford's *John Henry*), *Opportunity,* December 1931, 382. Brown dismisses Bradford's (white) version of John Henry, preferring to remember the more heroic figure he "met through the fine courtesy of Big Boy Davis, ex-coal miner, who told me of him on a winter evening, years ago, in a little cabin in the western foothills of Virginia."

61. W. Nikola-Lisa, "John Henry: Then and Now," *African American Review* 32 (Spring 1998): 51–56. Two of these writers have made John Henry more culturally "black," telling the story in rural black dialect or in jazz cadences, or showing him eating southern cuisine.

62. Julius Lester, *John Henry* (New York: Dial, 1994), n.p.; Lester quoted in Nikola-Lisa, "John Henry," 55–56.

63. Lomax, *Folk Songs of North America,* 553.

64. Courlander, *Negro Folk Music,* 76–78; Mel Watkins, *On the Real Side: Laughing, Lying, and Signifying* (New York: Touchstone, 1994), 464–68; Levine, *Black Culture,* 258, 427–33. Before Jim Jeffries's loss to Jack Johnson, the white heavyweight champ was thought to be upholding the racial superiority of the Anglo-Saxon; Johnson's 1910 victory over Jeffries ("the great white hope") refuted the theory so completely that boxing promoters did not allow a black man to fight for the heavyweight title for the next twenty-two years.

65. Quoted in Roger Abrahams, *Deep Down in the Jungle* (Hatboro, Pa.: Folklore Associates, 1964), 98–103.

66. Cited in Watkins, *On the Real Side,* 464.

67. Watkins, *On the Real Side,* 464; Levine, *Black Culture,* 429.

68. What Mikhail Bakhtin finds in novelistic discourse can also be found in popular music discourse. For example, the ethnomusicologist Ingrid Monson has shown how jazz musicians' common trope of "conversation" for jazz ensemble playing fits into Bakhtin's concept of internal dialogism. Monson, *Sayin' Something,* 87–93, 98–100, and esp. 208–15.

69. M. M. Bakhtin, *The Dialogic Imagination* (Austin: University of Texas Press, 1988), 314–26 and 415–20. On "dialogic criticism," see Lipsitz, *Time Passages,* 99–100, and Berman, *All That Is Solid Melts into Air,* 181–286.

70. Zora Neale Hurston, *The Sanctified Church* (Berkeley, Calif.: Turtle Island Press, 1984), 64. The Chicago banjoist Eddie Condon attributed the song to Tony Jackson, a legendary New Orleans pianist and composer of the first two decades of the century who never recorded; he remembered the title as "I've Got Elgin Movements in My Hips with Twenty Years' Guarantee." Eddie Condon with Thomas Sugrue, *We Called It Music* (New York: Da Capo, 1992 [1947]), 27.

71. See Hayden Carruth, "Good Ole Wagon," in *On Music,* ed. Daniel Halpern and Jeanne Wilmot Carter (Hopewell, N.J.: Ecco Press, 1994), 140–45.

72. John Edgar Wideman, preface to *Breaking Ice,* ed. Terry McMillan (New York: Viking, 1990), viii.

73. To cite a recent example, the jazz trombonist Tyrone Hill employs an instrumental technique he calls "multiphonics" in which he plays and hums a note simultaneously and produces overtones, buzzings, muted sounds, and "all kinds of notes." Hill was a member of the Sun Ra Arkestra for many years, and Sun Ra encouraged him to develop this method because "you got to do stuff like that to keep up with the electronics." Quoted from a concert of the Marshall Allen–Tyrone Hill Quartet, Ceremony Hall, Austin, Texas, April 11, 1999.

74. Sidran, *Black Talk*, xi; Larry Neal, *Visions of a Liberated Future* (New York: Thunder's Mouth, 1989), 113–17; Bayles, *Hole in Our Soul*, 92–93.

75. Sandra R. Lieb, *Mother of the Blues: A Study of Ma Rainey* (Amherst: University of Massachusetts Press, 1981), 29–30.

76. Houston A. Baker Jr., *Modernism and the Harlem Renaissance* (Chicago: University of Chicago Press, 1989), 92–93.

77. *The Collected Poems of Sterling A. Brown*, ed. Michael S. Harper (Chicago: TriQuarterly, 1989), 62–63; Davis, *Blues Legacies*, 139–41.

78. Keil and Feld, *Music Grooves*, 295–97.

79. Devotees of Yoruba-derived orisha religions such as Vodun claim their gods have to keep up with the times, and so they evolve with the human experience. See Andrew Apter, *Black Critics and Kings* (Chicago: University of Chicago Press, 1992), 154–60; Leslie G. Desmangles, *Faces of the Gods* (Chapel Hill: University of North Carolina Press, 1992), 93–99.

80. Ishmael Reed, *Mumbo-Jumbo* (New York: Harvest, 1972), 151.

81. Charles Nanry, "Jazz and Modernism: Twin-born Children of the Age of Invention," *Annual Review of Jazz Studies* 1 (1982): 146–54.

82. Gene Bluestein, *Poplore: Folk and Pop in American Culture* (Amherst: University of Massachusetts Press, 1994), 1–2.

83. Robert Goffin, "The Best Negro Jazz Orchestras," in Cunard, *Negro*, 183.

84. Whiteman, *Jazz*, 7 8; Mencken and Hiram Moderwell quoted in Moore, *Yankee Blues*, 108, 151.

85. Jazz will die, according to Berlin, only "when commuters no longer rush for trains . . . [or] when businessmen take afternoon siestas." Berlin quoted in Ogren, *Jazz Revolution*, 144; Daniel Mason, *The Dilemma of American Music* (New York: Macmillan, 1928), 158–59.

86. Godowsky quoted in Whiteman, *Jazz*, 192–94; Paul Lindemeyer, *Celebrating the Saxophone* (New York: Hearst, 1996), 38–45.

87. Sigmund Spaeth, *Music Is Fun* (Philadelphia: Blakiston, 1939), 219.

88. Eudora Welty, "Powerhouse," in *Hot and Cool: Jazz Short Stories*, ed. Marcella Breton (New York: Plume, 1990), 29–42. The term "powerhouse" also builds on the common primitivist connection linking African Americans with vitality or energy. Euro-Americans saw blacks as less civilized and more natural, believing they more easily "let go" of rationality. For a primitivist analysis of "Powerhouse," see Leland H. Chambers, "Improvising and Mythmaking in Eudora Welty's Powerhouse," in *Representing Jazz*, ed. Krin Gabbard (Durham, N. C.: Duke University Press, 1995), 54–69.

89. Balliett, *American Musicians*, 74–75.

90. Fats Waller, "Christopher Columbus," *American Songbook Series: Waller/ Razaf*, Smithsonian CD AD 048–21 (1994).

91. Crawford, *American Musical Landscape*, 219–20.

92. Eileen Southern, ed., *Readings in Black American Music* (New York: Norton, 1972). The readings from this book span three hundred years and feature eyewitness accounts from throughout the African diaspora. From slave traders' journals to European travel memoirs of the nineteenth century, nearly all contain stories of black ex tempore musical production that includes local sounds and improvised lyrics that comment on the narrator or traveler observing the scene.

93. Wilmot Alfred Fraser, "Jazzology: A Study of the Tradition in Which Jazz Musicians Learn to Improvise," Ph.D. diss., University of Pennsylvania, 1983, 194–95, 224.

94. Ralph J. Gleason, liner notes, Jimmie Lunceford, *Rhythm Is Our Business, Vol. 1 (1934–1935)*, Decca DL 79237 (n.d.); and Jimmie Lunceford, *Harlem Shout, Vol. 2 (1935–1936)*, Decca DL 79238, (n.d.), IJS.

95. Gleason, liner notes, *Harlem Shout*; George T. Simon, *The Big Bands* (New York: Schirmer, 1981), 329–33.

96. Gleason, liner notes, *Harlem Shout*.

97. Miller quoted in George T. Simon, *Glenn Miller and His Orchestra* (New York: Thomas Y. Crowell, 1974), 339.

98. Ayi Kwei Armah quoted in Chernoff, *African Rhythm*, xvii.

99. Burke, *Attitudes towards History*, 40.

100. Levine, *Unpredictable Past*, 185–86.

101. Duke Ellington, "From Where I Lie," in *Duke Ellington Reader*, 131; Robert Goffin, "The Best Negro Jazz Orchestras," in Cunard, *Negro*, 182.

Chapter 4

1. Jacquet was a renowned Texas tenor and his solo for the Lionel Hampton band's "Flying Home" (1942) is one of the most famous in jazz history. Jacquet played with the cream of the big bands in the mid-1940s, including Count Basie and Cab Calloway, and his emotive honking sax solos were a major influence on the sound of the tenor sax in rhythm and blues as it led up to rock and roll.

2. "The Power of Cohorts," *American Demographics* (December 1994): 22–31; see also "Name That Tune," *American Demographics* (August 1994): 22–27.

3. James J. Flink, *The Automobile Age* (Cambridge: MIT Press, 1990), 189–93.

4. H. L. Mencken, *Prejudices: Fourth Series* (New York: Knopf, 1924), 58.

5. See Roland Marchand, "The Designers Go to the Fair," *Design Issues* 8 (Fall 1991): 4–17, and 8 (Spring 1992): 22–40.

6. Segal, *Future Imperfect*, 102–10.

7. Roland Marchand, *Creating the Corporate Soul: The Rise of Public Relations and Corporate Imagery in American Big Business* (Berkeley: University of California Press, 1998), 301–11.

8. Ibid., 304. Similarly, in Hollywood, immigrant studio executives struggled with their new roles as cultural leaders to define American values and identity, resulting in such 1930s legacies as the films of Frank Capra and Walt Disney and John Ford's *The Grapes of Wrath* (1939). Robert Sklar, *Movie-Made America* (New York: Random House, 1975), 174–96.

9. Marchand, *Creating the Corporate Soul*, 204–48.

10. Geertz, *Interpretation of Cultures*, 208, 213–20.

11. Stowe, *Swing Changes*, 112–18. See also the chapter on swing in Philip H. Ennis, *The Seventh Stream:* (Manchester, N.H.: Wesleyan University Press), 113–28.

12. Cited in Meikle, *Twentieth Century Limited*, 155.

13. Goodman, *Kingdom of Swing*, 145–55, 197–201; Schuller, *Swing Era*, 3–23. See also James Lincoln Collier, *Benny Goodman and the Swing Era* (New York: Oxford University Press, 1988), 128–31. One explanation for the Palomar success is that West Coast radio audiences had been hearing Goodman's midnight broadcasts on the "Let's Dance" show in prime time and were familiar with their entire repertoire.

14. Robert Rydell, *All the World's a Fair* (Chicago: University of Chicago Press, 1984), 2–8.

15. *Official Guide: Book of The Fair, 1933* (Chicago: A Century of Progress, 1933), 11.

16. Lowell Tozer, "A Century of Progress, 1833–1933: Technology's Triumph Over Man," in *The American Culture*, ed. Hennig Cohen (Boston: Houghton Mifflin, 1968), 206.

17. Fritz Lang quoted in Peter Bogdanovich, *Fritz Lang in America* (New York: Praeger, 1969), 15, 124. See also Paul M. Jensen, *The Cinema of Fritz Lang* (New York: A. S. Barnes, 1969), 58–59, and Lotte Eisner, *Fritz Lang* (London: Secker and Warburg, 1976), 86, 91–93.

18. Aldous Huxley, *Brave New World* (New York: HarperCollins, 1989 [1932]); Dewey, *Individualism Old and New*, 24, 33–34, 125.

19. Bix, *Inventing Ourselves Out of Jobs*, 114–42.

20. Charles J. Maland, *Chaplin and American Culture* (Princeton University Press, 1989), 149–58; David Robinson, *Chaplin: His Life and Art* (New York: McGraw-Hill, 1985), 458–62.

21. Bix, *Inventing Ourselves Out of Jobs*, 43–79 and 143–203; Carroll Pursell, *The Machine in America: A Social History of Technology* (Baltimore: Johns Hopkins University Press, 1995), 249, 269.

22. "Science Will Liberate All Mankind in Next Century, Leaders Predict," *New York Times*, May 26, 1934, 1, 11.

23. Ibid., 1.

24. Roland Marchand, "Corporate Imagery and Popular Education: World Fairs and Expositions in the United States, 1893–1940," in David E. Nye and Carl Pederson, eds., *Consumption and American Culture* (Amsterdam: Free Press, 1991), 18–33.

25. Pursell, *Machine in America*, 230, 249, 268.

26. David E. Nye, *Electrifying America* (Cambridge: MIT Press, 1990), 150, 160–61, 331–35; William Gibson, "My Own Private Tokyo," *Wired*, September 2001: 21–22.

27. Adams, *Tempo of Life*, 31–33.

28. Dewey, *Art as Experience*, 139–40.

29. Robinson, *Chaplin*, 459. Chaplin described the figures of the tramp and the gamin as "the only two live spirits in a world of automatons. They really live" (459).

30. Dewey, *Art as Experience*, 139–41; Howard Mumford Jones, ed., *Letters of Sherwood Anderson* (Boston: Little, Brown, 1953), 279–85. Anderson sketched the first scene of the proposed play in a letter to an interested producer, Louis Greunberg.

31. Sherwood Anderson, *Puzzled America* (New York: Scribners, 1935), 29, 46, 147. See also his philosophical inquiry into these issues in "Machine Song," in Sherwood Anderson, *Perhaps Women* (New York: Liveright, 1931), 1–11.

32. Anderson, *Puzzled America*, 107–8.

33. Paul P. Appel, ed., *Homage to Sherwood Anderson* (New York: Paul A. Appel, 1970 [1941]), 49–52, 147–50. The author Ben Hecht claimed that Anderson was always searching for the lost American small-town soul that he himself had condemned in *Winesburg, Ohio* (1919); Hecht noted that Anderson did not spend much time in the 1930s in cities, or with immigrant workers.

34. *Perhaps Women* went virtually unreviewed, but Anderson recommended it to friends, writers, and philosophers throughout the decade as his boldest statement on worn-out men, the challenge of the machine, and the need to engage these issues at the individual and social levels (that is, not through political ideologies such as Marxism). Ray Lewis White, ed., *Sherwood Anderson's Memoirs: A Critical Edition* (Chapel Hill: University of North Carolina Press, 1969), 550–51. For letters referring to the book and/or these issues, see Jones, *Letters of Sherwood Anderson*, 237–43, 254–55, 282–85, 341–42, 375.

35. Besides Dewey, Anderson, and Mumford, these included Walter Lippmann, Edmund Wilson, and Stuart Chase, among others. See, for example, Wilson, "Walter Lippmann's 'A Preface to Morals'" in *The Uncollected Edmund Wilson*, ed. Janet Groth and David Castronovo (Athens: Ohio University Press, 1995), 108–16; Chase, *Men and Machines*, 272–78, and *Mexico* (New York: Literary Guild, 1931), 215–27, 318–27, in which he expresses his envy of "machineless men."

36. Anderson, *Puzzled America*, 147.

37. Smith, *Making the Modern*, 119–30, 185–94.

38. "Power—A Profile of Charles Sheeler," *Fortune*, December 1940, 73–83.

39. "Railroads on Parade" (review), *Variety*, November 4, 1939, 45. See also Douglas, *All Aboard!*, 376–78.

40. "Zephyr Makes World Record Run 1017 Miles at Average of 78 an Hour," *New York Times*, May 27, 1934, 1, 12; Geoffrey Freeman Allen, *Railways of the Twentieth Century* (New York: Norton, 1983), 72–77, 92–96.

41. Langdon Winner, *Autonomous Technology* (Cambridge: MIT Press, 1977), 36–38, 97; "Zephyr Makes World Record Run," 1, 12.

42. Allen, *Since Yesterday*, 182; see also Stover, *American Railroads*, 208, and Allen, *Railways of the Twentieth Century*, 92–96.

43. Meikle, *Twentieth Century Limited*, 162, 179; Stover, *American Railroads*, 206–7.

44. Meikle, *Twentieth Century Limited*, 96–98, 172–79, 183–85.

45. Tichi, *Shifting Gears*, 4–16.

46. Raymond Loewy, *Industrial Design* (London: 4th Estate, 1980), 77–93. See also Meikle, *Twentieth Century Limited*, 132–33, 155–60.

47. Douglas, *All Aboard!*, 377.

48. Kouwenhoven, *Half a Truth*, 93. For the role of the train in disseminating modernity to American small towns, see Stilgoe, *Metropolitan Corridor*; for the role of the train in global modernity, see Kern, *Culture of Time and Space*, 12, 23–24, 213–18.

49. W. Fred Cottrell, *The Railroader* (Palo Alto, Calif.: Stanford University Press, 1940), 82.

50. Stover, *American Railroads*, 200–203.

51. "Fortune Round Table—Transportation Policy and the Railroads," *Fortune*, August 1939, 50. Yet as successful as the streamliner trains were in revitalizing the railroad industry in the public eye, trains never regained their former prominence in American consciousness.

52. Kouwenhoven, *Half a Truth*, 129–42.

53. "Obsolete Men," *Fortune*, December 1932, 24–34, 91–94; see also Ralph Aiken, "More Machines and Less Men," *North American Review*, May 1931, 397–403, and "The Apex of Mass Production," *Literary Digest*, June 28, 1930, 27.

54. Elton Mayo, *The Human Problems of an Industrial Civilization* (New York: Macmillan, 1933), 182–83.

55. Langdon Winner, "When Technologies Die, Do We Mourn?" *Technology Review* 94 (November–December 1991): 74; Watty Piper, *The Little Engine That Could* (New York: Platt and Munk, 1986 [1930]).

56. Virginia Lee Burton, *Choo-Choo* (Boston: Houghton Mifflin, 1937) and *Mike Mulligan and his Steam Shovel* (Boston: Houghton Mifflin, 1939).

57. David R. Roediger, *The Wages of Whiteness* (London: Verso, 1991), 117–21; Lhamon, *Raising Cain*, 3–15, 44–54; Lott, *Love and Theft*, 6–7, 115–22.

58. Caponi, *Signifyin(g)*, 1–45.

59. Robert A. Coles and Diane Isaac, "Primitivism as a Therapeutic Pursuit: Notes Toward a Reassessment of Harlem Renaissance Lit," in *The Harlem Renaissance: Revaluations*, ed. Amritjit Singh, William S. Shiver, and Stanley Brodwin (New York: Garland, 1989), 3–12. See also Tracy Fessenden, "The Soul of America: Whiteness and the Disappearing of Bodies in the Progressive Era," in *Perspectives on Embodiment*, ed. Gail Weiss and Honi Fern Haber (New York: Routledge, 1999), 23–38.

60. Philip Rieff, *The Triumph of the Therapeutic: Uses of Faith after Freud* (New

York: Harper, 1966), 11, 15, 25. John Kasson suggests that the change from repression to release occurred a generation earlier at Coney Island; see Kasson, *Amusing the Million*, 5–12. Such a response should be seen within the context of the 150-year trajectory of the industrial revolution. As Christoph Asendorf summed up the difference between eighteenth- and nineteenth-century thought on bodies and machines: "The body as a mechanical object ha[d] been replaced by the machine as a bodily object." Asendorf, *Batteries of Life*, 44.

61. Mark Johnson, *The Body in the Mind: The Bodily Basis of Meaning, Imagination, and Reason* (Chicago: University of Chicago Press, 1987), xxxviii. For an overview of recent work on embodiment, see Weiss and Haber, *Perspectives on Embodiment*, especially Mark Johnson, "Embodied Reason" (81–102) and Thomas J. Csordas, "Embodiment and Cultural Phenomenology" (143–60); see also Johnson and Lakoff, *Philosophy in the Flesh: The Embodied Mind and Its Challenge to Western Thought* (New York: Basic Books, 1999), 3–7.

62. Dewey, *Art and Experience*, 162–69; Richard Shusterman, *Pragmatist Aesthetics* (New York: Oxford, 2000), 3–33.

63. See, for example, Hughes Panassie, *Hot Jazz: The Guide to Swing Music* (New York: M. Witmark, 1936); Winthrop Sargeant, *Jazz: Hot and Hybrid* (New York: Arrow Editions, 1938); Fredric Ramsey and Charles Edward Smith, eds., *Jazzmen* (New York: Harcourt, Brace, 1939); and Robert Goffin, *Jazz, from The Congo to the Metropolitan* (New York: Doubleday, 1944).

64. For reflections of several twentieth-century composers on the emergence of the importance of rhythm, see Michael Oliver, ed., *Settling the Score* (London: Faber and Faber, 1999), 110–24. For a contemporary analysis of the function of rhythm in music and its physiological effects, see Seashore, *Psychology of Music*, 138–48. For an interesting popular attempt to theorize rhythm as an element in art and culture, see Betty Lynd Thompson, *Fundamentals of Rhythm and Dance* (New York: A. S. Barnes, 1933), 1–24. *Times-Picayune* article cited in Lawrence Levine, *The Unpredictable Past* (New York: Oxford University Press, 1993), 220–21; Pleasants, *Agony of Modern Music*, 123. See the entire chapter in Pleasants entitled "The Crisis of Rhythm."

65. Rabinbach, *The Human Motor*, 172–76.

66. Ellington, "Duke Steps Out," 49–50.

67. John Cage, *Silences* (Hanover, N.H.: Wesleyan University Press, 1961), 8.

68. C. Scoby Strohman, interview, "Social Dancing: At the Cotton Club and the Savoy," an episode of *Eye on Dance*, broadcast March 11, 1985, WNYC-TV, New York, ARC Videodance, prod. Celia Ipiotis and Jeff Bush, courtesy Lincoln Center Dance Collection, New York Public Library.

69. See Dominick Cavallo, *Muscles and Morals: Organized Playgrounds and Urban Reform, 1880–1920* (Harrisburg: University of Pennsylvania Press, 1981). Stuart Chase spoke for many liberal intellectuals when he suggested dynamic play as the answer to monotony and fatigue, but he believed American workers made lousy choices: "routine, mechanized jobs . . . demand a righting of an outraged biological balance through some form of play . . . [but] prize fights, ball games, race courses, roller coasters, tabloid murder stories, gambling,

gin . . . [are] a blind rush from the monotony." Lilian Gilbreth, a Taylorist industrial engineer, found the evidence of assembly-line workers' enervation inconclusive, and her research lines up with postwar ethnographic work on assembly lines. Some men couldn't take the work; many felt great fatigue; some enjoyed the monotony; some didn't care, so long as each man had "more free time, all his own, that he may use as he pleases." Stuart Chase, "Play," in Beard, *Whither Mankind*, 346; Lilian M. Gilbreth, "Work and Leisure," in Charles Beard, ed., *Towards Civilization* (London: Longman, 1930), 232–52; Rabinbach, *Human Motor*, 217–24. The black vernacular phrase "work that body" refers to creative expression on the dance floor. One ethnomusicologist points out that "this use of 'work' . . . might be seen as an African-American inversion of the central concept of the Anglo-American work ethic." Kai Fikentscher, *"You Better Work!": Underground Dance Music in New York City* (Hanover, N.H.: Wesleyan University Press, 2000), 64.

70. On protests against Taylorism and on the House hearings, see Robert Kanigel, *The One Best Way: Frederick Winslow Taylor and the Enigma of Efficiency* (New York: Viking, 1997), 459–94, 533–39. For the General Motors workers, see Sidney Fine, *Sit-Down: The General Motors Strike of 1936–1937* (Ann Arbor: University of Michigan Press, 1969), 55–59. For Cold War unionized workers, see Charles R. Walker and Robert H. Guest, *The Man on the Assembly Line* (Cambridge: Harvard University Press, 1952), 8, 32, 51–52, 110, 117, 136–38, 152, and Ely Chinoy, *Automobile Workers and the American Dream* (Garden City, N.Y.: Doubleday, 1955), 70–73; see also O'Malley, *Keeping Watch*, 168–70.

71. The popularity of brass bands, also big, noisy, and powerful, was probably related to industrialization; but brass-band music was more a spectator form of martial music than a functional dance music except in New Orleans. William John Schafer, *Brass Bands and New Orleans Jazz* (Baton Rouge: Louisiana State University Press, 1977).

72. Jelly Roll Morton, "A Discourse on Jazz," in Gleason, *Jam Session*, 30–33; Handy, *Father of the Blues*, 252; Ellington, *Music Is My Mistress*, 413–15; Goodman, *Kingdom of Swing*, 189. See also Paul Berliner, *Thinking in Jazz* (New York: Oxford University Press, 1991), 351. Drummers built the standard trap set as we know it today between the world wars, adding the high-hat, tom-tom, cymbals, and wire brushes to create a lusher world of sound, to support soloists with different rhythms, and most important, in the words of the arranger Bill Challis, "to push big bands around." Bill Challis, interview by Ira Gitler, 1971, IJS, I:19–20. See also Cliff Leeman, interview by Milt Hinton, n.d., IJS, II:5. The role of the drummer as timekeeper is discussed in Theodore Dennis Brown, "A History and Analysis of Jazz Drumming to 1942," Ph.D. diss., University of Michigan, 1976, 201–3.

73. David Albert "Panama" Francis, interview by Milt Hinton, 1977, JOHP, IJS, II:52.

74. John Simmons, interview, IJS, I:12–13; Milt Hinton, interview by author, Jamaica, New York, August 22, 1996. John Simmons and Milt Hinton agreed on a total of four bassists that could be considered role models in 1930:

Wellman Braud (with Duke Ellington), Pops Foster (with Louis Armstrong), Walter Page (with Count Basie), and Steve Brown (with Jean Goldkette).

75. Eddie Durham quoted in Dance, *World of Count Basie*, 63.

76. Jimmy Crawford, interview by Stanley Crouch, n.d., JOHP, IJS, I:108.

77. Baby Dodds with Larry Gara, *The Baby Dodds Story* (Baton Rouge: Louisiana State University Press, 1992 [1959]), 1.

78. Cozy Cole, interview by William Kirchner, 1980, JOHP, IJS, IV:19–21.

79. Luigi Russolo, "The Art of Noises," in *Futurist Manifestos*, ed. Umbro Apollonio (New York: Viking, 1971), 75; Thompson, *Soundscape of Modernity*, 134–38. See also John Szwed, *Space Is the Place: The Lives and Times of Sun Ra* (New York: Pantheon, 1997), 134–40, 228–30.

80. Hart, *Drumming at the Edge*, 185.

81. Rose, *Black Noise*, 62–70; Margaret Thompson Drewal, *Yoruba Ritual: Performers, Play, Agency* (Bloomington: Indiana University Press, 1992), 2, 11.

82. Rose, *Black Noise*, 38–39.

83. Albert Murray uses the term "survival technology" specifically to refer to blues ritual, but also to any ritual strategy employed to confront a crisis. Murray, *The Blue Devils of Nada*, 53, 105.

84. Levine, *Black Culture*, 190–297.

85. Murray, *Stomping the Blues*, 6.

86. Karol Berger, *A Theory of Art* (New York: Oxford, 2000), vii–ix, 3–12; Shusterman, *Pragmatist Aesthetics*, 3–33; Murray, *Stomping the Blues*, 16.

87. Stearns, *Story of Jazz*, 140; Collier, *Benny Goodman*, 228.

88. Steven M. Friedson, *Dancing Prophets: Musical Experience in Tumbuka Healing* (Chicago: University of Chicago Press, 1996), 196.

89. A classic account is Hsio Wen Shih, "The Spread of Jazz and the Big Bands," in Albert McCarthy and Nat Hentoff, *Jazz* (New York: Da Capo, 1959), 171–87; see also Stowe, *Swing Changes*, 11–13. The jazz historian Thomas Hennessey sees in this massing of instruments into sections a reflection of the "interchangeable parts" of the American system of manufacturing. "By combining . . . the written harmonies of European classical music with the improvised African-American tradition, and harnessing the whole thing to a dance beat, Redman answered needs of musicians, dancers, [and] listeners." Hennessey, *From Jazz to Swing*, 88–89.

90. Schuller, *Swing Era*, 222–30; Collier, *Making of Jazz*, 188–92; Goodman, *Kingdom of Swing*, 138.

91. Mark C. Gridley, *Jazz Styles: History and Analysis* (Upper Saddle River, N.J.: Prentice Hall, 2000), 135.

92. Wingy Manone, quoted in Stowe, *Swing Changes*, 4; Dance, *World of Swing*, 1.

93. Murray, *Stomping the Blues*, 149–50. For a discussion of the elusive idea of playing behind or ahead of the beat, see Collier, *Benny Goodman*, 153–56.

94. Stowe, *Swing Changes*, 10.

95. Schuller, *Swing Era*, 248, 297–98.

96. The tenor saxophonist Budd Johnson defines a "flag-waver" as "one of

those long, hot tunes, and we just build and build and build and take it out."
Albert "Budd" Johnson, interview with Milt Hinton, March 1975, JOHP, IJS.

97. Orrin Keepnews, liner notes, *An Anthology of Big Band Swing, 1930–1955*, Decca Jazz CD GRD 2–629 (1993).

98. Collier, *Benny Goodman*, 225–28.

99. Shih, "Spread of Jazz," 183–84.

100. Collier, *Benny Goodman*, 141.

101. Lans Lamont quoted in Burt Korall, *Drummin' Men* (New York: Schirmer, 1990), 4–5. Benny Goodman's classically trained young pianist Mel Powell gave a very similar description of his first experience of seeing a big band—Goodman's orchestra at the Paramount Theater in New York City—in Tom Scanlan, *The Joy of Jazz: Swing Era 1935–1947* (Golden, Colo.: Fulcrum, 1996), 23–24.

102. See the comments of the trumpeter Harry Edison and the alto saxophonist Preston Love in Dance, *World of Count Basie*, 103, 151, and the interviews with John Simmons, Jimmy Crawford, Bill Challis, and Cliff Leeman, IJS.

103. Damon Runyon, "The Brighter Side," February 19, 1938, n.p., clipping file, Harvard Theater Collection, Pusey Library.

104. Benny Goodman, "Swing Back," *Pic*, January 9, 1940, n.p., Harvard Theater Collection, Pusey Library.

105. Quoted in Ross Firestone, *Swing, Swing, Swing* (New York: Norton, 1992), 241–42.

106. "University of Michigan Prof Defines Swing Music," *New York Amsterdam News*, September 14, 1940, 17.

107. Firestone, *Swing, Swing, Swing*, 241–42.

108. Seldes, *Seven Lively Arts*, 104.

109. Gama Gilbert, "Swing It! And Even in a Temple of Music," *New York Times Magazine*, January 16, 1938, 7, 21.

110. Challis, interview, JOHP, IJS, I:47–48; Joel Whitburn, *Joel Whitburn's Pop Memories 1890–1954* (Menomonee Falls, Wis.: Record Research Inc., 1986), 447–54.

111. Danny Barker, interview by Milt Hinton, April 1980, JOHP, IJS: III:2.

112. Ibid., 3. Barker recalled that big bands were known for their "very famous, very popular rhythm sections" of piano, bass, drum, and guitar. Musicians would ask of a given band, "Who is in the rhythm section?" or "Who was in McKinney's Cotton Pickers' rhythm section . . . or in the rhythm section with Fletcher [Henderson]?" See also Schuller, *Swing Era*, 225–27.

113. Ibid., 2–3.

114. Bechet, *Treat It Gentle*, 211.

115. Barker, interview, III:3.

116. Wilfrid Mellers, *Music in a New Found Land* (New York: Oxford University Press, 1987 [1964]), 314.

117. Count Basie quoted in Dance, *World of Count Basie*, xvii–xviii.

118. Charles Keil quotes this anecdote from an interview with Red Mitchell in *Music Grooves*, 192–93.

119. See Albert McCarthy, *Big Band Jazz* (New York: Da Capo, 1974), 189–93, and Schuller, *Swing Era*, 632–45.

120. Simon, *Big Bands*, 118–19.

121. Williams quoted in Dance, *World of Swing*, 71, 87.

122. Schuller, *Swing Era*, 637.

123. Carl Cons, "Who Said Casa Loma Can't Swing? Their 'Machine Jazz' in Fine Groove," *Downbeat*, November 1936, 1, 5, 9; "Sweet Music Carries Gray and Long," *Downbeat*, May 1940, 14, 18. See also "Glenn Gray's Gang Keeps Ahead of Crazes," *Metronome*, April 1939, 16. In 1936 Cons made a plea for the place of machine jazz: "In a machine age . . . may the idea be dared that a faultlessly coordinated organization working smoothly as one unit, both rhythmically and harmonically, can play an inspired and admired brand of swing?"

124. Ellington, "Duke Steps Out," 46–50.

125. Eddie Durham described the difference between white and black musical approaches in terms that belie any idea of a "right" way of playing. "[In] the white bands, the musicians play one or two tones, the vibrato tone and the straight tone. . . . And that's why any white musician can sit down and play in Glenn Miller's band or someplace else. But the black musician can get eight or ten different tones on his horn. . . . [W]hen he gets in a band, that's why it's hard for him [initially] to fit." The individualist must become part of a section, and you have to learn to be a team player; since you "got other[s] on the team with you, you've got to stay in line." Durham arranged for both the Basie band and the Glenn Miller Orchestra, and his perceptions support the belief that jazz instrumentalists incorporated the vocalizations of blues singing. Durham, interview, IJS, 49.

126. Norma Miller with Evette Jensen, *Swingin' at the Savoy* (Philadelphia: Temple University Press, 1996), 115.

127. Ibid., 313, 332; *The Essential Count Basie, Vol. 2*, Columbia CD CK 40835 (1987 [1939]).

128. Stearns, *Story of Jazz*, 211.

129. Hammond and Dugan, "An Early Black-Music Concert," 194.

130. Budd Johnson, interview, IJS.

131. Miller quoted in "'Rhythm Section Is My Only Worry'—Miller," *Downbeat*, January 1, 1940, 2, 19. See also Paul Eduard Miller, "Are White Bands Stealing Ideas from the Negro?" *Downbeat*, December 15, 1940, 5. In 1936, Paul Miller wrote that African American bands were the leaders in "innovation and creativity"; by late 1940, "America's big-name colored bands [were] no longer the box-office attractions they were a few years back." White bands were playing "Negroid music" and using "Negroid arrangers," so black bands were "no longer distinctive. . . . The whites were successfully stealing their stuff."

132. Goodman, *Kingdom of Swing*, 161–66.

133. For the importance of a white front man and the economic consequences for African American big bands, see Stowe, *Swing Changes*, 121–30.

134. Schuller, *Swing Era*, 11. See also Collier, *Benny Goodman*, 122–40;

Gridley, *Jazz Styles*, 86–88; and Martin Williams, *The Jazz Tradition* (New York: Oxford University Press, 1970), 54–62.

135. Attali, *Noise*, 64–67.

136. See the publicity photographs in Frank Driggs and Harry Lewine, eds., *Black Beauty, White Heat* (New York: Da Capo, 1995), 298, 303–5.

137. See, for example, Simon, *Big Bands*, 6–7, 37–39.

138. Stowe, *Swing Changes*, 35. Both photographic styles contrast sharply with the three types of publicity shots popular for 1920 jazz bands: musicians set up in diagonals, kneeling and pointing instruments in all directions; musicians mugging in a vaudeville style; musicians seated seriously on a stage with their instruments set carefully around them.

139. Quoted in *Duke Ellington Reader*, 94.

140. Simon, *Big Bands*, 3–11.

141. Collier, *Benny Goodman*, 188–95.

142. Brown, "History . . . of Jazz Drumming," 1–78; Korall, *Drummin' Men*.

143. See, for example, Mike Hennessey, *Klook: The Story of Kenny Clarke* (London: Quartet, 1990), 15–16; Sonny Greer, interview by Stanley Crouch, n.d., JOHP, IJS, I:46, IV:50–51; and Zutty Singleton, interview by Stanley Dance, n.d., JOHP, IJS: I:14–19.

144. Cozy Cole, interview with William Kirchner, 1980, JOHP, IJS, III:11–2. Bassist Milt Hinton claims that Cab Calloway replaced Leroy Maxey after hearing Gene Krupa; Krupa made Calloway realize the band needed a "drum soloist." See David Albert "Panama" Francis, interview with Milt Hinton, n.d., JOHP, IJS, I:42.

145. Ayo Bankole, Judith Bush, and Sadek H. Samaan, "The Yoruba Master Drummer," *African Arts* 8 (Winter 1975): 51–53, 77; Chernoff, *African Rhythm*, 91–113; Thompson, "Aesthetic of the Cool," 85–90.

146. Levine, *Black Culture*, 294–97; Mezzrow, *Really the Blues*, 143–64; Ogren, *Jazz Revolution*, 102–6, 151–53; Bruce H. Klauber, *The World of Gene Krupa: That Legendary Drummin' Man* (Ventura, Calif.: Pathfinder, 1990), 22.

147. Edmond Souchon, M.D., "King Oliver: A Very Personal Memoir," in Martin T. Williams, ed., *Jazz Panorama: From the Pages of Jazz Review* (New York: Crowell-Collier Press, 1962), 21–30.

148. Dodds, *Baby Dodds Story*, 35–36, 50, 59.

149. "Gene Krupa Tells His Ideas of Drumming," *Downbeat*, July 1936, 8; George Wettling, "A Dance Band Is as Good as Its Rhythm Section," *Downbeat*, January 15, 1942, 16.

150. John Hammond, "New York as Backward as Chi. In Swing Music," *Downbeat*, June 1935, 4; Goodman, *Kingdom of Swing*, 164; "Krupa Tells His Ideas," 8. On the function of the jazz drummer, see also Berliner, *Thinking in Jazz*, 132, 353. Krupa preached this sense of lightness (following Jo Jones's model) but he rarely achieved it with Goodman's band; his successors, Davey Tough and Big Sid Catlett, actually had a much lighter touch.

151. Wells, *Night People*, 70–71.

152. Stowe, *Swing Changes*, 11.

153. Ferguson, *Otis Ferguson Reader*, 71.

154. Leo Walker, *The Wonderful Era of the Great Dance Bands* (New York: Da Capo, 1990 [1964]), 221–31; Stowe, *Swing Changes*, 133–40; "Bands' Big Bonanza in '42 on Movie Screens," *Downbeat*, March 15, 1942, 6.

155. Stowe, *Swing Changes*, 33; Gridley, *Jazz Styles*, 86.

156. Bayles, *Hole in Our Soul*, 61–62.

157. Simon, *Big Bands*, 13.

158. Giedion, *Mechanization Takes Command*, v–vi.

159. Erenberg, "News from the Great Wide World," 493.

160. Ferguson, *Otis Ferguson Reader*, 73.

161. Basie quoted in Hentoff and Shapiro, *Hear Me Talkin' to Ya*, 304.

Chapter 5

1. "The Invisible Screw," program for dinner given by Thomas H. Bede in honor of Ernest K. Breech, President, Bendix Aviation Corporation, Le Perroquet Suite, The Waldorf Astoria, June 23, 1942. Thanks to Terry Monaghan for this reference, and for seeing the connections between this program and my thesis.

2. Henry Adams, *The Education of Henry Adams* (New York: Library of America/Vintage, 1990 [1907]), 352–55. For a still-useful discussion of Adams's influences and subsequent legacy with regard to Machine Age thought, see Thomas R. West, *Flesh of Steel: Literature and the Machine in American Culture* (Nashville: Vanderbilt University Press, 1967), 14–19.

3. Linda Mizejewski, *Ziegfeld Girl: Image and Icon in Culture and Cinema* (Durham, N.C.: Duke University Press, 1999), 151.

4. Burns Mantle, quoted in Samuel Milton Marks, "Settings By Joseph Urban," Ph.D. diss., University of Wisconsin, 1955, 482; Richard and Paulette Ziegfeld, *The Ziegfeld Touch* (New York: Abrams, 1992), 176–77.

5. The most useful overview of tap is Jerry Ames and Jim Siegelman, *The Book of Tap: Recovering America's Long Lost Dance* (New York: David McKay, 1977).

6. For several case studies that analyze the process by which specific technological inventions were disseminated into society through popular culture, from comics and dime novels to vaudeville and popular song, see the essays in Joseph J. Corn, ed., *Imagining Tomorrow* (Cambridge: MIT Press, 1986). For the specific example of the telephone, see Claude S. Fischer, *America Calling* (Berkeley: University of California Press, 1992).

7. Robert Luther Thompson, *Wiring a Continent* (Princeton, N.J.: Princeton University Press, 1947), 20–24; David E. Nye, *American Technological Sublime* (Cambridge: MIT Press, 1994), 33–43; David Noble, *The Religion of Technology* (New York: Knopf, 1997), 94.

8. This stage concept has since become a cliché in theater and film; it was most recently featured in *Sleepless in Seattle* (1993), where a map of the United States strung with what look like Christmas lights illustrated the phone lines.

9. Geraldine Maschio, "The Ziegfeld Follies: Form, Content, and Signifi-

cance of an American Revue," Ph.D. diss., University of Wisconsin, 1981, 70–75. Maschio's dissertation documents every Follies year by year and skit by skit (1907–25, 1927, 1931). In 1915 only 10 percent of Americans had phones in their homes; David E. Nye, *Consuming Power* (Cambridge: MIT Press, 1998), 6.

10. Mizejewski, *Ziegfeld Girl*, 146–47.

11. Maschio, "Ziegfeld Follies," 70–75. Important historical analyses of Ziegfeld include the biographies by Charles Higham, *Ziegfeld* (Chicago: Regnery, 1972), and Ziegfeld and Ziegfeld, *Ziegfeld Touch*, as well as Robert C. Toll, *The Entertainment Machine: American Show Business in the Twentieth Century* (New York: Oxford University Press, 1982), 182–89, 136–39, Eddie Cantor with David Freedman, *Ziegfeld, the Great Glorifier* (New York: Alfred H. King, 1934), and Marjorie Farnsworth, *The Ziegfeld Follies* (New York: Bonanza, 1956).

12. Though arguably the Follies constituted elite culture, its performers were drawn from all classes and ethnicities and the annual revues toured often. Ziegfeld began producing film versions of the Follies with the arrival of "talkies" (for example, *Glorifying the American Girl* [1929] and *Whoopee* [1930]). An epic film biography (or "biopic"), *The Great Ziegfeld* won the Academy Award for Best Picture in 1936.

13. Susan J. Douglas, "Amateur Operators and American Broadcasting: Shaping the Future of Radio," in Corn, *Imagining Tomorrow*, 45; see also Tichi, *Shifting Gears*.

14. Morton Eustis, "Fred Astaire—The Actor Dancer Attacks His Part," *Theatre Arts Monthly* 21 (May 1937): 378–79. Ironically, Astaire was Busby Berkeley's favorite dancer, but Berkeley recognized that their styles concerning dance on film were entirely different.

15. "1920 Follies Huge and Fast Moving," *New York Times,* June 23, 1920, 14. Ziegfeld's cultural influence was often overlooked in part because even his admirers perceived him as somewhat superficial and devoid of intellect. See Higham, *Ziegfeld*, 232–33.

16. Higham, *Ziegfeld*, 233.

17. Wilson wrote several essays about the Follies and entitled the first part of his memoir of the 1920s "The Follies." Edmund Wilson, *The American Earthquake: A Documentary of the Twenties and Thirties* (New York: Doubleday, 1958), 44–47, 50–52, 59–60, 88–89.

18. Gilbert Seldes, "Profiles—The Glorifier II," *New Yorker,* August 1, 1931, 20; Seldes, *Seven Lively Arts*, 133–34.

19. Seldes, *Seven Lively Arts*, 133–37. Friedrich Nietzsche brought the designations of "Apollonian" (order-making) and "Dionysian" (emotional abandon) into vogue in his treatise investigating the emergence of Greek dramatic forms, *The Birth of Tragedy from the Spirit of Music* (1872). The terms became common currency among intellectuals with regard to cultural patterns and behaviors.

20. Higham, *Ziegfeld*, 103; Cantor, *Ziegfeld*, 138; Ziegfeld and Ziegfeld, *Ziegfeld Touch*, 179.

21. Wilson, *American Earthquake*, 59.

22. Higham, *Ziegfeld*, 108; Maschio, "Ziegfeld Follies," 76–77.

23. Wilson, *American Earthquake*, 51.

24. Ziegfeld quoted in Derek and Julia Parker, *The Natural History of the Chorus Girl* (Indianapolis: Bobbs-Merrill, 1975), 96–97; Goddard quoted in Farnsworth, *Ziegfeld Follies*, 134.

25. Ziegfeld was renowned for his understanding of the sexual desires and fantasies of white American men. See J. P. McEvoy, "He Knew What They Wanted," *Saturday Evening Post*, September 10, 1932, 10–11.

26. Wilson, *American Earthquake*, 51 (emphasis added).

27. Quoted in Parker and Parker, *Natural History of the Chorus Girl*, 96–97; see also Mizejewski, *Ziegfeld Girl*.

28. Higham, *Ziegfeld*, 108; Ziegfeld and Ziegfeld, *Ziegfeld Touch*, 179. Where captains of industry such as Henry Ford subsumed human beings in the machine process, Ziegfeld's business allowed him, in effect, to "perform" technology for the public, like an aristocrat sharing his bounty with those less aesthetically fortunate. For example, Ziegfeld shared the thrill of night-time electric illumination with New York City pedestrians when he built what was then "the largest electric light sign in American history." Used to advertise the debut of Anna Held, his first wife and a renowned French musical-comedy star, the electric current required to light the sign was more than that used "to illuminate the Brooklyn Bridge . . . [It] could heat 150 rooms . . . [and] could cast a searchlight beam 30 miles." The sign was eighty feet long, forty-five feet high, and used 32,000 square feet of glass; the glass and metal weighed eight tons and required eleven miles of wire. The lights framing the words "Anna Held" comprised 2,300 "gas globes," and light seemed to "explode" around his wife's name in "leaping flame[s]." Higham, *Ziegfeld*, 67–68.

29. Maschio, "Ziegfeld Follies," 56, 66, 68.

30. Carolyn Marvin, "Dazzling the Multitude: Imagining the Electric Light as a Communications Medium," in Corn, *Imagining Tomorrow*, 206–8.

31. Photos of these women can be seen in Farnsworth, *Ziegfeld*, 172–73.

32. Seldes discusses Al Jolson and Fannie Brice in his perceptive essay, "The Daemonic in the American Theater," in *Seven Lively Arts*, 191–200.

33. Wilson, "The Finale at the Follies" (1925), in *American Earthquake*, 46–47. For a discussion of John Tiller's precision-training methods and the creation of the Tiller Girls, see Parker and Parker, *Natural History of the Chorus Girl*, 102–12.

34. Wilson, *American Earthquake*, 46.

35. Ibid., 46–47.

36. Ibid., 47.

37. "Ziegfeld Is Angry!," an advertising flyer for the Cotton Club, n.d., courtesy Harvard Theater Collection.

38. Maschio, "Ziegfeld Follies," 58–65.

39. Ibid., 87–89, 147, 152; Ethan Mordden, *Make Believe: The Broadway Musical in the 1920s* (New York: Oxford University Press, 1997), 87–89.

40. Seldes, *Seven Lively Arts*, 270.

41. Stearns and Stearns, *Jazz Dance*, 132–38; David Levering Lewis, *When Harlem Was in Vogue* (New York: Oxford University Press, 1981), 210; Barry Singer, *Black and Blue: The Life and Lyrics of Andy Razaf* (New York: Schirmer, 1992), 4; Parker and Parker, *Natural History of the Chorus Girl*, 146–48. Black jazz musicians often married chorines, and they had nothing but praise for their dancing, which they often claimed elicited better musical performances from the bands. Stearns and Stearns, *Jazz Dance*, 138–43; Malone, *Steppin' on the Blues*, 99–104.

42. Ruth Eleanor Howard, "Hollywood Talkies Are Dancing Now," *American Dancer* 3 (July 1929): 26–27.

43. Brenda Dixon Gottschild, *Digging the Africanist Presence in American Performance* (Westport, Conn.: Greenwood Press, 1996), 32.

44. Gilbert W. Gabriel, "Taps!—A Requiem," *Vanity Fair*, August 1929, 32. Gabriel was quick to point out the superiority of the human body to the machine: "You'll probably agree with me that motor car engines are a pretty monotonous task-master to the human thigh bone."

45. Ibid., 33.

46. Parker and Parker, *Natural History of the Chorus Girl*, 96–97; "Broadway at Large." See also the Radio City Music Hall web site, www.radiocity.com/b1e.html.

47. Farnsworth, *Ziegfeld*, 24–25.

48. Ibid., 22–25.

49. Seldes, "Profiles—The Glorifier II," 20.

50. Wayburn quoted in Maschio, "Ziegfeld Follies," 140; Cantor, *Ziegfeld*, 64. In the 1840s, the French drama teacher François Delsarte created a system of physical exercises that he believed mirrored spiritual energy in the body; he emphasized naturalistic movement, which was a break with the dramatic conventions of artifice and exaggeration. The Delsarte method was popular among actors and dancers in the early twentieth century. Ted Shawn, *Every Little Movement: A Book about Francois Delsarte* (Brooklyn: Dance Horizons, 1968), 2–11.

51. Veblen, *Theory of Business Enterprise*, 326.

52. McEvoy, "He Knew What They Wanted," 10–11.

53. Ziegfeld rarely chose "natural" beauties or those with perfect features or bodies. His female body-ideal (36–26–38) was voluptuous, sinuous, and "hip-py" compared to both the 1920s flapper (for example) or the current white American ideal; he often stated that "for perfection they [the hips] should be always two inches larger than the bosom." It was the *process*—the beautification—that turned his ideal females into cultural fantasies. For example, he preferred to sheath legs "in the finest silk and chiffon" than to have them bare; in other words, his aesthetic driving force was more "the art of intimation rather than disclosure." Farnsworth, *Ziegfeld*, 81, 84.

54. Higham, *Ziegfeld*, 107; Cantor, *Ziegfeld*, 34.

55. Lewis Mumford, *Technics and Human Development* (New York: Harvest, 1967), 188–94.

56. Maschio, "Ziegfeld Follies," 177–78.

57. Wayburn quoted in Maschio, "Ziegfeld Follies," 141. Even the term "The Great Glorifier" has the ring of a king's nickname; all accolades for the female-powered dynamo redounded to the male king of Broadway.

58. Veblen, *Theory of Business Enterprise,* 18–28; see also West, *Flesh of Steel,* 78–86.

59. Farnsworth, *Ziegfeld Follies,* 126; Higham, *Ziegfeld,* 235; Maschio, "Ziegfeld Follies," 178.

60. Mordden, *Make Believe,* 12–13.

61. Wilson, *American Earthquake,* 88–89; Maschio, "Ziegfeld Follies," 185.

62. Higham, *Ziegfeld,* 233.

63. Martin Rubin, *Showstoppers: Busby Berkeley and the Tradition of Spectacle* (New York: Columbia University Press, 1993), 1–6.

64. Ruby Keeler, Foreword to Tony Thomas, Jim Terry, and Busby Berkeley, *The Busby Berkeley Book* (Greenwich, Conn.: New York Graphic Society, 1973), 11.

65. Patrick Brian and Rene Gilson, "Busby Berkeley Interview," *Cahiers du Cinema in English* 2 (1966): 28.

66. Gary Lee Steinke, "An Analysis of the Dance Sequences in Busby Berkeley's Films," Ph.D. diss., University of Michigan, 1979, 42, 45.

67. Quoted in Brian and Gilson, "Busby Berkeley Interview," 35.

68. Cheney and Cheney, *Art and the Machine,* 4–21, 41–53.

69. Berkeley quoted in Lucy Fisher, "The Image of Woman as Image: The Optical Politics of Dames," *Film Quarterly* 30 (Fall 1976): 4.

70. Norbert Wiener, *The Human Use of Human Beings* (New York: Avon, 1967 [1950]), 254.

71. Rubin, *Showstoppers,* 122–23; Martin Rubin, "The Crowd, The Collective, and The Chorus: Busby Berkeley and the New Deal," in *Movies and Mass Culture,* ed. John Belton (New Brunswick, N.J.: Rutgers University Press, 1996), 59–92.

72. John Martin, "The Dance: New Musical Comedy Talent: Busby Berkeley's Direction Raises the Level of Our Stage Performances," *New York Times,* July 22, 1928, 21. For Martin, Berkeley was that rare artist working the middle ground between high and low culture. The cultured elites were mesmerized by the intricate rhythmic figures within his chorus lines, while Berkeley "overlay his multiple rhythms with acrobatic tricks and bits of external cleverness" for the more vulgar.

73. Ibid., 22, 61, 70–71.

74. Unlike Seldes and Gabriel, Martin did not recognize the influence of African American dance (and dancers) on Berkeley; the dances and rhythms of the Charleston and the Black Bottom were beneath comment. Martin did applaud the "greatly improved standards of pulchritude" among Broadway's chorus girls, a reference to the slimmer, more streamlined 1920s model. Ibid., 21.

75. Ibid., 21.

76. Berkeley prepared his dancers as he would an athletic team, diagramming the choreography like a coach explaining the plays. "I would gather the girls around a blackboard, and . . . explain the movements with diagrams. This always captured their interest . . . where the camera would be, where they would be. . . . " This procedure was especially helpful in doing the overhead shots of the complicated patterns. Berkeley quoted in Thomas and Terry, *Busby Berkeley Book*, 26, 62–63.

77. Rubin, *Showstoppers*, 51–53, 201fn87.

78. Ibid., 52.

79. "Even Broadway at Last Begins to Understand," *Journal of Electrical Workers and Operators* 27 (December 1928): 626.

80. Cantor, *Ziegfeld*, 10–11.

81. McEvoy, "He Knew What They Wanted," 11.

82. Ziegfeld and Ziegfeld, *Ziegfeld Touch*, 180; Mordden, *Make Believe*, 105; Rubin, *Showstoppers*, 34–35. Ziegfeld's innovative set designer, Joseph Urban, helped pioneer the settings of silent film by apprenticing himself to the new medium in 1920; Ziegfeld himself had no such dedication to craft. Urban pioneered set designs for Hearst, Fox Movietone, and Cosmopolitan Film throughout the 1920s. Marks, "Settings by Joseph Urban," 6, 118; Mordden, *Make Believe*, 20.

83. Such artisans included Urban, the leading set designer for the Metropolitan Opera House between 1917 and 1933, and Ned Wayburn, a renowned tap dancer who ran a chain of dancing schools; Irving Berlin and George Gershwin wrote for the Follies regularly.

84. Rubin, *Showstoppers*, 89–90; Ziegfeld and Ziegfeld, *Ziegfeld Touch*, 181; Mordden, *Make Believe*, 192–93. Berkeley showed little interest in going to Hollywood when first asked, but the producer Samuel Goldwyn tempted him with the promise of a hit show with Eddie Cantor as the star.

85. Rubin, *Showstoppers*, 114; Parsons quoted in Thomas and Terry, *Busby Berkeley Book*, 26, and see also 25, 30, 38–39; Mizejewski, *Ziegfeld Girl*, 137–85.

86. William Murray, "The Return of Busby Berkeley," *New York Times Magazine*, March 2, 1969, 26–27; 46, 48, 53–54; Steinke, "An Analysis of the Dance Sequences," 29–30, 162.

87. In the three consecutive production numbers that mark the end of *Footlight Parade*, the narrative moves from frivolous domestic pleasure to female spectacle to military drill (there is no relationship between the production numbers and the plot). First, "Honeymoon Hotel" is a fantasy of ritual communion in which all the hotel employees and several dozen couples provide a continuous sing-along for the newlyweds. Second, "By a Waterfall" displays a heavenly planet of cavorting aqua-babes in Dick Powell's dreams; the abundant women provide an interesting contrast to the monogamy of "Honeymoon Motel." Finally, in "Shanghai Lil," James Cagney's search for his whore-with-a-heart-of-gold ends up with the two of them on board an American battleship.

88. Thomas and Terry, *Busby Berkeley Book*, 46–47, 73–74, 124–25,

142–47. The authors point out that "minstrel shows and Negro music . . . [are] a popular motif in Berkeley's films."

89. The exception that proves the rule can be found in *Lady Be Good* (1941), in which Berkeley uses the acrobatic dance team the Berry Brothers to energize the movie. But their version of the film's featured ballad, "You'll Never Know," exaggerates black southern dialect, and the first shot focuses entirely on the younger Berry's huge, contorted mouth—an old minstrel trope, and an offensive one, especially in 1942.

90. Rubin, *Showstoppers,* 75.

91. Arthur Knight quoted in Steinke, "An Analysis of Dance Sequences," 41–42. Berkeley rejected the concept of dance as "physical expression" and strove instead to create "dance as a visual experience." Rubin, *Showstoppers,* 42.

92. Berkeley quoted in Patrick and Gilson "Busby Berkeley Interview," 28.

93. Rubin, *Showstoppers,* 42–43.

94. Ibid., 90–91.

95. Ibid., 52–53.

96. Berkeley quoted in Thomas and Terry, *Busby Berkeley Book,* 71.

97. Rubin, *Showstoppers,* 110; Berkeley quoted in *Busby Berkeley Book,* 71.

98. Nicole Amour, "The Machine Art of Dziga Vertov and Busby Berkeley," *Images* 5 (November 1997), www.imagesjournal.com.

99. Fisher, "The Image of Woman as Image," 3; Jack Cole quoted in Jerome Delamater, "Busby Berkeley: An American Surrealist," *Wide Angle* 1 (Spring 1976): 26.

100. Cole quoted in Delamater, "Busby Berkeley," 26; see also Jean-Louis Comolli, "Dancing Images," *Cahiers du Cinema in English* 2 (1966): 22–25.

101. Film scholars disagree on whether women lose their identity or are empowered by such collective power. One feminist scholar claims women lose their "individuation" through their look-alike quality, and through being "consumed in the creation of an . . . abstract design." In response, one historian of 1930s films suggests that set in context, the successful integration of chorus girls into larger patterns allowed Americans to "realize their [own] *harmonic* potential," and, in the finales, "celebrate collective action." Fisher, "The Image of Woman," 3–4; James Hay, "Dancing and Deconstructing the American Dream," *Quarterly Review of Film Studies* 10 (Spring 1985): 100.

102. Rubin, *Showstoppers,* caption of photograph no. 28. In two of Berkeley's most acclaimed films, *Footlight Parade* and *42nd Street*, the only character of any consequence is the troubled director; in both cases he suffers personally and economically from the effects of Broadway's demise, the Depression, and the rise of Hollywood musicals.

103. T. J. Jackson Lears, *Fables of Abundance* (New York: Basic Books, 1994).

104. Rubin calls this Berkeley trademark "controlled disorientation." As all stage conventions drop away—there is no stage, audience, or realistic setting—it "make[s] the viewer lose all sense of the proscenium frame-of-reference and effectively sever[s] spectacle space from the surrounding narrative space." Rubin contrasts "narrative space"—dramatic theatrical space based

on either the laws of physics or stage conventions—with "spectacle space, which can be expanded and transformed to include anything and to go anywhere, w[ith] complete freedom and arbitrariness." Rubin, *Showstoppers*, 118, 120. An analogy to Berkeley's "spectacle space" might be the artist M. C. Escher's textured dreamscapes.

105. The girls walk, stroll, and turn on what seem like a series of small Ferris wheels and carousels, themselves simply gearwheels reoriented for leisure.

106. Rubin, *Showstoppers*, 117–18.

107. Just as the locomotive as symbol and motive force facilitated American techno-progress (and adjustment to modernity), the subway's rhythms ground this fantasy in the interwar city.

108. Rubin, *Showstoppers*, 116. In other words, "I Only Have Eyes for You" is an artistic triumph for a 1930s artist trying to mediate the conflicting demands of the individual in a mass society, Berkeley's "most fluid mixture of mass spectacle and personalized, intimate romance."

109. Vidor's early experiments with putting the camera in motion during specific shots clearly influenced Berkeley; he explains the method behind this particular shot in his autobiography. King Vidor, *A Tree Is a Tree* (New York: Harcourt, Brace, 1953), 151–52; see also Raymond Durgnat and Scott Simmon, *King Vidor, American* (Berkeley: University of California Press, 1988), 79, and Rubin, "The Crowd, The Collective and the Chorus," 61–64.

110. The "city" here is a stage set seemingly derived from the architect Hugh Ferriss's renderings of skyscrapers (familiar now from the recent *Batman* movies), full of shadows, empty streets, and the suggestion of canyons. Here instead the usually dark foreboding buildings are lit from below and the streets are made lively by the peppy walk of the chorines.

111. For example, the black ball drops once and the women arrange themselves into an elaborate cake frosting set of concentric circles. In the outer circle, the women have their legs spread wide—white tops on the outer ring, black legs on the inner—while in the next inner circle, women lie on their sides inside the other women's legs. This pattern repeats until we get to a pinwheel center where women open and close their legs to a slower rhythm then those in the outer circle.

112. Rubin, "The Crowd, the Collective and the Chorus," 80.

113. From the original trailers for *Dames* (1934) and *Footlight Parade* (1933) as provided in the VHS copy of *Dames*.

114. Berkeley quoted in Thomas and Terry, *Busby Berkeley Book*, 38–39, 134.

115. Movie audiences probably made the connection, as the Bonus Marchers were burned out of their shantytowns in Washington, D.C., the year before by the United States military. See Rubin, "The Crowd, The Collective, and the Chorus," 72–74.

116. Thomas and Terry, *Busby Berkeley Book*, 61.

117. Mizejewski, *Ziegfeld Girl*, 138.

118. There are a few exceptions. For example, after James Cagney is reunited with Shanghai Lil (played by Ruby Keeler) in *Footlight Parade*, they tap-dance

their happiness—individually, one at a time—on a long wooden bar. Keeler taps out a standard military snare-drum pattern with her feet, bringing a sense of order to the chaotic bar scene; Cagney taps out Keeler's pattern first, then adds one of his own. Each then takes a "solo," and then they dance in tandem. There is more individual dancing in this minute of film than in nearly all of Berkeley's production numbers.

Chapter 6

1. "Fred Astaire: #1 Exponent," *Life*, November 25, 1941, 72–83; Chuck Green quoted in Judith Lynne Hanna, *The Performer-Audience Connection: Emotion to Metaphor in Dance and Society* (Austin: University of Texas Press, 1983), 47.

2. Malone, *Steppin' on the Blues*, 94–95; Paul Draper with Fran Avallone, *On Tap Dancing* (New York: Marcel Dekker, 1978), 12, 87; Ames and Siegelman, *Book of Tap*, 89; liner notes, *Eddie Brown's 'Scientific Rhythm'* (1990), dir. Sharon Arslanian, prod. Instructional Media Center, University of California at Riverside. Paul Draper was one of the few famous (and successful) tap dancers to produce a methodological approach to tap. Trained in ballet, Draper believed tap was a serious art ill-served by instructors, pedagogues and post-1950s dancers. Despite the valorization of his early ballet training, many of his statements reflect the values of African American artistic creation, including a deemphasis on striving for perfection and an aesthetic focus on "sound creation."

3. Hanna, *Performer-Audience Connection*, 51.

4. Le Corbusier, *When the Cathedrals Were White*, 160.

5. Stearns and Stearns, *Jazz Dance*, 184.

6. The Jazz musician Charlie Kniceley quoted in Trina Marx, *Tap Dance* (Englewood Cliffs, N.J.: Prentice-Hall, 1983), 66; Covan quoted in Stearns and Stearns, *Jazz Dance*, 178. Most swing bands had a favorite tap dancer: Ellington often traveled with Baby Laurence, and "Groundhog" (real name unknown) with Count Basie. A select few had songs named after them, such as the Count Basie Orchestra's "Shorty George," a song and dance step named after Shorty Snowden.

7. Ames and Siegelman, *Book of Tap*, 20–21.

8. Gabriel, "Taps!—A Requiem," 76; "The Talkies and Tap Dancing—As The Rooneys See It," *American Dancer* 3 (March–April, 1929): 22.

9. Pete Nugent quoted in *Stearns and Stearns*, 178. Gibson's statement merits reflection if one stops to imagine the foot speed necessary to imitate the fastest-talking person you may know, and to reflect that black oral storytelling is known for its rapid delivery.

10. For example, here are three examples of recordings on *Cotton Club Stars*, Stash LP ST124 (1984 [1929–37]), IJS: Bill Robinson accompanied by Irving Mills and his Hotsy-Totsy Gang, "Ain't Misbehavin'," recorded September 4, 1929; the Nicholas Brothers, "Wrap Your Cares in Rhythm and Dance" and "They Say He Ought to Dance," recorded December 6, 1937; and Buck and Bubbles, "Breakfast in Harlem," n.d. Bill Robinson recorded one of his

most famous sequences with Don Redman's orchestra, "Doin' the New Low Down," on *Doin' the New Low Down*, Hep LP 1004 (1984 [1932]). See also the interview with Kay Starr in Fred Hall, *More Dialogues in Swing* (Ventura, Calif.: Pathfinder, 1991).

11. Fred Astaire, *Steps in Time* (New York: Harper, 1959), 226–27; Miles Davis with Quincy Troupe, *Miles: The Autobiography* (New York: Simon and Schuster, 1989), 132. Many of big-band swing's finest drummers (Jo Jones, Buddy Rich, Sid Catlett, and Cozy Cole) were originally tap dancers.

12. Gabriel, "Taps!," 32, 76.

13. Ames and Sieglman, *Book of Tap*, 51–90.

14. Powell, Introduction to Ames and Siegelman, *Book of Tap*, x. Powell's teacher, Jack Donahue, was a renowned "hoofer" of the first quarter of the century and part owner of a chain of tap schools. The choreographer Don Saddler said he loved the hoofer genre, "because it says what we are as much as, say, corn bread." Keeler and Saddler quoted in Ames and Siegelman, *Book of Tap*, ix–xi, 109.

15. Thompson, *African Art in Motion*, 5, 7, 9; Cheryl Willis, "Tap Dance: Manifestation of the African Aesthetic," in *African Dance*, ed. Kariamu Welsh-Asante (Trenton, N.J.: Africa World Press, 1996), 145–59; for a 1930s analysis of the upward-flowing aesthetics of ballet, see John Martin, *Introduction to the Dance* (New York: Norton, 1939), 189–93, 212–13, 217–21.

16. Sally R. Sommer, "Hearing Dance, Watching Film," *Dance Scope* 14 (Fall 1980): 57.

17. Sandman Sims and Chuck Green quoted in *No Maps on My Taps*, dir. George Nieremberg, 1979; Draper, *On Tap Dancing*, 4, 129.

18. Astaire admired Bubbles much more than Robinson as a dancer. Letter, Fred Astaire to Marshall Stearns, March 27, 1961, Fred Astaire (vertical file), IJS. According to Bob Hope, Bubbles's "highly individual style of rhythm dancing shaped the style and success for many of the great dancers[,] from the Nicholas Brothers to Fred Astaire, Eleanor Powell, and the rest." Liner notes, *Bubbles, John W., That Is*, Vee-Jay 1109LP (1957).

19. Thomas Doherty, *Projections of War: Hollywood, American Culture, and World War II* (New York: Columbia University Press, 1993), 221–26; Malone, *Steppin' on the Blues*, 115.

20. Jack Donahue, "Hoofing," *Saturday Evening Post*, September 14, 1929, 29.

21. Hanna, *Performer-Audience Connection*, 48. The Irish dancer Jack Donahue remembered the corner streets of Boston filled with tap-dancing competitions at the turn of the twentieth century. Donahue, "Hoofing," 29, 233–35.

22. Stearns and Stearns, *Jazz Dance*, 49.

23. Similarly, "jig piano" was a common deprecatory name for ragtime; the "jig top" was a common term used by both blacks and whites to refer to the circus tent featuring African American music and dance. The tap dancer Leonard Reed, a barker in carnival shows in the early 1910s, recalled these terms in Rusty E. Frank, *Tap!: The Greatest Tap Dance Stars and Their Stories, 1900–1955* (New York: Morrow, 1990), 21.

24. Stearns and Stearns, *Jazz Dance*, 48–50. The story of the development of professional tap dancing is best told through its individual exemplars in Stearns and Stearns, *Jazz Dance*, 180–228.

25. John W. Bubbles quoted in Stearns and Stearns, *Jazz Dance*, 218. Ethel Waters, the highest-paid African American entertainer of the 1920s, was at first scared to play theaters "on the white time" because white audiences were formal and too quiet. Waters, *His Eye Is on the Sparrow*, 154, 157, 173–74. African American marching bands have long been famous among white Southerners—for their rhythmic power, humor, and dynamic motion, elements actively discouraged by white military-drill instruction. This tradition is carried on in the genre of "Stepping," a combination of military drill, choreographed dance, and verbal play performed in competition between black fraternities. See Malone, *Steppin' on the Blues*, 127–40 and 187–214.

26. Frank, *Tap!*, 21.

27. Willie Covan quoted in Frank, *Tap!*, 25. The Four Covans were one of only three black groups to headline white vaudeville before 1920; they starred in the breakthrough black musical, *Shuffle Along* (1921).

28. Stearns and Stearns, *Jazz Dance*, 17, 192–93; Astaire, *Steps in Time*, 227; Bob Thomas, *Astaire: The Man, the Dancer* (New York: St. Martin's, 1984), 107.

29. Collins quoted in Marx, *Tap Dance*, 17; Sims quoted in Ames and Siegelman, *Book of Tap*, 19–20. Sims perceived a sociological element as well: white dancers generally learned to tap dance in school, and from "counting"; black dancers learned on the street, from memorizing rhythmic patterns and stylizing the sounds of the city.

30. Kimberly Flynn, *Bring in 'da Noise, Bring in 'da Funk Study Guide* (New York: Public Theater, 1996), 18–19, 30.

31. Rosalind Wade with K. G. Newham, *Tap Dancing in 12 Easy Lessons* (Philadelphia: David McKay, n.d. [ca. 1935]), 58–64. Collection of IJS.

32. Ibid., 60–61.

33. "Bubbles," *New Yorker*, August 26, 1967, 21–23.

34. Eleanor Powell and Jimmy Slyde quoted in Ames and Siegelman, *Book of Tap*, ix, 119.

35. See, for example, Anne Schley Duggan, *Tap Dances* (New York: A. S. Barnes, 1936 [1932]), and *Tap Dances for School and Recreation* (New York: A. S. Barnes, 1935); Edith Ballwebber, *Tap Dancing: Fundamentals and Routines* (Chicago: Clayton F. Summy, 1930), and *Illustrated Tap Rhythms and Routines* (Chicago: Clayton F. Summy, 1933); Helen Frost, *Tap, Caper, and Clog* (New York: A. S. Barnes, 1932); and Marjorie Hillas, *Tap Dancing* (New York: A. S. Barnes, 1930).

36. "Realm of the Dance," *American Dancer* 2 (August 1928): 21.

37. See, for example, C. L. Green, "The Dance in Physical Education," *American Dancer* 1 (June 1927): 18–19, 39; Norma Gould, "At What Age Should Children Study Dancing?" *American Dancer* 1 (October 1927): 10; and H. A. Hemphill, "Dancing Is Best Exercise—Recommended by Football Coaches," *American Dancer* 2 (July 1928): 23.

38. Sharon Park Arslanian, "The History of Tap Dance in Education, 1920–1950," Ph.D. diss., Temple University, 1997, 213–29.

39. There were implied references to other theories of physical culture as well (for example, Delsarte, Emile Jacques Dalcroze, and F. M. Alexander).

40. Mary Jane Hungerford, *Creative Tap Dancing* (New York: Prentice-Hall, 1939), 3, 168.

41. Nearly all the manuals refer to "the Negro's" dances but none recognize an African American vernacular tradition; most discuss Scottish clogging at greater length. Many also feature prefaces from well-known male progressive educators equating tap dancing with the Greek "harmony between mind and body that made for beauty." See, for example, Jesse Fiering Williams, Preface to Duggan, *Tap Dances*, ix.

42. Ballwebber, *Illustrated Tap*, 7, 9; Ballwebber quoted in Arslanian, "History of Tap Dance in Education," 223.

43. Duggan, *Tap Dances*, vii–viii.

44. Ibid., ix.

45. Ibid., 9.

46. In all the manuals together there appear one photo and two diagrams of African American dancers.

47. Arslanian, "History of Tap Dance in Education," 236.

48. Susan McClary and Robert Walser, "Theorizing the Body in African-American Music," *Black Music Research Journal* 14 (Spring 1994): 75–84. "Once again we have the familiar pattern of African Americans developing an expressive form but having it register as significant for others only when it is picked up by 'genuine' artists with aesthetic know-how and non-profit integrity" (78).

49. Martin, *Introduction to the Dance*, 163; Reid Badger, *A Life in Ragtime* (New York: Oxford University Press, 1995), 99–100. The Castles established a precedent for dancing stars in American society, and especially for Fred Astaire and Ginger Rogers. Vernon Castle was Fred Astaire's idol, and the last Astaire/Rogers vehicle was *The Story of Vernon and Irene Castle* (1939). Vernon Castle's idol was the black drummer Buddy Gilmore, one of the musical stars of the Clef Club Orchestra. The conductor and composer James Reese Europe led the Clef Club Orchestra, and was also musical director for the Castles. Yet this biopic of the Castles' lives erased the contribution of both Europe and Gilmore. Europe was cofounder of the Clef Club, a musicians' organization that provided most of the music for New York City's social elite for the first two decades of the century. Irene Castle believed Europe invented the fox trot, and credits him with introducing the slower southern blues rhythm into social dance. Yet in the 1939 movie—for which Irene Castle was the major consultant—there are no black characters, there is no mention of African American dance, and there is no mention or representation of James Reese Europe.

50. Arslanian, "History of Tap Dance in Education," 230–50.

51. Stearns and Stearns, *Jazz Dance*, 220–28.

52. Thomas, *Astaire,* 130; John Mueller, *Astaire Dancing* (New York: Knopf, 1985), 120.

53. Thomas, *Astaire,* 116, 120–21; Graham Greene, "Follow the Fleet," *The Spectator,* April 24, 1936, 744. Adele Astaire, Fred's sister and long-time dancing partner, left the stage to become Lady Charles Cavendish, and lived the rest of her life as an intimate of British royalty.

54. Hay, "Dancing and Deconstructing the American Dream," 98–99.

55. Robert Sklar, *City Boys* (Princeton, N.J.: Princeton University Press, 1992), 1–9.

56. Quoted in Stearns and Stearns, *Jazz Dance,* 228.

57. Greene, "Follow the Fleet," 744.

58. Hermes Pan quoted in Thomas, *Astaire,* 98, 100.

59. Jane Goldberg, "John Bubbles: A Hoofer's Homage," *Village Voice,* December 4, 1978, 112; John W. Bubbles, interview with George Nierenberg, 1979, IJS; Letter, Astaire to Stearns, March 27, 1961, IJS.

60. According to Paul Whiteman, among musicians and partygoers on the West Coast during World War I, the other coast was called the "effete East."

61. Mueller, *Astaire Dancing,* 120.

62. An ocean liner's propeller was often several stories tall by itself, and was then built of cast metal, not chrome and ceramic. For an analysis of these machines and their relationship (or lack thereof) to a functioning ocean liner, I am indebted to Bill Pugsley.

63. In older factories, workstations were connected to a central generator through just such belt-driven mechanisms, often along the ceiling. A worker would simply throw a belt up to the electric cable and create a new workstation.

64. The machine rhythm is in triplets (in 12/8 time), and the workers' chant is in 4/4.

65. Peter Wood, "'Gimme the Kneebone Bent': African Body Language and the Evolution of American Dance Forms," in *The Black Tradition in American Modern Dance,* ed. Gerald E. Myers (Brooklyn, N.Y.: American Dance Festival, 1988), 8; Malone, *Steppin' on the Blues,* 9–22; Stearns and Stearns, *Jazz Dance,* 15.

66. Mueller, *Astaire Dancing,* 120.

67. In fact, the ship's bowels bear more of a resemblance to Raymond Loewy's high-tech office as displayed in the 1934 "Machine Art" exhibit than a ship's engine room. Certainly *Titanic* (1997), for example, provided a more realistic view of an ocean liner's lower decks.

68. A "break" is an improvisational challenge for the musician: all instruments drop out except one, which must maintain both rhythm and narrative interest until the rest of the band returns.

69. Mueller, *Astaire Dancing,* 120.

70. For an early example of this practice, see the discussion of the dancer William Henry Lane ("Master Juba") in Stearns and Stearns, *Jazz Dance,* 45.

71. A close analysis of an extended musical sequence in the Marx Brothers movie *A Day at the Races* (1937) also suggests the idea of a movement from folk to fine art, or from spirituals to swing.

72. Greg Sule Wilson, "Mr. Bojangles," *Village Voice,* October 1988, n.p. Clipping from Bill Robinson vertical file, IJS. Robinson was "half of the tap dance team that was the closest 1930s Hollywood would ever get to an interracial couple—that happy, gray-haired black man with the rolling eyes who danced down a flight of stairs with cute little Shirley Temple."

73. Beale Fletcher, *How to Improve Your Tap Dancing: For the Beginning, Intermediate, and Professional Dancer* (New York: A. S. Barnes, 1957), 116–17. Fletcher's book was widely used by professionals, and Stearns quotes his definition of the basic "time step" (the essential tap step). Fletcher's glossary of steps differs greatly from the 1930s tap manuals and reflects the Hollywood adaptation of a ballet-influenced tap for 1950s musicals.

74. Ibid.

75. Ballet was a "portrait of the ethereal"; its aesthetic goal was to display beauty emerging from suffering. Modern dance appropriated French and German expressionism to represent the everyday round of ordinary people and "parallel[ed] the movement of man as he works, plays, thinks, and struggles." Ibid.

76. Fletcher's 1957 plea for an American history in tap reflected the popularity of the Gene Kelly musicals of the time, but it was unusual for its time, as tap was otherwise in decline. Many important sources on tap were assembled in the 1970s at the height of the first tap revival on Broadway (after nearly thirty years of obscurity), a revival that saw Ruby Keeler in "No No Nanette" and a series of all-black revues (*Aint Misbehavin'*, *Eubie*, *The Wiz*). The current tap productions, however, enjoy a level of popularity and visibility unseen since the 1930s.

77. Elmo Terry-Morgan, "Noise/Funk: Fo' Real Black Theatre on 'Da Great White Way," *African American Review* 31 (Winter 1997): 677–87; Margo Jefferson, "'Noise' Taps a Historic Route to Joy," in *The Jazz Cadence of American Culture,* ed. Robert O'Meally (New York: Columbia University Press, 1998), 381–85.

78. Draper, *On Tap Dancing,* 90.

79. O'Connor quoted in *Ames and Siegelman,* 115.

80. Astaire claimed he worked hard to make his dances seem like second nature—to integrate the rhythms with a sense of effortlessness. In this way he reflected the value of "coolness" in African dance, though I am not claiming any direct influence. On "coolness" see Thompson, *African Art in Motion,* 43–45.

Chapter 7

1. Carl Van Vechten, "The Lindy Hop," in Paul Padgett, ed., *The Dance Writings of Carl Van Vechten* (New York: Dance Horizons, 1974), 38–40. Some scholars dismiss Van Vechten as a quintessential primitivist; see, for example, J. Michael Jarrett, "On Jazzology: A Rapsody," in Jon Michael Spencer, *Sacred Music of the Secular City* (Durham: Duke University Press, 1992), 189–92.

2. "The Lindy Hop," *Life,* August 23, 1943, 43–56.

3. Malone, *Steppin' on the Blues*, 13, 25–26; Stearns and Stearns, *Jazz Dance*, 13–14. For the importance of the circle motif in African American dance—from the ring shout to the minstrel dance-around—see Stuckey, *Slave Culture*, 53–80.

4. Roger Copeland and Marshall Cohen, eds., *What Is Dance?: Readings in Theory and Criticism* (New York: Oxford University Press, 1983), 426. The editors of this anthology declared that their goal was to reveal the process by which dancers and dance critics evolved a language for describing the human body in motion, a process which began, significantly, in the 1930s.

5. Van Vechten, *Dance Writings*, 39; Stearns and Stearns, *Jazz Dance*, 329.

6. Van Vechten, *Dance Writings*, 40.

7. Stearns and Stearns, *Jazz Dance*, 323–24. The dance scholar Terry Monaghan is responsible for the innovative scholarship in this area. Monaghan, "Did Lindbergh Really 'Lindy Hop' the Atlantic?" *Jazz, Jump, and Jive*, April–May 1999, 7–13.

8. William H. McNeill, *Keeping Together in Time: Dance and Drill in Human History* (Cambridge: Harvard University Press, 1995), 1–11.

9. McNeill, *Keeping Together in Time*, 8; Torgovnick, *Primitive Passions*, 3–15. Biologists have shown that stimulating eye and ear does alter brain-wave patterns, and anthropologists have observed how extended periods of dance, or rhythmically assisted trance, break down the brain's ability to distinguish the self from its environment.

10. Lucille Marsh, "A Survey of the Social Dance in America," *Journal of Health and Physical Education* 6 (November 1935): 62.

11. Robert P. Crease, "The Last of the Lindy Hoppers," *Village Voice*, August 25, 1987, 27–32; Robert P. Crease, "The Lindy Hop," in Gabbard, *Representing Jazz*, 224–25.

12. Ellis, *The Dance of Life*, 204–5, 323–31.

13. Sally Sommer, "Social Dance," in Eric Foner, ed., *A Reader's Companion to American History* (Boston: Houghton Mifflin, 1991), 262–63.

14. Sheila Walker, quoted in the documentary *Dancing: New Worlds, New Forms*, dir. and prod. Orlando Bagwell, RM Arts and BBC, 1993, Lincoln Center Dance Collection, New York Public Library. Such polyrhythmic articulation of the parts of the body has its basis in West and Central African cultural practice. For a set of useful definitions of dance styles between the world wars, see Richard Kislan, *Hoofing on Broadway* (New York: Prentice Hall, 1987).

15. Recruiting talent in the South in 1943 for the then-nascent Atlantic Records label, Stone distinguished a clear southern black affinity for the heavier beats of rhythm and blues than for the smooth, steady swing tempo. He also noted the absence of lindy hoppers on southern dance floors. Jesse Stone, interview by Chris Goddard, 1981, II: 113–14 and 131–32, and III: 73–75, IJS.

16. Murray, *Stomping the Blues*, 16–17, 20, 38, 189, 230; Malone, *Steppin' on the Blues*, 1–11 (quote on p. 2).

17. Stearns and Stearns, *Jazz Dance*, 323–34.

18. Gena Caponi-Tabery, "'Jump for Joy': The Jump Trope in African America, 1937–1941," *Prospects* 24 (1999): 521–74. According to the dance

historian Terry Monaghan, acrobatic air steps were not new to African American dance, but they had long been prohibited from dance halls because of their difficulty and danger. (Air steps were barred at many dance halls in the 1930s and 1940s.) It is more accurate to say Manning introduced air steps to the Savoy with the backing and approval of the Savoy management, and they quickly became a feature attraction of the dance hall's entertainment. Terry Monaghan, e-mail communication with author, June 6, 2002.

19. Robert Crease, "The Future of the Lindy and the New York Swing Dance Society: An Epilogue," in Norman Miller with Evette Jensen, *Swingin' at the Savoy* (Philadelphia: Temple University Press, 1996), 261. In the 1950s, American avant-garde dancers consciously drew on African dance movement and aesthetics to loosen up the rigid torsos of their classical training. Although the dancers recognized African dance as a separate tradition, with its own "aesthetic and social values" embodied in the polyrhythmic, undulating presentation of the body, their cultural borrowing was motivated by a desire to feel "closer to nature." The dancers were still invested in the mythology that held blacks to be so and their bodies thus "free of inhibitions." These dancers adapted African dance gestures such as "bent elbows and knees, its compartmented torso, its contrapuntal polyrhythms, its gravity-bound weight, and its sexual frankness." Sally Banes, *Writing Dancing in the Age of Postmodernism* (Hanover, N.H.: Wesleyan University Press, 1994), 62–66, 112–13. These African-derived dance gestures do not explain why the African *American* lindy hop was neither "gravity-bound" nor "sexually frank," or how it could become the American vernacular dance of the swing era. For American social dance in the 1930s, "the values of African-American music" were what the tempo of life called for: "its repetitions, its improvisatory structure, its oral transmission, its emphasis on rhythm over melody, and its emphasis on the body as an instrument." Audiences needed a renewal of "an appreciation of the body's concreteness." Sally Banes, *Greenwich Village 1963: Avant-Garde Performance and the Effervescent Body* (Durham: Duke University Press, 1993), 204–5.

20. Joel Dinerstein, "Lester Young and the Birth of Cool," in Caponi, *Signifyin(g)*, 239–76; see also Caponi-Tabery, "Jump for Joy." Caponi-Tabery shows how the "jump trope" in black culture in the 1930s reflected the social aspirations of African Americans in transition during the black migration: the birth of the jump shot in basketball, the creation of the "air steps" of the lindy hop, the jump trope in big-band songs ("One O'Clock Jump," "The Joint Is Jumpin'"), and the emergence of jump blues; see also Stearns and Stearns, *Jazz Dance*, 325.

21. Richard Wright and Edwin Rosskam, *12 Million Black Voices* (New York: Viking, 1941), 130.

22. Hurston, "Characteristics of Negro Expression," 62–63.

23. Emile Jacques-Dalcroze, *Eurhythmics, Art, and Education* (New York: A. S. Barnes, 1935), 226.

24. For two compelling arguments that African American musical innovation emerges from dance, see Stuckey, *Slave Culture*, 86–97, and Sidran, *Black Talk*, 20.

25. Crease, "Future of the Lindy," 256–61.

26. Later, lindy hoppers added such steps as the "jig walk" (where the woman hung around the man's neck as he walked forward), back-to-front mirroring movements, high leg kicks, and air steps (side to side, over the back, and over the head).

27. Frankie Manning quoted on videotape during dance session in Martha Batiuchok, "The Lindy," M.A. thesis, New York University, 1988.

28. Dancers quoted in *Oh, How We Danced* (1982), dir. John Belcher, Brian Jones, and Dorothy Jungels, Lincoln Center Dance Collection, New York Public Library. The documentary is an oral history of social dancing in the United States between the 1920s and 1950s. Lindy hopper and dance historian Ernie Smith quoted in the documentary *New World, New Forms;* see also Malone, *Steppin' on the Blues,* 100–104.

29. Stearns and Stearns, *Jazz Dance,* 321–27; "Rugcutters Find Harlem 'Heaven,'" *New York Amsterdam News,* April 8, 1939, 20. The Savoy manager Charles Buchanan referred to the ballroom as first and foremost a "community institution" that keeps "young people off the street" and only secondarily as a national institution.

30. "Savoy Begins Celebration of 14th Year, Nation's Leading Ballroom," *New York Amsterdam News,* March 9, 1940, 21; "Call Savoy Ballroom Nation's 'Workshop' For Swing World," *New York Amsterdam News,* June 22, 1940, 30, 33.

31. Leo Rosten writing under the name of Leonard Q. Ross, from *The Strangest Places* (1939), excerpt reprinted in David Meltzer, ed. *Reading Jazz* (San Francisco: Mercury, 1993), 153–55.

32. "Savoy Begins Celebration of 14th Year," 21.

33. Katrina Hazzard-Gordon, "Dancing to Rebalance the Universe," *Journal of Physical Education, Recreation, and Dance,* 62 (February 1991): 36–39, 48. Rosten was also impressed by the freedom of expression on display at the Savoy. He wanted to go up close to the dancers but did not know if there were rules and did not want to be seen as "square." He asked a young man watching if he could venture out without a partner. "Jes' suit yo'self, Mister," the man said, and this simple answer hit Rosten with the force of a new idea (or ideal). The man shouted after him, "'Jes' suit yo'self, Mister! We all does.'" Rosten wrote with admiration, "I have never forgotten that." Rosten seemed happily shocked by the informality, openness, and self-expression at the Savoy.

34. Ferguson, "Breakfast Dance, in Harlem," in *Otis Ferguson Reader,* 58–63 (emphasis added).

35. Malcolm X with Alex Haley, *The Autobiography of Malcolm X* (New York: Ballantine, 1992 [1964]), 53–154.

36. Ibid., 69, 74–78, 86.

37. Howard Johnson and Scoby Strohman refer to "the track" in "Social Dancing: At the Cotton Club and the Savoy," *Eye on Dance.* Other common animal metaphors in swing-era jazz culture included "chick" and "canary" for a woman, and "cat" for a man. See "Cab Calloway's Hepster Dictionary," an appendix to Calloway, *Of Minnie the Moocher and Me,* 252–61.

38. "Call Savoy Ballroom Nation's 'Workshop,'" 29–30, 33; "Lace up Your Boots and Dig This Jive!," *New York Amsterdam News,* March 2, 1940, 21.

39. "We're stomping at the Savoy" kicked off many radio broadcasts from the ballroom. See, for example, *Count Basie: The Golden Years, Vol. 1, 1937,* EPM Musique CD. The ballroom's national renown was also trumpeted by the songs "Savoy" and "Savoy Rhythm," the latter recorded as early as August 15, 1929, by the black territory band Roy Johnson's Happy Pals.

40. Russell Gold, "Guilty of Syncopation, Joy, and Animation: The Closing of Harlem's Savoy Ballroom," *Studies in Dance History* 5 (spring 1994): 50–64 (Razaf's poem is quoted on pp. 53–54); Terry Monaghan, "Mid-Life Crisis— The Six-Month Closure of the Savoy Ballroom in 1943," unpublished article.

41. E. M. von Hornbostel, "African Negro Music," *Africa* 1 (January 1928): 39–40. Hornbostel famously theorized that European classical music begins from "hearing" and African music "from motion" (i.e., dance). In other words, classical music is narratively based and assumes an audience of listeners; African music is propulsive and assumes an audience of dancers and participants.

42. Hazzard-Gordon, "Dancing to Rebalance the Universe," 36–39; see also Henry John Drewal and Margaret Thompson Drewal, *Gelede: Art and Female Power among the Yoruba* (Bloomington: Indiana University Press, 1990), 5, 18, 80. Robert Farris Thompson translates the word "ase" (pronounced ah-SHAY) as "the power to make things happen." Other approximations include "the vital force," "the power to bring things into existence," "calm execution," or simply "authority." Thompson, *Flash of the Spirit* (New York: Vintage, 1984), 5–9.

43. Malone, *Steppin' on the Blues,* 11, 24, 31.

44. West African kinesthetic continuity was kept alive in the South through the ring shout and social dance. Dance was also the preeminent recreation allowed by southern slaveholders, and there were many occasions for competitive dancing in which slaves shared knowledge and skills: in holiday and weekend dances, in corn shucking celebrations, and in urban festivals such as John Canoe and Pinkster. While blacks stood in a circle and watched individuals dance, they would often call out work-derived motions as steps. Hazzard-Gordon, "Dancing under the Lash," 106–7, and *Jookin',* 18–21.

45. For an analysis of the sociomusical function of the personal cry, from the field hollers of southern sharecroppers to that of urban street vendors, see James, *Stars in de Elements,* 16–34, and Sidran, *Black Talk,* 36–37 and 101–2.

46. Lopez, *Lopez Speaking,* 135–36.

47. Frankie Manning, interview, "Jazzing It Up," an episode of a public television news series *Eye on Dance,* WNYC, New York City, recorded April 7, 1988, prod. ARC Videodance, Celia Ipiotis, and Jeff Bush, Lincoln Center Dance Collection, New York Public Library.

48. Manning quoted in Batiuchok, "Lindy Hop"; Omofolabo S. Ajaji, *Yoruba Dance: The Semantic of Movement and Body Attitude in a Nigerian Culture* (Trenton, N.J.: Africa World Press, 1998), 35; Stearns, *Jazz Dance,* 15–16.

49. Johnson quoted in "Social Dancing: At the Cotton Club and the Savoy," *Eye on Dance.*

50. Smith quoted in the documentary *Dancing: New Worlds, New Forms.*

51. Smith quoted in Stearns and Stearns, *Jazz Dance,* 329–30.

52. "Lindy Hop," *Life,* 46–56.

53. Norma Miller quoted in Crease, "Last of the Lindy Hoppers," 30.

54. Manning, interview, "Jazzing It Up," *Eye on Dance.*

55. Stearns and Stearns, *Jazz Dance,* 328.

56. Stearns and Stearns, *Jazz Dance,* 328; Miller, *Swingin' at the Savoy,* 63.

57. Modern dancers actively ignored African American social dance styles until after World War II, when a new avant-garde revived elements of "primitivism" and brought a death knell to "the etherealized bodies of Euro-American culture." Banes, *Greenwich Village 1963,* 204–12.

58. Joann Kealiinohomoku, "An Anthropologist Looks at Ballet as a Form of Ethnic Dance," in Copeland and Cohen, *What Is Dance?,* 545.

59. Gabriel, "Taps!—A Requiem," 32, 76.

60. Isadora Duncan, "The Dance of the Future," in Copeland and Cohen, *What Is Dance?,* 263.

61. Singer, *Black and Blue,* 113–14.

62. Howard Spring, "Swing and the Lindy Hop: Dance, Venue, Media, and Tradition," *American Music* 15 (summer 1997): 183–208.

63. See Malone, *Steppin' on the Blues,* 98–102.

64. Robin Harris, "You Dance? Riches and Fame Wait!," *New York Daily News,* July 8, 1935, 3, 15; "Dance Champs to Get Prizes from Astaire," *New York Daily News,* August 27, 1935, 20; Jack Turcott, "Harvest Ball On Tonight," *New York Daily News,* August 28, 1935, 3, 33. The Loew's State Theater program featuring the Harvest Moon Ball champs proved so popular that by 1938 both the king and queen of the ball and division winners received two-week contracts. Roger Dakin, "20,000 Cheer Ball Finals at Garden," *New York Daily News,* September 1, 1938, 4; William Murtha, "20,000 Jam Garden to See Harvest Ball Final Winners," *New York Daily News,* August 28, 1941, 4–5.

65. A partial list of celebrities included the members of the New York Giants baseball team and former New York governor Al Smith (1935); Ginger Rogers, Bill Robinson, Jack Dempsey, and Milton Berle (1936); George Raft, Sonja Henie, Alice Faye, Jack Dempsey, Bert Lahr, Jack Haley, and Ray Bolger (1939); and Billy Rose, Irving Berlin, Babe Ruth, Ralph Bellamy, and James Cagney (1940).

66. Jack Turcott, "20,000 Hail Royal Couple of Dance At Harvest Ball," *New York Daily News,* August 29, 1935, 3.

67. William Murtha, "Fun-Bent 20,000 Jam Garden for 10th Harvest Moon Ball," *New York Daily News,* September 7, 1944, 4.

68. Turcott, "20,000 Hail Royal Couple of Dance," 3.

69. Front pages, *New York Daily News,* August 28, 1941, and August 27, 1942. The *Daily News* often added pages of photos to its usual centerfold spread to cover the event; in 1941, the half-page photo of the winning couple shared the front page with one of Hitler and the ex–French premier.

70. William Murtha, "20,000 See Engaged Couple Win Ball Title," *New York Daily News,* August 29, 1940, 4. In 1942, for example, the human-interest

angle was that the winning couple had promised their friends they would get married if they won. They did, and asked for a preacher when interviewed after their victory. In 1944 the winners had met only three weeks before, and the reporter played up the angle of a dawning romance. See, for example, "20,000 Jam Garden," 4, 10.

71. "Harvest Moon Ball Tonight—Got Tickets?," *New York Daily News*, August 28, 1935, 3, 33; Miller, *Swingin' at the Savoy*, 56–57, 72–75; Crease, "Last of the Lindy Hoppers," 29–30; Frankie Manning, taped interview by Terry Monaghan, October 18, 1998, London, England. Thanks to Terry Monaghan for use of this interview.

72. Progressive educators considered dancing an excellent form of recreation. Significantly, historians view the 1935 Harlem riot as the end of an era: David Levering Lewis refers to it as one unofficial ending of the Harlem Renaissance and its ideological drive to gain social equality through literary and artistic production; Malcolm X (inaccurately) marks the riot as the end of white tourism in Harlem. Lewis, *When Harlem Was in Vogue*, 305–6; Claude McKay, "Harlem Runs Wild," in Eric J. Sundquist, *Cultural Contexts for Ralph Ellison's "Invisible Man"* (Boston: Bedford/St. Martin's, 1995), 220–25. The Harvest Moon Ball changed markedly after the outbreak of World War II. All profits were then donated to "the aid of servicemen" via the USO, and beginning in 1942, coverage of the event was dominated by the presence of soldiers in special servicemens' divisions, and the *Daily News* played up competition between the branches of the armed forces. William Murtha, "Service Men Prove They Also Can Dance," *New York Daily News*, August 25, 1942, 25; Murtha, "Harvest Ball Finals Will Be Held Tonight," *New York Daily News*, September 8, 1943, 16; Howard Whitman, "22-Year-Olds Cop Crowns in Harvest Moon Finals," *New York Daily News*, September 9, 1943, 4, 17.

73. "Contest OKs Harlem Step," *New York Daily News*, July 14, 1935, 3, 22. Quote from Crease, "Last of the Lindy Hoppers," 29.

74. Jack Turcott, "100,000 Throng Mall and Dance Final Is Put Off," *New York Daily News*, August 16, 1935, 3, 21 (photos on 1, 26); Jack Turcott, "Harvest Moon First Garden Public Ball," *New York Daily News*, August 25, 1935, 3, 8; Jack Turcott, "Mayor, [Governor] Smith Harvest Moon Wallflowers," *New York Daily News*, August 25, 1935, 40.

75. Crease, "Last of the Lindy Hoppers," 30.

76. Malone, *Steppin' on the Blues*, 15–16.

77. Miller, *Swingin' at the Savoy*, 80–82.

78. Jack Turcott, "22,000 Cheer Victors in Harvest Moon Ball," *New York Daily News*, August 27, 1936, 24.

79. Jack Turcott, "'B'way All Agog over Harvest Ball Sellout," *New York Daily News*, August 28, 1937, 28. That year, the *Daily News* received "hundreds of commendatory telegrams" for their role in providing a stepping-stone for unknown dancers to become professional.

80. Roger Dakin, "Harvest Ball Champs Score in Stage Debut," *New York Daily News*, September 1, 1939, 4, 43.

81. Turcott, "B'way All Agog," 28.

82. Jack Turcott, "Six Harvest Ball Pairs Wow Stage," *New York Daily News*, August 27, 1937, 4.

83. Roger Dakin, "Theatre Hails Harvest Moon Ball Winners," *New York Daily News*, August 30, 1940, 4; Roger Dakin, "Ball Winners Triumph Again in Stage Show," *New York Daily News*, August 29, 1941, 35. Apparently the reporters used a boilerplate article that described how well the amateur champs fared in their professional debut. The dancers were always applauded for their lack of nervousness, for overcoming fatigue—even after a day of practice, a night of grueling competition, and 7 A.M. rehearsals—and for showing considerable poise when dancing alone on a Broadway stage. See, for example, Roger Dakin, "Ball Winners Pack Broadway Show," *New York Daily News*, September 2, 1938, 2.

84. William Murtha, "20,000 See Engaged Couple Win Ball Title," *New York Daily News*, August 29, 1940, 4.

85. "20,000 Jam Garden to See Harvest Moon Ball Final Winners," *New York Daily News*, August 28, 1941, 4–5. The named couples were Bill Dotson and Rebecca Brune, Walter Johnson and Mae Miller, James Outlaw and Alyce Pearson.

86. William Murtha, "20,000 See Ball Finals; Big Winners to Wed," *New York Daily News*, August 27, 1942, 4.

87. Jack Turcott, "23,500 Cheer Victors in Harvest Moon Ball, "*New York Daily News*, August 26, 1937, 26.

88. Leon James and Edith Matthews appear in a photo-spread in *New York Daily News*, August 29, 1935, 33; Greenwich and Gibson appear in *New York Daily News*, August 28, 1936, 32; Daniel and James are captured in "Lindy Hoppers," *New York Daily News*, August 26, 1937, 30. The photo of Norma Miller and George Ricker appears in Roger Dakin, "20,000 Cheer Ball Finals at Garden," *New York Daily News*, September 1, 1938, 4; the photo of Mildred Pollard and Albert Minns appears in the centerfold (p. 31) of the same edition. All three lindy hop teams appear in a photo with the caption "Lindy Hop," *New York Daily News*, September 2, 1938, 28–29. The Harvest Moon Ball winners for 1940 all appear in a group photograph. William Murtha, "Theatre Hails Harvest Moon Ball Winners," *New York Daily News*, August 30, 1940, 4.

89. "Two Good Dancers Say 'Hello,'" *New York Daily News*, August 27, 1936, 76; "Cheering a Champ," *New York Daily News*, September 7, 1944, 23. In 1936 the caption noted that "Ginger Rogers . . . leans from her box . . . to shake hands with Bill Robinson, Harlem's #1 tap dancer." Abe Lyman's photograph appears in "Harvest Moon Ball Tonight, Got Tickets?" *New York Daily News*, August 28, 1935, 3, 33.

90. "Billie Holiday to Be Harvest Moon Singer," *New York Daily News*, August 29, 1938, 37.

91. Monaghan, "Mid-life Crisis."

92. "22-Year-Olds Cop Crowns," *New York Daily News*, September 9, 1943, 4, 17. A year later, the competition's racial element resurfaced. With Cab Calloway as the swing band in 1944, "Harlem jive came back with a vengeance . . .

taking all three of the top spots." "20,000 Jam Garden," *New York Daily News*, September 7, 1944, 4, 10.

93. Cited in Spring, "Swing and the Lindy Hop," 199–201.

94. "Farewell to the Jitterbug? Teachers Enlist Irene Castle in War on Swing Dance Style," *Newsweek*, August 14, 1939, 30–31; "'Jitterbug' Dying Out, Dance Masters Agree," *New York Times*, August 1, 1939, 16; "When U.S. Went Dance Mad—Nostalgic Rogers-Astaire Recreates Castles' Reign," *Newsweek*, April 3, 1939, 30–31; "Boomps, Yips," *Time*, July 10, 1939, 31.

95. "The Lindy Hop," *Life*, 43–44; Crease, "Last of the Lindy Hoppers," 30–32.

96. James Weldon Johnson, *Along the Way* (New York: Viking, 1934), 363; see also James Weldon Johnson, *The Book of American Negro Spirituals* (New York: Viking 1925), 31–32. In his autobiography, Johnson wrote positively of the kind of "primitivism" that historians now usually dismiss as racist. Johnson was amused by the irony of white "attempt[s] to throw off the crusts and layers of inhibitions laid on by sophisticated civilization; striving to yield to the feel and experience of abandon; seeking to recapture a taste of primitive joy in life and living; trying to work their way back into that jungle that was the Garden of Eden" (363).

97. Crease, "Lindy Hop," in Gabbard, *Representing Jazz*, 224.

98. As a member of a Federal Writers Project program investigating religious cults in New York City, Dunham studied Afro-Christian worship and found the language and ideology "clearly and definitely Christian" but the pattern of motor behavior "almost . . . purely African" (and quite similar to worship she had seen in Haiti). At the time, these connections struck her with the force of revelations. The service featured "rhythmic percussion-type hand-clapping and foot-stamping," jumping and leaping, "conversion . . . in unknown tongues," and ecstatic possession ("self-hypnosis by motor-activity of the shoulders"). Katherine Dunham, "The Negro Dance," in *The Negro Caravan*, ed. Arthur P. Davis, Sterling A. Brown, and Ulysses Lee (New York: Arno/ New York Times, 1970 [1941]), 990–91, 994, 999.

99. Ibid., 997–98.

100. Black dance traditions were first appreciated for their entertainment value, but Dunham perceived a different sort of cultural dissemination when the cakewalk swept the nation along with ragtime in the late 1890s. When dancing the cakewalk, blacks interpolated other plantation dance styles (the Pas Mala, Walkin' the Dog, Ballin' the Jack), making it both contemporary and traditional, an experiential fusion of continuity and change. Dancers repeated this process with the Charleston in the 1920s.

101. Ibid., 1000.

102. Graham, "American Dance," 106.

103. *The Swing Era: How It Was to Be Young Then, 1940–1941* (New York: Time-Life, 1971), 10–22.

104. Les Back, "Nazism and the Call of the Jitterbug," in Helen Thomas, ed., *Dance in the City* (New York: St. Martin's, 1997), 194–95. The journalist

Richard Harding Davis recognized the totalitarian ethic in the German lock-step march as early as 1917, when he watched the German army march into Brussels. They were "not men marching, but a force of nature like a tidal wave. . . . Hour after hour passed and there was no halt, no breathing time, no open spaces in the ranks . . . uncanny, unhuman." They had "lost the human quality." Cited in Sullivan, *Our Times*, 438–39.

105. As W. T. Lhamon has recently shown, the same dance moves and kinesthetics displayed by Long Island slaves dancing for money on holidays at New York City markets in the early 1800s—those which excited T. D. Rice and other early blackface minstrels—still excited young white Americans in the videos of MC Hammer and Michael Jackson. Lhamon, *Raising Cain*, 218–26.

106. Salman Rushdie, *The Wizard of Oz* (London: British Film Institute, 1992), 44.

107. Roger Dakin, "20,000 Hail Winners in Harvest Moon Ball," *New York Daily News*, August 31, 1939, 4, 19; "Tie Smashes Precedent at Harvest Ball," *New York Daily News*, August 29, 1940, 4, 8; Stearns and Stearns, *Jazz Dance*, 323.

108. John Fricke, liner notes, *The Wizard of Oz*, Rhino Movie Music CD RS 71999 (n.d.); see also Rushdie, *Wizard of Oz*, 51.

Chapter 8

1. Histories of the Fair include Helen A. Harrison, ed., *Dawn of a New Day: The New York World's Fair 1939–40* (New York: Queens Museum/NYU Press, 1980); Rosemarie Haag Bletter, ed., *Remembering the Future: The New York World's Fair from 1939 to 1964* (New York: Rizzoli, 1989); and the documentary *The World of Tomorrow*, dir. Tom Johnson and Lance Bird (n.d.). The Fair is discussed at length in the following histories: Robert Rydell, *World of Fairs: The Century of Progress Expositions* (Chicago: University of Chicago Press, 1993), 115–56, 183–87; Susman, *Culture as History*, 211–29; Meikle, *Twentieth Century Limited*, 197–215; Roland Marchand, "The Designers Go to the Fair," *Design Issues* 8 (Fall 1991), 4–17, and 8 (Spring 1992), 22–40; Marchand, "Corporate Imagery and Popular Education," 18–33. Full-length photographic essays of the Fair include the following: Richard Wurts and Stanley Appelbaum, *The New York World's Fair 1939–1940* (New York: Dover, 1977); Larry Zim, Mel Lerner, and Herbert Rolfes, *The World of Tomorrow* (New York: Main Street Press, 1988); and Barbara Cohen, Steven Heller, and Seymour Chwast, *Trylon and Perisphere* (New York: Abrams, 1989). Well-researched reimaginings of the Fair include E. L. Doctorow, *World's Fair* (New York: Penguin/Plume, 1996), and David Gelernter, *1939: The Lost World of the Fair* (New York: Avon, 1995).

2. Trachtenberg, *Incorporation of America*, 230–31.

3. The dispersed enthusiasm for the 1940 Fair is noted at the end of the documentary *The World of Tomorrow*. Warren I. Susman was the film's historical consultant; the actor Jason Robards narrated.

4. Chester Himes's essay, *"Now* Is the Time" (1943), in *The Crisis* called for African American support of the American war effort and continual protest against unequal social treatment in the United States. Reprinted in Chester

Himes, *Black on Black* (Garden City, N.Y.: Doubleday, 1973), 219–23. Charlie Parker's composition "Now's the Time" (1946) echoed the vitality of this vernacular phrase among African Americans.

5. Wurts and Appelbaum, *New York World's Fair,* 112–13; Susman, *Culture as History,* 226–27.

6. Official Invitation to Opening Day Dedication, June 1, 1940, and Robert D. Kohn to Mrs. Eleanor Roosevelt, May 20, 1940, Box 366—American Common, Opening Day Dedication Program folder, New York World's Fair 1939–40 Archive, New York Public Library (archive hereafter cited as NYWF).

7. Milton Gordon, "Assimilation in American Life: Theory and Reality," in *Majority and Minority: The Dynamics of Racial and Ethnic Relations,* ed. Norman Yetman and C. H. Steele (Boston: Allyn and Bacon, 1971), 261–82; Michael Orni and Howard Winant, *Racial Formation in the United States* (New York: Routledge, 1994), 14–23, 48–50; Richard Alba, *Ethnic Identity: The Transformation of White America* (New Haven: Yale University Press, 1990), 1–5. For the language of the American Legion constitution, see http://www.users.qwest.net/~azal post61/pages/history.htm.

8. Press Release, American Common, n.d., New York City, World's Fair Negro Week Collection, Box 1, Press Releases Folder, Schomburg Center for Research in Black Culture, New York, New York (hereafter cited as Schomburg Center); "'Forty Fair Teems on Second Best Sunday," *New York Times,* September 23, 1940, 19–20.

9. Some reflections on this relationship can be found in John Dewey, *Freedom and Culture* (New York: Capricorn, 1939), 86–102, 175–76, and Reinhold Niebuhr, "Ten Years That Shook My World," *Christian Century,* April 26, 1939, repr. in *The Strenuous Decade: A Social and Intellectual Record of the Nineteen-Thirties,* ed. Daniel Aaron and Robert Bendiner (New York: Anchor, 1970), 493–98.

10. Grover Whalen, *Mr. New York* (New York: Knopf, 1955), 55–57; Cohen, Heller, and Chwast, *Trylon and Perisphere,* 47–50; Wurts and Appelbaum, 112–13.

11. Susman, *Culture as History,* 226.

12. Eduard C. Lindeman, "Dedication to the Wall of Fame" (speech), September 22, 1940, New York City, World's Fair Negro Week Collection, Shomburg Center; "'Forty Fair Teems on Second Best Sunday," 19–20.

13. Such an omission seems especially egregious in retrospect, as jazz and jazz dance then represented democracy and freedom in Europe, even in Nazi Germany and Stalinist Russia. See, for example, S. Frederick Starr, *Red and Hot: The Fate of Jazz in the Soviet Union* (New York: Limelight, 1985), 107–29, 157–203; Michael H. Kater, *Different Drummers: Jazz in the Culture of Nazi Germany* (New York: Oxford University Press, 1992), 29–69; and Levine, *Unpredictable Past,* 182–84. For an excellent short memoir of the clampdown on "Judeo-Negroid music" (the "Nazi epithet for jazz") inside Czechoslovakia, see Josef Skvorecky, "Red Music," in *Talking Moscow Blues* (New York: Ecco, 1988), 83–97.

14. "'Forty Fair Teems on Second Best Sunday," 19–20.

15. William Irwin Thompson, *The American Replacement of Nature* (New York: Doubleday, 1991), 52–53.

16. See, for example, Eric Foner, *The Story of American Freedom* (New York: Norton, 1999), 100–108, 131–32, 136–37, 276–79.

17. L. D. Reddick, "The Negro in the Building of America" (original manuscript), Box 366—American Common, Negro Week folder, NYWF. African American leaders who lent their name to the "National Committee for the Participation of Negroes in the 'American Common' World's Fair 1940" included W. E. B. Du Bois, A. Philip Randolph, Marian Anderson, Alain Locke, Adam Clayton Powell Jr., Walter White, and Mary McLeod Bethune. Du Bois gave the opening-day speech on "The Religious Genius of the American Negro." For a full review of the activities of Negro Week, see the *New York Times* listing of the Fair's daily activities, July 23–July 28, 1940. For a review of the opening day program, see "Nominees Invited to Speak at Fair," *New York Times,* July 24, 1940, 17; "Program Runs Rest of Week," *New York Amsterdam News,* July 27, 1940, 1, 24. The *New York Times* quoted Mayor Fiorello LaGuardia's speech lauding African American accomplishment since the end of the Civil War and quoted his claim that "more progress has been made [by blacks], during this comparatively short period, than has been achieved by any race in the entire history of the world."

18. Some scholars contend that the popularity of black cultural forms among whites derives from the maintenance of preindustrial values—improvisation, spontaneity, a looser sense of time—within African American cultural practices. See, for example, Lipsitz, *Time Passages,* 112–13, 238–41, and Eugene Genovese, *Roll, Jordan, Roll* (New York: Pantheon, 1974), 289–94. For an analysis of the cultural functions of humor, music, dance, body-centered public display, and masking within "black laughter," see Watkins, *On the Real Side,* 11–13, 40–41, and Levine, *Black Culture,* 298–366. The historian William Piersen calls this combination of survival technologies "a more subtle rebellion." See William Piersen, *Black Legacy* (Amherst: University of Massachusetts Press, 1993), 53–73.

19. Press Release from Geraldyn Dismond, National Committee for the Participation of Negroes in the American Common, July 21, 1940, World's Fair Negro Week Collection, Schomburg Center.

20. In the press release announcing Negro Week, Harvey Anderson, the director of the American Common, wrote that of all the presentations until that point, "we have realized [our goals and objectives] more closely in Negro Week than in any event thus far." Press Release of American Common, July 21, 1940, Box 366—American Common, Negro Week folder, NYWF.

21. The historical literature and photographic documentation of the New York World's Fair is extensive, but I have found only two stray mentions of the Savoy Ballroom exhibit, one photograph, and one drawing.

22. "Andrews Castigates Grover A. Whalen," *New York Amsterdam News,* March 25, 1939, 5.

23. Michael Eric Dyson, "Be Like Mike? Michael Jordan and the Pedagogy of Desire," in Caponi, *Signifying*, 408; Manning quoted in Batiuchok, "Lindy Hop." Judging by such works as Luis Valdez's *Zoot Suit* (1981), young Hispanic Americans and Asian Americans were equally enamored of the lindy hop.

24. Todd Gitlin, "World Leaders: Mickey et al.," *New York Times*, May 3, 1992, Sect. 2, 1, 30.

25. The First Lady's remarks introduced the Washington-produced show videotaped for public television. *In Performance*, PBS, KLRU-TV, Austin, Texas, September 16, 1998.

26. To name some well-known examples, on Broadway, *Bring in 'da Noise, Bring in 'da Funk, Jelly's Last Jam, Ain't Misbehavin', Swing!*; in movies, *Dirty Dancing, Grease, Flashdance, Footloose, Save the Last Dance*.

27. Susman, *Culture and Commitment*, 296; Marchand, "Designers Go to The Fair," 39–40.

28. Quoted in Joseph P. Cusker, "The World of Tomorrow," in Harrison, *Dawn of a New Day*, 4.

29. E. B. White, "A Reporter At Large—The New York World's Fair," *New Yorker*, May 13, 1939, 27.

30. Benjamin Franklin discussed the superiority of "the lovely white" complexion for a human being, and the historian Ronald Takaki has theorized its importance to the American Enlightenment in *Iron Cages* (New York: Oxford University Press, 1988), 17, 28–29; on streamlining, see Meikle, *Twentieth Century Limited*, 27.

31. Whalen, *Mr. New York*, 21–23, 203.

32. Bel Geddes designed "Futurama" for General Motors, and Dreyfuss designed "Democracity" inside the Perisphere and the "Demonstration Call Room" of the AT&T exhibit.

33. Whalen's opening-day speech was excerpted in the *New York Times*, May 1, 1939, 5.

34. Officials and spokesmen for Chicago's 1933 Century of Progress Exposition made many references to the need for Americans to "modernize" themselves, but the Midway was centrally placed on the exposition grounds, and monthly bulletins offered entire articles about the exhibits and rides, as well as the "rights" of Americans to some "jollification." There was also marked cooperation among political officials, investors, fair concessionaires, and union members. Robert Rydell cites Chicago's success as the trigger event for the decade's fairs: "Why were there so many fairs in the 1930s? Because the Chicago fair employed 22,000 people, boosted retail sales 19%, [and] made a $160,000 profit for investors." Investors poured money into the expositions in Dallas, San Diego, Cleveland, New York City, and San Francisco. Chicago's civic officials did not have any delusions about defining a new pattern of living. Rydell, *World of Fairs*, 121.

35. "First Royalty Visits the Fair," *New York Times*, May 2, 1939, 1, 16; "N.Y. Fair Finales to $15,000,000 Gross Receipts at the Gate," *Variety*, October 25, 1939, 1, 12. The *New York Times* reported opening-day complaints from tourists

concerning the expensive 75¢ admission: "The high prices in many of the eating places ... [are] prohibitive for persons of small or moderate means." In midsummer, *Variety* ran a front-page article with information culled from interviewing out-of-town visitors to the Fair. Visitors were intimidated by the size and expense of the Fair, and many said they went to the industrial exhibits and then to Broadway; the Fair was "too big and too costly" to see it all. "N.Y. Fair's Midway Beefs Biz Is Bad, but Tourists Have Their Own Reasons Why," *Variety,* July 5, 1939, 1, 55.

36. For a concise discussion of the Cartesian influences on the ideology of technological progress, see David Noble, *The Religion of Technology* (New York: Knopf, 1997), 143–71. Noble still credits Descartes with framing the mind/body problem as a battle between rational intellect against emotional experience: "'The body is always a hindrance to the mind in thinking'" (144). The philosophy of science over the last thousand years, Noble contends, has been to liberate the noble brain from the ignoble body. "In Cartesian terms, the development of a thinking machine was aimed at rescuing the immortal mind from its mortal prison" (142).

37. Whalen actively discouraged fairgoers from visiting the Amusement Area, though the impresario Billy Rose tried to explain the first rule of fairs to Whalen in 1938: "People wanted to eat ... to see nude or near-nude girls ... they wanted color and music, noise and entertainment." World's fairs were carnivals, Rose explained, and the anchor show should be an outdoor nude show (within the limits of the law). Earl Conrad, *Billy Rose: Manhattan Primitive* (New York: World, 1968), 121; Rydell, *World of Fairs*, 121–22, 137. In 1940 the Amusement Area was renamed "The Great White Way"; this use of Broadway's nickname only emphasizes other historical ironies.

38. Nearly the entire cartoon is shown in *The World of Tomorrow.*

39. Brooks Atkinson, "Going to the Fair," *New York Times,* May 14, 1939, sect. 11, 1. The only exhibits open were Aquacade, the exhibit featuring African pygmies, and the Savoy Ballroom. Atkinson expressed disappointment that "the amusements of tomorrow" would be "deformed animals, gangster busters and peep-shows"; he overheard someone joke that in the Amusement Area "an old-fashioned light bulb would be a sensation."

40. "Fair Labor Tie-ups Fought by Mayor," *New York Times,* May 24, 1939, 27; "Fair Has Its Busiest Week-end," *New York Herald Tribune,* May 22, 1939, 1, 6; "Work Is Rushed on Concessions in Play Area," *New York Herald Tribune,* May 26, 1939, 17; "Fair Steps Up Festivities for Long Week-end," *New York Herald Tribune,* May 27, 1939, 16; "Four Attractions Open in Fun Area," *Billboard,* July 1, 1939, 30, 68.

41. "World Fairs: New York, San Francisco" (special issue), *Architectural Forum* 70 (June 1939): 439.

42. For a discussion of the idealized male body of the 1930s, see Kenneth R. Dutton, *The Perfectible Body: The Western Ideal of Male Physical Development* (New York: Continuum, 1995), 67–72.

43. Marchand, "Designers Go to the Fair," 5, 8–9; on the background of

the cultural battle between artists and the machine, see Cheney, *Art and the Machine*, 3–6, 12, 55–95.

44. Alexander Calder, "A Water Ballet," *Theatre Arts Monthly* 23 (August 1939): 578–79.

45. Rosamond Gilder, "The Body of Atlas," *Theater Arts Monthly* 23 (August 1939): 580.

46. "Skin Drawing at the Fair—Strip Shows Top Grossers," *Billboard*, June 10, 1939, 3, 31; "Life Goes to the World's Fair," *Life*, July 3, 1939, 55–69.

47. "$600,000 to $1,000,000 of N.Y. Fair Corp. Coin Means Midway Must Get a Break," *Variety*, July 26, 1939, 1, 55; "4 New Shows Make World's Fair Zone Almost Complete," *Billboard*, June 24, 1939, 110.

48. Rydell, *World of Fairs*, 135–46.

49. Christina Cogdell, "The Futurama Recontextualized: Norman Bel Geddes's Eugenic 'World of Tomorrow,'" *American Quarterly* 52 (June 2000): 193–245.

50. Robards quoted in *The World of Tomorrow*.

51. The one exception was the corporate-funded "Railroads on Parade" exhibit, where thirty-five African Americans were employed as actors, singers, and extras to help enact the history of the railroads.

52. "Protest Bias against Race by G. Whalen," *New York Amsterdam News*, March 18, 1939, 1, 6; Adam C. Powell Jr., "Soap Box," *New York Amsterdam News*, April 1, 1939, 10; "Jail 4 World's Fair Pickets," *New York Amsterdam News*, April 8, 1939, 1, 6.

53. "Committee to Act on Discrimination at Fair Exposition," *New York Amsterdam News*, April 1, 1939, 11; "A Step in the Right Direction" (editorial), *New York Amsterdam News*, April 15, 1939, 10; "Committee in Move to Block Opening of Fair," *New York Amsterdam News*, April 29, 1939, 1, 5.

54. One member of the Greater New York Coordinating Committee explained, "We didn't want to force him to pass through a picket line. . . . We have no quarrel with the president. We blame Grover Whalen for the administration policy." "Picket Fair as FDR Speaks," *New York Amsterdam News*, May 6, 1939, 1, 3; see also "Fair Pickets, 300 Strong March through Times Square District," *New York Amsterdam News*, May 6, 1939, 3.

55. "Harlem Conference Sees 'Discrimination,'" *New York Herald Tribune*, May 7, 1939, n.p., clipping file, Center for American History, University of Texas at Austin. Perhaps the last word on the issue came from a gathering of speakers at a two-day conference called to discuss the lack of representation of Blacks at the New York World's Fair. Presenters included Richard Wright, Rachel Dubois of New York University's Sociology Department, and the *Esquire* magazine artist and writer E. Simms Campbell. The conference unanimously endorsed a resolution condemning "discrimination" by the Fair management and declared blacks in the future would hold "a higher place in the cultural and economic world of tomorrow than that to which he has been relegated by the World's Fair Corporation."

56. "Happy-Days-in-Dixie for Harlem Talent on Broadway," *Variety*,

March 29, 1939, 1; "Sepia Stars Have Busy Year on Air," *New York Amsterdam News,* January 7, 1939, 16. *Variety* reported that the WPA "Mikado" had eighty black performers, not counting "the musicians . . . because they're ofay," and Todd's "Mikado" had 112 performers. Keil, *Music Grooves,* 304.

57. "N.Y. Fair's Midway Beefs Biz Is Bad," 1, 55.

58. "N.Y. Fair Nixes Name Dance Bands," *Metronome,* May 1939, 7.

59. Roger Littleford, "On Flushing Front," *Billboard,* July 15, 1939, 31, 62; "Gate Average Takes a Rise in 10-Day Tilt," *Billboard,* July 22, 1939, 29, 62. See also "Goodman Swings Needed Coin into L. A. Symph Coffers, Whams Elite," *Variety,* August 9, 1939, 1, 47. The Golden Gate Centennial experienced a 25,000-person-a-day increase during Benny Goodman's four-day stint on that fair's "Treasure Island."

60. Grover Whalen contracted with the Music Corporation of America (MCA) for "the hiring of name bands" beginning the week of August 5, 1939. The board authorized $5,000 to construct a bandshell, and contracted with D. A. Werblin of MCA for $4,500 per week for the first two weeks (a trial period) for each band, and then $5,500 per week upon renewal and for the duration of the Fair. *Minutes of the Board of Directors of the New York World's Fair, Vol. III,* July 28, 1939, 1238–39. See also "MCA–World's Fair Deal on Fire for Orks to Hypo Gate," *Billboard,* July 22, 1939, 9.

61. "Swing Comes to the Fair," Pathé Newsreel, Ernie Smith Video Collection, Smithsonian Institution, Washington, D.C.

62. "Jitterbugs Up Fair Midway 20 to 500%, *Variety,* August 16, 1939, 1, 35.

63. "Fair's 2-Day Paid Gate 400,473 on Its First 50-Cent Weekend," *New York Herald Tribune,* August 7, 1939, 1, 11. Tommy Dorsey's big band played the following week.

64. "New Bands and 40¢, 8 PM Gate in Biz Area Kayoes N.Y. Fair's Midway Ops," *Variety,* September 20, 1939, 55. The final event of the 1939 season was a memorial concert for George Gershwin at the Mardi Gras Casino, a victory, of sorts, for swing culture; seating was provided for three thousand, and the concert was broadcast throughout the fairgrounds. "N.Y. Fair Finales to $15,000,000 Gross Receipts at the Gate," *Variety,* Oct. 25, 1939, 1, 12.

65. "NYWF Amusement Zone Represents Investment of $3 Million," *Variety,* June 14, 1939, 55.

66. "World's Fairs: New York, San Francisco," *Architectural Forum* 70 (June 1939): 439.

67. For Downes's appointment, see Box 1049—"Press Clippings" (folder), and internal memorandum, "Music Advisory Committee" (folder). "Fair Names Downes," *New York World-Telegram,* February 18, 1938, n.p.; "Fair Music Leader Named," *North Shore Daily Journal,* February 18, 1938, n.p. Members of the committee included the presidents of CBS and NBC; the directors of the New York Philharmonic Society, the Julliard School of Music, the Metropolitan Opera, the New York Public Library, and the Municipal Art Society; wealthy patrons such as Marshall Field, Mrs. Daniel Guggenheim, and vice-chairman Mrs. Vincent Astor; the editor of the *New York Herald Tribune;* and Walter Damrosch,

the conductor of the New York Philharmonic. The operas were arranged in co-operation with the Metropolitan Opera. For the role of the board of directors, see the meetings of November 28, 1939, and January 11, 1939, in *The Minutes of the Board of Directors, New York World's Fair 1939–40, Vol. I*, 93–94.

68. Olin Downes, "Music Festival Ushers in Season of Varied Cultural Programs," *New York Times*, May 1, 1939, 9.

69. Spaeth, *Music Is Fun*, 221–22. Ironically, Downes had written positively of jazz's international influence in the mid-1920s. See Henry O. Osgood, *So This Is Jazz* (New York: Dutton, 1926), 148–51.

70. "Fair Canceling Its Festival of Classical Music," *New York Herald Tribune*, May 25, 1939, 22–23; "Music Program Canceled by Fair," *New York Times*, May 25, 1939, 30; "Music Hall Changes to Popular Fare," *Billboard*, June 3, 1939, 30.

71. Whiteman's agent requested confirmation on May 16; Whiteman sent a desperate personal telegram a week later (addressing Downes as "Olin"), explaining that he needed some advance notice to set up a national radio hookup. Finally, on May 25, Gretl Urban, one of the fair's music supervisors, sent a curt telegram to Whiteman's agent advising him of Downes's resignation and the termination of their contract. "Sorry can make no contracts any kind for hall of music. Hall closes Monday night." Telegram, Frank Burke, Artists Management, Inc., to Olin Downes, May 16, 1939; telegram, Paul Whiteman to Olin Downes, May 24, 1939; telegram, Gretl Urban to Frank Burke, May 25, 1939. Box 173—"Jazz Orchestras, Theatre & Music, Participation," NYWF.

72. As *Variety* reflected in 1940, the first year's Fair seemed like "a publicity front for a chosen few" symbolized by their "tophats and cutaways." "N.Y. Fair Finales to $15,000,000 Gross Receipts at the Gate," *Variety*, October 25, 1939, 1, 12.

73. Most rejection letters contained a variation of the following line: "At the present time I am not engaging any dance orchestras for the music program at the Fair." Gretl Urban to Mr. F. Cornelis of The Melody Makers Club Orchestra of Belgium, March 21, 1939, Box 174—"Jazz Orchestras"; Kay Swift to William A. Burnham of Consolidated Radio Artists (representing Ferde Grofé), February 21, 1939, Box 173—"Jazz Orchs. F-H," NYWF. Swift told Burnham she admired Ferde Grofé's work, but she was not booking any popular music; Grofé later performed at the Ford exhibit with a new electronic keyboard.

74. Letter, Luckyeth Roberts to Grover Whalen, March 9, 1939, Box 173, NYWF.

75. "Luckey Roberts Set for Carnegie Hall," *New York Amsterdam News*, September 2, 1939, 17; "Charles [Luckey] Roberts Brings Harlem to Carnegie Hall," *New York Herald Tribune*, August 31, 1939, 29.

76. Miller, *Swingin' at the Savoy*, 133–34.

77. "Savoy Theatre on Fair Site Is Gala Spot," *New York Amsterdam News*, June 3, 1939, 3.

78. "Building Quivers as Jitterbugs Vie," *New York Times*, May 21, 1939, sect. 1, 40.

79. Gale made his first complaint in early July to the chairman of the Amusement Control Committee, who was sympathetic but could not convince the Fair's lawyers to compensate Gale. See "Gale Objects to Todd's Colored Show @ N.Y. Fair," *Variety,* July 5, 1939, 55. For the internal discussions, see Memorandum, H. M. Lammers, Chairman, Amusement Control Committee, to Legal Department, "Subject: Savoy Theater Complaint with Reference to Hot Mikado," July 17, 1939; handwritten note, "H. B." [unidentified] to Commander H. M. Lammers, July 30, 1939, internal memo, "Indebtedness to the Fair by Savoy Ballroom," August 9, 1939; internal memo, George P. Smith Jr. to James Hemingway, Legal Department, August 13, 1939; internal memo, Commander H. M. Lammers, Chairman, Amusement Control Committee, to Vice President, Fair Corporation, August 21, 1939. Box 975—"Gale Enterprises, Inc.," NYWF. An anonymous consultant to *Billboard* used Gale's experience to illustrate the Fair corporation's inconsistent business dealings: "What kind of ethical standards is this fair governed by? It has broken faith with and slapped the face of nearly everyone at one time or another." The columnist brought out a laundry list of offenses committed against the concessionaires (the lack of lighting, changing policy on nudity, and so on) and specifically asked for redress for Gale. "And what of the concessioner who has it written in his contract that there shall be no competing show and who was assured orally that he was to have an exclusive on a certain type of operation, only to have the fair, in its own theater, allow a production that definitely is competition to this man." "An Insider Looks at the Fair, Subject: The Board," *Billboard,* July 29, 1939, 28. On the closing in mid-August, see "Savoy Is Closed Tightly at Fair," *New York Amsterdam News,* August 12, 1939, 17; "Boone Resigns as Press Head; 2 Shows Close," *Billboard,* August 12, 1939, 28; "2 Girl Shows Fail to Pass Censors; Cuban Village Free," *Billboard,* August 19, 1939, 28; "Contractors Take over 2 Attractions," *Billboard,* August 26, 1939, 44.

80. "Music Hall Changes to Popular Fare," *Billboard,* June 3, 1939, 30.

81. "'Hot Mikado' Ends Stand," *New York Amsterdam News,* June 17, 1939, 17.

82. Meetings of July 20 and August 31, 1939, as recorded in the *Minutes of the Board of Directors, Vol. III,* 1939: 1085–86, 1128, 1236–37. For the 1940 season, Todd presented the comedians Abbott and Costello along with the singer and dancer Gypsy Rose Lee.

83. "A Few Notes about the Hot Michael Todd," *New York Times,* October 8, 1939, sect. 9, 1–2.

84. Ibid., 2. For example, Todd built soundstages in Hollywood in the late 1920s and ran a barely legal "school of bricklaying" in Chicago. Todd's first major theatrical success was a Midway act at the Century of Progress Exposition called the "Flame Dance," in which a female dancer dressed as a moth and whirled around a giant candle until her clothes caught fire and burned off, leaving her nearly naked. "I burnt up four dolls before I got [the hang of] it," Todd laughed in retrospect at this small obstacle. In the mid-1930s he created a department store exhibit called "Kute Kris Kringle" that netted him $200,000. Based on the "woman-in-a-fishbowl effect," Todd used reducing

lenses to show kids a live, seemingly miniaturized Santa Claus at work in his workshop. He set up a phone next to the peephole so kids could call Santa and tell him what they wanted for Christmas. The store would then call parents and pass along the information if they had the requested items in stock. "Cut-rate Showman," *Collier's*, September 7, 1940, 40–43; "Todd's New Orleans Village at N.Y. Fair Easily a No. 1 Midway Standout," *Variety*, May 22, 1940, 63.

85. Conrad, *Billy Rose*, 123–28.

86. Quoted in Polly Rose Gottlieb, *The Nine Lives of Billy Rose* (New York: Crown, 1968), 143.

87. "Billy Rose: The Bantamweight Colossus," *Theatre Arts Monthly* 29 (January 1945): 42–50. Rose brought the Ziegfeld Theater in 1945 and claimed he was living his dream to "produc[e] plays and spectacles in the Ziegfeld Theater for the rest of my life." The first production at the theater was entitled "The Seven Lively Arts," and was an attempt to highlight great American cultural contributions. The show starred Benny Goodman, Cole Porter, Hassard Short, Norman Bel Geddes, and Bert Lahr.

88. Kenneth R. Dutton, *The Perfectible Body: The Western Ideal of Male Physical Development* (New York: Continuum, 1995), 120–25, 153–59.

89. "Theatre Arts Gallery No. 1—Michael Todd," *Theatre Arts Monthly* 37 (July 1953): 80.

90. Brooks Atkinson, "The Hot Mikado," *New York Times*, March 14, 1939, 26.

91. Todd was also something of a marketing genius. For the first month, he tinkered with the structure and format of the show until he could turn a profit. He cut the two-act show to seventy minutes and one act; a few critics commented that the show lost nothing in the transition. He lowered the admission price from the off-Broadway high of $2.20 to 99¢, and finally to a 40¢ general admission price. He ballyhooed (literally yelled through a megaphone) at the back door of the Aquacade, imploring Billy Rose's customers to come see his show. Rose called Todd to a famous meeting at Lindy's Restaurant in midtown Manhattan, a summit dubbed "The Treaty of Lindy's" by the New York press, where Rose agreed to promote Todd's show to his customers in return for a quiet back door and Todd's reciprocal promotion. By September, the *New York Times* recognized Todd for his business acumen, moxie, and success.

Todd also tried to low-ball his actors and dancers, and became entangled in a debate with the actors' union. He pled a lack of profit at the Fair owing to low prices, and Equity agreed to the cut in pay until they discovered Todd was making a healthy profit. "Performer Trouble in Mikado," *New York Amsterdam News*, July 15, 1939, 16; "'Mikado' Business Slow," *New York Amsterdam News*, July 29, 1939, 17; "Equity Puts Screws on Show," *New York Amsterdam News*, August 5, 1939, 17.

92. "Michael Todd's 'Hot Mikado,'" *Variety*, March 29, 1939, 54.

93. "Todd's New Orleans Village 'Tap Day,'" *Time*, June 5, 1939, 40; Atkinson, "Hot Mikado," 26.

94. "Cut-Rate Showman," *Collier's*, September 7, 1940, 40–41. Todd's biographer used the same phrase as a title for his chapter on the World's Fair. Art

Cohn, *The Nine Lives of Michael Todd* (New York: Random House, 1958), 87–103; see also Michael Todd Jr. and Susan McCarthy Todd, *A Valuable Property: The Life Story of Michael Todd* (New York: Arbor, 1983), 43–65.

95. Mantle, "'Hot Mikado' Burns Up," 53; "Bill Robinson Fair's Big Star," *New York Amsterdam News,* September 23, 1939, 17.

96. Collier, *Duke Ellington,* 68–69.

97. Contemporary accounts differ as to the relative success of the seven-week run of *The Hot Mikado* on Broadway, before the Fair. A profile in *Collier's* claimed it could have run at the Broadhurst Theater for a year and half, for the show grossed $20,000 in its second week and apparently "Cole Porter saw it seven times." "Cut-Rate Showman," 40–41.

98. The lindy hoppers were a young, contentious group of teenagers, and once a backstage argument disrupted the smooth running of the show. Michael Todd fired them, and went out to hire some others. But Herbert "Whitey" White was one of the few assertive black impresarios of the time because he had a monopoly on the commodity of the lindy hop. Todd flew to Chicago looking for other first-rate lindy hoppers, but he returned without success and acted as if he had never fired the dancers in the first place. Stearns and Stearns, *Jazz Dance,* 331–32.

99. Ibid., 331.

100. "A Musical Comedy Parade," *Theatre Arts Monthly* 23 (June 1939): 397.

101. "Bill Robinson Fair's Big Star," 17; see also "'Hot Mikado' Preps for Highways," *New York Amsterdam News,* October 14, 1939, 20.

102. "Tap Day," 40. Most photos of Robinson feature his golden costume and his smile. "Frontispiece," *Theatre Arts Monthly* 23 (May 1939): 392; *Theatre Arts Monthly* 24 (September 1940): 687.

103. Atkinson, "Hot Mikado," 26; Todd's 'Hot Mikado," *Variety,* March 29, 1939, 54; "Broadway in Review—The Hot Mikado," *Theatre Arts Monthly* 23 (May 1939): 325–29.

104. Atkinson, "Hot Mikado," 26; Mantle, "'Hot Mikado' Burns Up"; "Todd's 'Hot Mikado' Comes to Broadway," *New York Amsterdam News,* April 1, 1939, 20. Ironically, Robinson was known to be abrasive among African Americans; he was known—with a mixture of fear and respect—as the Mayor of Harlem. Stearns and Stearns, *Jazz Dance,* 332.

105. "Cut-Rate Showman," 41; "Todd Was the Last of the Big Showmen," *New York Herald Tribune,* March 23, 1958, n.p., clipping file, "Michael Todd," Center for American History, University of Texas at Austin.

106. "A Few Notes about the Hot Michael Todd," 1–2.

107. Of the three production numbers in this show, one featured Mary Bruce's Harlem dance troupe. Bruce was a classically trained tap and ballet dancer who had taught the likes of Katherine Dunham. Her troupe was written up by the *New York Amsterdam News,* and noted specifically for "a precision and liveliness seldom seen above 110th Street." Todd and Hassard Short visited her school on a tip from the Apollo Theater owner Frank Schiffman and were so

impressed that "they signed her on the spot to produce a unit for their World's Fair venture." Todd mentioned neither Bruce nor her dancers in any publication; but in *Collier's* he stood proudly in front of the "Gay New Orleans" exhibit surrounded by five beautiful white dancers in *Gone With the Wind*–influenced period costume. "Mary Bruce Scores with Dance Group at the Fair," *New York Amsterdam News*, August 3, 1940, 10; "Mary Bruce Chorus Tops" and Bill Chase, "All Ears," *New York Amsterdam News*, February 18, 1939, 16–17.

108. "N.Y. World's Fair Debut," *Variety*, May 15, 1940, 54. *Variety's* preview of the 1940 Fair reflected back on the successes and failures of the 1939 Fair, noting that "Aquacade . . . was the lone b.o. [box office] boff on the midway last year, outside of Todd's 'Hot Mikado' in the Music Hall."

109. "'Hot Mikado' to Be Filmed," *New York Amsterdam News*, September 30, 1939, 16; "Bill Robinson Fair's Big Star," 17; "Todd's New Orleans Village," 63.

110. Abel Green, "War, Rain Hurt, but New York Fair Indicates How Showmanship Pays," *Variety*, July 10, 1940, 47.

111. White, "A Reporter At Large," 28.

Conclusion

1. Fredric Jameson, *Postmodernism, or The Cultural Logic of Late Capitalism* (Durham: Duke University Press, 1991), 36. For Jameson, steam power is the motive force of the first machine age, electricity the second, and electronics and nuclear energy the third.

2. Bambaataa quoted in Ulf Poschardt, *DJ Culture* (London: Quartet, 1998), 217.

3. Andrew John Ignatius Vontz, "The Strange Triumph of Electronic Music," *Salon*, June 19, 2002. The dominance of these forms forced the music industry to shift to "digital and computer-based recording equipment" much earlier than they might have.

4. Mihaly Csikszentmihalyi, *Flow: The Psychology of Optimal Experience* (New York: Harper and Row, 1990), 95, 98, 108–9.

5. Doug Stewart, "The Joint Is Jumping," *Smithsonian*, March 1999, 60–74.

6. Ibid., 70.

7. James Gleick, "Theories of Connectivity," *New York Times Magazine*, April 22, 2001, 64.

8. Bambaataa quoted in David Toop, *The Rap Attack* (Boston: South End, 1984), 130, and on Grandmaster Flash, 106–7; Rose, *Black Noise*, 63.

9. Both recordings can be found on the anthology *Chill Out!*, CD EX-257–2, Instinct (1993).

10. Bill Malone, *Country Music USA* (Austin: University of Texas Press, 1985), 7–8. "No other industrial phenomenon has held such a magnetic and romantic fascination for Americans . . . even though the automobile has had a greater impact on the breakdown of regional barriers. The railroad provided employment apart from agriculture, it offered the means of escape from unpleasant or unwanted responsibilities, and . . . transport[ed] people to alternative and presumably better economic opportunities. Even those . . . bound

to the land . . . could experience a vicarious satisfaction in identifying with this great symbol of industrial energy and with the tough, unfettered men who mastered it."

11. Arthur Bell, "The Ballad of John Henry," as heard on John Lomax, *The Ballad Hunter, Part 8: Railroad Songs,* Library of Congress, Music Division, Recording Laboratory AAFS L49–5, LC1977–86 (1958).

12. Hughes, *American Genesis,* 309.

13. Dunham, "Negro Dance," 1000.

14. Schuller, *Swing Era,* 4–5.

15. Ernie Smith, "Portrait of the Swing Era," in Miller, *Swingin' at the Savoy,* xxxiv, xxxvi.

16. Simon, *Glenn Miller and His Orchestra,* 429–30.

17. Cited in Erenberg, *Swingin' the Dream,* xi.

18. Martin Williams, "Fletcher Henderson," in *The Swing Era 1936–1937* (New York: Time-Life Books, 1972), 62.

19. Nelson George, *Hip-Hop America* (New York: Penguin, 1999). Queen Latifah's production of the hit comedy *Living Single* (and her film roles) and Ice Cube's *Fridays* films are only two prominent examples.

INDEX

Page numbers of illustrations are in italics.

whitefacing (of African American culture), 27–28, 173–76, 237, 249, 313, 332 n.74, 349 n.115

Whiteman, Paul, 50–52, 54, 57, 72, 130–31, 167, 181, 302

Whitey's Lindy Hoppers, 26, 250, 259, 278, 289, 303–10

Whitman, Walt, 34, 81–82, 122, 296

Wideman, John Edgar, 127

Williams, Bert, 136, 191, 192, 195

Williams, Cootie, 107, 117

Williams, Martin, 321–22

Williams, William Carlos, 39, 82

Wills, Bob, and His Texas Playboys, 73, 102

Wilson, Edmund, 188–90, 192–93

Wilson, Teddy, 173, 276

Winner, Langdon, 151

Wizard of Oz, The, 281–82

Wolfe, George F., 248

women and machines, 126–130, 147, 153–54, 190–202, 296–97; trains, 88–91, 173; "girls" as standardized parts of popular culture, 182–220

work songs, 46–47, 82–84, 120–21, 133–34, 337 n.59

world's fairs and international expositions, 27, 139–40, 143–50, 283–311, 391 n.2; as projection of national culture, 141–42; Columbian Exposition (1893), 294; Golden Gate Centennial (1939), 299. *See also* New York World's Fair; Chicago Century of Progress Exposition

World War II, 320–21

"Wreck of Old 97, The," 82

Wright, Richard, 256

Yoruba culture (West Africa), influence of, on African American vernacular culture, 129–30, 162, 251, 265, 355 n.79

Young, Lester, 108, 138, 171

Zephyr, the, 148–49, *152*, 154, 174. *See also* streamliner trains

Ziegfeld, Florenz, 87, 184–97, 219–20; as industrialist of popular culture, 198–202, 369 n.53; influence of, on Busby Berkeley, 202–7, 219–20; influence of, on Billy Rose and Michael Todd, 305, 397 n.87

Ziegfeld Follies, 12, 26, 87, 184–202, 247

"Ziegfeld walk," 189–90